Accelerated Land Reform, Mining, Growth, Unemployment and Inequality in South Africa

Nombulelo Gumata • Eliphas Ndou

Accelerated Land Reform, Mining, Growth, Unemployment and Inequality in South Africa

A Case for Bold Supply Side Policy Interventions

palgrave
macmillan

Nombulelo Gumata
South African Reserve Bank
Pretoria, South Africa

Eliphas Ndou
South African Reserve Bank
Pretoria, South Africa

Wits Plus, University of the Witwatersrand
Johannesburg, South Africa

School of Economic and Business Sciences
Johannesburg, South Africa

ISBN 978-3-030-30883-4 ISBN 978-3-030-30884-1 (eBook)
https://doi.org/10.1007/978-3-030-30884-1

This Palgrave Macmillan imprint is published by the registered company Springer Nature Switzerland AG.
The registered company address is: Gewerbestrasse 11, 6330 Cham, Switzerland

Preface

Should the South African Reserve Bank lower the current 3–6 per cent inflation target range and broaden the central bank mandate to include maximum employment (low unemployment rate) as well? This is a question posed by Kganyago (2017). Is there anything inherently wrong with the current flexible inflation targeting framework, such that there is an urgent need to move to another monetary policy framework such as nominal gross domestic product (NGDP) growth targeting, for example? In addition, how important are supply side policy interventions such as accelerated land reform, positive productivity growth and investment growth shocks in pursuing a dual mandate? Is there a role that lower-tier banks, such as the Postbank, mutual banks and co-operative banks can play in complementing the Land Bank development mandate? Can the financial regulatory landscape be adjusted to phase in a greater co-ordinated role and participation for lower-tier banks to support entrepreneurship, provision of housing finance and funding of small, medium and micro enterprises (SMMEs). Lastly, what does inclusive growth mean in the South African context?

This book answers these questions by assessing the role of supply side policy interventions in contributing to a lower inflation regime, increase potential output, increasing the output-employment intensities and aligning the banking sector to better serve these objectives. Furthermore, we evaluate whether the current flexible inflation targeting framework per se is the root cause of the current economic malaise in the country. To put context to the questions explored in the book, Fig. 1 shows that formal non-agricultural sector (formal) employment accounts for roughly 70 per cent of total employment. The agricultural sector employment accounts for 5.4 per cent of the non-formal employment, whereas the informal and private household sectors account for 17.5 per cent and 7.75 per cent, respectively. Thus, the non-formal and agricultural sectors contribute 30 per cent to the employment rate.

Nonetheless, the unemployment rate increased post-2009 and averaged 26 per cent and income inequality remains high at the aggregate level and along racial lines as shown in Fig. 2. The National Development Plan's (NDP) overarching goal is to eliminate poverty, reduce inequality

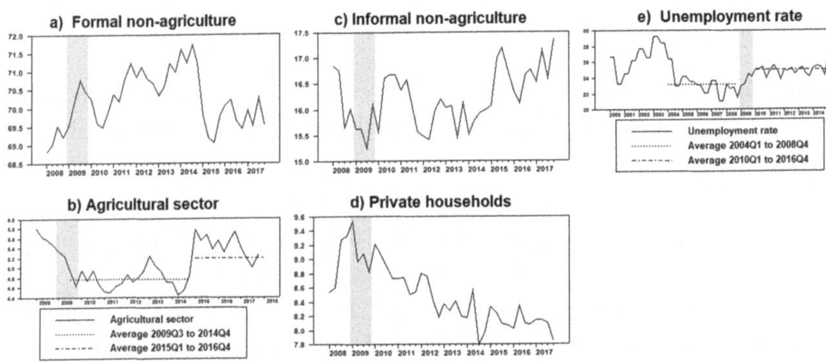

Fig. 1 Employment trends and the unemployment rate. (Source: Statistics South Africa and authors' calculations)

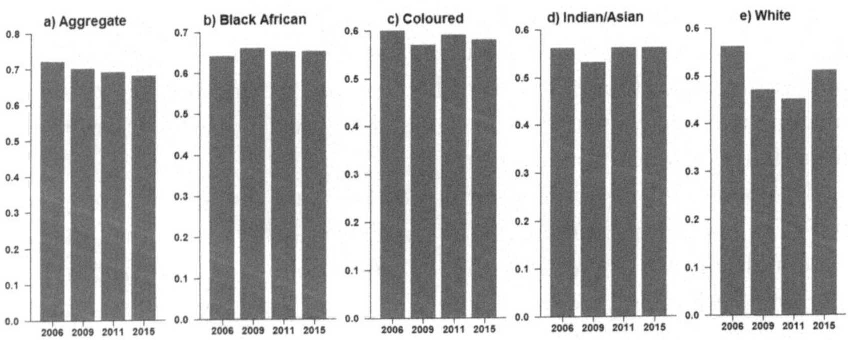

Fig. 2 Gini coefficient income per capita by race. (Source: Statistics South Africa)

from the current aggregate level of 0.68 to 0.6 by 2030. The NDP also has a goal to lower the unemployment rate to 6 per cent by 2030. With the unemployment rate having averaged 26 per cent post-2009, what are the policy implications of these targets? What needs to be done?

This book contributes to academic and policy research debates in this area by conducting empirical research on various relevant global, domestic and sector-specific aspects that are aimed at answering these questions. One of the major criticisms raised against the NDP is that the national planning commission did not provide an employment policy, comprehensive financial and macroeconomic policy framework within which these targets can be achieved. This book contributes to measures aimed at correcting for this omission in the NDP by providing empirical evidence on the interaction of foreign and domestic factors that influence the South African macroeconomy.

In particular, within the current discourse of *land expropriation without compensation and the willing buyer:willing seller land reform model*, the book addresses the interaction of the accelerated land reform policy with the objectives of financial, price and macroeconomic stability. From an economic and financial perspective, we argue that "*land expropriation without compensation*" also loosens a binding financial constraint on part of the public finances and can be a good deterrent of collusion in the market for farmland. Thus, correcting a big market failure with the current willing buyer:willing seller land reform policy. At the same time, the debate about the "*willing-seller:willing-buyer*" is intricately linked with asset prices and wealth channels of the monetary policy transmission mechanism to the degree that it interacts with and is influenced by the direction of housing and farmland prices. Furthermore, the accelerated land reform policy is a supply side policy intervention aimed at unleashing potential output, changing the ownership patterns in the economy, increasing participation in the economy, labour absorption and economic inclusion. By their very nature, supply side policy interventions tend to have larger and persistent shock effects on growth in investment, output and employment, labour participation, economic inclusion and lowering the Gini coefficient (income inequality). Evidence shows that the redistribution of land is a necessary but not a sufficient condition to bring about real economic empowerment and poverty alleviation. Post-settlement support should be an integral part of the policy output in order to achieve a long-term sustainable development outcome. Thus, policy interventions should be designed to ensure that post-settlement support cuts across all major land reform programmes, namely, redistribution, land tenure and restitution. In addition, policy interventions should provide a comprehensive post-settlement reconstruction and development programme plan.

Such supply side policy interventions will also deal with the monopoly, oligopoly and vertically integrated market structures in the agricultural sector that incentivise anti-competitive behaviour. Bold, well-structured and well-executed supply side policy interventions via the accelerated land reform policy can help bring about competition in the agricultural sector and sub-sectors such as the grains and poultry industries with benefits to the aggregate economy and consumers. Substituting imports with locally produced commodities and increasing area planted, for instance, can trigger a range of upstream and downstream multipliers with positive effects on the intensity of job creation in the agricultural sector far better than what the import tariffs and the exchange rate depreciations alone have been able to achieve.

To this end, we argue that changes to section 25 of the Constitution have a significant bearing on the current mandates of the South African Reserve Bank (SARB), namely, price and financial stability. As such, we treat the proposed changes to section 25 of the constitution as an empirical question in this book. In addition, as an empirical question, we argue that the balance sheet channel of the monetary policy transmission anchors the debate about how section 25 of the constitution is linked with section 224 of the constitution. In order to quantitatively monitor the progress of low and stable inflation, unemployment rate, maximum employment growth, inclusive growth and financial stability, the SARB mandate must be expanded. First, the book presents a robust case for a lower inflation target range of 2 to 4 per cent compared to the current 3 to 6 per cent target range. We dedicate a number of chapters that present empirical evidence showing that financial and macroeconomic stability is greatly improved and enhanced in a low inflation regime characterised by the inflation target range of 2 to 4 per cent.

Second, we argue that the low unemployment rate (maximum employment) mandate is already implied in the current flexible inflation targeting framework to the degree that the monetary policy's objective function tries to stabilise the inflation and real GDP growth deviations from the target. Thus, an explicit target of the low unemployment rate (maximum employment) is not inconsistent with the current flexible inflation targeting the monetary policy framework. We present robust aggregate and sectorial empirical evidence showing that real GDP growth is very closely related to employment via Okun's law or the employment of intensity of real economic activity, which is in turn closely linked to income and wealth inequality. We argue that a more comprehensive measure of welfare ought to include the unemployment rate, income and wealth inequality, the rationale being that the assessment of income and wealth inequality encompasses inclusive growth. But at the same time, they are specific in that they put a spotlight on the fact that economic growth can be seen as inclusive at the aggregate level and yet mask significant and growing income and wealth inequality at a disaggregated level.

Third, the key theme that cuts across the findings in the book is not only that a lower inflation target range compatible with higher and robust output and employment growth, but that the role of productivity at the aggregate and sectorial levels cannot be understated. Evidence contained in several chapters in the book indicates that positive labour productivity growth shocks lead to a significant decline in consumer price inflation and inflation expectations. Improved labour productivity growth tends to accentuate the decline in inflation expectations and is positive for real wages, output and employment growth.

Fourth, we dedicate chapter(s) in the book to address the debate that the inflation targeting monetary policy framework largely played a role in the slow recovery post-financial crisis. Critiques of the inflation targeting framework contend that a nominal GDP level or growth target (NGDPT) or even wage targeting would have performed far better than the flexible inflation targeting regime. We provide evidence showing that the SARB is still better off directly targeting inflation. Real GDP growth is higher when the gap between the NGDP growth and inflation is wider. During recessions inflation tends to exceed NGDP growth, resulting in lower real GDP growth. This suggests that a combination of lower inflation and high NGDP growth is needed to achieve high real GDP growth. In a comparison of the Taylor rule policy prescriptions of how the conduct of monetary policy would evolve under consumer price inflation and NGDP growth targets, we find that the repo rate would be aggressively tightened to bring NGDP growth to target. Monetary policy tightening and the associated costs of disinflation are heightened under the NGDP growth targets. Thus, we conclude that South Africa would be worse off under NGDP growth targeting compared to the current flexible inflation targeting framework. However, a higher target for NGDP growth implies a lower Taylor rule prescription. During the recession in 2009, the repo rate would have been much lower than the actual repo rate at the time.

The results imply a higher NGDP growth driven by, for instance, positive productivity and investment growth shocks as opposed to higher consumer price index (CPI) inflation is consistent with a lower policy rate. This is because positive productivity growth shocks exert opposing effects on NGDP growth and inflation. The NGDP growth increases in response to positive productivity growth shocks whereas inflation declines. Similarly, positive investment growth shocks exert minimal inflationary pressures. We conclude that a higher NGDP growth target is not inconsistent with a lower CPI inflation target. A lower inflation target and a higher NGDP growth target are not mutually exclusive. Alternatively, a higher NGDP growth target and a low inflation target satisfy the dual mandate of low and stable inflation, robust real output growth and maximum employment growth.

Nonetheless, we present a strong case to show that nominal and real wage growth are relevant variables that can be monitored within the mandates of price stability (low and stable inflation), financial stability and maximum employment (single-digit unemployment rate). There are no contradictions to the information and signals they convey to policymakers. The bottom line is that we need to lower the inflation target range (regime) and achieve higher productivity growth. It is the anchor for low and stable nominal variables such as nominal wage and GDP growth.

Evidence contained in the book arrives at the conclusion of a transition to a lower inflation targeting regime of 2 to 4 per cent and a pragmatic approach to target the unemployment rate of 5 per cent by 2030. We are of the opinion that the transition to a lower inflation targeting regime can be opportunistic and leverage on the current period of disinflation.[1] Despite the inflationary pressures due to the exchange rate depreciation and oil price shocks, we are currently experiencing what Orhapnides and Wilcox (1996) referred to as "*a good fortune of disinflationary shocks*", especially driven by very benign demand side pressures and abating levels of political and policy uncertainty.[2] Policymakers can be deliberate and adjust the inflation target range lower. This approach will also spill over to the wage and inflation expectations formation process and lower inflation expectations and wage inflation. Evidence presented in the book shows that the association between nominal wage inflation and consumer price inflation is responding positively and the nominal wage premium is compressing. The nominal wage inflation trend is declining and converging towards that of consumer inflation. Lowering the inflation target range will complement this downward trend and further reinforce the convergence of nominal wage inflation towards a lower inflation target band. Thus, the decline in trend inflation and a lower inflation regime (target range) will set the tone and anchor all other nominal variables.

Empirical evidence in Gumata and Ndou (2019) shows that capital flows play an integral role in the maintenance of price stability mainly via the exchange rate channel. The stability of the exchange rate is an important pillar in the achievement of the price stability mandate and contributes to the highest sustainable sectoral growth. This means that policy interventions aimed at dealing with the adverse effects of the exchange rate volatility have to be implemented. Furthermore, Gumata and Ndou (2019) show that bank credit conditions and bank credit risk are instrumental factors in the propagation of the effects of capital flow shocks on credit growth. Capital flow shocks loosen the credit and financial constraints banks operate in since they have an impact on excess capital adequacy ratio (CAR), excess liquid asset holdings of banks and loan loss provisions. Evidence in this book shows that international trade shocks and export growth matter for the sectoral employment intensities. The impact of commodity booms and busts, productivity, the exchange rate and volatility shocks on exports, investment, output and

[1] See Orhapnides and Wilcox (1996) the Opportunistic Approach to Disinflation.

[2] Ndou et al. (2019) show that the exchange rate pass-through (ERPT) has declined and become much lower post-2015. The decline in the ERPT post-2011 is consistent with muted demand side inflation pressures, low consumer and business confidence mitigating inflationary pressures.

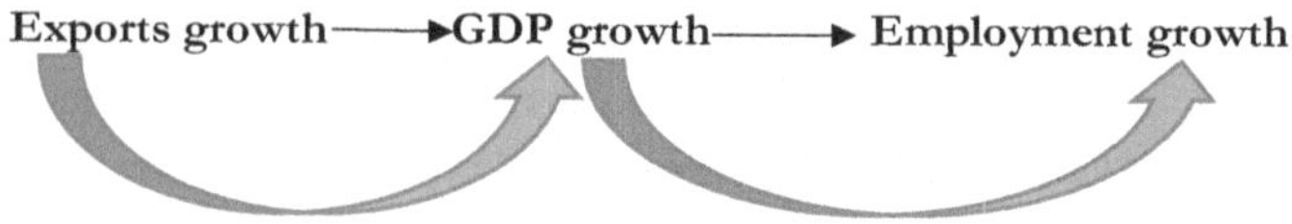

Fig. 3 The exports-led growth hypothesis. (Source: Adapted from Ancharaz 2011)

employment growth as shown in the analytical framework depicted in Fig. 3 demands policy co-ordination. Evidence contained in this book shows a robust association between exports growth, GDP growth and employment growth. Exports growth and commodity price booms are strongly associated with a high intensity of job creation, indicating the importance of the impact of trade, productivity growth and exchange rate shocks.

Furthermore, we establish that there is a dominance of the "*exports growth-led GDP growth*" hypothesis over the "*GDP growth-driven exports growth*" hypothesis, implying that exports growth is intensively associated with the impact of commodity price shocks on employment growth and less so with gross value added growth. Hence, the contribution of sectors such as mining and agriculture to GDP growth has been low. These sectors are exports growth–driven with very limited value added. The exports-led growth strategy is a necessary but insufficient condition for large-scale job creation. Hence, we conclude that there is a very strong and compelling case for beneficiation and greater value added along the value chains in the agricultural and mining sectors.

It is against the strong macrofinancial interlinkages between the impact of (i) capital flows on the exchange rate and its volatility and (ii) financial regulatory and macroprudential tools on the transmission of credit conditions, asset and commodity prices on real economic activity that the role of monetary, financial regulation and macroprudential policies in the attainment of price and financial stability and maximum employment (low unemployment) mandates is brought into sharp focus. As such, we argue that section 224 be rewritten to be clear as to what it means by price stability and explicitly include the financial stability mandate.

What do we mean by a pragmatic approach to single-digit unemployment rate? What rate of unemployment is the SARB to target? Figure 4(c) shows that at best the unemployment rate was at the lowest in 1996 at

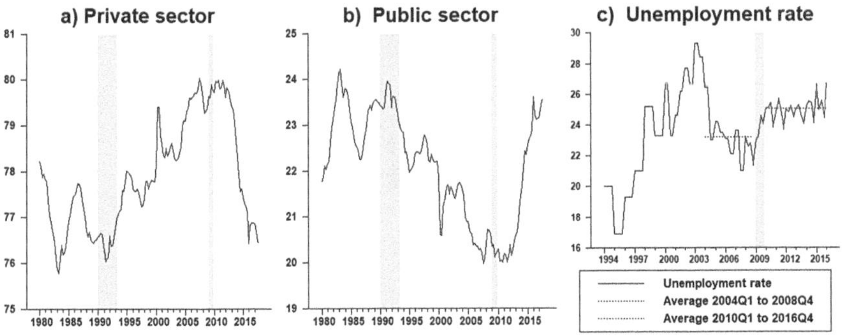

Fig. 4 Employment and unemployment rates. (Source: South African Reserve Bank and authors' calculations)

just above 16 per cent and recently at just above 22 per cent for the period 2003Q1 to 2008Q4. So, with the NDP unemployment rate targeted at 14 per cent by 2020 and 6 per cent by 2030, this means that there is a wide gap to close by 2030, taking into account that the unemployment rate rose to 29.1 per cent in 2019Q1.

Since we have no idea what the maximum (full) employment and the natural unemployment rate (alternatively, the lowest sustainable unemployment rate) is, we can infer from recent history that during the period 2004Q1 to 2007Q4 the South African economy grew at an average of 5.05 per cent and the formal non-agricultural sector employment intensity of GDP growth during this period was 2.99 per cent. Furthermore, we estimated that had real GDP and employment levels progressed along the linear trends post-2009 shown in Fig. 5, the level of real GDP would have been around R5 trillion and the level of formal non-agricultural employment would have been around 11 million.

This means that the economy would have added roughly 2 million jobs over the past ten years had the economy continued to add a constant net 35,000 jobs per quarter. These estimates exclude the non-formal agricultural sectors as shown in Fig. 6, where we provided robust empirical evidence showing that with the successful use of accelerated land reform as a policy intervention tool, this sector has a huge potential not only to contribute to large-scale employment creation, especially for youth, unskilled and low-skilled labour including those that the formal job market is highly unlikely to absorb, but can also serve the multiple

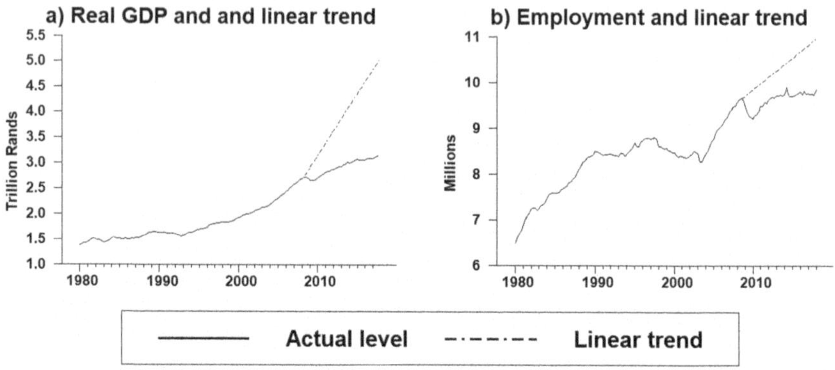

Fig. 5 Actual and trend real GDP and employment levels post-2009. (Source: South African Reserve Bank and authors' calculations)

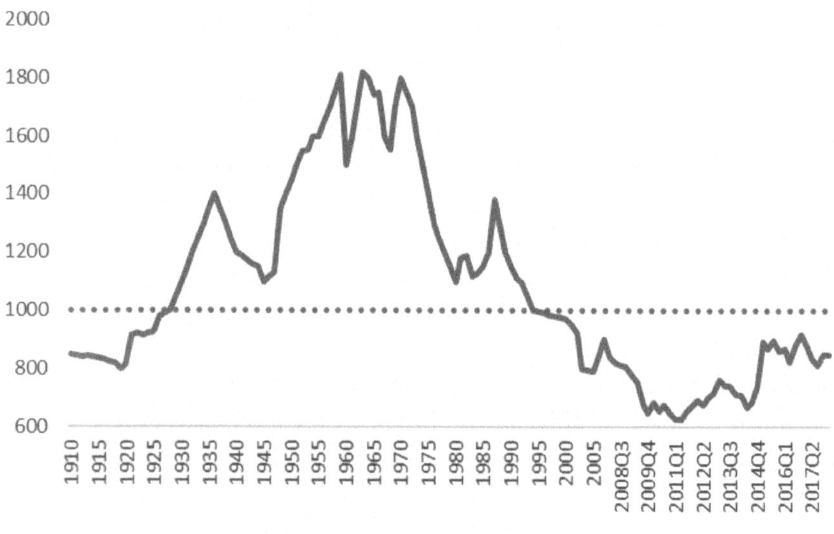

Fig. 6 Agricultural sector employment. (Source: BAFP 2011b and Statistics South Africa)

policy purposes of dealing with "*social justice and the social ills of hunger, poverty, inequality and unemployment*".

We dedicate a number of chapters in the book to deal with the role of accelerated land reform to grow and transform the agricultural sector, and thus contribute to the reduction of poverty and inequality.

Thus, a pragmatic approach implies the SARB be given a mandate to lower the unemployment rate by 10 percentage points to 16 per cent in the medium term and to below 10 per cent in the long run.[3] In the near and short term, the SARB should target to lower the unemployment rate by a maximum of 2 percentage points on an annual basis. This amounts to a lower unemployment rate by a cumulative 10 percentage points in 5 years and 20 percentage points in 10 years. The medium (five) to long-term (ten) years also allows policymakers to learn more about the unemployment rate (employment growth) responses to various shocks and the cyclical characteristics (cyclicality) in the employment creation and unemployment rate, and thus to fine-tune its policy operations to best support a lower inflation target, financial stability and low and stable unemployment rate (maximum employment growth). Furthermore, it allows the SARB the scope to deal with the criticism of the measurement of full employment and the natural rate of unemployment.

For instance, Yellen (2017) states that the Federal Reserve (Fed) expected the rapid decline in the unemployment rate would go below the Fed's estimate of the natural rate of unemployment or that full employment would lead to an increase in inflation. Brainard (2017) and Kashkari (2017) amongst others also raise the persistent disconnect (divergence) between the price stability and maximum (full) employment mandates in the US post-financial crisis. These authors show that the concept of maximum (full) employment is time-varying as the US economy has persistently surpassed estimates of maximum (full) employment without triggering higher consumer price and nominal wage inflation. Furthermore, these authors argue that had the US Fed stuck to the pre-crisis estimates of the maximum or full (un)employment rate target, additional workers might not have re-entered the labour force and the job market would have remained healthy. Krugman (2017) brings to the fore the fact that the US labour market has more than fully recovered to pre-crisis levels and yet there hasn't been a significant change in the skills of the workforce. Unemployment is lower than it was in 2007 and wage growth is still very low and benign. Similarly, Baker (2018) shows that

[3] The medium term is defined as three to five years and the long term is defined as eight to ten years. The near and short term are defined as one to three years.

the unemployment rates for workers without a high school degree hit a record low as less-educated workers continued to be biggest job gainers in post-global financial crisis recovery.

The critics of the NDP have highlighted that one major mistake the national planning commission made was that South Africa does not have an employment policy. This book contributes to the correction of this omission in the NDP by presenting empirical evidence showing that it is not only about the projections of employment numbers but the intricate interaction and co-ordination of a number of macroeconomic, trade, exchange rate and financial policies, regulatory and macroprudential policies, and the financial institutional design. Yes, the SARB should lower the inflation target range and target maximum employment growth (a low stable unemployment rate), as well as monitor and report on progress on inclusive growth. Productivity growth and investment growth shocks matter for output growth, employment growth and price stability. Hence, policy co-ordination becomes pertinent and binding, especially when the central bank mandate is expanded to explicitly include maximum employment over and above price and financial stability.

Pretoria, South Africa

Nombulelo Gumata
Eliphas Ndou

Reference

Ancharaz, V. 2011. Trade, Jobs and Growth in Africa: An Empirical Investigation of the Export-led Jobless Growth Hypothesis. *Mimeo*. Available at http://www.oecd.org/site/tadicite/48735521.pdf

Ancharaz, V., Mbekeani, K., and Brixiová, Z. 2011. Impediments to Regional Trade Integration in Africa. *African Development Bank Economic Brief*, 2(11).

Baker D. 2018. Economy Adds 157 000 Jobs in July, Little Evidence of Wage Pick Up in Wage Growth. Economist's View. https://economistsview.typepad.com/economistsview/unemployment/

BFAP. 2011a. South African Agricultural Baseline 2011.

BFAP. 2011b. The Contribution of the Agro-Industrial Complex to Employment in South Africa. Tech. Rep. June, The Bureau for Food and Agricultural Policy, Pretoria.

Brainard, L. 2017a. Understanding the Disconnect between Employment and Inflation with a Low Neutral Rate. Speech at The Economic Club of New York New York City, 5 September 2017.

Brainard, L. 2017b. Navigating the Different Signals from Inflation and Unemployment. Speech at the New York Association for Business Economics, New York City, 30 May 2017.

Gumata, N., and Ndou, E. 2019. *Capital Flows, Credit Markets and Growth in South Africa: The Role of Global Economic Growth, Policy Shifts and Uncertainties*. Palgrave Macmillan. ISBN 978-3-030-30887-2.

Kashkari, N. 2017. Why I Dissented at the March 2017 FOMC Meeting. https://www.minneapolisfed.org/news-and-events/messages/why-i-dissented.

Kganyago, L. 2017. Balanced and Sustainable Growth: The Role and Mandate of the SARB. A Lecture at the Unisa Graduate School of Business, 30 August 2017. https://www.bis.org/review/r170904a.pdf

Krugman, P. 2017. Inflation Targets Reconsidered. ECB Forum on Central Banking, May 2014 Monetary Policy in A Changing Financial Landscape. https://www.ecbforum.eu/uploads/originals/2014/pdf/speakers/PAPER_Paul_R_Krugman.pdf

Ndou, E., Gumata, N., and Tshuma, M.M. 2019. *Exchange Rate Pass Through, Second Round Effects and Inflation Process, Evidence from South Africa*. Palgrave Macmillan. ISBN 978-3-030-13931-5.

Orhapnides, A., and Wilcox, D. 1996. *The Opportunistic Approach to Disinflation*. Board of Governors of the Federal Reserve System. Finance and Economics Discussion Paper Series No. 96-24.

Yellen, J.L. 2017. From Adding Accommodation to Scaling It Back. Remarks by at The Executives' Club of Chicago, Chicago Hilton 720 S, Michigan Avenue, Chicago, IL. https://www.federalreserve.gov/newsevents/speech/files/yellen20170303a.pdf

Acknowledgements

We thank our colleagues at the South African Reserve Bank (various divisions within the Research Department), Statistics South Africa, Productivity South Africa (Leroi Raputsoane and Juliet Mashabela), The South African Chamber of Mines (Bongani Motsa), Agricultural Business Chamber (Agbiz) Wandile Sihlobo, South African Grain Information Service (SAGIS), Johannesburg Stock Exchange (JSE) Vuyo Mpumza, Professor Michael Aliber for providing data for farmland prices and Sandile Hlatshwayo for supplying data for the South African economic policy uncertainty index. We owe a great deal of gratitude to the anonymous reviewers. We also thank Thomas Doan at Estima Rats software for coding assistance and their courses.

Contents

List of Figures

List of Tables

1

Introduction

The South African National Development Plan (NDP) targets net 11 million new jobs or an unemployment rate of 6 per cent 2030 to increase the labour participation rate to 65 per cent. In addition, the NDP's overarching goal is to eliminate poverty, reduce inequality from the current aggregate level of 0.68 to 0.6. What needs to be done? This book contributes to academic and policy efforts to answer this question and forward concrete and implementable policy recommendations. This book is divided into six parts that are dedicated to answer this question.

- Part I deals with how the interaction between nominal wage inflation, consumer price inflation and the exchange rate appreciation and depreciation episodes influences output costs associated with disinflation.
- Part II evaluates the performance of the inflation targeting framework in South Africa and assesses whether nominal GDP growth targeting is a viable alternative.
- Part III estimates the output-employment intensities and the structural change indices. It decomposes overall productivity into changes of productivity within sectors and changes in the allocation of labour between sectors, alternatively structural change.

N. Gumata, E. Ndou, *Accelerated Land Reform, Mining, Growth, Unemployment and Inequality in South Africa*, https://doi.org/10.1007/978-3-030-30884-1_1

- Part IV deals with policy uncertainty, mining sector charter, exchange rate volatility, commodity price booms and busts, binding minimum wage increases and the mining sector.
- Part V addresses the policy of accelerated land reform in the agricultural sector and its implications for food security and affordability, price stability, output growth and employment growth, especially youth employment.
- Part VI deals with the interaction between the financial sector regulatory framework, the property rights clause and the South African Reserve Bank mandate.

We apply a variety of econometric techniques to capture the various aspects of the transmission of shocks into the South African economy. We test several hypotheses and the applicability of some theoretical models to determine whether they are agreeable and relevant for the South African economy. In all instances, we use various econometric techniques to assess the robustness of the empirical findings and the policy implications.

1.1 The Interaction Between Nominal Wage Inflation, Consumer Price Inflation and the Exchange Rate Appreciation and Depreciation Episodes Influences Output Costs Associated with Disinflation

This part of the book is premised on the inflation-wage spiral depicted in Fig. 1.1. The direct and indirect channels of transmission of the exchange rate depreciation affect labour markets, wage setting behaviour and consumer price inflation. The stages of the transmission channels indicate that the exchange rate depreciation shock (i) directly impacts nominal wage and consumer price inflation (first-round stage) via an increase in the import prices of input, production and finished goods and (ii) the inflationary changes are also transmitted into wage inflation via the indirect or second-round effects. Furthermore, inflation expectations play an important role in the link between nominal wage and consumer price inflation, alternatively, the wage-inflation spiral as shown in Fig. 1.1.

We find that nominal wage inflation and consumer price inflation display very similar disinflation episodes over time as shown in Fig. 1.2. Furthermore, the trends show that nominal wage inflation and consumer price inflation have trended downwards in a comparable fashion over

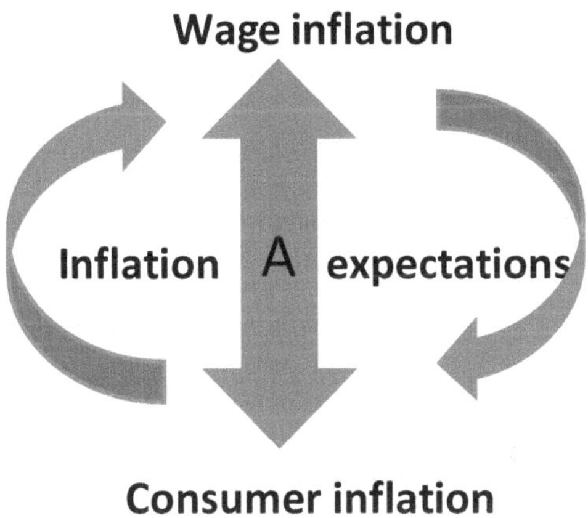

Fig. 1.1 Inflation-wage spiral relationship and the role of inflation expectations. (Source: Authors' drawing)

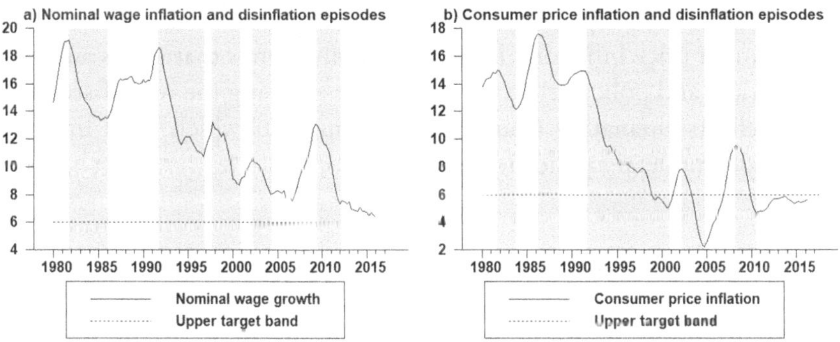

Fig. 1.2 Consumer and wage price inflationary and disinflation periods. (Note: Shaded areas represent the disinflation periods which are at least 2 percentage points lower than at the peak. The centred nine-quarter moving average inflation is expressed in per cent. Source: Authors' calculations)

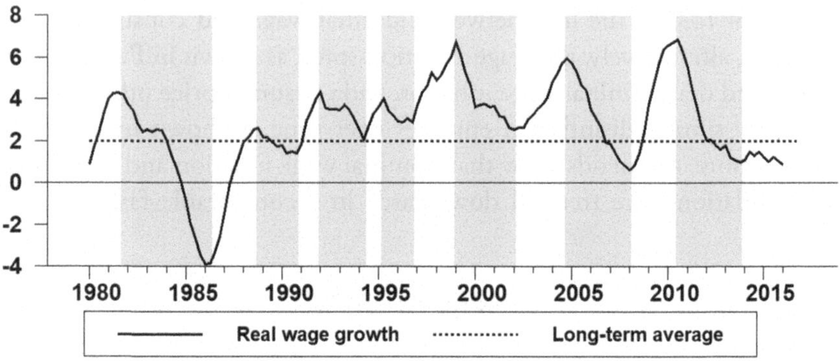

Fig. 1.3 Real wage inflationary and disinflation periods. (Note: Shaded areas refer to disinflation periods which are at least 2 percentage points lower than at the peak. The centred nine-quarter moving average inflation is expressed in per cent. Source: Authors' calculations)

time. The nominal wage inflation trend has declined significantly post the recession in 2009 and is approaching the upper band of the inflation targeting range.

Furthermore, Fig. 1.3 shows that real wage inflation has accordingly declined and has been persistently below the long-term average of 2.52 per cent since 2012Q1. This has narrowed the margin between nominal wage and consumer price inflation.

We conclude that the consideration of nominal wage growth does not necessarily imply a high level of inflation inertia or persistence compared to consumer price inflation. The policy implication is that this is another appropriate and policy-relevant approach at assessing the role of second-round effects emanating from the labour markets which is an integral part of the monetary policy formulation process.

1.2 An Evaluation of How the Inflation Targeting Framework Has Performed in South Africa

In light of prolonged deviations of real GDP growth and employment levels from linear trends post-2009 shown in Fig. 1.4, there has been a resurgence of arguments against the inflation targeting monetary policy framework. This part of the book chapter evaluates the performance of the inflation targeting regime in South Africa.

Insight from the relationship between output growth, output-gap and inflation (Phillips curve) shows that the relationship between the output-gap and inflation varies and this has been especially the case post-2009. Figure 1.5 shows that there are times during which both inflation and the output-gap move in the same direction, as well as times in which they diverge. The nature of shocks that drive inflation and the output-gap may at times move these variables in different directions. Pre-2009, the relationship between the output-gap and inflation was positive and steep but

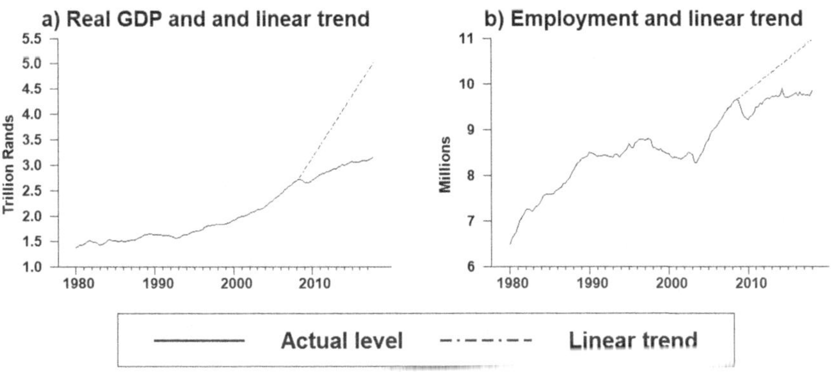

Fig. 1.4 Actual and trend real GDP and employment levels post-2009. (Source: South African Reserve Bank and authors' calculations)

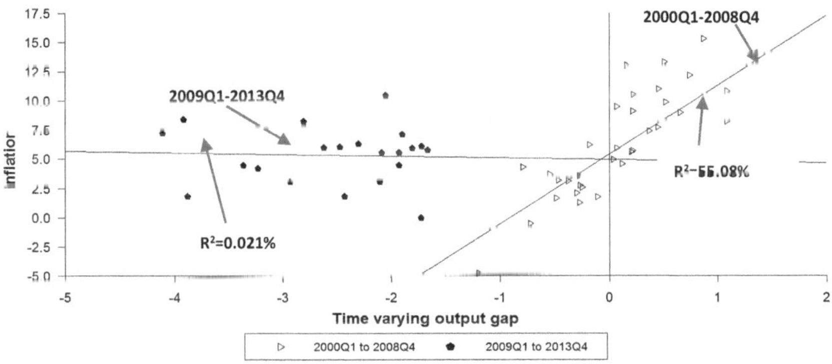

Fig. 1.5 Inflation and output-gap post-2009. (Source: Ndou and Gumata 2017)

it has been rather weak and slightly negative post-2009. These trends mean that the period post-2009 has been characterised by the simultaneous occurrence of a negative and widening output-gap and inflation deviations from the target band.

The flattening of the Phillips curve post-2009 implies that that inflation has become less responsive to resource slack (the output-gap) and is largely driven by other factors and shocks. Clarida (2019) states that a flatter Phillips curve is a proverbial double-edged sword. This is because it allows policymakers to support employment more aggressively during downturns as a sustained inflation breakout is less likely to occur when the Phillips curve is flatter. Nonetheless, a flatter Phillips curve also increases the cost economic output of reversing the unwelcome increases in longer-run inflation expectations. As a result, a flatter Phillips curve makes it more important that longer-run inflation expectations remain anchored at levels consistent with low and stable inflation. Furthermore, evidence shows that policymakers have considerable scope to engage in short-run demand management policies in the low inflation regime (when inflation is below 4.5) than in high inflation regime (when inflation is above 4.5). This is because there is a substantial degree of policy effectiveness in the low inflation regime and prices become more rigid as consumer price inflation moves below the 4.5 per cent inflation regime. Therefore, nominal demand shocks are unlikely to generate much inflation in the low inflation regime relative to the high inflation regime.

On the appropriateness of the current 3 to 6 per cent inflation target band, we demonstrate the importance of thresholds within the target range. Evidence shows that under different model specifications based on the economic growth theories, by the time the inflation rate hits 5 per cent, the economy has transitioned from a low to a high inflation regime as shown in Fig. 1.6. The transition functions within the current inflation target to capture the manner in which inflation moves from a low to a high inflation regime as it responds to certain shocks.

Furthermore, evidence shows that positive inflation shocks when inflation is between 0 and 3 per cent and below 4.5 per cent exert positive effects on GDP growth. This contrasts with negative effects exerted when inflation is above 6 per cent and 6.5 per cent, as GDP growth declines.

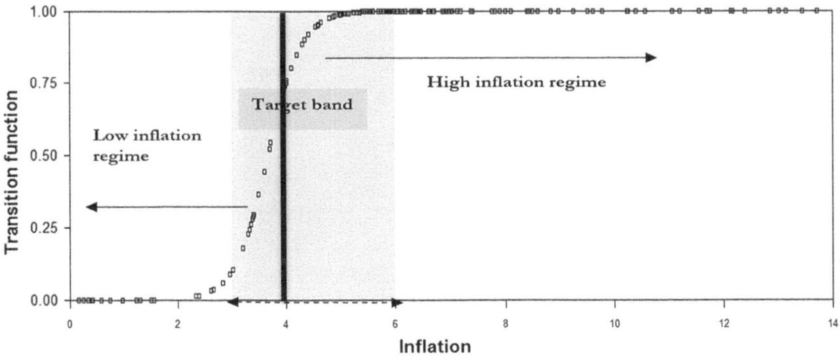

Fig. 1.6 The shape of the transition function for the inflation threshold. (Note: The vertical line in the shaded area denotes the estimated inflation threshold. Source: Ndou and Gumata 2017)

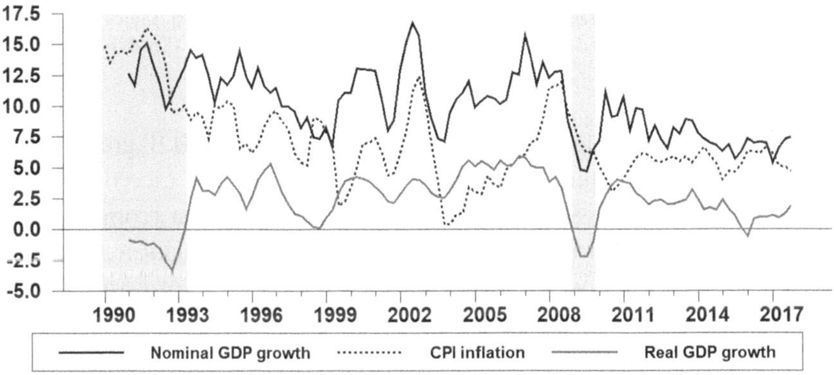

Fig. 1.7 Inflation, nominal and real GDP growth. (Note: The grey shaded areas denote the South African recessions. Source: South African Reserve Bank and authors' calculations)

These results imply that policymakers can exploit the inflation-output trade-off to their advantage when inflation is within certain thresholds within the current 3 to 6 per cent inflation target range. The transition functions of inflation from the low to the high inflation regime provide further evidence that a lower inflation target range of 2 to 4 per cent is consistent with a lower inflation regime.

On the issue whether nominal GDP (NGDP) growth targeting is a viable alternative to inflation targeting on South Africa, Fig. 1.7 shows that

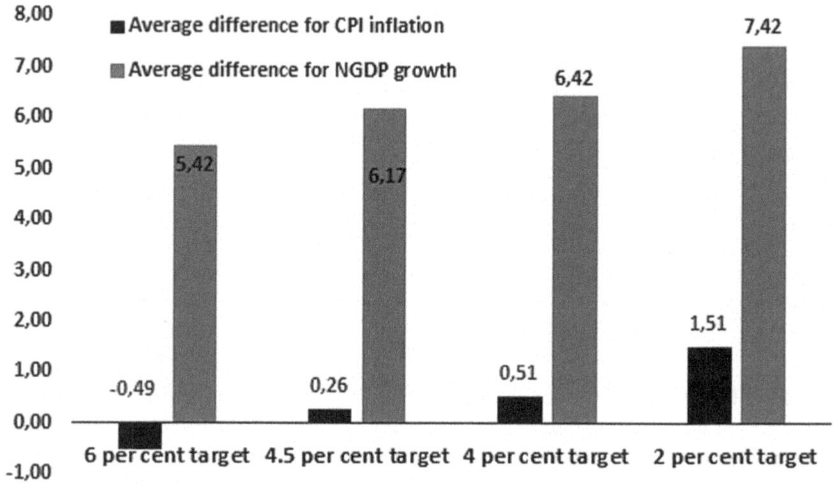

Fig. 1.8 Average differences between the actual repo rate and Taylor prescriptions for CPI inflation and NGDP growth under different targets. (Source: Authors' calculations)

real GDP growth is higher when the gap between the NGDP growth and inflation is wider. During recessions inflation tends to exceed NGDP growth resulting in lower real GDP growth. This suggests that a combination of lower inflation and high NGDP growth is needed to achieve high real GDP growth. When we compare the Taylor rule policy prescriptions of how the conduct of monetary policy would evolve under consumer price inflation and NGDP growth targets, we find that the repo rate would be aggressively tightened to bring NGDP growth to target as shown in Fig. 1.8. Monetary policy tightening and the associated costs of disinflation are heightened under the NGDP growth targets. Thus, we conclude that South Africa would be worse-off under NGDP growth targeting compared to the current flexible inflation targeting framework.

However, a higher target for NGDP growth implies a lower Taylor rule prescription. During the recession in 2009, the repo rate would have been much lower than the actual repo rate at the time. Similarly, towards the end of the sample between 2014Q1 and 2016Q4, the Taylor rule would have been the same as the actual repo rate if the South African Reserve Bank (SARB) was targeting 10 per cent NGDP growth and slightly lower if the target was 12 per cent.

Thus, the results imply a higher NGDP growth driven by for instance positive productivity and investment shocks as opposed to higher CPI inflation is consistent with a lower policy rate. This is because positive productivity shocks exert opposing effects on NGDP growth and inflation. The NGDP growth increases in response to positive productivity shocks whereas inflation declines. Similarly, positive investment shocks exert minimal inflationary pressures. We conclude that a higher NGDP growth target is not inconsistent with a lower CPI inflation target. A lower inflation target and a higher NGDP growth target are not mutually exclusive. Alternatively, a higher NGDP growth target and a low inflation target satisfy the dual mandate of low and stable inflation, real output growth and maximum employment growth.

1.3 A Lower Inflation Target Regime and Monetary Policy Credibility

To conclude the evaluation of the inflation targeting framework in South Africa, we assess the credibility of monetary policy conduct. Ndou et al. (2019) show that there are a number of ways in which the credibility of monetary policy conducted can be assessed. They use the Bordo and Siklos (2014, 2015), Lopez-Villavicencio and Mignon (2017) measures of credibility as shown in Fig. 1.9. Evidence indicates that monetary policy has become more credible during the inflation targeting period, especially

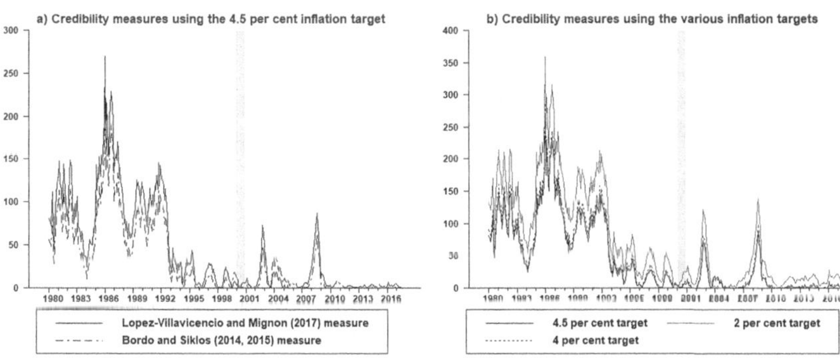

Fig. 1.9 Monetary policy credibility indicators. (Note: The grey shaded areas denote the South African recession. Source: Ndou et al. 2019)

post-2009. This is because the deviation of the inflation outcomes relative to the inflation target has been minimum, especially post-2009.

The conduct of monetary policy under the inflation targeting regime has fared in well and the credibility of monetary policy conduct has improved immensely and especially post-2009. This is because the deviation of the inflation outcomes relative to the inflation target has been minimum, especially post-2009. Evidence shows that it matters more where inflation outcomes are relative to the target itself. Economic agents' expectations of future inflation also matter. Post-2009, inflation outcomes have been more often than not, within the 3 to 6 per cent inflation target range. Nonetheless, viewed from the inflation expectations perspective, it seems that monetary policy conduct is less credible as inflation expectations have been largely "poorly" anchored during the inflation targeting period. This is despite the actual inflation outcomes relative to the inflation target as shown in Fig. 1.10.

Evidence indicates that the concurrence of the adverse supply shocks and positive inflation expectations shocks can have devastating effects on economic activity. The repo rate is adjusted aggressively due to a positive aggregate demand shock, and this translates into a quick decline in the response of inflation expectations. The simultaneous occurrence of adverse supply shocks and positive inflation expectations shocks that move economic variables in the same direction can have debilitating effects on economic

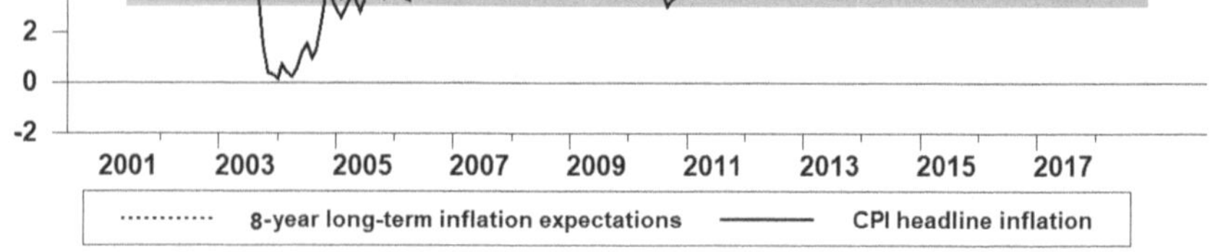

Fig. 1.10 Inflation and eight-year long-term inflation expectation. (Note: Shaded area denotes the inflation target band. Source: Gumata and Ndou 2017)

activity. This means that policymakers should take appropriate action when necessary to mitigate that expected prices do not become realised prices.

Thus, despite the divergence between the measures of credibility and inflation expectations, evidence shows that macroeconomic performance has been persistently robust in periods during which inflation has been between 2 and 4 per cent. These further bolster the case for lowering the inflation target range. Furthermore, it may also be the case that lowering the inflation target range is an indirect policy approach to anchor inflation and wage expectations lower in line with economic environments characterised by backward-looking inflation expectations processes. If the central bank manages to make the inflation target credible, in the sense of making economic agents' inflation expectations align with the inflation target, the stabilisation of inflation around its target becomes easier. This is because inflation outcomes are heavily affected by previous expectations of inflation. It becomes easier for policymakers to stabilise unemployment around its long-run sustainable rate. The trade-off between stability of inflation around the target and that of unemployment around its long-run sustainable rate becomes more favourable to policymakers when the conduct of monetary policy credible and inflation expectations are well anchored.

1.4 The Output-Employment Intensities and the Structural Change Indices

We estimate the output-employment intensities and find that the aggregate output-employment coefficients vary over time and were the lowest post-financial crisis. GDP growth above 2 per cent is associated with the highest growth in QES employment and, in particular, private sector employment growth. On the other hand, the doubling of output growth to 4 per cent and above results in a significant decline in the unemployment rate. At a sectorial level, evidence indicates that the most output growth employment intensity is generated by the construction sector followed by the transport, trade and finance sectors as shown in Fig. 1.11. For these sectors, a per cent growth in their output resulted in employment growth of between 0.7 per cent and 1 per cent in these sectors for the period 2000Q1 to 2016Q4.

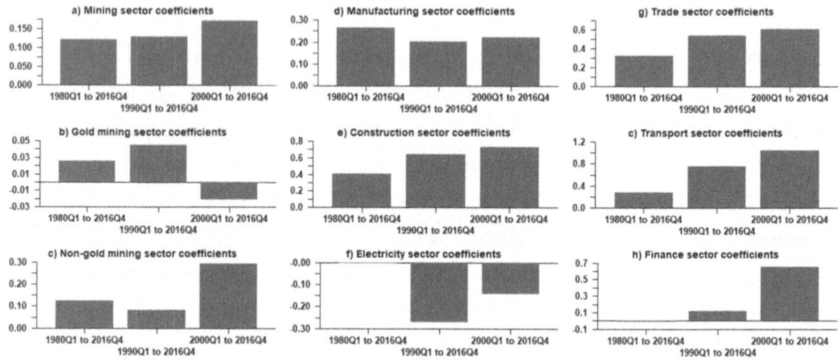

Fig. 1.11 Sectorial of the coefficients for the output-employment intensities. (Source: Authors' calculations)

The unemployment-employment relationship indicates that an increase in employment growth does lead to a decline in the unemployment rate. Thus, the unemployment rate moves less than one-for-one with employment growth and this worsened post-recession. The estimates indicate that a 1 percentage change (increase) in employment resulted in a −0.1-percentage point decline in the unemployment rate compared to a −0.4 percentage points decline pre-2007. The estimated delta coefficient of −0.4 percentage points raises the policy implications of whether it is sufficient to absorb new entrants into the labour market. More so because an increase in employment increases the returns to job search, which induces workers to enter the labour force and increase in the labour participation ratio. This means that policy interventions aimed at enhancing the labour absorption rate must focus on the transport, trade and finance, manufacturing and mining sectors. These measures will contribute to the objectives of maximum output and employment growth.

On the role of productivity, the McMillan and Rodrik (2011) show that changes in overall productivity can be disaggregated into changes of productivity within sectors and changes in the allocation of labour between sectors (or structural change) given by Eq. (1.1)

$$\Delta Y_t = \sum_{i=n} \theta_{i,t-k} \Delta y_{i,t} + \sum_{i=n} y_{i,t-k} \Delta \theta_{i,t} \tag{1.1}$$

Weighted sum of productivity growth within individual sectors also referred to as "within component of productivity growth"

Weighted sum of productivity growth effect on labour reallocation on different sectors also referred to as "structural change"

where Y_t is aggregate or economy-wide labour productivity, $y_{i,t}$ is specific sector labour productivity, $\theta_{i,t}$ is the share of employment in a specific sector i, the operator Δ denotes the change in labour productivity or employment shares between $t-k$ and t. The first decomposition term in Eq. (1.1) measures the "*within*" component of productivity growth, which is the weighted sum of productivity growth within individual sectors. The weights are the employment share of each sector at the beginning of the time-period. The second decomposition term measures "*structural change*" which is defined as the productivity growth effect on labour reallocation across different sectors of the economy. It measures the inner product of productivity levels with the change in employment shares across sectors at the end of the time-period. When the changes in employment shares are positively correlated with productivity levels, the structural change term will be positive. This means that structural change will increase economy-wide productivity growth.

Furthermore, the decomposition in Eq. (1.1) gives a better understanding of the productivity performance within individual sectors across economic activities. The analysis presents a comprehensive view as opposed to the partial analysis. For instance, a high rate of productivity growth within an industry can have implications for overall economic performance if the industry's share of employment shrinks rather than expands. Such that if the displaced labour ends up in activities with lower productivity, economy-wide growth will suffer and may even turn negative. In addition, McMillan and Rodrik (2011) indicate that the structural change component provides the direction of labour flows. In the case of growth-reducing (growth enhancing) structural change, the end-of-period relative productivity of sectors $\left(y_{i,t} / Y_t\right)$ is negatively (positively) related or correlated to the change in the sector employment share ($\Delta\theta_{\mathrm{i,y}}$).

We find that the labour productivity decomposition indicates that the structural change component has made negative contributions for the period 1990 to 2015 for the aggregate economy as opposed to the within component in Fig. 1.12. The sectoral decompositions shows that the "*structural change*" component has been growth reducing (negative contribution) especially for the (i) manufacturing; (ii) mining; (iii) electricity, gas and water and (iv) wholesale and retail trade, catering and accommodation sectors. On the other hand, the "*within*" component seems to have been the largest contributor especially for the (i) agricultural sector; (ii) wholesale and retail trade, catering and accommodation and (iii) finance, insurance, real estate and business service sectors. The evidence suggests that indeed the increased levels of market deregulation, various policy reforms aligned with the process of opening up the South African economy into a globalised world have benefitted the within component of labour productivity at the expense of the structural

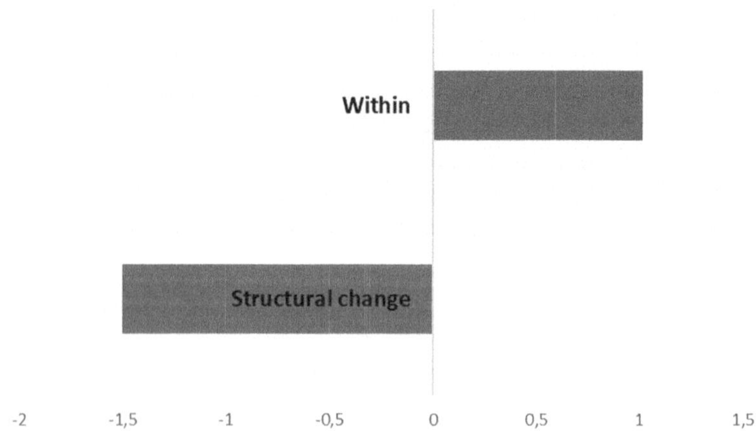

Fig. 1.12 McMillan and Rodrik (2011) decomposition. (Source: Authors' calculations)

component. The process of deregulation and globalisation has been highly beneficial to intra-sector productivity, but this was at the expense of structural changes within these sectors. Such trends manifest themselves in, for example, high concentration levels of very few firms and economic players within sectors with detrimental effects on competition, price formation, contribution to growth and employment.

1.5 The Exports-Led GDP Growth Hypothesis and the Stimulation of Economic and Employment Growth

Why is it the case that the mining sector accounts for more than a quarter of exports earnings but contributes so little to GDP and employment growth? Is it the case of the general observation that Africa's experience with the export-led strategy seems to be quite disappointing? Similarly, the agricultural sector is a net exporter and contributed 11.6 per cent to total exports as of 2017, making the sector a meaningful contributor to aggregate export earnings. But the agricultural sector gross value added (GVA) contribution averaged 2.67 per cent in the 2000s. We test the export-led growth hypothesis for the agricultural and mining sectors using the analytical framework depicted in Fig. 1.13.

The *"export-led growth" hypothesis* depicted in Fig. 1.4 is based on a two-step relationship between exports growth, GDP growth and employment growth. We establish whether exports have boosted GDP growth, and then examine if such growth has been job-creating. Within the exports and output growth nexus, the causality from exports to real output is the "exports-led GDP growth hypothesis" while the reverse causal flow from real output to exports is referred to as the "GDP growth-driven

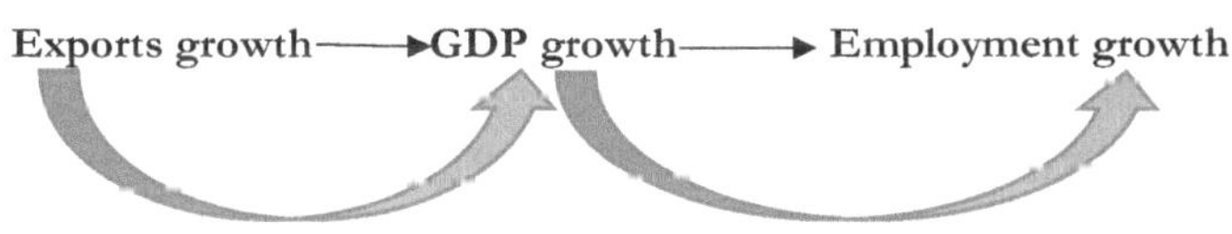

Fig. 1.13 The exports-led growth hypothesis. (Source: Adapted from Ancharaz 2011)

exports" hypothesis. The exports-led GDP growth hypothesis reflects the view that export-oriented policies help to stimulate economic growth.

We establish that for the mining sector at an aggregated and commodity sector level, exports growth responds more to aggregate GDP growth compared to the responses of GDP growth to aggregate and commodity sector exports growth. Thus, there is a prevalence of the "*GDP growth-driven exports growth*" hypothesis over the "*exports growth-led GDP growth*" hypothesis. But at the disaggregated commodity sector level, evidence confirms the validity of the dominance of the "*exports growth-led GDP growth*" hypothesis over the "GDP growth-driven exports growth" hypothesis. Evidence shows that exports growth is intensively associated with mining commodity employment growth and less so with mining commodity gross value added. Hence, the contribution of the mining sector to GDP has been on a circular decline and so low. The mining sector is an export-driven sector with very limited value add.

Furthermore, evidence indicates that private sector non-agriculture employment growth generated by positive shocks to GDP growth far exceeds and persists compared to that due to positive shocks to exports growth. Thus, we reject the "*export-led jobless growth*" hypothesis. Positive shocks to exports growth do induce positive effects on GDP and employment growth. But these positive effects are not persistent and do not result in intensive employment growth. Hence, the export-led strategy seems to be quite disappointing. Export-led growth is a necessary but insufficient condition for job creation in the mining sector. This means that there is a strong case for beneficiation especially for the commodity sectors. Exports growth is intensively associated with aggregate and commodity sector employment growth and less so with aggregate and commodity sector GVAs (output). By its very nature, minerals beneficiation implies an increase in value-added and a bigger role for the manufacturing sector in GDP.

The policy implication is that strategies aimed at investing in the value chains for these mining commodity sectors, developing new export markets and cushioning the sector against the cyclicality and severe slumps in global demand and commodity prices will support the mining sector as a "*sunrise industry*". The coal, metal ores, platinum group and other commodity sectors, which include the diamonds, copper, chrome and manganese will underpin the mining as a "*sunrise*" industry. These sectors will play an instrumental role in the employment creation and meeting the unemployment targets set out in the NDP. Commodity prices play an instrumental role in the sectors that will underpin mining as a "*sunrise*" industry; we argue that this places a sense of urgency on the exchange rate policy, the design of the proposed sovereign wealth fund, the co-ordination of the trade and other macroeconomic policies.

With respect to the agricultural sector, we establish that exports growth leads to employment intensity in the agricultural sector compared to increased gross value added post-2009 in stark contrast to what was the case, for instance, during the 1990s. The results show that the dominant effects are due to exports growth. The agricultural sector employment growth responds more to exports growth compared to output growth. The implication is that farmers are more responsive to exports demand and this increases the employment growth intensity in the agricultural sector. The "*output growth-driven exports growth*" hypothesis and strategy best explains developments in the agricultural sector. Trade openness and the export-oriented growth strategy augers well for the agricultural sector output, employment and labour productivity growth. In addition, food commodity price booms (busts) result in an increase (decline) in exports, output and employment growth. Food commodity price booms propagate (amplify) the effects of the positive and negative shocks throughout the sector. Nonetheless, although South Africa is doing relatively well in terms of food availability and quality (quantitatively and qualitatively), this does not directly imply food affordability.

1.6 Import Competition, the Effectiveness of Import Tariffs and Exchange Rate Depreciation in Selected Agricultural Sector Industries

What are the effects of exposure to import competition on the agricultural sector? First, we establish that the agricultural sector mostly imports rice, wheat, meat (largely poultry which accounts for more than 90 per cent of total imported meat), palm oil and alcoholic beverages (whiskies, rum, gin and other alcoholic beverages). Second, the breakdown of imports by country of origin shows that a large share of imports originates from Argentina, Indonesia and Brazil. Collectively, the products and the countries of origin account for 20 per cent of imports, respectively. The results from the Autor et al. (2016) approach used to assess the impact of import competition due to the importation of wheat, soybeans, meat and sunflower seeds on the agricultural sector employment show that a higher degree of import penetration has negative effects on the agricultural sector output and employment growth. However, the prices of, for instance, fresh versus frozen chicken portions and wheat clearly indicate that the imposition of import tariffs is not the ideal and effective tool to deal with prices, competition, output and employment growth in these agricultural sub-sectors. For instance, the divergence and the margin between the domestic and import price of chicken portions continued to widen despite the various rounds of import tariffs imposed. A similar picture emerges in the case of the wheat price which is largely determined by international factors. South Africa is a small player in the wheat market and cannot significantly affect international prices.

Evidence in the book implies that in the case of the poultry sector, the poultry sector is characterised by the oligopoly and vertically integrated market structure is incentivising anti-competitive behaviour. In such cases there is a clear and wide gap that policy interventions via the land reform policy can help close. This is the case with evidence of monopoly market structure in the agricultural sector in general. A well-structured and executed land reform policy strategy can help bring about competition in the agricultural sector and sub-sectors such as the poultry industry with benefits to the aggregate economy and consumers. In addition, substituting imports with locally produced commodities can trigger a range of upstream and downstream multipliers with positive effects on the intensity of job creation in the agricultural sector. Structural reforms and changes in the wheat and poultry market structure via land reform policy as a strategic tool can have the desired effects far more than what the import tariffs and exchange rate depreciation have been able to achieve. The strategy of using the accelerated land reform policy augers well with the argument that feed costs constitute 60 per cent of a chicken company's total costs.

1.7 Can Accelerated Land Reform Help Reduce Poverty and Inequality?

Data shows that recipients of child income support grants constitute almost 70 per cent of people receiving social income grants. At the same time, the recipients of the child income support grants constitute more than 70 per cent of social income grants across all provinces. Thus, despite being smaller in value of pay-out, it means that an increase in social income grants will disproportionality benefit recipients of child support grants. Figure 1.14 shows that mothers between ages 20–24 years, 25–29 years and 30–34 years were responsible for 25.5 per cent, 26.2 per cent and 21.3 per cent of reported births, respectively, in 2017.

Furthermore, data shows that children and women bore the brunt of the adverse effects of extreme poverty. At the same time, the age groups 15 to 34 years also constitute youth unemployment. Figure 1.15 shows that the age group 15–24 years had the highest unemployment rate, lowest absorption and labour participation rates in 2018Q2. Thus, data implies that the age groups 15 to 24 accounted for a larger share of births

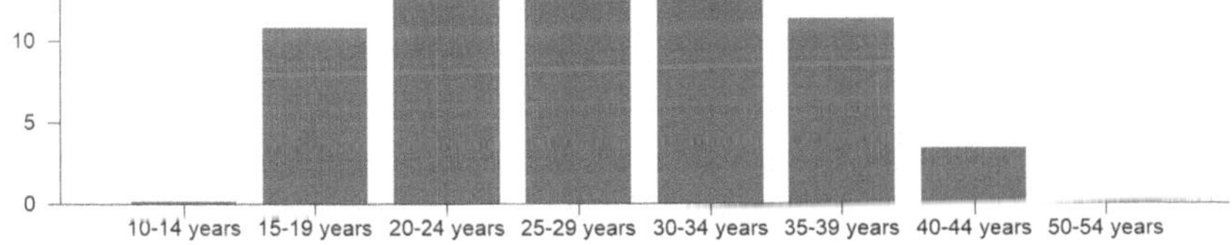

Fig. 1.14 Age distribution of reported births in 2017. (Source: Statistics South Africa)

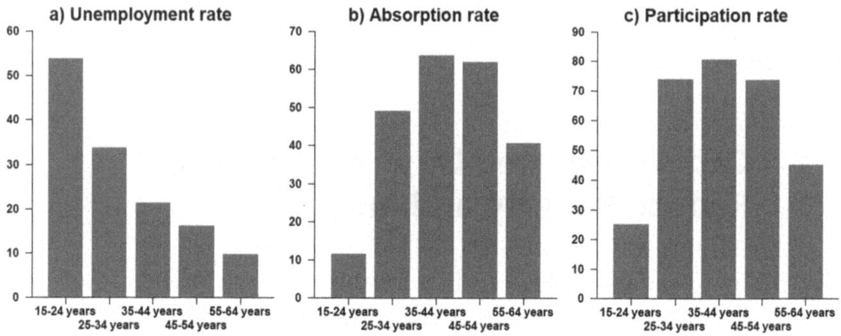

Fig. 1.15 Age distribution of unemployment, absorption and labour participation rates. (Source: Statistics South Africa)

in 2017. Simultaneously, this age group has the highest unemployment rate, lowest absorption and participation rates. We argue that this is where the "*vicious circle of exclusion, unemployment and poverty*" lies and therefore there is a strong and compelling case for *bold and decisive supply side policy* interventions to target and break the persistent negative effects of race, gender, unemployment and poverty.

We find that compared to the demand side policy interventions such as an increase in social income grants and the binding minimum wage, accelerated land reform policies as supply side policy interventions are broader; unleash potential GDP; and contribute to changing the ownership patterns in the economy, increasing participation in the economy and labour absorption economic inclusion, and lowering of the Gini coefficient (income inequality). But we establish that as demand side policy interventions, social income grants and the binding minimum wage reinforce each other, especially in cases where targeted part of the population is employed and earns a minimum wage. Figure 1.16 shows that an increase in the binding minimum wage persistently reinforces the effects of the increase in social income grants on the Gini coefficient.

An increase in social income grants has more persistent positive effects when accompanied by an increase in the binding minimum wage. Thus, a desirable policy intervention is that which complements an increase in social income grants with employment opportunities that pay a minimum wage. Furthermore, we find that there was a direct impact of social income grants in displacing the agricultural sector as a key source of income in the

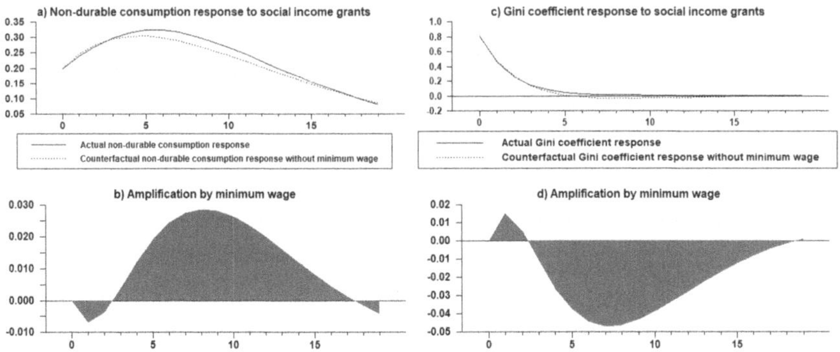

Fig. 1.16 Responses to positive shocks to social income grants and amplifications by the minimum wage. (Source: Authors' calculations)

rural areas. This means that social income grants acted as supplementary income and largely replaced reliance on the agricultural sector as a source of income. The expansion in social income grants contributed to the decline in the reliance on the agricultural sector as a key source of income. Although, social income grants as a demand side policy intervention achieve their set objective of increasing consumption expenditure and improving the capacity of households to spend, they fail dismally in terms of solving the long-term effects low growth, high unemployment, high poverty rates and diversifying sources of income for rural communities.

Accelerated land reform and an increase in hectares planted lead to an increase in the agricultural sector output, investment and employment, and they lower the Gini coefficient. Nonetheless, we provide robust empirical evidence that the policies of accelerated land reform and expropriation of land without compensation on their own are necessary but insufficient conditions to reduce unemployment poverty and inequality. The policies of accelerated land reform and expropriation of land without compensation must be accompanied by the productive utilisation of land as captured in the Land and Agricultural Development Bank Act (2002), a wholistic approach to post-settlement support and favourable trade policies. These supportive policy interventions include, for example, provision of persistent investment in supportive infrastructure, ample funding for housing, sanitation, agricultural development and revolution, innovation, productivity, profitability and so on.

1.8 Do the Land Redistribution and Increase in Hectares Planted Policies Complement Each Other?

Accelerated land redistribution and an increase in hectares (area) planted are broader supply side policy interventions aimed at dealing with the problem of perennial poverty, income and wealth inequality at a much broader level. They are supply side policy interventions aimed at unleashing potential GDP, changing the ownership patterns in the economy and increasing participation in the economy, labour absorption and economic inclusion. Land enters the production function as a primary resource with multifactor effects. In addition, it is not only the agricultural sector that stands to benefit from accelerated land reform and an increase in area (hectares) planted, but a number of sectors such as manufacturing, exports, transport, wholesale and retail trade, catering, accommodation and tourism, finance and insurance services, community and social services.

The policy of accelerated land reform and an increase in hectares planted are aimed at creating a class of entrepreneurs and self-employed people through the formation of co-operatives, small and medium enterprises. These policy interventions also present a channel through which employment can be created. Accelerated land reform and an increase in hectares (area) planted might not have a direct and instantaneous impact on poverty and inequality as such but may work via a number of channels to affect output, investment, exports and employment growth, poverty and inequality. This, therefore, implies that there are additional channels, such as the exchange rate, asset price, collateral and wealth effects and Tobin's Q involved in the transmission of the shocks to accelerated land reform and increase in hectares planted into the real economy. Furthermore, accelerated land reform and an increase in hectares (area) planted contribute to food security and affordability which in turn can be channelled to support sustainable school nutrition systems to offer more alternative nutritious foods and further alleviate poverty. For instance, Gordon and Ruffini

(2018) show that the impact of school-based child nutrition services extends beyond the academic gains. It has a potential to improve a range of student outcomes extending beyond test scores. Thus, accelerated land reform and an increase in hectares (area) planted policy interventions are ultimately aimed at lowering poverty and inequality, but they are expected to have a different impact on growth in output, investment, exports, employment, labour participation and absorption.

Evidence in the book shows that the Gini coefficient declines and remains depressed across horizons in response to positive hectares (area) planted shock and the agricultural sector employment growth remains positive. In addition, the positive land redistribution shock amplifies the decline in the Gini coefficient and the increase in the agricultural sector employment growth. Similarly, a positive land redistribution shock to land redistribution increases employment growth and lowers the Gini coefficient in Fig. 1.17, and these effects are propagated by the increase in hectares (area) planted.

Thus, we conclude that the policy of land redistribution and increase in hectares (area) planted policies are complementary policy tools that reinforce each other. A combination of these supply side policy tools exerts the desired effects on the agricultural sector employment growth and leads to a decline in the Gini coefficient.

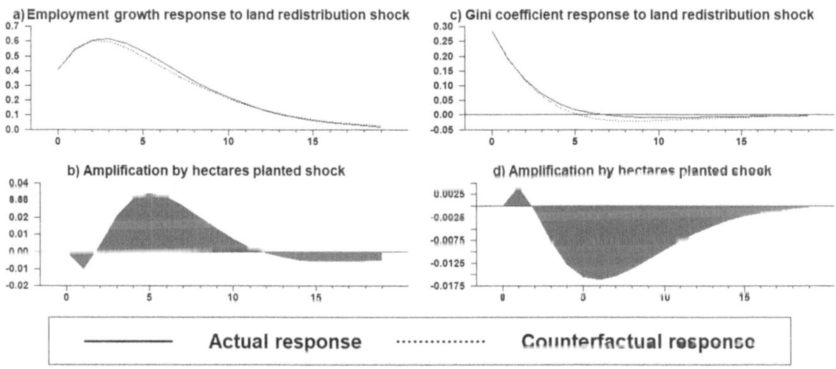

Fig. 1.17 Responses to positive land redistribution and propagation by hectares (area) planted shocks. (Source: Authors' calculations)

1.9 What Does the Accelerated Land Reform Policy Imply for Youth Unemployment?

We explore the impact of positive shocks to the agricultural sector on youth employment. This is important because within the accelerated land reform policy and land expropriation without compensation discourse, there has been much talk about the role of the agricultural sector in absorbing a large share of youth for gainful employment, thus leveraging on the "*youth dividend*". Evidence shows that there is a positive association between growth in employment in the agricultural sector and youth employment. The bilateral relationships in Fig. 1.18 indicate that the variation in the agricultural sector employment is associated with an increase of 46 per cent in the 15 to 24 years and 51 per cent in the 25 to 34 years. At the same time, youth employment increases when lead by increases in aggregate agricultural sector employment.

Furthermore, Fig. 1.19 shows that employment growth for all age groups increases in response to a positive shock to the agricultural employment growth. But the agricultural employment growth for the age group 15 to 24 years increases more, followed by that of the 25 to 34 years age group. This implies that youth employment benefits from positive shocks to the agricultural sector. Thus, policies aimed at growing the agricultural sector such as accelerated land reform and support for the agricultural

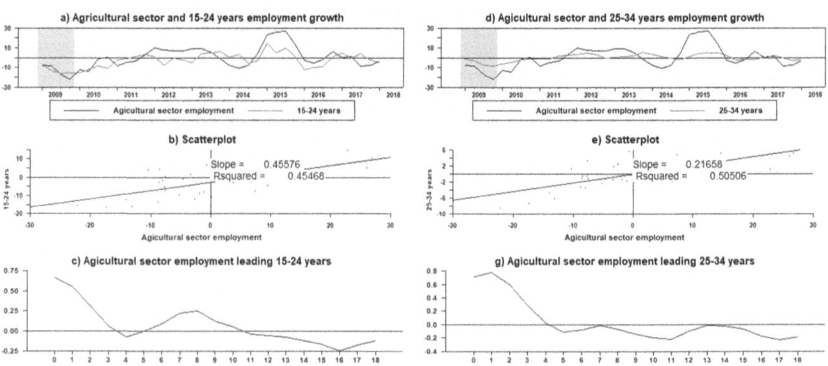

Fig. 1.18 Agricultural sector and youth employment. (Source: Statistics South Africa and authors' calculations)

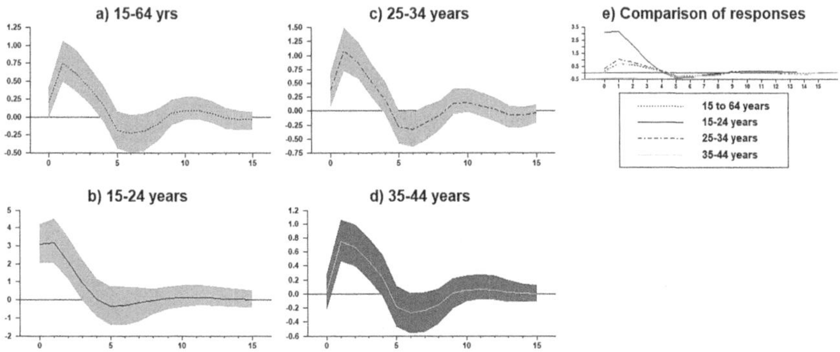

Fig. 1.19 Responses to agricultural sector employment. (Source: Authors' calculations)

sectors in various forms such as investment in irrigation, research and development will benefit employment creation especially the absorption and participation of youth (new entrants) in the labour markets. Such a policy strategy will also lead to increased rural labour absorption and participation and lower the unemployment rate in the so-called rural provinces.

The accelerated land reform policy has to be mindful of the country's gender disparities so that it can help reduce the degree of gender inequality. Data shows that women constitute only 23 per cent of land redistribution beneficiaries between 1994 and 2016. Women are a minority of beneficiaries in a majority of provinces and make up less than one quarter of beneficiaries of land redistribution as shown in Fig. 1.20. What can policymakers do to change this trend and increase the participation of women, especially in the rural areas in agriculture? We argue in the book that there is a case to be explicit and clear as to what "*equitable basis*" in section 25(5) means when it comes to redressing gender imbalances in the accelerated land redistribution policy. At the same time, at the policy level, the ownership of land and participation of women in the agricultural sector should be encouraged, enforced and supported via legislation as is the case with the Land and Agricultural Development Bank. Such legislation and laws should be complemented by setting up mechanisms through which the implementation is monitored and evaluated against set objectives and targets.

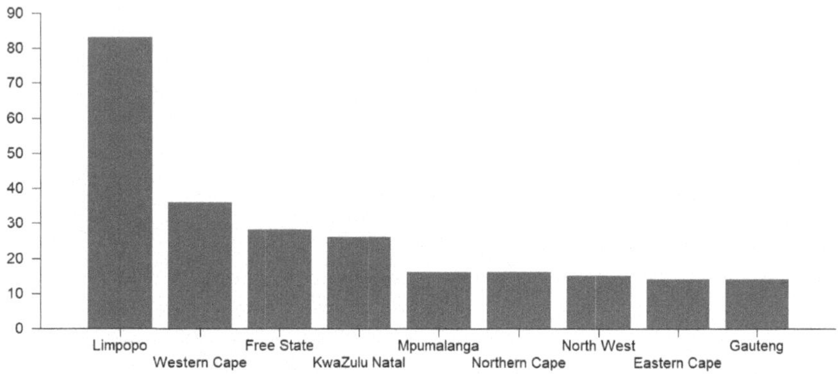

Fig. 1.20 Percentage of women beneficiaries in land reform between 1994 and 2016. (Source: Umrabulo No. 43, 2018)

Vast literature in this area indicates that different forms of approaches to land reform have had different effects in addressing gender, class and poverty. As a result, land acquisition and the choice of land for redistribution model have implications for the impact of land reform on gender, class and poverty. For instance, Netshipale et al. (2007) present evidence showing that the changes in land redistribution policies over time resulted in significant differences in beneficiary participation among land redistribution models. The implementation outcomes of land redistribution indicate that the Settlement Land Acquisition Grant (SLAG) model benefitted the poor while the Land Redistribution for Agricultural Development Phase 1 (LRAD1), Land Redistribution for Agricultural Development Phase 2 (LRAD2) and Proactive Land Acquisition Strategy (PLAS) models benefitted mostly other social classes. Therefore, the approach to accelerated land redistribution has to pay attention not only to gender but also class which is a proxy for poverty. We have shown that poverty is also disproportionately distributed along racial lines.

What should policymakers do to make sure that the gains in the gender distribution in the agricultural employment are accelerated? What does this mean for accelerated land reform? Jacobs et al. (2003) state that the LRAD programme was designed and promoted as a flagship programme through a class of black commercial farmers, the so-called *emerging black farmers*. We argue that with respect to addressing the gender and class imbalances on land ownership and participation in the agricultural sector, intentional programmes such as these must be designed and implemented. Policies that are intentionally designed to increase the participation *of women, especially from rural and poor* backgrounds, have to be designed, implemented and evaluated to assess their success rate. We also stated that McKinsey & Company (2015) and BFAP (2011) show that the Eastern Cape, KwaZulu-Natal and Limpopo provinces present significant opportunities for the agricultural sector. Thus, such a scheme can be guided by the areas identified and the employment matrix presented in BFAP (2011) to also address aspect related to size and scale for the involvements of targeted beneficiaries.

1.10 The Role of Investment and Productivity Shocks on Output and Employment Growth

A recurring theme in the evidence presented in the book are the spill-over effects of investment and productivity growth shocks on output and employment growth. For instance, we establish that the average gross value added contribution by the agricultural sector was at 3.12 per cent in the 1960s compared to 2.67 per cent in the 2000s. The contribution of gross fixed capital formation (investment) by the agricultural sector has also been on a persistent decline since the 1960s. It contributed more than 10 per cent to aggregate investment in the 1960s compared to an average of 3.24 per in the 2000s as shown in Fig. 1.21.

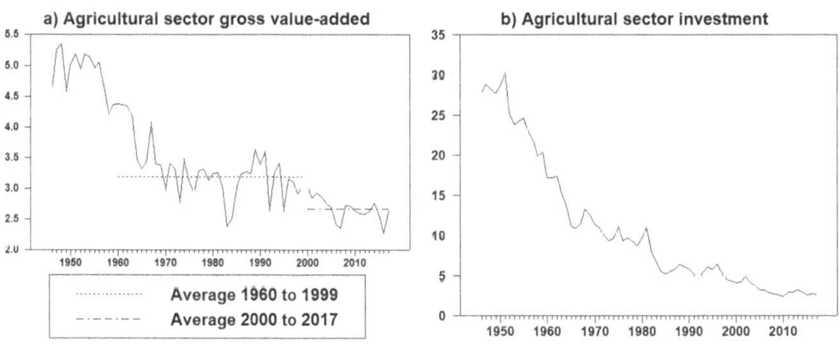

Fig. 1.21 Agricultural sector contribution to aggregate gross value added and investment. (Source: South African Reserve Bank and authors' calculations)

We find that positive agricultural sector employment growth increases more than output growth in response to positive shocks to the agricultural investment growth, implying that output growth tends to be labour intensive (creates more employment). At the same time, labour productivity improves. Thus, increasing investment growth and expanding investment in activities such as irrigation, research and development agriculture will improve the agricultural sector GDP and employment growth. Investment growth exerts effects similar to those of a technological change shock of productivity growth. Furthermore, the results for a positive shock to area cultivated in the former homelands indicate that agricultural output, employment and labour productivity increase. This means that bringing underutilised land in the former homelands and communal areas will make a significant and meaningful difference in the agricultural sector contribution to growth, employment and labour productivity. But increasing investment alone is not sufficiently large enough to boost agricultural sector output, employment and labour productivity. In fact, the results show that bringing in underutilised land in the former homelands and communal areas more than doubles the response of the agricultural sector output growth, employment and labour productivity growth.

Similarly, we establish that an investment-led strategy is superior in the mining sector. Nonetheless, investment growth is a necessary but insufficient condition. Commodity prices are an important part of a thriving mining sector. A combination of an increase in commodity prices and demand for mining exports augers well for mining investment. In particular, we find that persistent shocks, especially of positive shocks to commodity prices, lead to persistently higher levels of mining investment as opposed to non-persistent shocks. Furthermore, our results concur with findings in Fornero and Kirchner (2014) showing that agents learn over time about the true persistence of the commodity shock. If the persistence of a commodity price shock turns out to be high, then higher expected returns of capital especially in the commodity sector can trigger an investment boom that has important spill-over effects on investment in other sectors and the rest of the economy. The findings reinforce policy implications of establishing a sovereign wealth fund as an instrument for long-term planning and management of mineral resources.

1.11 Impact of Binding Minimum Wage Shocks in the Mining and Agricultural Sectors

We dedicate a number of chapters in the book to assess the sectorial impact of an increase in the binding minimum wage. A binding minimum wage increased from a low R2000 per month in 2001 to R10,000 per month in 2016. At this level, the minimum wage in the mining sector is more than double the National Minimum Wage of R3500. We find that that there are differences in the responses to an increase in the minimum at the aggregate and disaggregated mining sector. Employment growth declines across sectors and the decline is severe at the aggregate level. At the disaggregated level, the decline in other mining sector employment is statistically insignificant compared to the gold and coal mining sectors. Unit labour costs decline across sectors and this is on account of the increase in labour productivity. Labour productivity increases in response to an increase in the minimum wage especially in the coal and other mining sectors. An increase in the minimum wage in the mining sector pushes employment and labour productivity growth in different directions. This is especially the case for the coal mining and other mining sectors.

Thus, the impact of an increase in the binding minimum wage in the mining sector is best characterised by the institutional model which assumes that firms respond to an increase in the minimum wage by improving their overall efficiency though two channels, namely, (i) reducing organisational inefficiencies and or (ii) increasing the productivity of employees. The pass-through of an increase in the minimum wage and labour costs into higher prices is neutralised by the increase in efficiency. The mining sector mainly adjusts via the employment and labour productivity growth channels. This means that the mining sector curtails employment growth, that is, the sector employs less people than otherwise would have been the case in the absence of a binding increase in the minimum wage. But at the same time the mining sector increases labour productivity to adjust and neutralise the impact of the increase in the minimum wage on employment growth. The imposition of a higher minimum wage in the mining sector does not necessarily destroy jobs but may hinder the intensity of job creation. Labour productivity gains are used as the channel to neutralise and cushion employment losses (direct layoffs) in the sector.

From a policy perspective, policymakers have to pay attention to such idiosyncratic adjustment mechanisms to increases in the binding minimum wage especially when the mining sector is earmarked as a "sunrise industry" which is meant to contribute meaningfully to high and sustainable employment growth. In addition, setting up a sovereign wealth fund as an instrument for long-term planning and management of mineral resources will also assist the sector to adjust to such binding wage shocks. This is over and above broadening the scope of employee incentives beyond the reliance on just increases in the binding minimum wages.

On the other hand, we find the agricultural sector output, the minimum wage and employment increase in response to positive shocks to labour productivity. This implies that the agricultural sector conforms to the wage efficiency hypothesis. The increases in labour productivity growth shocks are transmitted via an increase in output, wages and employment growth in the agricultural sector. Furthermore, positive shocks to the minimum wage exert the similar effects as those of a food commodity price bust and monetary policy tightening on employment. However, the increase in the minimum wage does not result in a decline in the agricultural sector output as opposed to the effects exerted by the food commodity price bust and monetary policy tightening. The agricultural sector output growth is unaffected by the increase in the minimum wage as farmers decrease the rate of employment but increase the rate of hours worked.

The comparison of the effects of food commodity price busts, exports growth slumps, monetary policy tightening and the increase in the minimum wage indicate that exports growth slumps are the most potent channel through which the negative effects of factors such as a slowdown in global demand and droughts are transmitted to the agricultural sector. The employment decline due to the minimum is far miniscule compared to that induced by a slump in exports growth and the monetary policy tightening.

Furthermore, the net effects of all the shocks indicate that the concurrence of all these shocks has a devastating effect on the agricultural sector output and employment growth. The implication is that the concurrence of the implementation of a binding minimum wage, commodity price bust, exports growth slump and monetary policy tightening exert severe and persistent negative effects on the agricultural sector. Employment losses do occur due to the increase in the binding minimum wage, but these are far muted compared to those due to exports growth slumps and monetary policy tightening. Thus, global demand, food commodity prices and the balance sheet channel of the monetary policy transmission matter for the agricultural sector.

Evidence shows that positive shocks to the minimum wage result in an increase in the capital-labour ratio. This implies that farmers not only increase hours worked in response to an increase in the binding minimum wage, but they also increase the rate at which the capital replaces labour in the production process, hence there is no decline in output. Thus, hours worked and the introduction of labour-reducing practices explain the adjustment through which the agricultural sector adjusts to a binding minimum wage in line with the institutional model which assumes that firms respond to an increase in the minimum wage by improving their overall efficiency through two channels, namely, (i) reducing organisational inefficiencies and/or (ii) increasing the productivity of employees. The adjustment process also results in the substitution of workers with capital.

1.12 The Role of the Land Bank, Postbank and Lower-Tier Banks

In this book, we argue that in order to make a success of the accelerated land reform policy, we need to rethink the institutional arrangements and the financing of the land reform policy and agricultural sector. This is especially important within the context of accelerated land reform, productive use of redistributed land and the agricultural revolution envisaged in the 2018 State of the Nation address by the president and the vision contained in the NDP. In addition, we argue that the issue of funding models and institutional design is not only applicable to the agricultural sector but also to the funding of small and medium enterprises and housing as they form part and parcel of a successful land reform and redistribution policy, alternatively, what Moseneke (2014) refers to as the democratic consolidation achieving urban and rural land equity.

We present evidence that the relative size of the Land Bank size and funding of the agricultural sector by commercial banks constitute between 1 per cent and 2 per cent of the banking sector. The Land Bank is unable to meet its developmental mandate of bridging the gaps where the perceived risk of transactions exceeds the appetite of commercial bank funders such as development projects, financing farmers with limited assets to offer as security (collateral) under the current funding model and institutional design. To the effect that the Land Bank reports that it had to relinquish profits and use direct lending channels in order to subsidise the interest rates to emerging farmers. Furthermore, the business and funding models of the Land Bank are very similar to those of commercial banks. There is not much differentiation between the Land Bank and other commercial bank funding models and loan rates.

Thus, there is a role that agricultural co-operatives can play in complementing the Land Bank especially in development funding for the agricultural sector value chain. This is especially important given the fact that specialised institutions to serve the agricultural sector can be better organised to price and manage the risks posed by new entrants in the agricultural sector at the scale envisaged by the land reform policy and the agricultural revolution.

First, the Land Bank in essence is a state Bank. This means that the government will have to capacitate the Land Bank in various ways so that the set objectives in the Land and Development Bank Act are fully achieved. One of the ways in which the Land Bank can be capacitated is via a persistent and incremental injection of cash over a prolonged period of time. This is over and above the implementation and enforcement of a rigorous financial and prudential regulatory environment to make sure that the risks faced by the bank are well managed and that the new business model to support the accelerated land reform policy, rural development and agricultural revolution is sustainable over the long run. This is particularly important given results showing that investment growth takes the biggest knock and employment growth remains depressed for a prolonged period. Investment, innovation and employment growth form part of the core mandate of the Land Bank, namely, (i) sustainability, productivity, competitiveness, investment, innovation and profitability of famers, (ii) agricultural entrepreneurship and job creation and (iii) the development of thriving rural financial systems.

Second, based on the size of the balance sheet, we cannot speak of the financial landscape and lower-tier banks without the inclusion of the Postbank. The Postbank is a fully fledged bank which is mandated to offer a range of financial services, in particular to rural and low-income communities that have little or no access to banking facilities and financial services. The Postbank reports that over and above offering banking and financial services to social income grant recipients, in 2005 it became the leading provider of Mzansi accounts in South Africa with more Mzansi account holders than any other bank, which include the big four banks. The Postbank is a significant player in the banking and financial system and provides essential financial services to households in the lower income categories. This is financial inclusion and, in part, the fulfilment of the mandate of financial innovation and the development of thriving rural financial systems which is at the core of accelerated land reform. The Postbank reports that it has over 2000 post offices across the country. This is a massive footprint which should be leveraged on to fundamentally change the rural economies.

Third, the co-operative banks, although few and small, are growing and profitable. In addition, there were 24 co-operative financial institutions (CFIs) across the country, with assets to the tune of R142 million, R115 million deposits and have extended loans to the amount of R94 million. We are of the opinion that co-operative financial institutions subject to some regulatory requirements have the potential to become fully fledged co-operative banks. Therefore, they are the feeding pipeline to expanding lower-tier banks across the country. This means that with full adherence to the regulatory requirements and sufficient support, the number of co-operative banks can easily grow to more than ten spread across the country. In turn, the sustainable growth of co-operative banks will contribute to the growth and increase in the number of mutual banks. Hence, we argue that to bridging the gaps where the perceived risk of transactions exceeds the appetite of commercial funders for entrepreneurs, small and medium enterprises (SMEs) and housing to clients with limited assets to offer as collateral, the Postbank, co-operative and mutual banks have a big role to play.

However, this means that the regulatory and reporting environment has to change and be aligned to the changing banking and financial landscape. To this effect, the provision for the South African Reserve Bank to be the sole supervisor of lower-tier banks including primary and secondary co-operative banks is in accordance with the rigorous financial regulation of the banking and financial section in line with the financial stability mandate. Such regulatory changes include agricultural co-operatives that are interested in establishing banking services for their members using their existing branch networks, especially in rural areas. Agricultural co-operatives held almost 10 per cent of farm debt in 2017.

The regulatory interventions aimed at encouraging co-operative banks and co-operative financial institutions to adapt to risk-based approaches, adherence to appropriately designed and sophisticated capital-adequacy requirements is consistent with Corbae and Levine (2018) who show that economies can avoid the fragility costs of competition by enhancing bank governance and tightening leverage requirements. Corbae and Levine (2018) find that the monetary transmission mechanism is materially shaped by bank competition because bank lending responds more aggressively to central bank-induced changes in interest rates in more competitive environments. Regulations that improve bank governance boost efficiency and financial stability.

Furthermore, a financial regulatory approach that natures co-operative financial institutions to become fully fledged co-operative banks can contribute to the decentralisation of the distribution of banks and concentration of the banking system. Flogel and Gartner (2018) show that Germany has a decentralised system not only regarding the distribution of banks, but also its financial and political system more generally. Flogel and Gartner (2018) show that decentralised banks, which are predominantly regional savings banks and co-operative banks, account for most lending to business and have extended lending compared to centralised big banks.

1.13 The Balance Sheet Channel, Contractionary Effects of Exchange Rate Depreciations and the Import Substitution Strategy

In this book, we dedicate a number of chapters to assess the balance sheet effects of the R/US$ exchange rate depreciation. We find that the balance sheet channel tends to make currency depreciations to exert contractionary effects. For instance, mining investment declines and remains depressed in response to a real exchange rate depreciation shock. Foreign debt increases, and intermediate imports decline as well. Foreign debt and intermediate imports are more responsive to the real exchange rate, indicating that the balance sheet channel is more active and adjusts more. Real exchange rate depreciation shocks are transmitted more via the balance sheet items of foreign debt and the import of intermediate goods which are largely representative of inputs to the production process and investment. But investment growth and foreign debt are more responsive to a decline in commodity prices. Investment growth and foreign debt remain depressed for a longer period compared to the import of intermediate goods.

The results affirm the centrality of the balance sheet channel in transmitting negative shocks to commodity prices, demand for mining commodities and exchange rate depreciation. The impact of the decline in commodity prices on mining investment, foreign debt and intermediate imports is characteristic of the transmission via the wealth and nominal net worth balance sheet channels. The contractionary effects of commodity price declines; real and R/US$ exchange rate depreciation are mainly transmitted via the balance sheet of firms, wealth and nominal net worth. Thus, the interaction of the exchange rate dynamics and balance sheet effects are key channels that drive business cycle in the mining sector; they are highly complemented and propagated by commodity price cycles and how persistent they are.

For the agricultural sector, evidence shows that the R/US$ exchange rate depreciations and appreciations exert asymmetric balance sheet effects. The R/US$ exchange rate depreciations (appreciations) are associated with the increase (decline) in the importation of agricultural sector goods. For instance, a persistent R/US$ exchange rate depreciation can result in a prolonged increase in the importation of consumption goods by between 4 and 6 years.

At the same, the exchange rate depreciation (appreciation) shocks result in an increase (decline) in the food value chain with negative (positive) effects on headline inflation. In addition, positive and negative shocks to the white maize price exert opposite effects on food price and headline inflation. On a net basis, even though the R/US$ exchange rate appreciation dampens the grain price inflation, net effects do not result in immediate and significantly lower food and headline inflation. But they assist in containing inflationary pressures.

We establish similar exchange rate balance sheet channel effects in the agricultural sector as those in the aggregate economy and the mining sector. We find that the R/US$ exchange rate depreciation shock results in a sharper decline in the importation of intermediate and capital goods compared to consumption goods. In addition, imports of intermediate and capital goods are more responsive to the R/US$ exchange rate volatility, in particular permanent volatility, compared to the consumption goods. Thus, the contractionary effects due to sharp and persistent exchange rate depreciation due to the balance sheet effects induced by the importation of intermediate goods for investment and the production process are present in the agricultural sector as well.

However, at a disaggregated (micro) level, we find that policy interventions via the increase of domestic production of poultry and wheat and the R/US$ depreciation are superior in dampening the rate of the importation of white meat and wheat, compared to the imposition of import tariffs and the R/US$ depreciation. The policy implication is that an increase in the production of domestic white meat and wheat by increasing the area planted works via the import substitution channel to dampen imports. On the other hand, the R/US$ depreciation works via the price channel to achieve the same effects. Thus, we conclude that there is a compelling case to pursue an import substitution strategy via the increase of domestic white meat, fertiliser and wheat production to deal with the issues related to the distortions imposed by the increased degree of import penetration.

Such a strategy will have a significant impact on the rate of importation of consumption goods in the agricultural sector. We establish the same policy implications with respect to the importation of intermediate goods, especially the fertilisers. The imposition of tariffs and the exchange rate depreciation alone cannot solve structural market flaws and failures of these industries. As a medium- to long-run policy intervention, an increase in the domestic production of white meat and fertiliser and area planted for wheat is the most effective policy to deter the high degree and substitute imports. There is a need to pursue the import substitution strategies to industrialisation as envisaged in the 2018 State of the Nation address, the land reform policy and agricultural revolution. This is consistent with the McMillan and Rodrik (2011) assertion that whatever contribution globalisation has made in different countries, evidence shows that its effects depend heavily on local circumstances, choices made by domestic policymakers and domestic growth strategies. "One important difference among countries is the degree to which they are able to manage the downside effects posed by the process of globalisation". Evidence in this chapter clearly shows that high degrees of import penetration exert downside effects of the process of globalisation on the agricultural sector and policy interventions should be put in place to neutralise these effects.

1.14 The Impact of Financial Regulations and Macroprudential Tools on the Funding of the Agricultural Sector Growth

Figure 1.22 shows that on average between 2008Q1 and 2014Q4, banks have extended 1.69 per cent of total bank credit to the agricultural sector compared to 43.28 per cent to the households' sector and 16.65 per cent to the financial intermediation and insurance sectors. Thus, is there scope to use financial regulations and macroprudential tools on the funding of the agricultural sector growth?

We find that the lowering of the banks' excess capital adequacy ratio (CAR) is another channel through which the banking and financial

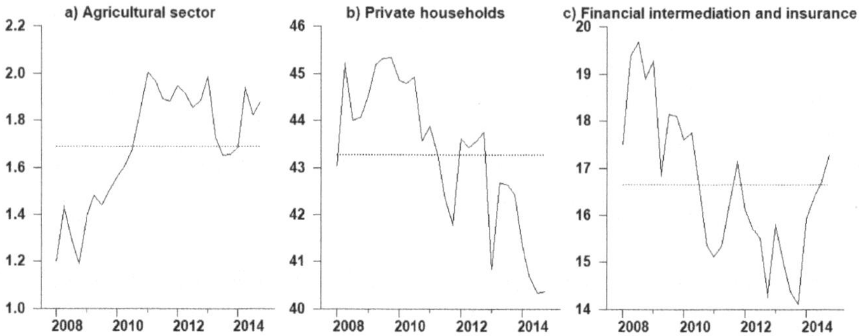

Fig. 1.22 Sectoral distribution of bank credit. (Source: South African Reserve Bank and authors' calculations)

regulations can be used to support the accelerated land reform policy and the agricultural revolution as envisaged in the National Development Plan. We establish that risk weighted assets and the credit share of the agricultural sector by the banking sector increase in response to a negative shock to excess CAR. Thus, the loosening of the CCyB is effectively an accommodative monetary policy stance and the injection of liquidity in the real economy to support investment spending, output and employment growth. This is another channel through which the banking and financial regulations can be used to support the accelerated land reform policy and the agricultural revolution as envisaged in the National Development Plan.

Furthermore, lowering excess CAR leads to an increase in the credit share of the agricultural sector by commercial banks which has a positive effect on the agricultural sector output growth, investment growth and employment growth. Thus, the loosening of excess CAR and increasing the credit share allocated to the agricultural sector the agricultural sector growth supports activity in the agricultural sector. In addition, different magnitudes of negative shocks to excess CAR have incremental benefits for the agricultural sector credit share by the banking sector, output growth, investment growth and the employment growth. Thus, we have established robust evidence that an increase in the balance sheet of the Land Bank, changes to the banking and financial regulations to open up space for the Postbank, mutual banks and co-operative banks (lower-tier banks) will largely benefit the supply of credit to the agricultural sector and benefits that accrue to accelerated land reform. This means that a multi-institutional approach to funding accelerated land reform and the agricultural sector is a prudent risk-based long-term approach to make sure that the agricultural sector and the value chain is sustainable for the long run.

1.15 The Interaction Between the Financial Sector Regulatory Framework, Property Rights Clause and the South African Reserve Bank Mandate

How then does the country quantitatively measure, evaluate and monitor the progress of developing the rural financial system, food security and affordability and job creation? We argue that in order to align and co-ordinate policies and quantitatively measure, evaluate and monitor the progress, the South African Reserve Bank (SARB) will play a much more meaningful role. In the current form, the price and financial stability mandates of the South African Reserve Bank "*exist in order to exist*" and are not anchored on other broader social welfare objectives. This has implications for the mandate and the monetary policy framework of the SARB. In its current form, section 224(1) must change and the monetary policy framework under which the South African Reserve Bank operates also must change.

References

Ancharaz, V. 2011. *Trade, Jobs and Growth in Africa: An Empirical Investigation of the Export-Led Jobless Growth Hypothesis*. African Development Bank.

Autor, D.H., Dorn, D., and Hanson, G.H. 2016. *The China Shock: Learning from Labour Market Adjustment to Large Changes in Trade*. NBER Working Paper 21906.

BFAP. 2011. The Contribution of the Agro-Industrial Complex to Employment in South Africa. Tech. Rep. June, The Bureau for Food and Agricultural Policy, Pretoria.

Bordo, M., and Siklos, P. 2014. *Central Bank Credibility, Reputation and Inflation Targeting in Historical Perspective*. NBER Working Papers 20693.

Bordo, M.D., and Siklos, P.L. 2015. *Central Bank Credibility Before and After the Crisis*. NBER Working Paper No. 21710.

Clarida, R.H. 2019. The Federal Reserve's Review of Its Monetary Policy Strategy, Tools, and Communication Practices. Speech given at The Bank of Finland Conference on Monetary Policy and Future of Economic and Monetary Union, Helsinki, Finland.

Corbae, D., and Levine, R. 2018. Competition, Stability, and Efficiency in Financial Markets. http://faculty.haas.berkeley.edu/ross_levine/Papers/JH091418.pdf

Flogel, F., and Gartner, S. 2018. *The Banking Systems of Germany, the UK and Spain from a Spatial Perspective: The German Case*. IAT Discussion Paper, No. 18/04.

Fornero, J., and Kirchner, M. 2014. *Learning About Commodity Cycles and Savings-Investment Dynamics in a Commodity Exporting Economy*. Working Papers Central Bank of Chile WP 727.

Gordon, N.E., and Ruffini, K.J. 2018. *School Nutrition and Student Discipline: Effects of Schoolwide Free Meals*. NBER Working Paper No. 24986.

Gumata, N., and Ndou, E. 2017. *Bank Credit Extension and Real Economic Activity in South Africa: The Impact of Capital Flow Dynamics, Bank Regulation and Selected Macro-Prudential Tools*. Palgrave Macmillan. ISBN 978-3-319-43550-3.

Jacobs, P., Lahiff, E., and Hall, R. 2003. Land Redistribution. Programme for Land and Agrarian Studies School of Government University of the Western Cape. http://www.plaas.org.za/sites/default/files/publicationspdf/ELARSA%2001.pdf.

Land and Agricultural Development Bank Act. 2002. 10 June 2002. Government Gazette No. 23506. Vol. 444. Cape Town.

Lopez-Villavicencio, A., and Mignon, M. 2017. Exchange Rate Pass Through in Emerging Countries: Do the Inflation Environment, Monetary Policy Regime and Central Bank Behaviour Matter? *Journal of Money and Finance*, 79(C), 20–38. Elsevier.

McKinsey and Company. 2015. *South Africa's Big Five: Bold Priorities for Inclusive Growth*. Johannesburg: McKinsey Global Institute.

McMillan, M.S., and Rodrik, D. 2011. *Globalisation, Structural Change and Productivity Growth*. NBER Working Paper 17143.

Moseneke, D.C.J. 2014. Reflections on South African Constitutional Democracy—Transition and Transformation. Keynote address at the Mistra-

Tmali-UNISA Conference 20 Years of South African Democracy: So Where to Now? The University of South Africa, 12 November 2014.

National Development Plan 2030. 2012. *Our Future-Make it Work*. National Planning Commission. Sherino Printers. ISBN: 978-0-621-41180-5.

Ndou, E., and Gumata, N. 2017. *Inflation Dynamics in South Africa: The Role of Thresholds, Exchange Rate Pass-Through and Inflation Expectations on Policy Trade-offs*. Palgrave Macmillan. ISBN 978-3-319-46701-6.

Ndou, N., Gumata, N., and Tshuma, M.N. 2019. *Exchange Rate, Second Round Effects and Inflation Process: Evidence from South Africa*. Palgrave Macmillan. ISBN 978-3-030-13931-5.

Netshipale, A.J., Oosting, S.J., Raidimi, E.N., Mashiloane, M.L., and De Boer, I.J.M. 2007. Land Reform in South Africa: Beneficiary Participation and Impact on Land Use in the Waterberg District. *NJAS Wageningen Journal of Life Sciences*, 83, 57 66.

State of the Nation Address. 2018. Making Your Future Work Better—Learning from Madiba. Delivered by President Cyril Ramaphosa During a Joint Sitting of the Two Houses of Parliament (National Assembly and the National Council of Provinces). https://www.gov.za/speeches/state-nation-address-2018

Umrabulo. 2018. Lets' Talk. Umrabulo No. 43, August 2018. https://www.anc1912.org.za/umrabulo-43-2018.

Part I

The Interaction Between Nominal Wage Inflation, Consumer Price Inflation and the Exchange Rate Appreciation and Depreciation Episodes and their Influence on Output Costs Associated with Disinflation

2

Does the Consideration of Nominal Wage Growth Imply a High Level of Inflation Inertia or Persistence Compared to Consumer Price Inflation?

Learning Objectives

- Whether the sacrifice ratios or the cumulative output and employment losses resulting from a one-percentage-point reduction in consumer price inflation are different to those associated with the decline in nominal wage inflation.
- Assess the extent to which output growth and employment growth are constrained by disinflationary policies.
- Explore whether the nominal wage and consumer price inflation disinflation episode effects on GDP growth and employment growth are comparable and synchronised.
- Understand whether the Ball (1994) approach and Harding and Pagan (2002b) dating cycle technique to estimate the magnitudes and durations of sacrifice ratios arrive at similar conclusions.
- Describe how the repo rate responds prior to disinflation episodes.

N. Gumata, E. Ndou, *Accelerated Land Reform, Mining, Growth, Unemployment and Inequality in South Africa*, https://doi.org/10.1007/978-3-030-30884-1_2

2.1 Introduction

Ndou et al. (2017) show that within the nexus of disinflationary costs, sacrifice ratios and inflation persistence lies the credibility of the inflation target. These authors corroborate vast literature and empirical evidence showing that the lack of credibility of the inflation target is also an important source of inflation persistence itself. In addition, literature shows that the existence of multiple price rigidities (or frictions) can be a contributing factor that compromises the credibility of monetary policy. This chapter extends work done in Ndou et al. (2017) by considering the role of nominal and real wage disinflation episodes over and above those in consumer price inflation. Does the consideration of the (un)employment growth in the objective function of the Monetary Policy Committee (MPC) introduce increased inflation persistence via nominal wage inflation growth? Do the consumer and nominal wage inflation disinflation episodes coincide? Furthermore, what are the magnitudes of the cumulative losses of output from its trend and sacrifice ratios associated with a 1 per cent permanent reduction in consumer and nominal wage inflation during each disinflation episode?

The consideration of the (un)employment growth in the monetary policy objective function implies that the implications of the key labour market indicators for the monetary policy stance must be well understood. We contribute to the discussion of the adoption of an extended (expanded) mandate by the MPC by showing the behaviour of consumer and nominal wage inflation persistence during disinflation periods and whether these episodes coincide. In addition, we fill academic and policy research gaps by showing how consumer and nominal wage inflation persistence relate to output losses and sacrifice ratios during the disinflation episodes. Furthermore, the analysis fills research and policy research gaps by showing the evolution of nominal wage inflation and its role in determining inflationary pressures from the labour markets.[1] This is especially the case given the historical background presented in Fig. 2.1 which shows that nominal wage price inflation as opposed to consumer price

[1] It is also noteworthy that an understanding of the evolution of nominal wage inflation over the disinflation episodes is an indirect way of assessing the role of second round effects to the degree that they are approximated by nominal wage price inflation.

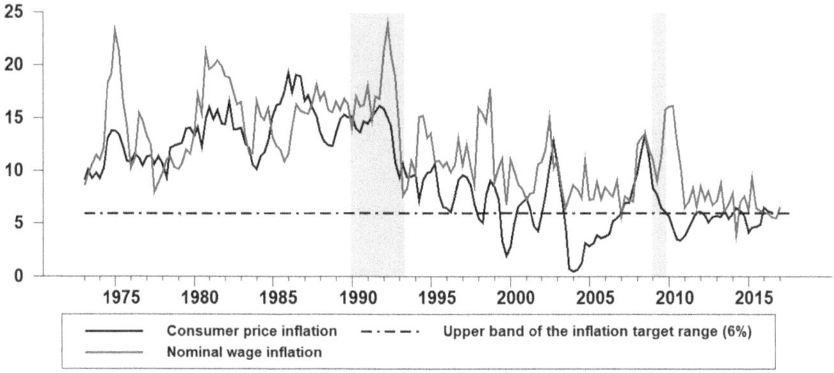

Fig. 2.1 Consumer and nominal wage price inflation. (Note: The grey shaded areas denote the South African recessions. Source: South African Reserve Bank and authors' calculations)

inflation has been persistently above the 6 per cent inflation threshold. This happens even though consumer price inflation has been in and out of the 3–6 per cent inflation target range.

2.2 Why Does This Analysis Matters?

2.2.1 The Rejection of the Unemployment Invariance Hypothesis

South Africa has long grappled with the problem of jobless growth and low labour participation rates alongside nominal wage inflation that is persistently above the upper threshold of the 3–6 per cent inflation target band.

However, Gumata and Ndou (2017) establish that the long-run unemployment rate does impact the labour force participation rate. The authors establish that policies that increase labour force participation will impact the unemployment rate, contrary to the suggestions of the "*unemployment invariance hypothesis*". Hence, they conclude that this indicates the presence of the discouraged worker effect channel. Furthermore, the labour force participation rate can act as one of the labour market reform tools that neutralises inflationary pressures and risks emanating for labour market dynamics, thus minimise the necessary adjustments on the policy rate.

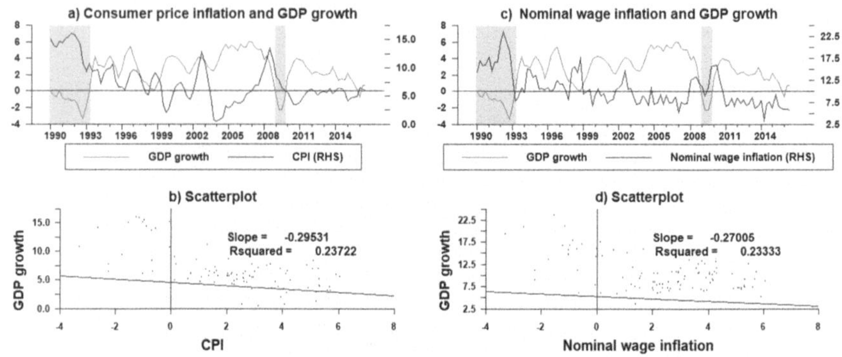

Fig. 2.2 Consumer and nominal wage price inflation and GDP growth. (Note: The grey shaded areas denote the South African recessions. Source: South African Reserve Bank and authors' calculations)

2.2.2 High Inflation Is Bad for Economic Growth

Ndou et al. (2017) show that there is a strong feedback link between inflation outcomes, inflation expectations and excess wage growth (nominal wage growth in excess of the 6 per cent inflation threshold). At the same time, inflation expectations shocks induce cyclicality in the wage-setting process. This suggests that allowing inflation expectations to remain high has unintended consequences, such as the inability to anchor wage growth within the inflation target band. The authors present evidence showing that the achievement of low and sustainable inflation and well-anchored inflation expectations minimises the amplification of second-round effects.

Figure 2.2 shows a negative association between nominal wage and consumer price inflation and GDP growth. The R-square shows that both nominal wage and consumer price inflation explain around 23 per cent of the variation in GDP growth over the sample period from 1990Q1 to 2016Q4.[2]

Furthermore, the cross-correlations in Fig. 2.3 confirm the negative relationship but with varying strengths across sub-samples. The results suggest that high nominal wage and consumer price inflation results in a decline in GDP growth for at least five quarters. The severity of the negative association was stronger during the 1990s.

[2] We establish a negative relationship between nominal wage and consumer price inflation and employment growth in Fig. 2.15 in the Appendix.

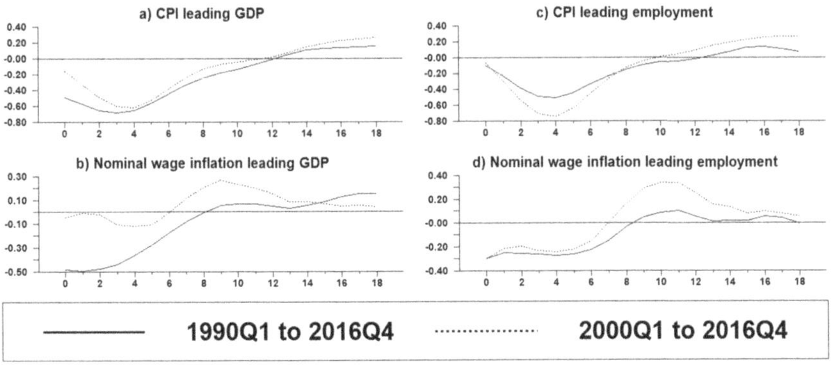

Fig. 2.3 Nominal wage and consumer price inflation leading GDP growth and employment growth. (Source: Authors' calculations)

These stylised facts therefore establish early evidence to the effect that a disinflationary policy stance is necessary to minimise the adverse effects of inflation on GDP growth and employment growth. In addition, the prolonged negative effects of the increase in nominal wages and consumer price inflation suggest that inflation persistence matters as well. As a result, we explore the role of the persistence of nominal wage and consumer price inflation persistence on the output and employment costs and sacrifice ratios in later sections.

2.2.3 The Short-Run Phillips Curve

Similarly, we establish a negative relationship between nominal wage and consumer price inflation and the unemployment rate in Fig. 2.4. The stylised facts imply that there is a trade-off (Phillips curve) between nominal wage, consumer price inflation and the unemployment rate.

2.2.4 Increased Labour Productivity Matters

We establish a positive association between the GDP growth and employment growth and labour productivity growth. At the same time, labour productivity growth is negatively associated with the unemployment rate as expected in Fig. 2.5.

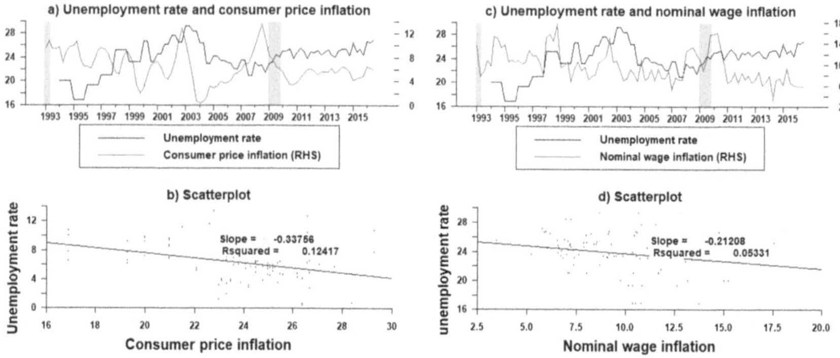

Fig. 2.4 Unemployment rate, consumer price and nominal wage inflation. (Note: The grey shaded areas denote the South African recessions. Source: Authors' calculations)

Fig. 2.5 (Un)employment rate, GDP growth and labour productivity growth. (Note: The grey shaded areas denote the South African recessions. Source: Authors' calculations)

Literature and empirical evidence emphasise the positive effects of containing inflation on long-term output growth. But the recessionary effects brought about by a disinflationary policy stance are likely to constrain output growth and employment growth. To what extent is output growth and employment growth constrained by a disinflationary policy? Are the nominal wage and consumer price inflation disinflation episode effects on GDP growth and employment growth comparable and synchronised?

We use two approaches to establish the duration and dates during which the disinflation episodes have occurred and the duration of such episodes. First, similar to Ndou and Gumata (2017), we use the Ball (1994) approach to estimate the magnitudes of sacrifice ratios. The Ball approach has been extensively used and is widely preferred to select disinflation episodes than estimating the sacrifice ratio from a Phillips curve.[3] Second, we use is the Harding and Pagan (2002b) approach. It is one of the classical cycle dating techniques that are typically used to study cycles in real economic activity. We use the Harding and Pagan (2002b) dating cycle technique to identify the turning points in the output growth, employment growth, nominal wage, real wage and consumer price inflation.[4] The approach also serves as a robustness analysis for the episodes identified by the Ball (1994) approach.

2.3 What Are Sacrifice Ratios and Why They Matter?

The sacrifice ratio can be defined as the cumulative output loss resulting from a one-percentage-point reduction in the inflation rate.[5] Alternatively, sacrifice ratios refer to the degree to which demand must be reduced to achieve a given reduction in the inflation rate. This measures the extent to which real output is forgone to reduce trend inflation by one percentage point.[6] Ball (1994) asserts that quantifying output losses of disinflation episodes is important because disinflation tends to be a major cause of recessions in advanced economies. However, not all episodes of elevated inflation are associated with an overheating economy or demand. There are cases highly dominated by external factors and supply side shocks. This is why we extend the analysis of sacrifice ratios and output losses due to disinflationary episodes by exploring the role of nominal wage inflation.

Nonetheless, irrespective of the sources of inflationary pressures, empirical evidence shows that lower inflation (price stability) contributes

[3] Vast literature has recently shown the current disconnect and the weak relationship between inflation, output and (un)employment growth. See for instance Yellen (2017), Brainard (2017), Kashkari (2017) amongst others.

[4] Harding and Pagan (2002a) extend the BB algorithm developed by Bry and Boschan (1971).

[5] See Ndou and Gumata (2017) for further reading.

[6] We apply the same definition to the measurement of the sacrifice ratios and disinflation episodes based on nominal wage inflation.

to raising potential growth particularly, in relation to relative prices and lowering the inflation risk premium. Hence, we also explore the role of nominal wage inflation and the effects of the disinflation episodes on employment growth as well.

2.4 The Ball (1994) and Harding and Pagan (2002b) Approaches to Disinflation

We use two approaches to establish the dates during which the disinflation episodes have occurred and the duration of such episodes. First, similar to Ndou and Gumata (2017), we use the Ball (1994) approach to estimate the magnitudes of sacrifice ratios. The Ball approach has been extensively used and is widely preferred to select disinflation episodes than estimating the sacrifice ratio from a Phillips curve. Methodologically, the Ball (1994) approach identifies the disinflation episode to occur only when trend inflation declines by at least 2 percentage points from its peak. The 2 per cent threshold separates significant aggregate demand shifts from those of fluctuations arising from other shocks. This assumes that monetary policy accounts for all cyclical output variation. The peak of inflation is identified at time *t*, and it occurs when trend inflation at time *t* exceeds the preceding four quarters and those in the subsequent quarters. A trough occurs when inflation at time *t* is lower than in the preceding four quarters and the following four quarters.

The Harding and Pagan approach is one of the classical cycle dating techniques that are typically used to study cycles in real economic activity. We use the Harding and Pagan (2002b) dating cycle technique that has been used in various empirical studies to identify the turning points in the log-level and growth rates of the series that constitute the financial cycle.[7] The approach also serves as a robustness analysis for the episodes identified by the Ball (1994) approach. The key features of the cyclical phases are their duration, amplitude and slope as shown in Fig. 2.6. The duration for recessions (downturns) is defined as the number of quarters (months) between the peak and the trough. In turn, the duration for upturns is defined as the time

[7] Harding and Pagan (2002a) extend the BB algorithm developed by Bry and Boschan (1971).

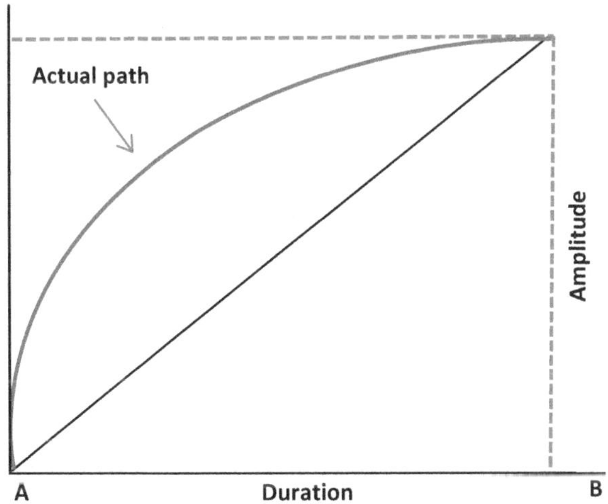

Fig. 2.6 Key features of the cyclical phases. (Source: Authors' drawing adapted from Harding and Pagan (2002a))

it takes to attain the level at the previous peak after the trough. Disruptions (booms) correspond to the bottom (top) 25 per cent of downturns (upturns) in terms of amplitude.

The Harding and Pagan (2002a) dating cycle technique requires a search for the maxima and minima over a given period of time. Then, it selects pairs of adjacent, locally absolute maxima and minima that meet certain censoring rules. For example, for (Y_t) at time t the Bry-Boschan algorithm detects a peak at date t if Eq. (2.1) is satisfied.

$$\left\{\left(\Delta_t\, Y_t,\ldots,\Delta Y_t\right)>0,\quad \left(\Delta Y_{t+1},\ldots,\Delta_k Y_{t+k}\right)<0\right\} \tag{2.1}$$

The algorithm detects a trough at date t if Eq. (2.1) is satisfied

$$\left\{\left(\Delta_k\, Y_t,\ldots,\Delta Y_t\right)<0,\quad \left(\Delta Y_{t+1},\ldots,\ \Delta_k Y_{t+k}\right)>0\right\} \tag{2.2}$$

where Δ_k is $\Delta_k Y_t = Y_t - Y_{t-k.}$ The Harding and Pagan (2002b) approach suggests $k = 2$ for quarterly data and $k = 5$ for monthly data. The approach discards turning points within six months of the beginning or end of the series. The Bry-Boschan algorithm then develops a procedure for ensuring that peaks and troughs alternate. It imposes that in the presence of a double trough, the lowest value is chosen, whereas, in the presence of a double peak, the highest value is chosen. The censoring rules are also imposed on the minimum duration of phases. The algorithm specifies that a phase must last at least six months and that a complete cycle from peak to peak must last at least 15 months. Alternatively, it requires the duration of a complete cycle to be at least five quarters and of each phase to be at least two quarters.

2.5 Actual Output and Employment Relative to Trend Output and Employment During Consumer and Wage Disinflation Episodes

To identify the consumer price and nominal wage disinflation periods, the study uses quarterly (Q) data from 1970Q1 to 2017Q2 sourced from the South African Reserve Bank database. The trends for consumer and nominal wage inflation are extracted from the actual inflation rates by using the nine-quarter centred moving averages of quarterly consumer and nominal wage inflation. This smoothing technique eliminates the influence of supply shocks which lead to temporary inflation departures from trend. Figure 2.7 shows that nominal wage and consumer price inflation have six disinflation episodes over the sample period 1973Q1 to 2017Q2. The period 1991Q1 to 2006Q4 marked the prolonged period of disinflation in nominal and consumer price inflation.

However, it is also noticeable that although the two variables present very similar disinflation episodes over the sample period, the duration and amplitude of the disinflation episodes differ slightly. Furthermore, the trends show that nominal wage and consumer price inflation have trended downwards over the sample period. It is noticeable that the nominal wage inflation trend has declined significantly post the recession in

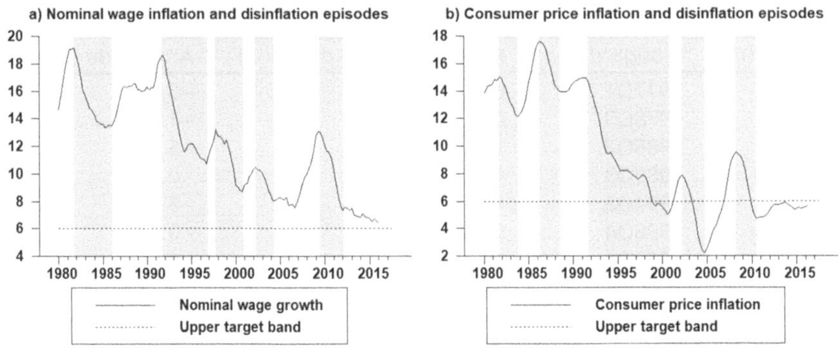

Fig. 2.7 Consumer and wage price inflationary and disinflation periods. (Note: Shaded areas represent the disinflation periods which are at least 2 percentage points lower than at the peak. The centred nine-quarter moving average inflation is expressed in per cent. Source: Authors' calculations)

2009 and is approaching the upper band of the inflation targeting range. At the same time, the consumer price inflation trend has been persistently just below the 6 per cent inflation threshold in Fig. 2.7. In addition, Table 2.1 shows that some durations of nominal wage inflation tend to be longer than those of the consumer price inflation. The longest disinflation episode for nominal wage inflation being that during 2009Q2 to 2014Q1 with the amplitude of −6.27 per cent decline in nominal wage inflation. This is closely followed by the period 1991Q4 to 1994Q2 with an amplitude of −6.61 per cent.

On the other hand, in Table 2.2 the longest period of disinflation in consumer price inflation occurred during the period 1991Q3 to 1995Q2 with the amplitude of −6.77 per cent, 2002Q2 to 2004Q4 with the amplitude of 5.63 per cent and 2008Q2 to 2010Q4 with an amplitude of −4.61 per cent.

How do the episodes of nominal wage and consumer price inflation established above compare to those in the real wage? We calculate the real wage as the nominal wage inflation less actual consumer inflation. Figure 2.8 shows that real wage inflation has had eight disinflation episodes compared to the six episodes established for nominal wage and

Table 2.1 Duration and amplitude of nominal wage inflation peaks and troughs

Peak dates	Trough dates	Peak-to-trough (duration)	Amplitude (%)
1975Q3	1977Q1	6	−5.06
1977Q3	1978Q3	4	−1.43
1981Q4	1985Q2	14	−5.83
1988Q3	1989Q3	4	−0.53
1991Q4	1994Q2	10	−6.61
1995Q4	1996Q4	6	−0.72
1997Q4	2000Q4	12	−4.30
2002Q2	2004Q4	8	−2.28
2005Q1	2006Q4	7	−0.88
2009Q2	2014Q1	19	−6.27

Source: Authors' calculations

Table 2.2 Duration and amplitude of consumer price inflation peaks and troughs

Peak dates	Trough dates	Peak-to-trough (duration)	Amplitude (%)
1975Q3	1977Q2	7	−1.43
1981Q4	1983Q4	8	−2.82
1986Q2	1989Q1	11	−3.69
1991Q3	1995Q2	15	−6.77
1995Q4	1997Q2	6	−0.68
1997Q4	2000Q3	11	−2.87
2002Q2	2004Q4	10	−5.63
2008Q2	2010Q4	10	−4.61
2012Q3	2013Q1	2	−0.02
2013Q4	2014Q4	4	−0.54

Source: Authors' calculations

consumer price inflation. In addition, we establish that the 1970s and 1980s had severe contraction in the real wage.

Nonetheless, it is evident in Fig. 2.8 and Table 2.3 that real wage growth has had two severe disinflation episodes in succession during the period 2004Q4 to 2008Q1 and 2010Q3 to 2013Q4. In addition, real wages have been consistently growing below the long-term average of 2.52 per cent since 2012Q1, and it is the first time in history that such a trend in real wage growth has been observed. This means that the wage premium above the inflation rate has narrowed.

Furthermore, Table 2.3 shows that 2004Q4 to 2008Q1 and 2010Q3 to 2013Q4 had the longest duration in recent history and the amplitudes of −5.19 per cent and 5.76 per cent, respectively. The trends in nominal

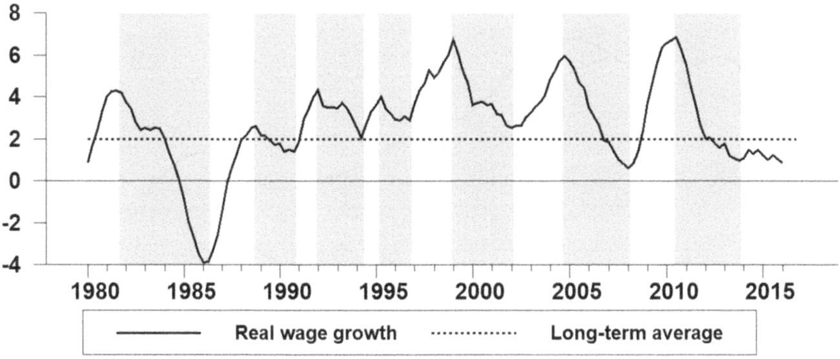

Fig. 2.8 Real wage inflationary and disinflation periods. (Note: Shaded areas refer to disinflation periods which are at least 2 percentage points lower than at the peak. The centred nine-quarter moving average inflation is expressed in per cent. Source: Authors' calculations)

Table 2.3 Duration and amplitude of real wage inflation peaks and troughs

Peak dates	Trough dates	Peak-to-trough (duration)	Amplitude (%)
1974Q4	1978Q3	15	−6.70
1981Q3	1982Q4	5	−1.90
1983Q3	1986Q2	11	−7.24
1988Q4	1990Q4	8	−1.23
1992Q1	1994Q2	9	−2.14
1995Q2	1996Q2	4	−1.10
1999Q1	2000Q1	4	−2.79
2000Q3	2002Q1	6	−1.28
2004Q4	2008Q1	13	−5.19
2010Q3	2013Q4	13	−5.76
2014Q4			

Source: Authors' calculations

wage and consumer price inflation in Fig. 2.9 are highly synchronised although the starting points differ in some episodes as was the case in the early 1980s. In addition, it is evident that the trends were on a prolonged downward trend in the late 1980s to 2004. The downward trend resumed in 2011 to date.

Last, the observed trend in real wage growth brings to the fore the role of inflation volatility and persistence and whether it stabilises within the target band. Hence, in the empirical section we explore, the role of inflation persistence on disinflationary costs on GDP growth and employment growth.

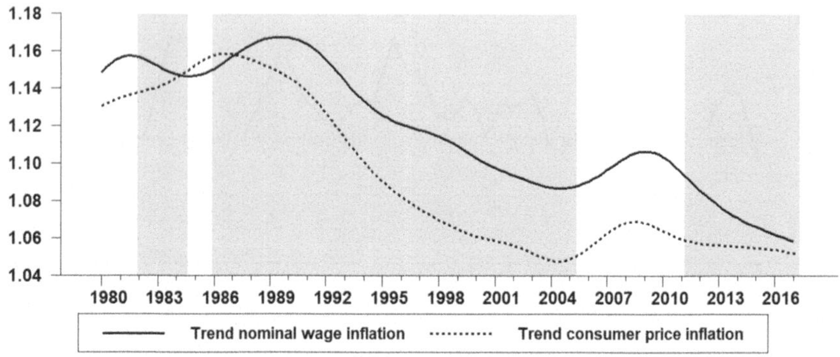

Fig. 2.9 Trend nominal wage and consumer price. (Note: Shaded areas refer to disinflation periods which are at least 2 percentage points lower than at the peak. The centred nine-quarter moving average inflation is expressed in per cent. Source: Authors' calculations)

2.6 How Does Trend Output and Employment Behave During the Nominal Wage and Consumer Price Disinflation Episodes

We explore the association of trend and actual output and employment with the disinflation episodes in nominal wage and consumer price disinflation episodes. It is noticeable that in all the nominal wage and consumer price disinflation episodes, output and employment levels are below trend in Fig. 2.10. This suggests that there are output and employment costs incurred during disinflation episodes.[8]

Nonetheless, it is evident that the severity of output and employment costs incurred during the disinflation episodes differs as shown in Table 2.4. Figure 2.11 presents a comparison of the GDP and employment costs associated with nominal wage and consumer price inflation disinflation episodes. We measure the costs as those periods during which GDP growth and employment growth show negative deviation from trend during the nominal wage and consumer price disinflation episodes.

[8] We calculate the output and employment costs as the average decline in output and employment growth during the disinflation episode.

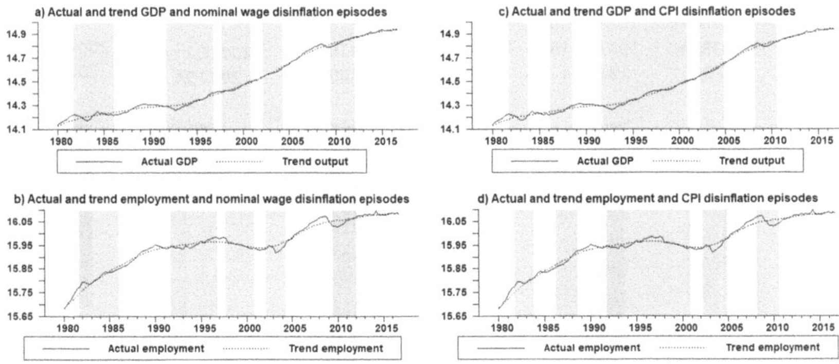

Fig. 2.10 Actual and trend output and employment over nominal wage and consumer price disinflation episodes. (Note: Shaded areas refer to disinflation periods which are at least 2 percentage points lower than at the peak. The centred nine-quarter moving average inflation is expressed in per cent. Source: Authors' calculations)

Table 2.4 Duration and amplitude of output and employment peaks and troughs

CPI disinflation dates	GDP cost	Employment cost	Wage disinflation dates	GDP cost	Employment cost
1975Q3 to 1977Q4	−1.51	−1.71	1975Q3 to 1978Q3	−0.68	0.24
1981Q4 to 1983Q4	−2.07	−2.40	1981Q4 to 1986Q1	0.01	0.43
1986Q2 to 1989Q3	−1.45	−0.91	1991Q4 to 1996Q4	−0.68	−0.23
1991Q4 to 2000Q4	−2.69	−0.68	1997Q4 to 2000Q4	−0.21	0.03
2002Q2 to 2004Q4	−0.64	−2.17	2002Q2 to 2004Q2	−0.81	−1.25
2008Q2 to 2011Q3	−1.63	−1.65	2009Q3 to 2012Q1	−0.72	−0.99

Source: Authors' calculations

Table 2.4 and Fig. 2.11 show the deviations of the means for the periods of disinflation. The results show that indeed the nominal wage and consumer price disinflation episodes exert different costs on GDP growth and employment growth.

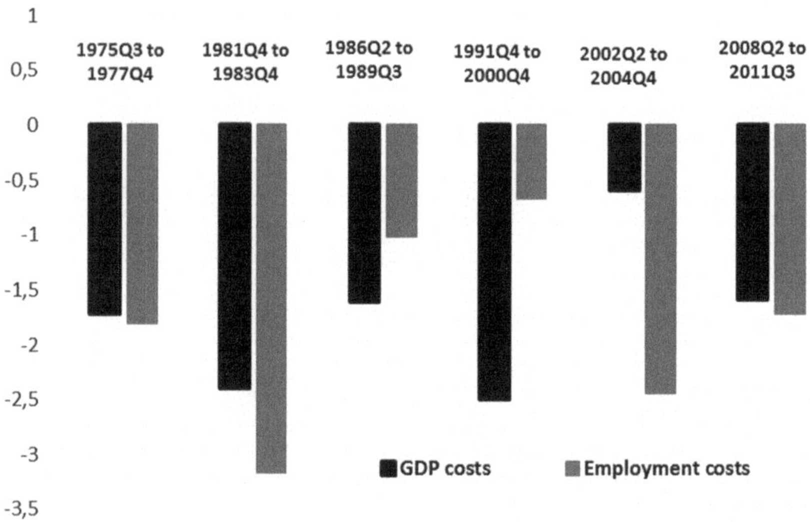

Fig. 2.11 GDP and employment costs and consumer price disinflation episodes. (Source: Authors' calculations)

Irrespective of whether we assess the output and employment costs associated with nominal wage and consumer price disinflation in Table 2.4 and Fig. 2.11, the employment costs are much higher compared to output costs. In some instances, such as was the case during 2002Q2 to 2004Q4, the employment costs associated with the disinflation episodes were more than double those on output.

The period 1981Q4 to 1983Q3 was the costliest in terms of the mean negative deviations of GDP and employment growth from trend. The period was more costly in particular for employment growth which deviated by 3.2 percentage points from trend. Furthermore, the disinflation episode for the period 2002Q2 to 2004Q4 was more costly in terms of employment growth with a mean negative deviation of 2.4 percentage points. Similarly, the recent disinflation episode during 2008Q2 to 2011Q3 was more costly for employment growth compared to GDP growth at 1.7 per cent and 1.6 per cent, respectively.

2.7 How Do Cyclical Output and Employment Perform During the Disinflation Episodes?

So far, the analysis in this chapter has shown that output and employment tend to deviate from trend during disinflation episodes. Furthermore, employment losses tend to be higher compared to output losses. However, the average costs calculated in the earlier section differ to the sacrifice ratios. Hence, this section uses the Ball (1994) approach to calculate the sacrifice ratios associated with the identified disinflation episodes. The Ball (1994) approach relies on two main assumptions regarding the path of trend output and when it returns to actual output. The assumptions state that (i) output is at its trend at the peak of inflation; (ii) it returns to trend four quarters after the end of the disinflation episode; and (iii) trend output grows log-linearly between these periods. Therefore, trend output follows a straight line connecting the beginning point of disinflation to a year after disinflation. The sacrifice ratio is then calculated as the sum of the deviations between the fitted line for trend output and employment and the log of output and employment. This is then divided by the change in trend nominal wage and consumer price inflation over the course of the episode.

First, Fig. 2.12 shows that the disinflation episodes tend to be associated with the negative output and employment gaps although there are

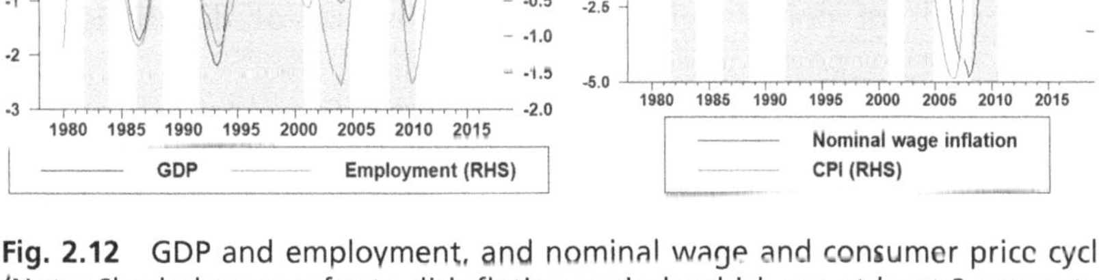

Fig. 2.12 GDP and employment, and nominal wage and consumer price cycles. (Note: Shaded areas refer to disinflation periods which are at least 2 percentage points lower than at the peak. The centred nine-quarter moving average inflation is expressed in per cent. Source: Authors' calculations)

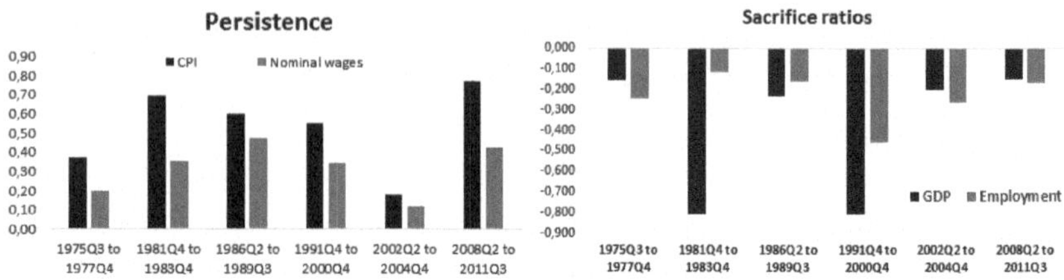

Fig. 2.13 Persistence and sacrifice ratios. (Source: Authors' calculations)

lags in this relationship. At the same time, the cyclical troughs show that employment growth is more responsive compared to output growth corroborating results discussed in the earlier section.

Furthermore, it is evident that the nominal wage formation process lags (responds with a lag) that in the consumer price inflation process consistent with the fact that the wage formation process follows an adaptive process. This adaptive adjustment process is clearly in the peaks and troughs during the period 1998Q1 and 2000Q4, 2004Q2 and 2007Q2 and 2009Q3 and 2013Q4. In addition, Ndou et al. (2017) show that the inflation persistence coefficients are associated with higher magnitudes of sacrifice ratios. Meaning that a 1 per cent reduction in inflation leads to output losses.[9] The higher the size of the inflation persistence coefficient, the higher the output sacrifice ratio. This means that in the presence of high persistence, an aggressive policy stance may lead to large output losses and this is prevalent in backward-looking price formation expectations environment. In addition, inflation persistence matters more in cases where the inflation expectations formation is dominated by the price formation process of simply averaging past inflation, particularly if past inflation outcomes are high. Mayes and Chapple (2009) show that this may lead to increased costs of disinflation and may indeed require longer periods of policy tightening given any size of disinflationary pressures.

Figure 2.13 shows that consumer price inflation has a higher degree of persistence compared to nominal wage inflation and that the sacrifice

[9] Positive sacrifice ratio values suggest that during that disinflation episode, a reduction in inflation led to an improvement in output.

ratios are higher for employment compared to GDP in the inflation targeting regime. Last, we show the magnitudes and persistence of the deviation of output and employment from trend during disinflation episodes in Fig. 2.16 and nominal wage and consumer price inflation trends in Fig. 2.17 in the Appendix. It is evident that for the 2008Q2–2011Q4 period, output losses were very large and the inflation trend was flat a year after the disinflation period compared to the episodes.

2.8 How Does the Policy Rate Change During the Disinflation Episodes?

The analysis in this chapter has shown that output and employment tend to deviate from trend during disinflation episodes. Furthermore, employment losses tend to be higher compared to output losses. This may be associated with the magnitudes and duration of the policy responses aimed at disinflation. Hence, we conclude this analysis by examining the repo rate responses during the disinflation episodes. Figure 2.14 shows that indeed the periods of disinflation are preceded by the repo rate tightening

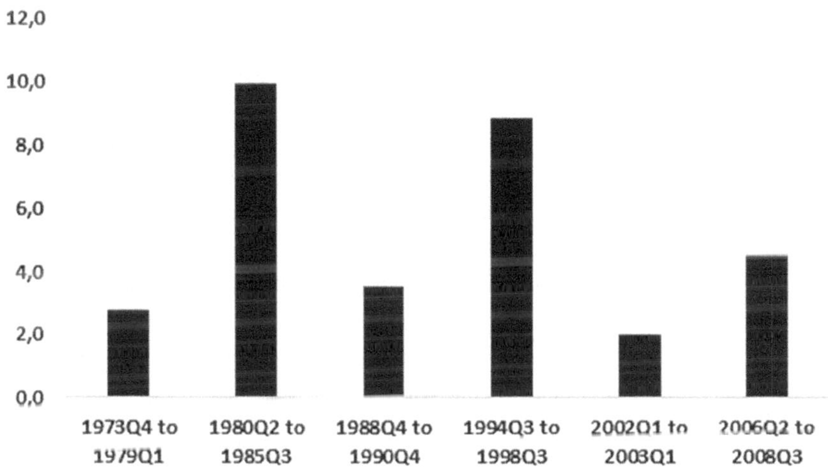

Fig. 2.14 Repo rate increases preceding disinflation episodes. (Source: Authors' calculations)

cycles. It is also evident that the degree to which the policy rate is tightened is related to the disinflation costs. For instance, the change of the repo rate from trough to peak for the period 1980Q2 to 1985Q3 preceded the period that was associated with the most-costly disinflation episodes in Figs. 2.11 and 2.13. Similarly, the period 1994Q3 to 1998Q3 is associated with the costly output growth disinflation episode. The results are consistent with Mayes and Chapple (2009) that heightened inflationary pressures and persistence may lead to increased costs of disinflation and may require longer periods of policy tightening given any size of disinflationary pressures.

On the contrary, during the period 2002Q1 to 2003Q1, the repo rate increase from trough to peak was the lowest on record at a total 2 percentage points but it is associated with the most-costly disinflation episode in terms of employment growth contraction. This evidence reinforces the earlier evidence in Gumata and Ndou (2017) showing that the repo rate is a blunt tool and that there are cases where macroprudential tools can be used as complementary tools to neutralise the adverse effects on GDP growth and employment growth. The implication of the high employment costs associated with disinflation episodes and policy responses compared to output, is that employment growth is more responsive to disinflation policies. This means that policies aimed at the disinflation of wage and consumer price inflationary pressures should pay attention to the accentuated spill-over effects of such policies on employment growth.

Therefore, in the eventuality of an expanded mandate of the Bank, special attention has to be afforded to the impact of the disinflation policy tools on the objectives of output and employment growth.[10] In addition, it is evident that the costliest disinflation episodes are those that are associated with consumer price inflation compared to nominal wage price inflation. Meaning that the consumer price inflation adjustment costs are costlier than those in nominal wage inflation in line with the theoretical predictions of nominal wage rigidities.

[10] Alternatively, when pursuing the mandates of price and growth stability and maximum employment.

2.9 Conclusion and Policy Implications

This chapter explored whether the consideration of nominal wage growth would imply a high level of inflation inertia or persistence compared to consumer price inflation. First, we establish that nominal wage and consumer price inflation have six disinflation episodes over the sample period 1973Q1 to 2017Q2. However, the duration and amplitude of the disinflation episodes differ slightly. Second, the trends show that nominal wage and consumer price inflation have trended downwards over the sample period. The nominal wage inflation trend has declined significantly post the recession in 2009 and is approaching the upper band of the inflation targeting range.

Furthermore, real wage inflation has had eight disinflation episodes compared to the six episodes established for nominal wage and consumer price inflation. In addition, real wages have been consistently growing below the long-term average of 2.52 per cent since 2012Q1. It is the first time in history that such a trend in real wage growth has been observed. This has narrowed the margin between nominal wage and consumer price inflation. Hence, we conclude that the nominal wage and consumer price inflation disinflation episode effects on GDP growth and employment growth are comparable and synchronised.

Evidence in this chapter shows that the consideration of nominal wage growth does not necessarily imply a high level of inflation inertia or persistence compared to consumer price inflation. The policy implication is that this is another appropriate and policy-relevant approach at assessing the role of second-round effects emanating from the labour markets which is an integral part of the monetary policy formulation process. Furthermore, we establish that there are output and employment costs incurred during disinflation episodes. The repo rate tightening precedes all the disinflationary episodes. The employment costs associated with disinflationary episodes are much higher compared to output costs and in some instances were more than double those on output. The policy implication is that there is a case for the consideration of other macroprudential tools that complement the repo rate in neutralising the adverse effects of disinflation on GDP growth and employment growth.

Appendix

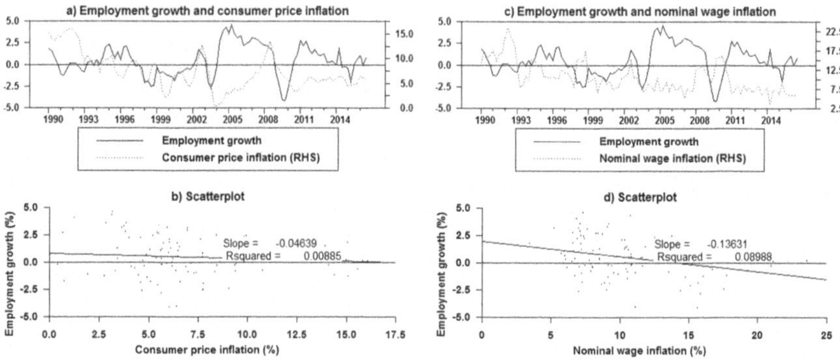

Fig. 2.15 Consumer and nominal wage price inflation and employment growth. (Source: Authors' calculations)

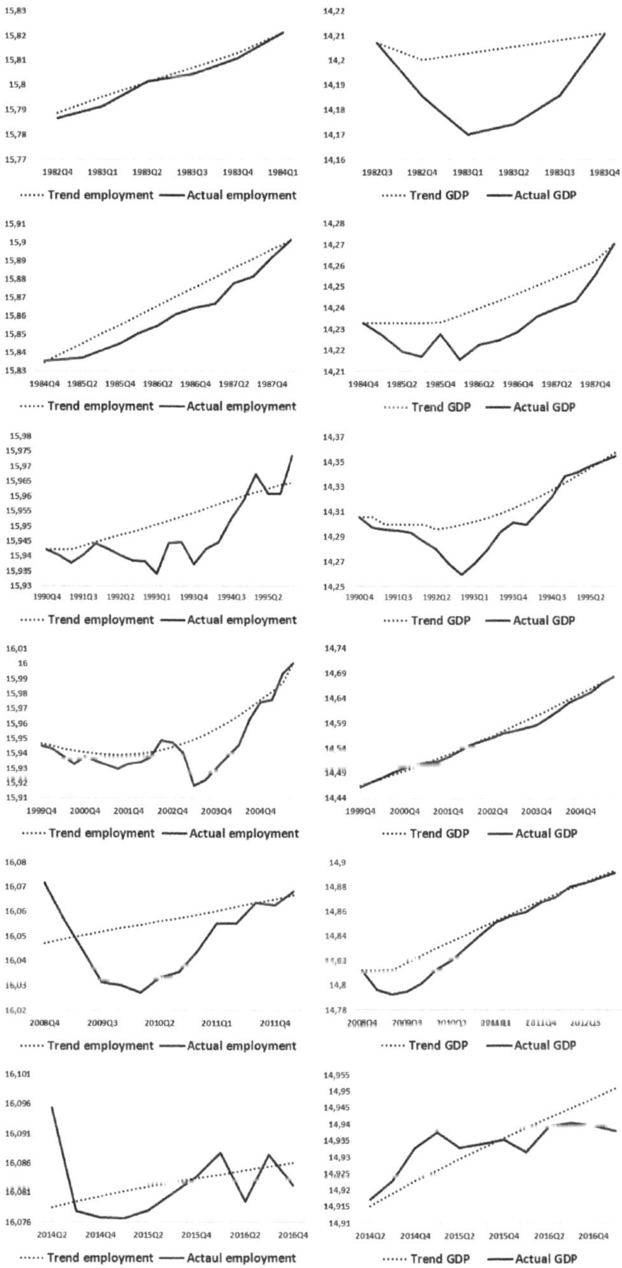

Fig. 2.16 Output and employment deviations from trend during disinflation episodes. (Source: Authors' calculations)

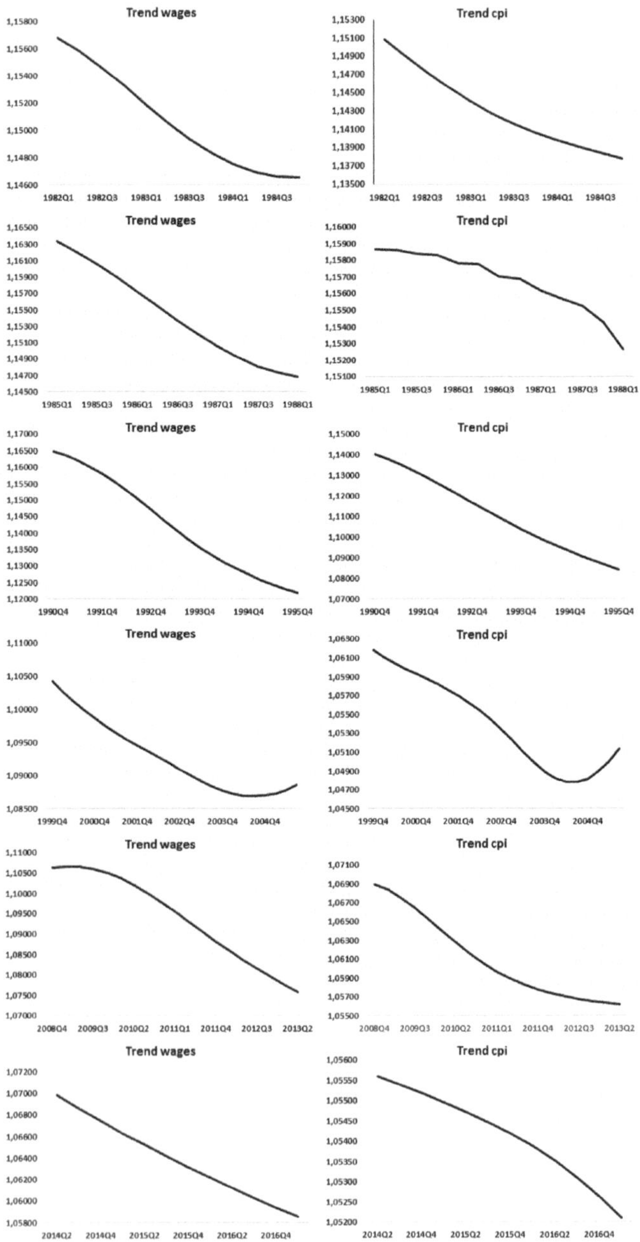

Fig. 2.17 Trend nominal wage and consumer price inflation during disinflation episodes. (Source: Authors' calculations)

References

Ball, L. 1994. What Determines the Sacrifice Ratio? In N. G. Mankiw (ed.), *Monetary Policy*. University of Chicago Press, pp. 155–82.

BFAP. 2011a. South African Agricultural Baseline 2011.

BFAP. 2011b. The Contribution of the Agro-Industrial Complex to Employment in South Africa. Tech. Rep. June, The Bureau for Food and Agricultural Policy, Pretoria.

Brainard, L. 2017a. Understanding the Disconnect between Employment and Inflation with a Low Neutral Rate. Speech at The Economic Club of New York New York City, 5 September 2017.

Brainard, L. 2017b. Navigating the Different Signals from Inflation and Unemployment. Speech at the New York Association for Business Economics, New York City, 30 May 2017.

Bry, G., and Boschan, C. 1971. *Cyclical Analysis of Time Series: Selected Procedures and Computer Programs*. NBER Books. ISBN 0-87014-223-2.

Gumata, N., and Ndou, E. 2017. *Bank Credit Extension and Real Economic Activity in South Africa: The Impact of Capital Flow Dynamics, Bank Regulation and Selected Macro-prudential Tools*. Palgrave Macmillan. ISBN 978-3-319-43550-3.

Hall, S.G., Henry, S.G.B., and Wilcox, J.B. 1989. *The Long-run Determination of the UK Monetary Aggregates*. Discussion Paper Series, No. 41, Bank of England.

Hall, S.G., Hondroyiannis, G., Swamy, P.A.V.B., and Tavlas, G. 2008. *A Portfolio Balance Approach to Euro Area Money Demand in a Time Varying Environment*. Bank of Greece.

Harding, D., and Pagan, A. 2002a. A Comparison of Two Business Cycle Dating Methods. *Journal of Economics Dynamics and Control*, 27, 1681–90.

Harding, D., and Pagan, A. 2002b. Dissecting the Cycle: A Methodological Investigation. *Journal of Monetary Economics*, 49, 365–81.

Kashkari, N. 2017. Why I Dissented at the March 2017 FOMC Meeting. https://www.minneapolisfed.org/news-and-events/messages/why-i-dissented.

Mayes, D., and Chapple, B. 2009. The Costs and Benefits of Disinflation: A Critique of the Sacrifice Ration. *Reserve Bank of New Zealand Bulletin*, 58(March), pp. 9–22. Reserve Bank of New Zealand.

Ndou, E., and Gumata, N. 2017. *Inflation Dynamics in South Africa: The Role of Thresholds, Exchange Rate Pass-through and Inflation Expectations on Policy Trade-offs*. Palgrave Macmillan. ISBN 978-3-319-46701-6.
Ndou, E., Gumata, N., and Ncube, M. 2017. *Global Economic Uncertainties and Exchange Rate Shocks*. Palgrave Macmillan. ISBN 978-3-319-62279-8.
Yellen, J.L. 2017. From Adding Accommodation to Scaling It Back. Remarks by at the Executives' Club of Chicago Chicago Hilton 720 S. Michigan Avenue Chicago, IL. https://www.federalreserve.gov/newsevents/speech/files/yellen20170303a.pdf.

3

Wage and Consumer Price Inflation During Exchange Rate Appreciation and Depreciation Episodes

Learning Objectives

- Assess whether the exchange rate depreciation and appreciation shocks affect nominal wage and consumer inflation differently.
- Explore the propagation effects of permanent exchange rate volatility on nominal wage and consumer price inflation.
- Assess the impact of positive nominal wage and consumer price inflation shocks on output growth, employment growth and the repo rate.
- Establish whether inflation regimes demarcated by the 4 per cent CPI threshold play a role on the effects of consumer price inflation shocks on output growth, employment growth and the repo rate.
- Assess whether the real wage inflation regimes demarcated by the 2 per cent real wage threshold play a role on the effects of consumer price inflation shocks on output growth, employment growth and the repo rate.
- Explore what the 2 per cent real wage inflation threshold implies for labour productivity.

N. Gumata, E. Ndou, *Accelerated Land Reform, Mining, Growth, Unemployment and Inequality in South Africa*, https://doi.org/10.1007/978-3-030-30884-1_3

3.1 Introduction

This chapter extends the analysis in Chap. 2 by exploring the nominal wage and consumer price inflation during the Rand per US dollar (R/US$) exchange rate appreciation and depreciations. Ndou and Gumata (2017) show that a persistently rising exchange rate volatility shock leads to a pronounced positive correlation between inflation and output-gap volatilities, also known as the Taylor curve (policy frontier). In addition, the inflation and output-gap volatilities increase due to a higher level of the exchange rate volatility, meaning that that the policy frontier curve shifts outwards. Consumer price inflation and the output-gap are the key variables in the central bank objective function or loss minimisation function under the flexible inflation targeting framework. The inclusion of the mandate of maximum (full) employment in the central bank objective function requires a good understanding of the main labour market indicators such as nominal wage inflation. Hence, this chapter explores whether the responses of nominal wage and consumer price inflation differ to the R/US$ exchange rate appreciation and depreciation shocks. In addition, we explore whether permanent R/US$ exchange rate volatility amplifies or neutralises the impact of the exchange rate appreciation and depreciations. This is because the exchange rate shocks may be transmitted via the volatility channel before impacting nominal wage and consumer price inflation.

At the same time, nominal wage and consumer price inflation have a bilateral relationship via the consumer price and wage-inflation spiral effects. To ascertain the different macroeconomic effects of nominal wage and consumer price inflation, we explore their shock effects on output growth, employment growth and the repo rate to stem the expectations-wage-consumer price inflation spiral. Cognisant of the role of threshold effects and inflation regimes in the transmission of shocks, we further establish whether inflation regimes demarcated by the 4 per cent CPI inflation threshold play a role on the effects of consumer price inflation shocks on output growth, employment growth and the repo rate. Furthermore, in light of the recommendations that central banks should target wage inflation, we assess whether the real wage inflation regimes demarcated by the 2 per cent real wage threshold play a role on the effects of consumer price inflation shocks on output growth, employment growth and the repo rate. The analysis concludes by determining the implications for labour productivity.

3.2 The Link Between the Exchange Rate, Nominal Wages and Consumer Price Inflation

Figure 3.1 shows the direct (first round) and the indirect (second round) impacts of nominal wage and consumer inflation. For instance, in Fig. 3.1, the exchange rate depreciation directly impacts the labour supply and demand curves in the exporting, importing and import substituting sectors. The exchange rate depreciation makes domestic exports cheaper relative to the rest of the world and thus more competitive. The resulting price competitiveness is expected to result in increased demand for domestic exports thus increasing the demand for labour which in turn increases wage inflation. Similarly, in cases where the exchange rate depreciation increases imported inputs and production costs, the transmission of an increase in production will increase nominal wage and consumer price inflation. Alternatively, the exchange rate depreciation can increase the price of imported goods and production costs, thus reducing the quantity of labour demand and wage inflation in importing sectors. The exchange rate depreciation effect impacts the cost of imported capital, intermediate goods and technology which are complements to domestic labour; the decline in the quantity used can also reduce the demand for labour and affect wage inflation.

However, output growth and labour demand can increase in import substituting sectors thus resulting in an increase in the demand for labour and wage inflation. Thus, the direct and indirect channels of transmission of the exchange rate depreciation affect labour markets, wage setting behaviour and consumer price inflation. To summarise, the stages of the transmission channels show that (i) the exchange rate depreciation shock directly impacts nominal wage and consumer price inflation (first-round stage) via an increase in the import prices of input, production and finished goods, and (ii) the inflationary changes are also transmitted into wage inflation via the indirect or second-round effects.

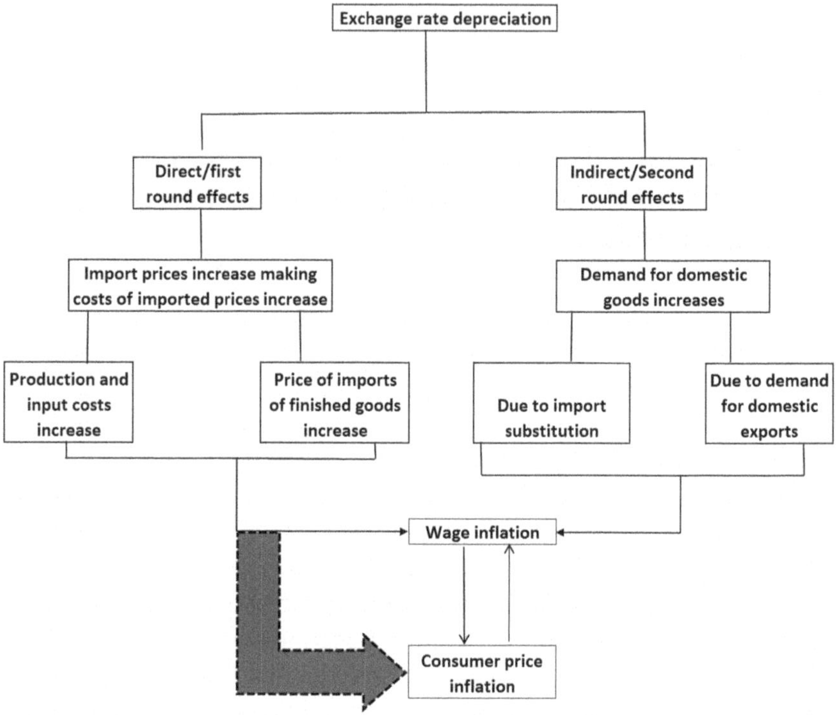

Fig. 3.1 Direct and indirect transmission of the exchange rate depreciation shocks to wage inflation. (Source: Authors' drawing and adapted from Lafleche (1996–1997))

We show the role of inflation expectations in the link between nominal wage and consumer price inflation, alternatively, the wage-inflation spiral in Fig. 3.6. We estimate a bilateral VAR model that includes nominal wage and consumer price inflation. The data is on a quarterly (Q) basis and spans the period 2000Q1 to 2017Q4. The VAR model is estimated using 2 lags and 10,000 Monte Carlo draws. The shock is a one standard deviation shock. Figure 3.2 shows that nominal wage inflation increases more in response to positive consumer price inflation shocks. In addition, consumer price inflation increases in response to positive nominal wage shocks. But it is evident in Fig. 3.2(c) that nominal wage inflation peaks at high level compared to consumer price inflation.

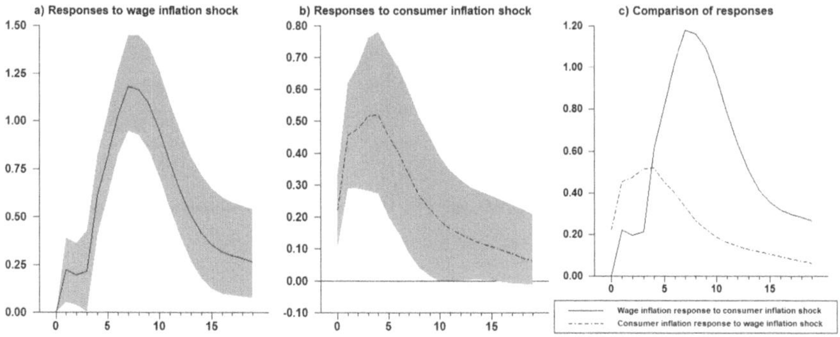

Fig. 3.2 Nominal wage and consumer price inflation responses. (Note: The grey shaded area bands denote the 16th and 84th percentile confidence bands. Source: Authors' calculations)

3.3 The Exchange Rate, Nominal Wage and Consumer Price Inflation

What about the responses of nominal wage and consumer price inflation to the exchange rate depreciation shocks? Are they significantly different? We show the lead lag relationships in Fig. 3.3(b) and (d) using the cross-correlations. The results show that consumer price and nominal wage inflation increase when preceded by the R/US$ exchange rate depreciation. These findings possibly indicate that the direct (first round) impact of the exchange rate effects is most likely more muted on nominal wage inflation.

We estimate VAR models which include the R/US$ exchange rate changes, depreciation, appreciations, consumer price and nominal wage inflation to assess the empirical validity of the results in the previous sections. The R/US$ exchange rate depreciation (appreciation) indicates positive (negative) R/US$ exchange rate changes only. We create two dummy variables that take on the values of the R/US$ exchange rate (i) depreciation and zero otherwise, and (ii) appreciation and zero otherwise. The intention is to assess the different impact of the exchange rate appreciation and depreciations on nominal wage and consumer price inflation.

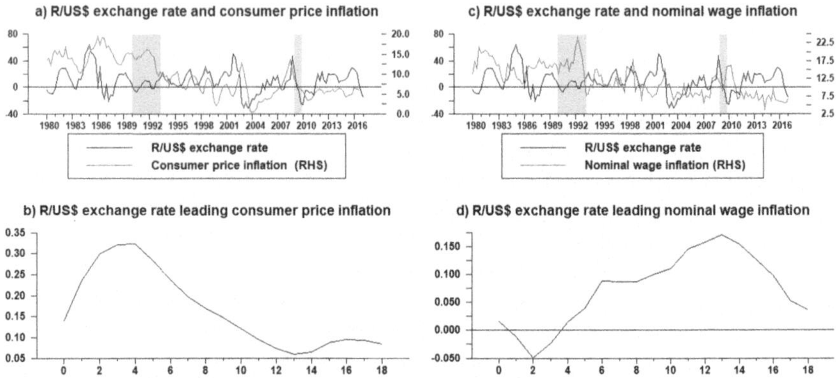

Fig. 3.3 Lead relationship between the R/US$ exchange rate changes, nominal wage and consumer price inflation. (Note: The grey shaded areas denote the South African recessions. Source: South African Reserve Bank and authors' calculations)

The dummy variables enter the VAR separately. The VAR models are estimated for the period 2000Q1 to 2017Q4 and include 2 lags and 10,000 Monte Carlo draws. The shocks are a one standard deviation shock.

The results in Fig. 3.4 indicate that the R/US$ exchange rate shocks push nominal wage and consumer price inflation in the same direction albeit at different magnitudes and timing. For instance, Fig. 3.4(c) shows that the direct impact of the R/US$ exchange rate appreciation and depreciation shocks is bigger on consumer price inflation compared to nominal wage inflation. The direct (first-round) effects of the R/US$ exchange rate changes are more pronounced on consumer price inflation compared to nominal wage inflation.

The nominal wage inflation responses are muted compared to those of consumer price inflation, and they are very unresponsive (sluggish) in the year after the shock indicating the differences in the inflation processes that inform both variables, such as the degree of wage indexation by unions over a three-year period. For instance, Fig. 3.5 shows that at peak, consumer price inflation increases by 0.57 percentage points after three quarters due to the R/US$ depreciation compared to 0.44 percentage points in the case of nominal wage inflation.

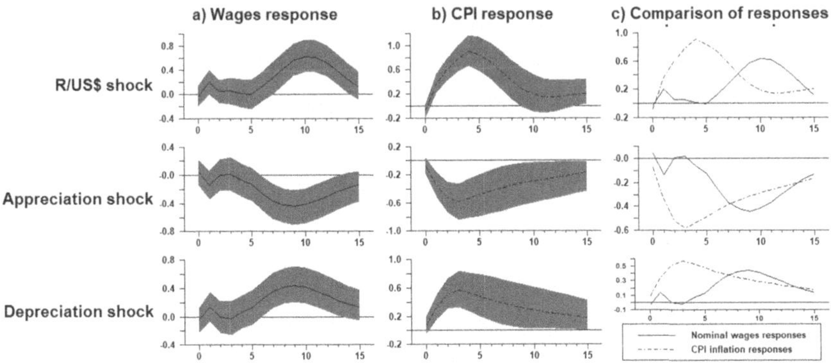

Fig. 3.4 Responses of nominal wages and inflation to R/US$ exchange rate shocks. (Note: The grey shaded area bands denote the 16th and 84th percentile confidence bands. Source: Authors' calculations)

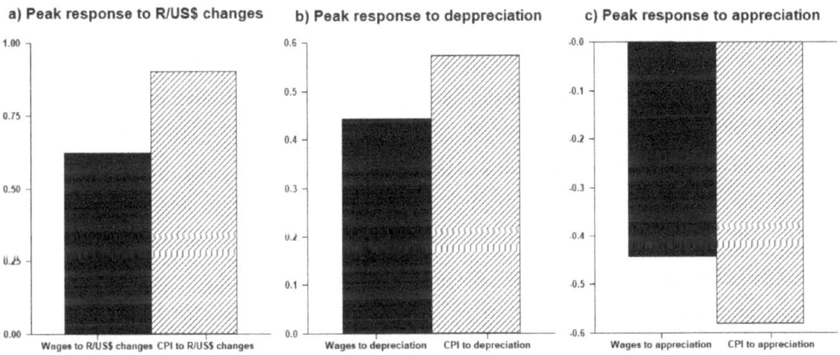

Fig. 3.5 Peak responses of nominal wages and consumer price inflation to R/US$ exchange rate shocks. (Source: Authors' calculations)

These differences are also evident in cases where the changes in the R/US$ changes are not distinguished into appreciation and depreciation shocks, where consumer price and nominal wage inflation increase by 0.9 percentage points after four quarters and 0.62 percentage points after ten quarters, respectively. Similarly, R/US$ exchange rate appreciation shocks exert more downward pressure at peak response on consumer price inflation compared to nominal wage inflation.

3.4 Are the Macroeconomic Shock Effects and Monetary Policy Responses to Nominal Wage and Consumer Prices Different?

So far, we have presented evidence that shows that the peak and sizes of nominal wage and consumer price inflation are different to the R/US$ exchange rate changes. Do positive nominal wage and consumer price inflation shocks exert the same effects on macroeconomic variables such as output and employment growth? In addition, do positive nominal wage and consumer price inflation shocks elicit the same monetary policy response? Furthermore, are the shock effects of nominal wage and consumer price inflation shocks different depending on the inflation regime? To answer these questions, we estimate VAR models for the period 2000Q1 to 2017Q4. We estimate VAR models specified as:

1. Model one which includes consumer price inflation, GDP growth, employment growth and repo rate
2. Model two which includes nominal wage inflation, GDP growth, employment growth and repo rate
3. Model three which includes the consumer price inflation dummy, GDP growth, employment growth and the repo rate
4. Model four which includes the nominal wage inflation dummy, GDP growth, employment growth and the repo rate

For the nominal wage and consumer price inflation regimes, we create two dummy variables to delineate high and low nominal wage and consumer price inflation regimes. The high (low) consumer price inflation periods equal the values of inflation above (below) 4 per cent and zero otherwise. Similarly, the high (low) nominal wage inflation regimes equals the values of nominal wage inflation above (below) 4 per cent and zero otherwise. The VAR models are estimated using 2 lags chosen by AIC and 10,000 Monte Carlo draws. All growth rates are at annual rate. The shocks are a one standard deviation shock.

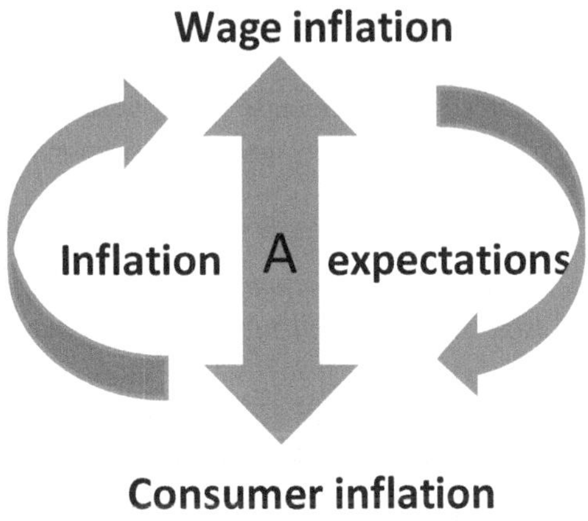

Fig. 3.6 Inflation-wage spiral relationship and the role of inflation expectations. (Source: Authors' drawing)

The estimated models are specified in such a way that we assess the validity of the theoretical assertions about the impact of consumer price inflation and nominal wage inflation on real economic variables and the policy rate. For instance, theoretically an increase in nominal wages is expected to increase labour absorption as an increase in the wage rate entices economic agents to enter the labour market. In addition, positive labour force participation shocks are expected to increase output and employment growth but lower inflation. This is because the supply side policies which increase the labour force participation rate are expected to shift the long-run supply curve function to the right and increase the long-run equilibrium output whilst lowering the price inflation. In this instance, the wage rate plays a dual role (i) of allocating jobs and (ii) affecting the behaviour of workers by influencing physical productivity, work effort and morale and determines the quality of the labour hiring pool or the probability of acceptance of a firm's employment offer.

However, there is a threshold beyond which wage inflation can result in an inflation-wage spiral, especially when taking into account the role of inflation expectations as shown in Fig. 3.6. The bilateral relationship between the consumer price and nominal wage inflation as indicated by the arrow A in Fig. 3.6 indicates the consumer price and wage-inflation spiral effects and the role of inflation expectations. Inflation expectations play a role in transmitting consumer price inflation shocks to nominal wage inflation. As a result, an increase in consumer price inflation is expected to result in a decline output and employment growth but elicit an increase in the repo rate to stem the expectations-wage-consumer price inflation spiral.

The results in Fig. 3.2 already showed that nominal wage inflation increases more (almost more than double) in response to positive consumer price inflation shocks. We concluded that this evidence indicates that the transmission of the second-round effects of the exchange rate depreciation shocks is likely to be more pronounced and persistent. The results in Fig. 3.7 indicate that indeed positive nominal wage and consumer price inflation shocks exert different effects on output and employment growth. Positive shocks to consumer price inflation (nominal wage inflation) result in a decline (increase) in output and employment growth. A comparison of the effects of the consumer price inflation shocks shows that employment growth declines more compared to output growth in Fig. 3.7(a) and (b) row (c).

On the other hand, positive shocks to nominal wage and consumer price inflation exert different effects on the repo rate. The repo rate increases in response to an increase in consumer price and nominal wage

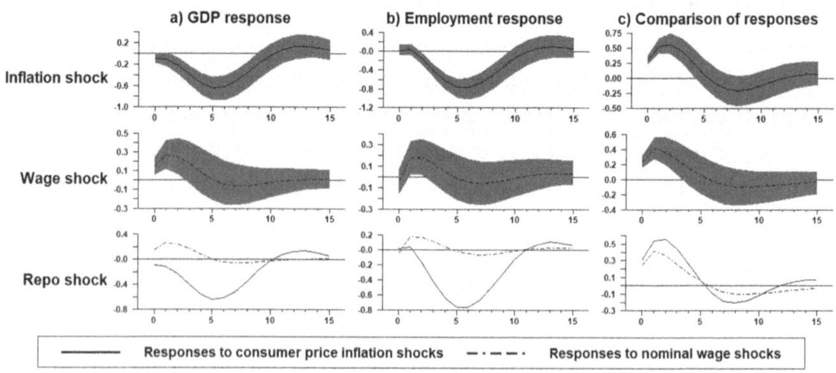

Fig. 3.7 Responses to nominal wage and consumer price inflation shocks. (Note: The grey shaded area bands denote the 16th and 84th percentile confidence bands. Source: Authors' calculations)

inflation in Fig. 3.7(row c). But it is also evident that increases in consumer price inflation exert more upward pressure on the repo rate compared to nominal wage inflation shocks.

3.4.1 Do Inflation Regimes Play a Role on the Effects of Nominal Wage and Consumer Price Inflation Shocks?

To answer this question, we estimate VAR models for the period 2000Q1 to 2017Q4. The intention is to assess the impact of the role of inflation regimes, alternatively, where consumer price inflation is relative to the target range. The results in Fig. 3.8 indicate that indeed inflation regimes relative to the 4 per cent consumer price inflation exert asymmetric responses to output and employment growth. Output and employment growth decline due to positive inflation shocks in the high inflation regime (inflation above 4 per cent) compared to low inflation regimes (inflation below 4 per cent). The results also show that inflation regimes have a bearing on the repo rate responses. Low inflation regimes result in a decline in the repo rate largely because the inflationary pressures are very muted.

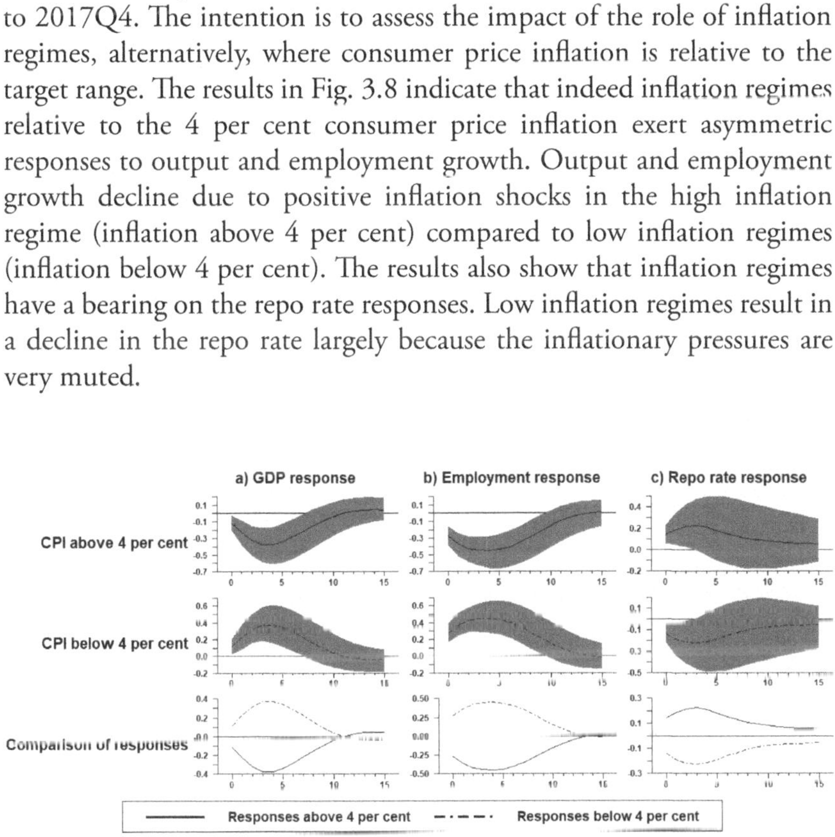

Fig. 3.8 Responses to consumer price inflation shocks above and below 4 per cent. (Note: The grey shaded area bands denote the 16th and 84th percentile confidence bands. Source: Authors' calculations)

These results concur with the evidence showing that there is a high level of macroeconomic stability during periods of low inflation regimes (inflation below 4 per cent).

3.4.2 What About Real Wage Inflation Threshold?

Does the real wage inflation threshold exert different effects on output growth, employment growth and the repo rate? Theoretically, the real wage can increase due to improvements in labour productivity or nominal wage growth that is higher than actual inflation outcomes. Thus, the impact of an increase on the real wage on output and employment growth will depend on whether the increase is induced by productivity gains or a low inflation environment. In cases where increases in labour productivity exceed (below) inflation, the impact on output and employment growth is expected to be net positive (negative). This is because nominal wage inflation is positively related to labour productivity. Thus, if labour productivity increases at a slower pace compared to nominal wages, this is expected to result in an inflationary environment. In addition, a slower pace of labour productivity growth is expected to have a dampening effect on output and employment growth aligned to the negative impact of inflation on these macroeconomic variables. Since the effects of labour productivity and inflation exert different effects on output and employment growth, they are expected to elicit different monetary policy responses depending on the inflation regimes.

These two opposing effects work via the unit labour costs. Where a decline in labour productivity increases business costs as unit labour costs increases squeeze on profit margins resulting in firms increasing prices more rapidly and exerting upward pressure on inflation. It is also possible that slower labour productivity growth can dampen aggregate demand which might neutralise some of the demand-driven inflationary pressures. Vast empirical evidence[1] shows that in the short- to medium-term, the net impact of the two opposing effects of productivity growth and inflation on real wages is *higher* inflation, largely due to the slowdown in

[1] See for instance Yellen (2005), Cochrane (2015), Chien and Arias (2015) amongst others.

labour productivity growth. This is because labour productivity growth plays an integral role in output growth, employment growth and dis-inflation, alternatively price stability.

To assess the impact of positive shocks to real wages, we estimate a VAR model which includes real wage growth, GDP growth, employment growth and repo rate. We showed in the previous chapter that real wage inflation has been subdued below 2 per cent since 2012. Does it matter where real wage inflation is at for output growth, employment growth and the repo rate responses? To analyse the role of the real wage inflation regimes, we create two dummy variables for periods during which real wage inflation is above (below) 2 per cent and zero otherwise. Similar to the previous section, we refer to periods of wage inflation above (below) 2 per cent as high (low) real wage regimes.

The results in Fig. 3.9 indicate that it does matter where real wage inflation is at, for the response of output growth, employment growth and the repo rate responses. Output growth and employment growth increase in the low real wage regime (real wage inflation below 2 per cent) compared to the high real wage regime (real wage inflation above 2 per cent). These results are consistent with the theoretical predictions of the different impact of labour productivity growth and inflation play in driving increases in real wage growth and in turn output and employment growth.

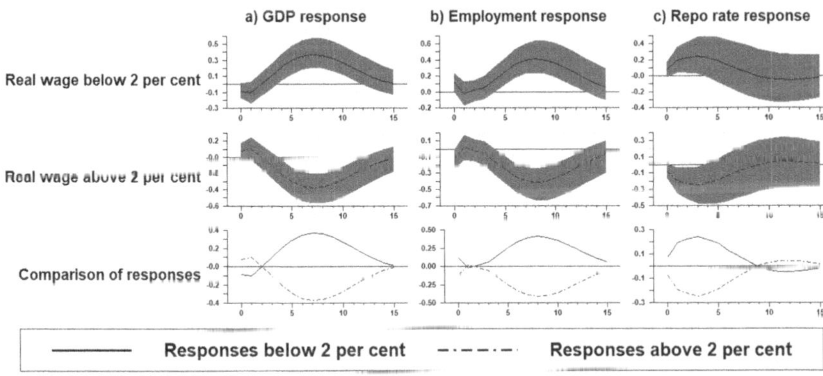

Fig. 3.9 Responses to real wage shocks above and below the 2 per cent threshold. (Note: The grey shaded area bands denote the 16th and 84th percentile confidence bands. Source: Authors' calculations)

At the same time, if real wage growth is largely driven by rapid inflation, nominal wage adjusts more than labour productivity and the inflationary pressures induce a monetary policy tightening via the increase in the repo rate.

Thus, as much as the real wage growth regime matters, the drivers of the increase in real wage also matter for the response of output and employment growth and the repo rate. In addition, even if the South African Reserve Bank were to target wage inflation as argued by Scott Sumner (1995), it would have to pay a great deal of attention to the performance of labour productivity growth to the degree it impacts output growth, employment growth and inflation. In this regard, Gumata and Ndou (2017) established that a positive labour productivity growth shock leads to a significant decline in consumer price inflation and inflation expectations. Improved labour productivity growth tends to accentuate the decline in inflation expectations. In addition, the labour productivity shock moves inflation and GDP growth in opposite directions, indicating a policy trade-off rather than a shift on the Taylor curve.

3.5 Do Exchange Rate Volatility Components Propagate the Impact of the R/US$ Exchange Rate Changes on Nominal Wage and Consumer Price Inflation?

We established in the earlier sections that the R/US$ exchange rate changes exert different effects on nominal wage and consumer price inflation. But we did not explore the role of the exchange rate volatility channel. We explore the role of the exchange rate volatility because the R/US$ exchange rate changes are more often accompanied by volatility. We decompose the exchange rate volatility components into the overall, transitory and permanent components. Furthermore, evidence in later chapters of the book shows that the nominal (NEER) and real (REER) effective exchange rates are comparable. This means that they can be used interchangeably in the estimations of the impact of the exchange rate volatility. Because the exchange rate changes are most often than not accompanied by volatility, this section assesses whether the exchange rate volatility components propagate or amplify the impact of the exchange rate depreciation and appreciation on nominal wage and consumer price inflation.

We estimate a number of counterfactual VAR models which include nominal wage inflation, consumer price inflation, the permanent exchange rate volatility component and the R/US$ depreciation and appreciation dummy variables as described earlier. We consider the impact of permanent volatility because we showed that it tends to have persistent effects compared to the transitory exchange rate volatility. The dummy variables enter the VAR models separately. The approach to estimate the exchange rate volatility components is explained in Ndou et al. (2017). The data used is quarterly (Q) from 2000Q1 to 2017Q4. The model is estimated using 2 lags and 10,000 Monte Carlo draws. The counterfactual responses show the responses when the channel of interest is not included in the model. The amplification effects due to this channel are the difference between the actual and the counterfactual response.

The results in Figs. 3.10 and 3.11 indicate that permanent exchange rate volatility shocks tend to propagate the effects of the R/US$ exchange rate depreciation and neutralise the impact of the exchange rate appreciation. The impact of the amplification of the exchange rate depreciation and appreciation shock is more pronounced on consumer price inflation.

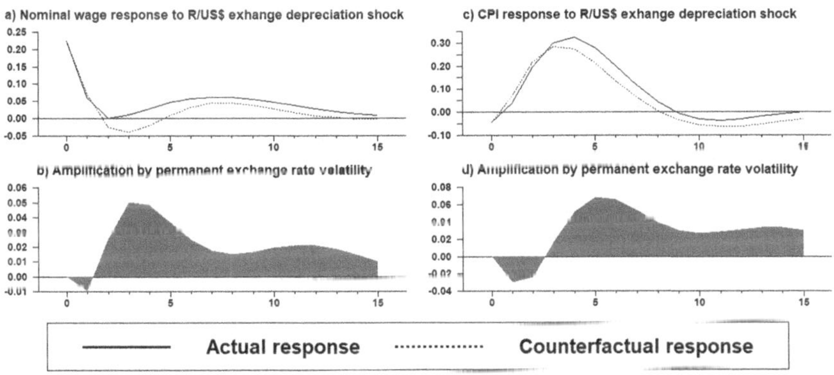

Fig. 3.10 Responses to R/US$ exchange rate depreciation shocks and amplification by permanent exchange rate volatility shocks. (Source: Authors' calculations)

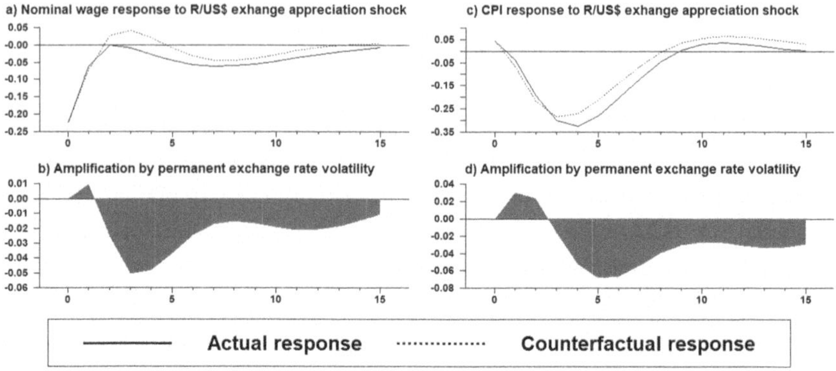

Fig. 3.11 Responses to R/US$ exchange rate appreciation and amplification by permanent exchange rate volatility shocks. (Source: Authors' calculations)

The policy implication of the results is that policy interventions to deal with the exchange rate volatility to neutralise its impact during the R/US$ exchange rate appreciation and depreciation episodes will greatly contribute to the price stability mandate.

3.6 Conclusion and Policy Implications

What is the nature of the association between the exchange rate, nominal wage and consumer price inflation? First, evidence in this chapter shows that nominal wage inflation increases more (almost more than double) in response to positive shocks to consumer price inflation. Second, the R/US$ exchange rate shocks push nominal wage and consumer price inflation in the same direction albeit at different magnitudes and timing. The direct impact of the R/US$ exchange rate changes has more impact on consumer price inflation compared to nominal wage inflation. Third, the R/US$ exchange rate depreciation and appreciation shocks exert more immediate effects on consumer price inflation compared to nominal wage inflation. Fourth, permanent exchange rate volatility shocks tend to propagate the effects of the R/US$ exchange rate depreciation and neutralise the impact of the appreciation. The impact of the amplification of the exchange rate depreciation and appreciation is more pronounced on consumer price inflation. The policy implication of the results is that policy interventions to deal with the exchange rate volatility to neutralise its impact during the R/US$ exchange rate appreciation and depreciation episodes will greatly contribute to the price stability mandate. This is especially important given the fact that the transmission of the second-round effects of the exchange rate depreciation inflationary shocks is more pronounced and persistent.

Furthermore, positive shocks to nominal wage and consumer price inflation exert different effects on output and employment growth. Positive shocks to consumer price inflation (nominal wage inflation) result in a decline (increase) in output and employment growth. A comparison of the effects of the consumer price inflation shocks shows that employment growth declines more compared to output growth. The repo rate increases in response to an increase in consumer price and nominal wage inflation. But evidence shows that increases in consumer price inflation exert more upward pressure on the repo rate compared to nominal wage inflation shocks.

In addition, periods of low inflation regimes, alternatively when consumer price inflation is above (below) 4 per cent, exert asymmetric responses to output and employment growth. Output growth and employment growth decline due to positive inflation shocks in the high inflation regime (inflation above 4 per cent) compared to low inflation regimes (inflation below 4 per cent). The results also show that inflation regimes have a bearing on the repo rate responses. Low inflation regimes result in a decline in the repo rate largely because the inflationary pressures are very muted.

Similarly, we establish that it does matter where real wage inflation is at for output growth, employment growth and the repo rate responses. Evidence shows that output and employment growth increase in the low real wage regime (real wage inflation below 2 per cent) compared to the high real wage regime (real wage inflation above 2 per cent). These results are consistent with the theoretical predictions of the different impact labour productivity growth and inflation play in driving increases in real wage growth and in turn output growth and employment growth. Evidence shows that if real wage growth is largely driven by rapid inflation, nominal wages adjust more than labour productivity growth. In turn, the inflationary pressures induce a monetary policy tightening via the increase in the repo rate.

Therefore, as much as the real wage growth regimes and thresholds matter, the drivers of the increase in real wages also matter for the response of output and employment growth and the repo rate to inflation shocks.

The policy implication is that policymakers have pay a great deal of attention to the performance of labour productivity growth to the degree it impacts output growth, employment growth and inflation. This is in line with empirical evidence showing that positive labour productivity growth shocks lead to a significant decline in consumer price inflation and inflation expectations. Improved labour productivity growth tends to accentuate the decline in inflation expectation. In addition, a labour productivity shock moves inflation and GDP growth in opposite directions, indicating a policy trade-off rather than a shift on the Taylor curve.

References

Chien, Y., and Arias, M.A. 2015. Lagging Long-Term Wage Growth. *Economic Synopses* (14), Federal Reserve Bank of St. Louis.

Cochrane, J. 2015. Wages and Inflation. The Grumpy Economist. John Cochrane's Blog. https://johnhcochrane.blogspot.com/2015/06/wages-and-inflation.html.

Gumata, N., and Ndou, E. 2017. *Bank Credit Extension and Real Economic Activity in South Africa: The Impact of Capital Flow Dynamics, Bank Regulation and Selected Macro-prudential Tools*. Palgrave Macmillan. ISBN 978-3-319-43550-3.

Lafleche, T. 1996–97. The Impact of Exchange Rate Movements on Consumer Prices. *Bank of Canada Review*, 1996–1997(Winter), 21–32.

Ndou, E., and Gumata, N. 2017. *Inflation Dynamics in South Africa: The Role of Thresholds, Exchange Rate Pass-through and Inflation Expectations on Policy Trade-offs*. Palgrave Macmillan. ISBN 978-3-319-46701-6.

Ndou, E., Gumata, N., and Ncube, M. 2017. *Global Economic Uncertainties and Exchange Rate Shocks*. Palgrave Macmillan. ISBN 978-3-319-62279-8.

Silver, S., and Sumner, S. 1995. Nominal and Real Wage Cyclicality During the Interwar Period. *Southern Economic Journal*, 61(3), 588–601. January.

Sumner, S. 1995. Using Monetary Policy to Target a Nominal Wage Index. *Journal of Economics and Business*, 47(2), 205–15. May.

Yellen, J. 2005. Productivity and Inflation. Speech at the Economic Summit at the Stanford Institute for Economic Policy Research in Palo Alto, California. FRBSF Economic Letter Number 2005-04.

Part II

An Evaluation of the Performance of the Current Inflation Targeting Framework in South Africa and Whether Nominal GDP Growth Targeting is a Viable Alternative

4

An Evaluation of How the Inflation Targeting Framework Has Performed in South Africa

Learning Objectives

- Evaluate the performance of the inflation targeting framework in South Africa.
- Assess the credibility of monetary policy conduct relative to the 3 to 6 per cent inflation target range.
- Discuss shifts in the Taylor curve.
- Evaluate the locations of different policy regimes on constant Taylor curve.
- Discuss the fiscal policy relative to the inflation target range.
- Evaluate the Taylor gaps and real house and stock price booms.

4.1 Introduction

In Chap. 31 we recommended that the South African Reserve Bank (SARB) mandate be expanded to explicitly include a mandate for maximum employment, a target for a low unemployment rate and monitor income inequality. At the same time, we recommended that the inflation target band be lowered from the current 3 to 6 per cent to 2 to

N. Gumata, E. Ndou, *Accelerated Land Reform, Mining, Growth, Unemployment and Inequality in South Africa*, https://doi.org/10.1007/978-3-030-30884-1_4

4 per cent. We also argued that these changes should be accompanied by an overhaul in the monetary policy framework and the expansion of monetary policy tools to assist the SARB to achieve its expanded mandate. However, we were silent about the assessment of the flexible inflation targeting framework currently in place. In light of prolonged deviations of real GDP growth and employment levels from linear trends post-2009 shown in Fig. 4.1, there has been a resurgence of arguments against the inflation targeting monetary policy framework. This chapter evaluates the performance of the inflation targeting regime in South Africa.

In advanced economies the debate about the adequacy of the current monetary policy frameworks was also fuelled by the persistent underperformance or undershooting of inflation targets and very subdued wage inflation. Furthermore, in the United States (US), the rapid decline in the unemployment rate is expected to go below the US Federal Reserve Bank (US Fed) estimate of the natural rate of unemployment or full employment. This has not led to an increase in consumer price and nominal wage inflation and has resulted in a persistent disconnect (divergence) between the price stability and maximum (full) employment mandates of the US Fed post-financial crisis. These developments have confirmed that the concept of maximum (full) employment is time varying as the US economy has persistently

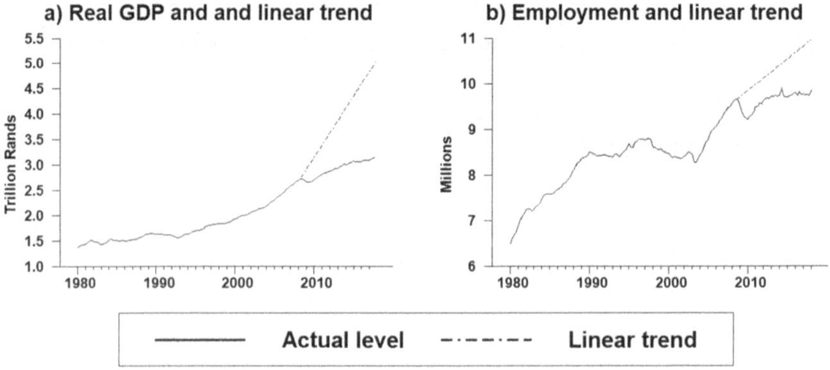

Fig. 4.1 Actual and trend real GDP and employment levels post-2009. (Source: South African Reserve Bank and authors' calculations)

surpassed estimates of maximum (full) employment without triggering higher consumer price and nominal wage inflation.

In the euro area, the European Central Bank (ECB) has engaged in various unconventional monetary policy tools so as to assist it to achieve its price stability mandate. The ECB engaged in large-scale asset purchases (LSAPs) to restore financial stability following the euro area sovereign crisis. Evidence shows that the ECB has been successful in restoring stability and the yields have declined thus creating fiscal space through which policymakers can manoeuvre and support economic activity and employment growth. Furthermore, Lenza and Slacalek (2019) find evidence to the effect that quantitative easing (QE) in the euro area by stimulating economic activity and asset prices positively affected household employment, income and wealth. The authors find that the effects of the LSAPs by the ECB also had an effect in income inequality mostly by reducing the unemployment rate for poorer households and increasing the wages of the employed. In addition, LSAPs also helped to reduce net wealth inequality slightly through its positive impact on house prices.[1]

In the case of South Africa, the argument is that had the economy corrected and output continued to grow at the pre-crisis linear trend, the level of real GDP would have been around R5 trillion and the level of formal non-agricultural employment would have been around 11 million. This means that the economy would have added roughly 2 million jobs over the past ten years had the economy continued to add a constant net 35,000 jobs per quarter. But is the flexible inflation targeting monetary policy framework to blame for the persistent subdued real economic activity post-2009?

4.2 Insight from Inflation and Output Trade-offs

The inflation targeting framework was adopted in 2000 in South Africa. The target range has been at 3–6 per cent since then. Ndou et al. (2013) use the relationship between the Taylor curve and macroeconomic

[1] See also Ampudia and Van den Heuvel (2019).

performance. They find that a negative relationship or the inflation-output growth trade-off holds. The negative relationship indicates a negative trade-off between inflation and the output-gap conditional volatilities. They also find that periods of a positive trade-off tend to be followed by a slowdown in economic growth. The implication being that periods of sub-optimal monetary policy may have adverse effects on economic growth. To visualise the shifts in the Taylor curve, the authors produce the Taylor curve shifts in Fig. 4.2.

The Taylor curve shifts in Fig. 4.2 show that the adoption of inflation targeting generally coincided with a prolonged period of macroeconomic stability. They also establish evidence of a negative trade-off in the later parts of 1990s prior to the formal adoption of inflation targeting, thus confirming that the trade-off between output and inflation volatility started before the formal implementation of the framework. This period was also characterised by prolonged disinflation.

The authors show that the average conditional volatilities for the output-gap and inflation shifted inwards between 2000Q1 and 2007Q2

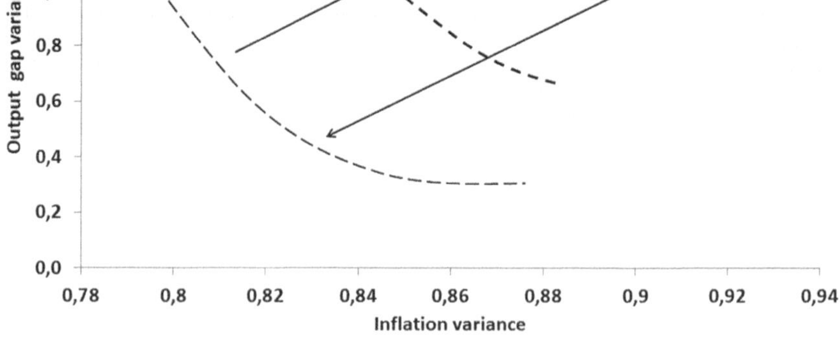

Fig. 4.2 Shifts in the South African Taylor curves. (Source: Ndou et al. (2013))

but shifted outwards between 2007Q3 and 2012Q3 in Fig. 4.2. The Taylor curve shifted inward as the lower inflation volatility for any given level of output volatility was achieved. However, the period post-financial crisis and the recession was characterised by an increase in the variance of the output-gap and inflation, thus shifting the Taylor curve outwards for the period 2007 to 2012.

Furthermore, Ndou et al. (2013) show how the South African Reserve Bank's (SARB) preferences in terms of the stabilisation of inflation relative to output has evolved as shown in Fig. 4.3.

They show that the SARB seems to have reasonably adjusted policy settings in response to the deviation of inflation from target and the deviation of output from potential in balanced way. These findings are aligned to what the flexible inflation targeting framework is about. They find that policy settings across regimes were positioned above point B which is consistent with the SARB placing equal weights on both the conditional volatilities of inflation and the output-gap in the loss function. The locations of different regimes gradually shifted downwards from point A which implies the bank placed more weight on stabilising inflation consistent with strict inflation targeting. In addition, using the Taylor principle, Ndou et al. (2013) establish that the conduct of monetary policy in South Africa varied in line with changes in the monetary policy regimes as shown in Fig. 4.4.

The Taylor principle dictates that $\theta_1 / (1 - \theta_3 - \theta_4)$ must exceed unity for a well-designed counter-inflationary monetary policy response. When it is less than one, this implies that monetary policy authorities allow the real interest rate to fall in the presence of a positive inflation shock. They fail to reject the null hypothesis of $\theta_1 = 0$ for the larger part of the period pre-2000. The Taylor principle is found to hold since 1999, except for a brief period in 2009 during the recession. They conclude that the results of the Taylor principle post-2000 suggest that the monetary policy conduct during the inflation targeting period was optimal, compared to the pre-inflation targeting period.

The results for the deviation from the Taylor principle in 2009 indicate that the argument by Sumner (2012) that because of inflation fears

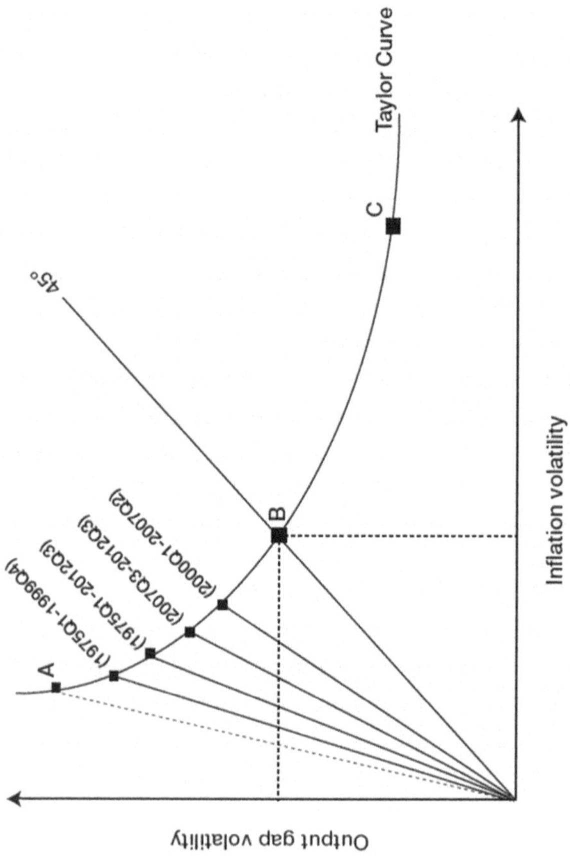

Fig. 4.3 Locations of different policy regimes on constant Taylor curve. (Source: Ndou et al. (2013))

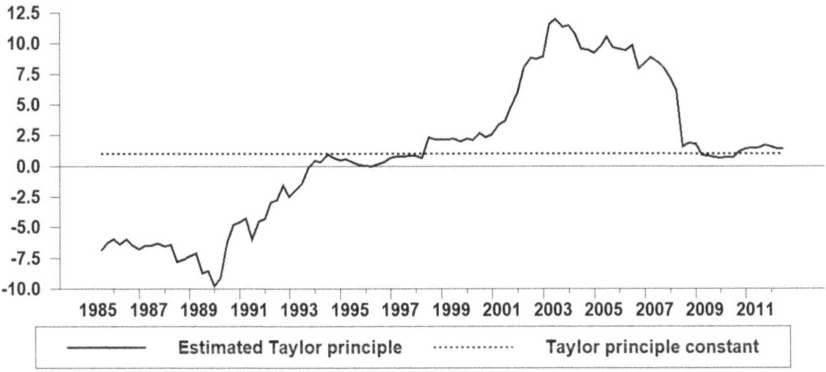

Fig. 4.4 Taylor principle in South Africa. (Note: The dotted line represents one as cut-off for the assessment of optimal monetary policy settings. Any points above the dotted line confirm the validity of Taylor principle and that the conduct of monetary policy was optimal. Anything below the dotted line indicates sub-optimal monetary policy conduct. Source: Ndou et al. (2013))

central banks did not provide enough monetary stimulus in late 2008 is not completely true. The real interest rates were negative for the best part of the period post-2009, and this case also coincided with the largest countercyclical fiscal stimulus which saw large increases in government spending and debt. Thus, it is not completely true to suggest that the inflation targeting framework has been rigid and only concentrated on stabilising the inflation volatility at all cost. Policymakers, true to the mandate of flexible inflation targeting, have also paid attention to the output-gap variability.

4.3 Evidence from Disinflation Episodes and Output Costs

With regard to the output costs of disinflation, Ndou and Gumata (2017) establish that the longest disinflation episode occurred between 1991Q1 and 2001Q3 with trend inflation declining by 9.05 percentage points. This was flowed by the 2002Q2 to 2005Q4 period which saw a further

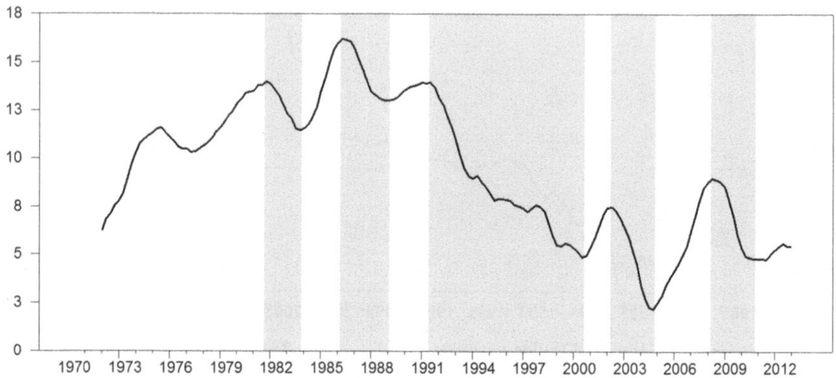

Fig. 4.5 Inflation and disinflation periods. (Note: Shaded areas refer to disinflation periods which are at least 2 percentage points lower than at the peak. The centred nine-quarter moving average inflation is expressed in per cent. Source: Ndou and Gumata (2017))

decline of 5.33 per cent in the inflation trend in and 4.18 per cent during 2008Q2 to 2011Q4 as shown in Fig. 4.5.

Figure 4.6 shows how actual output in relation to trend output performed during the disinflation periods. In four of the five identified episodes, actual output was below trend output indicating that periods of disinflation are associated with output slowing down below trend. Disinflation policies tend to result in output costs in the short run.

They present two contrasting trends of disinflation output costs and inflation persistence during the inflation targeting framework. They show that the period 2002Q2–2005Q4 was associated with the lowest disinflation output costs and inflation persistence compared to large output costs for the 2008Q2–2011Q4 period after the financial crisis and the recession in Fig. 4.7.

The post-crisis inflation targeting regime is associated with larger magnitudes of inflation persistence. The higher the size of the inflation persistence coefficient, the higher the output sacrifice ratio. This means that the high degree of inflation persistence during the inflation targeting period

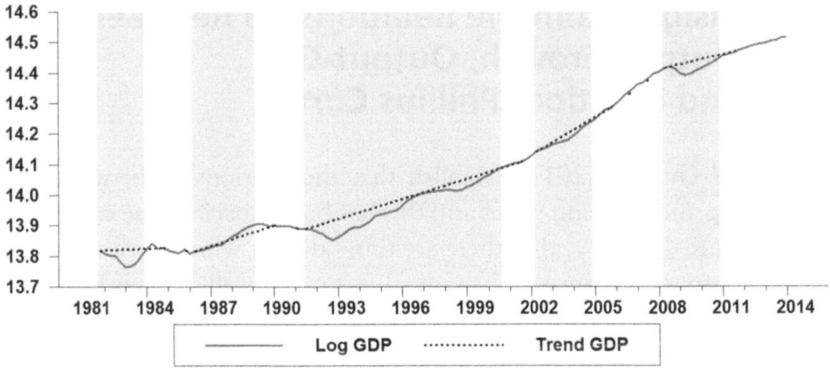

Fig. 4.6 Actual and trend output during disinflation episodes. (Note: The shaded areas refer to disinflation periods. Source: Ndou and Gumata (2017))

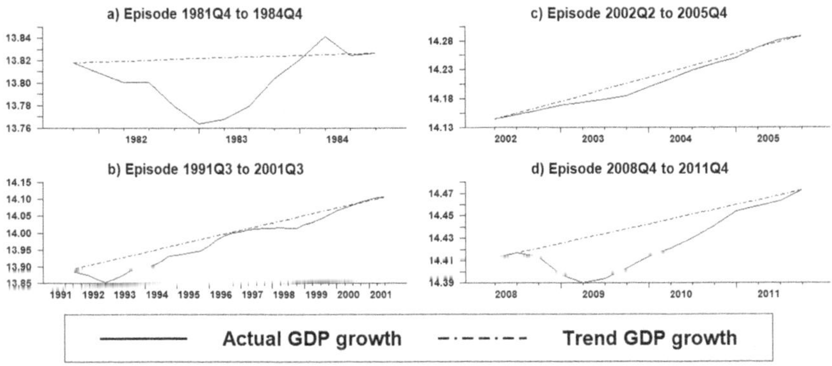

Fig. 4.7 Actual and trend GDP growth during disinflation episodes. (Source: Ndou and Gumata (2017))

has required an aggressive monetary policy stance thus leading to large output losses. High degrees of inflation persistence are prevalent in backward-looking price formation expectations environment.

4.4 Insight from the Relationship Between Output Growth, Output-Gap and Inflation (Phillips Curve)

Ndou and Gumata (2017) establish that the relationship between the output-gap and inflation varies and this has been especially the case post-2009. Figure 4.8 shows that there are times during which both inflation and the output-gap move in the same direction, as well as times in which they diverge. The nature of shocks that drive inflation and the output-gap may at times move these variables in different directions. Pre-2009, the relationship between the output-gap and inflation was positive and steep, but it has been rather weak and slightly negative post-2009. These trends mean that the period post-2009 has been characterised by the simultaneous occurrence of a negative and widening output-gap and inflation deviations from the target band.

The flattening of the Phillips curve post-2009 as shown in Fig. 4.8 implies that inflation has become less responsive to resource slack (the output gap). Hence there is a noticeable change in the dynamic relationship between inflation and the output-gap. Clarida (2019) states that a

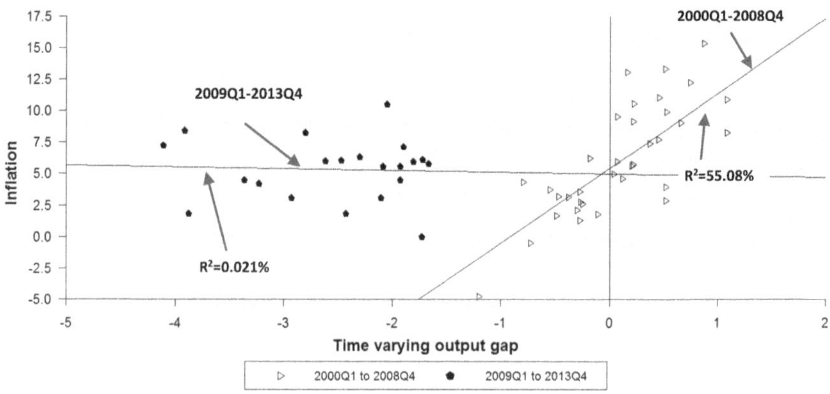

Fig. 4.8 Inflation and output-gap post-2009. (Source: Ndou and Gumata (2017))

flatter Phillips curve is a proverbial double-edged sword. This is because it allows policymakers to support employment more aggressively during downturns as a sustained inflation breakout is less likely to occur when the Phillips curve is flatter. Nonetheless, a flatter Phillips curve also increases the cost economic output of reversing the unwelcome increases in longer-run inflation expectations. As a result, a flatter Phillips curve makes it all the more important that longer-run inflation expectations remain anchored at levels consistent with low and stable inflation.

4.5 The Existence of Thresholds Within the Current Inflation Target Range

Within the debate about the appropriateness of the current 3 to 6 per cent inflation target range, Ndou and Gumata (2017) provide evidence showing the impact of various shocks and the importance of the thresholds within the target range. The authors use the transition functions within the current inflation target to capture the manner in which inflation moves from a low to a high inflation regime as it responds to certain shocks. The authors show that positive inflation shocks when inflow is between 0 and 3 per cent, and below 4.5 per cent exert positive effects on GDP growth. This contrasts with negative effects exerted when inflation is above 6 per cent and 6.5 per cent, as GDP growth declines. These results imply that policymakers can exploit the inflation-output trade-off to their advantage when inflation is within certain thresholds within the current 3 to 6 per cent inflation target range.

To further demonstrate the importance of thresholds within the current inflation target range, they provide evidence showing that under different specifications based of the economic growth theories, by the time the inflation rate hits 5 per cent, the economy has transitioned from a low to a high inflation regime in Fig. 4.9. The transition functions of inflation from the low to the high inflation regime in Fig. 4.9 provide further evidence that a lower inflation target range of 2 to 4 per cent is consistent with a lower inflation regime.

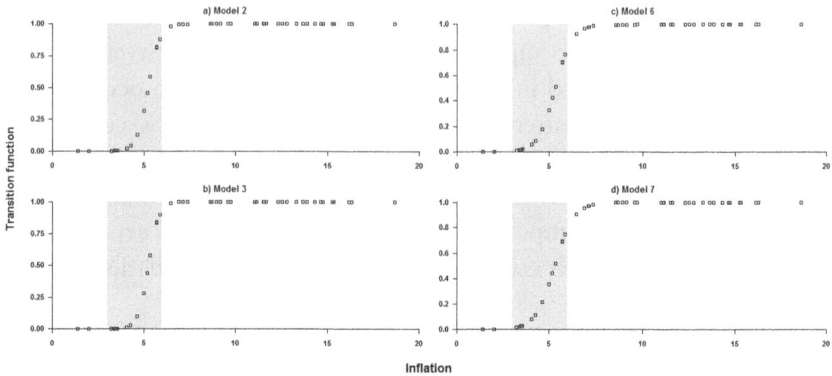

Fig. 4.9 The transition functions of various inflation threshold models. (Note: The shaded portion denotes the 3–6 per cent target band. Source: Ndou and Gumata (2017))

4.6 The Inflation Target Range and Thresholds Matter for the Pass-Through of Shocks

The authors also present vast empirical evidence showing that the target range and inflation regimes matter for the pass-through of the R/US$ exchange rate. For instance, they show that the degree of the R/US$ exchange rate and the pass-through to import prices depends on the relative position of inflation within the target range. They present evidence showing that the transition in the R/US$ exchange rate pass-through (ERPT) from a low to a high inflation regime occurs at 4 per cent in Fig. 4.10. Evidence shows that by the time inflation reaches 6 per cent, we are already in a higher inflation regime. In terms of the magnitudes of the R/US$ ERPT to inflation in different inflation regimes, they estimate that the ERPT increases from 0.51 per cent in the low inflation regime to 0.54 per cent in the higher inflation regime.

Furthermore, they show that the amplification magnitudes induced by inflation differ when inflation is (i) above and below 6 per cent, (ii) between 3 and 6 per cent and (iii) below 4.5 per cent in Fig. 4.11. The

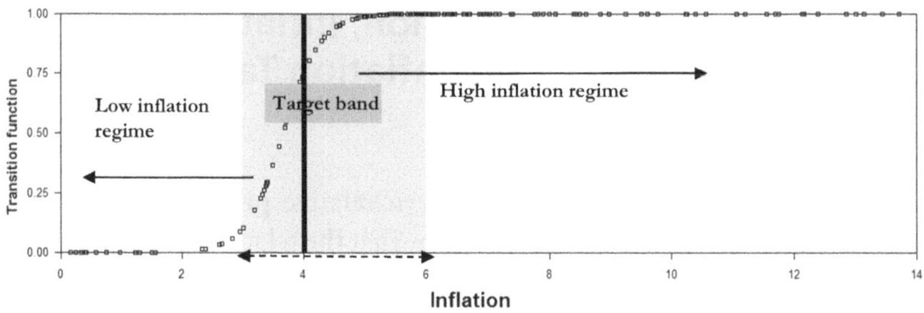

Fig. 4.10 The shape of the transition function for the inflation threshold. (Note: The vertical line in the shaded area denotes the estimated inflation threshold. Source: Ndou and Gumata (2017))

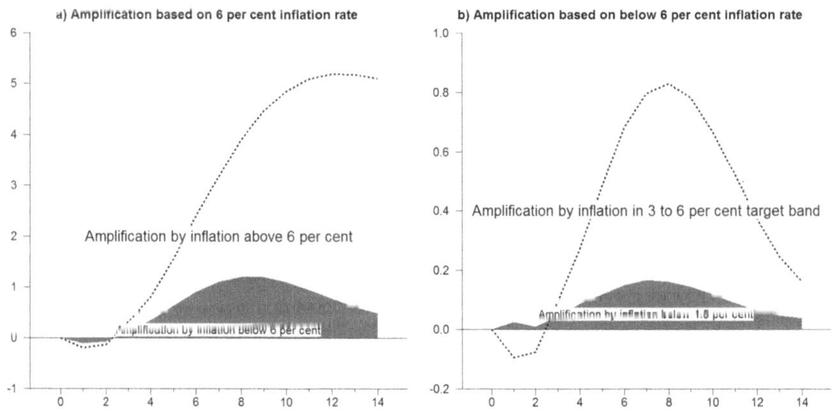

Fig. 4.11 Import price amplification effects based on the level of inflation. (Source: Ndou and Gumata (2017))

cumulative propagating ability of inflation is much lower and almost diminished when inflation is below 4.5 per cent compared to when it is above and just below 6 per cent. They conclude that the level of inflation within the target range matters and the enforcement of price stability weakens the propagating abilities of inflation.

4.7 Relative Price Dispersion, Inflation and the Role of the Inflation Target Range

With respect to the relationship between relative price dispersion and inflation, Ndou and Gumata (2017) show that the relative price dispersion increases more as the rate of inflation increases.

They show in Fig. 4.12 that relative service price dispersion is minimised at a monthly inflation rate of 0.473 per cent or annual inflation of 5.8 per cent for the period 2000M2 to 2011M12, which is within the current inflation target range. They conclude that the period of inflation targeting contributed to the decline in the inflation threshold for the relative services price dispersion.

4.8 Monetary Policy Conduct and Asset Price Booms and Busts

Asset price booms and busts are an important aspect of the conduct of monetary policy to the degree that they influence the price formation process and inflation expectations. With respect to the conduct of

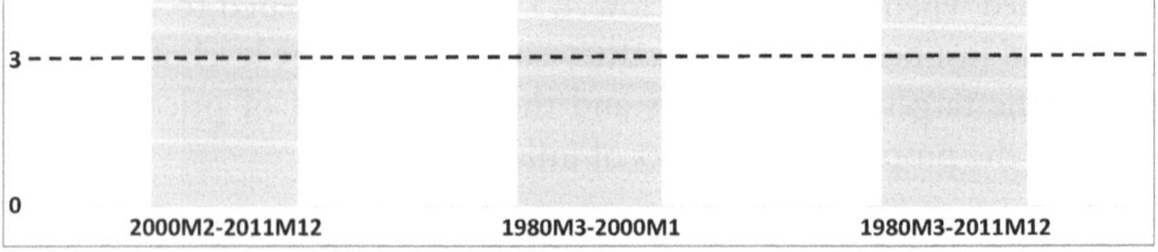

Fig. 4.12 Points at which the inflation rate minimises relative service price dispersion. (Source: Ndou and Gumata (2017))

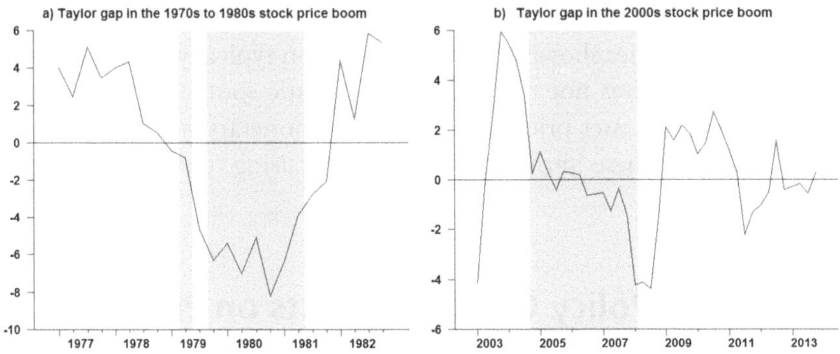

Fig. 4.13 Taylor gaps during costly stock price booms. (Note: Shaded areas refer to periods of costly stock price booms. Source: Ndou and Gumata (2017))

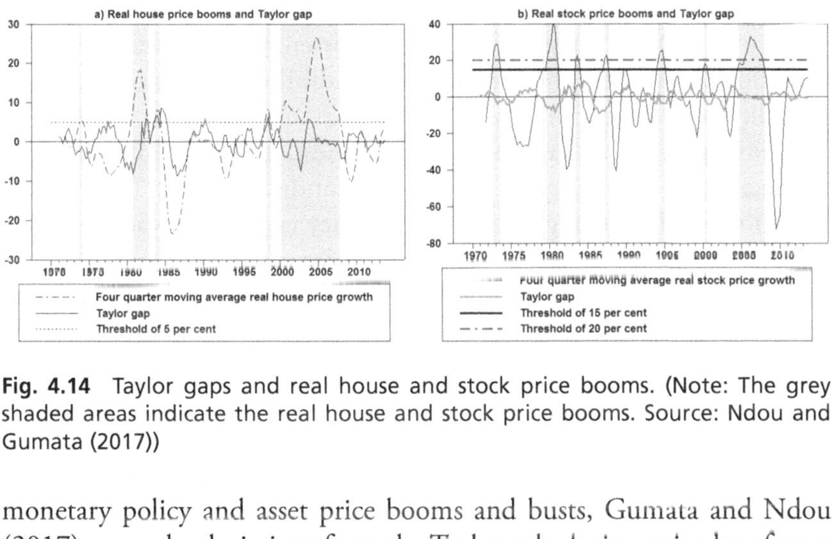

Fig. 4.14 Taylor gaps and real house and stock price booms. (Note: The grey shaded areas indicate the real house and stock price booms. Source: Ndou and Gumata (2017))

monetary policy and asset price booms and busts, Gumata and Ndou (2017) assess the deviations from the Taylor rule during episodes of asset price booms and busts. They analyse the interaction of nominal interest rates, real interest rates, inflation-gap and the output-gap to assess whether monetary policy was accommodative during these costly boom episodes.

In Figs. 4.13 and 4.14, they show that monetary policy was highly accommodative during the late 1970s and early 1980s real equity and house price booms, but this was not necessarily the case during these booms under the inflation targeting period. Their results corroborate various other studies showing that with inflation typically under control, monetary policy was not the main or systematic source of the excesses that led to recent asset price booms. Rather, monetary policy effectively accommodated these growing imbalances, raising the risk of damaging busts.

4.9 Fiscal Policy Conduct Effects on Price Stability and the Inflation Targeting Regime

Theory is unequivocal about the existence of the causal connection between fiscal discipline and inflation. For instance, Mishkin and Savastano (2001) suggest that the worsening in fiscal solvency conditions may affect the central bank credibility to control inflation. In addition, De Mendonca and Da Silva (2016) show that fiscal discipline is important for low and stable inflation. These authors show the importance of credibility in fiscal policy conduct matters. Ndou et al. (2019) show that strong (weak) fiscal policy credibility leads to a significant exchange rate appreciation (depreciation) and reduces (increases) inflation and inflation expectations. In addition, the exchange rate appreciates more due to a persistently rising fiscal credibility shock compared to a non-persistent shock. The decline in inflation is larger due to a persistently rising fiscal policy credibility shock compared to a non-persistent shock. This means that a persistent increase in fiscal policy credibility is necessary to support exchange rate appreciations and inflation declines.

The authors present evidence showing that fiscal policy credibility neutralises the transmission of exchange rate depreciation shocks to inflation and inflation expectations especially in high inflation regimes. High fiscal policy credibility dampens the pass-through of exchange rate depreciation shocks. Thus, fiscal policy credibility plays an important role in neutralising the transmission of exchange rate depreciation shocks, dampens inflation expectations and assists monetary policy in achieving the price stability mandate.

With respect to the impact of fiscal policy credibility shocks on the ERPT to consumer price inflation, Ndou et al. (2019) show evidence that fiscal policy credibility shocks lower the ERPT. The decline in the ERPT is bigger in the low inflation regimes compared to the high inflation regimes. In addition, the positive fiscal policy credibility shock leads to more fluctuations in the ERPT in the low inflation regimes (when inflation is below 6 per cent). The authors argue that this evidence shows that fiscal discipline is important in reducing the level of ERPT and the effects are magnified in low inflation regime. Furthermore, the decline in the ERPT is bigger due to persistent improvements in fiscal policy credibility. This means that the improvement in fiscal policy credibility is an important channel that helps in reducing the degree of the ERPT. Weak fiscal policy credibility post-2012 led to an increase in the ERPT, thus neutralising the impact of fiscal credibility in lowering the ERPT. These findings reinforce the fact that strong fiscal policy credibility matters for the achievement of the price stability mandate. In addition, low inflation regimes matter for the transmission of fiscal shocks to prices and the real economy.

4.10 The Role of Economic Policy Uncertainty and Channels of Transmission into the Domestic Economy

The period post-2009 was characterised by heighted economic policy uncertainty as shown in Fig. 4.15.

Caldara et al. (2014) shows that uncertainty shocks have a significant macroeconomic impact in situations where they elicit a tightening of credit and financial conditions. In addition, Farmer (2011) shows that not only do market participant's expectations or beliefs exert an independent influence on economic activity, they also select equilibrium. Ndou

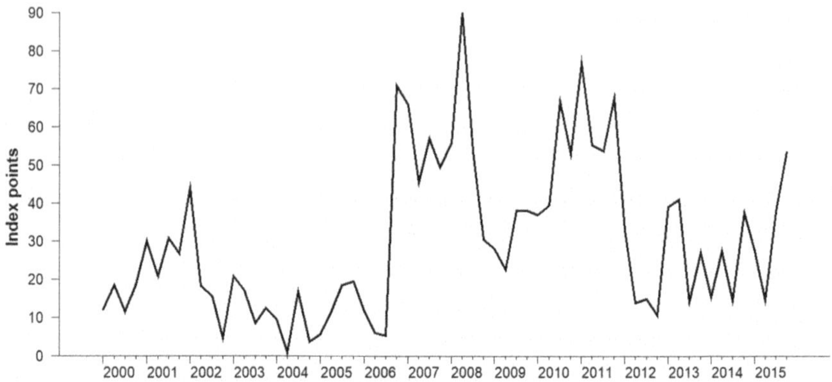

Fig. 4.15 The South African policy uncertainty index. (Source: Hlatshwayo and Saxegaard (2016))

et al. (2019) explore the role of domestic policy uncertainty and how it is transmitted into real economic activity and might partly explain subdued economic activity post-2009 despite the conduct of highly expansionary monetary and fiscal policies. The authors provide evidence showing that policy uncertainty indirectly accentuates adverse economic effects by acting as a propagation channel to various shocks. In addition, elevated economic policy uncertainty may neutralise the effects of looser monetary policy settings and exchange rate depreciations.

With respect to inflation uncertainty, the authors show that together with other uncertainty measures in Fig. 4.16, it contributed negatively and resulted in muted consumption expenditure growth. Inflation uncertainty drags consumption expenditure and worsens its decline due to adverse economic shocks. Hence, the prevalence of inflation uncertainty has adverse effects on consumption expenditure and price stability matters.

They conclude that uncertainty should be minimised as it directly and adversely affects economic activity and indirectly propagates other shocks.

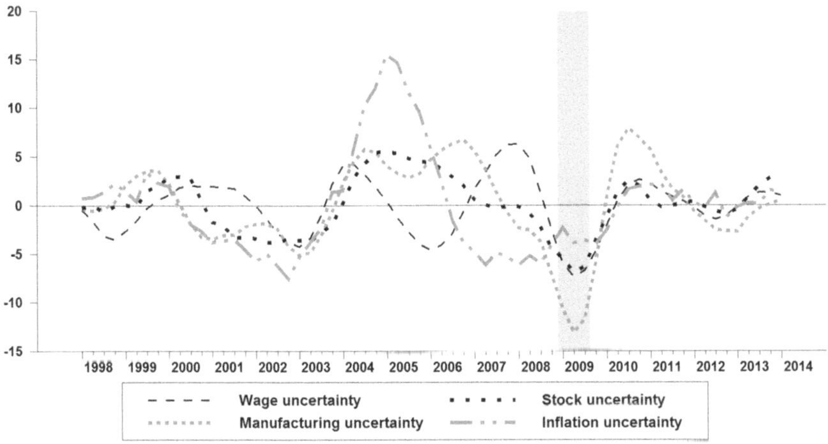

Fig. 4.16 Contributions of various forms of uncertainty to consumption expenditure growth. (Note: The grey shaded portion refers to recession in 2009. Source: Ndou et al. 2019)

4.11 How Has the Credibility of Monetary Policy in South Africa Evolved?

To conclude the evaluation of the inflation targeting framework in South Africa, we assess the credibility of monetary policy conduct. Ndou et al. (2019) show that there are a number of ways in which the credibility of monetary policy conducted can be assessed. They use the Bordo and Siklos (2014, 2015), Lopez-Villavicencio and Mignon (2017) measures of credibility as shown on Fig. 4.17. Evidence indicates that monetary policy has become more credible during the inflation targeting period, especially post-2009. This is because the deviation of the inflation outcomes relative to the inflation target have been minimum, especially post-2009.

However, another measure of monetary policy credibility is how well anchored inflation expectations are. Figure 4.18 shows that the eight-year break-even inflation rates as a proxy for long-term inflation expectations have been largely close to 6 per cent since 2007. Similarly, Fig. 4.19 shows current and one-year ahead BER expectations of nominal wage and salary increases have been in excess of 6 per cent. The trends presented in

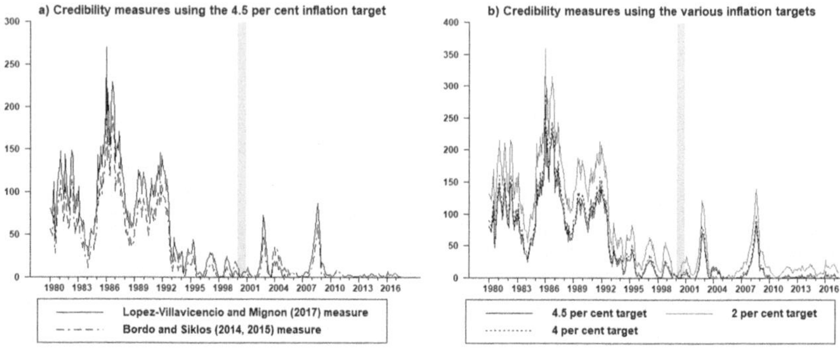

Fig. 4.17 Monetary policy credibility indicators. (Note: The grey shaded areas denote the South African recession. Source: Ndou et al. 2019)

Figs. 4.18 and 4.19 suggest that economic agents have undertaken a view that future inflation will be persistently around (and even slightly above) 6 per cent, contrary to what the Lopez-Villavicencio and Mignon (2017) and Siklos (2014, 2015) measures of credibility in Fig. 4.17 suggest about policy conduct. There is a persistent disconnect between policy conduct, inflation outcomes and inflation expectations.

Thus, viewed from the inflation expectations perspective, it seems that monetary policy conduct is less credible as inflation expectations have been largely "poorly" anchored during the inflation targeting period. This is despite the actual inflation outcomes relative to the inflation target. Ndou and Gumata (2017) find evidence indicating that the concurrence of the adverse supply shocks and positive inflation expectations shocks can have devastating effects on economic activity. The repo rate is adjusted aggressively to a positive aggregate demand shock and this translates into a quick decline in the response of inflation expectations. The policy implication is that financial market participants do indeed believe that the monetary policy authority deals decisively with positive aggregate demand shocks. Hence, monetary policy conduct may have earned credibility in dealing with demand-driven inflationary shocks.

But the results differ in relation to the policy responses due to supply shocks and positive inflation shocks. Irrespective of the fact that positive inflation expectations shocks and the adverse supply shocks lead to a persistent rise in inflation expectations and the depreciation in the

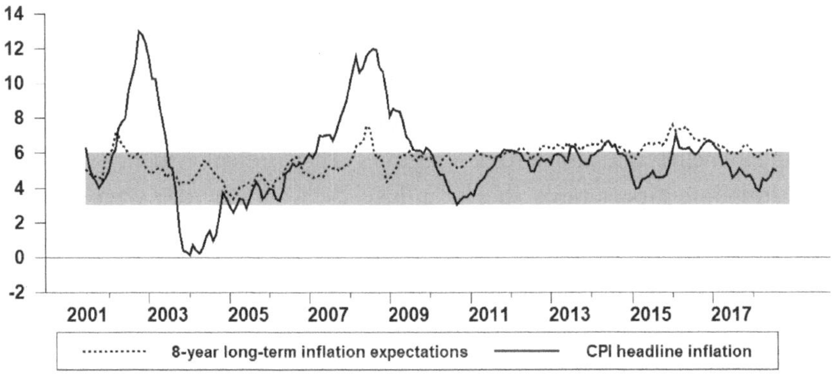

Fig. 4.18 Inflation and eight-year long-term inflation expectation. (The eight-year long-term inflation expectations are derived from the difference between the yields of the R186 nominal and the R197 inflation-indexed bonds. Note: Shaded area denotes the inflation target band. Source: South African Reserve Bank and authors' calculations)

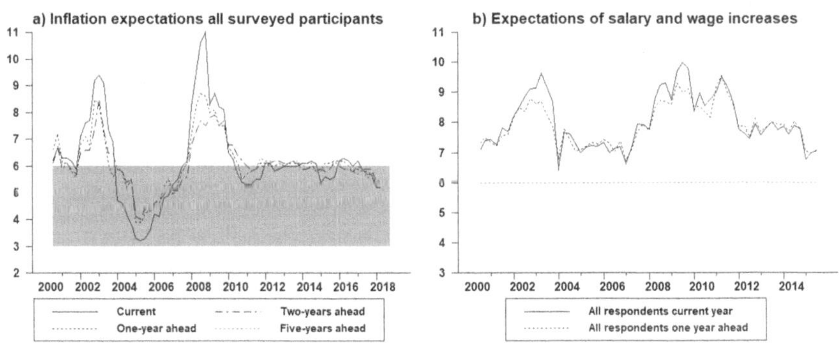

Fig. 4.19 Inflation expectations and expected salary and wage increases. (Source: South African Reserve Bank and authors' calculations)

exchange rate, agents have learned that policy is "partially accommodative" to these shocks. Ndou and Gumata (2017) argue that, from a policy perspective, the findings reinforce the view that the concurrence of adverse supply shocks and positive inflation expectations shocks that tend to move economic variables in the same direction and this can have debilitating effects on economic activity. This means that policymakers should take appropriate action when necessary to mitigate that expected prices do not become realised prices.

However, Ndou and Gumata (2017) present evidence that inflation expectations are affected by a constant learning process and economic agents do update beliefs and adjust to new regimes. They present evidence showing that inflation expectations shocks induce cyclicality in the wage setting process and there are downward rigidities in the labour market which may be largely on account of the prevalence of inflation-indexed labour contracts which last for multiyear periods. They conclude that allowing inflation expectations to remain high has the unintended consequences as policy initiatives may not be able to anchor wage growth within the inflation target band. Achieving sustainable desirable inflation outcomes and well anchored inflation expectations requires policymakers to engage on a persistent drive of "moral suasion" with price setters to discourage the perpetual behaviour of wage indexation outside the inflation target band.

Thus, evidence presented in this chapter indicates that the inflation targeting framework has performed fairly well despite the divergence between the measures of credibility. Macroeconomic performance has been robust and persistent under the inflation targeting framework, especially in periods during which inflation has been between 2 and 4 per cent. Which further bolsters the case for lowering the inflation target range. Although, the period post-2009 has been marred by poor macroeconomic performance, the conduct of monetary policy has been credible when assessed from the inflation outcomes perspective. It may also be the case that lowering the inflation target range is an indirect policy approach to anchor inflation and wage expectations lower in line with economic environments characterised by backward-looking inflation expectations processes.

4.12 Conclusion and Policy Implications

How has the inflation targeting framework performed in South Africa? This chapter evaluated the performance of the inflation targeting framework in South Africa from several perspectives. Insight from the inflation and output-gap trade-off indicates that the Taylor curve shifted inwards between 2000Q1 and 2007Q2 as lower inflation volatility for any given level of output volatility was achieved. Furthermore, evidence shows that the SARB seems to have reasonably adjusted policy settings in response to the deviation of inflation from target and the deviation of output from potential in balanced way. These findings are aligned to what the flexible inflation targeting framework is about. Insight from the relationship between output growth, output-gap and inflation shows that the Phillips curve has become flatter post-2009. The relationship between the output-gap and inflation has been rather weak and slightly negative post-2009. These trends mean that the period post-2009 has been characterised by the simultaneous occurrence of a negative and widening output-gap and inflation deviations from the target band.

Furthermore, within the debate about the appropriateness of the current 3 to 6 per cent inflation target range, evidence shows that there are thresholds within the current inflation target band where policymakers can exploit the inflation-output trade-off to their advantage. These inflation thresholds lie between 2 and 4 per cent. In addition, evidence shows that various measures of the credibility of monetary policy conduct indicate that monetary policy has become more credible during the inflation targeting period, especially post-2009. This is because the deviation of the inflation outcomes relative to the inflation target has been minimum, especially post-2009. Thus, evidence presented in this chapter indicates that the inflation targeting framework has performed fairly well and the macroeconomic performance has been robust under the inflation targeting framework, especially in periods during which inflation has been between 2 and 4 per cent.

References

Ampudia, M., and Van den Heuvel, S.K. 2019. *Monetary Policy and Bank Equity Values in a Time of Low and Negative Interest Rates*. Finance and Economics Discussion Series 2019-064. Board of Governors of the Federal Reserve System, Washington.

Bordo, M., and Siklos, P. 2014. *Central Bank Credibility, Reputation and Inflation Targeting in Historical Perspective*. NBER Working Papers 20693.

Bordo, M.D., and Siklos, P.L. 2015. *Central Bank Credibility Before and After the Crisis*. NBER Working Paper No. 21710.

Caldara, D., Fuentes-Albero, C, Gilchrist, S., and Zakrajsek, E. 2014. *The Macroeconomic Impact of Financial and Uncertainty Shock*. Board of Governors of the Federal Reserve System International Finance Discussion Papers No. 1166.

Clarida, R.H. 2019. The Federal Reserve's Review of Its Monetary Policy Strategy, Tools, and Communication Practices. Remarks at "The Bank of Finland Conference on Monetary Policy and Future of EMU [Economic and Monetary Union]" Helsinki, Finland.

De Mendonca, H.F., and Da Silva, R.T. 2016. Fiscal Effects from Inflation Targeting: The Brazilian Experience. *Applied Economics*, 41(7), 885–97. Taylor & Francis Journals.

Farmer, R.E.A. 2011. *Confidence, Crashes and Animal Spirits*. NBER Working Paper No. 14846.

Gumata, N., and Ndou, E. 2017. *Bank Credit Extension and Real Economic Activity in South Africa: The Impact of Capital Flow Dynamics, Bank Regulation and Selected Macro-prudential Tools*. Palgrave Macmillan. ISBN 978-3-319-43550-3.

Hlatshwayo, S., and Saxegaard, M. 2016. *The Consequences of Policy Uncertainty: Disconnects and Dilutions in the South African Real Effective Exchange Rate-Export Relationship*. IMF Working Paper WP/16/113.

Lenza, M., and Slacalek, J. 2019. Quantitative Easing Did Not Increase Inequality in the Euro Area. *ECB Research Bulletin No. 54*. https://www.ecb.europa.eu/pub/economic-research/resbull/2019/html/ecb.rb190129.en.pdf

Lopez-Villavicencio, A., and Mignon, M. 2017. Exchange Rate Pass Through in Emerging Countries: Do the Inflation Environment, Monetary Policy Regime and Central Bank Behaviour Matter? *Journal of Money and Finance*, 79, 20–38. Elsevier.

Mishkin, F.S., and Savastano, M.A. 2001. *Monetary Policy Strategies for Latin America*. NBER Working Paper No. 7617.

Ndou, E., and Gumata, N. 2017. *Inflation Dynamics in South Africa: The Role of Thresholds, Exchange Rate Pass-through and Inflation Expectations on Policy Trade-offs*. Palgrave Macmillan. ISBN 978-3-319-46701-6.

Ndou, E., Gumata, N., Ncube, M., and Olson, E. 2013. *An Empirical Investigation of the Taylor Curve in South Africa*. African Development Bank Working Paper No. 189.

Ndou, E., Gumata, N., and Tshuma, M.M. 2019. *Exchange Rate Pass Through, Second Round Effects and Inflation Process, Evidence from South Africa*. Palgrave Macmillan. ISBN 978-3-030-13931-5.

Siklos, P.L. 2014. Boom and Bust Cycles in Emerging Markets: How Important is the Exchange Rate. *Journal of Macroeconomics*, 56(C), 172–87. Elsevier.

Siklos, P.L. 2015. *Has Monetary Policy Changes? How the Crisis Shifted the Ground Under Central Banks*. Rimini Centre for Economic Analysis Working Paper Series 18-10.

Sumner, S. 2012. The Case for Nominal GDP Targeting. Mercatus Center at George Mason University. https://papers.ssrn.com/sol3/papers.cfm?abstract_id=3255027

5

Is There a Case for Nominal GDP Growth Targeting in South Africa and Abandoning Inflation Targeting?

Learning Objectives

- Assess whether there is a case for nominal GDP growth targeting in South Africa.
- Establish the shifts in the inflation gap and NGDP growth gaps overtime.
- Determine the Taylor rule prescriptions for consumer price inflation and NGDP growth under different target rates.
- Understand what happens to the Taylor rule prescriptions under NGDP growth target rates.

5.1 Introduction

Post the financial global crisis, the debate for changes in the monetary policy frameworks ranged from (i) abandoning the flexible inflation targeting monetary policy framework, (ii) increasing the inflation targets, (iii) targeting nominal wage inflation, (iv) targeting the price level or (v) targeting the level or growth rate of nominal GDP (NGDP). The thrust

N. Gumata, E. Ndou, *Accelerated Land Reform, Mining, Growth, Unemployment and Inequality in South Africa*, https://doi.org/10.1007/978-3-030-30884-1_5

of the arguments to change the monetary policy frameworks is that the inflation targeting monetary policy framework is not robust enough and has serious flaws and failed during the recent financial crisis. For instance, Sumner (2012) argues that because of inflation fears, the United States Federal Reserve Bank (US Fed) did not provide enough monetary stimulus in late 2008, thus allowing the largest decline in nominal spending since the 1930s. This adverse demand shock intensified the effects of the financial crisis and led to high unemployment. He argues that NGDP targeting (i) would have greatly reduced the severity of the recession, (ii) eliminated the need for fiscal stimulus, (iii) made it much easier for politicians to resist calls for bailouts of private sector firms, (iv) made asset price bubbles slightly less likely to occur, (v) assured low inflation on average and (vi) reduced the severity of the business cycle. We test the validity of these claims in this chapter using the South African data with especial emphasis on the period of the inflation targeting framework. We ask: Is there a case for NGDP targeting in South Africa and abandoning the inflation targeting? Would the South African Reserve Bank (SARB) be worse-off if it was targeting nominal GDP?

We contribute to the academic and policy discussions in this area by doing one-to-one comparison of how NGDP targeting would have fared in South Africa relative to the current inflation targeting framework. Similar to the analysis conducted in Chap. 4 on the evaluation of the inflation targeting regime through shifts in the Taylor curve over time, we estimate shifts in the consumer price inflation (CPI) and NGDP gap volatilities over time. In addition, to get a sense of how the conduct of monetary policy would have evolved under the NGDP growth target versus the CPI inflation target, we estimate the Taylor rule prescriptions and compare them to the current monetary policy stance under different targets. This comparison of the Taylor rule prescriptions enables us to understand how monetary policy would have reacted to the NGDP growth and CPI variables as policy targets. Alternatively, does the NGDP growth target imply that we must target the same growth rate as that of CPI inflation in South Africa or is it equivalent to a higher growth rate?

5.2 What Is Nominal GDP Targeting?

The idea of an NGDP growth target was initially proposed in the 1980s[1] as an alternative to the money supply targets which were failing as nominal anchors for monetary policy. It was resurrected post-financial crisis as an alternative to the inflation targeting monetary policy framework.[2] The NGDP is total nominal income in the economy. Similar to inflation targeting, NGDP targeting can be formulated in terms of either levels or rates of change (growth rates). The targeting of the NGDP level or growth means that the inflation target falls off and instead the central bank targets the total amount of nominal spending in the economy. Whereas price-level targeting and nominal income targeting are closely related.[3]

Sumner (2012) defines NGDP growth targeting as a single target that can also satisfy the dual mandate since NGDP growth is the sum of inflation and real growth, and the latter depends on the state of employment. The author argues that a stable path of NGDP growth would tend to stabilise employment more effectively than an inflation target. This is because the employers' ability to meet their wage bills depends more on NGDP growth than on the rate of inflation. Thus, NGDP growth targeting is a better way to keep aggregate nominal wages close to equilibrium and stabilise employment growth. Similarly, Hatzius (2011) shows that nominal GDP is equal to the price level multiplied by real GDP, and real GDP in turn is very closely related to employment via "Okun's law", alternatively, the output-employment rate of intensity. Thus, there is a lot of common ground between an NGDP growth target and a standard Taylor rule in which the desired stance of monetary policy depends on the deviations of inflation and unemployment from their target rates.

Furthermore, it is argued that NGDP growth targeting has the advantage of limiting asset market instability given that asset price bubbles tend to form when NGDP growth is higher than average. In this regard, Sumner (2012) argues that the big advantage of NGDP growth

[1] See Meade (1978), Tobin (1980a, b, 1983).

[2] See, for instance, Romer (2012), Krugman (2014), Hatzius (2011), Woodford (2012), Sumner (2014), Beckworth (2016), Frankel (2012), Bhandari and Frankel (2017), Koenig (2013), Sheedy (2014).

[3] See Bullard (2019).

targeting shows up on the downside because financial-market crises are highly correlated with falling NGDP growth and are almost certainly made worse by it. In relation to the Fisher debt-deflation and NGDP targeting, it is argued that there exists an optimal stochastic rate of inflation, consistent with that obtained under NGDP growth targeting, that supports the efficient allocation of resources, alternatively, optimal risk sharing in the absence of complete asset markets.

Within the monetary policy frameworks, the robustness of the set target (objective) relates to the ability of monetary policy authorities to hit the target ex-post under various shocks. In particular, the argument is that the NGDP level or growth target is robust to adverse supply shocks such as productivity and commodity price shocks. This is because it allows the impact of the shock to be automatically divided between some loss of price stability and some loss on the output objective. The deviation of inflation from target and output from potential are the two variables in the monetary policy objective function, and the monetary policy authorities aim to minimise the loss function. This contrasts with the inflation targeting regime where an adverse shock implies a tight monetary policy thereby, needlessly worsening the fall in output as shown in Fig. 5.1. As such, the proponents of NGDP growth targeting argue that it is best suited for emerging market economies which are highly vulnerable to aggregate supply shocks and terms-of-trade shocks.

In Fig. 5.1, the supply shock that moves the aggregate supply curve from AS intersection with aggregate demand curve AD at point A to the intersection of adverse supply shock AS curve at point C results in lower output losses under the NGDP target compared to point B under inflation targeting. This is because under the NGDP targeting framework, the effects of the adverse AS shock fall equally on output and inflation. It is argued that this is a better outcome compared to that under the inflation targeting framework, where the effects of an adverse aggregate supply or terms-of-trade shocks fall more on output at point B largely because of the impact of tightening monetary policy shocks.

But it is also noteworthy that inflation is higher under NGDP targeting at point C compared to point B under inflation targeting. Thus, indeed the results under NGDP targeting are consistent with the desired effects of generating inflation. In responding to an adverse supply shock

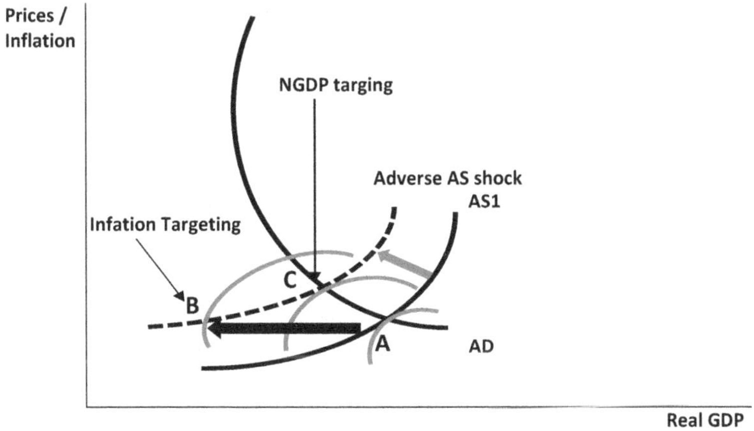

Fig. 5.1 Illustration of how NGDP targeting delivers better outcomes than inflation targeting. (Source: Authors' drawings and adapted from Frankel (2018))

under NGDP targeting, inflation is allowed to increase and the adjustment in economic growth is less severe compared to the outcome under inflation targeting. This then probably is the key aspect that differentiates the monetary policy responses under the flexible inflation targeting framework. Because even though the first round or direct impact of aggregate supply and terms-of trade shocks are automatically accommodated, constrained discretion implies that poorly anchored inflation expectations demand monetary policy response or tightening so as to contain the wage-inflation spiral and the build-up of inflationary pressures.

Under the NGDP targeting, it is unclear what the role of inflation expectations is given that economic agents do not observe NGDP growth but prices and price changes (inflation). Furthermore, Bullard (2019) states that with price-level targeting or nominal income targeting, policymakers would worry about past misses of targets and would try to correct for these misses in such a way that you would stay on a path for the price level or a path for nominal GDP. On the other hand, compared to the price-level targeting or nominal GDP targeting, the Inflation targeting framework is forward looking.

5.3 What Is the Nature of the Inflation and NGDP Volatilities in South Africa?

This section starts the empirical analysis by adopting the methodology in Ndou et al. (2013) to assess the nature of the of the inflation and NGDP volatilities in South Africa. We use data for inflation and NGDP for the sample period 1980Q1 to 2017Q3. First, we start by showing the correlation between the inflation and NGDP gap volatilities for the sub-samples 1980Q1–1999Q4, 2000Q1–2007Q2 and 2007Q3–2017Q3 in Fig. 5.2.

The correlations show that the association between NGDP and inflation gap has changed over the years, whereas it was positive during the sub-sample 1980Q1 to 1999Q4, it changed and became negative during the sub-samples 2000Q1 to 2007Q2 and 2007Q3 to 2017Q3. Thus, the period post-2007Q2 was characterised by an increase in the inflation volatility as shown in Fig. 5.3.

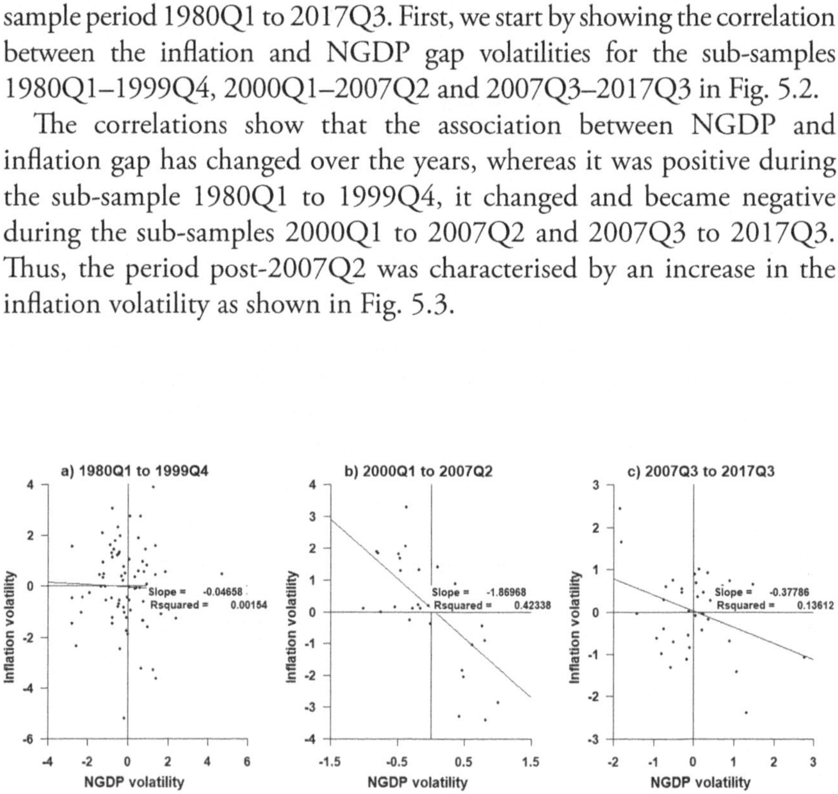

Fig. 5.2 Relationship between inflation and NGDP gap volatilities. (Source: Authors' calculations)

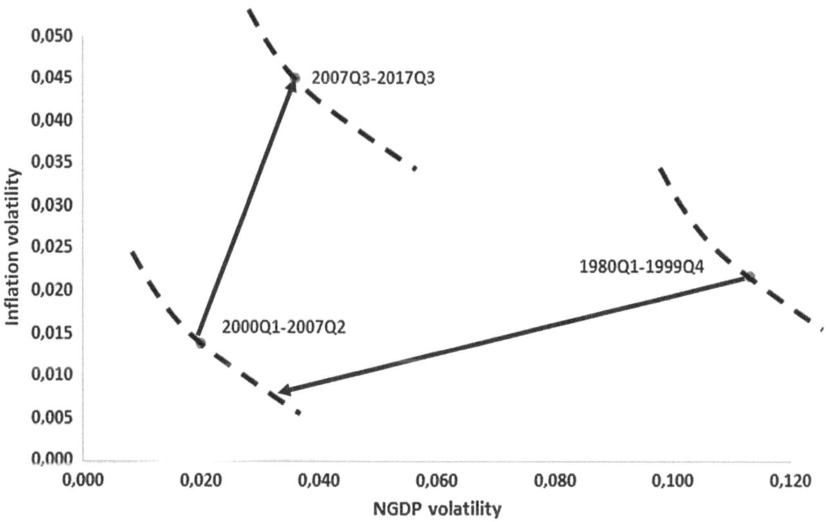

Fig. 5.3 Shifts in the inflation and NGDP gap volatilities. (Source: Authors' calculations)

5.4 Inflation and Repo Rate Responses to Positive NGDP Growth Shocks

This assesses the responses of inflation and the repo rate to positive NGDP growth shocks. We start by showing the evolution and association of CPI inflation and the NGDP growth over time. Figure 5.4 shows that there is a positive relationship between CPI inflation and NGDP growth. In Fig. 5.4(b) NGDP growth explains 39 per cent of the variation in CPI inflation. In addition, compared to CPI inflation, NGDP growth has hardly remained within the 3 to 6 per cent inflation during the sample period.

To assess the responses of inflation and the repo rate to positive NGDP shocks, we estimate VAR models that include inflation, repo rate and NGDP growth. The data is quarterly (Q) and the sample starts in 1980Q1 to 2017Q3. The VAR models are estimated using 2 lags and 10,000

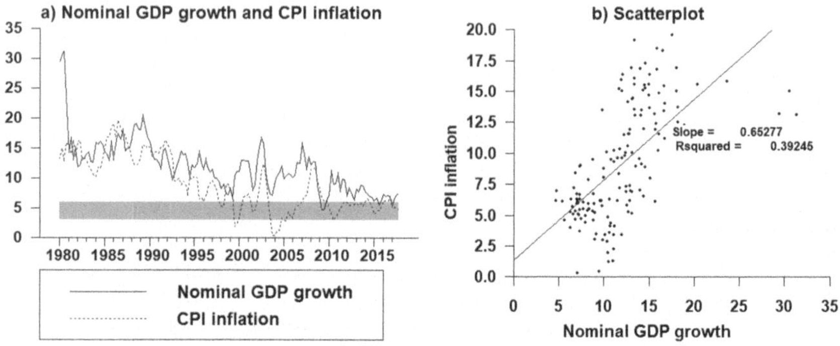

Fig. 5.4 Association between NGDP growth and CPI inflation. (Note: The grey shaded area denotes the 3 to 6 per cent inflation target band. Source: Authors' calculations)

Monte Carlo draws. The shock is a one standard deviation shock. The results in Fig. 5.5 show that inflation and the repo rate increase in response to positive NGDP growth shocks.

5.5 Taylor Rule Prescriptions Using NGDP Growth and CPI Inflation Under Different Inflation Target Bands

If inflation and the repo rate increase in response to positive NGDP shocks as shown in Fig. 5.5, what does this mean for the conduct of monetary policy? To answer this question, we assess how the Taylor rule prescriptions indicate the repo rate should respond to NGDP growth and CPI inflation under different inflation target bands. As stated earlier we conduct a one-to-one comparison of NGDP growth and CPI under different targets to assess whether the NGDP growth target implies targeting the same growth rate as that of CPI inflation in South Africa or is it equivalent to a higher growth rate. We assess the Taylor rule prescriptions implied by the (i) 6 per cent target, (ii) 4.5 per cent target, (iii) 4 per cent target and (iv) 2 per cent target.

In the estimations of the Taylor rule prescriptions, we assume that (i) the SARB aims to keep the real repo rate at 2 per cent and (ii) apply a

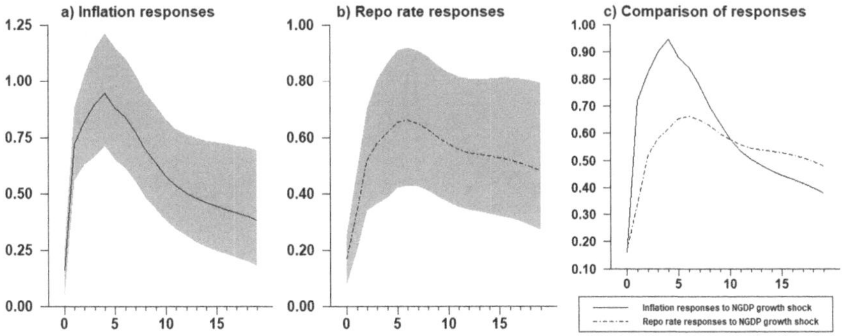

Fig. 5.5 Inflation and repo rate responses to positive NGDP growth shocks. (Note: The grey shaded area bands denote the 16th and 84th percentile confidence bands. Source: Authors' calculations)

weight of 0.5 on the output-gap, and (iii) we do not smooth the interest rate smoothing coefficient (i.e. the interest rate smoothing coefficient is set at zero). We define the real repo rate as the current nominal repo rate less current CPI inflation. The CPI inflation rate is measured as changes in the CPI index over four quarters. We use the 6 per cent, 4.5 per cent, 4 per cent and 2 per cent targets, the weight on the output-gap and the interest rate smoothing coefficient to estimate various versions of the Taylor rule in Eq. (5.1)

$$Repo\ rate_t = \rho\ repo\ rate_{t-1} + (1-\rho)\left[\left(r_t^* + \pi_t^*\right) + 1.5\left(\pi_t - \pi_t^*\right) + \beta gap_t\right], \quad (5.1)$$

where $Repo\ rate_t$ is the current repo rate, $repo\ rate_{t-1}$ is the repo rate lagged by one quarter, ρ is the interest rate smoothing parameter, β is the weight on the output-gap, r_t^* is the real repo rate, π_t is the CPI inflation rate, π_t^* is the inflation target rate and gap_t is the output-gap. The output-gap is derived using the Hodrick-Prescott filter. We use real GDP growth rate over four quarters. The data used in the estimations is quarterly (Q) and the sample spans the period 1980Q1 to 2017Q4. In estimations where we derive the Taylor rule prescriptions using the NGDP growth rate, we replace CPI inflation with NGDP growth in Eq. (5.1).

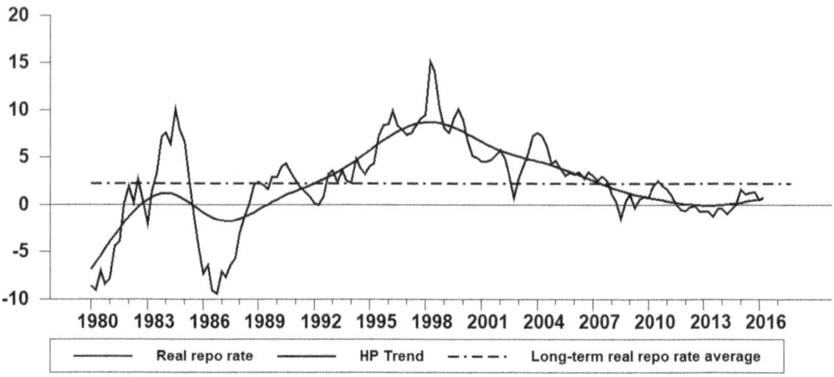

Fig. 5.6 Real repo rate. (Source: Authors' calculations)

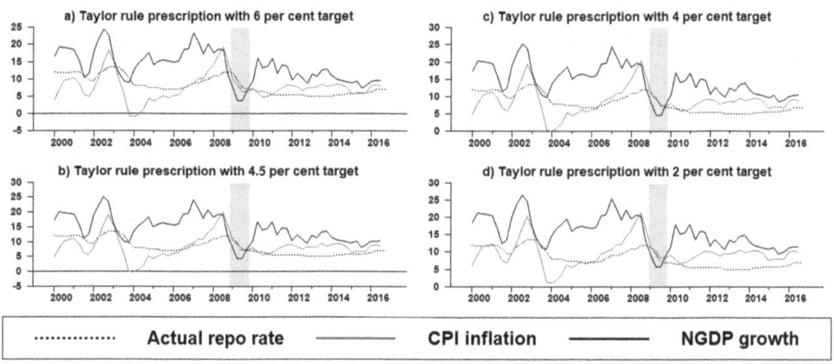

Fig. 5.7 Taylor rule prescriptions for CPI inflation and NGDP growth under different targets. (Note: The grey shaded area denotes the South African recession. Source: Authors' calculations)

The use of the 2 per cent real repo rate is not arbitrary. It is derived from the long-term sample average of the real repo rate from 1980Q1 to 2017Q4 as shown in Fig. 5.6. The estimated real repo rate mean for the sample period is 2.28 per cent.

We show the results from 2000Q1 to 2017Q4. The results in Fig. 5.7 show that if the SARB followed the Taylor rule prescriptions, the repo rate would have been higher when targeting NGDP growth across targets.

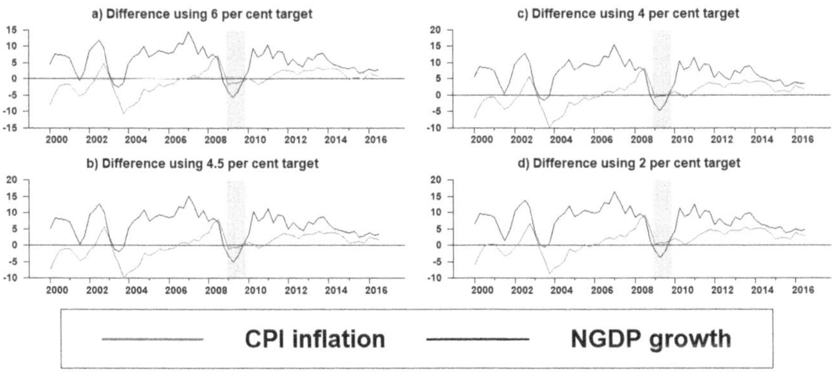

Fig. 5.8 Differences between the actual repo rate and Taylor prescriptions for CPI inflation and NGDP growth under different targets. (Note: The grey shaded area denotes the South African recession. Source: Authors' calculations)

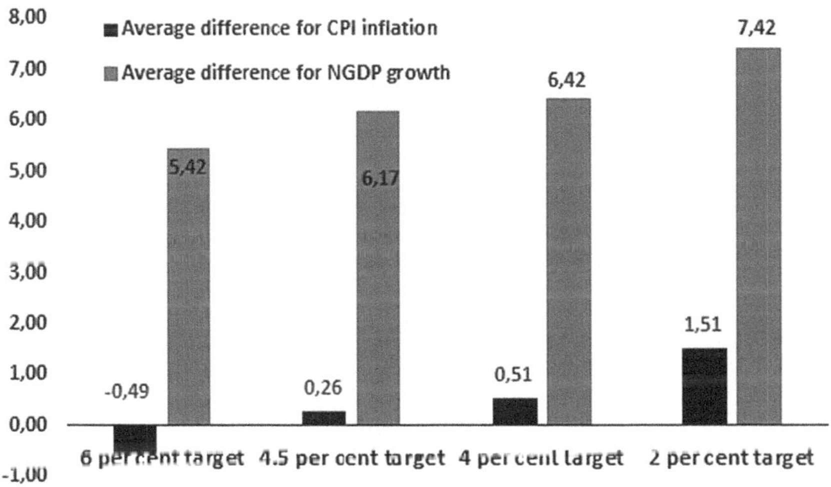

Fig. 5.9 Average differences between the actual repo rate and Taylor prescriptions for CPI inflation and NGDP growth under different targets (Source: Authors' calculations)

On average, the repo rate would have been 5 percentage points higher under the NGDP growth targeting framework compared to 1.5 percentage points under the inflation targeting framework under all the targets in Figs. 5.8 and 5.9.

The results in Fig. 5.9 show that the target matters for the conduct of monetary policy. For instance, if the SARB was targeting 6 per cent, the repo rate would have been 5.42 percentage points higher on average for the sample period 2000Q1 to 2017Q4 than the current repo rate. This is compared to 0.49 percentage points lower if the SARB targeted 6 per cent CPI inflation. The average difference between the current repo rate and what it would be if we followed the Taylor rule prescriptions widens as the target for NGDP growth and CPI inflation declines to 2 per cent. This evidence means that the repo rate would be aggressively tightened to bring NGDP growth to target.

This evidence is consistent with Creamer and Botha (2017) who establish that the inflation targeting framework minimises the loss central bank function to a great extent compared to NGDP growth targeting when considering an open economy. Thus, monetary policy tightening and the associated costs of disinflation are heightened under the NGDP growth targeting. Thus, we conclude that South Africa would be worse-off under NGDP growth targeting compared to the current flexible inflation targeting framework.

5.6 What Happens When the NGDP Growth Target Is Increased?

Could the estimates of the Taylor rule prescriptions imply that a higher NGDP growth target is consistent with a lower repo rate? This is important given that NGDP is the sum of all nominal spending in the economy. Thus, NGDP growth can be influenced by an increase in total spending due to (i) an increase in prices (i.e. inflation) or (ii) an increase or excess demand or output growth in the economy. The two components of NGDP, namely, inflation and nominal demand or output growth, influence the direction of NGDP growth. To assess whether a higher NGDP growth is consistent with a lower repo rate, we estimate the Taylor rule prescriptions under the targets of (i) 10 per cent and (ii) 12 per cent. The results in Figs. 5.10 and 5.11 show that the target used to estimate the Taylor rule prescriptions for NGDP growth matter for the monetary policy response.

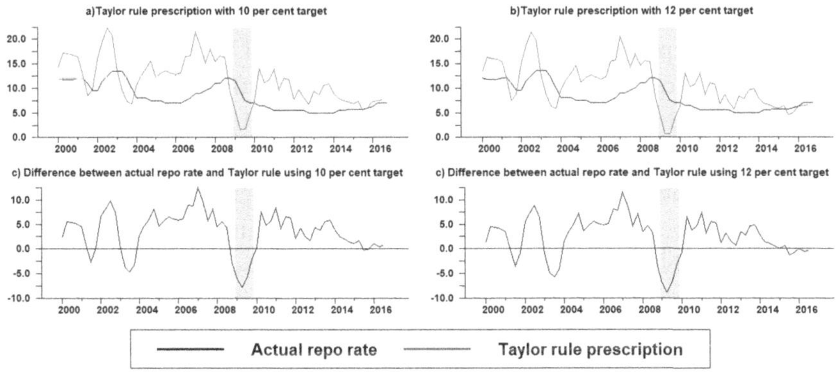

Fig. 5.10 Taylor rule prescriptions for NGDP growth under higher targets. (Note: The grey shaded area denotes the South African recession. Source: Authors' calculations)

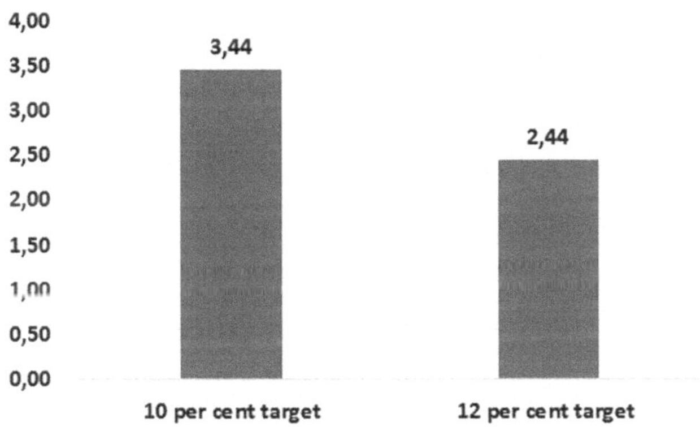

Fig. 5.11 Average differences between the actual repo rate and Taylor prescriptions for NGDP growth under higher targets. (Source: Authors' calculations)

A higher target for NGDP growth implies a lower Taylor rule prescription. During the recession in 2009, the repo rate would have been much lower than the actual repo rate at the time. Similarly, towards the end of the sample between 2014Q1 and 2016Q4, the Taylor rule would have been the same as the actual repo rate if the SARB was targeting 10 per cent NGDP growth and slightly lower if the target was 12 per cent.

Thus, the results imply that a high NGDP growth target is consistent with a lower repo rate. This means that a higher NGDP growth driven by, for example, positive productivity growth and investment growth shocks as opposed to higher CPI inflation is consistent with a lower policy rate. This is because positive productivity growth shocks exert opposing effects on NGDP growth and inflation. NGDP growth increases in response to positive productivity shocks whereas inflation declines. This means that in the case of NGDP growth, output growth increases more and benefits from the decline in inflation and this mutes the policy rate responses to inflationary pressures. Thus, positive productivity shocks neutralise the role of inflationary pressures in NGDP growth. Similarly, positive investment shocks exert minimal inflationary pressures. These results concur with the Sumner (2012) argument that under NGDP targeting the productivity shock is offset by an opposite and equally unexpected decline in the inflation rate.[4] Thus, we conclude that a higher NGDP target is not inconsistent with a lower CPI inflation target. Positive productivity shocks that push NGDP growth higher and CPI inflation lower are necessary to dampen the rate at which the repo rate responds to inflationary shocks. A lower inflation target and a higher NGDP growth target are not mutually exclusive.[5]

5.7 Conclusion and Policy Implications

Would South Africa be worse-off under NGDP growth targeting compared to the current flexible inflation targeting framework? Furthermore, is a higher NGDP growth target consistent with a lower repo rate? We establish that on average, the repo rate would have been 5 percentage points higher under the NGDP growth targeting framework compared to 1.5 percentage points under the inflation targeting framework under the 6 per cent, 4.5 per cent, 4 per cent and 2 per cent target rates. This means that, if the SARB was targeting NGDP growth, it would have had to be more

[4] We explore the responses of NGDP growth to labour productivity shocks in Chap. 6.

[5] We empirically explore whether a higher NGDP growth target is consistent with the 3 to 6 per cent inflation target and the possibility of the dual mandate to achieve maximum employment growth and a low unemployment rate in Chap. 7.

aggressive in tightening monetary policy to contain inflationary pressures and bring NGDP growth to these target rates.

Furthermore, the Taylor curve, alternatively, the trade-off between the volatilities of the inflation and NGDP growth gaps suggests that inflation volatility increased more post-2007Q4 when the Taylor curve shifted outwards. This is compared to a benign inflation volatility shift when considering the trade-off between the inflation and real GDP growth gap volatilities. Thus, the SARB would be worse-off targeting NGDP growth as opposed to the inflation under the current flexible inflation targeting framework. Hence, we conclude that there is currently no strong and compelling case for NGDP growth targeting in South Africa.

However, the results considering higher NGDP growth target rates indicate that it is consistent with a lower repo rate. This means that a higher NGDP growth driven by productivity shocks as opposed to higher CPI inflation is consistent with a lower policy rate. This is because positive productivity shocks exert opposing effects on NGDP growth and inflation. Thus, positive productivity shocks neutralise the role of inflationary pressures in NGDP growth. Hence, we conclude that a higher NGDP target is not inconsistent with a lower CPI inflation target. Positive productivity shocks that push NGDP growth higher and CPI inflation lower are necessary to dampen the rate at which the repo rate responds to inflationary shocks. A lower inflation target and a higher NGDP growth target are not mutually exclusive.

References

Bean, C. 1983. Targeting Nominal Income: An Appraisal. *The Economic Journal*, 93, 806–19.

Beckworth, D. 2016. The Financial Stability Case for a Nominal GDP Target. *Cato Journal*, 39(2), 419–47. https://www.cato.org/cato-journal/springsummer-2019/financial-stability-case-nominal-gdp-target.

Bhandari, P., and Frankel, J.A. 2014a. *The Best of Rules and Discretion: A Case for Nominal GDP Targeting in India*. CID Working Paper No. 284.

Bhandari, P., and Frankel, J.A. 2014b. *The Best of Rules and Discretion: A Case for Nominal GDP Targeting in India*. CID Working Paper No. 284, Harvard

Kennedy School. https://www.hks.harvard.edu/sites/default/files/centers/cid/files/publications/faculty-working-papers/284_Frankel_IndiaGDP.pdf.
Bhandari, P., and Frankel, J.A. 2015. *Nominal GDP Targeting for Developing Countries*. Working Paper 20898. http://www.nber.org/papers/w20898.
Bhandari, P., and Frankel, J.A. 2017. *Nominal GDP Targeting for Developing Countries*. NBER Working Paper No. 20898.
Bullard, J. 2018. Speech: A Primer on Price Level Targeting in the U.S. Slides. www.stlouisfed.org/from-the-president/speeches-and-presentations.
Bullard, J. 2019. James Bullard Discusses NGDP Targeting. Federal Reserve Bank of St. Louis. St. Louis Fed Timely Topics Podcast that was released April 19, 2019. https://www.stlouisfed.org/publications/regional-economist/second-quarter-2019/bullard-nominal-gdp-targeting?
Creamer, K., and Botha, T.R. 2017. Assessing Nominal GDP Targeting in the South African Context. *Central Bank Review*, 17 (1), March 2017, 1–10. https://www.sciencedirect.com/science/article/pii/S1303070116300506?via%3Dihub.
Du Plessis, S., and Rietveld, M. 2013. *Should Inflation Targeting be Abandoned in Favour of Nominal Income Targeting?* University of Stellenbosch Economic Working Papers: 12/13.
Frankel, J. 1995. The Stabilizing Properties of a Nominal GNP Rule. *Journal of Money, Credit and Banking*, 27(2), 318–34.
Frankel, J. 2012. Central Banks Can Phase in Nominal GDP Targets Without Damaging the Inflation Anchor. *VoxEU*, December 19.
Frankel, J. 2013. Nominal GDP Targets without Losing the Inflation Anchor. In L. Reichlin and R. Baldwin (eds.), *Is Inflation Targeting Dead: Central Banking after the Crisis*. Centre for Economic Policy Research: London, 90–94.
Frankel, J. 2018. The Case for (and Drawbacks of) Nominal GDP Targets. Paper Prepared for Brookings Institution Conference, "Should the Fed Stick with the 2 Percent Inflation Target or Rethink It?" Hutchins Center on Fiscal and Monetary Policy Monday, January 8, 2018.
Hassan, S., and Loewald, C. 2013. *Nominal GDP Targeting and the Monetary Policy Framework*. South African Reserve Bank Working Paper WP 1305.
Hatzius, J. 2011. The Case for a Nominal GDP Level Target. US Economics Analyst, Goldman Sachs Global ECS Research, October.
Hoelle, M., and Peiris, U. 2013. *On the Efficiency of Nominal GDP Targeting in a Large Open Economy*. Krannert Working Paper Series, Paper No. 1273.
Koenig, E.F. 2013. Like a Good Neighbor: Monetary Policy, Financial Stability, and the Dis-tribution of Risk. *International Journal of Central Banking*, 9(2), 57–82. https://www.ijcb.org/journal/ijcb13q2a3.htm.

Krugman, P. 2014. Inflation Targets Reconsidered. ECB Forum on Central Banking, May 2014 Monetary Policy in A Changing Financial Landscape. https://www.ecbforum.eu/uploads/originals/2014/pdf/speakers/PAPER_Paul_R_Krugman.pdf

Meade, J. 1978. The Meaning of Internal Balance. *The Economic Journal*, 88, 423–35.

Ndou, E., Gumata, N., Ncube, M., and Olson, E. 2013. *An Empirical Investigation of the Taylor Curve in South Africa*. African Development Bank Working Paper No. 189.

Romer, D. 2012. What Have We Learned about Fiscal Policy from the Crisis. In *In the Wake of the Crisis: Leading Economists Reassess Economic Policy*. Chap. 6, 1st ed., vol. 1. The MIT Press, pp. 57–66.

Sheedy, K.D. 2014. Debt and Incomplete Financial Markets: A Case for Nominal GDP Targeting. *Brookings Papers on Economic Activity*, Spring 2014. https://www.brookings.edu/wp-content/uploads/2014/03/2014a_Sheedy.pdf.

Summers, H., Wessel, D., and Murray, J.D. 2018. Rethinking the Fed's 2 Per cent Inflation Target: A Report from the Hutchins Center on Fiscal and Monetary Policy at Brookings. https://www.brookings.edu/wp-content/uploads/2018/06/ES_20180607_Hutchins-FedInflationTarget.pdf.

Sumner, S. 1995. Using Monetary Policy to Target a Nominal Wage Index. *Journal of Economics and Business*, 47 (2), 205–15.

Sumner, Scott. 2012. The Case for Nominal GDP Targeting. Mercatus Center, George Mason University.

Sumner, S. 2014. Nominal GDP Targeting: A Simple Rule to Improve Fed Performance. *Cato Journal*, 34, 315–37.

Svensson, Lars E.O. 2003. What is Wrong with Taylor Rules? Using Judgment in Monetary Policy through Targeting Rules. *Journal of Economic Literature*, 41, 426–77.

Svensson, Lars E.O. 2009. Flexible Inflation Targeting—Lessons from the Financial Crisis. Speech at BIS, 21 September.

Tobin, J. 1980a. Stabilization Policy Ten Years After. *Brookings Papers on Economic Activity*, 1, 19–72.

Tobin, J. 1980b. *Asset Accumulation and Economic Activity*. Basil Blackwell: Oxford.

Tobin, J. 1983. Macroeconomics under Debate. Mitsui Lecture, University of Birmingham, England, March, reprinted in Tobin [1996b], pp. 203–36.

Woodford, M. 2012. *Methods of Policy Accommodation at the Interest-Rate Lower Bound*. Columbia University.

6

How Does Nominal GDP Growth Respond to Various Shocks

Learning Objectives

- Determine the responses of nominal GDP (NGDP) growth and inflation to positive monetary base shocks.
- Explore the responses of NGDP growth and inflation to aggregate demand, aggregate supply and loan supply shocks.

6.1 Introduction

Chapter 5 concluded that a lower inflation target and a higher nominal GDP (NGDP) growth target are not mutually exclusive, because positive productivity shocks exert opposing effects on NGDP growth and inflation. This chapter extends the analysis on the merits of NGDP targeting in South Africa by assessing how NGDP growth responds to various shocks. How does NGDP growth respond to positive narrow money supply (monetary base) shocks? Does NGDP growth respond differently to aggregate demand, aggregate supply and loan supply shocks? Sumner (2012) argues that because of inflation fears, the Fed did not provide enough monetary stimulus in late 2008, thus allowing the largest decline

N. Gumata, E. Ndou, *Accelerated Land Reform, Mining, Growth, Unemployment and Inequality in South Africa*, https://doi.org/10.1007/978-3-030-30884-1_6

in nominal spending since the 1930s. Furthermore, the proponents of NGDP growth targeting argue that it differs in how it responds to productivity or supply shocks. We contribute to academic and policy research by exploring how NGDP responds to various financial and macroeconomic shocks.

6.2 How Does NGDP Growth and Inflation Respond to Monetary Base Growth Shocks?

This section starts by testing how NGDP growth and inflation respond to positive narrow money supply growth (monetary base) shocks. We estimate a VAR model that includes NGDP growth, inflation and the monetary base. The data is on a quarterly (Q) basis for the period 1980Q1 to 2017Q4. The VAR model is estimated using 2 lags and 10,000 Monte Carlo draws. The shock is a one standard deviation to the monetary base growth. The results in Fig. 6.1 show that positive monetary base growth shocks result in an increase in NGDP growth and inflation. In addition, NGDP growth increases more than inflation in Fig. 6.1(c).

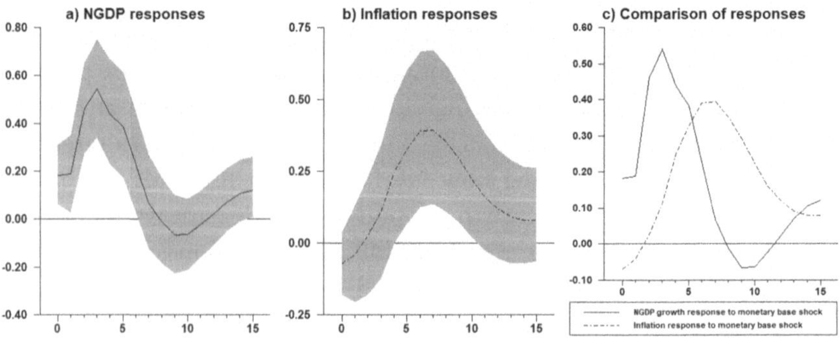

Fig. 6.1 NGDP growth and inflation responses to positive monetary base shocks. (Note: The grey shaded area bands denote the 16th and 84th percentile confidence bands. Source: Authors' calculations)

6.3 The Identification of Various Structural Shocks by Sign Restriction Approach

The proponents of NGDP growth targeting argue that it differs in how it responds to productivity or supply shocks. To assess the validity of this claim, this section assesses whether NGDP growth and inflation respond differently to aggregate supply shocks. We use the sign restriction approach to correctly identify the various structural shocks. First, how is an adverse aggregate supply shock identified and what distinguishes it from, for example, an adverse monetary policy, aggregate demand and loan supply shock? In Table 6.1 we show the signs we impose in the sign-restricted VAR models to distinguish and identify the adverse monetary policy, aggregate supply shock, and aggregate demand and loan supply shocks.

An adverse aggregate supply shock moves output and prices in opposite directions as shown by the signs in Table 6.1 column 3. As a result, because adverse aggregate supply shocks pose risks to the inflation outlook, an inflation targeting central bank reacts to an adverse aggregate supply shock by increasing the nominal interest rate. Thus, within an inflation targeting regime, an adverse aggregate supply shock not only moves inflation and output in different directions, but it also elicits a contractionary monetary policy response via an increase in the policy rate. On the other hand, Table 6.1 column 2 shows that a contractionary monetary policy shock leads to an unexpected rise in the policy rate and other short-term interest rates. This has a negative effect on real output, prices and the lending rate as bank interest rates are tied to the short-term interest rates. To distinguish between a contractionary monetary policy shock and an adverse aggregate supply shock, inflation is expected to decline following a negative monetary policy shock, whereas an adverse aggregate supply shock results in an increase in inflation.

Table 6.1 Identification scheme for various adverse shocks

	Monetary policy	Aggregate supply	Aggregate demand	Loan supply
Policy rate	+	+	–	+
Lending rate	+	+	–	+
Inflation/NGDP growth	?	?	?	?

Source: Authors' calculations

An adverse credit supply (loan supply) shock in column 5 Table 6.1 is similar to a contractionary monetary policy shock. Both shocks result in an increase in lending rates but can have a different effect on the quantities of credit. Barnett and Thomas (2013) show that credit supply shocks tend to be associated with quantity rationing effects which are absent under a monetary policy shock. This is because under an adverse loan supply shock, the balance sheet channel of the monetary policy transmission mechanism largely via the role of the quality of balance sheets (non-performing loans), wealth and asset price channels plays a potent role.

What are aggregate demand shocks and how are they identified? A negative aggregate demand shock is identified by assuming that output and prices move in the same direction in Table 6.1. The central bank reacts to a negative aggregate demand shock by lowering the nominal interest rate. This leads to a decline in the lending rate. In turn, the decline in the policy and lending rates due to an adverse shock to aggregate demand is expected to stimulate credit demand and supply. However, Bean et al. (2010) show that the impact of accommodative monetary policy can be neutralised by the negative effects on an adverse aggregate demand shock which result in a fall in loan demand as aggregate income falls.

6.4 NGDP and Inflation Responses to Aggregate Supply Shocks?

One of the key arguments in favour of NGDP growth targeting is that it distributes the impact of supply shocks on both inflation and output growth as opposed to inflation targeting which mostly penalises output growth. We explore the responses of NGDP growth and inflation to various supply shocks to assess the differences. We use rand oil prices, commodity prices including gold, labour productivity and the R/US$ exchange rate as variables that represent supply shocks. In this case because we are assessing the impact of positive shocks, with respect to the R/US$, it means that we are assessing the impact of the depreciation of the exchange rate. All growth rates are at an annual rate. The shock is one standard deviation shock. The VAR models are estimated using 2 lags and 10,000 Monte Carlo draws. The results in Fig. 6.2 show that positive oil

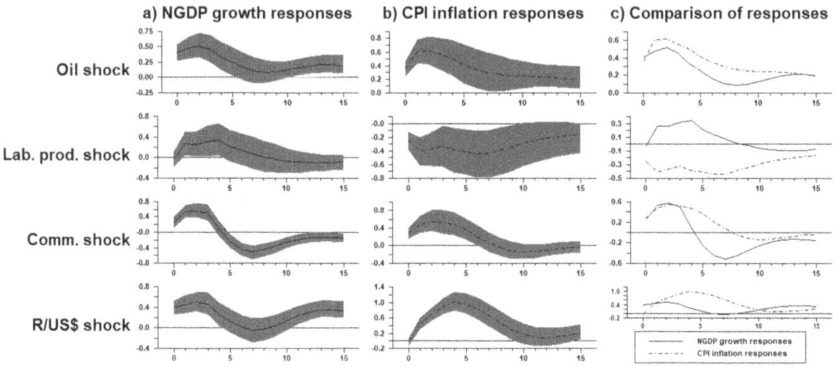

Fig. 6.2 NGDP growth and inflation responses to various aggregate supply shocks. (Note: The grey shaded area bands denote the 16th and 84th percentile confidence bands. The oil shock = oil price shock, Lab. prod. Shock = labour productivity shock, Comm. Shock = commodity price shock and the R/US$ shock = R/US$ exchange rate shock. Source: Authors' calculations)

and commodity price shocks exert similar effects on NGDP growth and inflation, but they tend to have a more persistent effect on inflation. Similarly, the R/US$ exchange rate depreciation has pronounced and persistent effects on inflation compared to NGDP growth.

On the other hand, the results indicate that positive shocks to labour productivity exert opposing effects on NGDP growth and inflation. NGDP growth increases whereas inflation declines due to positive labour productivity shocks. This means that in the case of NGDP growth, output growth increases more and benefits from the decline in inflation due to a positive labour productivity shock. These results concur with Sumner (2012) argument that under NGDP targeting the productivity shock is offset by an opposite and equally unexpected change in the inflation rate.

6.5 How Does NGDP and Inflation Respond to Aggregate Demand Shocks?

We stated earlier that aggregate demand shocks are identified by assuming that output and prices move in the same direction in Table 6.1. In cases of, for example, a negative aggregate demand shock, the central bank reacts by lowering the nominal interest rate. This leads to a decline in the lending rate. In turn, the decline in the policy and lending rates due to an adverse shock to aggregate demand is expected to stimulate credit demand and supply. However, Bean et al. (2010) show that the impact of accommodative monetary policy can be neutralised by the negative effects on an adverse aggregate demand shock which result in a fall in loan demand as aggregate income falls. Furthermore, Sumner (2012) states that an NGDP targeting regime responds to demand shocks or changes in velocity in exactly the same way as an inflation targeting regime. In both cases the money supply adjusts to fully offset any sudden change in velocity. The NGDP targeting accommodates shifts in money demand and produces the same long-run rate of inflation as inflation targeting.

We estimate VAR models that include nominal wage growth, unit labour costs, household consumption expenditure growth, gross fixed capital formation growth and government expenditure growth as indicators of various aggregate demand shocks. All growth rates are at annual rates. The shock is a one standard deviation shock. The VAR models are estimated using 2 lags and 10,000 Monte Carlo draws.

The results in Fig. 6.3 indicate that positive demand shocks push NGDP growth and inflation in the same direction. Positive aggregate

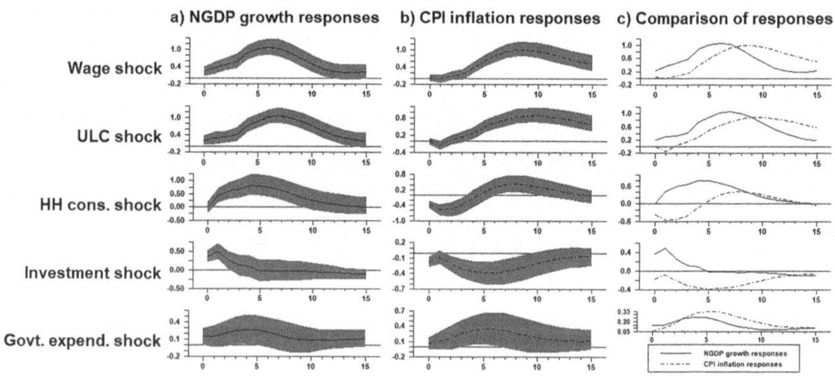

Fig. 6.3 NGDP growth and inflation responses to various aggregate demand shocks. (Note: The grey shaded area bands denote the 16th and 84th percentile confidence bands. Wage shock = nominal wage growth shock, ULC shock = unit labour costs shock, HH cons shock = household consumption growth shock, Investment shock = gross fixed capital formation growth shock and Govt. expend. shock = government expenditure growth shock. Source: Authors' calculations)

demand shocks are particularly pronounced and persistent on NGDP growth. It is also notable that of all positive aggregate demand shocks, investment growth shocks exert the least inflationary consequences. In addition, positive government expenditure growth shocks exert more pressure on inflation compared to NGDP growth. Whereas positive household expenditure growth shocks have a contemporaneous positive effect on NGDP growth compared to the delayed effects on inflation.

6.6 NGDP and Inflation Responses to Credit or Loan Supply Shocks?

To conclude the analysis in this chapter, this section explores the responses of NGDP growth and inflation to various forms of positive credit, loan supply financial conditions and credit risk shocks. We showed in Table 6.1 that an adverse loan or credit supply shock is similar to a contractionary monetary policy shock. Both shocks result in an increase in lending rates but can have a different effect on the quantities of credit supplied. This is because credit supply shocks tend to be associated with quantity rationing effects which are absent under a monetary policy shock. This is because under an adverse loan supply shock, the balance sheet channel of the monetary policy transmission mechanism largely via the role of the quality of balance sheets (non-performing loans), wealth and asset price channels plays a potent role.

To assess the role of credit supply shocks, we use credit growth, non-performing loans as a ratio of total loans, the lending rate spread and the financial conditions index (FCI) in the VAR estimations. In this case a positive shock to non-performing loans is equivalent to worsening of the quality of the balance sheets. Whereas an adverse shock to FCI implies that financial conditions are tightening. The FCI used in the estimations is estimated in Gumata et al. (2012). Similarly, a positive to the lending rate spread implies tightening in credit and lending conditions. The lending spread is the difference between the repo rate and the weighted lending rate. The results in Fig. 6.4 show that all adverse loan supply shocks dampen NGDP growth and inflation, but the effects are especially nega-

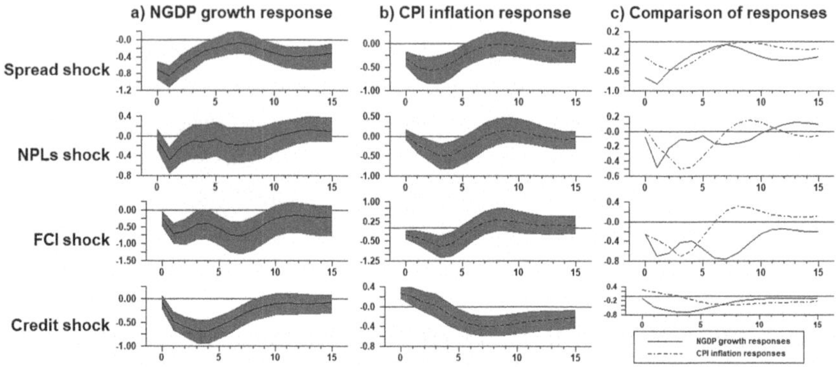

Fig. 6.4 NGDP growth and inflation responses to various loan supply shocks. (Note: The grey shaded area bands denote the 16th and 84th percentile confidence bands. Spread shock = lending spread shock, NPLs shock = non-performing loans shock, FCI shock = financial conditions index shock, credit shock = credit growth shock. Source: Authors' calculations)

tive for NGDP growth. All growth rates are at annual rates. The shock is a one standard deviation shock. The VAR models are estimated using 2 lags and 10,000 Monte Carlo draws.

The results in Fig. 6.4 show that all adverse (positive) loan supply shocks dampen NGDP growth and inflation, but the effects are especially negative for NGDP growth.

6.7 Conclusion and Policy Implications

This chapter explored the responses of NGDP growth and inflation to various financial and macroeconomic shocks. We find that NGDP growth increases more due to positive monetary base shocks compared to inflation. In addition, positive aggregate demand shocks push NGDP growth and inflation in the same direction. Positive aggregate demand shocks have a particularly pronounced and persistent effect on NGDP growth. Investment growth shocks exert the least inflationary consequences.

On the other hand, positive shocks to labour productivity exert opposing effects on NGDP growth and inflation. NGDP growth increases whereas inflation declines due to positive labour productivity growth shocks.

This means that in the case of NGDP growth, output growth increases more and benefits from the decline in inflation due to a positive labour productivity growth shock. All adverse (positive) loan supply shocks dampen NGDP growth and inflation, but the effects are especially negative for NGDP growth.

References

Barnett, A., and Thomas, R. 2013. *Has Weak Lending and Activity in the United Kingdom been Driven by Credit Supply Shocks?* Bank of England Working Paper No. 482.

Bean, Charlie. 1983. Targeting Nominal Income: An Appraisal. *The Economic Journal*, 93, 806–19.

Bean, C., Paustian, M., Penalver, A., and Taylor, T. 2010. Monetary Policy after the Fall. Paper Presented at the Federal Reserve Bank of Kansas City Annual Conference, Jackson Hole, Wyoming, August 28, 2010. https://www.kansascityfed.org/publicat/sympos/2010/Bean_final.pdf.

Bhandari, P., and Frankel, J. 2014a. *The Best of Rules and Discretion: A Case for Nominal GDP Targeting in India*. CID Working Paper No. 284.

Bhandari, P., and Frankel, J. 2014b. *The Best of Rules and Discretion: A Case for Nominal GDP Targeting in India*. CID Working Paper No. 284, Harvard Kennedy School. https://www.hks.harvard.edu/sites/default/files/centers/cid/files/publications/faculty-working-papers/284_Frankel_IndiaGDP.pdf.

Bhandari, P., and Frankel, J.A. 2015. *Nominal GDP Targeting for Developing Countries*. Working Paper 20898. http://www.nber.org/papers/w20898.

Blanchard, Olivier, Dell'Ariccia, Giovanni, and Mauro, Paolo. 2010. *Rethinking Macroeconomic Policy*. IMF Staff Position Note, 12 February.

Creamer, K., and Botha, T.R. 2017. Assessing Nominal GDP Targeting in the South African Context. *Central Bank Review*, 17(1), March 2017, 1–10. https://www.sciencedirect.com/science/article/pii/S1303070116300506?via%3Dihub.

Du Plessis, S., and Rietveld, M. 2013. *Should Inflation Targeting be Abandoned in Favour of Nominal Income Targeting?* University of Stellenbosch Economic Working Papers: 12/13.

Frankel, J. 1995. The Stabilizing Properties of a Nominal GNP Rule. *Journal of Money, Credit and Banking*, 27(2), 318–34.

Frankel, J. 2012. Central Banks Can Phase in Nominal GDP Targets Without Damaging the Inflation Anchor. *VoxEU*, December 19.

Frankel, J. 2013. Nominal GDP Targets without Losing the Inflation Anchor. In L. Reichlin and R. Baldwin (eds.) *Is Inflation Targeting Dead: Central Banking after the Crisis.* Centre for Economic Policy Research: London, pp. 90–94.

Frankel, J. The Case for (and Drawbacks of) Nominal GDP Targets. Capital Formation and Growth, Harvard Kennedy School, Harvard University. https://www.brookings.edu/wp-content/uploads/2017/12/frankel-slides.pdf

Gumata, N., Klein, N., and Ndou, E. 2012. *A Financial Conditions Index for South Africa.* IMF Working Paper WP/12/196.

Hassan, S., and Loewald, C. 2013. *Nominal GDP Targeting and the Monetary Policy Framework.* South African Reserve Bank Working Paper WP 1305.

Hatzius, J. 2011. The Case for a Nominal GDP Level Target. US Economics Analyst, Goldman Sachs Global ECS Research, October.

Hoelle, M., and Peiris, U. 2013. *On the Efficiency of Nominal GDP Targeting in a Large Open Economy.* Krannert Working Paper Series, Paper No. 1273.

Ndou, E., and Gumata, N. 2017. *Inflation Dynamics in South Africa: The Role of Thresholds, Exchange Rate Pass-through and Inflation Expectations on Policy Trade-offs.* Palgrave Macmillan. ISBN 978-3-319-46702-3.

Ndou, E., Gumata, N., Ncube, M., and Olson, E. 2013. *An Empirical Investigation of the Taylor Curve in South Africa.* African Development Bank Working Paper No. 189.

Summers, H., Wessel, D., and Murray, J.D. 2018. Rethinking the Fed's 2 per cent Inflation Target: A Report From the Hutchins Center on Fiscal and Monetary Policy at Brookings. https://www.brookings.edu/wp-content/uploads/2018/06/ES_20180607_Hutchins-FedInflationTarget.pdf

Sumner, S. 1995. Using Monetary Policy to Target a Nominal Wage Index. *Journal of Economics and Business*, 47(2), 205–15.

Sumner, Scott. 2012. The Case for Nominal GDP Targeting. Mercatus Center, George Mason University.

Svensson, Lars E.O. 2003. What Is Wrong with Taylor Rules? Using Judgment in Monetary Policy through Targeting Rules. *Journal of Economic Literature*, 41, 426–77.

Svensson, Lars E.O. 2009. Flexible Inflation Targeting—Lessons from the Financial Crisis. Speech at BIS, 21 September.

Woodford, M. 2012. *Methods of Policy Accommodation at the Interest-Rate Lower Bound.* Columbia University.

7

Are High NGDP Growth Targets Consistent With a Dual Mandate of Low Inflation and Maximum Employment Growth and a Low Unemployment Rate?

Learning Objectives

- Determine whether high NGDP growth targets are consistent with the 3 to 6 per cent inflation target range and the possibility of the dual mandate to achieve maximum employment growth and a low unemployment rate.
- Explore the role of the exchange rate channel and the nominal wage channel in transmitting high NGDP growth shocks to inflation.
- Assess the role of the exchange rate channel in transmitting high NGDP growth shocks to inflation expectations in different inflation regimes.
- Determine the role of the exchange rate channel in dampening or propagating inflationary pressures and the impact on the repo rate response to positive inflation shocks.

N. Gumata, E. Ndou, *Accelerated Land Reform, Mining, Growth, Unemployment and Inequality in South Africa*, https://doi.org/10.1007/978-3-030-30884-1_7

7.1 Introduction

Chapter 5 showed that a high nominal GDP (NGDP) growth target is consistent with a lower repo rate. This chapter determines whether high NGDP growth targets are consistent with the 3 to 6 per cent inflation target range. In addition, we assess how the NGDP target impacts the employment growth and the unemployment rate. We start by exploring the responses of NGDP growth to positive inflation shocks and vice versa. NGDP is the sum of all spending in the economy, and it is influenced by an increase in total spending due to an increase in prices (i.e. inflation) or increased nominal demand (output) in the economy as shown in Fig. 7.1. The two components of NGDP, namely inflation and nominal demand (output), influence the direction of NGDP growth.

The trends in Fig. 7.1 show that real GDP growth is higher when the gap between the nominal GDP growth and inflation is wider. During recessions inflation tends to exceed nominal GDP growth resulting in lower real GDP growth. This suggests that a combination of lower inflation and high nominal GDP growth is needed to achieve high real GDP growth. This evidence based on trend analysis suggests that high nominal and real GDP growth targets cannot be achieved if inflation is not tightly

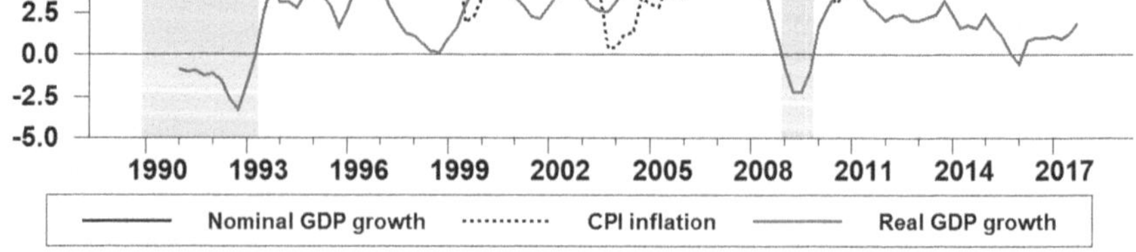

Fig. 7.1 Inflation, nominal and real GDP growth. (Note: The grey shaded areas denote the South African recessions. Source: South African Reserve Bank and authors' calculations)

controlled. That is, high inflation rates are not consistent with high nominal and real GDP growth rates. Alternatively, a lower inflation target and a high nominal and real GDP growth targets are not mutually exclusive. Based on these observations, this chapter examines the extent to which a high NGDP target impacts employment growth and the unemployment rate. In addition, we examine how the responses of inflation are impacted by the different inflation targeting bands. In the assessment of the responses to high NGDP targets, we include factors that are identified as risks to the inflation outlook, such as positive nominal wage growth, the nominal effective exchange rate (NEER) and inflation expectations shocks.

Sumner (2012) defines NGDP targeting as a single target that can also satisfy the dual mandate since NGDP growth is the sum of inflation and real growth, and the latter depends on the state of employment. The author argues that a stable path of NGDP growth would tend to stabilise employment more effectively than an inflation target. This is because the employers' ability to meet their wage bills depends more on NGDP growth than on the rate of inflation. Thus, NGDP growth targeting is a better way to keep aggregate nominal wages close to equilibrium and stabilising employment growth. Similarly, Hatzius (2011) shows that nominal GDP is equal to the price level multiplied by real GDP, and real GDP in turn is very closely related to employment via Okun's law, alternatively, the output employment rate of intensity. Thus, there is a lot of common ground between an NGDP growth target and a standard Taylor rule in which the desired stance of monetary policy depends on the deviations of inflation and unemployment from their target rates.

Furthermore, it is argued that NGDP growth targeting has the advantage of limiting asset market instability given that asset price bubbles tend to form when NGDP growth is higher than average. In this regard, Sumner (2012) argues that the big advantage of NGDP growth targeting shows up on the downside because financial-market crises are highly correlated with falling NGDP and are almost certainly made worse by it. In relation to the Fisher debt-deflation and NGDP targeting, it is argued that there exists an optimal stochastic rate of inflation, consistent with that obtained under NGDP growth targeting, that supports the efficient allocation of resources, alternatively, optimal risk sharing in the absence of complete asset markets.

7.2 Where Does the NGDP Threshold Lie?

We begin analysis by looking at NGDP growth statistics and where the threshold occurs. The average mean of NGDP growth between 1991Q1 and 2017Q4 is about 10.166044. The STAR tests reject the linearity assumptions which indicate the presence of non-linearity in the evolution of NGDP growth. The results hold when using the one-, two- and three-quarter delay parameters in the estimations. We apply the Balke (2000) threshold techniques using NGDP growth, employment growth and the unemployment rate in the model. The Balke (2000) threshold techniques find a threshold closer to 10 per cent. We also apply the Tsay (1998) threshold test, which regresses NGDP growth on a constant and the first 4 lags. We find a threshold of around 10 per cent. Hence, we apply 10 per cent as the NGDP growth threshold in the analysis.

7.3 The Effects of NGDP Growth on Employment Growth and the Unemployment Rate

This section begins by estimating (i) a bivariate VAR model which includes NGDP growth and employment growth; (ii) a bivariate VAR model which includes NGDP growth and the unemployment rate; (iii) a three-variable VAR model which includes NGDP growth, employment growth and the unemployment rate and (iv) a four-variable VAR model which includes NGDP growth, employment growth, the unemployment rate and consumer price inflation. In all models, the exogenous variables include a constant and a recession dummy. The models are estimated using 2 lags and 10,000 Monte Carlo draws. The shock is a one standard deviation shock to NGDP growth.

Figure 7.2 shows that employment growth rises significantly for nearly a year and the unemployment rate declines significantly for nearly a year. This evidence indicates that positive NGDP growth increases employment growth and lowers the unemployment rate. This finding is robust to different model specifications. However, in Fig. 7.2(d), consumer price

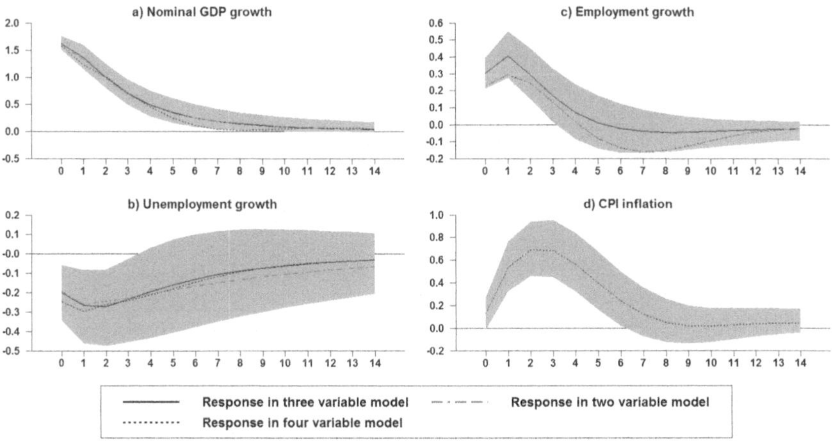

Fig. 7.2 Inflation, employment growth and the unemployment rate responses to positive NGDP growth shocks. (Note: The grey shaded bands denote the 16th and 84th percentile confidence bands. Source: Authors' calculations)

inflation increases, and such an increase poses a threat to the price stability mandate. These models did not assess the effects of NGDP growth when distinguishing between high and low NGDP growth regimes. In addition, these models did not assess the influence of the inflation targeting band on the reaction of the inflation rate. Hence, in the sections we show the influence of high NGDP growth on inflation when taking into account high inflation regimes (when inflation excess 6 per cent) and low inflation regimes (when inflation is between 3 and 6 per cent).

7.4 The Impact of Positive NGDP Growth Shocks: Perspective from the Employment Growth and the Unemployment Rate

We separate the NGDP growth into high and low regime thresholds based on the 10 per cent NGDP growth threshold. The high NGDP growth regime (NGDP_high) dummy equals to the values of NGDP growth above 10 per cent and zero otherwise. The low NGDP growth

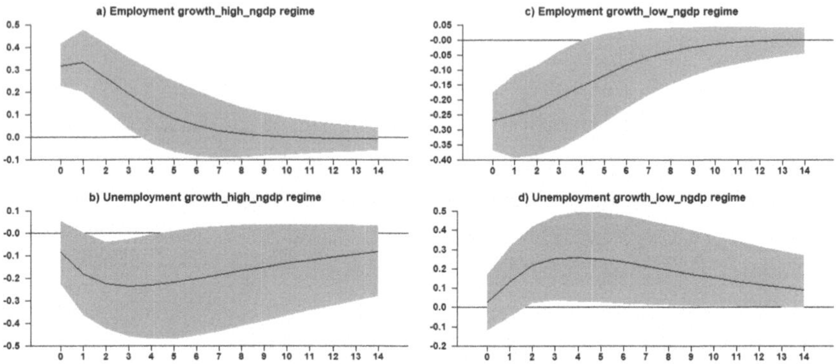

Fig. 7.3 Employment growth and the unemployment rate responses to positive NGDP growth shocks. (Note: The grey shade bands denote the 16th and 84th percentile confidence bands. Source: Authors' calculations)

regime (NGDP_low) dummy equals to the values of NGDP growth below 10 per cent and zero otherwise. These dummy variables are included separately in the models. The first model estimated includes the NGDP_high dummy, employment growth and the unemployment rate. The second model includes the NGDP_low dummy, employment growth and unemployment rate.

The results based on the NGDP growth regimes in Fig. 7.3 show that employment growth rises significantly due to a positive NGDP growth shock when NGDP growth exceeds 10 per cent. On the other hand, the unemployment rate declines due to a positive NGDP growth shock when NGDP growth exceeds 10 per cent. This contrasts with positive NGDP growth shock when NGDP growth is below 10 per cent. The results show that employment growth declines and the unemployment rate increases. These findings imply that the NGDP growth threshold matters for the effects of NGDP growth on employment growth and the unemployment rate. These results are robust to the different model specifications.

7.4.1 Perspective from Consumer Price Inflation Regimes

To determine if the inflation targeting framework matters, we examine the role of inflation regimes in responding to positive NGDP

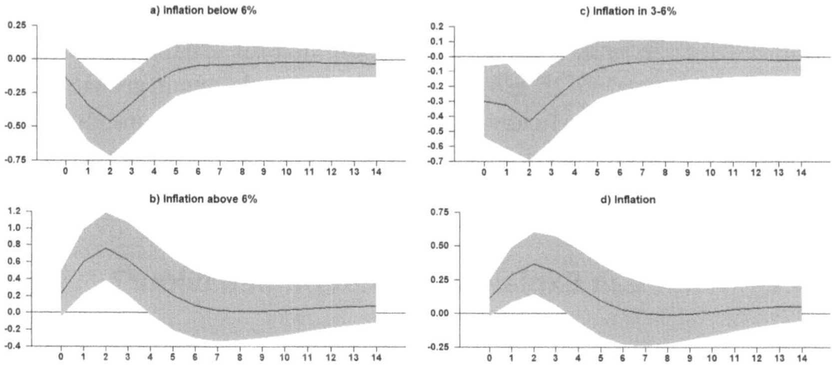

Fig. 7.4 Inflation responses to positive NGDP growth shocks under different inflation regimes. (Note: The grey shade bands denote the 16th and 84th percentile confidence bands. Source: Authors' calculations)

growth when above 10 per cent. We separate the inflation regimes into (i) below 6 per cent, (ii) above 6 per cent and (ii) between 3 and 6 per cent. We separate these regimes by creating three dummy variables. Each inflation dummy in each target band equals to the value of inflation in each band and zero otherwise. We estimate VAR models which include the NGDP_high dummy, employment growth, the unemployment rate and the inflation dummy as endogenous variables. The exogenous variables include a constant and recession dummy. The model is estimated using 2 lags and 10,000 Monte Carlo draws. The shock is a one standard deviation to NGDP growth.

Figure 7.4 shows that the response of inflation to positive NGDP growth shocks depends on where inflation is relative to the 3 to 6 per cent target band. For instance, inflation declines when (i) it is below 6 per cent and (ii) within the 3–6 per cent inflation target band. This contrasts with the increase in inflation when inflation is above the 6 per cent threshold. These findings imply that the inflation regimes and the inflation target matter for the response of inflation positive NGDP growth shocks when it is above 10 per cent. Thus, a low inflation target is not inconsistent with a high NGDP growth target.

There are policy implications that can be derived from the preceding findings. First, these findings reveal that NGDP growth targeting on its own is not the best optimal to achieve high employment growth and a low unemployment rate because inflation may increase to high levels in South Africa. Second, these results suggest that an expanded mandate which includes real GDP growth, maximum employment growth (low unemployment rate) and a low inflation target is the appropriate approach monetary policy can take to macroeconomic stabilisation. A lower inflation target and a higher NGDP growth target are not mutually exclusive.

7.4.2 What Can Explain the Inflation Behaviour?

We include nominal wage growth and the nominal effective exchange rate (NEER) in the preceding VAR models. These nominal wage and exchange rate channels are the main channels through which first and second round inflationary pressures are transmitted. In addition, these channels are key drivers of upside risks to the inflation outlook. As a result, we show how inflation responds to positive nominal wage growth and NEER shocks depending on the inflation regimes. In Fig. 7.5, nominal wage growth rises due to positive NGDP growth shocks in the high NGDP growth regime. In addition, the exchange rate appreciates, and this dampens the inflationary pressures

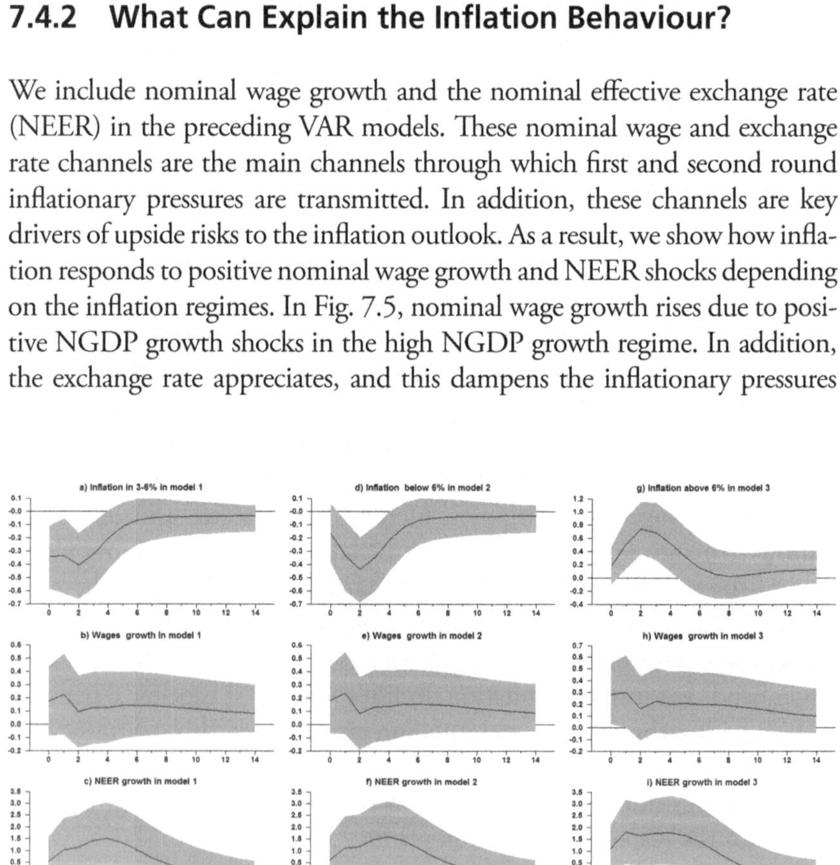

Fig. 7.5 Nominal wage growth and NEER responses to positive NGDP growth shocks under different inflation regimes. (Note: The grey shade bands denote the 16th and 84th percentile confidence bands. Source: Authors' calculations)

in Models 1 and 2 when inflation is below 6 per cent and between 3 and 6 per cent. The muted wage growth and the accompanying exchange rate appreciation imply that inflationary pressures are minimised and even contained even though NGDP growth is above 10 per cent.

On the other hand, the results of the Model 3 where inflation is above 6 per cent (high inflation regime) indicate that inflation increases as the exchange rate appreciation is not enough to dampen the increase in nominal wages and inflation. Thus, the inflation regimes matter for the transmission of nominal wage and exchange rate shocks in the high NGDP growth regimes. A low inflation regime is not inconsistent with a high NGDP growth regime.

7.4.3 The Role of the Exchange Rate Channel

We estimate various counterfactual VAR models to determine the role of the exchange rate channel in transmitting high NGDP growth shocks to inflation in various inflation regimes. The models include the NGDP_high dummy, employment growth, the unemployment rate and the inflation dummy. The NEER growth enters the model as an endogenous variable. The exogenous variables include a constant and recession dummy. The recession dummy is equal to one during the recession and zero otherwise. The model is estimated using 2 lags and 10,000 Monte Carlo draws. The counterfactual response is calculated by shutting off the exchange rate channel.

The cumulative responses of inflation are shown in Fig. 7.6 and show that the exchange rate appreciation accentuates the decline in inflation when it is below 6 per cent and when within the 3–6 per cent target range. In addition, the exchange rate appreciation dampens the increase in inflation when it is above 6 per cent. This evidence reveals the potency of the exchange rate channel in the transmission of high NGDP growth shocks.

7.4.4 The Role of the Nominal Wage Growth Channel

We show the role of nominal wage growth channel in transmitting positive NGDP growth shocks to inflation in inflation regimes. The counterfactual

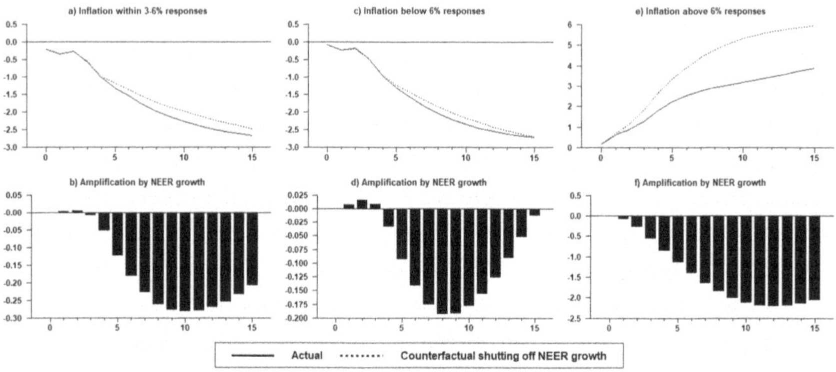

Fig. 7.6 Cumulative actual and counterfactual inflation responses to positive NGDP growth shocks and the role of the exchange rate. (Source: Authors' calculations)

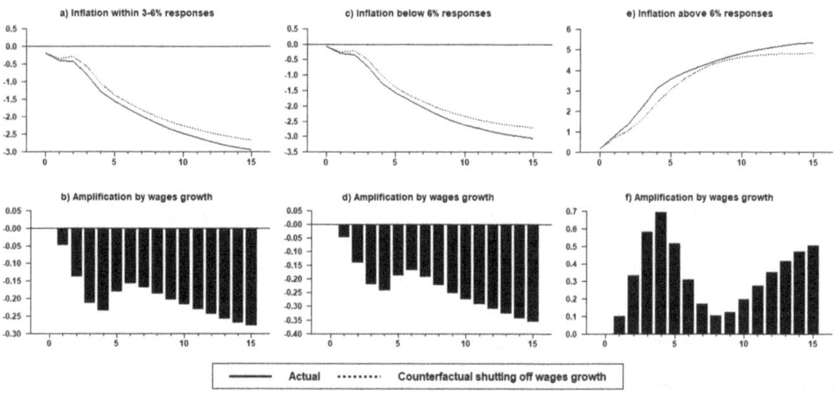

Fig. 7.7 Cumulative actual and counterfactual inflation responses to positive nominal GDP growth shocks and role of nominal wage growth. (Source: Authors' calculations)

nominal wage growth is calculated by shutting off nominal wage growth in transmitting positive NGDP growth shocks to inflation.

Figure 7.7 shows that nominal wage growth accentuates the decline in inflation when inflation is below 6 per cent and when it is within the 3–6 per cent inflation target range. This contrasts with the amplification of high NGDP growth shocks when inflation is above 6 per cent. This shows that low nominal wage growth in the low inflation regime helps in minimising inflationary pressures.

7.4.5 The Role of the Inflation Expectation Channels

This section examines the role of inflation expectations in transmitting high NGDP growth shocks to inflation in different inflation regimes. We replace consumer price inflation with inflation expectations (inflation_exp). We use the current, one-year ahead and two-year ahead inflation expectations. The results in Fig. 7.8 show that a positive NGDP growth shock leads to the exchange rate appreciation and a decline in inflation expectations. This minimises the increase in nominal wage growth.

Thus, the exchange rate appreciation and muted increases in nominal wage inflation result in a decline in inflation expectations response to high NGDP growth regimes. These results suggest that an expanded mandate which caters for price stability and maximum employment growth is consistent with high NGDP growth regimes.

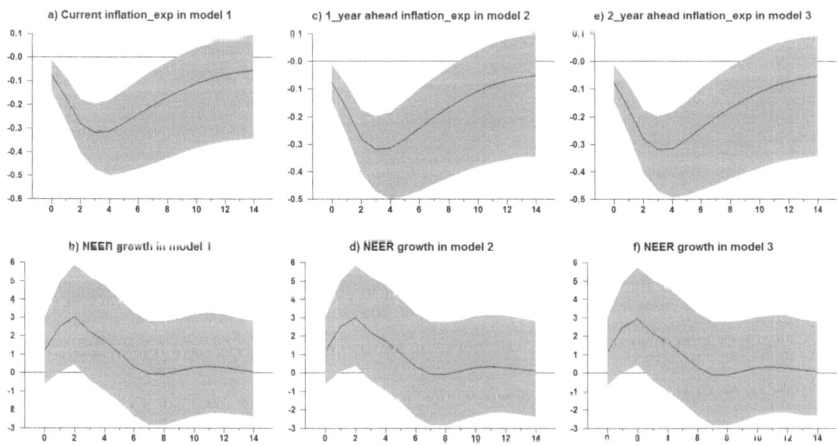

Fig. 7.8 Inflation expectations responses to positive NGDP growth shock in the high NGDP growth regime. (Note: The grey shade bands denote the 16th and 84th percentile confidence bands. Source: Authors' calculations)

7.5 What Are the Implications for the Conduct of Monetary Policy?

We assess the monetary policy stance based on the response of the repo rate in different inflation regimes. The responses are based on the three VAR models specified in the earlier sections. The results in Fig. 7.9 show that in all models, the repo rate rises significantly over two periods. This suggests that positive NGDP growth shocks in the high NGDP growth regime do not lead to persistently tight monetary policy stance. This is because unexpected increases in nominal GDP growth above the 10 per cent threshold lead to the exchange rate appreciation which dampens inflationary pressures.

We further show the role of the exchange rate channel in mitigating the inflationary pressures and dampening the repo rate responses to inflation by estimating a counterfactual VAR model. This approach is meant to demonstrate the role of the exchange rate channel in the transmission of positive NGDP growth shocks to policy rate responses to inflation. Figure 7.10 shows that the repo rate is tightened less than the actual response when the exchange rate channel is allowed to operate in

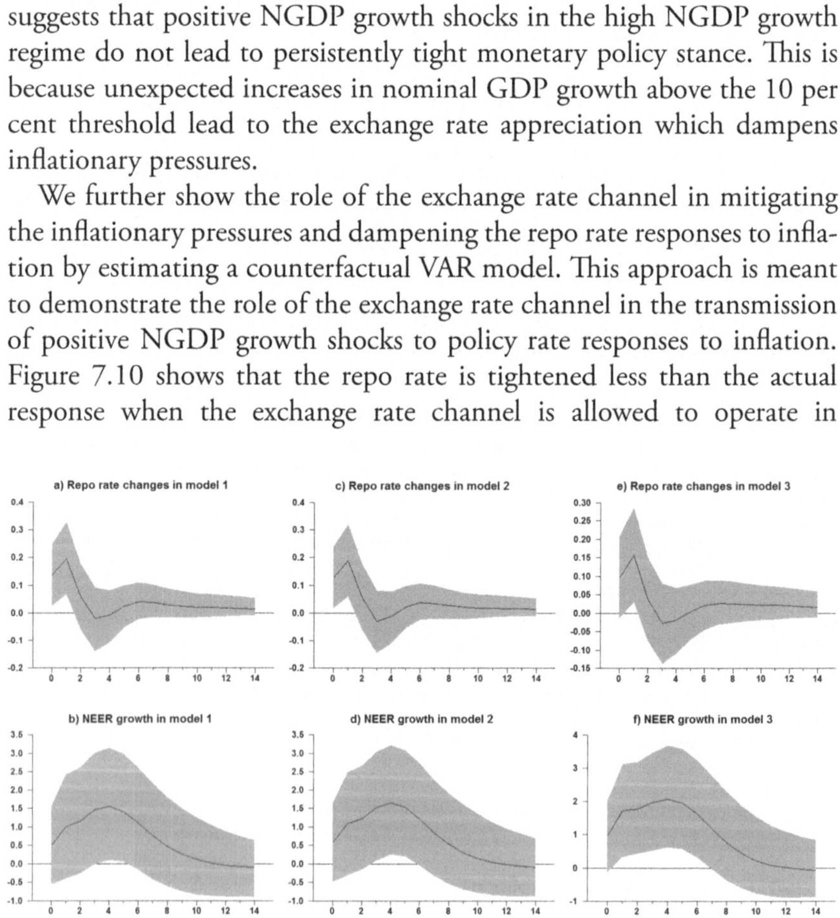

Fig. 7.9 Repo rate responses to positive NGDP growth shocks in the high NGDP growth regime. (Note: The grey shade bands denote the 16th and 84th percentile confidence bands. Source: Authors' calculations)

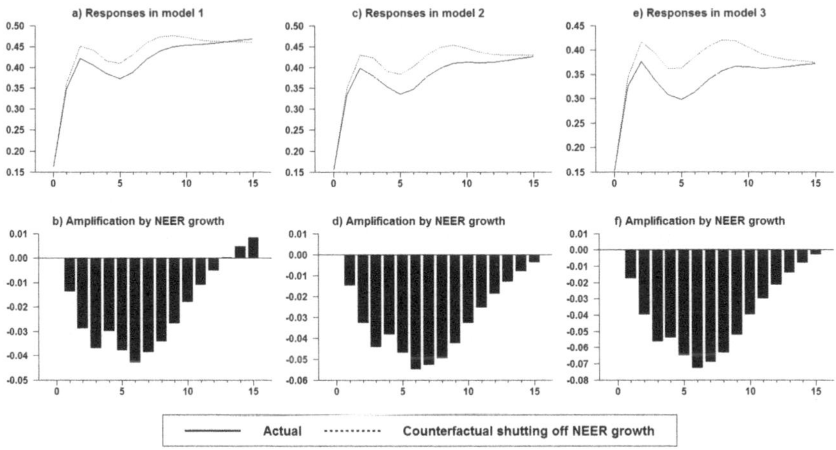

Fig. 7.10 Cumulative repo rate responses to positive NGDP growth shocks in the high NGDP growth regime. (Source: Authors' calculations)

the models compared to when it is shut off. The results show that the exchange rate appreciation dampens the pace of the policy rate tightening to inflation shocks.

7.6 Conclusion and Policy Implications

Are high NGDP growth targets consistent with low inflation and the dual mandate of maximum employment growth and a low unemployment rate? We find that employment growth rises significantly due to a positive NGDP growth shock when NGDP growth exceeds 10 per cent. On the other hand, the unemployment rate declines more due to a positive NGDP growth shock when NGDP growth exceeds 10 per cent. These findings imply that the NGDP growth threshold matters for the effects of NGDP growth on employment growth and the unemployment rate. In addition, the response of inflation to positive NGDP shocks depends on where inflation is relative to the 3 to 6 per cent target band. Inflation declines when in low inflation regimes. These findings imply that the inflation regimes and the inflation target matter for the response of inflation positive NGDP growth shocks when it is above 10 per cent.

The exchange rate appreciation and muted increases in nominal wage inflation also result in a decline in the inflation expectations response in high NGDP growth regimes.

The policy implication of the results is a low inflation target is not inconsistent with a high NGDP growth target. Furthermore, low inflation regimes and the exchange rate channel play an important role in neutralising inflationary shocks and dampening the response of the repo rate to inflation shocks in the high NGDP growth regime. Thus, in the South African, NGDP growth targeting alone is inadequate and should be accompanied by the price stability framework. Otherwise, inflation rises above the 6 per cent threshold of the target band due to positive NGDP growth shocks. This means that a dual mandate must give equal weighting to price stability, output growth and maximum employment growth. An expanded mandate in South Africa which includes a low inflation target, high real GDP growth and maximum employment growth (low unemployment rate) is the appropriate approach monetary policy can take to macroeconomic stabilisation. A lower inflation target and a higher NGDP growth target are not mutually exclusive.

References

Balke, N. 2000. Credit and Economic Activity: Credit Regimes and Nonlinear Propagation of Shocks. *The Review of Economics and Statistics*, 82(2), 344–49. MIT Press, May.

Bean, Charlie. 1983. Targeting Nominal Income: An Appraisal. *The Economic Journal*, 93, 806–19.

Bhandari, P., and Frankel, J. 2014a. *The Best of Rules and Discretion: A Case for Nominal GDP Targeting in India*. CID Working Paper No. 284.

Bhandari, P., and Frankel, J. 2014b. *The Best of Rules and Discretion: A Case for Nominal GDP Targeting in India*. CID Working Paper No. 284, Harvard Kennedy School. https://www.hks.harvard.edu/sites/default/files/centers/cid/files/publications/faculty-working-papers/284_Frankel_IndiaGDP.pdf.

Bhandari, P., and Frankel, J.A. 2015. *Nominal GDP Targeting for Developing Countries*. Working Paper 20898. http://www.nber.org/papers/w20898.

Blanchard, Olivier, Dell'Ariccia, Giovanni, and Mauro, Paolo. 2010. *Rethinking Macroeconomic Policy*. IMF Staff Position Note, 12 February.

Bullard, J. 2019. James Bullard Discusses NGDP Targeting. https://www.stlouisfed.org/publications/regional-economist/second-quarter-2019/bullard-nominal-gdp-targeting?

Creamer, K., and Botha, T.R. 2017. Assessing Nominal GDP Targeting in the South African Context. *Central Bank Review*, 17(1), March 2017, 1–10. https://www.sciencedirect.com/science/article/pii/S1303070116300506?via%3Dihub.

Du Plessis, S., and Rietveld, M. 2013. *Should Inflation Targeting be Abandoned in Favour of Nominal Income Targeting?* University of Stellenbosch Economic Working Papers: 12/13.

Frankel, J. 1995. The Stabilizing Properties of a Nominal GNP Rule. *Journal of Money, Credit and Banking*, 27(2), 318–34.

Frankel, J. 2012. Central Banks Can Phase in Nominal GDP Targets without Damaging the Inflation Anchor. *VoxEU*, December 19.

Frankel, J. 2013. Nominal GDP Targets without Losing the Inflation Anchor. In L. Reichlin and R. Baldwin (eds.), *Is Inflation Targeting Dead: Central Banking after the Crisis*. Centre for Economic Policy Research: London, pp. 90–94.

Frankel, J. *The Case for (and Drawbacks of) Nominal GDP Targets. Capital Formation and Growth*. Harvard Kennedy School, Harvard University. https://www.brookings.edu/wp-content/uploads/2017/12/frankel-slides.pdf.

Hassan, S, and Loewald, C. 2013. *Nominal GDP Targeting and the Monetary Policy Framework*. South African Reserve Bank Working Paper WP 1305.

Hatzius, J. 2011. The Case for a Nominal GDP Level Target. US Economics Analyst, Goldman Sachs Global ECS Research, October.

Hoelle, M., and Peiris, U. 2013. *On the Efficiency of Nominal GDP Targeting in a Large Open Economy*. Krannert Working Paper Series, Paper No. 1273.

Summers, H., Wessel, D., and Murray, J.D. 2018. Rethinking the Fed's 2 per cent Inflation Target: A Report from the Hutchins Center on Fiscal and Monetary Policy at Brookings. https://www.brookings.edu/wp-content/uploads/2018/06/ES_20180607_Hutchins-FedInflationTarget.pdf.

Sumner, S. 1995. Using Monetary Policy to Target a Nominal Wage Index. *Journal of Economics and Business*, 47(2), 205–15.

Sumner, Scott. 2012. The Case for Nominal GDP Targeting. Mercatus Center, George Mason University.

Svensson, Lars E.O. 2003. What Is Wrong with Taylor Rules? Using Judgment in Monetary Policy through Targeting Rules. *Journal of Economic Literature*, 41, 426–77.

Svensson, Lars E.O. 2009. Flexible Inflation Targeting—Lessons from the Financial Crisis. Speech at BIS, 21 September.

Tsay, R.S. 1998. Testing and Modeling Multivariate Threshold Models. *Journal of the American Statistical Association*, 93(443), 1188–202. September.

Woodford, M. 2012. *Methods of Policy Accommodation at the Interest-Rate Lower Bound*. Columbia University.

Part III

The Output-Employment Intensities and the Structural Change Indices

8

What Is the Nature of the Output-Employment-Unemployment Nexus in South Africa? Evidence from Various Approaches to Okun's Law

Learning Objectives

- Establish how the output growth intensity of employment creation, alternatively, Okun's Law at the aggregate and sectorial level has evolved.
- Determine the implications of the employment-output intensity and the unemployment-employment relationship for the labour force participation rate.
- Establish the implications of ratio α/β for the output growth consistent with a stable employment (unemployment) rate.
- Examine the evolution of the sectorial output growth intensity of employment creation.

8.1 Introduction

Gumata and Ndou (2019) showed the existence of the *output–inflation* trade-off and that it is dependent on the inflation regimes. The authors showed that the South African data supports the new Keynesian hypothesis which implies that demand policy interventions are less effective in

N. Gumata, E. Ndou, *Accelerated Land Reform, Mining, Growth, Unemployment and Inequality in South Africa*, https://doi.org/10.1007/978-3-030-30884-1_8

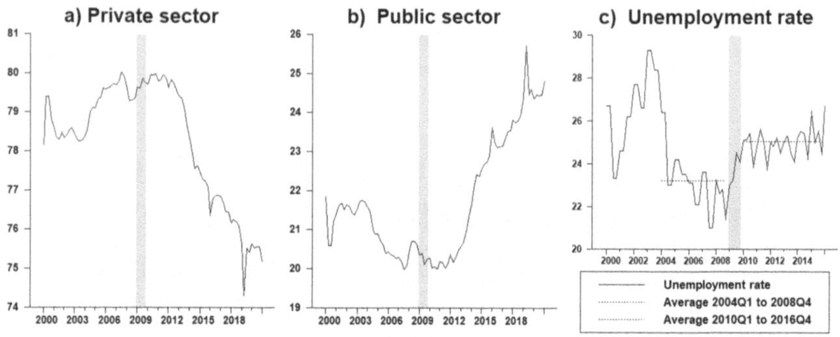

Fig. 8.1 Employment and unemployment rates. (Note: The shaded areas denote the South African recession. Source: South African Reserve Bank)

countries with high trend inflation and where prices are less rigid. The effectiveness of demand management policies depends on the price rigidities. The policy effectiveness is more pronounced below the mid-point (4.5 per cent) of the inflation target band. The authors provide evidence showing that the amplification effects are pronounced when inflation is below 4.5 per cent than when it is just anywhere below the 6 per cent inflation threshold. Furthermore, a nominal demand policy shock that affects nominal demand will have a bigger effect on real output in a low inflation regime than in a high inflation regime, when considering the role of nominal wage growth which is the price aspect of the labour markets. This chapter extends the analysis by exploring the *output-growth intensity of employment* creation, alternatively, the Okun's Law. How has the intensity of the ability of output growth to create jobs evolved?

First, Fig. 8.1(a) and (b) shows that the contribution of the private and public sectors on QES employment tend to be countercyclical.[1] Post-2010 the decline in private sector employment was countered by public sector employment. Nonetheless, this was insufficient to lower the unemployment rate in Fig. 8.1(c). It is also noteworthy that even as the contribution of the private sector employment was increasing in the 1990s, the

[1] They move in different directions.

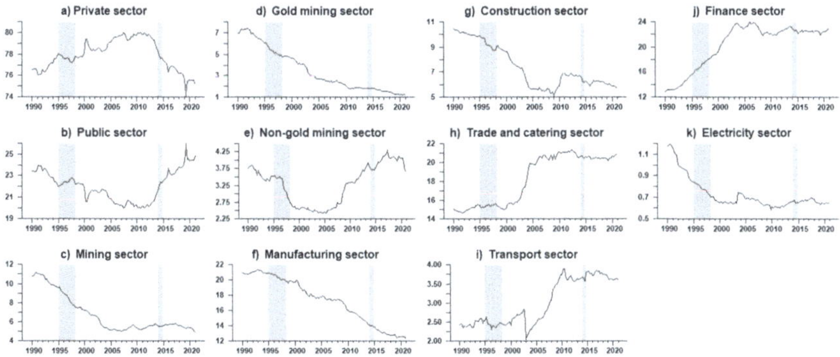

Fig. 8.2 Sectorial contributions to formal private sector employment. (Note: The shaded areas denote the South African recessions. Source: South African Reserve Bank)

unemployment rate was also increasing and only started to respond and decrease in 2003Q1. In addition, Fig. 8.1(b) and (c) show that for a prolonged period pre-2009, the private sector was the main driver of employment growth as opposed to the public sector.

Figure 8.2 shows that much of the private sector employment in the 1990s up to 2014 was mainly due to the contributions of the financial, transport and retail sectors. The construction and the electricity sectors also made positive contribution post-2010. On the other hand, the mining sector has been driven by the non-gold mining sector especially post-2000, but this had not been able to increase the contribution of the sector to the levels of between 16 per cent and 12 per cent recorded during the mining boom of the early 1980s.[2] In addition, it is evident from the trends in Fig. 8.2 that the contribution of the non-gold mining employment to total private and formal non-agriculture employment remained positive post-2009. What could explain this momentum despite (i) the domestic recession, (ii) heightened policy uncertainty in the industry including the electricity outages and the implementation of the minimum

[2] It is noteworthy that the increased contribution of the mining sector in the 1980s coincided with that of the electricity sector in line with the discoveries and surge in global commodity prices in the early 1980s. We explore the role of commodity and asset price booms and busts in later chapters of this book.

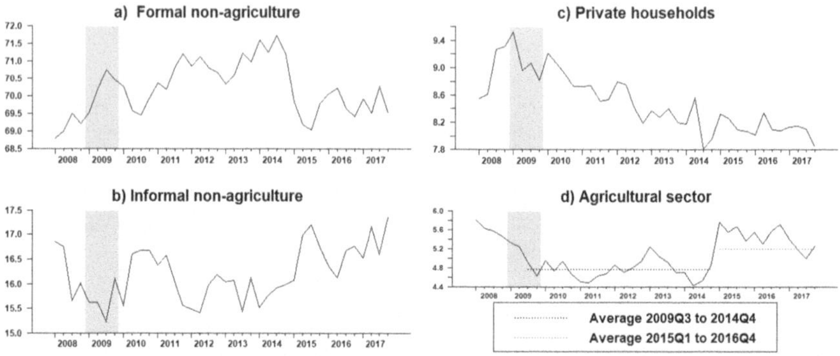

Fig. 8.3 QLFS employment. (Note: The shaded areas denote the South African recession. Source: South African Reserve Bank and Statistics South Africa)

wage of R7500 across the board in 2010 and (iii) subdued global demand and commodity prices?[3]

On the contrary, the manufacturing sector contribution has been on a secular decline since the 1990s. This is in stark contrast to the trend displayed by the financial sector which has been on a persistently rising trend during the sample period. Do these sectorial shifts in the contributions of employment have a meaningful impact on the employment intensity of output growth?

At the same time, the QLFS sectorial employment trends in Fig. 8.3 indicate that post-2014 the formal non-agricultural sector contribution declined whilst the informal non-agriculture and agricultural sector contributions increased.[4] Nonetheless, this was not enough to lower the unemployment rate in Fig. 8.1 and increase the contribution of the private sector to aggregate employment growth.

It is against this background that this chapter starts the empirical analysis of the employment dynamics, which will give more insights on the consideration of targeting maximum employment (the maximum employment mandate) alongside low and stable inflation. The analysis begins by exploring the aggregate and sectorial employment intensity of output growth. In addition, the analysis takes cognisance of the fact that

[3] These aspects are explored in later chapters of this book.

[4] Data for the QLFS employment is only available from 2008Q1.

Yellen (2017), Brainard (2017a) and Kashkari (2017) amongst others raise the persistent disconnect (divergence) between the price stability and maximum (full) employment mandates in the United States (US) post-financial crisis.[5] These authors show that the concept of maximum (full) employment is time varying as the US economy has persistently surpassed estimates of maximum (full) employment without triggering higher consumer price and nominal wage inflation. Furthermore, these authors argue that had the US Fed stuck to the pre-crisis estimates of the maximum or full (un)employment rate target, additional workers might have not re-entered the labour force and yet the job market remained healthy.

Gumata and Ndou (2017) show that the South African labour market conditions and labour market reforms as supply side policies are useful in impacting the relationship between unemployment and job adverts. At the same time, price stability benefits too. Furthermore, labour market reforms work via their influence on the labour demand and wage settings. The authors reject the "*unemployment invariance hypothesis*", suggesting that policies which stimulate investment or improve innovation and technology or change the size of the labour force will have an effect in changing the unemployment rate in the long run. Hence, various policy interventions in the labour market can be used to mitigate the "*discouraged worker effects*". This means that various policy interventions can enhance the labour absorption rate.

8.2 Alternative Approaches to the Estimation of the GDP-Employment-Unemployment Growth Relationship

This section presents a brief discussion of the methodologies used to estimate various versions of the Okun's Law to test the degree to which the output growth intensity of employment creation has varied over time.

[5] The puzzle is why inflation has been persistently low at a time when estimates place the economy at or near full employment. Hence, the argument that the Phillips curve has weakened (flattened) post-financial crisis as inflation and nominal wages have tended to change relatively little as the unemployment rate has fallen considerably. Thus Brainard (2017a) argues that with the Phillips curve appearing to be a less reliable guidepost than it has been in the past, the anchoring role of inflation expectations and lowering financial imbalances remains critically important.

Ball et al. (2013) state that the Okun's Law is part of models in which shifts in aggregate demand cause changes in output, which in turn lead firms to hire and fire workers. As such, in these models, when unemployment is high, it can be reduced through nominal demand stimulus policies. The models assume that there exist some long-run levels of output, employment and unemployment, and that shifts in aggregate demand cause output to fluctuate around its potential.[6] These output movements due to aggregate demand shifts cause firms to hire and fire workers and thus change the (un)employment rate. On the other hand, changes in employment move the unemployment rate in the opposite direction.

The Okun's Law relationship can be expressed as in Eqs. (8.1), (8.2) and (8.3)

$$E_t - E_t^* = \gamma\left(Y_t - Y_t^*\right) + \eta_{t,}\ \gamma > 0 \quad \textit{employment equation}, \tag{8.1}$$

$$U_t - U_t^* = \delta\left(E_t - E_t^*\right) + \mu_{t,}\ \ \delta < 0 \quad \textit{unemployment equation}, \tag{8.2}$$

$$U_t - U_t^* = \beta\left(Y_t - Y_t^*\right) + \varepsilon_{t,}\quad \beta < 0 \quad \textit{Okun's Law}, \tag{8.3}$$

where E_t in the *employment equation* Eq. (8.1) is the log of employment, Y_t is the log of output, U_t is the unemployment rate in the *unemployment equation* Eq. (8.2) and the $*$ signifies a long-run level. The coefficient β in the Okun's Law depends on the coefficients for:

1. γ which is the response of employment to output
2. δ which is the response of unemployment to employment

These coefficients in the un(employment) relationships in Eqs. (8.1) and (8.2) underlie the Okun's Law. Ball et al. (2013) indicate that γ is affected by the decisions that firms take in adjusting labour and capital as inputs in the production function. Since it can be costly to adjust employment, firms tend to accommodate short-run output fluctuations by, for example, adjusting the number of hours per worker and workers' produc-

[6] In this case Ball et al. (2013) state that "potential output" is synonymous with long-run output and the "natural rate" refers to the long-run unemployment. The long-run level of employment and the natural rate of unemployment are determined by the size of the labour force and frictions in the labour market.

tivity. On the other hand, the coefficient for δ is expected to be less than one in absolute value. Ball et al. (2013) state that this is because unemployment moves less than one-for-one with employment. In addition, an increase in employment increases the returns to job search, which induces workers to enter the labour force (increase in the labour participation ratio). Hence, these procyclical movements in the labour force tend to partly offset the effects of employment on the unemployment rate.

In addition, the coefficient for $\beta = \gamma\delta$ in the Okun's Law is expected to be less than the coefficient γ in the employment equation in absolute value. Furthermore, Ball et al. (2013) show that the coefficient is expected to depend on the adjustment costs of employment, which include (i) technological costs such as training (ii) costs created by employment protection laws and (iii) the number of workers who are marginally attached to the labour force, entering and exiting the labour market as employment fluctuates. The error term $\varepsilon_t = \mu_t + \delta\eta_t$ captures factors such as changes in productivity and the labour force participation rate that shift the unemployment-output relationship. When the error term ε_t is small, this means that the Okun's Law fits well.

8.2.1 Different Versions of the Employment-Output Intensity Relationship

We use three alternative approaches of estimating Okun's Law on quarterly. In addition, this chapter takes the approach that while a stable Law can fit the data at the aggregate level, the sectorial breakdown can deliver heterogenous coefficients that can provide more information about the nature of the relationship between growth and employment. Alternatively, the sectorial employment intensity of growth can convey more information than the aggregate levels. As such, we estimate sectorial Okun's Laws coefficients as well.

First, we estimate the *difference version of employment-output intensity relationship* which captures the contemporaneous correlation between output growth and movements in employment and unemployment and employment as shown in Eqs. (8.4) and (8.5).

$$\Delta E_t = \alpha + \beta \Delta Y_t + \omega_t, \tag{8.4}$$

$$\Delta U_t = \alpha + \beta \Delta Y_t + \omega_t, \tag{8.5}$$

where Δ is the change from the previous period. Thus, Eqs. (8.4) and (8.5) estimate how output growth varies simultaneously with changes in the employment rate, and unemployment with changes in employment. For Eqs. (8.4) and (8.5), the parameter β is referred to as the "*Okun's coefficient*" (the employment-output intensity coefficient) and is expected to be negative (positive) indicating that rapid output growth (employment growth) is associated with a decrease (increase) in the unemployment (employment) rate. At the same time, Knotek (2007) indicates that the ratio α/β in Eqs. (8.4) and (8.5) gives the rate of output growth consistent with a stable employment (unemployment) rate. Alternatively, it represents how quickly the economy would need to grow to maintain a given level of employment (unemployment).

Second, we estimate the gap version of employment-output intensity which connects the level of employment to the gap between potential and actual output. Where the Y_t^* and E_t^* are estimated via the Hodrick-Prescott (HP) filter with a smoothing parameter of $\lambda = 1600$ for quarterly data. The gap version of Okun's is represented in Eq. (8.6).

$$\Delta E_t = \alpha + \beta \left(Y_t - Y_t^* \right) + \omega_t, \tag{8.6}$$

where α can be interpreted as the employment rate associated with full employment and β is expected to be positive indicating that rapid output growth is associated with an increase in the employment rate.

Third, we estimate the dynamic version of output-employment intensity to test for the persistence of output growth or the output-gap. Knotek (2007) indicates that the dynamic version of Okun's Law suggests that both past and current output can impact the current level of employment (unemployment). A common form for the dynamic version of Okun's Law is presented in Eq. (8.7).

$$\Delta E_t = \alpha + \beta_1 Y_t + \beta_2 Y_{t-1} + \beta_3 Y_{t-2} + \beta_4 E_{t-1} + \beta_5 E_{t-2}, \tag{8.7}$$

where current real output growth, past real output growth and past changes in the employment (unemployment) rate are included as explanatory variables on the right side of the Eq. (8.7). The variables on the right hand of Eq. (8.7) would then explain the current change in the employment (unemployment) rate. The dynamic version of Okun's Law not only captures the contemporaneous correlation between changes in the employment (unemployment) rate and real output growth but is not as restrictive in terms of the timing of the connection between output growth and changes in employment (unemployment).

8.3 How Has the GDP-Employment-Unemployment Growth Relationships Evolved?

This section estimates Eqs. (8.1), (8.2) and (8.3) in levels (logs) and log changes to assess how the employment and unemployment equations in relation to output and the employment-unemployment relation have evolved overtime. The sample size spans the period 1993Q1 to 2016Q4 due to data availability for the unemployment data. The data is sourced from the South African Reserve Bank database. We use the Hodrick-Prescott filter to estimate E^{*}, U^{*} and Y^{*} to estimate the *gap version of Okun's Law*. On the other hand, we use the annual (4Q changes) log changes Δ of employment, unemployment and output to estimate the *difference version of Okun's Law*.

First, we show the fit of the Okun's Law relationships between (i) $U_t - U_t^*$ and $Y_t - Y_t^*$ and (ii) $E_t - E_t^*$ and $Y_t - Y_t^*$ in Fig. 8.4. The scatterplots in Fig. 8.4 suggest that on a bilateral basis, the data confirms the apriori theoretical relationships since there is a negative relationship between the unemployment rate and output growth, whereas there is a positive relationship between employment and output growth. Nonetheless, the strength of the relationships differs significantly as shown by the *R*-squares. There is a weak (strong) relationship between unemployment (employment) and output growth. Furthermore, there are periods which are characterised by several outliers from the linear

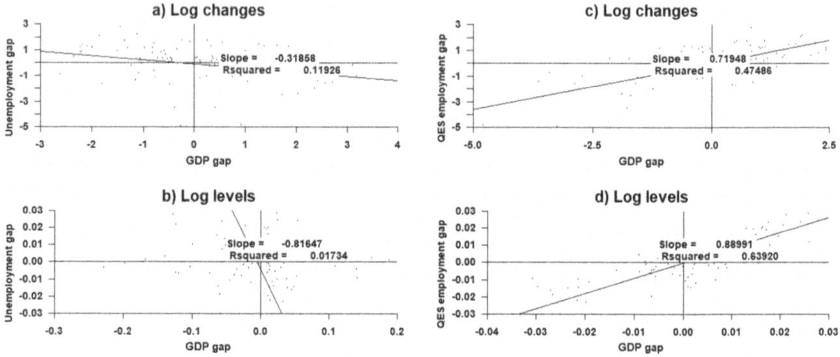

Fig. 8.4 The employment-output relationships. (Source: Authors' calculations)

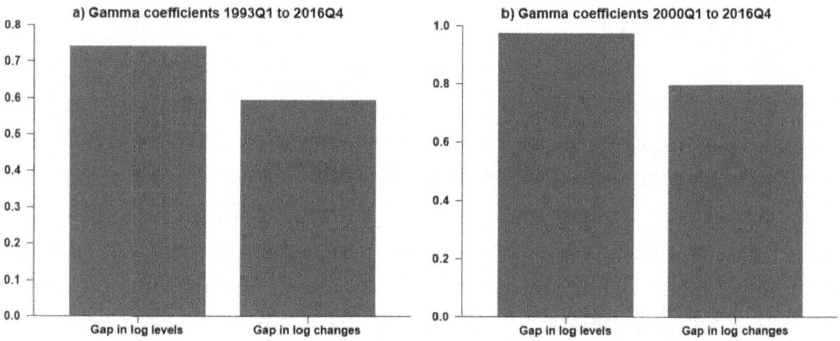

Fig. 8.5 The evolution of output-employment coefficients. (Note: The estimates in logs are based the HP filter of $\lambda = 1600$. The coefficients based on data in log changes are percentage changes over four quarters. Source: Authors' calculations)

regression line, suggesting that these un(employment) and output growth relationships are non-linear. These are early indications that the intensity of the output-un(employment) rate and growth differs and is characterised by a very low labour absorption and participation rates.

The results for Eq. (8.1) for the employment to output (gamma (γ) coefficients) presented in Fig. 8.5 (a) and (b) are positive as expected and vary between 0.5 per cent and 1 per cent. The coefficients are the highest for the period 2000Q1 to 2016Q4, meaning that employment growth was the highest and most responsive during this period. Furthermore, the estimated coefficients also indicate that the relationship between employment and GDP growth is time varying and the period 2000Q1 to 2016Q4 presented the highest intensity of employment growth per one per cent growth in output. The results are consistent with Gali et al. (2011) who refer to such episodes as those of the strong job creation and robust employment growth which tend to be associated with selected cyclical recoveries. On the other hand, the delta (δ) coefficients which is the response of unemployment to employment for the unemployment-employment (Eq. (8.2)) in Fig. 8.6 (a) and (b) indicate that an increase in employment growth does lead to a decline in the unemployment rate at varying degrees.

The delta coefficient varies between −0.1 per cent and −1.57 per cent over the entire sample period. The rate at which the unemployment rate is responsive to employment growth declined significantly post-2007Q1 to a mere 0.1 percentage point. This is consistent with Gordon (2010), Meyer and Tasci (2012) who suggest that the Okun's Law coefficient rates are time varying and most of the recessions tend to be followed by "jobless recoveries"[7] when unemployment does fall as much as predicted by

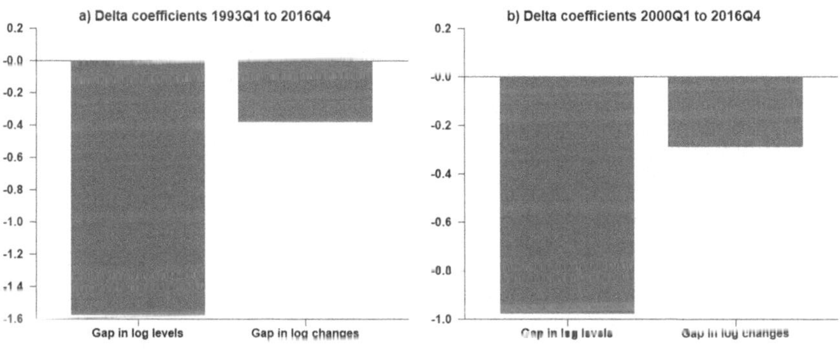

Fig. 8.6 The evolution of unemployment-employment coefficients. (Note: The estimates in logs are based the HP filter of $\lambda = 1600$. The coefficients based on data in log changes are percentage changes over four quarters. Source: Authors' calculations)

[7] The issue of "jobless recoveries" and "export-led jobless growth" are addressed in later chapters of this book.

Okun's Law. The estimated delta (δ) coefficients mean that a 1 percentage change (increase) in employment resulted in a −0.1 percentage point decline in the unemployment rate compared to −0.4 percentage points decline pre-2007.

The period of the highest intensity of output growth on employment growth was associated with a modest −0.4 percentage points reduction in the unemployment rate for every 1 per cent increase in employment growth. The sign and direction of the results is comparable to those in Mankiw (2012) who establish that a 1 per cent deviation of output from potential causes an opposite change in unemployment of half a percentage point for the US (Fig. 8.6).

However, in Fig. 8.6 (a) and (b) the estimated delta coefficient of −0.4 percentage points for South Africa compares unfavourably with −0.73 per cent for the United States in Ball et al. (2013). In addition, the estimated delta coefficient of −0.4 percentage points in Fig. 8.6 raises the policy implications of whether it is sufficient to absorb new entrants into the labour market. More so because an increase in employment increases the returns to job search, which induces workers to enter the labour force and increase in the labour participation ratio.

Similarly, the "*Okun's (β) coefficient*" in Eq. (8.3) in Fig. 8.7 indicates that the employment intensity of output growth is time varying and was the lowest post-financial crisis. The results are comparable to Ball et al. (2013) who establish a coefficient of −0.15 for Japan, −0.45 for the United States and −0.85 for Spain. The authors show that these varying "*Okun's (β) coefficients*" reflect differences in labour markets, such as the prevalence of temporary employment contracts in Spain for example. Nonetheless, Ball et al. (2013) conclude that fluctuations in unemployment are primarily caused by shifts in aggregate demand and that deviations from Okun's Law occur, but they are usually modest in size and short-lived. Figure 8.8 shows the stability of the coefficients for γ, δ and β coefficients in Eqs. (8.1), (8.2) and (8.3) over a 20-quarter rolling window. The confidence bands are based on the 95 per cent confidence intervals.[8]

[8] See Tables 8.3 and 8.4 in the Appendix for the point estimates for γ, δ, β and $\beta = \gamma\delta$.

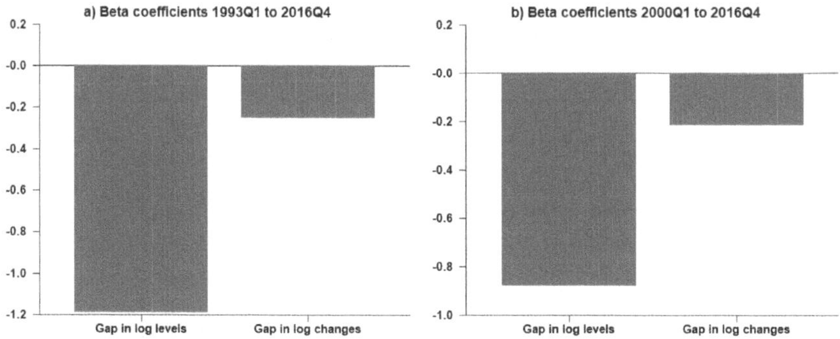

Fig. 8.7 The evolution of unemployment-output coefficients. (Note: The estimates in logs are based on the HP filter of $\lambda = 1600$. The coefficients based on data in log changes are percentage changes over four quarters. Source: Authors' calculations)

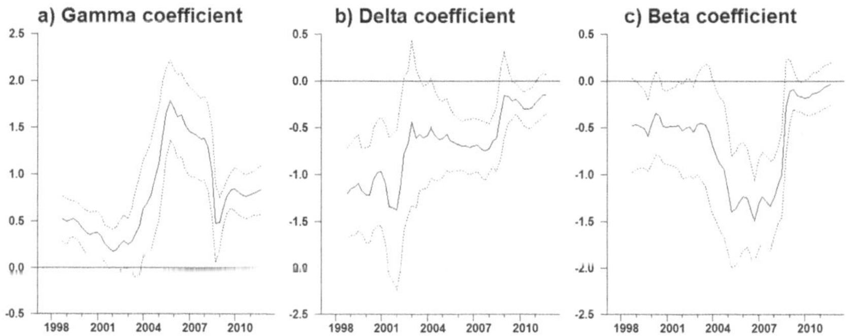

Fig. 8.8 The stability of the coefficients for γ, δ and β coefficients. (Note: The rolling coefficients are based on data in log changes (percentage change over four quarters). Source: Authors' calculations)

8.4 How Quickly Would Output Typically Need to Grow to Maintain a Given Level of Employment Growth and Unemployment Rate?

This section estimates the ratios for c/γ and c/β, where c is the constant and γ and β are the coefficients which are derived from Eqs. (8.1) and (8.3) and present the rate of output growth consistent with a stable

Table 8.1 Estimates of the ratios for c/β and α/β coefficients

	QES employment and GDP growth			Private sector employment and GDP growth		
	c	β	c/β	c	β	c/β
1980Q1 to 2016Q4	0.07	0.41	0.17	0.21	0.51	0.41
1990Q1 to 2016Q4	0.69	0.48	1.44	1.00	0.57	1.77
2000Q1 to 2016Q4	1.46	0.72	2.04	2.35	0.92	2.55

Source: Authors' calculations. The coefficients are based on data in log changes (percentage change over four quarters)

employment growth and unemployment rate. Alternatively, they capture the rate at which the economy would typically need to grow to maintain a given level of unemployment. Knotek (2007) indicates that the ratio α/β in Eqs. (8.4) and (8.5) gives the rate of output growth consistent with a stable employment (unemployment) rate. We also present the ratio of c/δ derived from Eq. (8.2) which relates the unemployment rate with employment growth in Table 8.1.

Similar to the IMF (2010), we find that the coefficients have risen over time in Table 8.1. First, the coefficient for c indicates that zero real output growth at any given point was associated with a decline of between 0.07 and 2.35 per cent in QES and private sector employment growth for the sample period 1980Q1 to 2016Q4.

Second, the β coefficients for QES and private sector employment growth suggest that GDP growth of between 1.5 per cent and 2 per cent is associated with employment growth of between 0.5 per cent and 1 per cent, respectively. Third, the α/β coefficients suggest that GDP growth above 2 per cent is associated with the highest growth in QES and, in particular, private sector employment growth. On the other hand, the coefficients derived using the official unemployment rate in Table 8.2 corroborate those in Table 8.1 and indicate that GDP growth above 2 per cent and in particular the doubling of output growth to 4 per cent and above results in a significant decline in the unemployment rate.

Table 8.2 Estimates of the β coefficients for the unemployment rate

	Unemployment rate and GDP		
	c	β	c/β
1993Q1 to 2016Q4	0.608	−0.294	2.067
2000Q1 to 2016Q4	0.393	−0.205	1.918
2007Q1 to 2016Q4	0.759	−0.198	3.824

Source: Authors' calculations. The coefficients are based on data in log changes (percentage change over four quarters)

8.5 The Sectorial Estimates of the Okun's Law Estimates

We stated earlier that the results based on aggregated data can musk the variation at a sectorial level. Hence this section estimates the sectorial "*Okun's coefficients*". We use sector gross value added (GVA) growth and sector employment growth given the fact that there is no data for sector unemployment rates. As a result, this section only deals with the sector employment intensity of sector GVA (output) growth. The results in Fig. 8.9 and Table 8.5 indicate that the sizes and signs of the coefficients vary over time. First, the mining sector including the disaggregation into gold and non-gold mining employment intensity vary between 0.12 per cent and 0.29 per cent. But it is evident that the gold mining sector employment has declined significantly for the period 2000Q1 to 2016Q4. The negative coefficient suggests that despite an increase in GVA (output growth), there has been a decline in employment growth, alternatively, "jobless growth". Nonetheless, it is evident that the non-gold mining sector employment intensity increased and more than doubled over the sample period. The negative sign on the coefficient for the gold mining sector is consistent with findings in earlier chapters showing that the gold mining sector is a sunset industry. Evidence shows that the gold mining sector is very unresponsive to the mining sector exports growth, GVA (output growth) and investment growth. In addition, we showed in earlier chapters that the gold mining sector contribution to GVA (output) and employment is on a secular decline.

Second, we establish a negative persistent employment intensity for the energy (electricity) sector in Fig. 8.9 and Table 8.5. In addition, evidence in earlier chapters shows that the contribution of the energy sector to formal private sector employment has been on a decline since the late 1980s, this

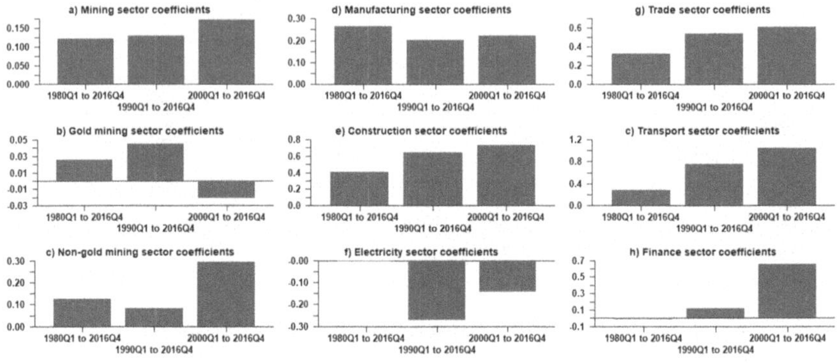

Fig. 8.9 Sectorial of the coefficients for the output-employment intensities. (Source: Authors' calculations)

despite the evidence that the 1980s were a period of high industrialisation in South Africa and the massive investment in electricity generation post-2009. Furthermore, evidence in earlier chapters shows that the coal mining GVA (output growth) generates more employment compared to the metal ores and the platinum group sectors. If the South African economy has been dependent on electricity that is generated via coal which is supposedly labour intensive and yet the electricity β coefficient is persistently negative, what does that mean for other energy sources? In addition, what does this mean for the policies that seek to diversify energy sources in South Africa? The finding of the persistently negative employment intensity of the electricity sector GVA (output growth) casts doubt on the assertion that massive investment in this sector *per se* is going to lead to high levels of employment.

Third, we find that even though the manufacturing sector contribution to employment growth has been on a circular decline similar to that of the electricity sector, the employment intensities of the sectors are vastly different. The employment intensity of the manufacturing sector has been fairly stable between 0.22 per cent and 0.26 per cent. This means that a 1 per cent increase in the manufacturing sector GVA (output growth) results in roughly 0.3 per cent employment growth in that sector compared to a persistent decline found in the electricity sector.

Fourth, the results in Fig. 8.9 and Table 8.5 suggest that most output growth employment intensity is generated by the construction sector followed by the transport, trade and finance sectors. For instance, a per cent growth in these sector GVAs (output) resulted in employment growth of between 0.7 per cent and 1 per cent in these sectors for the period 2000Q1 to 2016Q4. These employment intensity estimates compare favourably to those of the manufacturing and mining sectors. These results are consistent with those in Gumata and Ndou (2017) showing that financial sector liberalisation, deregulation and capital flow surges episodes have had a disproportionate distributional effect on the sectorial GVAs and have benefitted sectors that have proved to be negative on productivity and less job intensive. At the same time, they lead to sectoral employment reallocation in the non-tradable sectors, in particular the financial services and construction sectors. The sectors that tend to benefit are those that are sensitive to asset price booms[9] such as the construction and financial sectors at the expense of productive sectors and productivity growth. Similarly, Cecchetti and Kharroubi (2012) argue that when the financial sector grows more quickly, productivity tends to grow disproportionately slower in industries with higher research and development intensity.[10]

To conclude the analysis in this section, we estimate a VAR model to establish the robustness of the linear point estimates of the output-employment intensities shown in Fig. 8.10. The VAR model includes aggregate GDP growth, employment growth for the (i) manufacturing sector; (ii) construction sector; (iii) wholesale and retail trade, catering and accommodation sector; (iv) transport, storage and communication sector; and (v) finance, insurance, real estate and business services sector and endogenous variables. The recession dummy which takes on the value of one for the periods during which the recession occurs and zero otherwise enters the model as an exogenous variable. The VAR model is estimated using quarterly data (Q) for the sample starting from 2000Q1 to 2016Q4. The model is estimated using 2 lags and 10,000 Monet Carlo draws. The shock is a one-unit shock to aggregate GDP growth.

[9] Asset prices such as house and equity prices. Furthermore, Ndou et al. (2017) show that the economic sectors reflect heterogeneous responses to the REER appreciation shock. The manufacturing sector is highly sensitive to REER movements and declines following the REER appreciation shock. This reflects the dominating impact between the expenditure switching effects and the production costs hypothesis. These effects may be associated with trade exposure of the manufacturing sector to low cost imports and competitors as opposed the dominance of the benefits of reduced input costs of imported input materials in this sector.

[10] The policy implication is that credit and financial booms in general are not growth-enhancing.

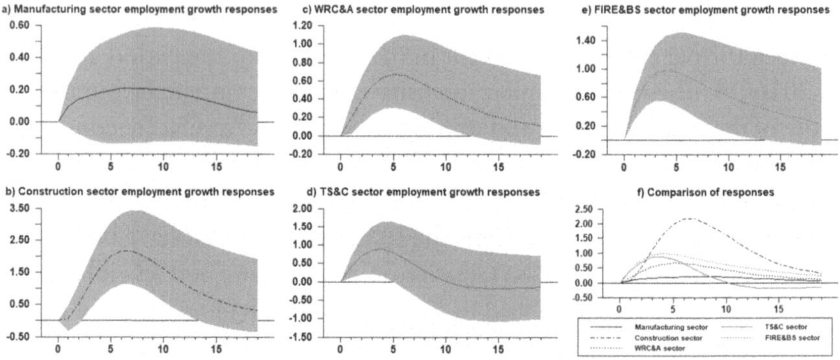

Fig. 8.10 Sectorial employment responses to positive GDP growth shocks. (Note: The grey shaded areas denote the 16th and 84th percentile confidence bands. WRC&A = Wholesale and retail trade, catering and accommodation sector; TS&C = Transport, storage and communication sector; FIRE&BS = Finance, insurance, real estate and business services sector. Source: Authors' calculations)

The results in Fig. 8.10 (f) concur with earlier point estimates and show that the employment growth in the (i) construction sector followed by the (ii) finance, insurance, real estate and business services sector; (iii) transport, storage and communication sector and the (iv) wholesale and retail trade, catering and accommodation sector are more responsive to positive GDP growth shocks.

8.6 Conclusion and Policy Implications

How has the intensity of aggregate and sectorial output growth to create jobs evolved? Evidence shows that the output-employment coefficients varying over time was the lowest post-financial crisis. GDP growth above 2 per cent is associated with the highest growth in QES employment and, in particular, private sector employment growth. On the other hand, the doubling of output growth to 4 per cent and above results in a significant decline in the unemployment rate. At a sectorial level, evidence indicates that the most output growth employment intensity is generated by the construction sector followed by the transport, trade and finance sectors. For these sectors, a per cent growth in their output resulted in employment growth of between 0.7 per cent and 1 per cent in these sectors for the period 2000Q1 to 2016Q4.

The unemployment-employment indicate that an increase in employment growth does lead to a decline in the unemployment rate. But the unemployment rate moves less than one-for-one with employment growth and this worsened post-recession. The estimates indicate that a 1 percentage change (increase) in employment resulted in a −0.1 percentage point decline in the unemployment rate compared to a −0.4 percentage points decline pre-2007. The estimated delta coefficient of −0.4 percentage points raises the policy implications of whether it is sufficient to absorb new entrants into the labour market. More so because an increase in employment increases the returns to job search, which induces workers to enter the labour force and increase in the labour participation ratio. This means that policy interventions aimed at enhancing the labour absorption rate must focus on the construction, transport, trade and finance, manufacturing and mining sectors. These measures will contribute to the objectives of maximum output and employment growth.

Appendix

Table 8.3 Point estimates of the γ, δ, β and $\beta = \gamma\delta$ coefficients (data in logs levels)

	Data in logs				
	γ	δ	β	$\gamma\delta$	Is $\beta = \gamma\delta < \gamma$?
1980Q1 to 2016Q4	0.62**	−1.57**	−1.19**	−0.98	No
1990Q1 to 2016Q4	0.74**	−0.98**	−0.88**	−0.72	Yes
2000Q1 to 2016Q4	0.97**	−0.92**	−1.16**	−0.90	Yes

Source: Authors' calculations
*/**/*** significance at 1 per cent/5 per cent and 10 per cent

Table 8.4 Point estimates of the γ, δ, β and $\beta = \gamma\delta$ coefficients (data in log changes)

	Log changes				
	γ	δ	β	$\gamma\delta$	Is $\beta = \gamma\delta < \gamma$?
1980Q1 to 2016Q4	0.48	−0.38	−0.25	−0.18	Yes
1990Q1 to 2016Q4	0.59	−0.29	−0.22	−0.17	Yes
2000Q1 to 2016Q4	0.80	−0.11	−0.03	−0.08	Yes

Source: Authors' calculations
*/**/*** significance at 1 per cent/5 per cent and 10 per cent

Table 8.5 Sectorial of the coefficients for the output-employment intensities

	Mining	Gold mining	Non-gold mining	Manufacturing	Construction	Electricity	Trade and catering	Transport	Finance
1980Q1 to 2016Q4	0.12	0.03	0.12	0.26	0.41	−0.01	0.32	0.28	−0.01
1990Q1 to 2016Q4	0.13	0.04	0.08	0.20	0.64	−0.27	0.54	0.75	0.12
2000Q1 to 2016Q4	0.17	−0.02	0.29	0.22	0.73	−0.14	0.61	1.04	0.66

Source: Authors' calculations

References

Ball, L.M., Leigh, D., and Loungani, P. 2013. *Okun's Law: Fit at Fifty?* NBER Working Paper 18668.

Brainard, L. 2017a. Understanding the Disconnect between Employment and Inflation with a Low Neutral Rate. Speech at The Economic Club of New York New York City, 5 September 2017.

Brainard, L. 2017b. Navigating the Different Signals from Inflation and Unemployment. Speech at the New York Association for Business Economics, New York City, 30 May 2017.

Cecchetti, S.G., and Kharroubi, E. 2012. *Reassessing the Impact of Finance on Growth*. BIS Working Papers No. 381.

Gali, J. 2010. *The Return of the Wage Phillips Curve*. NBER Working Paper 15758.

Gali, J. 2011. *Unemployment Fluctuations and Stabilization Policies: A New Keynesian Perspective*. MIT Press: Cambridge, MA. ISBN 978-0-262-01597-4.

Gali, J., Smets, F., and Wouters, R. 2011. *Unemployment in an Estimated New Keynesian Model*. NBER Working Paper 17084.

Gali, J., Smets, F., and Wouters, R. 2012. *Slow Recoveries: A Structural Interpretation*. NBER Working Paper 18085.

Gordon, Robert J. 2010. Okun's Law and Productivity Innovations. *American Economic Review: Papers & Proceedings*, 100 (2), 11–15.

Gumata, N., and Ndou, E. 2017. *Bank Credit Extension and Real Economic Activity in South Africa: The Impact of Capital Flow Dynamics, Bank Regulation and Selected Macro-prudential Tools*. Palgrave Macmillan. ISBN 978-3-319-43550-3.

Gumata, N., and Ndou, E. 2019. *Capital Flows, Credit Markets and Growth in South Africa: The Role of Global Economic Growth, Policy Shifts and Uncertainties*. Palgrave Macmillan. ISBN 978-3-030-30887-2.

IMF World Economic Outlook. 2010. Unemployment Dynamics During Recessions and Recoveries: Okun's Law and Beyond. Chapter 3, April. https://www.imf.org/external/pubs/ft/weo/2010/01/

Kashkari, N. 2017. Why I Dissented at the March 2017 FOMC Meeting. https://www.minneapolisfed.org/news-and-events/messages/why-i-dissented.

Knotek, E.S. 2007. How Useful is Okun's Law? *Economic Review*, 4, 73–102. Federal Reserve Bank of Kansas City, Kansas City, KS.

Mankiw, N. Gregory. 2012. *Principles of Macroeconomics*, 6th edition. Mason, OH: South-Western Cengage Learning.

Meyer, Brent, and Tasci, Murat. 2012. An Unstable Okun's Law, Not the Best Rule of Thumb. Economic Commentary, June 7.

Ndou, E., Gumata, N., and Ncube, M. 2017. *Global Economic Uncertainties and Exchange Rate Shocks*. Palgrave Macmillan. ISBN 978-3-319-62279-8.

Yellen, J.L. 2017. From Adding Accommodation to Scaling It Back. Remarks by at The Executives' Club of Chicago Chicago Hilton 720 S. Michigan Avenue Chicago, IL. https://www.federalreserve.gov/newsevents/speech/files/yellen20170303a.pdf

9

The Impact of Structural Change on the South African Economy: Evidence from the Structural Change Indices

Learning Objectives

- Assess whether structural change causes growth or the other way around.
- Construct gross value added, employment and investment structural change indices.
- Assess whether the McMillan and Rodrik (2011) "structural change" component been positive for the South African economy.

9.1 Introduction

This chapter explores the theme of sectorial displacement effects but with special emphasis on the role of structural change. What has been the role of structural change in the South African economy? Previous chapters have shown that the South African economy has undergone multiple shocks ranging from large exchange rate depreciations and appreciations; credit, housing and commodity price booms and busts; and heightened policy and political uncertainty. It is therefore very possible that these events and shocks have changed the structure of the economy. Connolly

N. Gumata, E. Ndou, *Accelerated Land Reform, Mining, Growth, Unemployment and Inequality in South Africa*, https://doi.org/10.1007/978-3-030-30884-1_9

and Orsmond (2011) show that structural change indices (SCIs) can give an indication of the effects of various shocks on the structure of the economy. Furthermore, Dietrich (2009) indicates that economic growth is often associated with structural change in economic sectors measured either in terms of employment or in terms of output. This is premised on the existence of the interrelation between economic growth and structural change. Nonetheless, the direction of causality as to whether economic growth determines structural change or the other way around is still an open empirical question.

It is against this background that this chapter (i) estimates the SCIs for nominal and real sectoral gross value added, employment and investment; (ii) tests the direction of causality, whether it runs from structural changes to economic growth or vice versa; and (iii) assesses whether the "*structural change*" component has been positive or growth reducing for the South African economy.

9.2 Brief Literature Review

Theoretically, structural changes in the economy occur due to (i) preference changes of demand, (ii) sectoral-specific productivity gains, alternatively the "*productivity hypothesis*" and (iii) other significant shocks. The demand side or the preference changes hypothesis postulates that consumer preferences influence the demand of goods and services consumed by economic agents, and this has an influence in the distribution of goods and services across economic sectors. The change in consumer preferences ensures that the distribution of the demand for goods and services across sectors does not remain constant as income rises. Changes in consumer preferences change with increases in income and affect the structure of the economy. In this instance, Diao et al. (2017) show that in contrast to the East Asian experience, none of the recent growth accelerations in Latin America and Africa was driven by rapid industrialisation. The authors find that the recent growth accelerations in the 2000s were based on either rapid within-sector labour productivity growth or growth-increasing structural change originating from the demand side of the economy.

Recent literature shows that other significant shocks such as the recent global financial crisis, capital flow surge episodes and low global real interest rate shocks also impact productivity and the sectoral distribution of value added and employment. For instance, Cette et al. (2016) shows that lower long-term real interest rates were responsible for lower productivity growth. On the other hand, Borio et al. (2015) find that fast credit growth leads to lower productivity growth. The main argument being that lower interest rates encourage more entrepreneurs to create firms and risk taking leading to banks financing investments by less efficient firms. Capital inflow surges push interest rate down and reduce average productivity in the economy by lowering the bar for less productive entrepreneurs.

Furthermore, these effects are compounded by a consumption boom in which tradable goods are imported and non-tradable goods are produced by small and inefficient firms. To this effect, Kalantzis (2014) shows that shares of non-tradable goods in domestic output typically increase following episodes of capital inflows and that these shifts towards non-tradable goods may be responsible for low average productivity. Kalantzis (2014) and Benigno et al. (2015) show that capital inflows boost non-tradable output such as services and construction and these sectors tend to have lower productivity than manufacturing and other trade sectors. Benigno et al. (2015) found evidence of reallocation of labour out of manufacturing, which is largely a tradable sector during the capital inflows episode. Such shift has severely dampened aggregate productivity growth in many countries even as resources within sectors have improved.

Gumata and Ndou (2017) tested the hypothesis that a lower real interest rate leads to weaker labour productivity growth and find that positive (increase) real interest rate shock increases labour productivity growth. But the impact of real interest rates has changes post the financial crisis. A positive real interest rate shock post-2008 has a weaker impact on labour productivity growth than a similar shock that increased labour productivity pre-2008. Furthermore, gross capital inflows have an impact on the amplification role gross capital inflows play in transmitting positive real rates shock to labour productivity growth. The authors conclude that low and even negative real rates post-2008 may have contributed to low productivity growth and impacted the manner in which capital inflow surge shocks transmit real interest rate shocks.

In addition, Gumata and Ndou (2017) establish that capital inflow surge shocks lead to sectoral employment reallocation. Capital flow surge episodes are linked to the expansion of employment shares in the non-tradable sectors, in particular, the financial services and construction sectors. However, the positive responses are at the expense of sectors that produce tradable goods, in particular, the manufacturing and mining sectors. An unexpected positive net portfolio flow volatility shock significantly reduces the gross value added of the manufacturing, agriculture, construction sectors and productivity growth. But the financial sector employment and gross fixed capital formation increase following a capital flow surge episode shock. The major recipient and sector that gains the most during episodes of capital flow surges is the financial sector. Large capital inflows also coincide with a shift of both labour and capital out of the manufacturing sector. The reallocation of investment is a general feature of large capital inflows.

9.3 Methodology of Measurement of Structural Change

A large body of recent empirical research uses indices of structural transformation to assess the hypotheses that economic growth determines structural change or changes in the economic structure influence growth. This approach is premised on the theoretical assertions that high-growth countries are typically those that have experienced substantial *growth-enhancing structural change*. This is especially the case when labour and other resources move from less productive to more productive activities resulting in economic growth even if there is no productivity growth within sectors (McMillan and Rodrik 2011). But the direction of causality as to whether economic growth determines structural change or changes in the economic structure influence growth is still an open empirical question. This is because economic growth brings about complementary changes in various aspects of the economy. In turn, these changes affect the economic growth processes.

Furthermore, McMillan and Rodrik (2011) find that structural change has typically been growth reducing in countries with a relatively large share of natural resources in exports. The authors state that this is explained by the variation in the contribution of structural change to overall labour productivity.[1] The larger the share of natural resources in exports, the smaller the scope of productivity-enhancing structural change. The key factor being that minerals and natural resources do not generate much employment, unlike manufacturing industries and related services.[2] The authors find that even though these "enclave" sectors typically operate at very high productivity, they cannot absorb the surplus labour from other sectors such as agriculture.[3]

On the other hand, Duarte and Restuccia (2010) and Herrendorf et al. (2014) find structural change to be a fundamental driver of long-term development in advanced economies. While Dietrich (2009) shows that there is bi-directional causality between aggregate economic growth and structural change for the Germany, Japan, the UK and the US.

There is no universally accepted measure of the rate of structural change. But Stamer (1998) and Connolly and Orsmond (2011) postulate that the SCI indicator measuring the speed of structural change must fulfil the following characteristics and conditions for a SCI with X_{it} as the share of the sector i at time t.

- The index must be equal to zero if the sectoral composition is unchanged.

$$SCI_{[s,y]} = 0 \leftrightarrow X_{is} = X_{it} \quad \forall i \in \{1,\ldots,n\}$$

[1] Labour productivity growth in an economy can be achieved (i) within economic sectors through capital accumulation, technological change or reduction of resource misallocation across firms and (ii) labour mobility across sectors, from low-productivity sectors to high-productivity sectors thus increasing overall labour productivity in the economy.

[2] See evidence in part four of the book on the role of the mining sector contribution to exports earnings, investment, output and employment growth.

[3] The role of the agricultural sector in aggregate growth and employment is explored in later chapters of this book.

- The structural change between two points at any given time must be independent of the direction and only the extent of change is regarded (symmetry). This means that the SCI only depends on the amount of changes and it is the same regardless whether it is measured from s to t or from t to s.

$$SCI_{[s,t]} = SCI_{[t,s]}$$

- The structural change of one period cannot be greater than the sum of the calculated structural change of at least two subperiods (triangle inequality).

$$S_{[s,t]} \leq S_{[s,q]} + S_{[q,t]} \quad for\, s < q < t$$

- The structural change index shall be a dispersion measure.
- The structural change index shall consider the weight (size) of the sectors.

Dietrich (2009) indicates that the norm of absolute values (NAV)[4] fulfils all conditions except condition 4 which means that the NAV is not a measure of dispersion. Hence, several studies often cite this as a disadvantage of the NAV given that huge movements in a few sectors can have the same impact on the index value as fewer changes of many sector. This can therefore lead to the underestimation of the degree of the structural change indices.

1. We use the NAV to estimate the SCIs following Dietrich (2009), Connolly and Lewis (2010) and Cortuk and Singh (2013). The NAV is represented in Eq. (9.1)

[4] The NAV is also referred to as the Michaely index (Michaely 1962) or Stoikov index (Stoikov 1966).

$$SCI = 0.5 \times \sum_{i=1}^{n} \left[X_{i,t} - X_{i,t-20} \right] \tag{9.1}$$

where $X_{i,t}$ is the moving average share of the sector nominal or real GVA, investment or employment relative to total nominal or real GVA, investment or employment over five years (20 quarters) to capture the medium-to long-term changes. We use the Henderson filter which is a cantered filter to calculate the moving averages.[5]

Dietrich (2009) indicates that the SCI in Eq. (9.1) leads to a range of the NAV between zero and unity. The interpretation of the SCI is such that the amount of structural change equals exactly the share of the movements of the sectors as a percentage of the whole economy. Such that, if the structure remains unchanged, the SCI is equal to zero. But if all sectors in the economy change, which implies that the whole economy has a total change, the SCI is equal to unity.

9.4 Structural Change Indices

This section estimates several nominal and real sectors' gross value added, investment and employment SCIs. There are eight sectors for nominal and real gross value added, employment and investment SCIs, namely, (i) agriculture; (ii) mining; (iii) manufacturing; (iv) construction; (v) wholesale and retail trade, catering and accommodation; (vi) transport, storage and communication; (vii) finance, insurance, real estate and business service; and (viii) electricity, gas and water. The sample size uses quarterly data (Q) that spans the period 1980Q1 to 2016Q4 and the data is sourced from the South African Reserve Bank, Statistics South Africa databases. The long-term agricultural sector employment data is sourced from BFAP (2011). The trends for sector labour productivity growth rates are shown in Fig. 9.9 in the Appendix. Figure 9.10 in the Appendix shows that evolution of the sector shares of employment over time.

[5] The Henderson filter which is a centred filter whose lag coefficients are selected to minimise the sum of squared third differences of the lag coefficients for the class of symmetric lag polynomials which pass third order polynomials through without change.

9.4.1 Nominal and Real Gross Value Added Structural Change Indices

This section discusses the estimated nominal and real sector gross value added SCIs using the NAV approach shown in Eq. (9.1). Figure 9.1 shows the evolution of the nominal gross value added sector SCIs.[6]

The results suggest that the structural changes were increasing in the mining sector especially during the 2000s compared to the agricultural sector which has remained largely dormant. The results of the agricultural sector indicate that there needs to be structural change the most from the point of view of efficient resource allocation. These results are consistent with those in Ando and Nassar (2017). Similarly, the structural changes for the manufacturing sector have remained negative for large part of the sample period in Fig. 9.1(b) compared to the construction and the electricity, gas and water sectors. On the other hand, Fig. 9.1(c) shows that finance, insurance and real estate; and transport, storage and communication sectors underwent high levels of structural changes during the late 1990s and early 2000s, but the rate of change has since declined.

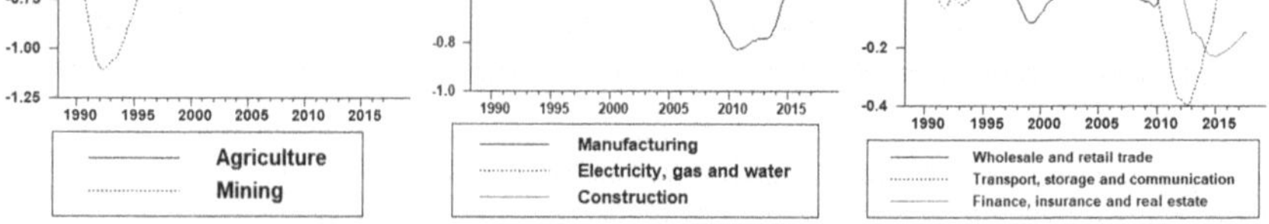

Fig. 9.1 Nominal gross value added structural change indices. (Source: Authors' calculations)

[6] The results for the real gross value-added are shown in Fig. 9.8.

9.4.2 Employment Structural Change Indices

This section complements the previous results by estimating the structural change indices for employment. We use the same approach to generate the sector employment structural change indices in Fig. 9.2. The results concur with those on Fig. 9.1 and indicate that there have been structural changes in the agricultural sector post-2014[7] and the mining sector employment especially in the non-gold mining sectors post-2000.

The manufacturing sector employment SCI index has remained dormant mirroring the trend of the nominal gross value added in Fig. 9.1. On the other hand, employment SCI for the electricity, gas and water sectors has remained largely flat around zero indicating that the structure of the employment in the sector has remained largely unchanged. The finance, insurance and real estate and wholesale and retail trade, catering and accommodation sectors underwent high levels of structural change in their employment compared to the transport, storage and communication sectors in Fig. 9.2(c).

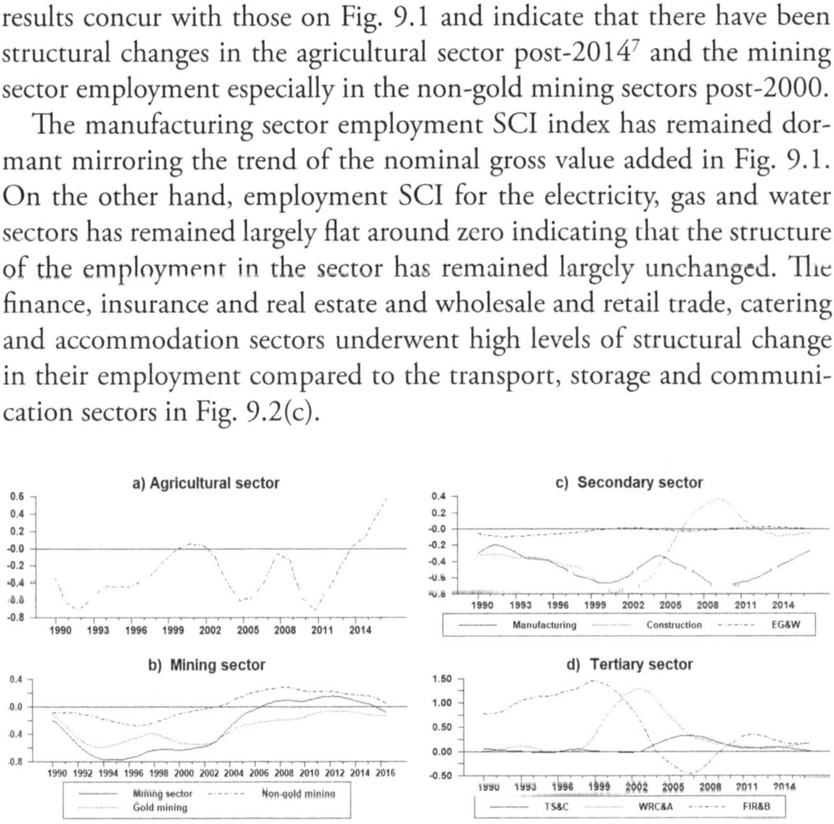

Fig. 9.2 Employment structural change indices. (Note: EG&W = Electricity, gas and water; TS&C = Transport, storage and communication; WRC&A = Wholesale and retail trade, catering and accommodation; FIR&B = Finance, insurance, real estate and business. Source: Authors' calculations)

[7] We explore the agricultural sector employment dynamics, the role of land reform and redistribution as forms of policy interventions to address the structural issues in the agricultural sector in further detail in later chapters.

9.4.3 Investment Structural Change Indices

This section concludes the discussion of the structural change indices by estimating the investment indices. Figure 9.3 shows consistent with the dormant structural changes in the agricultural sector; investment has been very low as well. This contrasts with the trends in the mining sector which have been high, albeit very cyclical.

The SCI for the manufacturing sector mirrors the nominal gross value added and employment trends especially post-2000. This contrasts with the electricity, gas and water sectors which have seen a considerable structural change in investment post-2000 in Fig. 9.3(b). Similarly, the transport, storage and communication sectors have seen considerable structural changes in investment. On the other hand, Fig. 9.3(c) shows that the structural change for investment in the finance, insurance and real estate declined, especially post-2009.

9.5 Causality Between Sectoral Growth and Sectoral Structural Change Indices

Literature on economic development asserts that development entails structural change. However, using the Granger causality tests in a panel environment, Dietrich (2009) shows that there is heterogeneous and

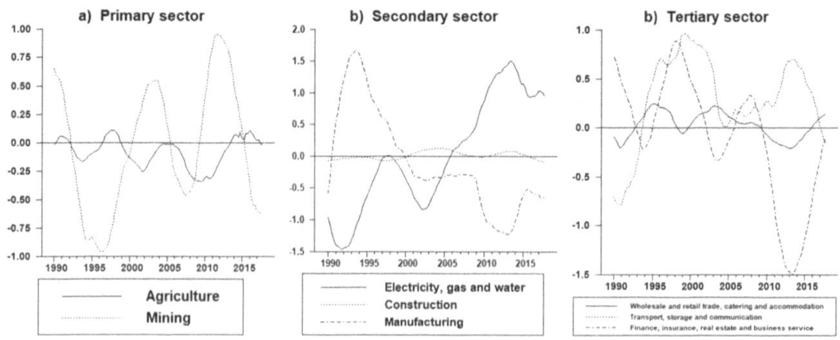

Fig. 9.3 Sector investment SCIs using the NAV approach. (Source: Authors' calculations)

bi-directional causality between economic growth and structural change measured in terms of employment and value added SCIs for seven OECD countries. Rather than use the Granger causality tests to assess the direction of causality between the sectorial value added and investment SCIs on sectorial growth and employment, we estimate various VAR models. We assess what happens when there are positive SCI shocks to sectoral output and employment growth. The SCIs are for the value added and investment. The intention is to assess and compare the responsiveness to the sectoral output and employment growth to structural changes in value added and investment. We use the value added and investment SCIs estimated using the NAV approach, sectoral output and employment growth. The sample for the estimations spans the period 1990Q1 to 2017Q4 and the growth rates are at annual rate. The models were estimated using 2 lags and 10,000 Monte Carlo simulations. The shock is a one standard deviation shock.

First, Fig. 9.4(a) and (d) show that the agricultural and mining sector output growth increase in response to positive shocks to the SCIs. At peak response the agricultural and mining sector output growth response increases by 3 and 2.5 percentage points, respectively. The comparison of the sector output growth and SCI responses shows that the output growth responses far exceed those of the SCIs. This implies that there is very limited bi directional causality, the strength of the

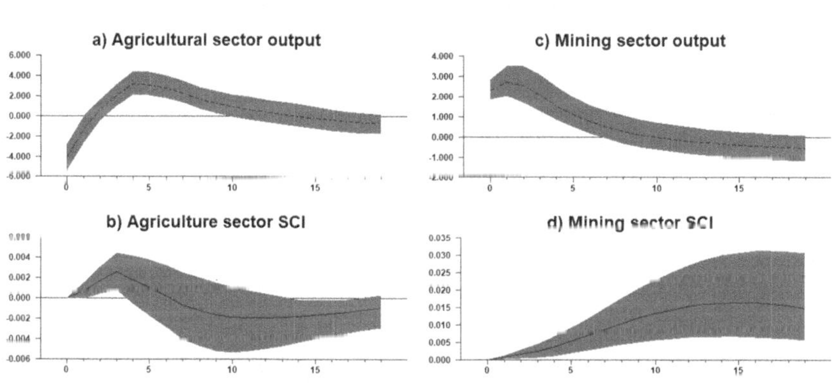

Fig. 9.4 Agricultural and mining sector responses to positive shocks. (Note: The grey shaded area bands denote the 16th and 84th percentile confidence bands. Source: Authors' calculations)

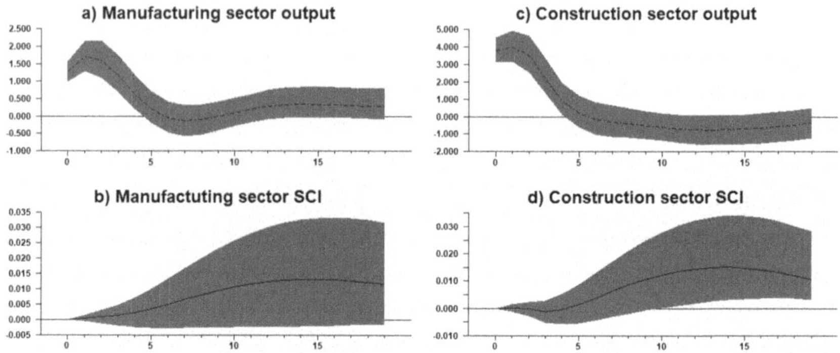

Fig. 9.5 Manufacturing and construction sector responses to positive shocks. (Note: The grey shaded area bands denote the 16th and 84th percentile confidence bands. Source: Authors' calculations)

causality and positive responses is in the direction SCIs to sector output growth. The implication is that the sector structural changes lead to sector output growth. There is very limited positive response the other way around.

Similarly, Fig. 9.5 shows that the manufacturing and construction sector output growth responses to positive shocks to SCIs far exceed those of the SCIs in response to positive shocks to sector output growth.

In fact, the responses of the SCIs in Fig. 9.5(b) and (d) are largely insignificant, especially for the manufacturing sector, indicating that the direction of causality runs from structural change to manufacturing and construction sector output growth. Thus, structural changes lead to output growth in the manufacturing and construction sectors.

The responses for the (i) wholesale and retail trade, catering and accommodation and (ii) transport, finance, insurance, real estate and business service sectors also indicate that the direction of causality runs from structural changes to sector output growth in Fig. 9.6.

Last, Fig. 9.7 shows a similar pattern of responses for the (i) electricity, gas and water and (ii) finance, insurance, real estate and business service sectors. Output growth responses in these sectors far exceed those of the SCIs. Thus, we conclude that sectoral output growth increases in response to positive shocks to sectoral structural change indices. Structural change overwhelmingly leads to output growth compared to the other way

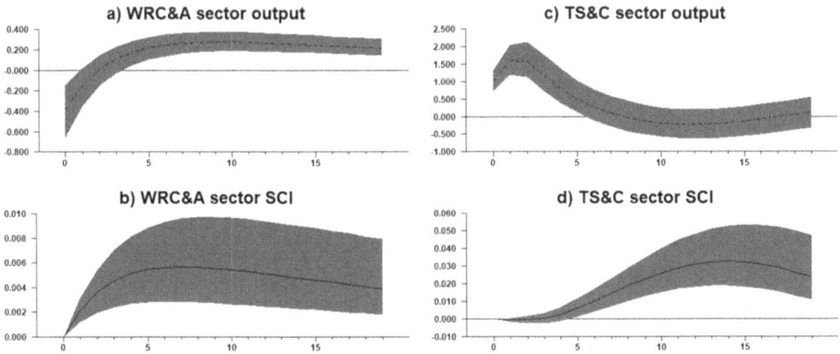

Fig. 9.6 WRC&A and TS&C sector responses to positive shocks. (Note: WRC&A = Wholesale and retail trade, catering and accommodation sectors; TS&C = Transport, storage and communication sector. The grey shaded area bands denote the 16th and 84th percentile confidence bands. Source: Authors' calculations)

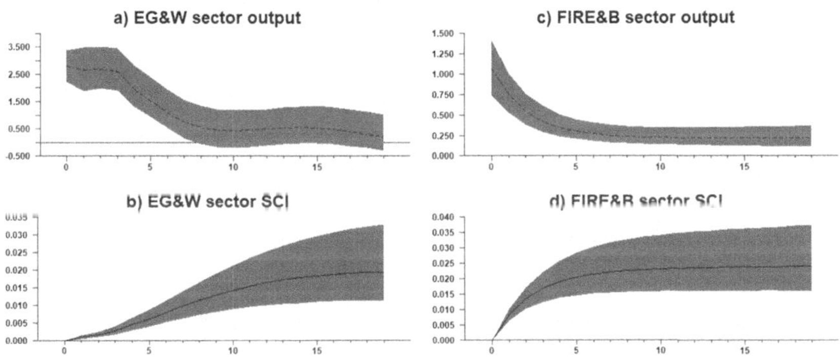

Fig. 9.7 EG&W and FIRE&B sector responses to positive shocks. (Note: EG&W = electricity, gas and water; and FIRE&B = finance, insurance, real estate and business service sectors. The grey shaded area bands denote the 16th and 84th percentile confidence bands. Source: Authors' calculations)

around. There is a strong unidirectional relationship between structural change as proxied by the SCIs and sector output growth. We find very weak evidence that sector output growth causes and speeds up structural change. The policy implications derived from this section concur with those implied by the McMillan and Rodrik (2011) decomposition that structural reforms across sectors are necessary to induce output growth. Output growth induced by structural change can lead to higher economic growth rates, rising income and changes to the demand side and employment shares of the economy.

9.6 Conclusion and Policy Implications

This chapter explored whether structural change causes growth. First, this chapter constructs the sector structural change indices and establishes that the structural changes were increasing in the mining sector especially during the 2000s compared to the agricultural sector which has remained largely dormant. The results for the agricultural sector indicate that there needs to be structural change especially from the point of view of efficient resource allocation. Similarly, the structural changes for the manufacturing sector have remained negative for large part of the sample period. On the other hand, finance, insurance and real estate; and transport, storage and communication sectors underwent high levels of structural changes during the late 1990s and early 2000s, but the rate of change has since declined.

Second, we establish overwhelming evidence that structural change causes growth. There is weak evidence suggesting that growth causes structural change. Sector output growth responses exceed those of the structural change indices. Structural change overwhelmingly leads to output growth compared to the other way around. We establish very weak evidence that sector output growth causes and speeds up structural change.

The "*structural change*" component has been growth reducing for the South African economy indicating that the direction of labour flows is negatively correlated with labour productivity in individual sectors. The implications for the aggregate economy have been such that displaced labour ends up in activities with lower productivity, informality and unemployment. Hence the economy-wide growth suffers and may even turn negative.

Appendix

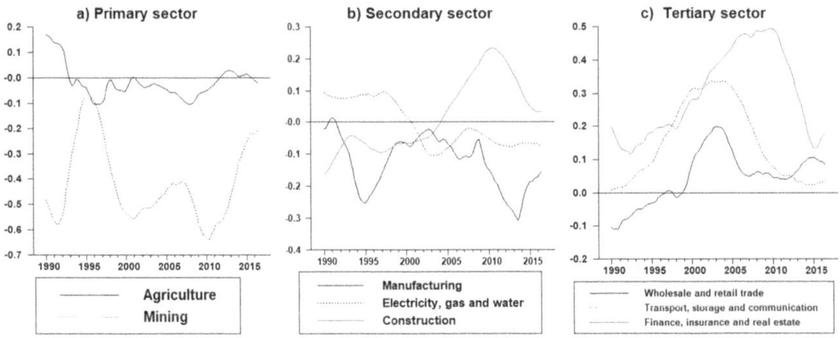

Fig. 9.8 Real gross value added structural change indices. (Source: Authors' calculations)

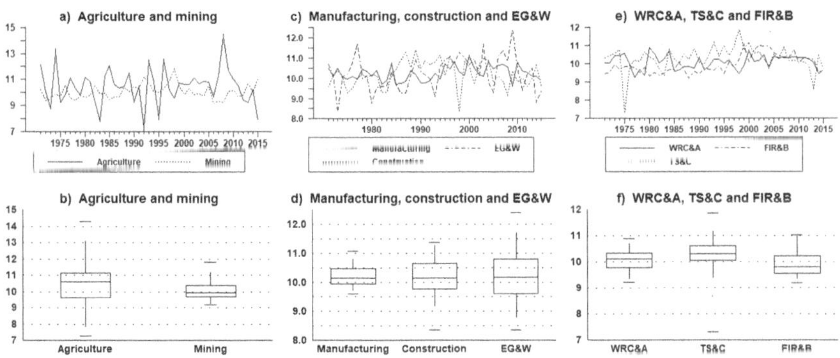

Fig. 9.9 Sector labour productivity growth rates. (Note: EG&W = electricity, gas and water; WRC&A = Wholesale and retail trade, catering and accommodation sectors; TS&C = Transport, storage and communication sector; and FIRE&B = finance, insurance, real estate and business service sectors. Source: Productivity SA and authors' calculations)

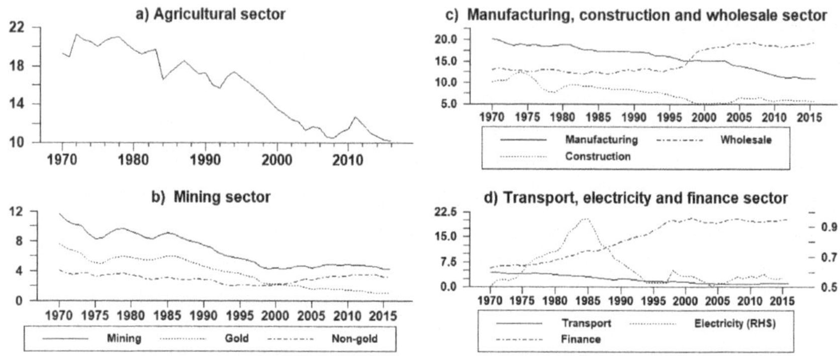

Fig. 9.10 Sector shares of employment. (Source: South African Reserve Bank, BFAP 2011 and authors' calculations)

References

Ando, S., and Nassar, K. 2017. *Indexing Structural Distortion: Sectoral Productivity, Structural Change and Growth*. IMF Working Paper. WP/17/205.

Ansari, M.R., Mussida, C., and Pastor, F. 2013. Note on Lilien and Modified Lilien Index. *Stata Journal*, 14(2), 398–406.

Benigno, G., Converse, N., and Fornaro, L. 2015. *Large Capital Inflows, Sectoral Allocation, and Economic Performance*. International Finance Discussion Papers 1132. https://doi.org/10.17016/IFDP.2015.1132

BFAP. 2011. The Contribution of the Agro-Industrial Complex to Employment in South Africa. Tech. Rep. June, The Bureau for Food and Agricultural Policy, Pretoria.

Borio, C., Kharroubi, E., Upper, C., and Zampolli, F. 2015. *Labour Reallocation and Productivity Dynamics: Financial Causes, Real Consequences*. BIS Working Papers No. 534.

Campos, Nauro F., De Grauwe, Paul, and Ji, Yuemei. 2017. *Structural Reforms, Growth and Inequality: An Overview of Theory, Measurement and Evidence*. CESifo Working Papers ISSN 2364-1428.

Cecchetti, S.G., and Kharroubi, E. 2012. *Reassessing the Impact of Finance on Growth*. BIS Working Paper No. 381.

Cette, G., Fernald, G., and Mojon, B. 2016. *The Pre-Great Recession Slowdown in Productivity*. Federal Reserve Bank of San Francisco Working Paper 2016-08.

Connolly, E., and Lewis, C. 2010. Structural Change in the Australian Economy. *RBA Bulletin*, September, 1–10.

Connolly, E., and Orsmond, D. 2011. *The Mining Industry: From Bust to Boom.* Research Discussion Paper 2011-08.

Cortuk, O., and Singh, N. 2013. Analyzing the Structural Change and Growth Relationship in India: State-level Evidence. *Economic Letters,* 110(3), 178–81. Elsevier, March.

Diao, X., McMillan, M., and Rodrik D. 2017. *The Recent Growth Boom in Developing Economies: A Structural Change Perspective.* NBER Working Paper No. 23132

Dietrich, A. 2009. Does Growth Cause Structural Change, or is it the Other Way Around? A Dynamic Panel Data Analysis for Seven OECD Countries. *Jena Research Papers in Economics.* http://econpapers.repec.org/paper/jrpjrp-wrp/2009-034.htm, accessed February 10, 2010.

Driver, Ciaran IV, and Saw, Chit-Wei. 1996. Performance of Structural Change Indices: Analysis Using Real and simulated Data. *Applied Economics Letters,* 3 (3), 187–88.

Duarte, M., and Restuccia, D. 2010. The Role of the Structural Transformation in Aggregate Productivity. *The Quarterly Journal of Economics,* 125(1), 129–73. February.

Gumata, N., and Ndou, E. 2017. *Bank Credit Extension and Real Economic Activity in South Africa: The Impact of Capital Flow Dynamics, Bank Regulation and Selected Macro-prudential Tools.* Palgrave Macmillan. ISBN 978-3-319-43550-3.

Herrendorf, B., Rogerson, R., and Valentinyi, A. 2014. Handbook of Economic Growth. *Growth and Structural Transformation,* 2, 855–941.

Kalantzis, Y. 2014. *Financial Fragility in Small Open Economies: Firm Balance Sheets and the Sectoral Structure.* Banque de France Working Paper 505.

Kalantzis, Y., and Thubin, C. 2017. *The Causes of Deindustrialisation in France.* Banque De France Eco Notepad.

Lilien, D.M. 1982. Sectoral Shifts and Cyclical Unemployment. *Journal of Political Economy,* 90, 777–93.

Los, B., Timmer, M.P., and De Vries, G.J. 2015. How Global are Global Value Chains? A New Approach to Measure International Fragmentation. *Journal of Regional Science,* 55(1), 66–92.

McMillan, M.S., and Rodrik, D. 2011. *Globalisation, Structural Change and Productivity Growth.* NBER Working Paper 17143.

Michaely, M. 1962. *Concentration in International Trade.* North Holland: Amsterdam.

Pages, Carmen. ed. 2010. *The Age of Productivity*. Inter-American Development Bank: Washington, DC.

Silva, E.G., and Teixeira, A.A.C. 2008. Surveying Structural Change: Seminal Contributions and a Bibliometric Account. *Structural Change and Economic Dynamics*, 19, 273–300.

Stamer, M. 1998. Interrelation between Subsidies, Structural Change and Economic Growth in Germany, A Vector Autoregressive Analysis. *Konjunkturpolitik*, 44 (3), 231–53.

Stoikov, V. 1966. Some Determinants of the Level of Frictional Unemployment: A Comparative Study. *International Labour Review*, 93, 530–49.

Timmer, M.P., Eurmban, A.A., Los, B., Stehrer, R., and De Vries, G.J. 2014. Slicing Up Global Value Chains. *Journal of Economic Perspectives*, 28 (2), 99–118.

10

The Impact of Structural Change on the South African Economy: Evidence from the McMillan and Rodrik (2011) Labour Productivity Decomposition Approach

Learning Objectives

- Estimate the McMillan and Rodrik (2011) labour productivity decomposition approach to the "within" and "structural change" components.
- Assess whether the McMillan and Rodrik (2011) "structural change" component has been positive for the South African economy.

10.1 Introduction

This chapter estimates the McMillan and Rodrik (2011) labour productivity decomposition approach to the "within" and "structural change" components. McMillan and Rodrik (2011) decompose labour productivity into "*within*" and "*structural change*" components and show that structural transformation, alternatively, the "*structural change*" component, largely differentiates successful countries from unsuccessful ones. The authors show that the difference between growth in Asia, Latin America and Africa can be explained by the variation in the contribution of structural change to overall labour productivity.

N. Gumata, E. Ndou, *Accelerated Land Reform, Mining, Growth, Unemployment and Inequality in South Africa*, https://doi.org/10.1007/978-3-030-30884-1_10

The supply side or the "*productivity hypothesis*" assumes that different technical progress in the sectors is a major determinant of structural change. Because different levels of technical progress or technical knowledge within economic sectors results in improvements in the sectoral production processes, it induces a shift in the composition and contributions of different sectors to economic growth. Faster productivity growth within and across economic sectors results in the movement of labour within and across sectors. The rate at which this occurs can be beneficial to the aggregate economy. McMillan and Rodrik (2011) find that structural change has contributed to overall growth and high-productivity employment opportunities have expanded thus lowering the unemployment rate in China, India and some other Asian countries. However, in many instances, labour has moved in the wrong direction, from more productive to less productive economic activities, including high levels of informality in economic activity in many countries in Latin America and Africa.

Cecchetti and Kharroubi (2012) examine the impact of the size and growth of the financial system on productivity growth at the level of aggregate economies. They find that at low levels, a larger financial system goes hand in hand with higher productivity growth. This is because as the financial system develops, it reduces transaction costs, raises investment and improves the distribution of capital and risk across the economy. Thus, through the transactions costs and investment channels, the financial system and financial development improve growth. But there is a threshold beyond which a large financial sector is associated with lower growth. In addition, the impact of faster growth in finance on growth measured in either employment or value added and real productivity growth tends to be bad. This is because financial booms are inherently bad for trend growth. It is against this background that this chapter estimates the "*within*" and "*structural change*" components of labour productivity and the impact of relative sector labour productivity on sector employment shares and what happens to the displaced workers.

10.2 Decomposition Approach

McMillan and Rodrik (2011) show that changes in overall productivity can be disaggregated into changes of productivity within sectors and changes in the allocation of labour between sectors (or structural change) given by Eq. (10.1)

$$\Delta Y_t = \sum_{i=n} \theta_{i,t-k} \Delta y_{i,t} + \sum_{i=n} y_{i,t-k} \Delta \theta_{i,t} \tag{10.1}$$

Weighted sum of productivity growth within individual sectors also referred to as "within component of productivity growth"

Weighted sum of productivity growth effect on labour reallocation on different sectors also referred to as "structural change"

where Y_t is aggregate or economy-wide labour productivity, $y_{i,t}$ is specific sector labour productivity, $\theta_{i,t}$ is the share of employment in a specific sector i, the operator Δ denotes the change in labour productivity or employment shares between $t-k$ and t. The first decomposition term in Eq. (10.1) measures the "*within*" component of productivity growth, which is the weighted sum of productivity growth within individual sectors. The weights are the employment share of each sector at the beginning of the time-period. The second decomposition term measures "*structural change*" which is defined as the productivity growth effect on labour reallocation across different sectors of the economy. It measures the inner product of productivity levels with the change in employment shares across sectors at the end of the time-period. When the changes in employment shares are positively correlated with productivity levels, the structural change term will be positive. This means that structural change will increase economy-wide productivity growth.

Furthermore, the decomposition in Eq. (10.1) gives a better understanding of the productivity performance within individual sectors across economic activities. The analysis presents a comprehensive view as opposed to the partial analysis. For instance, a high rate of productivity growth within an industry can have implications for overall economic performance if the industry's share of employment shrinks rather than expands. Such that if the displaced labour ends up in activities with lower productivity, economy-wide growth will suffer and may even turn negative. In addition, McMillan and Rodrik (2011) indicate that the structural change component provides the direction of labour flows. In the case of growth-reducing (growth-enhancing) structural change, the end-of-period relative productivity of sectors $\left(y_{i,t} / Y_t\right)$ is negatively (positively) related or correlated to the change in the sector employment share ($\Delta\theta_{i,y}$).

10.3 Selected Trends

This section estimates the McMillan and Rodrik (2011) labour productivity decomposition in Eq. (10.1). The data for labour productivity used is sourced from Productivity South Africa and is on an annual basis from 1970 to 2015. Whereas the data for employment is sourced from Statistics South Africa and the South African Reserve Bank databases. We start by showing the index levels of the sectoral labour productivity in Fig. 10.1.[1] The comparison of labour productivity levels across sectors shows that the mining sector has the highest level of productivity, followed by the manufacturing, wholesale and finance sectors. Furthermore, data shows that the growth rate in the mining sector labour productivity has performed much better in comparison to other sectors.

Nonetheless, the sectoral labour productivity as per cent of total labour productivity, alternatively the relative share of sector labour productivity or the labour productivity gaps[2] in Fig. 10.2, show that the contribution of the mining sector labour productivity declined from high levels of 20 per cent in the early 2000s to around 10 per cent post-2009. The large

[1] The growth rates are shown in Fig. 10.12 in the Appendix.

[2] McMillan and Rodrik (2011) define the productivity gaps as the differences in average labour productivity.

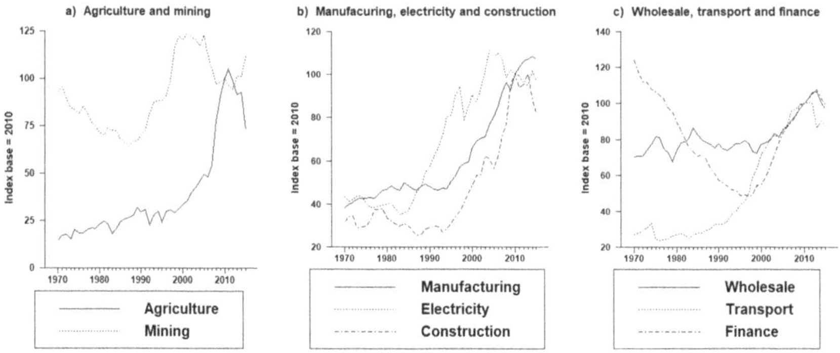

Fig. 10.1 Sector labour productivity levels. (Source: Productivity SA and authors' calculations)

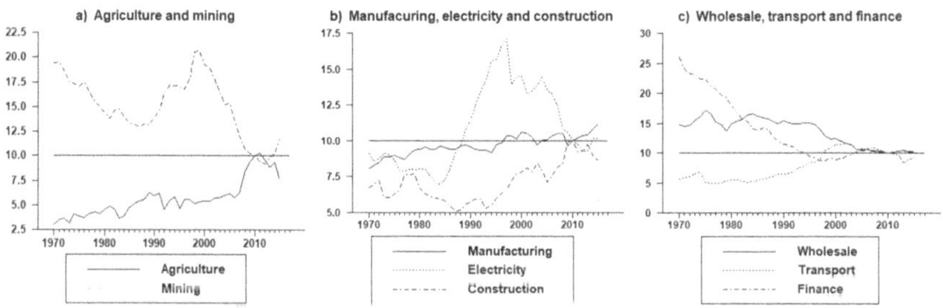

Fig. 10.2 Sectoral labour productivity as per cent of total labour productivity. (Source: Productivity SA and authors' calculations)

labour productivity gap between the agricultural sector and the mining sector in Fig. 10.2(a) declined post-2015 and the sector contributions converged to 10 percentage points. This was mainly due to the fact that the agricultural sector contribution increased whilst that of the mining sector declined.

A similar pattern is evident in Fig. 10.2(b) with respect to the (i) electricity, gas and water, (ii) construction and the (iii) manufacturing sectors. The labour productivity gaps between these sectors have converged towards the 10 percentage level, largely due to the fact that the contribution of the construction sector increased whereas that of the electricity, gas and water sector declined. The manufacturing sector contribution has largely remained around 10 per cent.

On the other hand, the (i) finance, insurance, real estate and business and (ii) wholesale and retail trade, catering and accommodation sector contributions have declined, whilst the transport, storage and communication sectors have increased. This resulted in the convergence of the sectors' contributions to the 10 percentage level.

What do the trends of the sector labour productivity share gaps in Fig. 10.2 imply for output and labour growth? As stated earlier, labour productivity gaps measure the persistent differences in output (GDP) per worker and efficiency in the allocation of labour between sectors. McMillan and Rodrik (2011) show that developing economies are characterised by large productivity gaps across different sectors of the economy and even among firms and plants within the same industry. Inter-sectoral labour productivity gaps are indicative of the allocative inefficiencies that reduce overall labour productivity and are a key feature of underdevelopment. But they tend to diminish as a result of sustained economic growth. Nonetheless, these labour productivity gaps (allocative inefficiencies) are important and potential engines of growth. Because they imply that labour and other resources can move from less productive to more productive sectors and activities of the economy, especially labour-absorbing sectors of the economy.

The trends shown in Fig. 10.2 and the marginal productivity of labour[3] in Fig. 10.3 show that the gaps are largely wide and imply that growth-enhancing structural change in the economy and across sectors can be an important contributor to overall economic growth. McMillan and Rodrik (2011) indicate that high-growth countries are characterised by substantial growth-enhancing structural change. We explore the labour productivity decomposition into the "*within*" and "*structural change*" components in the section.

[3] Based on the Cobb-Douglas production function specification where the average productivity multiplied by the labour share is the marginal productivity of labour.

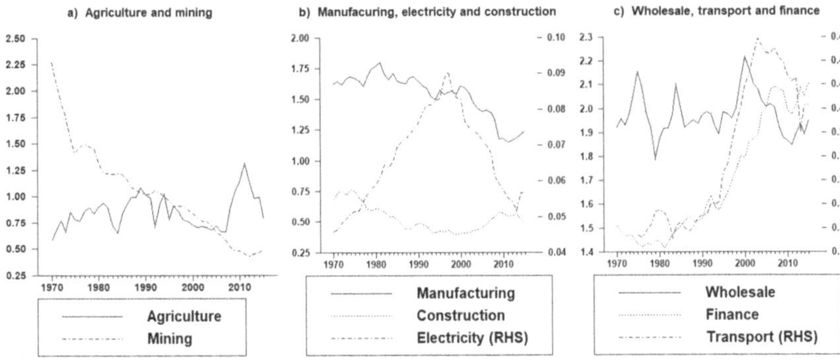

Fig. 10.3 Sectoral marginal labour productivity. (Source: Productivity SA and authors' calculations)

10.4 McMillan and Rodrik (2011) Decomposition Approach: The Decomposition of Labour Productivity into the "Within" and "Structural Change" Components

Equation (10.1) presented the McMillan and Rodrik (2011) decomposition of labour productivity. First, labour productivity can be decomposed to the "*within*" component of productivity growth, which is the weighted sum of productivity growth within individual sectors. The weights are the employment share of each sector at the beginning of the time-period. In this case, productivity can grow within economic sectors through capital accumulation, technological change, high levels of investment in research and development and the reduction of the resource misallocation across sectors and plants. In addition, labour can move across sectors, from low-productivity sectors to high-productivity sectors, thus increasing overall labour productivity in the economy. In this instance, Cecchetti and Kharroubi (2012) show that at low levels, a larger financial system is compatible with higher productivity growth. However, there are threshold effects beyond which a large banking sector and a higher level of credit are associated with lower growth measured as either employment or value added. In addition, financial booms have a negative effect on real productivity growth. Gumata and Ndou (2017) provide evidence that capital inflow surge shocks lead to sectoral employment reallocation and the expansion of employment shares in the non-tradable sectors, in particular, the financial services and construction sectors. The positive responses are at the expense of sectors that produce tradable goods, in particular, the manufacturing and mining sectors.

Similarly, Benigno et al. (2015) find that episodes of large capital inflows capital are associated with the reallocation of labour out of the manufacturing sector. The labour reallocation associated with large capital inflows is large during a period of low international interest rates. Large capital inflows are associated with an expansion of non-tradable sectors, such as services and construction, and this is at the expenses of the tradable sectors including agricultural products and manufactured goods. The authors also find that the share of both employment and investment allocated to the manufacturing sector drops during episodes of large capital inflows. In addition, the reallocation of labour occurs specifically during episodes of abundant international liquidity and in cases where governments do not offset capital inflows through substantial purchases of foreign assets. As such, the authors establish that accumulating reserves during the period in which capital inflows are unusually large appears to limit the extent of labour reallocation.

At the same time, Ndou and Gumata (2017) show that increases in labour productivity play an important role in dampening inflationary pressures directly and indirectly via the propagation effects. Labour productivity and unit labour costs exert opposite effects on size of the adjustments of the repo rate to positive inflation shocks. Positive and persistent labour productivity growth shocks lower inflation for prolonged periods. In addition, a positive labour productivity growth shock leads to a significant decline in inflation expectations. The implication is that inflationary pressures and expectations would subside more when there are persistent improvements in labour productivity growth.

Second, labour productivity can be decomposed to the "*structural change*" component which is defined as the productivity growth effect on labour reallocation across different sectors of the economy. It measures the inner product of productivity levels with the change in employment shares across sectors at the end of the time-period. When the changes in employment shares are positively (negatively) correlated with productivity levels, the structural change term will be positive (negative). This means that structural change will increase (decrease) economy-wide productivity growth.

McMillan and Rodrik (2011) indicate that the speed with which this structural transformation takes place is the key factor that differentiates successful countries from unsuccessful ones. The authors find that large share of the difference between growth in Asia, Latin America and Africa can be explained by the variation in the contribution of structural change to overall labour productivity. Their finding shows that in many Latin American and Sub-Saharan African countries, the structural change component has largely played a role of reducing as opposed to increasing economic growth since 1990. What does the South Africa data suggest? Figure 10.4 shows the McMillan and Rodrik (2011) decomposition for South Africa. The labour productivity decomposition shows that the structural change component has made negative contributions for the period 1990 to 2015 for the aggregate economy as opposed to the within component.

Figure 10.5 presents the McMillan and Rodrik (2011) sectoral decompositions and shows that the "*structural change*" component has been

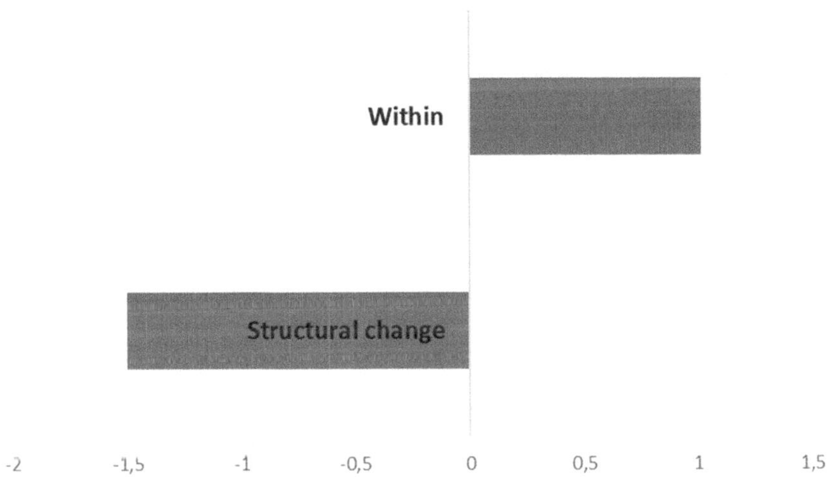

Fig. 10.4 McMillan and Rodrik (2011) decomposition for aggregate labour productivity. (Source: Authors' calculations)

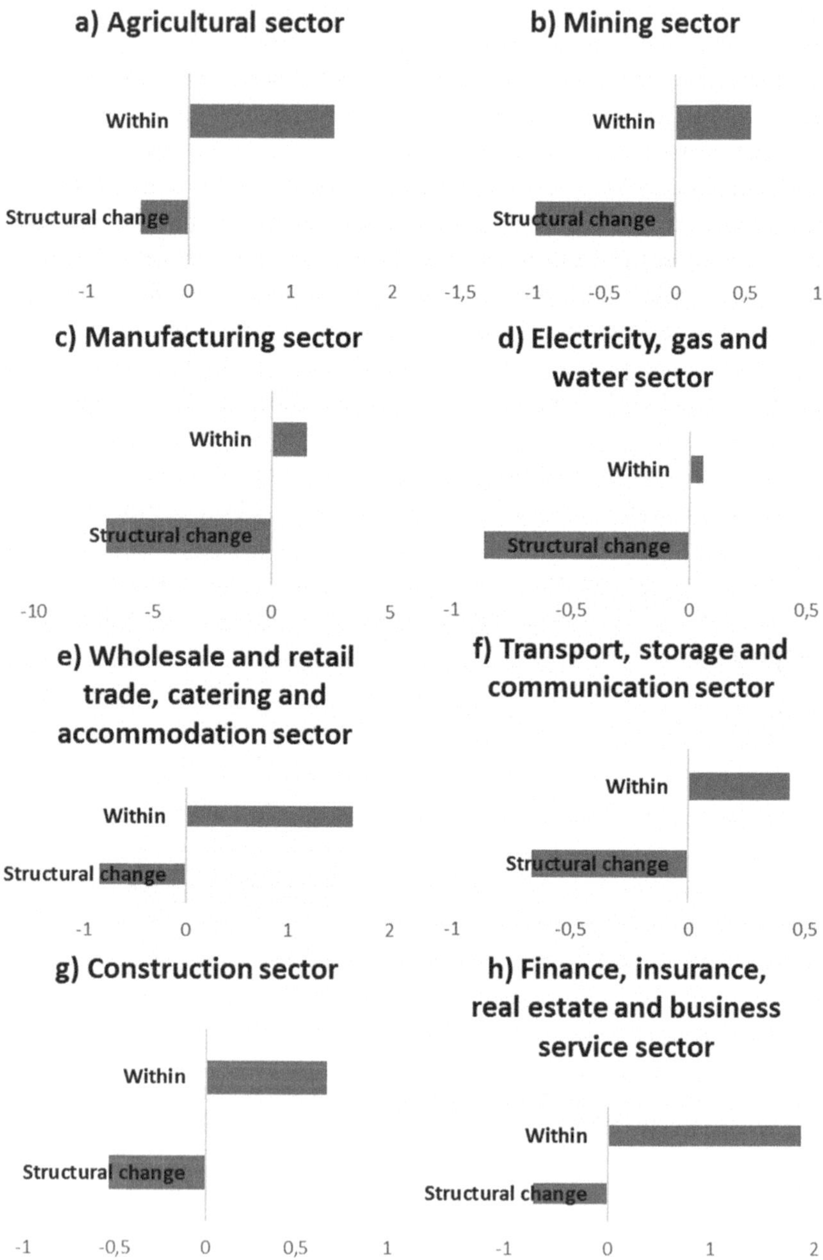

Fig. 10.5 McMillan and Rodrik (2011) decomposition for sectoral labour productivity. (Source: Authors' calculations)

growth reducing (negative contribution) especially for the (i) manufacturing; (ii) mining; (iii) electricity, gas and water; and (iv) wholesale and retail trade, catering and accommodation sectors.

On the other hand, the "*within*" component seems to have been the largest contributor especially for the (i) agricultural sector[4]; (ii) wholesale and retail trade, catering and accommodation; and (iii) finance, insurance, real estate and business service sectors. The evidence suggests that indeed the increased levels of market deregulation and various policy reforms aligned with the process of opening up the South African economy into a globalised world have benefitted the within component of labour productivity at the expense of the structural component. The process of deregulation and globalisation has been highly beneficial to intra-sector productivity, but this was at the expense of structural changes within these sectors. Such trends manifest themselves in, for example, high concentration levels of very few firms and economic players within sectors with detrimental effects on competition, price formation, contribution to growth and employment.[5]

Furthermore, the "*within*" component is largely a reflection of the employment shares and productivity growth rates within sectors although in different directions. For instance, the "*within*" component of labour productivity accounts for a large share in the (i) wholesale and retail trade, catering and accommodation and (ii) finance, insurance, real estate and business service sectors in line with the increase in the employment shares of these sectors. The rapid growth in the "*within*" productivity component has more than offset the negative contribution from the "*structural change*" component, especially for the two sectors. But the implications for the aggregate economy have been such that displaced labour ends up in activities with lower productivity, informality and unemployment. Hence the economy-wide growth suffers and may even turn negative. These results concur with findings in Diao et al. (2017) that the recent growth accelerations (during the 2000s) were based on

[4] The role of deregulation in the agricultural sector and export-oriented policies is explored in detail in later chapters of this book.

[5] These conclusions nonetheless do not downplay the role of commodity prices booms and busts, and exchange rates as was shown in earlier chapters for the mining sector, which in part are outcomes of open economies and a globalised world economy. The role of commodity price booms and busts and the exchange rate on the agricultural sector is explored in later chapters of this book.

either rapid within-sector labour productivity growth or growth-increasing structural change, but rarely both at the same time. The recent growth accelerations were largely driven from the demand side of the economy as opposed to rapid industrialisation. The policy implication is that there is much needed growth-enhancing structural change within sectors of the South African economy. These results corroborate those of the SCI estimates in the earlier sections.

In addition, the results of the labour productivity decomposition presented in Figs. 10.4 and 10.5 concur with those in McMillan and Rodrik (2011) showing that although the period 1990 to 2005 was characterised by high levels of globalisation effects on developing countries, it seems different countries have handled the stresses and opportunities it presents differently. McMillan and Rodrik (2011) observe that the diverse outcomes of the impact of globalisation on different countries suggest that the consequences of globalisation depend on the manner in which countries integrate into the global economy. The authors conclude that it is noteworthy that countries such as China, India and some other Asian countries have benefitted more from globalisation. In these countries structural change has contributed to overall growth, and high-productivity employment opportunities have expanded, thus lowering the unemployment rate. On the contrary, countries in Latin America and Sub-Saharan Africa have not benefitted much from globalisation. The impact of globalisation seems to have resulted in the structural changes that have not benefitted growth and employment. In many instances, labour has moved in the wrong direction, from more productive to less productive economic activities, including high levels of informality in economic activity.

10.5 Has the Structural Change Component Been Positive for the South African Economy?

We stated earlier that McMillan and Rodrik (2011) indicate that when changes in employment shares are positively (negatively) correlated with productivity levels, this term will be positive (negative), and structural change will increase (decrease) economy-wide productivity growth.

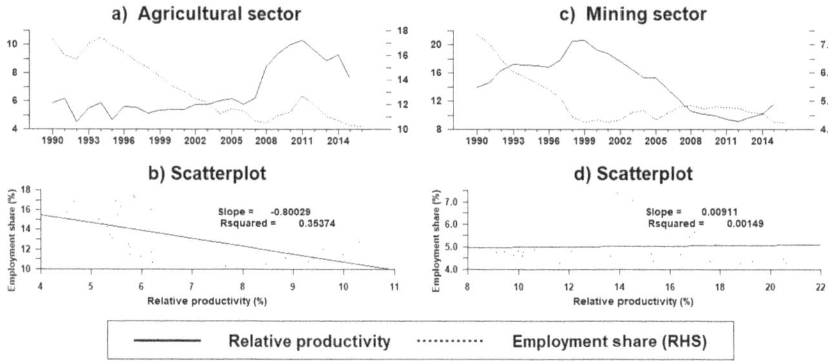

Fig. 10.6 The impact of structural change on the agricultural and mining sectors. (Source: Authors' calculations)

In addition, McMillan and Rodrik (2011) indicate that the structural change component provides the direction of labour flows. In the case of growth-reducing (growth-enhancing) structural change, the end-of-period relative productivity of sectors $\left(y_{i,t}/Y_t\right)$ is negatively (positively) related or correlated to the change in the sector employment share $(\Delta\theta_{i,y})$. Figure 10.6 shows that there is a negative relationship between the changes in the labour productivity and the employment shares in the agricultural sector. The relationship is slightly positive for the mining sector.

Similarly, Figs. 10.7, 10.8 and 10.9 establish a negative correlation between the end-of-period relative productivity for the (i) manufacturing; (ii) electricity, gas and water; (iii) construction; (iv) wholesale and retail trade, catering and accommodation; (v) transport; and (vi) finance, insurance, real estate and business service sectors and the respective employment shares.

Thus, we conclude that the structural change component has been growth reducing for the South African economy. The growth-reducing structural change component indicates that the direction of labour flows is negatively correlated with (end-of-period) labour productivity in individual sectors.

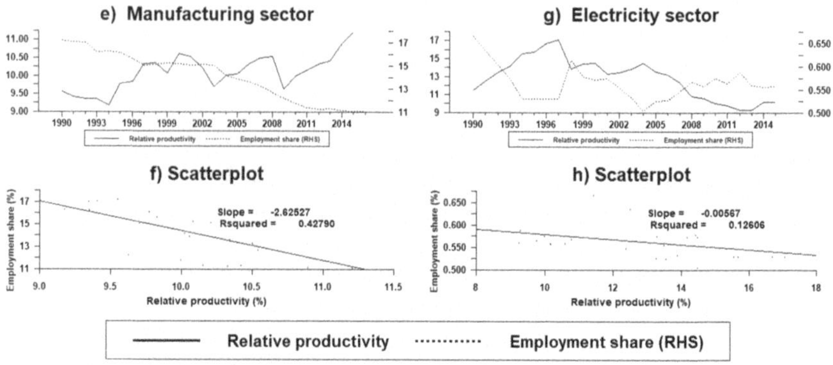

Fig. 10.7 The impact of structural change on the manufacturing, electricity, gas and water sectors. (Source: Authors' calculations)

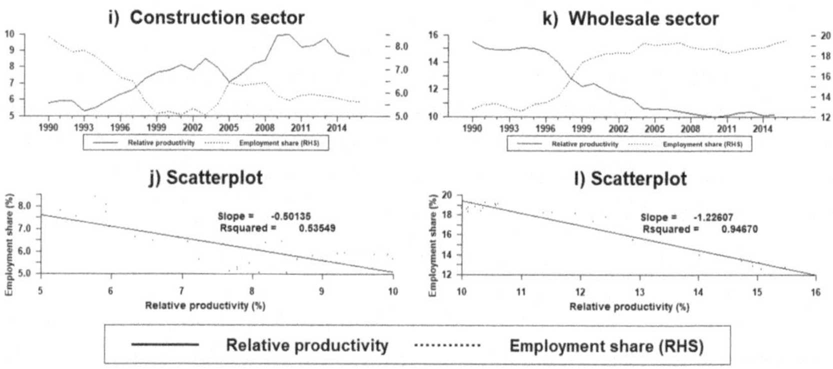

Fig. 10.8 The impact of structural change on the construction, wholesale and retail trade, catering and accommodation sectors. (Source: Authors' calculations)

10.6 What Happens to the Displaced Workers Due to Positive Shocks to Relative Labour Productivity?

To conclude this chapter, this section assesses what happens to displaced workers due to large inter-sectoral productivity gaps and growth-reducing sector structural change. We established in the earlier sections that the sectoral structural changes have been largely growth reducing and the direction of labour flows is negatively correlated with labour productivity

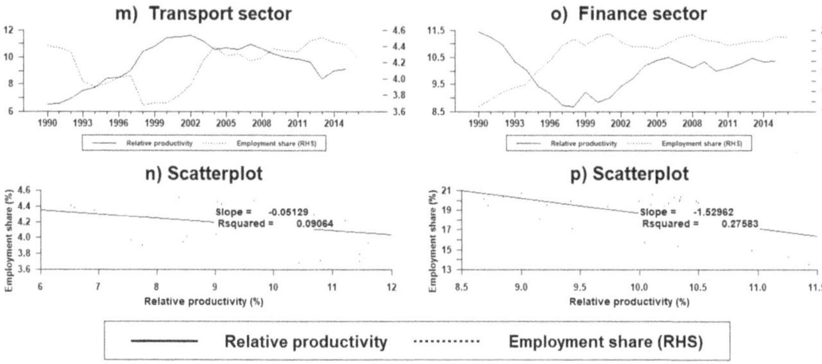

Fig. 10.9 The impact of structural change on the transport, finance, insurance, real estate and business service sector. (Source: Authors' calculations)

in individual sectors. McMillan and Rodrik (2011) state that in economies that don't exhibit large inter-sectoral productivity gaps or high and persistent unemployment, labour displacement does not have important implications for economy-wide productivity. On the other hand, in developing economies, characterised by large inter-sectoral productivity gaps, high and persistent unemployment, it is expected that displaced workers would end up in even lower-productivity economic activities and the informal sector.

In addition, McMillan and Rodrik (2011) raise the issue of worker displacement within the context of vast empirical studies that have shown that intensified competition brought about by trade liberalisation forced manufacturing industries to become more productive largely via the mechanism of "industry rationalisation" where the least productive firms exit the industry whilst the remaining firms shed "excess labour".[6] The authors show that in the case of Latin America, displaced workers may have ended up in less productive activities, such as the informal economy. What is the case for the South African economy?

First, Fig. 10.10 shows that the formal non-agricultural sector employment accounts for roughly 70 per cent of employment. The agricultural sector employment accounts for 5.4 per cent of the non-formal employment whereas the informal and private households' sectors account for 17.5 per cent and 7.75 per cent, respectively. Thus, the non-formal

[6] We explore the impact of trade liberalisation on the agricultural sector in later chapters.

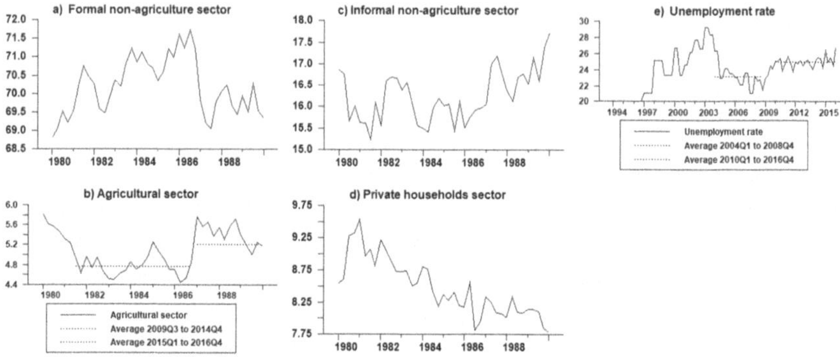

Fig. 10.10 Employment trends and the unemployment rate. (Source: Statistics South Africa and authors' calculations)

agricultural sectors contribute 30 per cent to the employment rate. At the same time, the unemployment rate has been persistently above 20 per cent since 2000 and increased post-2009 to average 26 per cent. These are early indications that the majority of "excess labour" shed due to trade and financial liberalisation since the 1990s ended up in the informal sector and unemployed.

For the empirical analysis, we estimate a number of VAR models to assess what happens to sectoral employment shares when there is a positive sector relative labour productivity shock. The VAR models include the sector employment share and relative labour productivity. Each sector's responses are estimated in separate VAR models. The VAR models include 2 lags and 10,000 Monte Carlo draws. The sample uses annual data (A) that spans the period 1990 to 2017 due to the availability of the labour productivity data. Figure 10.11 shows that positive shocks to relative sector labour productivity result in the decline in the employment shares of the various sectors, albeit at differing degrees.

Indeed, the results in Fig. 10.11 concur with those in the earlier sections showing that the "*structural change*" component has resulted in the flow of labour in the wrong direction. The question left unanswered is what happens to the workers who are thereby displaced. The results are in line with the observations in McMillan and Rodrik (2011) that the rationalisation of manufacturing industries has in most instances come at the expense of inducing growth-reducing structural change. Hence, the persistent unemployment rates and increasing levels of the informal sector.

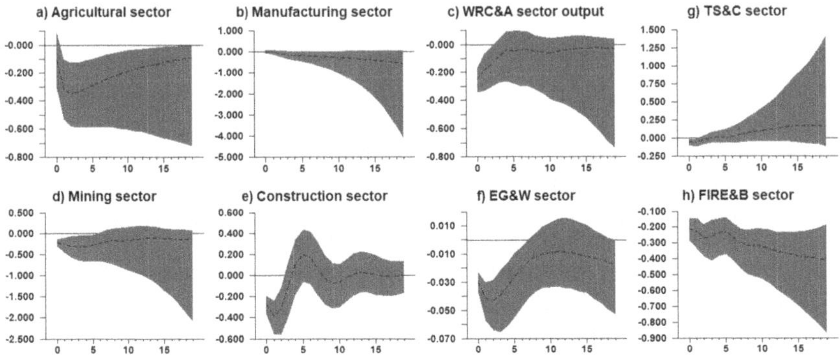

Fig. 10.11 Sector employment share responses to sector relative labour productivity. (Note: The band denotes the 16th and 84th percentile confidence bands. WRC&A = wholesale and retail trade, catering and accommodation sectors; EG&W = electricity, gas and water; TS&C = transport, storage and communication; and FIRE&B = finance, insurance, real estate and business service sectors. The grey shaded area bands denote the 16th and 84th percentile confidence bands. Source: Authors' calculations)

10.7 Conclusion and Policy Implications

This chapter estimated the McMillan and Rodrik (2011) labour productivity decomposition into "*within*" and "*structural change*" components. Evidence shows that the "*structural change*" component has made negative contributions for the period 1990 to 2015 for the aggregate economy as opposed to the "*within*" component. The "*structural change*" component has been growth reducing for the South African economy. At a sector level, the "*within*" component seems to have been the largest contributor especially for the (i) agricultural sector; (ii) wholesale and retail trade, catering and accommodation; and (iii) finance, insurance, real estate and business service sectors. The rapid growth in the "*within*" productivity component has more than offset the negative contribution from the "*structural change*" component, especially for the two latter sectors. The "*structural change*" component has been growth reducing for the South African economy indicating that the direction of labour flows is negatively correlated with labour productivity in individual sectors. The implications for the aggregate economy have been such that displaced labour ends up in activities with lower productivity, informality and unemployment. Hence the economy-wide growth suffers and may even turn negative.

The policy implications of the findings in this chapter are that the recent growth accelerations during the 2000s based on rapid "*within-sector*" labour productivity growth were also largely driven from the demand side of the economy as opposed to rapid industrialisation. Increased levels of market deregulation and various policy reforms aligned with the process of opening up the South African economy into a globalised world have benefitted the "*within*" component of labour productivity at the expense of the "*structural change*" component. The process of deregulation and globalisation has been highly beneficial to intra-sector productivity, but this was at the expense of structural changes within these sectors. Such trends manifest themselves in, for example, high concentration levels of very few firms and economic players within sectors with detrimental effects on competition, price formation, contribution to growth and employment. The rationalisation of manufacturing industries has in most instances come at the expense of inducing growth-reducing "*structural change*". Hence, the persistent unemployment rates and increasing levels of the informal sector. This means that there is much needed growth-enhancing structural change within sectors of the South African economy.

Appendix

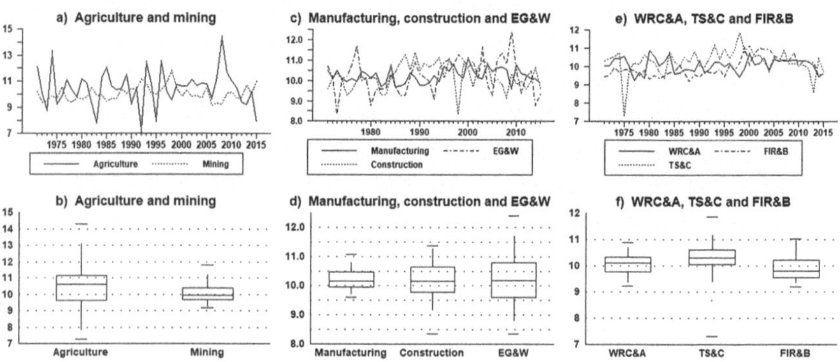

Fig. 10.12 Sector labour productivity growth rates. (Note: EG&W = Electricity, gas and water; TS&C = Transport, storage and communication; WRC&A = Wholesale and retail trade, catering and accommodation sectors; TS&C = Transport, storage and communication; and FIRE&B = finance, insurance, real estate and business service sectors. Source: Productivity SA and authors' calculations)

References

Ando, S., and Nassar, K. 2017. *Indexing Structural Distortion: Sectoral Productivity, Structural Change and Growth*. IMF Working Paper. WP/17/205.

Ansari, M.R., Mussida, C., and Pastor, F. 2013. *Note on Lilien and Modified Lilien Index*. IZA DP No. 7198. February 2013.

Benigno, G., Converse, N., and Fornaro, L. 2015. *Large Capital Inflows, Sectoral Allocation, and Economic Performance*. International Finance Discussion Papers 1132. https://doi.org/10.17016/IFDP.2015.1132.

BFAP. 2011. The Contribution of the Agro-Industrial Complex to Employment in South Africa. Tech. Rep. June, The Bureau for Food and Agricultural Policy, Pretoria.

Borio, C., Kharroubi, E., Upper, C., and Zampolli, F. 2015. *Labour Reallocation and Productivity Dynamics: Financial Causes, Real Consequences*. BIS Working Papers No. 534.

Campos, Nauro F., De Grauwe, Paul, and Ji, Yuemei. 2017. *Structural Reforms, Growth and Inequality: An Overview of Theory, Measurement and Evidence*. CESifo Working Papers ISSN 2364-1428

Cecchetti, S.G., and Kharroubi, E. 2012. *Reassessing the Impact of Finance on Growth*. BIS Working Paper N0. 381.

Connolly, E., and Orsmond, D. 2011. *The Mining Industry: From Bust to Boom*. Research Discussion Paper 2011-08.

Cortuk, O., and Singh, N. 2013. Analyzing the Structural Change and Growth Relationship in India: State-level Evidence. *Economic Letters*, 110(3), 178–81. Elsevier, March.

Diao, X., McMillan, M., and Rodrik, D. 2017. *The Recent Growth Boom in Developing Economies: A Structural Change Perspective*. NBER Working Paper No. 23132.

Dietrich, A. 2009. Does Growth Cause Structural Change, or is it the Other Way Around? A Dynamic Panel Data Analysis for Seven OECD Countries, Jena Research Papers in Economics, http://econpapers.repec.org/paper/jrpjrpwrp/2009-034.htm, accessed February 10, 2010.

Driver, Ciaran IV, and Saw, Chit-Wei. 1996. Performance of structural Change Indices: Analysis Using Real and Simulated Data. *Applied Economics Letters*, 3 (3), 187–88.

Gumata, N., and Ndou, E. 2017. *Bank Credit Extension and Real Economic Activity in South Africa: The Impact of Capital Flow Dynamics, Bank Regulation and Selected Macro-prudential Tools*. Palgrave Macmillan. ISBN 978-3-319-43550-3.

Herrendorf, B., Rogerson, R., and Valentinyi, A. 2014. *Handbook of Economic Growth, Growth and Structural Transformation*. Vol. 2. Elsevier, pp. 855–941.

Kalantzis, Y., and Thubin, C. 2017. *The Causes of Deindustrialisation in France*. Banque De France Eco Notepad.

Lilien, D.M. 1982. Sectoral Shifts and Cyclical Unemployment. *Journal of Political Economy*, 90, 777–93.

Los, B, Timmer, M.P., and De Vries, G.J. 2015. How Global are Global Value Chains? A New Approach to Measure International Fragmentation. *Journal of Regional Science*, 55(1), 66–92.

McMillan, M.S., and Rodrik, D. 2011. *Globalisation, Structural Change and Productivity Growth*. NBER Working Paper 17143.

Ndou, E., and Gumata, N. 2017. *Inflation Dynamics in South Africa: The Role of Thresholds, Exchange Rate Pass-through and Inflation Expectations on Policy Trade-offs*. Palgrave Macmillan. ISBN 978-3-319-46701-6.

Pages, Carmen ed. 2010. *The Age of Productivity*. Inter-American Development Bank: Washington, DC.

Silva, E.G., and Teixeira, A.A.C. 2008. Surveying Structural Change: Seminal Contributions and a Bibliometric Account. *Structural Change and Economic Dynamics*, 19, 273–300.

Stamer, M. 1998. Interrelation between Subsidies, Structural Change and Economic Growth in Germany, A Vector Autoregressive Analysis. *Konjunkturpolitik*, 44 (3), 231–53.

Timmer, M.P., Eurmban, A.A., Los, B., Stehrer, R., and De Vries, G.J. 2014. Slicing Up Global Value Chains. *Journal of Economic Perspectives*, 28 (2), 99–118.

Part IV

Policy Uncertainty, Mining Sector Charter, Exchange Rate Volatility, Commodity Price Booms and Busts, Binding Minimum Wage Increases and the Mining Sector

11

How Has the Intensity of the Ability of Commodity-Specific Output Growth to Create Jobs Evolved? Implications for the Mining Sector as a "Sunrise Industry"

Learning Objectives

- Establish the evolution of the output-employment intensity of the non-gold commodity mining sectors gross value added (GVA).
- Explore which non-gold commodity mining sectors will underpin mining as a "sunrise" industry.
- Establish the relationship between sector-specific commodity prices, output and employment.

11.1 Introduction

The President in his 2018 state of the nation address set out a vision of the mining sector as a "*sunrise industry*" as opposed to the current narrative of a "*sunset industry*".[1] Nonetheless, the trends in Fig. 11.1(c) indicate that the contribution of the mining sector to aggregate gross value

[1] "The mining sector is another area that has massive unrealised potential for growth and job creation. We need to see mining as a sunrise industry" https://www.parliament.gov.za/state-nation-address-cyril-ramaphosa president

N. Gumata, E. Ndou, *Accelerated Land Reform, Mining, Growth, Unemployment and Inequality in South Africa*, https://doi.org/10.1007/978-3-030-30884-1_11

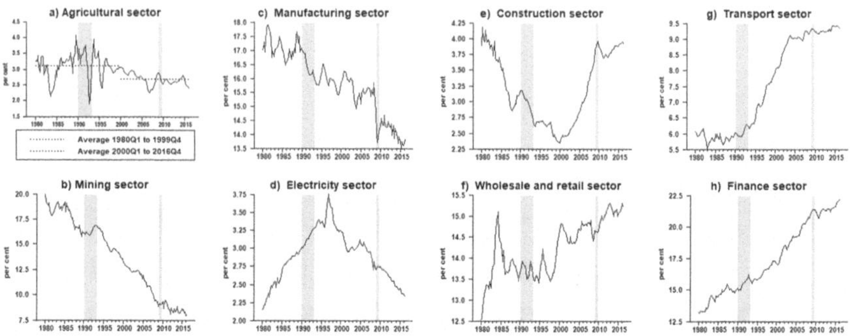

Fig. 11.1 Sectorial contributions to total gross value added. (Source: South African Reserve Bank and authors' calculations)

added (GVA) has been on a secular decline and seems to have stabilised around 8 per cent since 2010.[2] But further disaggregation of the mining sector by commodity in Figs. 11.2 and 11.3 indicates that the main contributing commodities to the primary sector GVA (output) and employment are non-gold sectors, in particular, coal, platinum group and metal ores.

Chapter 8 explored the output growth intensity of employment creation at an aggregated level for all sectors. Evidence showed that the sectorial output-employment[3] indicate the most output growth employment intensity is generated by the construction sector followed by the transport, trade and finance sectors. This chapter extends the analysis on the output-employment intensities by analysing the mining sector at a disaggregated level by commodity. We ask: How has the intensity of the ability of commodity-specific output growth to create jobs evolved? Which commodity sectors will underpin mining as a "*sunrise*" industry?

Figure 11.2 shows that metal ores, platinum group and coal are the biggest contributors to the primary sector GVA. Combined, the three sectors constitute more than 60 per cent to the primary sector GVA in Fig. 11.2(f).

[2] Connolly and Orsmond (2011) refer to this as the period during which mining was dismissed as emblematic of Australia's "old economy", with prices for key resource exports at their lowest levels in real terms for a century.

[3] Also referred to as the "Okun's coefficients"

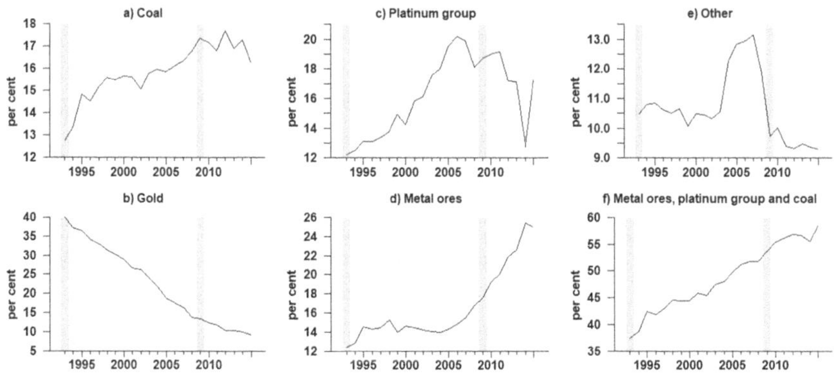

Fig. 11.2 Contributions of various commodity sectors to primary sector gross value added. (Source: Statistics South Africa and authors' calculations)

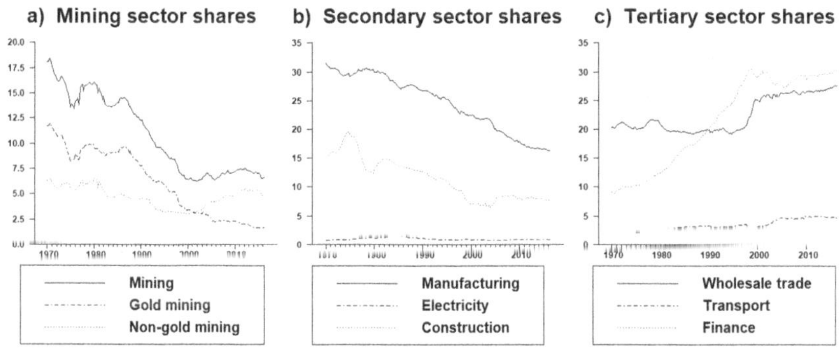

Fig. 11.3 Sectorial contributions to formal private sector employment. (Source: South African Reserve Bank and authors' calculations)

In addition, Fig. 11.3 shows that at an aggregate level, non-gold industries contribute more to employment growth in the formal non-agricultural sector compared to the gold mining sector. This is particularly the case post-2000. The National Development Plan (NDP) targets net 11 million new jobs or an unemployment rate of 6 per cent 2030 so as to increase the labour participation rate to 65 per cent. This means that the mining sector must play a meaningful role in job creation that even spills over to the manufacturing where the NDP targets to create a million jobs

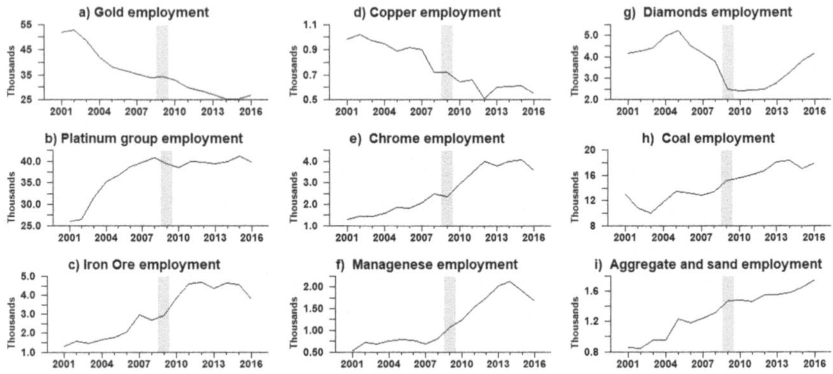

Fig. 11.4 Mining employment by mining commodity. (Source: South African Chamber of Mines and authors' calculations)

by 2030. The South African Chamber of Mines estimates that the coal industry inputs into the basic iron and steel industry constitute up 9.3 per cent and thus contributes indirectly to this sector. Similarly, the coal sector via the procurement of local goods and services indirectly contributed to creating and maintaining jobs mainly in the transport and storage sectors. The petroleum, chemicals, rubber and plastic industries are also major beneficiaries of the coal industry.

The disaggregation of employment levels by commodity in Fig. 11.4 shows that within the non-gold mining industry, the biggest employers are the platinum group, iron ore, coal, diamonds, chrome and manganese. Nonetheless, even though the contribution of gold mining is on a secular decline, in Fig. 11.2, it still employs more than a 100,000 people which constitutes just above 25 per cent of total mining employment in Fig. 11.5.

Thus, the trend analysis indicates that the non-gold mining sectors will be strong pillars of the strategy to make the mining sector a "sunrise" industry. In particular, the platinum group, coal, metal ores, chrome and manganese. The diamonds, chrome, manganese and copper commodity sectors contribute between 2 per cent and 5 per cent to mining employment. In the empirical section we only focus on the platinum group, coal and metal ores sectors due to data availability for GVA (output). We lump the diamonds, chrome, manganese and copper commodity sectors

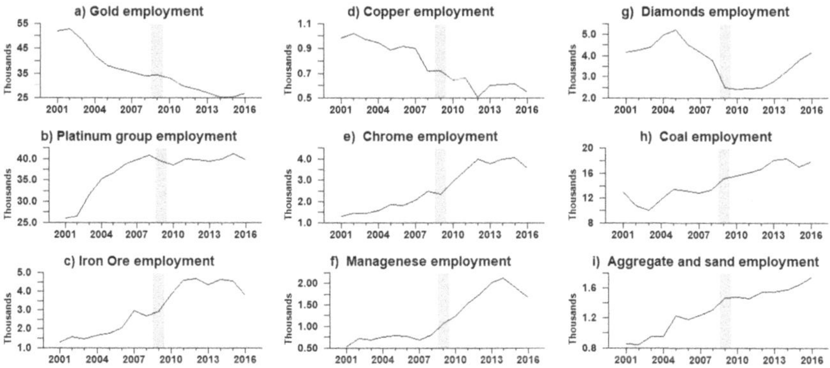

Fig. 11.5 Contributions to mining employment by mining commodity. (Source: South African Chamber of Mines and authors' calculations)

under others due to unavailability of disaggregated data. We assess how intensive the GVA (output) growth-employment nexus has evolved over the sector-specific commodity price cycles.

11.2 Is There a Case for a Special Treatment of Coal Mining Within the Mining Sector and Energy Mix Policy?

This section starts by analysing the case for the special treatment of the coal mining sector within the mining sector and energy mix policy. Figure 11.2 (a) and 11.5 (h) show that the contribution of coal mining to the primary sector GVA (output) and employment in the mining sector has doubled since 1993 and 2001, respectively. Furthermore, statistics show that coal mining is the fourth largest commodity sector by contribution to the mining sector. Hence, the Chamber of Mines National Coal Strategy argues a case for coal mining to continue to play an important role in the economy for the foreseeable future despite its declining profile and negative impact on the environment.[4]

[4] The report shows and argues that the electricity sector, the liquid fuels manufacture sector and the basic iron and steel industry are the three industries that will be adversely affected by the implemen-

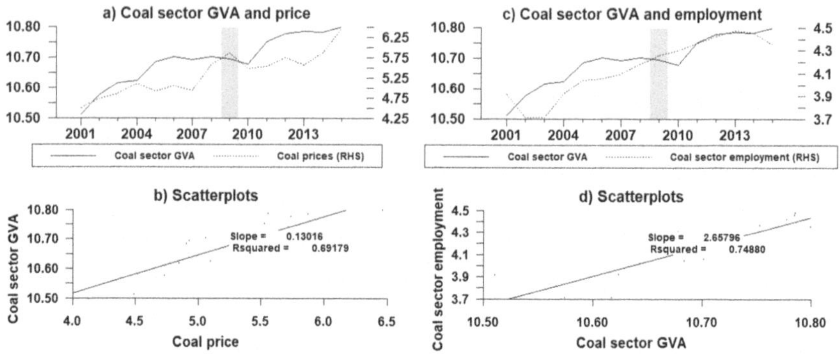

Fig. 11.6 Coal mining GVA, employment and prices (logs). (Note: The grey shaded areas denote the South African recession. Source: South African Chamber of Mines and authors' calculations)

Figure 11.3(h) shows that coal mining employment more than doubled and increased from 40,000 in 2002 to around 80,000 in 2016. Furthermore, Fig. 11.6 shows that coal mining GVA, employment and prices are positively associated.[5] The variation in coal prices explains around 69 per cent of changes in coal mining GVA. On the other hand, changes in coal GVA explain around 75 per cent variation in the coal mining sector employment. This means that an increase in coal prices has positive effects on the coal mining sector output growth and in turn employment growth. In addition, the Chamber of Mines reports that in 2016, the coal industry spent R60 billion on the procurement of goods and services, most of it locally. This contributed to creating and maintaining jobs in other industries. Indirectly, the coal industry created 173,093 jobs mainly in the transport and storage sector where almost 120,000 jobs were created representing 69 per cent.

The coal industry has huge spill-over effects for the transport industry.[6] These results are aligned to the findings in Chap. 8 where the sectorial

tation and enforcement of strict environmental laws in South Africa. Together, these three sectors account for more than 80 per cent of domestic coal demand in terms of value and approximately 70 per cent in terms of volumes. Indirectly, the coal industry is responsible for creating and sustaining over 170,000 jobs outside the coal industry.

[5] Figure 11.12 shows the evolution of the platinum, iron ore and coal prices.

[6] For further details, see http://www.chamberofmines.org.za/component/jdownloads/send/25-downloads/535-coal-strategy-2018

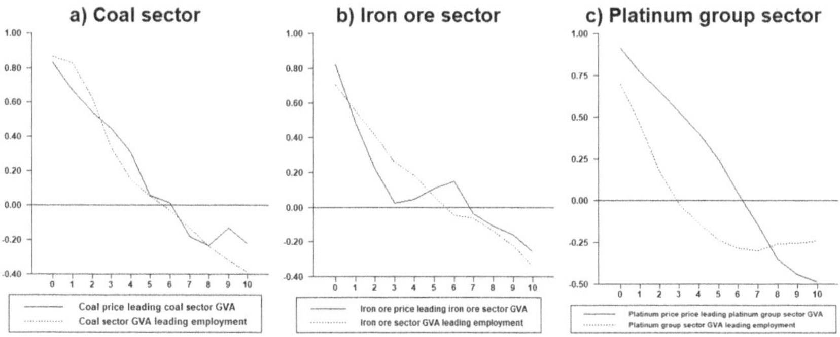

Fig. 11.7 Mining sector GVAs, employment and prices lead-lag relationships (logs). (Source: Authors' calculations)

"*Okun's coefficients*" show that the most output growth employment intensity is generated by the construction sector followed by the transport, trade and finance sectors. Evidence showed that an unexpected 1 per cent growth in transport, trade and finance sector GVA (output) resulted in employment growth of between 0.7 per cent and 1 per cent in these sectors for the period 2000Q1 to 2016Q4. The lead relationships in Fig. 11.7(a) confirm the relationships established in Fig. 11.6 and indicate that the coal price results in a prolonged increase in the coal mining sector GVA (output). At the same time, the increase in the coal mining sector GVA (output) results in a persistent increase in the coal mining sector employment in Fig. 11.7(a).[7]

11.3 The Metal Ores Commodity Sector

The stylised facts in Fig. 11.8 indicate that the variation in metal ore prices explain around 68 per cent of changes in the metal ores GVA (output). Similarly, changes in the metal ores GVA (output) explain about 50 per cent of changes in employment in the metal ores sector. Thus, the

[7] The South African Chamber of Mines shows that coal export prices are the leading indicator for net investment. A sustained increase in export prices is soon followed by higher net investment. Globally, coal prices are determined by demand and supply, whereas the benchmark price for domestically consumed coal is set by Eskom and has historically always been lower than the export price.

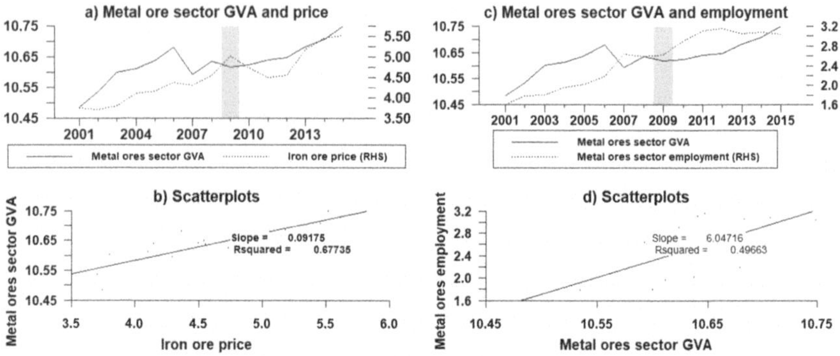

Fig. 11.8 Metal ores mining GVA, employment and prices (logs). (Note: The grey shaded areas denote the South African recession. Source: South African Chamber of Mines and authors' calculations)

metal ore commodity prices have a positive influence on the metal ore sector GVA (output) and employment growth although the intensity of the positive association differs.

The lead-lag relationship established in Fig. 11.7(b) corroborates the relationships established in Fig. 11.8 that metal ores prices have a positive effect on the metal ores mining sector GVA (output) which in turn leads to a persistent increase in employment in that sector. Nonetheless, on a comparative basis, the coal mining sector GVA explains a higher proportion of employment growth within coal mining compared to that explained by the iron ore sector GVA (output) in the metal ores sector employment growth. These are early indications that the coal mining GVA (output) is far more employment intensive and generates more employment creation per unit variation compared to the metal ores sector.

11.4 The Platinum Group Commodity Sector

Similar to the previous sections, we start by looking at the stylised facts for the platinum group mining sector. Figure 11.9 shows that changes in the platinum prices explain around 84 per cent of the variation in the

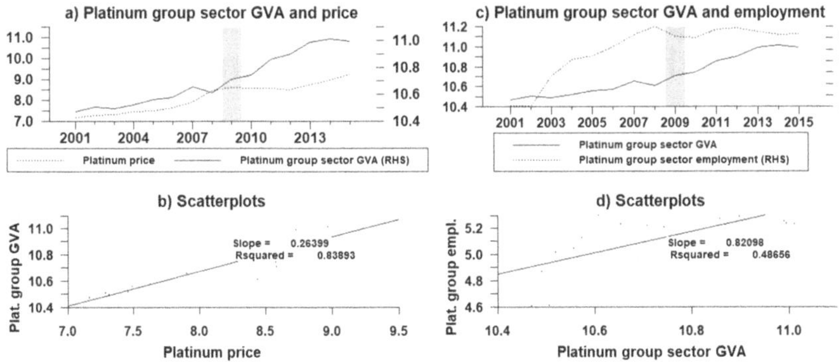

Fig. 11.9 Platinum group mining GVA, employment and prices (logs). (Note: Plat = platinum and emply. = employment. The grey shaded areas denote the South African recession. Source: South African Chamber of Mines and authors' calculations)

platinum group sector GVA (output). This implies that the platinum group sector GVA (output) is highly sensitive to platinum prices. At the same time, the platinum group sector GVA (output) explains around 49 per cent of changes in the platinum group sector employment.

The lead-lag relationships in Fig. 11.7 confirm that the platinum price leads to a prolonged increase the platinum group GVA (output) and this result in an increase in employment in that section. But, the platinum group GVA (output) is far more sensitive and responsive to price developments compared to employment levels. This implies that an increase in platinum prices are positive for the platinum group sector and induce producers to intensify production, but this does not necessarily lead to a persistent accelerated increase in employment levels. As was the case with the metal ores sector, the platinum group GVA (output) explains a lower proportion of changes in employment compared to the coal sector. Thus, on a comparative basis, based on the stylised facts, coal mining GVA (output) generates more employment compared to the metal ores and the platinum group sectors. Hence, we conclude that there is a case for a special treatment of coal mining within the mining sector and energy mix policy.

11.5 Output-Employment Estimates for the Commodity Sector Mining

This section uses the same approaches used in Chap. 8 to estimate the specific commodity sector GDP-employment growth relationship. Since there is no data on the sectoral unemployment rates, we only focus on the specific commodity sector GDP-employment growth relationship, alternatively, the employment equation as shown in Eq. 11.1. This is a component of Okun's Law.

$$E_t - E_t^* = \gamma\left(Y_t - Y_t^*\right) + \eta_{t,}\ \gamma > 0 \quad \textit{employment equation}, \quad (11.1)$$

where E_t in the *employment equation* Eq. (11.1) is the log of commodity sector employment, Y_t is the log of commodity output (GVA) and the $*$ signifies a long-run level. The coefficient for γ is the response of employment to output. The coefficient is expected to be positive (negative) indicating that rapid output growth is associated with an increase (decrease) in employment growth. The estimations are conducted for the sample period 2001Q1 to 2016Q4 due to availability of data. The data is sourced from the Statistics South Africa and the South African Chamber of Mines databases.

Figure 11.10 shows the evolution of the output-employment coefficients for the coal, metal ores and platinum group commodity sectors.[8] The results show that the coal mining and metal ores commodity sector GVAs (output) are indeed employment intensive. Although the rate of employment intensity has declined post-2009, the commodity sector remains a better employment creator than the platinum group commodity sector this trend has persisted post-2009. The coal mining sector employment creation intensity per 1 per cent of GVA (output) increase is more persistent than the metal ore and platinum group commodity sectors.

We estimate several bivariate-VAR models which include the commodity sector category GVA (output) and employment in log levels and

[8] We show the evolution of the Okun's coefficients in log changes in Fig. 11.14 in the Appendix.

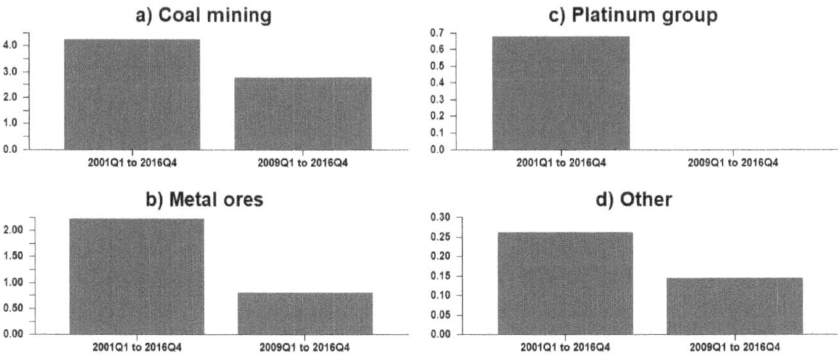

Fig. 11.10 The evolution of output-employment coefficients in equations (log levels). (Source: Authors' calculations)

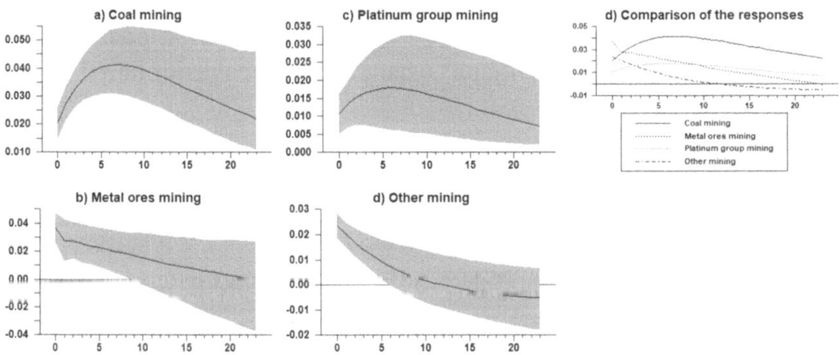

Fig. 11.11 Employment responses to commodity sector GVAs (log levels). (Note: The grey shaded bands denote the 16th and 84th percentile error bands. Source: Authors' calculations)

changes. The estimates using changes are to test for the robustness of the point estimated derived from the output-employment linear regressions. The commodity sector categories are the coal mining, metal ores mining and the platinum group mining sector. The models are estimated using 2 lags and 10,000 Monte Carlo draws. The data in log levels and log changes is used separately in different models. The results in Fig. 11.11 suggest that the output-employment coefficients are robust. Changes in the coal mining sector GVA (output) are associated with more employment creation compared to the metal ores, platinum group and other commodity sectors. The comparison of the responses in Fig. 11.11(d) indicates that the positive effects of the coal mining GVA (output) employment intensity tend to be more persistent as well in comparison to the metal ores and platinum group commodity sectors. These results further solidify the case for a special dispensation for the coal mining commodity sector within the mining sector and energy mix policy.

Furthermore, the South African Chamber of Mines shows that the coal mining sector is an important foreign exchange earner. Export sales have traditionally accounted for between 40 per cent and 45 per cent of total coal sales. The direction of South African coal exports was affected by the strict implementation of the Kyoto Protocol by European countries, which sought to enforce the mandatory reduction of GHG emissions. Hence, policymakers must take these considerations into account when the country becomes a signatory of international accords such as that of the climate change and environmental laws amongst others.

11.6 Conclusion and Policy Implications

How has the intensity of the ability of commodity-specific output growth to create jobs evolved? First, we establish that metal ores, platinum group and coal are the biggest contributors to the primary sector GVA (output). Combined, the three sectors constitute more than 60 per cent of the primary sector GVA (output). Second, the disaggregation of employment levels by commodity shows that within the non-gold mining industry, the biggest employers are the platinum group, iron ore, coal, diamonds, chrome and manganese. However, the data trends show that even though the contribution of gold mining is on a secular decline, it still employs more than a 100,000 people. This constitutes just above 25 per cent of total mining employment. Thus, it is not all doom and gloom for the gold mining industry.

Third, evidence shows that the variation in coal prices explains around 69 per cent of changes in coal mining GVA (output). On the other hand, changes in coal GVA (output) explain around 75 per cent variation in coal mining employment. This means that an increase in coal prices has positive effects in coal mining output growth and in turn employment growth. The Chamber of Mines reports that the coal industry indirectly created 173,093 jobs mainly in the transport and storage sector via spending and the procurement of goods and services mostly sourced locally. This evidence is corroborated by earlier findings in Chap. 8 showing that the sectorial "Okun's coefficients" suggest that the most output growth employment intensity is generated by the construction sector followed by the transport, trade and finance sectors. Evidence showed that a per cent growth in transport, trade and finance sector GVA (output) resulted in employment growth of between 0.7 per cent and 1 per cent in these sectors for the period 2000Q1 to 2016Q4.

Fourth, evidence shows that the platinum group, metal ores and coal mining industry GVAs (output) are very sensitive to sector-specific commodity prices. But, the coal mining sector GVA (output) generates more employment compared to the metal ores and the platinum group sectors. The Okun's Law estimates suggest that changes in coal mining GVA (output) are associated with more employment compared to the metal ores and platinum group commodity sectors. The comparison of the responses indicates that the positive effects of the coal mining GVA employment intensity tend to be more persistent as well in comparison to the metal ores and platinum group commodity sectors. Furthermore, the South African Chamber of Mines shows that the coal mining sector is an important foreign exchange earner. Export sales have traditionally accounted for between 40 per cent and 45 per cent of total coal sales. Hence, we conclude that there is a case for a special treatment of coal mining within the mining sector and energy mix policy. This can be supported by the co-ordination of the trade and other macroeconomic policies. The South African Chamber of Mines has identified that the growth markets for coal mining exports are likely to be in Asia, in countries such as India, Pakistan, Malaysia, Taiwan, Bangladesh, South Korea and Sub-Saharan Africa because of electricity shortages which are likely to increase appetite for coal. Hence, they suggest the exploration of these export markets for growth for South African coal as there is no scope for further growth in Europe, especially countries in the European Union because of environmental laws. In addition, the Chamber has identified technology as another export risk factor, other than environmental laws.

Fifth, the other sectors which include the diamonds, copper, chrome and manganese are non-negligible and contribute between 2 per cent and 5 per cent to mining employment. The diamonds, chrome and manganese commodity sectors have been making positive contributions to the mining sector post-2009. Combined, these commodity sectors employ more than 50,000 people. Evidence show that the other commodity sector GVA (output) is employment intensive and compares favourably to the platinum group especially post-2009. The coal, metal ores, platinum group and other commodity sectors will underpin the mining as a "*sunrise*" industry. In addition, these sectors will play an instrumental role in the employment creation and meeting the unemployment targets set out in the National Development Plan. Needless to mention that this will enable the South Africa Reserve Bank to achieve its expanded mandate of supporting the highest sustainable level of GDP growth and maximum employment.

The mining sector in general competes with other sectors such as agriculture, manufacturing (industrial), tourism and housing for land use. The findings in this chapter strongly indicate that, while trade-offs between the prioritisation of land use by sectors and the environmental damage considerations exist, policy decisions should seriously consider the GDP growth, employment growth and developmental implications as well. These considerations extend to the country being a signatory of international accords such as that of the climate change and environmental laws such as the enforcement of environmental laws in the form of a carbon tax, amongst others. The design of policies should strive to foster the co-existence of the sectors especially in cases where the spill-over effects are large and straddle across the national mandates of sustainable growth, maximum employment and development in general.

Furthermore, the fact that commodity prices play an instrumental role in these sectors that will underpin mining as a "*sunrise*" industry places a sense of urgency on the exchange rate policy, the design of the proposed sovereign wealth fund, the co-ordination of the trade and other macroeconomic policies.

Appendix

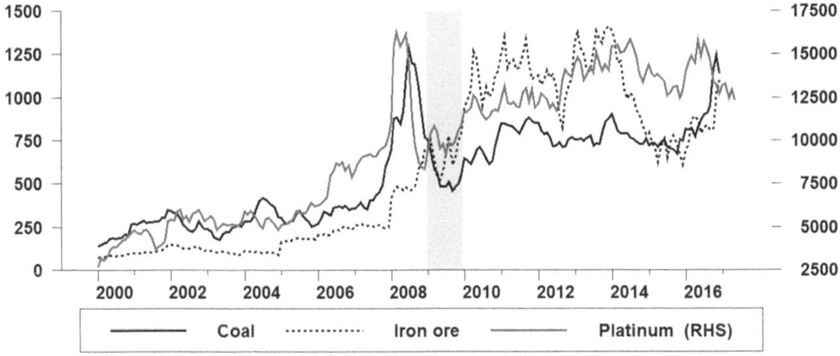

Fig. 11.12 Platinum, iron ore and coal prices. (Note: The grey shaded areas denote the South African recession. Source: International Monetary Fund Commodity Prices database and South African Reserve Bank)

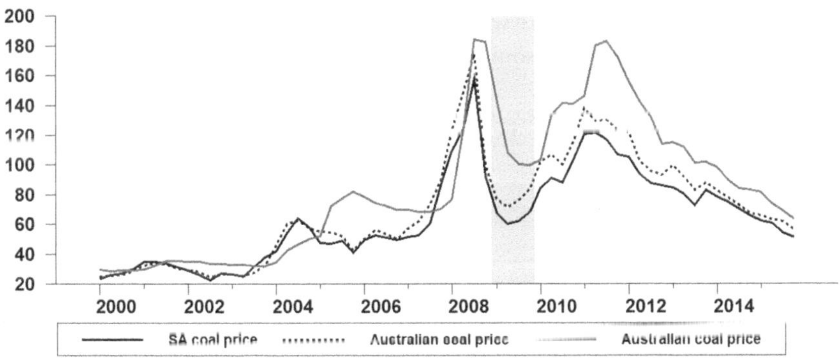

Fig. 11.13 Comparison of coal prices. (Note: The grey shaded areas denote the South African recession. Source: International Monetary Fund Commodity Prices database)

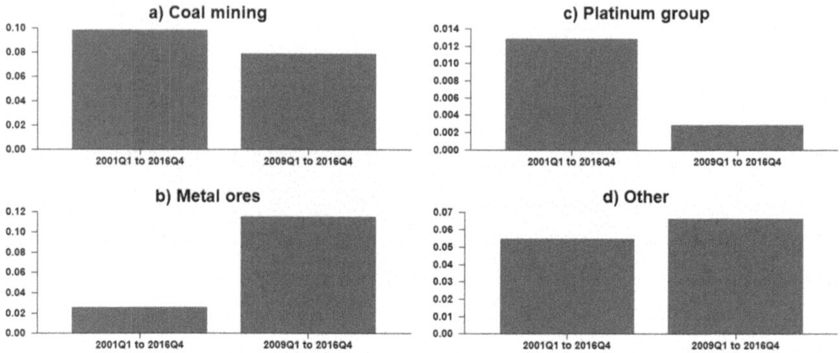

Fig. 11.14 The evolution of output-employment coefficients in equations (log changes). (Source: Authors' calculations)

References

Connolly, E., and Orsmond, D. 2011. *The Mining Industry: From Bust to Boom.* Research Reserve Bank of Australia. Discussion Paper 2011-08.

The South African Chamber of Mines. 2018. The National Coal Strategy for South Africa 2018. https://www.mineralscouncil.org.za/special-features/604-national-coal-strategy-for-south-africa.

12

Is Export-Led Growth a Necessary but Insufficient Condition for Job Creation in the Mining Sector? Does This Mean That There Is a Strong Case for Beneficiation?

Learning Objectives

- Establish the prevalence of the "exports growth-led GDP growth hypothesis" or the "GDP growth-driven exports growth" hypothesis using aggregate and commodity mining sector-specific data.
- Explore whether export-led GDP growth is a necessary but insufficient condition for employment creation in the aggregate mining sector and commodity-specific sectors.
- Assess what the results of the export-led GDP growth hypothesis imply for mineral beneficiation.
- Establish whether the South Africa data supports the "export growth-led jobless growth" hypothesis.

12.1 Introduction

Chapter 11 found that the coal, metal ores, platinum group and other commodity sectors[1] will underpin the mining as a "*sunrise*" industry. In addition, these sectors will play an instrumental role in employment

[1] The other sectors which include the diamonds, copper, chrome and manganese are *not non-negligible* and contribute between 2 per cent and 5 per cent to mining employment.

N. Gumata, E. Ndou, *Accelerated Land Reform, Mining, Growth, Unemployment and Inequality in South Africa*, https://doi.org/10.1007/978-3-030-30884-1_12

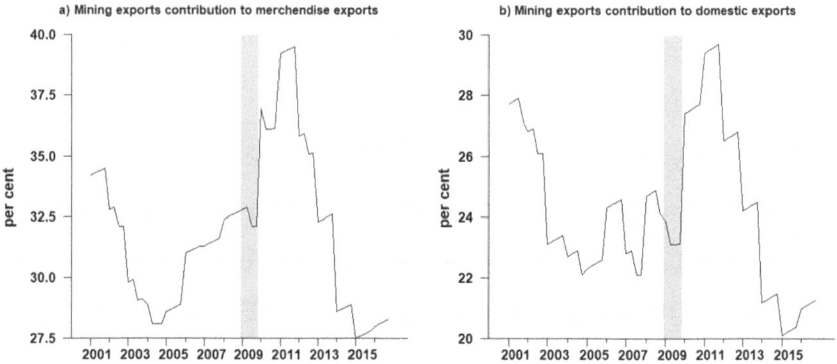

Fig. 12.1 Mining exports contributions. (Note: The grey shaded area denote the South African recession. Source: South African Chamber of Mines)

creation and meeting the unemployment rate targets set out in the National Development Plan. At the same time, this will enable the South Africa Reserve Bank to achieve its expanded mandate of supporting the highest sustainable level of GDP growth and maximum employment. This chapter extends the analysis of the mining sector as a *"sunrise" industry*. We ask whether the export-led growth strategy is a necessary but insufficient condition for employment creation in the mining sector. Does this mean that there is a strong case for minerals beneficiation?

Figure 12.1 shows that the mining sector contributes more than 27 per cent and 20 per cent to merchandise exports and total domestic exports, respectively. But Fig. 12.2(a) and (b) show that the mining sector contributes around 7.5 per cent to GDP and employment. Why is it the case that the mining sector accounts for more than a quarter of exports earnings but contributes so little to GDP and employment? Are these trends aligned to the general observation that Africa's experience with the export-led strategy seems to be quite disappointing? For instance, Ancharaz (2011) indicates that Africa's impressive growth performance in recent years has not generated significant employment opportunities, especially for the youth. Much of the growth has been driven by exports of natural resources that offer limited potential for job creation. Evidence suggests the prevalence of the "export growth-led jobless growth" hypothesis.

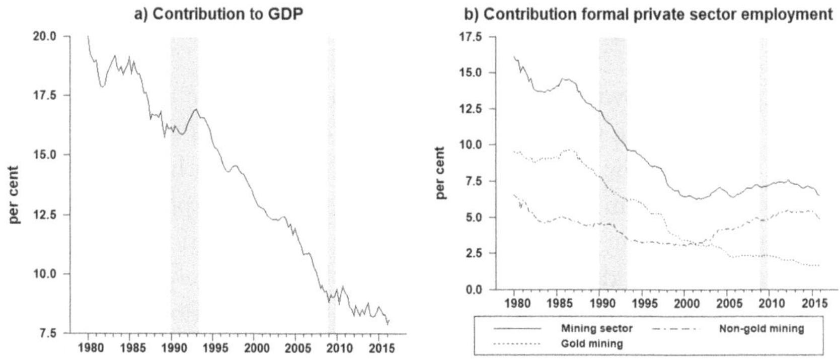

Fig. 12.2 Sectoral contributions to total gross value added. (Note: The grey shaded areas denote the South African recessions. Source: South African Reserve Bank and authors' calculations)

While exports have been an important factor in Africa's recent economic growth, this growth has not been job-creating to a degree needed to tackle unemployment and promote inclusive development in Africa.

Leautier and Hanson (2013) observe that strong economic growth caused by higher exports in capital-intensive extractive sectors does not necessarily create better prospects for the employment-intensive sectors like agriculture. Furthermore, Sachs and Warner (2001) present evidence of a *"curse of natural resources"* where countries with great natural resource wealth tend to grow more slowly than resource-poor countries. Hence, resource-abundant countries tended to be high-price economies and, perhaps as a consequence, miss out on export-led growth. This chapter empirically tests the hypothesis of export-led growth in the aggregate and specific commodity mining sectors to assess whether there is a strong case for beneficiation.

The National Development Plan (NDP) targets net 11 million new jobs or an unemployment rate of 6 per cent 2030 so as to increase the labour participation rate to 65 per cent. This means that the mining sector has to play a meaningful role in job creation that even spills over to the manufacturing where the NDP targets to create a million jobs by 2030. This implies that strategies such as mineral beneficiation will play an important role in the mining sector spill-over effects to other sectors.

12.2 The Export-Led Growth Hypothesis

The export-led growth hypothesis states that exports are one of the key factors of economic growth. Empirically, the broad idea that the export sector might be the driving force behind episodes of high growth is mainly derived from the amazing benefits created by export-led growth in Asia.[2] This Asian experience triggered high expectations for Africa. Furthermore, the idea that labour would benefit largely from export growth is the foundation upon which trade liberalisation is founded. Literature shows that since the production for exports is believed to be more labour-intensive than the production for the domestic market, better allocation of resources based on the country's comparative advantage would stimulate economic activity and job growth as larger outputs necessitate more labour participation. Nonetheless, Awokuse (2006) show that empirical evidence linking exports to economic growth has been mixed and inconclusive. Ancharaz (2011) indicates that a general observation that Africa's experience with the export-led strategy seems to be quite disappointing.

Literature states that the exports growth can be a catalyst for output growth: (i) directly, as a component of aggregate output and (ii) indirectly through the efficient resource allocation, greater capacity utilisation, exploitation of economies of scale and stimulation of technological improvement due to foreign market competition. In addition, exports provide foreign exchange that allows for the increased levels of imports of capital goods and intermediate goods that in turn raise the growth of capital formation and thus stimulate output growth. Furthermore, export growth through an expanded market base allows for the exploitation of economies of scale for open economies and promotes the transfer and diffusion of technical knowledge in the long run. Thus, Awokuse (2006) indicate that the export-led growth hypothesis implies that the rate of export growth will lead to economy-wide efficiency and productivity growth.

---

[2] This is especially the case for the so-called miracle growth of the four Tigers of South East Asia and China.

12.2.1 Analytical Framework

To test the export-led growth hypothesis, we use the analytical framework depicted in Fig. 12.3. The *"export-led growth" hypothesis* depicted in Fig. 12.3 is based on a two-step relationship between exports growth, GDP growth and employment growth. First, we need to determine whether exports growth has boosted GDP growth, and then examine if such growth has been employment intensive (job-creating).

Awokuse (2006) suggests that within the exports and output growth nexus, literature states that the causality from exports to real output is the "exports-led GDP growth hypothesis" while the reverse causal flow from real output to exports is referred to as the "GDP growth-driven exports" hypothesis. The exports-led GDP growth hypothesis reflects the view that export-oriented policies help to stimulate economic growth.

12.3 Data and Stylised Facts

Studies exploring the export-led growth hypothesis include aggregate and commodity-specific gross value added, private and mining sector gross fixed capital formation, private sector and commodity-specific mining employment and commodity prices in their models. We use foreign output shock represented by global GDP and imports growth. For the analysis of China-specific growth shocks, we replace global GDP and imports growth with the Chinese GDP and imports growth.

In the analysis, the terms-of-trade variable reflects the possible linkages of the real exchange rates (and the possible effects of restrictive trade policy such as tariff and non-tariff barriers) and real output. The foreign

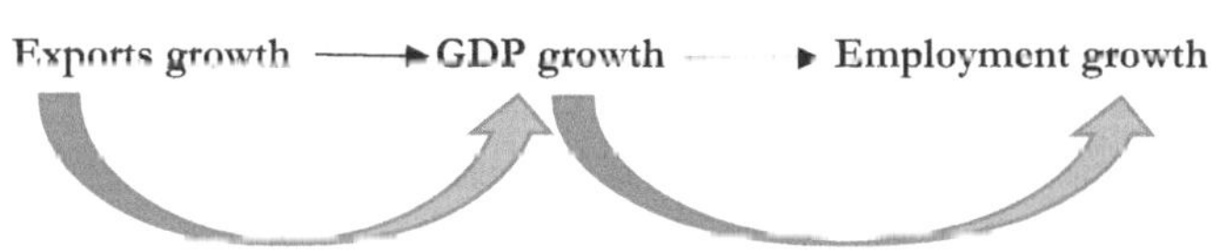

Fig. 12.3 The exports-led growth hypothesis. (Source: Adapted from Ancharaz 2011)

output controls for export growth not influenced by domestic price competitiveness or productivity, but by growth in the rest of the world. The data is sourced from the South African Chamber of Mines, International Monetary Fund, South African Reserve Bank and Statistics South Africa databases. The sample is on a quarterly (Q) basis and spans the period 2000Q1 to 2016Q4. All growth rates are at annual rate.

12.3.1 Aggregate Exports, GDP, Employment and Investment Growth

This section starts the analysis by conducting various stylised facts to establish the nature of the relationship between exports growth, GDP growth, employment growth and investment growth. We start the analysis by showing the trends in aggregate exports growth, GDP growth and employment growth. The scatterplot in Fig. 12.4 shows that there is a positive relationship between GDP and exports growth. In Fig. 12.4(b) exports growth explains around 45 per cent of the variation in GDP growth. Nonetheless, the cross-correlation in Fig. 12.4(c) shows a transitory positive effect when GDP growth lead exports growth. These results are early indications of the potential bi-directional causality between exports growth and GDP growth. We formally conduct the Granger cau-

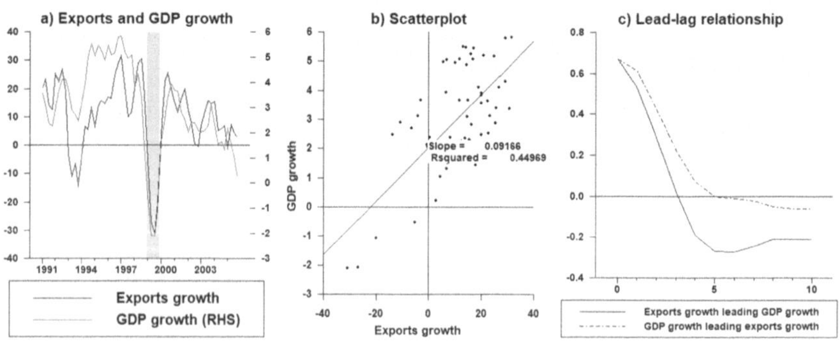

Fig. 12.4 Exports and GDP growth relationship. (Note: The grey shaded areas denote the South African recession. Source: South African Reserve Bank and authors' calculations)

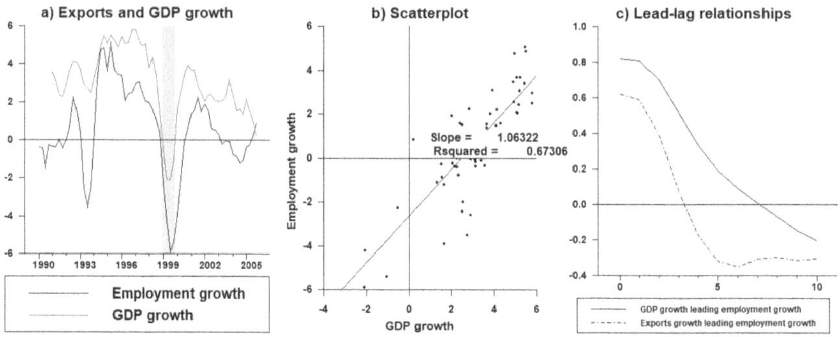

Fig. 12.5 Exports, GDP and employment growth relationship. (Note: The grey shaded areas denote the South African recession. Source: South African Reserve Bank and authors' calculations)

sality tests in later sections to test the prevalence of the "*exports growth-led GDP growth hypothesis*" or the "*GDP growth-driven exports growth*" hypothesis. The results are an early indication of that adverse commodity price, and minerals exports growth stocks tend to have severe negative effects on economic activity. We explore the effects of various shocks in the empirical section.

Figure 12.5(b) shows that GDP growth and employment growth are positively associated, and GDP growth explains around 67 per cent of the variation in employment growth. Furthermore, the lead relationships in Fig. 12.5(c) indicate that employment growth increases and persists when led by GDP growth compared to exports growth. This shows the direct link between GDP growth and employment growth. It is therefore undeniable that GDP growth is an intermediary through which exports growth leads to employment growth.

The R^2 in Fig. 12.6(b) shows that investment growth explains around 38 per cent of the variation in GDP growth. This evidence suggests that exports growth provide foreign exchange, and this affects imports of capital goods and intermediate goods that in turn impact capital formation and output growth. We empirically explore evidence of the balance sheet effects of the mining sector from the investment growth in Chap. 14.

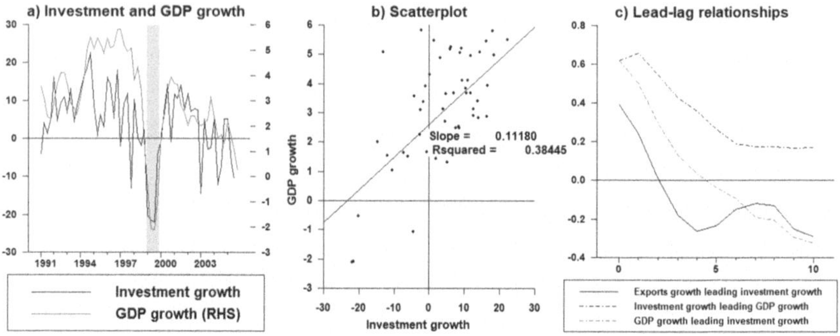

Fig. 12.6 Exports, GDP and investment growth relationship. (Note: The grey shaded areas denote the South African recession. Source: South African Reserve Bank and authors' calculations)

12.3.2 Evidence from Granger Causality Tests

The Granger causality tests in Table 12.1 indicate that there is bi-directional causality between exports growth and GDP growth. The data suggests the presence of both the "*exports-led growth*" hypothesis and the "*GDP growth-driven exports growth*" hypothesis.

Furthermore, this evidence confirms the existence of the exports, GDP, investment and employment growth nexus. This confirms earlier results of the "export-led job growth" hypothesis. The increase in exports growth will lead to investment-led economy-wide efficiency and productivity growth. The causality tests confirm that although investment growth does not necessarily cause exports, it leads to GDP growth and employment growth.

12.3.3 Mining Exports, GDP, Employment and Investment Growth

This section explores whether the stylised facts and hypothesis established at the aggregate level are also confirmed at the mining sector level. Figure 12.1 showed that the mining sector contributes more than 27 per cent and 20 per cent to merchandise exports and total domestic exports,

Table 12.1 Granger causality tests

Null hypothesis	Probability	Decision
Exports growth does not Granger cause GDP growth	0.0142***	Yes, exports growth causes GDP growth
Exports growth does not Granger cause employment growth	0.0127***	Yes, exports growth causes employment growth
Exports growth does not Granger cause investment growth	0.0476***	Yes, exports growth causes investment growth
GDP growth does not Granger cause exports growth	0.0149***	Yes, GDP growth causes exports growth
GDP growth does not Granger Cause employment growth	0.0206***	Yes, GDP growth causes employment growth
GDP growth does not Granger Cause investment growth	0.0010***	Yes, GDP growth causes investment growth
Investment growth does not Granger cause exports growth	0.5998	No, investment growth does not cause exports growth
Investment growth does not Granger cause GDP growth	0.0364***	Yes, investment growth causes GDP growth
Investment growth does not Granger cause employment growth	0.0515***	Yes, investment growth does not cause employment growth

Source: Authors' calculations
Note: ***/**/* indicate rejection of the null hypothesis at the 1/5/10 per cent level of significance

respectively. At peak post-2009, the mining sector contributed almost 40 per cent and 30 per cent to merchandise exports and total domestic exports, respectively.

The analysis starts with the coal mining sector. Figure 12.7 shows that coal exports growth, output growth and employment growth are positively associated. Coal exports growth explains almost 17 per cent of the variation in coal mining output growth, whereas it explains around 20 per cent of the variation in the coal mining sector employment growth.

Furthermore, Fig. 12.7(c) shows that coal mining exports growth leads to higher and more persistent effect on employment growth. The implication is that exports growth matters for the coal mining sector output growth and employment growth. A similar trend emerges in Fig. 12.8 when we assess the lead lag relationships between iron ore, platinum group metals (PGMs) and other minerals commodity exports growth and employment growth in those sectors. Nonetheless, it is evident that

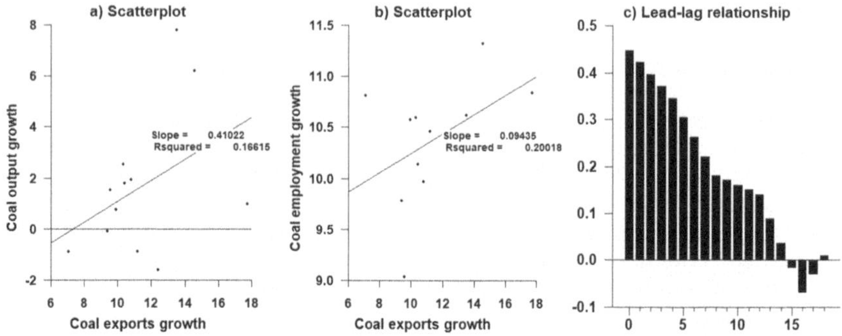

Fig. 12.7 Coal exports, GVA and employment growth relationship. (Source: Statistics South Africa, South African Chamber of Mines and authors' calculations)

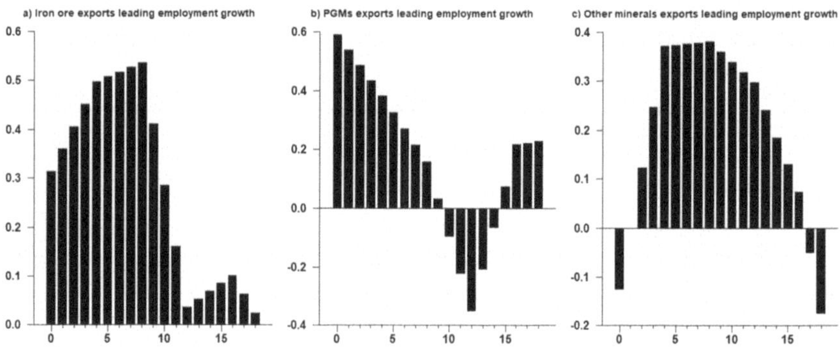

Fig. 12.8 Iron ore, PGMs and other mineral commodity exports and employment growth relationship. (Note: PGMs = platinum group metals. Source: Statistics South Africa, South African Chamber of Mines and authors' calculations)

the platinum group metal effects are highly cyclical. We show the lead-lag relations with output growth in Fig. 12.14 in the Appendix.

Overall, we conclude that mining commodities and sectors specifically geared at the exports markets have a significant leading positive effect on the mining sector output growth and employment growth. The South African Chamber of Mines shows that between 80 and 90 per cent of production is exported with the exception for coal where roughly 40 per cent is used for domestic consumption for energy production.[3]

12.4 Is There a Prevalence of the "*Exports-Led Growth*" Hypothesis Over the "*Growth-Driven Exports*" Hypothesis?

The key question raised in this chapter is whether export-led growth results in employment (job) creation in the mining sector. The stylised facts in the earlier sections suggest that this is the case for mining sector as opposed to the aggregate (broader) economy where we find that there is bi-directional causality from exports growth and GDP growth. This section tests for the prevalence or dominance of the exports growth versus the GDP growth channels in the broader economy and the mining sector in particular. We estimate a number of VAR models which include the data discussed in the earlier section. The first model estimated follows the ordering of the variables as shown in Fig. 12.3 and includes aggregate exports growth, GDP growth and private sector employment growth. The models are estimated using 2 lags and 10,000 Monte Carlo draws. The sample uses quarterly data and spans the period 2000Q1 to 2016Q4. The shocks are a one standard deviation. We do reverse ordering of the variables in the model to test for the robustness of the results.

The results in Fig. 12.9(e) indicate that exports growth responds more, and the positive effects tend to be persistent due to GDP growth compared to the responses of GDP growth to exports growth. At peak, exports growth increase by 4.2 percentage points due to a positive GDP growth shock. This exceeds the increase of 0.31 percentage points in GDP growth due to a positive exports growth shock in Fig. 12.10. Thus, we conclude that the "*GDP growth-driven exports growth*" hypothesis is stronger than the "*exports growth-led GDP growth hypothesis*". These results are robust

---

[3]This special dispensation for the coal mining industry possibly explains the high intensity and persistence of employment in this sector. The guaranteed domestic demand and price cushions the coal mining sector from the other external factors that influence commodity prices.

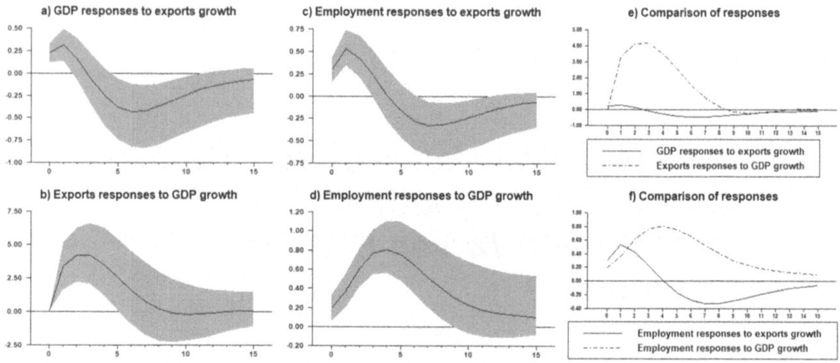

Fig. 12.9 Responses to GDP and exports growth. (Note: The grey shaded area bands denote the 16th and 84th percentile confidence bands. Source: Authors' calculations)

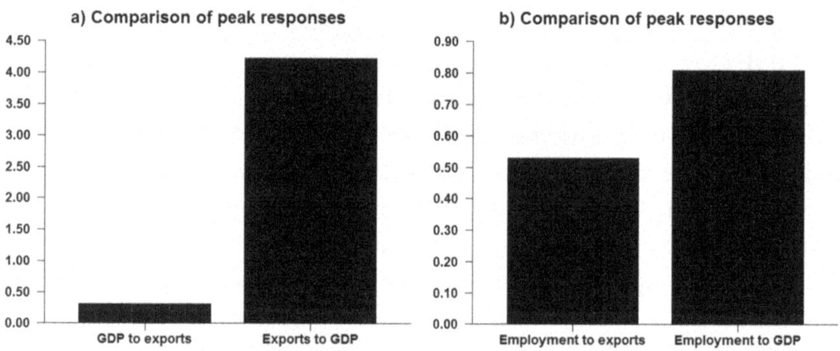

Fig. 12.10 Comparison of peak responses. (Source: Authors' calculations)

and corroborate earlier findings established in the stylised facts and the Granger causality tests.

Furthermore, evidence indicates that private sector non-agriculture employment growth generated by positive GDP growth shock far exceeds and persists compared to that due to positive exports growth shock. At peak response, employment growth increases by 0.81 percentage points due to a positive GDP growth shock compared to 0.53 percentage points due to a positive exports growth shock in Fig. 12.10. In addition, the slump in exports growth results in a pronounced decline in employment growth.

Thus, we conclude that exports growth exerts very limited positive effects on GDP growth. The direct impact of exports growth on employment growth confirms the findings in Ancharaz (2011) that Africa's experience with the export-led strategy seems to be quite disappointing. The impressive exports growth performance in recent years has not generated significant and persistent employment opportunities. Nonetheless, we reject the "*export-led jobless growth*" hypothesis. This is because positive exports growth shocks do increase GDP growth and employment growth. But the increase is not persistent and do not result in intensive employment growth. Hence, the export-led strategy seems to be quite disappointing.

The results imply that exports growth contributes very little to GDP growth. But GDP growth tends to stimulate exports growth more. Theory suggests that exports growth is positively dependent on foreign growth (income). We proxy foreign growth (income) with foreign GDP growth and global import growth by assessing the impact of G7 and the Chinese GDP growth and global import growth on South African exports growth. The results may imply the indirect role of foreign growth and import demand spill-over effects on the South African GDP growth. Gumata and Ndou (2019) showed that BRICS GDP growth shocks are a source of global GDP growth shocks and an amplifier of responses to GDP growth shocks. The BRICS GDP growth amplify the effects of adverse economic shocks such as the global financial crisis and uncertainty. In addition, commodity price shocks lead to positive responses of G7 growth and that BRICS, EMEs (excluding China) and BIITS amplify the effects of positive commodity shock on G7 economies.

There are channels which may explain the weak influence of exports growth on GDP growth. These channels link the role of the exchange rate depreciation and its volatility on exports growth. Ndou et al. (2017) show that the failure of the real exchange rate depreciation shock to stimulate economic growth via the exports channel is due to the domination of the contractionary exchange rate depreciation effects on the real investment growth channel. In addition, the beneficial effect of the real and nominal exchange rate depreciation shock on exports growth may be neutralised by the contractionary effects of the real exchange rate depreciation on investment and economic growth. Thus, when confronted by the large exchange rate depreciation shocks, policymakers need to understand the role of the balance sheet channel and the contractionary effects of large depreciations on investment and output growth. These effects far outweigh those of competitiveness and exports growth. The balance sheet channel is a drag on investment following depreciation. Hence, there is need for a serious re-assessment of the exchange rate policy.

The volatility of the exchange rate offsets or neutralises the effects of the depreciation to a large degree. The exchange rate risk has negative effects on export revenue. Hence, policy directed at a systematic depreciation of the exchange rate to stimulate the exports performance may not yield successful results as part of the depreciation effects are offset by the exchange rate risk.

12.4.1 Does the "*Exports-Led Growth*" Hypothesis Hold in the Mining Sector?

This section tests the "*exports-led growth*" hypothesis for the aggregate mining and commodity sector. We estimate a number of VAR models which include output, exports and employment growth data for aggregate mining and the commodity sectors, namely, coal, platinum group, metal ores and other minerals and commodities. We show the peak effects in Fig. 12.11. The results in the second column of Fig. 12.11 show that across minerals commodities in the mining sector, the "exports-led growth" hypothesis dominates the "GDP growth-driven exports" hypothesis in Fig. 12.11(b), (d), (f), (h) and (j). Employment growth in the mining sector is largely driven by exports growth. This is contrary to evidence established for aggregate GDP growth, exports growth and employment growth. These results concur with the fact that the South African mining sector is an export-driven industry with very little value add. As such, targeted interventions in the mining sector can lead to increased output growth and employment growth.

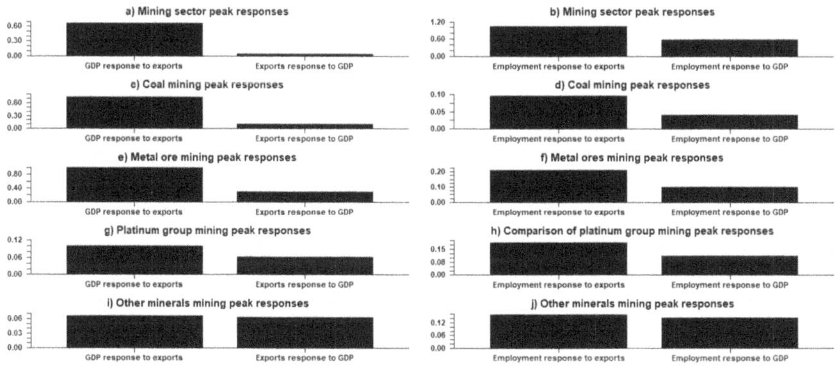

Fig. 12.11 Comparison of peak responses to mining and commodity output and exports growth. (Source: Authors' calculations)

12.4.2 The Role of Foreign Demand

This section explores the role of foreign GDP growth by assessing the impact of G7 GDP growth and China GDP growth on South African exports growth. We include the GDP growth for the G7 economies and China in the estimation of the VAR model. These variables are included separately in the models. Figure 12.12(c) and (e) shows that South African GDP growth and exports respond more to G7 GDP growth and China GDP growth.

At peak response, the South African GDP growth and exports growth responses are almost half the peak responses due to G7 GDP growth. The results underpin the importance of China GDP growth for South African economic activity.

12.4.3 Is Foreign Demand a Catalyst for Mining Exports, Output and Employment Growth?

To differentiate the analysis for aggregate South African GDP growth responses to positive foreign GDP growth, we use global and the Chinese imports growth to assess the responsiveness of South African commodity exports growth. Furthermore, we include commodity prices in the analy-

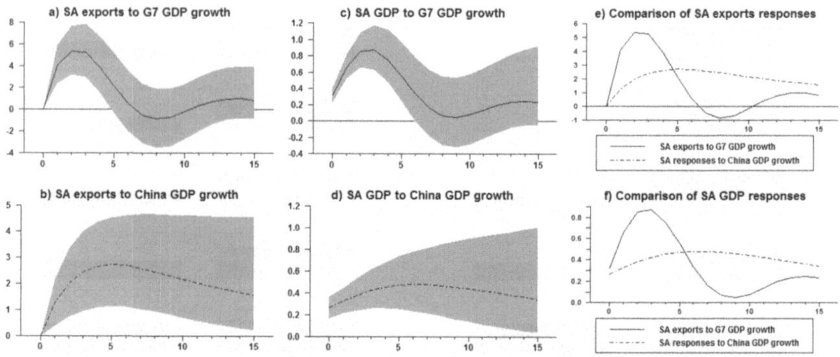

Fig. 12.12 Comparison of South African GDP and exports responses to positive G7 and Chinese GDP growth shocks. (Note: The grey shaded area bands denote the 16th and 84th percentile confidence bands. Source: Authors' calculations)

sis to assess their role. We assess the impact of positive global GDP growth and the Chinese imports growth shocks on aggregate mining and commodity sectors, namely, coal, platinum group, metal ores and other minerals and commodities. Various VAR models are estimated which include commodity prices, GVAs, exports and employment growth of the different commodity sectors. The commodity sector specific variables are included individually in the estimations. First, the VAR models are estimated to derive the response shown in Fig. 12.13(a) and (b). Second, various counterfactual VAR models are estimated to derive the propagations effects of commodity prices in Fig. 12.13(c). The counterfactual VAR models estimate the actual and counterfactual responses in the presence and absence of the commodity price channel. Thereafter, the difference between the actual and counterfactual responses is calculated to derive the propagations effects of the commodity price channel in Fig. 12.13(c).

The results in Fig. 12.13 show that world and China import growth are important for mining commodity exports. The results in Fig. 12.13(a) concur with reports by the South African Chamber of Mines that the bulk (around 45 per cent) of South African coal exports are destined to India. This direction of South African coal exports is because Europe as a traditional coal export market declined as the Netherlands, Belgium and

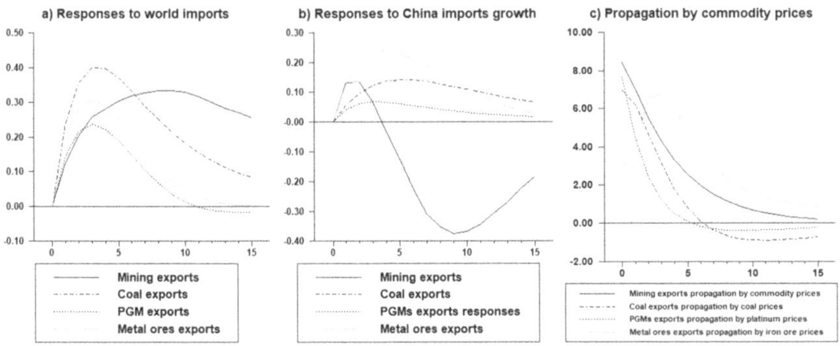

Fig. 12.13 Comparison of commodity mining exports responses to world and China imports growth shocks and amplification by commodity prices. (Source: Authors' calculations)

the UK started to implement strict compliance to environmental laws to comply with the Kyoto Protocol. Positive shocks to the Chinese imports growth accounts for almost half of the responses of mining commodities to world import growth and this is particularly the case for metal ores exports.

At the same time, commodity prices play an important role in propagating the positive global imports growth shocks in Fig. 12.13(c). Thus, we conclude that commodity prices are catalysts for the transmission of positive foreign demand shocks on mining exports growth, output growth and employment growth.

Do the results present a strong case for minerals beneficiation? Yes, we conclude that there is a strong case for minerals beneficiation especially for the mining commodity sectors. We establish that exports growth is intensively associated with mining commodity employment growth and less so with mining commodity output growth. Hence, the contribution of the mining sector to GDP growth has been on a circular decline and so low. The mining sector is an export-driven sector with very limited value add. By the very nature, the strategy of minerals beneficiation implies an increase in the value added and a bigger role of the manufacturing sector in GDP.

12.5 Conclusion and Policy Implications

This chapter explores whether there is a prevalence of the "*exports growth-led GDP growth*" hypothesis over the "*GDP growth-driven exports growth*" hypothesis. At the aggregate and commodity sector level, evidence suggests that exports growth responds more to aggregate GDP growth compared to the responses of GDP growth to aggregate and commodity sector exports growth. For instance, at peak, exports growth increase by 4.2 percentage points due to a positive shock to GDP growth compared to an increase of 0.31 percentage points in GDP growth due to a positive shock to exports growth. Thus, we conclude that there is a prevalence of the "*GDP growth-driven exports growth*" hypothesis over the "*exports growth-led GDP growth*" hypothesis. These results are robust and corroborate findings established by the Granger causality tests.

On the other hand, evidence for the mining and specific commodity sectors confirms the validity of the dominance of the "*exports growth-led GDP growth*" hypothesis over the "GDP growth-driven exports growth" hypothesis. Evidence shows that exports growth is intensively associated with mining commodity employment growth and less so with mining commodity output growth. Hence, the contribution of the mining sector to GDP growth has been on a circular decline and so low. The mining sector is an export-driven sector with very limited value add.

Furthermore, evidence indicates that private sector non-agriculture employment growth generated by positive shocks to GDP growth far exceeds and persists compared to that due to positive shocks to exports growth. At peak response, employment growth increases by 0.81 percentage points due to positive shocks to GDP growth compared to 0.53 percentage points due to a positive shock to exports growth. Thus, we reject the "*export-led jobless growth*" hypothesis. Positive shocks to exports growth do induce positive effects on GDP and employment growth. But these positive effects are not persistent and do not result in intensive employment growth. Hence, the export-led strategy seems to be quite disappointing. Export-led growth is a necessary but insufficient condition for job creation in the mining sector.

Does this mean that there is a strong case for beneficiation? Yes, evidence leads us to arrive at a conclusion that there is a strong case for minerals beneficiation especially for the commodity sectors. We establish that exports growth is intensively associated with aggregate and commodity sector employment growth and less so with aggregate and commodity sector output growth. Hence, the contribution of the mining sector to GDP growth has been on a circular decline and very low. By the very nature, minerals beneficiation implies an increase in value added and a bigger role for the manufacturing sector in GDP. The policy implication is that strategies aimed at investing in the value chains for these mining commodity sectors, developing new export markets and cushioning the sector against the cyclicality and severe slumps in global demand and commodity prices will support the mining sector as a "*sunrise industry*".

Appendix

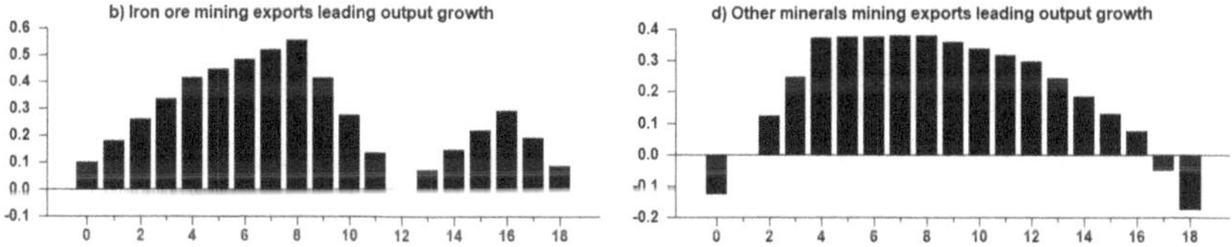

Fig. 12.14 Coal, iron ore, PGMs and other mineral commodity exports and output growth relationship. (Note: PGMs = platinum group metals. Source: Statistics South Africa, South African Chamber of Mines and authors' calculations)

References

Agosin, M. R. 2007. *Export Diversification and Growth in Emerging Economies.* Working Paper No. 233.

Ahmed, S., Appendino, M., and Ruta, M. 2015. *Global Value Chains and the Exchange Rate Elasticity of Exports.* IMF Working Paper WP/15/252.

Ancharaz, V. 2011. An Empirical Investigation of the Export-led Jobless Growth Hypothesis. African Development Bank.

Awokuse, T.O. 2006. Is the Export-Led Growth Hypothesis Valid for Canada? *The Canadian Journal of Economics*, 36(1) (Feb., 2003), 126–36.

Connolly, E., and Orsmond, D. 2011. *The Mining Industry: From Bust to Boom.* Research Reserve Bank of Australia. Discussion Paper 2011-08.

Eyraud, L. 2015. *End of the Super-cycle and Growth of Commodity Producers: The Case of Chile.* IMF Working Paper WP/15/242.

Fornero, J., and Kirchner, M. 2014. *Learning About Commodity Cycles and Savings-Investment Dynamics in a Commodity Exporting Economy.* Working Papers Central Bank of Chile WP 727.

Giles, J.A., and Williams, C.L. 2000. Export-Led Growth: A Survey of the Empirical Literature and Some Non-causality Results. Part 1. *Journal of International Trade & Economic Development*, 9, 261–337.

Gumata, N., and Ndou, E. 2019. *Capital Flows, Credit Markets and Growth in South Africa: The Role of Global Economic Growth, Policy Shifts and Uncertainties.* Palgrave Macmillan. ISBN 978-3-030-30887-2.

Heiko, H. 2008. *Export Diversification and Economic Growth.* Working Paper of the Commission on Growth and Development.

Leautier, F., and Hanson, K.T. 2013. Jobless Economic Growth in Africa: Is there a Role for Agriculture? *Journal of African Development*, 15(2), 1–17. African Finance and Economic Association (EFEA).

Michaely, M. 1977. Exports and Economic Growth: An Empirical Investigation. *Journal of Development Economics*, 4, 49–53.

Ndou, E., Gumata, N., and Ncube, M. 2017. *Global Economic Uncertainties and Exchange Rate Shocks.* Palgrave Macmillan. ISBN 978-3-319-62279-8.

Park, J.H., and Prime, P.B. 1997. Export Performance and Growth in China: A Cross Provincial Analysis. *Applied Economics*, 29, 1353–63.

Sachs, J.D., and Warner, A.M. 2001. The Curse of Natural Resources. *European Economic Review*, 45, 827–38.

13

The Impact of Mining Commodity Price Booms and Sharp Exchange Rate Depreciation Episodes on Mining Output and Employment Growth

Learning Objectives

- Establish commodity mining boom and bust episodes.
- Explore whether the commodity mining booms and busts coincide with sharp R/US$ exchange rate deprecations and appreciations and capital flow surge and sudden stop episodes.
- Establish whether South Africa missed out on recent commodity price booms.
- Explore the implications of the concurrence of commodity price booms and sharp R/US$ exchange rate depreciations on mining sector output and employment growth.

13.1 Introduction

Earlier chapters showed the important role commodity prices play in the propagation of positive to global demand and output growth shocks to domestic mining exports growth, output growth and employment growth in the sectors that will be pillars for mining as a "*sunrise*" industry. Evidence

N. Gumata, E. Ndou, *Accelerated Land Reform, Mining, Growth, Unemployment and Inequality in South Africa*, https://doi.org/10.1007/978-3-030-30884-1_13

showed that commodity mining exports have a persistent positive effect on mining output growth and employment growth. Nonetheless, we also noted the cyclicality induced by global demand and commodity price shocks. This chapter extends the analysis on the mining sector by exploring the role of sharp exchange rate depreciations, mining asset and commodity price booms and bust episodes in explaining severe output losses and employment growth slumps. In addition, this chapter explores whether South Africa missed out on recent commodity price booms.

Figure 13.1 shows that commodity prices explain 73 per cent of the variation in mining exports growth. Mining exports growth increases when lead by commodity prices in Fig. 13.1(c). This means that commodity price developments are important to the mining sector. Evidence in earlier chapters showed that the mining sector is such a significant contributor to export earnings and that export-oriented policy interventions and minerals beneficiation will assist in improving the intensity of the mining sector contribution to aggregate output growth and employment creation. If that is the case, what are the implications of the concurrence of mining asset and commodity price booms? Furthermore, what is the impact of the concurrence of sharp and persistent exchange rate depreciations and mining commodity price booms on mining output growth and employment growth? Do sharp exchange rate depreciation

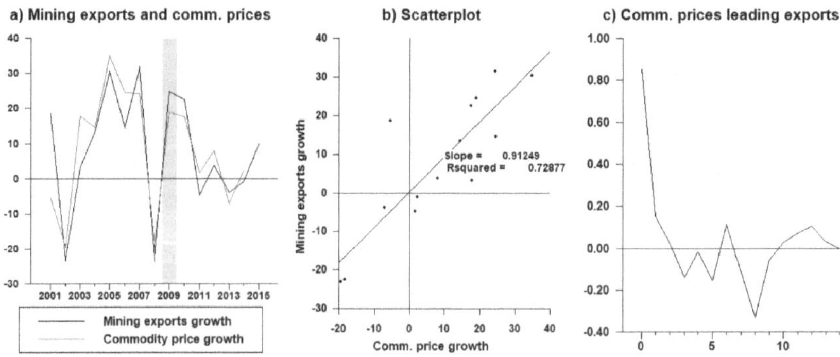

Fig. 13.1 Mining exports and commodity prices. (Note: Comm. prices = commodity prices. Grey shaded areas denote the South African recession. Source: South African Chamber of Mines, South African Reserve Bank and authors' calculations)

shocks propagate the effects of mining asset price busts? In essence, the question we are asking is whether there is an exchange rate depreciation dividend on the mining sector output growth and employment growth.

13.2 The Identification of Booms and Busts

This section starts by discussing the approaches used to identify periods of commodity price booms and busts. We use two techniques, namely:

1. Threshold techniques, namely, Fatas et al. (2009) and Borgy et al. (2009), to date episodes of asset price booms and busts
2. The Bry-Boschan (BBQ) algorithm and Harding and Pagan (2002b) approaches to date turning points, calculate the amplitude, duration and synchronisation of cycles

Fatas et al. (2009) and Borgy et al. (2009) use moving averages to define periods of booms and busts. Periods of booms (busts) are identified when the 4-quarter or 12-month moving average of the financial variable exceeds (are below) some growth rate threshold. Borgy et al. (2009) set the threshold for the boom (bust) at 15 (−15) per cent of the four-quarter moving average of the financial variable. Bordo and Jeanne (2002) set the thresholds for the boom (bust) 20 (−20) per cent. The boom (bust) 20 (−20) per cent episodes are comparable to positive (negative) one standard deviation from trend as done in some band-pass filter techniques.

The classical cycle dating techniques are typically used to study cycles in real economic activity. However, Pagan and Sossounov (2003) and Cashin et al. (2002) have applied these dating methods in empirical research into asset markets such as equity and commodity prices. The classical business cycle dating techniques are based on Burns and Mitchell (1946) who laid the methodological foundation for the analysis of business cycles in the US. We use the Harding and Pagan (2002b) dating cycle technique to identify the turning points.[1]

[1] Harding and Pagan (2002a) extend the BB algorithm developed by Bry and Boschan (1971).

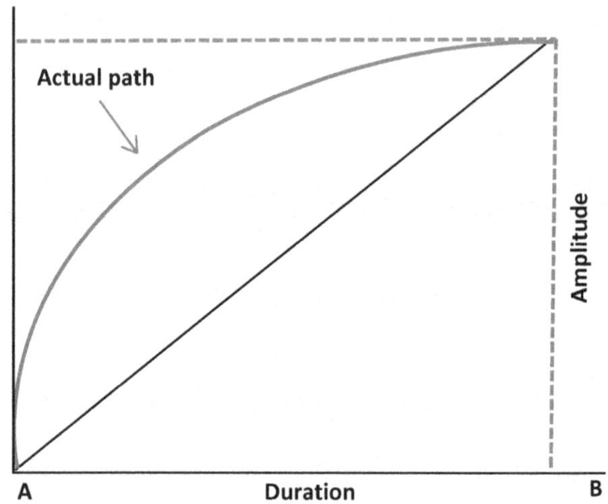

Fig. 13.2 Key features of the cyclical phases. (Source: Adapted from Harding and Pagan (2002a))

The Harding and Pagan (2002a) dating cycle technique requires a search for maxima and minima over a given period. Then, it selects pairs of adjacent, locally absolute maxima and minima that meet certain censoring rules. The Bry-Boschan algorithm then develops a procedure for ensuring that peaks and troughs alternate. It imposes that in the presence of a double trough, the lowest value is chosen, whereas, in the presence of a double peak, the highest value is chosen. The censoring rules are also imposed on the minimum duration of phases. The key features of the cyclical phases are their duration, amplitude and slope as shown in Fig. 13.2. The *duration* for recessions (downturns) is defined as the number of quarters (months) between *the peak and the trough*. In turn, the duration for upturns is defined as the time it takes to attain the level at the previous peak after the trough. Disruptions (booms) correspond to the bottom (top) 25 per cent of downturns (upturns) in terms of amplitude.

Downturns (upturns) refer to episodes other than disruptions (booms). A credit downturn (or upturn) is accompanied with a housing bust (boom), if it starts at the same time or after the beginning of an ongoing housing episode. The *amplitude* is the absolute distance between *the trough (peak) and peak (trough).*

13.3 Measuring the Synchronisation of Cycles: The Harding and Pagan Approach

To examine the extent of *cyclical co-movement or synchronisation across mining asset and commodity price cycles,* we use the concordance index developed by Harding and Pagan (2002b) and the cross-correlation techniques. There is strong perfect positive synchronisation (SPPS) between two series or cycles S_{it} and S_{jt} when the conditions in Eqs. (13.1a) and (13.1b) are satisfied.

$$\left(\Pr\left[S_{it}=1, S_{jt}=0\right]\right)=0. \tag{13.1a}$$

$$\left(\Pr\left[S_{it}=0, S_{jt}=1\right]\right)=0. \tag{13.1b}$$

On the other hand, there is strong perfect negative synchronisation (SPNS) when the conditions in Eqs. (13.2a) and (13.2b) are satisfied.

$$\left(\Pr\left[S_{it}=1, S_{jt}=0\right]\right)=1. \tag{13.2a}$$

$$\left(\Pr\left[S_{it}=0, S_{jt}=1\right]\right)=1. \tag{13.2b}$$

Cycles are independent or strongly non-synchronised (SNS) when the two series or cycles S_{it} and S_{jt} are independent. The series are perfectly procyclical (countercyclical) if the index is equal to zero (unity). The concordance index provides a measure of the fraction of time the two series or cycles S_{it} and S_{jt} are in the same phase of their respective cycles. This is different to directly focusing on the turning points of the variables as a degree of synchronisation. The concordance index measures the probability that the cycles of the variables will coincide. To construct the concordance cycle, a dummy variable S_{it} is created for each variable i. The dummy variable takes the value of one when the cycle is going through an upward phase and zero otherwise. Then the *concordance index* is constructed as the probability that cycles are simultaneously going through the same phases.

The concordance index has a maximum value of 1 and a minimum value of 0. The value of 1 occurs when $S_{it} = S_{jt}$ and zero when $S_{it} = \left(1 - S_{jt}\right)$ takes the values of 0. Similarly, when $\hat{\sigma} S_{it} S_{ij} = \hat{\sigma}^2_{S_{it}}$, $\hat{\rho}_S = 1$ means that the concordance is equal to one. When $\hat{\rho}_S = -1$, the concordance index is equal to zero. This means that when the phases coincide the concordance index is equal to 1 and when the phases are in opposite direction, the index is equal to zero.

In cases when there is no synchronisation between the phases over the entire sample period, the index takes the value of 0.5. In addition, to definitively conclude about the synchronisation of cycles, the correlation tests and coefficients p_{ij} between the dummy variables is computed. The correlation test ascertains whether I_c is statistically different from 0.5. The test is for the null hypothesis $p_{ij} = 0$ against the alternative $p_{ij} \neq 0$ for pairs of cycles. We also use the cross-correlation plot between the pairs of cycles. Over and above the dates of the cycles, the most important statistics in relation to synchronisation and the concordance index are $\hat{I}_S, \hat{\rho}_S, \hat{\mu}_S$.

13.4 Identification of Booms and Bust Episodes Based on the Threshold Techniques

This section identifies (i) boom episodes for mining commodity and asset prices and (ii) periods of sharp R/US$ exchange rate depreciation. The sample size spans the period 1994Q1 to 2017Q4 depending on the availability of the data. The data is sourced from the South African Reserve

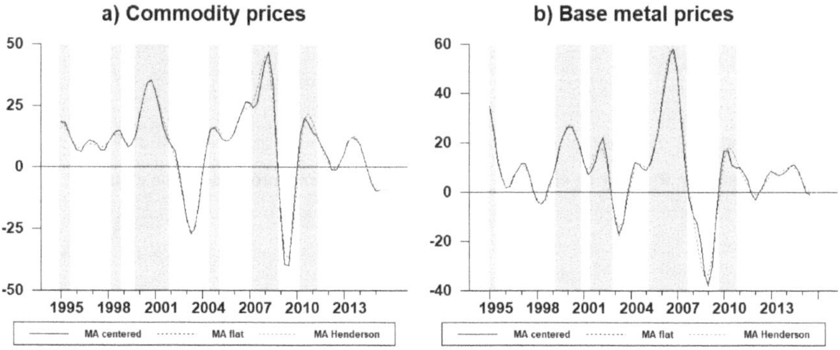

Fig. 13.3 Identified boom episodes for base metal and commodity prices. (Source: South African Reserve Bank, Reserve Bank of Australia and authors' calculations)

Bank, Reserve Bank of Australia, IMF and South African Chamber of Mines databases. As stated in the earlier section, we use the Fatas et al. (2009) and Borgy et al. (2009) to date episodes of mining commodity and asset price booms and busts.

Figure 13.3 shows the identified boom episodes for commodity and base metal prices. We identify six boom episodes for South African commodity prices and five episodes for base metal prices. Although the boom episodes tend to be highly synchronised, their duration and amplitudes differ. The aspects of the synchronisation, duration and amplitude of mining commodity prices, asset prices and the R/US$ exchange rate are explored in detail in the next sections.

Largely due to the fact that Fig. 13.3 indicates the significant role played by the R/US$ in determining the trend and trajectory of commodity prices. We also date the boom and bust episode for mining equity prices, different commodity prices and sharp R/US$ exchange rate depreciation and appreciation episodes.[2] In Fig. 13.4 the grey shaded episodes are equivalent to episodes when the R/US$ depreciated by more than 15 per cent.

[2] Figure 13.19 shows the stylised facts between the R/US$ exchange rate, platinum, coal and iron ore prices. There is a positive relationship between the R/US$ exchange rate and these commodity prices. The lead relationships indicate that changes in the R/US$ exchange rate lead to an increase in platinum, iron ore and coal prices.

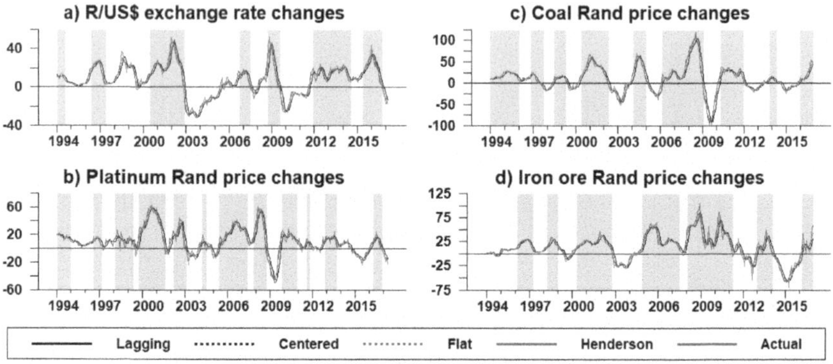

Fig. 13.4 The exchange rate of the R/US$, platinum, coal and iron ore prices. (Note: Grey shaded areas in Fig. 13.4(a) are equivalent to R/US$ exchange rate depreciations more than 15 per cent. The grey shaded areas in Fig. 13.4(b), (c) and (d) are equivalent to periods of commodity price increases above 15 per cent. Source: South African Reserve Bank, Reserve Bank of Australia and authors' calculations)

Figure 13.4 shows that we identify seven episodes of the R/US$ exchange rate depreciation above the 15 per cent threshold. The recent exchange rate depreciation during 2011Q3 to 2014Q2 is the longest in duration in recent history, and it was shortly followed by a sharp depreciation that exceeded the 20 per cent threshold for a considerable period. The period between 2011Q3 and 2016Q3 marked the longest R/US$ exchange rate depreciation in recent history.

Figure 13.4(b), (c) and (d) show that the platinum, coal and iron ore prices have several boom episodes which are very different in peak and amplitude.

In addition, these mining commodity price boom episodes do not necessarily coincide with each other, nor do they necessarily coincide with the exchange rate depreciations. Nonetheless, it is evident that the mining commodity price boom that started in the early 2000s up to the end of 2002 coincided with the exchange rate depreciation. This episode is in contrast with the mining commodity price booms that started in 2005Q3 to 2008Q4 and the period post-2009Q1. The difference being that the trough and the correction in 2009 was the severest on record and coincided with a severe exchange rate appreciation.

Post-financial crisis and the recession in 2009, the trajectories of the mining commodity price boom episodes are less synchronised with each other and with the exchange rate depreciation. It is also evident that the iron ore prices did not suffer a severe correction in 2009, as was the case with the other commodity prices. The appreciation of the exchange rate in 2017 resulted in the correction and commodity prices are moving in different directions.[3] Contrary to the platinum price moving in the opposite direction (declining) to the appreciation of the exchange rate, the iron ore and coal prices are moving in the same direction and increasing.[4] The increase in the iron ore and coal prices is occurring at the same time as the appreciation of the exchange rate.

We stated earlier that commodity price booms tend to be associated with asset price booms. Using the aggregate mining, gold mining and platinum share price returns as commodity mining sector asset prices, we establish the boom episodes as shown in Fig. 13.5. There have been several boom episodes and the prolonged boom occurred between 2005 and 2008. The boom post-2009 was very brief in comparison. It is also evident that the platinum shares dominate the evolution of the aggregate mining share price returns.

Literature shows that often, asset and commodity price boom episodes are accompanied by severe and prolonged credit growth booms. Figure 13.6 shows that this is indeed the case. The commodity price and asset price boom episodes in Figs. 13.4 and 13.5 of during 2004 and 2008 were highly synchronised with the credit boom episodes of aggregate and sectoral credit shown in Fig. 13.6. Nonetheless, the period post-2009 is different as the commodity price and asset price booms have not been accompanied by any boom episode in credit growth.

[3] See trends shown in Fig. 13.13.

[4] What does this mean? We estimate a number of three variable VAR models to assess the sensitivity of the commodity sector output and employment growth to the R/US$ appreciations and depreciations. We create two dummy variables (i) which takes the value of the R/US$ appreciation and zero otherwise and (ii) which takes on the value of the R/US$ depreciation and zero otherwise. At any given point, the VAR model includes output and employment growth for non-gold mining or platinum or coal or metal ores or the R/US$ exchange rate depreciation or appreciation dummy variable. A comparison of the peak responses based on commodity mining sectors is shown in Fig. 13.20.

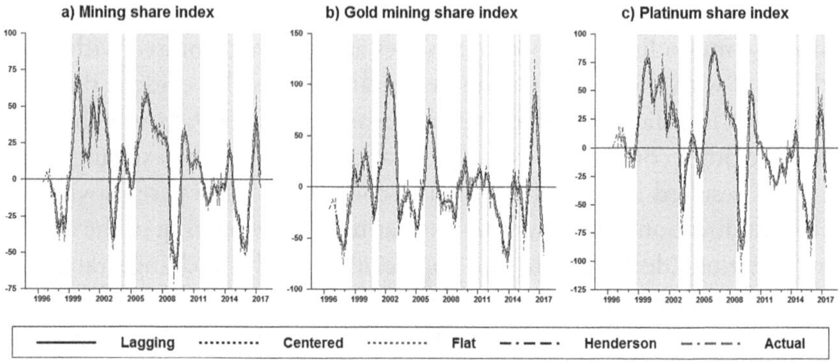

Fig. 13.5 Mining equity price booms and busts. (Source: South African Reserve Bank and authors' calculations)

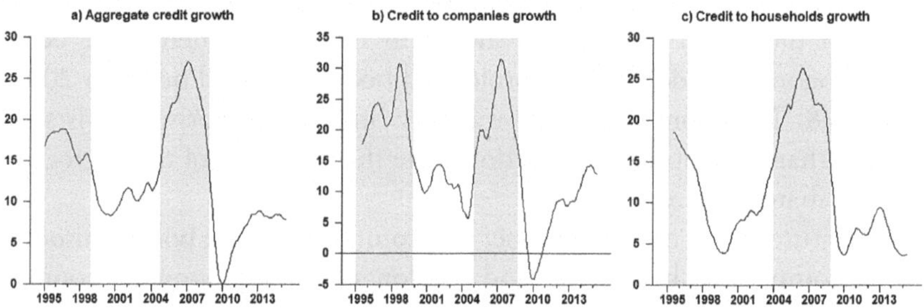

Fig. 13.6 Total and sectorial credit booms episodes. (Source: South African Reserve Bank and authors' calculations)

13.5 How Do Sharp Exchange Rate Appreciations and Depreciations Coincide with Capital Flow Surges and Sudden Stop Episodes?

This section uses the classification of capital flow episodes identified in Forbes and Warnock (2011). The authors distinguish between capital flow waves according to (i) sudden stops that occur when foreign capital inflows suddenly slow or stop, (ii) surges which happen when foreign capital inflows increase rapidly, (iii) retrenchment which occur when domestic investors liquidate their foreign investments and (iv) capital flight which occurs when domestic investors send large amounts of capital abroad. This classification also means that domestic investors are not cut off from global capital markets.

Similar to the approach followed in Gumata and Ndou (2019), we generate dummy variables that capture the capital flow episodes separately. We set the dummy variables equal to one for the period identified by Forbes and Warnock (2011) and zero otherwise. This is done for each capital flow wave episode, namely, a sudden stop episode and capital inflow surge episodes. Evidence in Gumata and Ndou (2019) showed that a capital flow surges shock leads to the R/US$ exchange rate appreciation. In contrast, heightened VIX[5] and sudden stop shocks, respectively, lead to the R/US$ exchange rate depreciation on impact by about 5 percentage points within 2 quarters. Hence, we assess the evolution of the R/US$ exchange rate over episodes of capital flow surges and sudden stops.

Figure 13.7(a) shows that periods of capital flow surges do indeed coincide with the R/US$ exchange rate appreciation, whilst Fig. 13.7(b) shows that periods of capital flow sudden stops coincide with the R/US$ exchange rate depreciations.

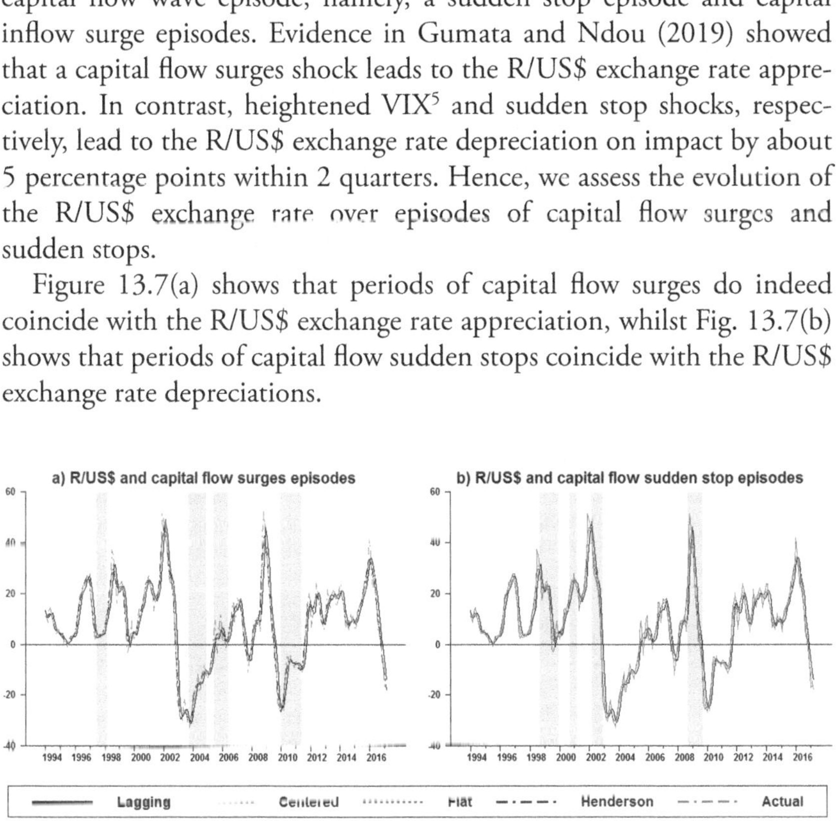

Fig. 13.7 The R/US$ exchange rate and the capital flow episodes. (Source: South African Reserve Bank and authors' calculations)

[5] VIX is the CBOE Volatility Index used to measure of the stock markets' expectations of volatility implied by the S&P500 index options.

13.6 Do Capital Flow Surge and Sudden Stop Episodes Coincide with the Equity and Commodity Price Booms and Busts?

The channels through which the R/US$ exchange rate depreciation and appreciation is transmitted into the macroeconomy are diverse and include the equity and commodity prices channels. In addition, funding for firms also comes in the form of capital inflows; hence we show the performance of the mining equity prices over capital flow surges and sudden stop episodes. Figure 13.8 shows that similar to the R/US$ exchange rate, mining share prices coincide with the capital flow episodes.

The trend analysis so far shows that the R/US$ exchange rate changes and capital flow episodes dominate the evolution of the mining sector share prices. Hence in the empirical section, we assess the propagation effects of sharp R/US$ exchange depreciation effects on commodity mining output and employment growth. The intention is to see whether they reinforce each other in the same direction or counter each other effects.

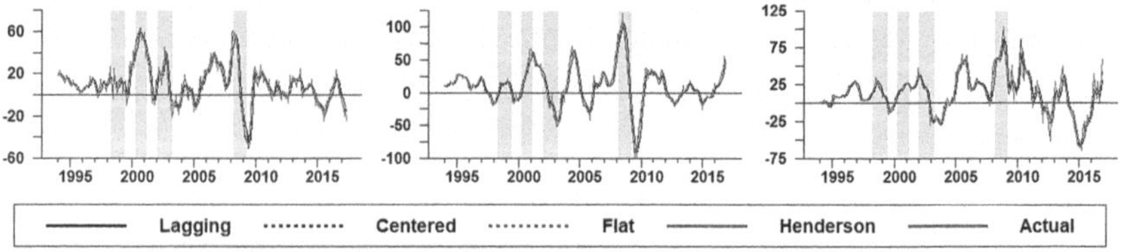

Fig. 13.8 Mining commodity prices, capital flow surges and sudden stop episodes. (Source: South African Reserve Bank and authors' calculations)

13.7 Did South Africa Miss Out from the Commodity Price Super Cycle?

To answer this question, we use the international commodity mining price index in US$, Australian$ and SDR and assess the performance of South African mining exports. We use the boom episodes identified in the earlier sections and assess the evolution of these different measures of commodity prices. First, Fig. 13.9(a) shows that all measures of commodity prices are highly synchronised over the identified commodity price booms.

Second, Fig. 13.9(b), (c) and (d) show that South African commodity prices are positively associated with international commodity prices. The R-squares indicate that the international commodity prices explain around 18 per cent and more of the variation in South African commodity prices. Third, the cross-correlations in Fig. 13.10 indicate that the lead relationships between all commodity prices is high indicating a high level of co-movement over the commodity price cycles.

Last, we assess the performance of South African commodity exports in relation to the Australian resource commodity exports. Figure 13.11 shows that South African and Australian exports performed very well

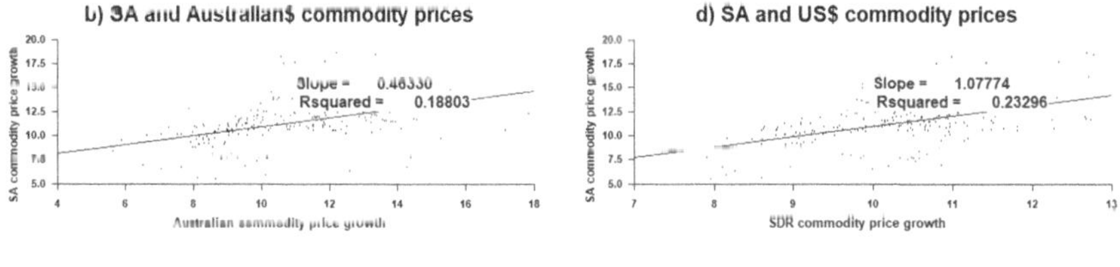

Fig. 13.9 South African and international commodity prices over commodity price booms. (Note: Shaded areas denote the South African recession. Source: South African Reserve Bank, Reserve Bank of Australia and authors' calculations)

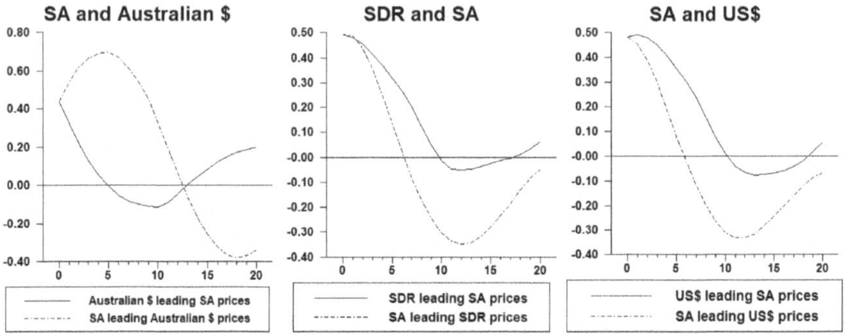

Fig. 13.10 South African and international commodity prices cross-correlations. (Source: South African Reserve Bank, Reserve Bank of Australia and authors' calculations)

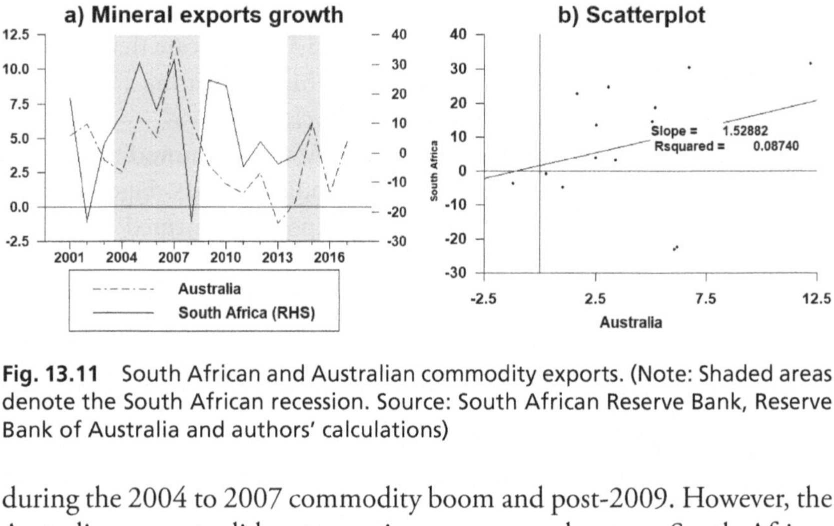

Fig. 13.11 South African and Australian commodity exports. (Note: Shaded areas denote the South African recession. Source: South African Reserve Bank, Reserve Bank of Australia and authors' calculations)

during the 2004 to 2007 commodity boom and post-2009. However, the Australian exports did not experience a severe slump as South African exports did during the global financial crisis. Thus, we conclude that South Africa did not miss out on the commodity price booms contrary to the popular narrative. South Africa participated and benefitted from the recent commodity price booms. Nonetheless, it is very possible that South Africa could have performed even better in taking advantage and managing its commodities given the diverse basket of its mineral resources that are exported.

These results reinforce the findings that strategies aimed at investing in the value chains for mining commodity sectors, the development of new export markets and cushioning the sector against the cyclicality and severe slumps in global demand and commodity prices will support the mining sector as a "*sunrise industry*". The highly cyclical nature of commodity prices and sensitivity to global demand demands a focused strategic approach to managing the mining sector. At the same time, it is necessary that such a strategy forms an integral part of the exchange rate policy and the operationalisation of the unemployment targets in the National Development Plan, the design of the proposed sovereign wealth fund and the co-ordination of the trade and other macroeconomic policies.

13.8 The Sector Mining Output Losses Due to Commodity and Asset Price Busts and Sharp Exchange Rate Appreciations and Depreciations

This section estimates the mining output losses due to mining commodity and asset price busts. We use the Fatas et al. (2009) and Borgy et al. (2009) threshold approaches to date episodes of asset price busts. We identify three bust episodes for South African commodity prices and base metal prices in Fig. 13.12. This contrasts with the identified busts when we consider specific commodity prices in Fig. 13.13. Nonetheless, it is evident that the bust in 2009 was the most severe in comparison to the 2003 episode.

Figure 13.13 shows that the mining commodity price busts are not necessarily synchronised. This was particularly the case during 2005 to 2006 when there was a clear divergence between the trends of platinum, iron ore and coal prices. This was again the case in 2009 when iron ore prices did not experience a bust as was the case with platinum and coal prices. Nonetheless, the downward trend was reversed and there are clear and wide divergences that have emerged since 2017. Platinum prices are in a bust phase compared to the boom episode experienced by the iron ore and coal prices.

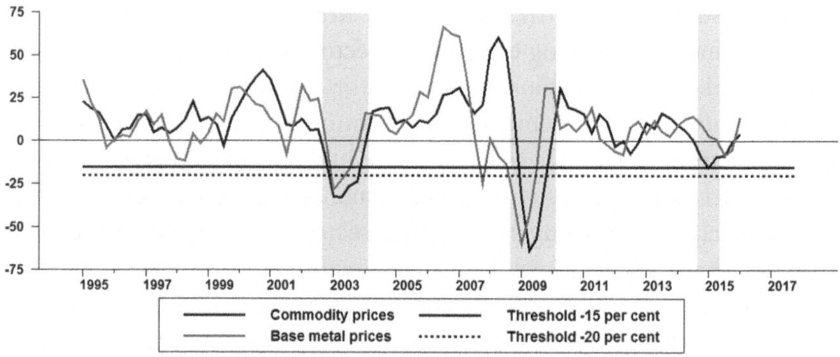

Fig. 13.12 Commodity and base metal price bust episodes. (Note: The grey shaded areas denote commodity price bust episodes. Source: South African Reserve Bank and authors' calculations)

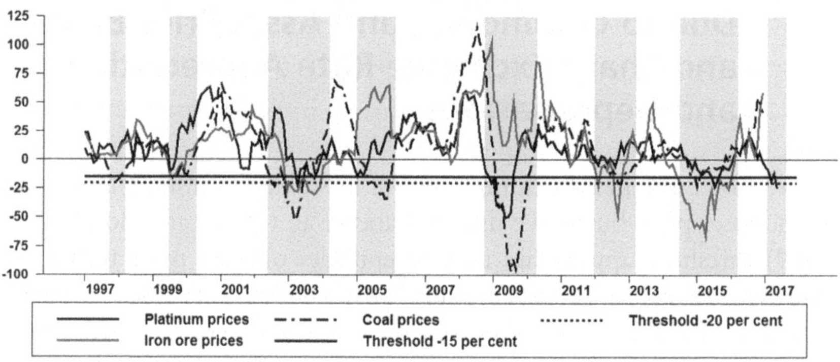

Fig. 13.13 Commodity price bust episodes. (Note: Shaded areas denote the South African recession. Source: South African Reserve Bank and authors' calculations)

Figure 13.14 presents the results for the bust episodes in the mining commodity equity prices. Similar to the trends observed in the commodity prices, we establish that there are periods when they diverge as was the case in 2001 and the early part of 2007 when the platinum prices dominated the developments in the mining stock price index.

The mining commodity equity price bust episodes are highly synchronised. Nonetheless, platinum stock prices tend to experience severe bust episodes as was the case in 2009 and 2015. In addition, we establish that

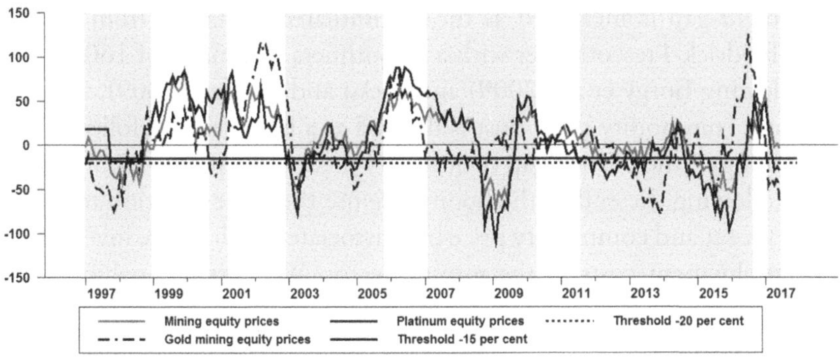

Fig. 13.14 Mining commodity stock price bust episodes. (Note: Shaded areas denote the South African recession. Source: South African Reserve Bank and authors' calculations)

both the gold mining and platinum stock prices are in a bust episode since January 2017.

13.9 What Happens to the Mining Sector Output, Investment and Employment Growth During Assets and Commodity Price Bust Episodes?

To answer this question, this section estimates the degree to which the identified commodity and asset (equity) price busts are associated with severe output (gross value added), investment (gross fixed capital formation) and employment growth. We estimate the economic costs associated with commodity and equity price bust episodes, the duration of the commodity and equity price bust episodes, the average commodity and equity price declines and the size of the output-gaps, investment-gap and employment-gap. The calculations are based on the estimated periods when the asset and commodity price bust occurred based on the four-quarter moving averages and the deviations of output, investment and employment from its potential trend based on the Hodrick-Prescott filter.[6] The cumulative widening in the output-gap, employment-gap and

[6] See Fatas et al. (2009) for further details.

investment-gap is measured as the accumulated deviation from a one-sided Hodrick-Prescott filter with a smoothness parameter of 1600.

Following Borgy et al. (2009) and Alessi and Detken (2009), a costly asset and commodity price bust is defined as a boom that is followed by a widening of the output-gap of at least 3 percentage points within three years following the end of the boom. We use the same criterion to assess a costly asset and commodity price bust associated with severe investment and employment costs in the mining sector. We start by analysing the impact of costly asset and commodity price booms on aggregate mining sector and non-gold sectors. Table 13.1 shows the results for the aggregate mining sector.

Evidence shows that although the commodity price bust during 2009Q1 to 2009Q4 was relatively short in comparison to that during 2002Q4 to 2004Q1, the mean decline in commodity prices, output investment and employment was more severe. The commodity price bust during 2014Q4 to 2016Q1 was also costly in terms of the negative effects on mining output and investment. Furthermore, the results show that the mining commodity price busts exert disproportionate effects and investment and employment growth bears the brunt of the busts.

Table 13.1 Estimated mining output, investment and employment costs associated with commodity price busts

Dates of bust	Duration in quarters (Q)	Mean commodity price changes (%)	Mining output-gap (%)	Mining investment-gap (%)	Mining employment-gap (%)
2002Q4 to 2004Q1	6	−24.79	−1.11	−3.71	−1.60
2009Q1 to 2009Q4	4	−44.71	−3.60	−13.70	−5.18
2012Q1 to 2012Q4	4	−1.78	−1.61	−22.62	−5.61
2014Q4 to 2016Q1	6	−9.02	−2.83	−14.37	−2.27

Source: Authors' calculations

13.9.1 Which Mining Commodity Sectors Are More Responsive to Commodity and Asset Price Busts?

This section explores the sensitivity of the selected mining commodity price gross value added (GVAs) and employment-gaps to sector-specific commodity and asset price busts. Due to data availability, we only analyse the platinum group metals (PGMs), coal and iron ore commodity sectors. We apply the same approach as used to analyse the aggregate mining sector. Table 13.2 shows that the platinum mining commodity sector fortunes have not changed meaningfully post-global financial crisis and recession. The mean platinum price bust phases in 2008Q4 to 2009Q3 and 2016Q4 to 2017Q2 exerted the most severe negative effects of output and employment growth.

Table 13.3 shows that the coal mining sector also had a severe price bust during 2008Q3 to 2009Q3 although it affected output growth more than employment. Nonetheless, the output and employment costs are much less severe when compared to those in the platinum sector.

Table 13.2 Estimated platinum mining busts and associated output and employment costs

Dates of bust	Duration in quarters (Q)	Mean platinum price changes (%)	Mean platinum stock price changes (%)	Platinum mining output-gap (%)	Platinum mining employment-gap (%)
2003Q2 to 2003Q4	3	−10.23	−18.23	−2.97	−10.88
2008Q4 to 2009Q3	4	−38.75	−13.04	−4.93	−6.74
2014Q4 to 2016Q1	5	−8.31	−8.00	−8.62	−6.19
2016Q4 to 2017Q2	3	−19.29		−26.54	−3.10

Source: Authors' calculations

Table 13.3 Estimated coal prices busts, the output and employment gaps

Dates of bust	Duration in quarters (Q)	Mean coal price changes (%)	Coal mining output-gap (%)	Coal mining employment-gap (%)
2004Q2 to 2005Q4	6	−20.20	−1.24	−11.66
2006Q4 to 2007Q2	2	−25.52	−2.03	−4.80
2008Q3 to 2009Q3	4	−60.50	−3.07	−1.96
2010Q4 to 2012Q3	7	−17.86	−3.52	−2.46

Source: Authors' calculations

Table 13.4 Estimated iron ore prices busts, the output and employment gaps

Dates of bust	Duration in quarters (Q)	Mean iron ore price changes (%)	Metal ores mining output-gap (%)	Metal ores mining employment-gap (%)
2001Q4 to 2002Q4	4	−2.42	−0.89	−9.83
2005Q4 to 2007Q4	8	−25.97	−2.85	−9.76
2008Q4 to 2009Q2	2	−15.12	−3.66	−16.41
2010Q2 to 2012Q3	9	−10.66	−0.99	−7.37
2013Q3 to 2015Q1	6	−44.20	−1.02	−6.05

Source: Authors' calculations

Last, Table 13.4 concurs with the earlier results for the platinum and coal sectors. The impact of the iron ore price busts tends to be most felt on employment growth.

Thus, the results in this section show that the cyclicality in mining commodity and asset price boom and bust episodes has severe costs on the mining sector. However, not all mining sector asset and commodity price busts are costly. Furthermore, the costs of the mining asset and commodity price busts differ across mining sector commodities. These findings further reinforce those evidence in earlier chapters indicating that policy interventions need to manage the cyclicality and impact commodity prices on mining output and employment growth.

The three commodity sectors, namely coal, platinum and metal ores, were identified as the sectors that will underpin mining as a "*sunrise*" industry. The strategies and policy interventions in the mining sector should pay attention to (i) the cyclicality of the specific commodity prices; (ii) the duration and amplitudes of the commodity price cycles; (iii) the synchronicity and coincidence of commodity price cycles, capital flow episodes and those of the R/US$ exchange rate; and (iv) the impact of commodity price busts on mining output, investment and employment growth. Understanding the impact of sector-specific commodity price cycles on the mining variables will enhance the awareness of the mining sector dynamics and that it is not a one-size-fits-all approach in terms of the design of policy interventions. There is a need for a centralised policy approach to the mining sector and its role in the economy.

13.10 Episodes of Financial Cycle Boom Episodes and the Amplification Effects on Credit and GDP

To analyse the propagation effects of (i) large sharp R/US$ exchange rate depreciation and appreciations, (ii) commodity price boom and busts on mining commodity output and employment growth, we estimate various VAR models. We complement the techniques used to date boom episodes and the correlation of mining commodity booms. The models include a dummy variable that captures the commodity prices growth boom episodes, mining GDP growth, mining employment growth and the R/US$ exchange rate dummy variable. The dummy variable captures periods of the R/US$ exchange rate deprecation above 10 per cent. The commodity price boom episode dummy variable captures periods during which commodity price growth exceed the 15 per cent increase threshold. The propagation or restraining (stifling) abilities of the specific channel are determined by the gap between actual and counterfactual responses when the variable is active and shut off in the model.

To estimate the effects on the specific commodity mining sectors, we replace the aggregate commodity price, mining output and employment with platinum, coal and iron prices, output and employment. The sectorial VAR models include the commodity price dummy for the boom episode, the R/US$ exchange rate depreciation dummy, output and employment growth for the specific mining commodity sector. The VAR models are estimated for the period 2000Q1 to 2015Q4 and have 2 lags chosen by AIC and the impulse are generated from 10,000 Monte Carlo draws.

In earlier sections, we showed that commodity price booms tend to coincide with R/US$ exchange rate depreciations. Thus, we explore the degree to which the R/US$ depreciation episodes above 10 per cent propagate the commodity price booms effects on output and employment growth. Figure 13.15(a) and (c) shows that non-gold mining output and employment respond positively to a commodity price boom. But the R/US$ exchange rate depreciation propagates the positive effects of the commodity price boom on employment growth in Fig. 13.14(d).

Figure 13.16 presents the results for the platinum mining sector and shows that the R/US$ exchange rate depreciation exerts different propagation effects of a platinum price boom on platinum output and employment growth. The results indicate that the concurrence of a platinum price boom episode and the R/US$ exchange rate depreciation is propagated more on employment growth as opposed to output growth.

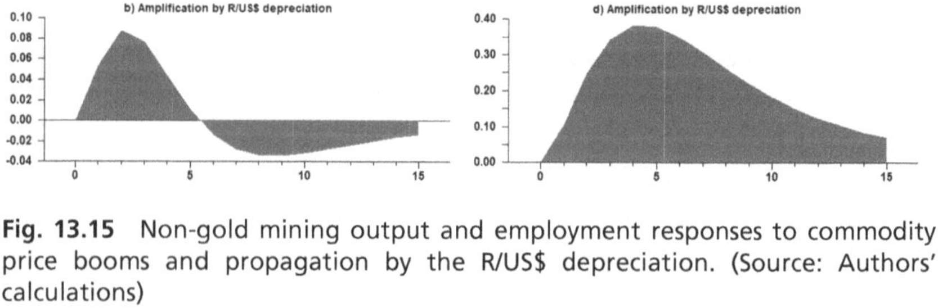

Fig. 13.15 Non-gold mining output and employment responses to commodity price booms and propagation by the R/US$ depreciation. (Source: Authors' calculations)

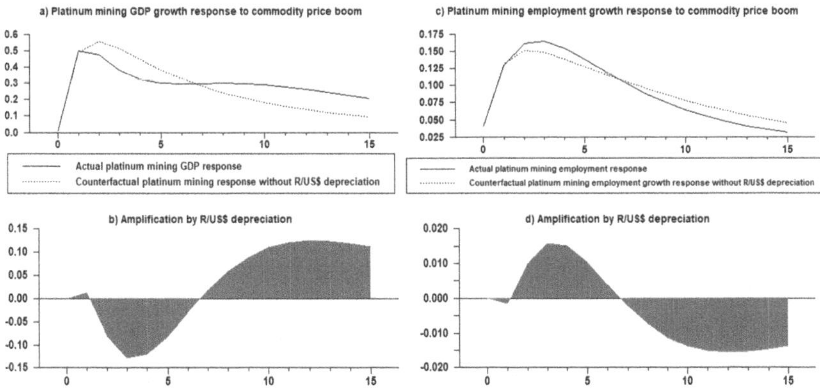

Fig. 13.16 Platinum mining output and employment responses to commodity price booms and propagation by the R/US$ depreciation. (Source: Authors' calculations)

A similar trend emerges in Figs. 13.17 and 13.18, the positive effects of a concurrence of a coal and metal ores price boom are propagated more on employment growth compared to output growth.

The results in this section concur with the evidence showing that the sector-specific commodity prices exert different effects on output and employment growth.

Earlier evidence showed that the platinum and coal sector employment growth is more responsive to positive shocks to the platinum and coal prices as opposed to output growth. These trends are contrary to the metal ores mining sector. Thus, the results of the concurrence of commodity price booms and sharp exchange rate depreciations do not benefit the mining sector gross value added (output growth). These findings corroborate the evidence in showing that employment growth in the mining sector is largely driven by exports growth contrary to evidence established for aggregate GDP growth, exports and employment. The South African mining sector is an export-driven industry with very little value add. Sharp R/US$ exchange rate depreciations shocks do not incentivise the mining sector to improve gross value add (output growth). Sharp exchange rate depreciation episodes are not good for the mining sector output growth.

Therefore, we conclude that a minerals beneficiation strategy which implies an increase in value added and a bigger role for the manufacturing

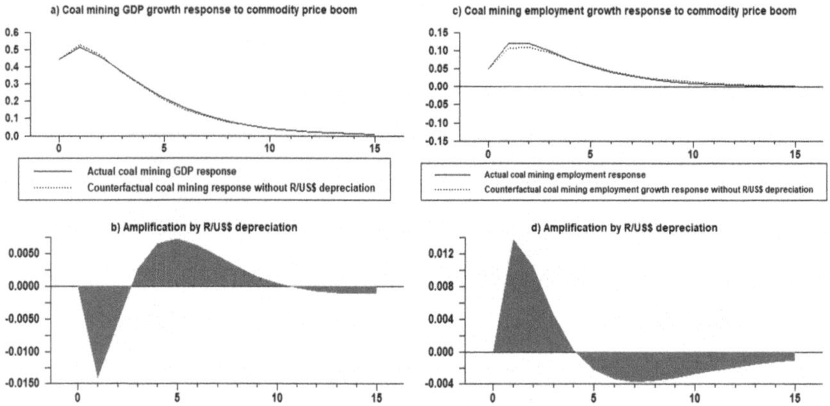

Fig. 13.17 Coal mining output and employment responses to commodity price booms and propagation by the R/US$ depreciation. (Source: Authors' calculations)

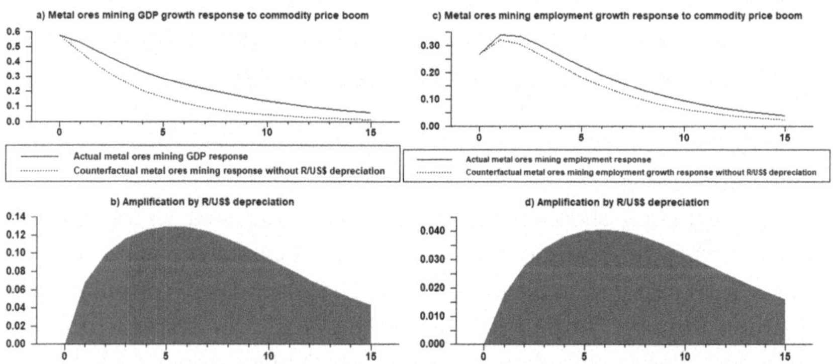

Fig. 13.18 Metal ores mining output and employment responses to commodity price booms and propagation by the R/US$ depreciation. (Source: Authors' calculations)

sector in GDP will improve the contribution of the mining sector to aggregate output growth. At the same time, policy interventions should also take into account the role of the exchange rate, strategies that cushion the sector against the cyclicality and severe slumps in global demand and commodity prices in supporting the mining sector as a "sunrise industry".

13.11 Conclusion and Policy Implications

This chapter starts by establishing the periods during which mining asset and commodity price booms and busts occurred and whether they are necessarily synchronised with each other and sharp R/US$ exchange rate appreciations and depreciation. First, we establish that mining asset and commodity prices have had a number of boom episodes. The prolonged boom occurred between 2005 and 2008. The boom post-2009 was very brief in comparison. Although the boom episodes tend to be highly synchronised, their duration and amplitudes differ. But the platinum shares dominate the evolution of the aggregate mining share price returns. Second, the evolution of the R/US$ exchange rate is dominated by periods of prolonged and persistent depreciations. We identify seven episodes of the R/US$ exchange rate depreciation above the 15 per cent threshold. The recent exchange rate depreciation during 2011Q3 to 2014Q2 is the longest in duration in recent history, and it was shortly followed by a sharp depreciation that exceeded the 20 per cent threshold for a considerable period. Third, periods of capital flow surges (capital flow sudden stops) coincide with the R/US$ exchange rate appreciation (depreciation). Similar to the R/US$ exchange rate, mining share prices coincide with the capital flow episodes. The R/US$ exchange rate changes and capital flow episodes dominate the evolution of the mining sector share prices.

Did South Africa miss out on recent commodity price booms? Evidence in this chapter leads us to conclude that South Africa did not miss out on the commodity price booms contrary to the popular narrative. South Africa participated and benefitted from the recent commodity price booms. Nonetheless, it is very possible that South Africa could have performed even better in taking advantage and managing its commodities given the diverse basket of its mineral resources that are exported.

Do sharp exchange rate depreciations propagate the effects of mining asset busts? First, we establish that mining commodity price busts exert disproportionate effects. Mining investment and employment growth bears the brunt of the busts. Second, evidence shows that mining output and employment respond positively to a commodity price boom. But the R/US$ exchange rate depreciation propagates the positive effects of the commodity price boom more on employment growth. Thus, we conclude that the exchange rate depreciation dividend is disproportionate on mining output and employment. This is because sharp R/US$ exchange rate depreciations do not incentivise the mining sector to improve gross value add. In essence, sharp exchange rate depreciation episodes are not good for the mining sector output growth.

From a policy perspective, these results reinforce the findings that strategies aimed at investing in the value chains for mining commodity sectors, the development of new export markets and cushioning the sector against the cyclicality and severe slumps in global demand and commodity prices will support the mining sector as a "*sunrise industry*". The highly cyclical nature of commodity prices and sensitivity to global demand, demand a focused strategic approach to managing the mining sector. At the same time, it is necessary that such a strategy forms an integral part of the exchange rate policy and the operationalisation of the unemployment targets in the National Development Plan, the design of the proposed sovereign wealth fund and the co-ordination of the trade and other macroeconomic policies. Understanding the effects of the synchronicity and coincidence of commodity price cycles, capital flow episodes and those of the R/US$ exchange rate will yield better policy interventions for mining output, investment and employment growth.

Appendix

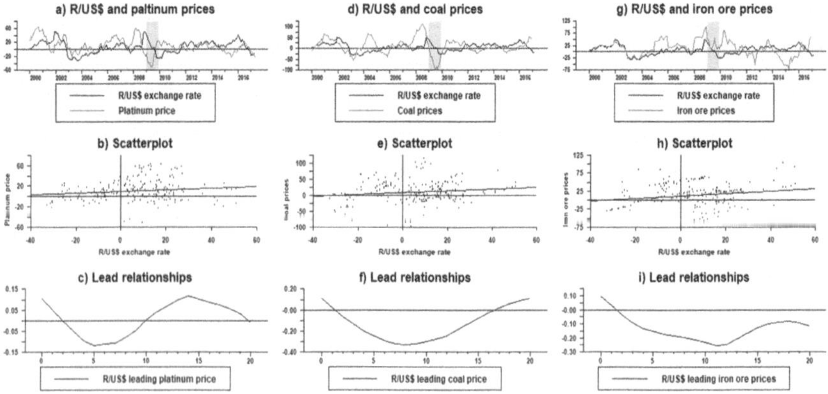

Fig. 13.19 R/US$ exchange rate and selected commodity prices. (Note: Grey shaded areas denote the South African recession. Source: South African Reserve Bank, Reserve Bank of Australia and authors' calculations)

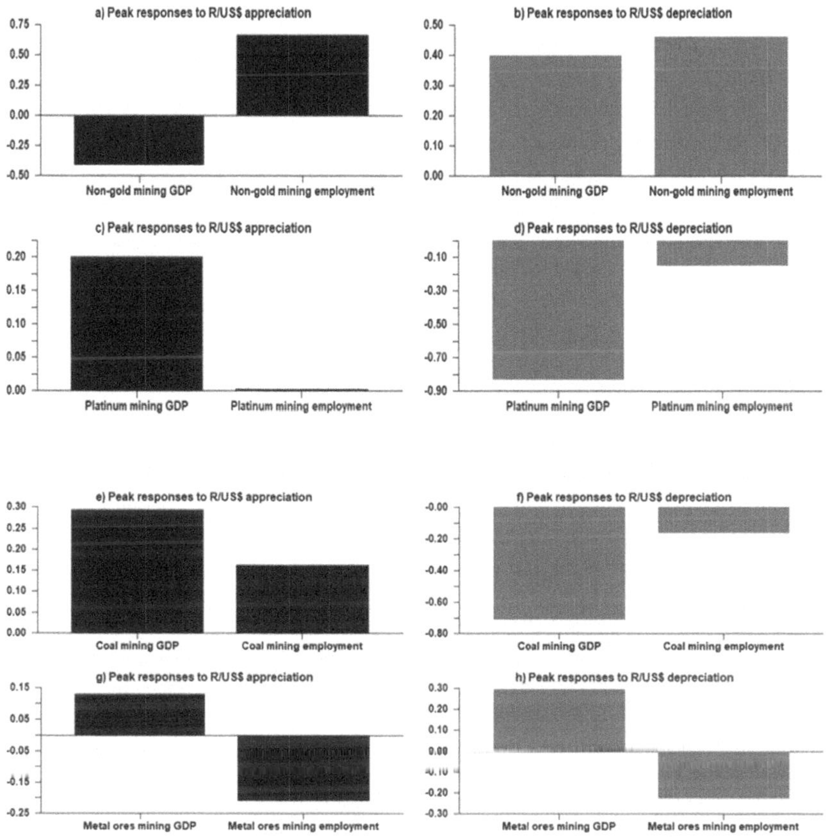

Fig. 13.20 Mining commodity output and employment peak responses to R/US$ exchange rate appreciations and depreciations. (Source: Authors' calculations)

References

Alessi, L., and Detken, C. 2009. *Real Time' Early Warning Indicators for Costly Asset Price Boom/Bust Cycles a Role for Global Liquidity*. ECB Working Paper Series No. 1039.

Ball, L., and Mankiw, N.G. 1994. Asymmetric Price Adjustment and Economic Fluctuations. *Economic Journal, Royal Economic Society*, 104(423), 247–61.

Ball, L., and Romer, D. 1989. Are Prices Too Sticky? *Quarterly Journal of Economics*, 104(3), 507–24.

Ball, L., and Romer, D. 1990. Real Rigidities and the Non-neutrality of Money. *Review of Economic Studies*, 57(2), 183–203.

Blanchard, O., and Quah, D. 1989. The Dynamic Effects of Aggregate Demand and Supply Disturbances. *The American Economic Review*, 79, 655–73.

Bordo, M.D., and Jeanne, O. 2002. Monetary Policy and Asset Prices: Does "Benign Neglect" Make Sense? *International Finance*, 5(2), 139–64.

Borgy, V., Laurent, C. and Jean-Paul, R. 2009. *Asset Price Boom Bust Cycles and Credit: What is the Scope of Macro Prudential Regulation*. Working Paper. Bank of International Settlements: Basel. December.

Bry, G., and Boschan, C. 1971. *Cyclical Analysis of Time Series: Selected Procedures and Computer Programs*. NBER Book Series. ISBN 0-87014-223-2.

Burns, A.F., and Mitchell, W.C. 1946. *NBER in NBER Book Series Studies in Business Cycles*. ISBN 0-870-14085-X.

Cashin, P., and McDermott, J.C. 2002. *The Long-Run Behavior of Commodity Prices: Small Trends and Big Variability*. IMF Working Papers WP/02/68.

Cashin, P., Céspedes, L.F., and Sahay, R. 2002. *Commodity Currencies and the Real Exchange Rate*. Central Bank of Chile Working Papers No. 236.

Fatas, A., Kannan, P., Rabanal, P., and Scott, A. 2009. Lessons from Asset Price Fluctuations for Monetary Policy. In *World Economic Outlook*. International Monetary Fund. September 2009.

Forbes, K.J., and Warnock, F.E. 2011. *Capital Flow Waves: Surges, Stops, Flight, and Retrenchment*. NBER Working Paper No. 17351.

Gumata, N., and Ndou, E. 2019. *Capital Flows, Credit Markets and Growth in South Africa The Role of Global Economic Growth, Policy Shifts and Uncertainties*. Palgrave Macmillan. ISBN 978-3-030-30887-2.

Harding, D., and Pagan, A. 2002a. A Comparison of Two Business Cycle Dating Methods. *Journal of Economic Dynamics and Control*, 27, 1681–90.

Harding, D., and Pagan, A. 2002b. Dissecting the Cycle: A Methodological Investigation. *Journal of Monetary Economics*, 49, 365–81.

Pagan, R.A., and Sossounov, K.A. 2003. A Simple Framework for Analysing Bull and Bear Markets. *Journal of Applied Econometrics*, 18(1), 23–46. John Wiley & Sons, Ltd.

14

The Role of the Exchange Rate on Investment Growth in the Mining Sector: Evidence from the Balance Sheet Hypothesis

Learning Objectives

- Establish whether there is a balance sheet channel transmitting negative commodity price shocks (i.e. demand for mining commodities) and the exchange rate depreciation shocks into the mining sector investment, foreign debt and intermediate imports.
- Explore the impact of contractionary effects of large real exchange depreciations versus large commodity price busts.
- Assess the impact of persistent and non-persistent commodity price shocks on mining investment, foreign debt and intermediate imports.
- Explore whether there is asymmetry in the transmission of different magnitudes of exchange rate depreciation shocks and sharp commodity price declines to mining investment.

14.1 Introduction

Earlier chapters showed that commodity prices play an important role in the mining sector output, investment and employment growth. Furthermore, evidence so far shows that sharp R/US$ exchange rate

N. Gumata, E. Ndou, *Accelerated Land Reform, Mining, Growth, Unemployment and Inequality in South Africa*, https://doi.org/10.1007/978-3-030-30884-1_14

depreciation shocks exert disproportionate effects on the mining sector output, investment and employment growth. The exchange rate depreciation dividend is disproportionate on mining output and employment. This is because sharp R/US$ exchange rate depreciations do not incentivise the mining sector to improve gross value add. Sharp exchange rate depreciation episodes are not good for the mining sector output growth. This chapter extends the analysis on the impact of the exchange depreciation and appreciation on the mining sector by assessing the role of the balance sheet channel.

Ndou and Gumata (2017) established that the contractionary effects of the R/US$ exchange rate depreciation are mainly transmitted via the balance sheet effects.[1] This presents trade-offs for the exports-led growth versus investment-led growth approaches. The authors conclude that, in cases when a choice must be made in line with the vision and objectives of the National Development Plan (NDP), an investment-lead strategy seems superior. Is this the case for the mining sector? Earlier chapters showed that despite the mining sector being a key export earner, its contribution to aggregate GDP and employment growth is poor. Hence, this chapter explores the role of investment growth and the balance sheet hypothesis in the mining sector.

Figure 14.1(c) indicates that the contribution of mining investment to aggregate and private sector investment declined between 2003Q1 and 2006Q4 but has since recovered and is at levels above the long-term average of 10 per cent which is comparable to the period pre-financial crisis. In fact, the contribution of mining investment growth to aggregate investment and private sector investment has been consistently above 10 per cent since 2009. The trend in mining investment is in direct opposite of aggregate investment.

Of interest as well is the observation that the contribution of mining investment growth to aggregate and private sector investment does not present a gloomy picture as expected in an industry reported to be plagued by heightened levels of policy uncertainty. Furthermore, Connolly and

---

[1] The contractionary effects of large real exchange rate depreciation can occur due to the cost of inputs and foreign currency-denominated debt resulting in foreign currency mismatches on balance sheets of firms.

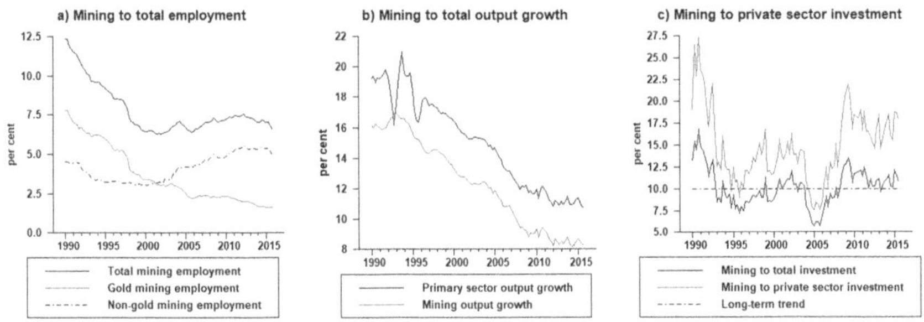

Fig. 14.1 Mining sector contribution to aggregate output, investment and employment growth. (Source: South African Reserve Bank and authors' calculations)

Orsmond (2011) show that the South African mining investment-to-GDP ratio compares favourably with those in Australia, Canada, US, China and India. Mohammad (2017) documents that prices of Australian resource exports nearly doubled between 2005 and 2011. The rapid rise in commodity prices resulted in mining investment increasing from an average of around 2 to 3 per cent of GDP before 2005 to a peak exceeding 9 per cent of GDP in 2013. But a 35 per cent decline in commodity prices since 2011 led to a decline in the terms-of-trade between 2011 and 2016. Similarly, mining investment declined to 4.5 per cent of GDP by 2016.

In addition, Connolly and Orsmond (2011) observe that the prolonged period of low investment in the mining sector during the 1990s meant that the mining industry was not in a strong position to quickly increase supply when global demand for commodities finally picked up strongly in 2003. As shown in Fig. 14.2(a), the ratio of mining investment to nominal GDP was below the long-term average of 1.76 per cent and only increased during 2005 but has since declined during 2014.

A similar trend is observed in Fig. 14.2(b) with respect to the contribution of the mining sector investment to total investment. Figure 14.15 shows that the increase in mining investment during 2005 and 2014 was comparable to level recorded during the 1970s and 1980s commodity

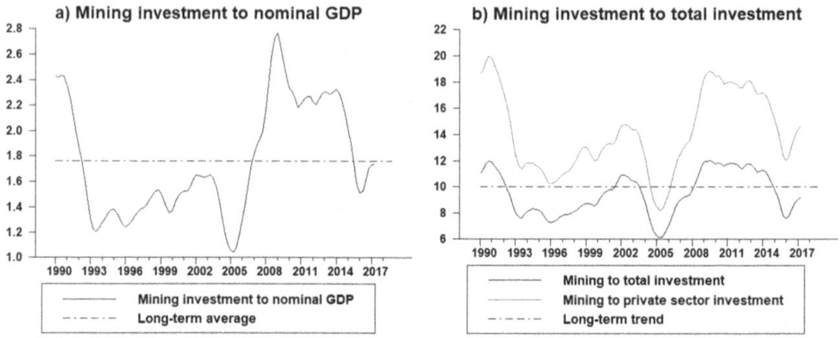

Fig. 14.2 Mining investment as a ratio of nominal GDP, aggregate and private sector investment (1990Q1 to 2018Q4). (Source: South African Reserve Bank and authors' calculations)

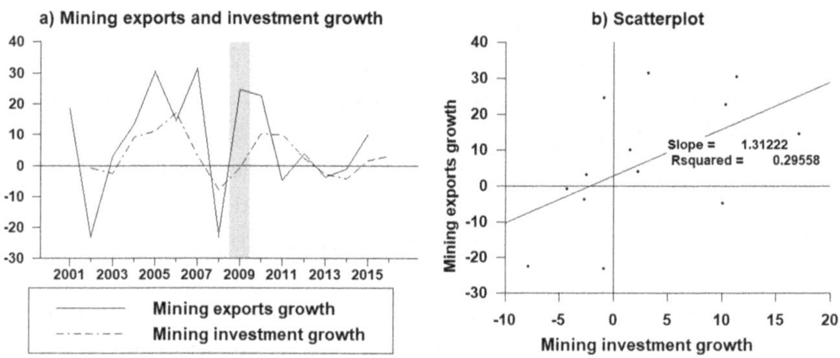

Fig. 14.3 Mining exports and investment growth relationship. (Note: The grey shaded area denotes the South African recession. Source: South African Reserve Bank and authors' calculations)

price booms. The same trend was observed in terms of mining investment as a ratio of total and private sector investment which recorded high levels of 25 per cent. On the other hand, Fig. 14.3 shows that mining exports and investment growth are positively associated. Mining investment growth explains around 30 per cent of the variation in mining exports.

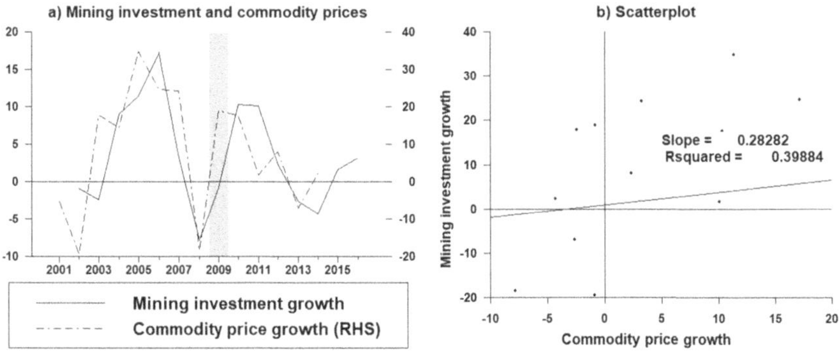

Fig. 14.4 Mining investment growth and commodity prices relationship. (Note: The grey shaded area denotes the South African recession. Source: South African Reserve Bank and authors' calculations)

Figure 14.4 also shows that commodity prices explain around 40 per cent of the variation in mining investment growth. An increase in commodity prices incentivises mining investment growth. This means that a concurrence of an increase in commodity prices and demand for exports augers well for mining investment. We explore the relative importance of positive shocks to these variables in the empirical section. We empirically explore the interaction between the exchange rate depreciation, commodity price declines and the balance sheet effects.

14.2 Literature Review

Literature shows that the presence of foreign currency-denominated debt can reverse the expansionary impact of exchange rate depreciations as theoretically postulated in the standard Mundell-Fleming framework. Krugman (1999), Aghion et al. (2001, 2003) and Céspedes et al. (2004) use the open economy Bernanke-Gertler-Gilchrist framework to show that, in the presence of foreign currency debt, currency depreciations may be contractionary. Kohler (2016) shows that the private sector companies in emerging market economies are often vulnerable to external shocks due to foreign currency-denominated liabilities, which can give rise to balance sheet effects.

The trust of the argument on the interaction of the exchange rate dynamics and the balance sheet effects is that procyclical exchange rate dynamics and balance sheet effects can give rise to boom-bust cycles. A currency appreciation makes firms' balance sheets with foreign currency debt appear more solid although they tend to be highly leveraged. This often coincides with the boom phase of the commodity price boom and the widening of the current account position. When the exchange rate eventually corrects and depreciates, the contractionary balance sheet effects set in and this results in a decline in the domestic firms' nominal net worth. This is how the exchange rate exerts a procyclical effect that interacts with foreign currency debt to generate and propagate a boom-bust cycles.

Several studies such as Galindo et al. (2003), Janot et al. (2008) and Kearns and Patel (2016) confirm that exchange rate devaluations are more likely to have a negative effect on output and growth in countries with high external debt burdens. Exchange rate devaluations can have a contractionary impact in countries with heavy liability dollarisation. The presence of dollar debt exerts threshold effects beyond which it reduces the expansionary effect of currency depreciations.[2] Galindo et al. (2003) establish that in countries that do not have foreign currency debt such as the US, a 10-per cent exchange rate depreciation is associated with an increase in growth of approximately 0.7 percentage points. Whereas countries where all the external debt is in foreign currency, such as most emerging market economies, a 10-per cent exchange rate depreciation is associated with a decrease of 1.6 percentage points in growth. [3]

Bruno (2018) finds that the US dollar exchange rate emerges as a determinant of global value chains (GVCs) activity. A stronger dollar is associated with tighter credit conditions and subdued GVC activity. As a

[2] It can even exert negative effects.

[3] Nonetheless, studies show that if firms were perfectly hedged, currency depreciations should not have any relevant negative balance sheet consequences.

result, exports from an emerging economy may fall when its currency depreciates against the dollar. This is because GVCs play a prominent role in global trade and lie at the intersection of (i) the financing requirement for working capital and (ii) the prevalence of US dollar invoicing in global trade.

Avdjiev et al. (2018) find that a stronger dollar is associated with lower growth in dollar-denominated cross-border bank flows and lower real investment in emerging market economies. The broad dollar index is the most relevant exchange rate for real investment. This highlights that dollar lending by global banks fluctuates with the broad dollar index and underlies the prevalence of the credit supply mechanism. The authors conclude that the policy implication of these findings is that a stronger dollar has real macroeconomic effects that go in the opposite direction to the standard trade channel. Whereas a stronger dollar would normally benefit those countries that export to the US, the dampening effect of the dollar on investment may offset any benefits that accrue from the trade channel. The financial channel actually dominates the traditional trade channel.

On the other hand, Rey (2015) Bruno and Shin (2015 and 2016) amongst others have placed a strong focus on the role of the global financial cycle driven by risk appetite and monetary policy in advanced economies. The interaction between the exchange rate and firms' balance sheets is also referred to as the "financial channel" of exchange rate developments. Kearns and Patel (2016) show that if the exchange rate of a global funding currency which is typically the US dollar, depreciates against the domestic currency, balance sheets of domestic firms improve and the currency mismatch is less heightened. This in turn stimulates domestic investment and increases the demand for further external credit. Thus, currency appreciation against global funding currencies increases the supply and reduces the cost of foreign lending. This tends to boost interest-sensitive domestic spending. On the other hand, the exchange rate depreciation results in a contraction in financial conditions and economic activity. Therefore, currency appreciations which improve the balance sheets of foreign currency-indebted firms induce an investment boom.

14.3 The Contractionary Effects of Large Real Exchange Depreciations Versus Large Commodity Price Busts

We start the empirical analysis by exploring whether there are different effects exerted by large real exchange rate depreciations and commodity price busts on balance sheets and mining investment growth. Evidence in earlier chapters showed that commodity price busts tend to be associated with large exchange rate depreciations. First, Fig. 14.5 shows the relationship between the various measures of the exchange rates, namely, the R/US$, nominal effective exchange rate (NEER) and the real effective exchange rate (REER). We inverted the NEER and REER so that they are interpreted in the same way as the R/US$, that is, an increase is equivalent to a depreciation and a decline is equivalent to an appreciation. The sample starts in 1990M1 to 2018M2. The data is sourced from the South African Reserve Bank database.

The trends in Fig. 14.5 indicate that all the Rand exchange rate measures are positively associated and that after a prolonged period of depreciation since 2011, the exchange rate appreciated by 20 per cent in 2017

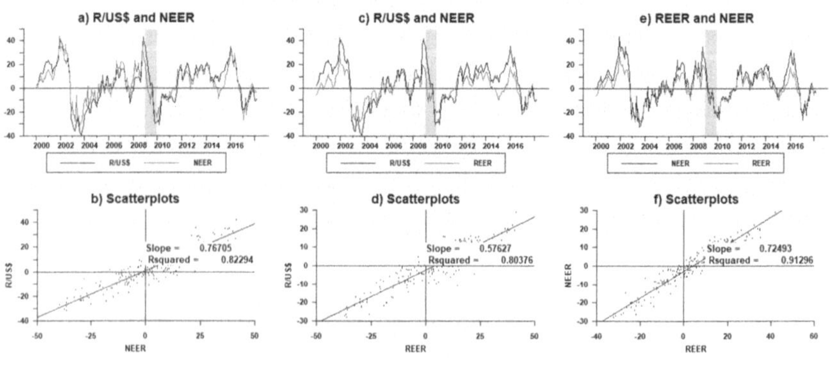

Fig. 14.5 Exchange rates. (Note: The grey shaded area denotes the South African recession. Source: South African Reserve Bank and authors' calculations)

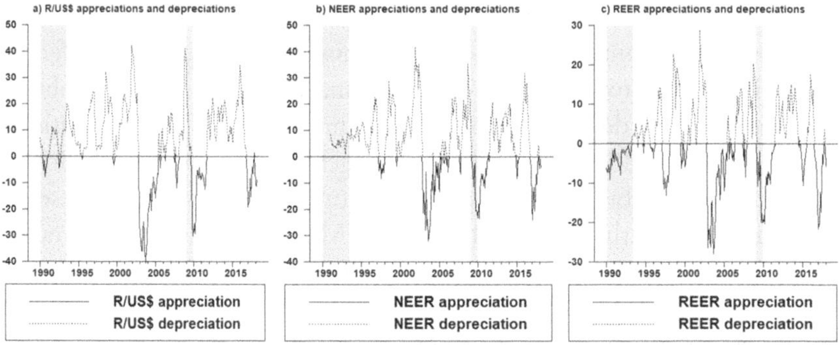

Fig. 14.6 Exchange rate appreciations and depreciations. (Note: The grey shaded area denotes the South African recession. Source: South African Reserve Bank and authors' calculations)

on a bilateral and weighted basis. In addition, Fig. 14.6 shows that episodes of the exchange rate depreciation of more than 10 per cent are a common occurrence across exchange rates.

14.3.1 What Is the Impact of Large Real Exchange Rate Depreciations Compared to Those Induced by Severe Commodity Price Busts?

This section estimates several VAR models to assess and compare the impact of sharp real exchange rate depreciations and commodity price busts on mining output, investment, private foreign debt and intermediate imports. We define sharp real exchange rate depreciations and commodity price busts as those that are 10 per cent and above. We create the following dummy variables where (i) the REER takes on the depreciation values above 10 per cent and zero otherwise; (ii) the R/US$[4] exchange rate takes on the depreciation values above 10 per cent and zero otherwise; and (iii) commodity price takes on the values of the decline above 10 per cent and zero otherwise. The VAR models include mining sector

[4] Serena and Sousa (2018) use the country-specific bilateral exchange rates to the US dollar and focus mainly on exchange rate depreciations.

investment, foreign debt, intermediate imports and the various dummy variables. The dummy variables enter the models individually in different estimations. The growth rates are at an annual rate. The size of the shock is a one standard deviation shock. The sample size for the estimations spans the period 2003Q1 to 2016Q3 largely due to the availability of data for foreign debt. The data is sourced from the South African Reserve Bank and the South African Chamber of Mines databases. The models are estimated with 2 lags and 10,000 Monte Carlo draws.

Figure 14.7 shows that mining investment declines and remains depressed in response to a real exchange rate depreciation shock. Foreign debt increases, and intermediate imports decline as well. A comparison of the responses in Fig. 14.7(c) shows that foreign debt and intermediate imports are more responsive to the real exchange rate, indicating that the balance sheet channel is more active and adjusts more. Thus, the real exchange rate depreciation shocks are transmitted more via the balance sheet items of foreign debt and the import of intermediate goods which are largely representative of inputs to the production process and investment. The results using the bilateral R/US$ exchange rate depreciation in Fig. 14.16 are similar to those generated using the REER. Therefore, we conclude that the responses to the exchange rate depreciation are robust to the measure of the exchange rate used in the model.

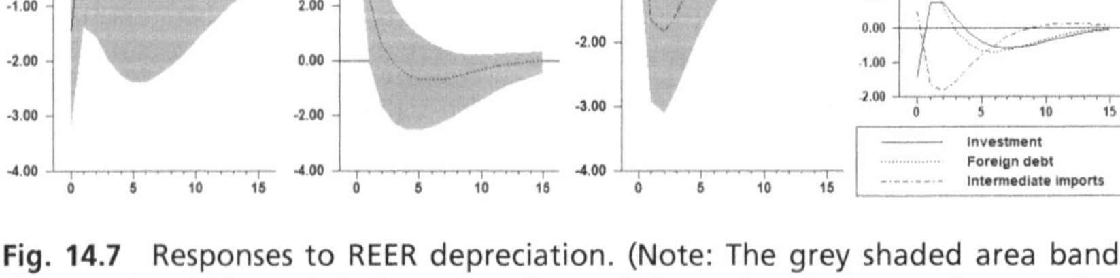

Fig. 14.7 Responses to REER depreciation. (Note: The grey shaded area bands denote the 16th and 84th percentile confidence bands. Int. = intermediate imports. Source: Authors' calculations)

Are the responses of investment, foreign debt and intermediate imports different to a decline in commodity prices? Figure 14.8 shows that investment growth and foreign debt are more responsive to a decline in commodity prices. Investment growth and foreign debt remain depressed for a longer period compared to the import of intermediate goods in Fig. 14.8(c).

To conclude the analysis in this section, Fig. 14.9 shows a comparison of investment, foreign debt and intermediate imports peak responses to real exchange rate depreciation shock and unexpected commodity price

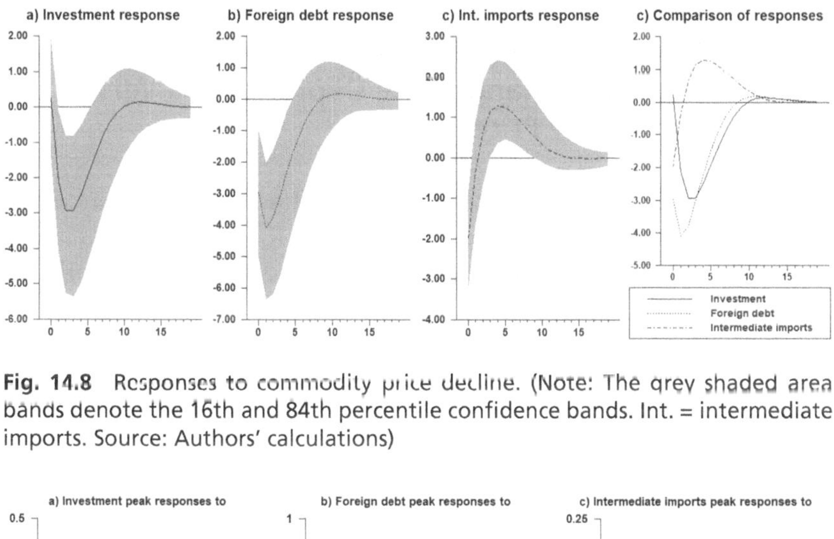

Fig. 14.8 Responses to commodity price decline. (Note: The grey shaded area bands denote the 16th and 84th percentile confidence bands. Int. = intermediate imports. Source: Authors' calculations)

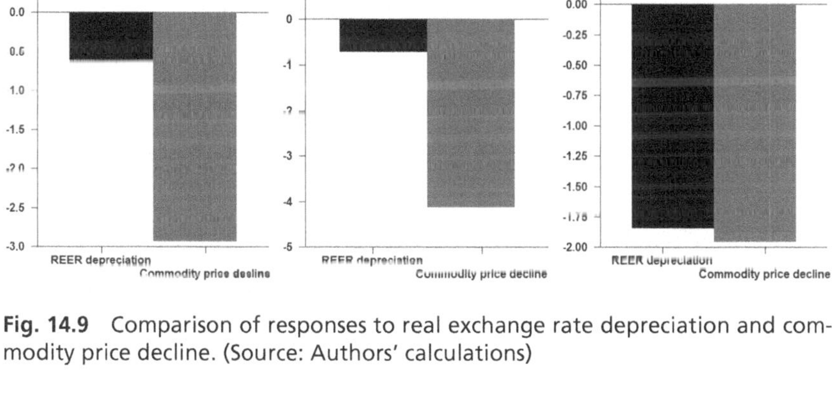

Fig. 14.9 Comparison of responses to real exchange rate depreciation and commodity price decline. (Source: Authors' calculations)

declines. The comparison of peak responses in Fig. 14.9 affirms the centrality of the balance sheet channel in transmitting negative commodity prices shocks such as the decline in demand for mining commodities and exchange rate depreciation shocks. The impact of the decline in commodity prices on mining investment, foreign debt and intermediate imports is characteristic of the transmission via the wealth and nominal net worth balance sheet channels. Thus, we conclude that the contractionary effects of commodity price declines and real and R/US$ exchange rate depreciation shocks are mainly transmitted via the balance sheet of firms, wealth and nominal net worth.

14.3.2 How Different Is the Variance Induced by the Real Exchange Rate Depreciations Versus Commodity Price Declines?

To answer this question, this section estimates three VAR models to assess which shock between the exchange rate (REER, R/US$) depreciation and commodity price shocks explains the greatest variation in mining investment, foreign debt and intermediate imports. The VAR models are specified as those in earlier sections. The results in Fig. 14.10 show that all shocks explain a higher variation in investment and foreign debt.

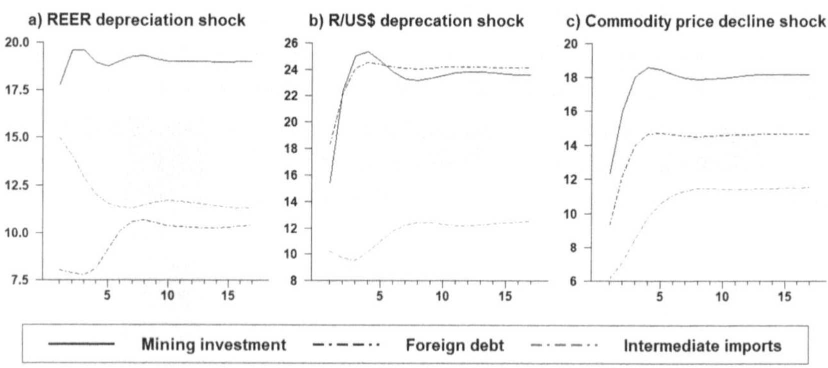

Fig. 14.10 Variations in the fluctuation in mining investment, foreign debt and intermediate imports due to exchange rate and commodity price depreciation. (Source: Authors' calculations)

Thus, the results confirm that the transmission of the contractionary effects of the exchange depreciation shocks and unexpected commodity price declines are mainly via the wealth and nominal net worth balance sheet channels.

14.3.3 How Does Mining Investment Respond to Commodity Prices, Foreign Debt and Intermediate Imports?

This section extends the analysis by comparing the responses of mining investment to positive commodity prices, foreign debt and intermediate imports shocks. Similar to the previous sections, we estimate several VAR models with the REER, R/US$ and commodity prices. But in this case, the shocks of interest are commodity prices, foreign debt and intermediate imports. The VAR models include the mining sector investment growth, foreign debt, intermediate imports and the various dummy variables. The dummy variables as explained in the earlier section enter the models individually in different estimations. The growth rates are at an annual rate. The size of the shock is a one standard deviation shock.

The results in Fig. 14.11 show that as expected, mining investment growth increases in response to foreign debt and intermediate imports.

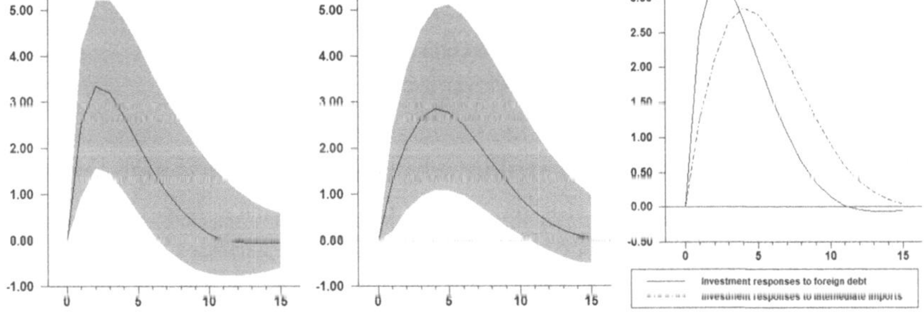

Fig. 14.11 Mining investment responses to positive foreign debt and intermediate imports shocks in model with REER depreciation dummy. (Note: The grey shaded area bands denote the 16th and 84th percentile confidence bands. Source: Authors' calculations)

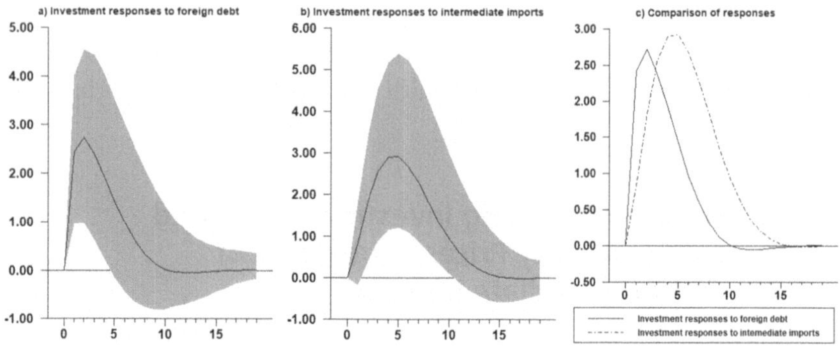

Fig. 14.12 Mining investment responses to positive foreign debt and intermediate imports shocks in model with commodity price increase. (Note: The grey shaded area bands denote the 16th and 84th percentile confidence bands. Source: Authors' calculations)

But the comparison of responses in Fig. 14.11(c) shows that investment responds more to foreign debt shock which shows the significance and importance of funding. We show the responses in the model with the R/US$ in the Appendix (Fig. 14.17), and they indicate that the responses of mining investment are robust to changes in the specification of the model.

Similarly, Fig. 14.12 shows that mining investment responds positively to foreign debt and intermediate imports in the model with increases in commodity prices. Thus, we conclude that the balance sheets of firms are important transmitters of shocks to mining investment.

14.3.4 The Impact of Persistent and Transitory Commodity Price Shocks

Fornero and Kirchner (2014) explore why despite sustained high levels of commodity prices during the recent commodity price booms, current account balances of several commodity-exporting countries deteriorated. They find this is because agents have imperfect information and learn about the persistence of commodity price shocks. At first, agents believe that the increase in commodity prices is temporary but then eventually revise their expectations upward as they are surprised by higher than forecasted price levels. This induces a gradual increase in domestic investment driven by investment in the commodity sector. But this results in a decline in domestic savings; hence the current account declines over time.

Vast research has established that the patterns of the trade account adjustments of commodity-exporting countries have differed. Some countries' current account adjustments have conformed to the predictions of the Harberger-Laursen-Metzler (HLM) effect.[5] On the other hand, the adjustments of some countries' trade balances have been best described by the inter-temporal approach to the current account or the so-called Obstfeld-Razin-Svenson effect.[6] Ndou and Gumata (2017) showed that the South African data supports the HLM effect. The results showed that a 10 per cent increase in the terms-of-trade leads to nearly 1.5 per cent increase in the trade balance. The terms-of-trade shock takes two years to die off, suggesting that the shock is transitory. Furthermore, the responses suggest that the adjustment of the trade account is characterised by the dominance of the consumption-smoothing effect over the investment effect. This is consistent with the view that agents largely perceive the positive terms-of-trade shock as transitory and it therefore does not incentivise them to alter the capital stock (Kent 1997).

Against this background, this section explores what the different impact of persistent, and non-persistent commodity price scenarios would mean for mining investment growth. As shown in Fig. 14.13, we explore cases of a non-persistent shock which dies off quickly and a persistent shock which takes time to die off. We again assess the different impact of non-persistent and persistent positive shocks to commodity prices. In this case we create a dummy variable that assumes the positive values of commodity prices and zero otherwise. The VAR model includes commodity prices, mining sector investment, intermediate imports and foreign debt. The intention is to assess the different impact of persistent and non-persistent positive

[5] The HLM effect suggests that an exogenous increase in terms-of-trade leads to an improvement in the country's trade balance if the marginal propensity to consume is lower than one.

[6] This approach predicts that the adjustment of the current account to a positive shock to terms-of-trade will differ, depending on whether agents perceive it to be persistent or transitory. If perceived to be transitory, rational economic agents will save the bulk of the temporary income gains. However, if agents perceive the shock to be permanent, income gains will almost immediately and entirely be spent. Hence, at any given point, the trade account adjustment will reflect either the dominance of the consumption smoothing effect over the investment effect or vice versa (Kent and Cashin 2003).

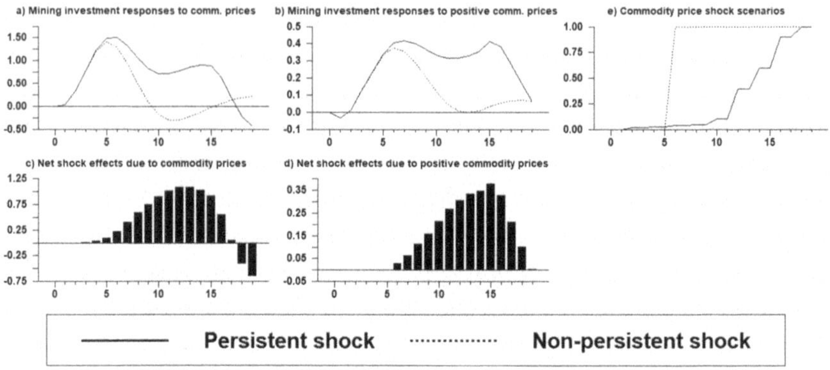

Fig. 14.13 Mining investment responses to persistent and non-persistent commodity price depreciation. (Note: Comm = commodity prices. Source: Authors' calculations)

shocks to (i) commodity prices and (ii) periods during which commodity prices are increasing and whether these exert different effects on the mining sector investment. One model includes all phases of commodity prices, whereas the other model includes the dummy variables that take only positive values of commodity prices.

The results in Fig. 14.13(a) and (b) show that persistent shocks, in particular of positive shocks to commodity prices, lead to persistently higher levels of mining investment as opposed to non-persistent shocks. Therefore, our results indicate that the findings in Fornero and Kirchner (2014) are valid for the South African economy as well. Agents learn over time about the true persistence of the commodity shock. If the persistence of a commodity price shock turns out to be high, then higher expected returns of capital especially in the commodity sector can trigger an investment boom that has important spill-over effects on investment in other sectors and the rest of the economy.

14.3.5 The Asymmetric Transmissions of Shocks to Mining Investment

This section uses the Kilian and Vigfusson (2011) approach to test for the asymmetric transmission of real exchange rate depreciation and commodity price decline shocks to mining investment. The Kilian and Vigfusson (2009) approach uses an impulse-response-based Wald test to distinguish between shocks of different magnitudes. The Kilian and Vigfusson approach analyses non-linear impulse response functions calculated by simulating the effects of different magnitudes of shocks at time t. The approach tests the null hypothesis that symmetric response functions to a positive shock should be equal to the vector of impulse responses to a negative shock. The Kilian and Vigfusson (2011) algorithm computes impulse response functions by Monte Carlo integration. We estimate several VAR models as done in earlier sections using the Kilian and Vigfusson approach to assess the asymmetric effects of real exchange rate depreciation, R/US$ depreciation and unexpected commodity price declines of different magnitudes on mining investment growth.

The results in Fig. 14.14 show that larger exchange rate depreciation shocks and unexpected commodity price declines result in more pronounced declines in mining investment. Thus, the exchange rate depreciation shocks and unexpected commodity price declines exert asymmetric contractionary effects on mining investment growth.

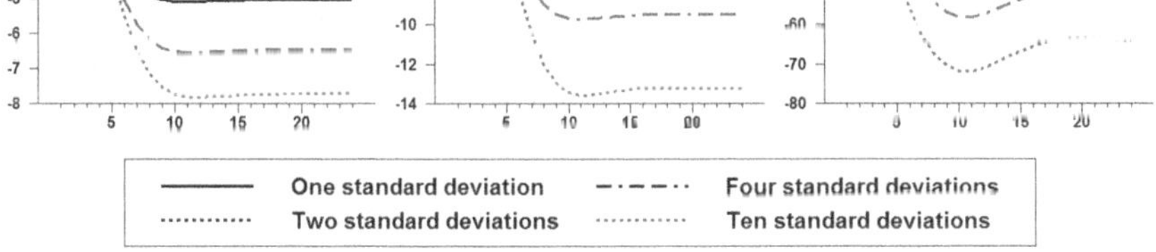

Fig. 14.14 Mining investment responses to different magnitudes of exchange rate depreciation shocks and unexpected commodity price declines. (Source: Authors' calculations)

14.4 Conclusions and Policy Implications

This chapter explored whether there is a balance sheet channel transmitting the negative shocks to commodity prices, demand for mining commodities and exchange rate depreciation into the mining sector investment, foreign debt and intermediate imports. Evidence in this chapter indicates that mining investment declines and remains depressed in response to a real exchange rate depreciation shock. Foreign debt increases, and intermediate imports decline as well. Foreign debt and intermediate imports are more responsive to the real exchange rate, indicating that the balance sheet channel is more active and adjusts more. Thus, the real exchange rate depreciation shocks are transmitted more via the balance sheet items of foreign debt and the import of intermediate goods which are largely representative of inputs to the production process and investment.

Are the responses of investment, foreign debt and intermediate imports different to a decline in commodity prices? We find that investment growth and foreign debt are more responsive to a decline in commodity prices. Investment growth and foreign debt remain depressed for a longer period compared to the import of intermediate goods. The results affirm the centrality of the balance sheet channel in transmitting negative shocks to commodity prices, demand for mining commodities and exchange rate depreciation. The impact of the decline in commodity prices on mining investment, foreign debt and intermediate imports is characteristic of the transmission via the wealth and nominal net worth balance sheet channels. The contractionary effects of commodity price declines, real and R/US$ exchange rate depreciation are mainly transmitted via the balance sheet of firms, wealth and nominal net worth.

Is an investment-led strategy superior in the mining sector? Yes, evidence in this chapter shows that investment growth is a necessary but insufficient condition. Commodity prices are an important part of a thriving mining sector. A combination of an increase in commodity prices and demand for mining exports augers well for mining investment. In particular, we find that persistent shocks, especially of positive shocks to commodity prices, lead to persistently higher levels of mining investment as opposed to non-persistent shocks. Furthermore, our results concur with findings in Fornero and Kirchner (2014) showing that agents learn over time about the true persistence of the commodity shock. If the persistence of a commodity price shock turns out to be high, then higher expected returns of capital especially in the commodity sector can trigger an investment boom that has important spill-over effects on investment in other sectors and the rest of the economy.

The findings reinforce earlier recommendations of the need to establish a sovereign wealth fund as an instrument for long-term planning and management of mineral resources. In addition, the findings that the balance sheet effects tend to make currency depreciations contractionary further corroborate earlier policy recommendations for an exchange rate policy. The interaction of the exchange rate dynamics and balance sheet effects are key channels that drive the business cycle in the mining sector. In turn, these are highly complemented and propagated by commodity price cycles.

Appendix

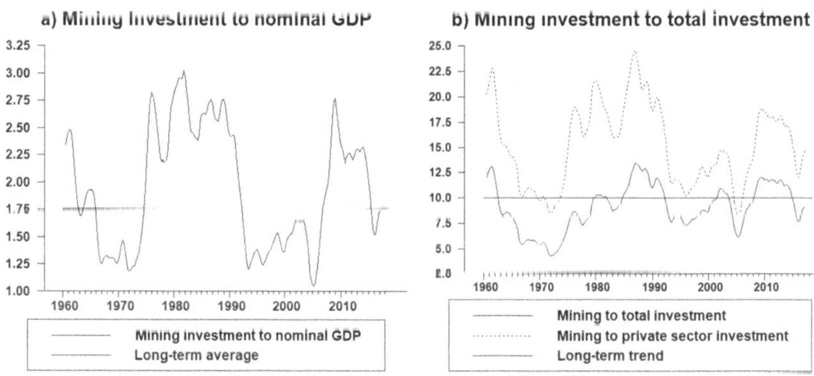

Fig. 14.15 Mining investment as a ratio of nominal GDP, aggregate and private sector investment (1960Q1 to 2018Q4). (Source: South African Reserve Bank and authors' calculations)

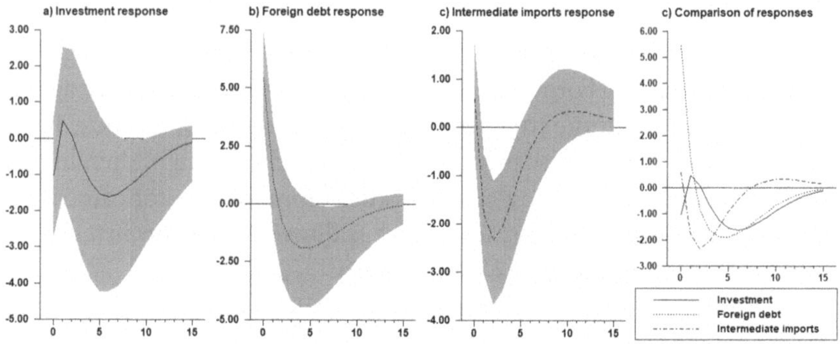

Fig. 14.16 Responses to R/US$ depreciation. (Note: The grey shaded area bands denote the 16th and 84th percentile confidence bands. Source: Authors' calculations)

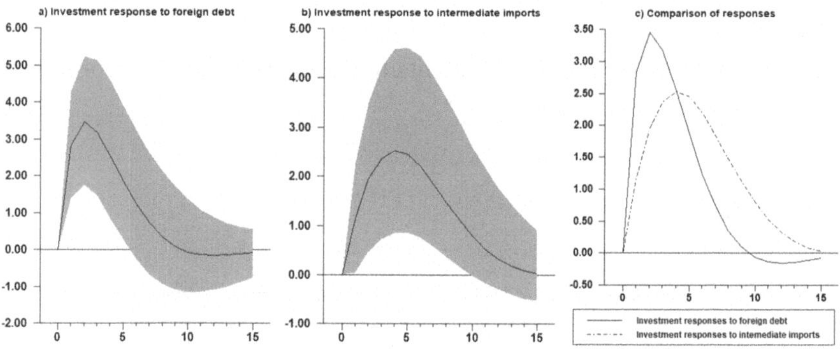

Fig. 14.17 Mining investment responses to foreign debt and intermediate imports in model with R/US$. (Note: The grey shaded area bands denote the 16th and 84th percentile confidence bands. Source: Authors' calculations)

References

Aghion, P., Bacchetta, P., and Banerjee, A. 2001. Currency Crises and Monetary Policy in a Credit-Constrained Economy. *European Economic Review*, 45, 1121–50.

Aghion, P., Bacchetta, P., and Banerjee, A. 2003. A Corporate Balance-Sheet Approach to Currency Crises. *Journal of Economic Theory*, 119, 6–30.

Avdjiev, S., Bruno, V., Koch, C., and Shin, H.S. 2018. *The Dollar Exchange Rate as a Global Risk Factor: Evidence from Investment*. BIS Working Papers No. 695.

Bebczuk, R., Galindo, A.J., and Panizza, U. 2007. *An Evaluation of the Contractionary Devaluation Hypothesis.* Working Paper 582, Inter-American Development Bank.

Blecker, R.A., and Razmi, A. 2007. The Fallacy of Composition and Contractionary Devaluations: Output Effects of Real Exchange Rate Shocks in Semi-Industrialised Countries. *Cambridge Journal of Economics*, 32, 83–109.

Bruno, V., Kim, Se-Jik and Shin, H.S. 2018. *Exchange Rates and the Working Capital Channel of Trade Fluctuations.* BIS Working Papers No. 694.

Bruno, V., and Shin, H.S. 2015. Capital Flows and the Risk-Taking Channel of Monetary Policy. *Journal of Monetary Economics*, 71, 119–32.

Bruno, V., and Shin, H.S. 2016. Cross-Border Banking and Global Liquidity. *Review of Economic Studies*, 82(2), 535–64.

Céspedes, L.F., Chang, R., and Velasco, A. 2004. Balance Sheets and Exchange Rate Policy. *American Economic Review*, 94, 1183–93.

Connolly, E., and Orsmond, D. 2011. *The Mining Industry: From Bust to Boom.* Discussion Paper 2011-08, Research Reserve Bank of Australia.

Fornero, J., and Kirchner, M. 2014. *Learning About Commodity Cycles and Savings-Investment Dynamics in a Commodity Exporting Economy.* Working Papers Central Bank of Chile WP 727.

Galindo, A., Panizza, U., and Schiantarelli, F. 2003. Debt Composition and Balance Sheet Effects of Currency Depreciation: A Summary of the Micro Evidence. *Emerging Markets Review*, 4, 330–39.

Janot, M.M., Garcia, M.G.P., and Novaes, W. 2008. *Balance Sheet Effects in Currency Crises: Evidence from Brazil.* Working Paper 162, Banco Central do Brasil.

Kearns, J., and Patel, N. 2016. Does the Financial Channel of Exchange Rates Offset the Trade Channel? *BIS Quarterly Review.*

Kent, C. 1997. *The Response of the Current Account to Terms of Trade Shocks: A Panel-data Study*. Reserve Bank of Australia RBA Discussion Papers RDP 9705.

Kent, C., and Cashin, P. 2003. *The Response of the Current Account to Terms of Trade Shocks: Persistence Matters.* IMF Working Paper No WP/03/143.

Kilian, L., and Vigfusson, R.J. 2009. *Pitfalls in Estimating Asymmetric Effects of Energy Price Shocks.* CEPR Working Paper 7284.

Kilian, L., and Vigfusson, R.J. 2011. Are Responses of the U.S. Economy Asymmetric in Energy Price Increases and Decreases? *Quantitative Economics*, 2, 419–53.

Kohler, K. 2016. *Currency Devaluations, Aggregate Demand, and Debt Dynamics in an Economy with Foreign Currency Liabilities*. Working Paper No. 78, Institute for International Political Economy Berlin.

Krugman, P. 1999. Balance Sheets, the Transfer Problem, and Financial Crises. *International Tax and Public Finance*, 6, 459–72.

Luc Eyraud, L. 2015. *End of the Super-cycle and Growth of Commodity Producers: The Case of Chile*. IMF Working Paper WP/15/242.

Mohammad, A. 2017. *Labor Market Adjustment to Shocks in Australia*. IMF Working Paper WP/17/124.

Ndou, E., and Gumata, N. 2017. *Inflation Dynamics in South Africa: The Role of Thresholds, Exchange Rate Pass-through and Inflation Expectations on Policy Trade-offs*. Palgrave Macmillan. ISBN 978-3-319-46701-6.

Rey, H. 2015. *Dilemma Not Trilemma: The Global Financial Cycle and Monetary Policy Independence*. NBER Working Paper No. 21162.

Serena, J.M., and Sousa, R. 2018. *Does Exchange Rate Depreciation have Contractionary Effects on Firm-level Investment? The Implications of Alternative Types of Bond Financing*. European Stability Mechanism Working Paper Series No. 26.

15

The Role of the Exchange Rate Volatility Shocks on the Mining Sector

Learning Objectives

- Estimate different components of the exchange rate volatilities for the nominal effective exchange rate, real effective exchange rate and the R/US$ exchange rate.
- Assess the impact of overall and permanent exchange rate volatility on mining exports, investment, output and employment growth.
- Estimate the thresholds for mining investment as a ratio of nominal GDP, mining investment as a ratio of total investment and mining investment as a ratio of private sector investment.
- Assess the impact of the estimated mining investment thresholds on output and employment growth.

15.1 Introduction

Earlier chapters showed that the balance sheet effects tend to make currency depreciations contractionary. Furthermore, the exchange rate balance sheet effects are highly complemented and propagated by commodity

N. Gumata, E. Ndou, *Accelerated Land Reform, Mining, Growth, Unemployment and Inequality in South Africa*, https://doi.org/10.1007/978-3-030-30884-1_15

price cycles and how persistent they are. This chapter extends the analysis on the exchange rate effects by exploring the role of different components of the exchange rate volatility on the mining sector exports, investment, output and employment growth.[1] Ndou et al. (2017)[2] establish that the volatility of the exchange rate and the resulting exchange rate and exports risks offset or neutralise the effects of the depreciation to a large degree. They find that the exchange rate risk has negative effects on exports revenue. Hence, a policy directed at a systematic depreciation of the exchange rate to stimulate the exports performance may not yield successful results because part of the depreciation effects is offset by the exchange rate risk. The authors conclude that the exchange rate risk matters, and policy interventions aimed at the exchange rate should also address this aspect. What is the impact of exchange rate volatility on mining exports, investment, output and employment growth?

Figure 15.1 shows the relationship between the estimated exchange rate volatility components for the R/US$ exchange rate, nominal effective exchange rate (NEER) and real effective exchange rate. In earlier chapters

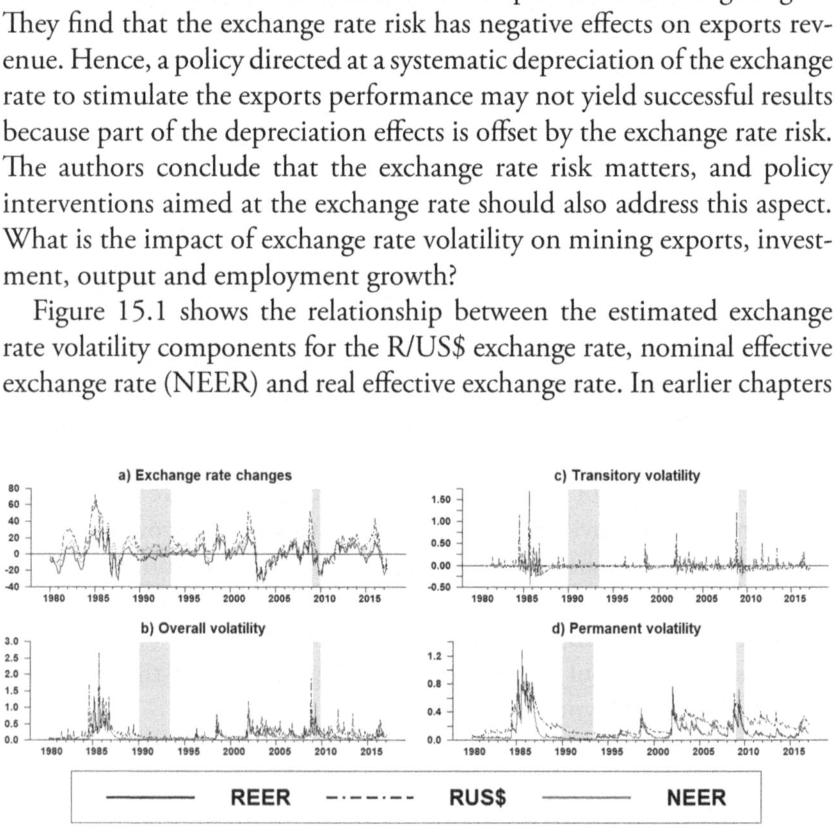

Fig. 15.1 Exchange rate changes and components of volatility. (Note: The grey shaded areas denote the South African recessions. Source: South African Reserve Bank and authors' calculations)

[1] We use the same approach used in Chaps. 9, 15 and 18 of Ndou et al. (2017) to calculate the different components of the exchange rate volatility.

[2] See Chaps. 18 and 23.

we established that the different measures of the exchange rate are highly correlated. The trends of the volatility components showed in Fig. 15.1 confirm this. The three measures of the exchange rate volatility indicate that all the three measures of volatility are very similar. Thus, we use the R/US$ exchange rate volatility components in the empirical section.

15.2 Why Does Exchange Rate Volatility Matter?

Arize (1996) shows that risk-averse exporters will reduce their export activity by switching sources of supply and demand or change prices to minimise their exposure to adverse effects of exchange rate risk. This may render exchange rate, foreign currency intervention policies and trade policies that are aimed at stabilising the export market ineffective especially when policymakers ignore the stability and level of real exchange rate. Figure 15.2 shows a schematic diagram of the channels of transmission of exchange rate volatility. The channels of focus in this chapter are captured in the first and second columns which deal with the influence of hedging risk and risk aversion of investors.

Channel one suggests that the hedging risks of future exchange rate fluctuations may lead firms to set higher prices, including charging a risk premium. As a result, the higher prices would lower the aggregate consumptions. According to Chang (2011), the second channel suggests that short-run fluctuations in the exchange rate may have negative effects at the microeconomic level. The negative effects arise when higher exchange rate volatility leads to an increase in costs for risk-averse investors. Increased risk aversion may lead to lower investment, output and fewer jobs created. This suggests that heightened exchange rate volatility will induce more uncertainties and transactions costs, and this leads to a decline in output.

Bahmani-Oskooee and Hanafiah Harvey (2015) argue exchange rate uncertainty and volatility may have significant short- and long-run effects on domestic consumption. The exchange rate uncertainty and volatility are an important cause of business cycle fluctuations including via the consumption and investment channels which are key component of aggregate

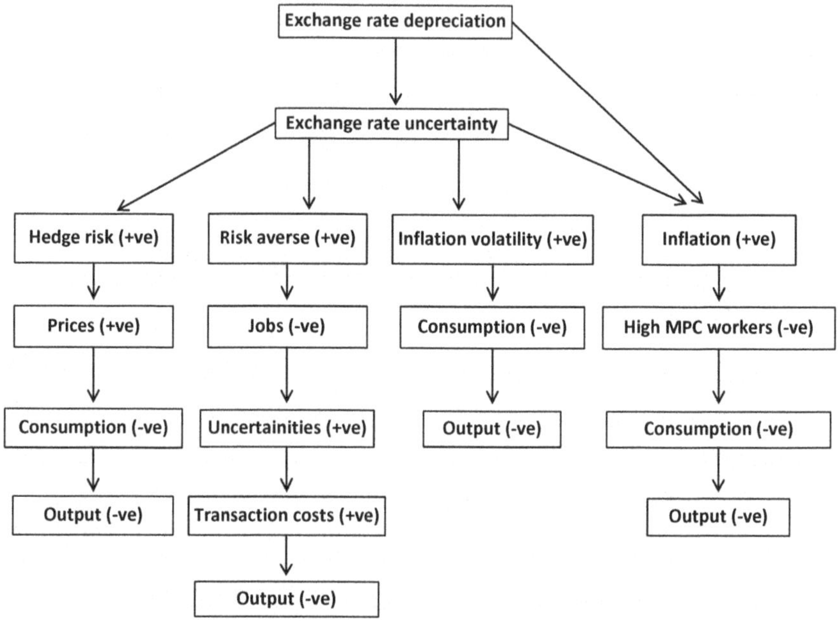

Fig. 15.2 Transmission of exchange volatility shocks. (Note: (+ve) imply positive effect, (–ve) imply negative effect. Source: Authors' drawing)

demand. The long-run negative effects of exchange rate uncertainty and volatility imply that it is harmful for economic growth. The exchange rate volatility could lower trade, and this eventually lowers production which may lead to a rise in the unemployment rate.

The policy implication is that heightened exchange rate volatility can have adverse effects on the nation's economy especially in the event of exogenous shocks. Hausmann et al. (2006) found that swings in the exchange rate have an impact on wealth effects and these effects depend on the perceived persistence of the volatility shocks. Volatility induces uncertainty in the production decision process, and this can impact economic growth. In addition, the exchange rate volatility has an impact on planning decisions and can alter economic prospects. Grossmann et al. (2014) suggest that policymakers focus on the high frequency components of volatility rather than on overall volatility as an intermediate target when trying to reduce the exchange rate volatility.

15.3 Thresholds for Mining Investment Growth

Earlier chapters showed that the ratio of mining investment to nominal GDP was below the long-term average of 1.76 per cent and only increased during 2005. In addition, the contribution of the mining sector investment to total investment increased to levels above the long-term average of 10 per cent around 2005. The increase in mining investment during 2005 and 2014 was comparable to levels recorded during the 1970s and 1980s commodity price booms. The same trend was observed in terms of mining investment as a ratio of total and private sector investment which recorded high levels of 25 per cent. Bonciani and Van Roye (2013) showed that volatility and uncertainty tend to have larger but significant effects during periods of economic and financial distress. The authors point out the importance of non-linearities and the likelihood of linear regime dependencies when analysing these volatility and uncertainty shocks. Furthermore, Fig. 15.1 shows that the exchange rate volatilities increased post-2009. Hence, we assess the responses of mining investment, output and employment.

We establish the thresholds at which (i) the ratio of mining investment to nominal GDP, (ii) the contribution of mining investment to total investment and (iii) mining investment to private sector investment occur. We use the Balke (2000) approach to establish the thresholds.[3] The data spans period 1990Q1 to 2016Q4 and is sourced for the South African Reserve Bank database. All growth rates are at annual rate. The estimated VAR model includes the mining sector output (GVA), mining sector employment, commodity prices and mining sector gross operating surpluses. We include the (i) the ratio of mining investment to nominal GDP, (ii) the contribution of mining investment to total investment and (iii) mining investment to private sector investment individually in the model to establish their thresholds. The established thresholds are shown in Table 15.1 and Fig. 15.3. The thresholds show that mining investment as a ratio of nominal GDP occurs at 1.9 which is slightly above the long-term average of 1.76 established in earlier chapters.

Similarly, the thresholds for the mining investment as a ratio of total and private sector investment are established at 11.6 and 17.8, respectively.

[3] See Balke (2000) for details.

Table 15.1 Mining sector investment thresholds

	Mining investment as a ratio of nominal GDP	Mining investment as a ratio of total investment	Mining investment as a ratio of private sector investment
Balke (2000) threshold	1.9	11.6	17.8

Source: Authors' calculations

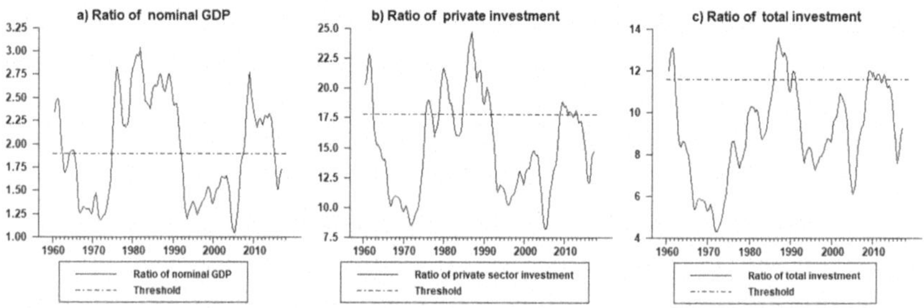

Fig. 15.3 Mining investment and estimated thresholds. (Source: South African Reserve Bank and authors' calculations)

The thresholds are above the long-term average levels of 9.48 and 14.2 established in earlier chapters. These thresholds delineate the high and low investment regimes. They can be used to assess what happens to mining sector output and employment in these two different mining investment regimes.

The trends shown in Fig. 15.3 show that all measures of mining investment are below the estimated investment ratio thresholds.

15.4 What Is the Impact of the Exchange Rate Volatilities on Mining Investment, Output and Employment Growth?

To answer this question, this section estimates several VAR models which include the exchange rate volatility mining investment, output and employment growth. The models include the estimated overall and permanent exchange rate volatility components. These exchange rate volatil-

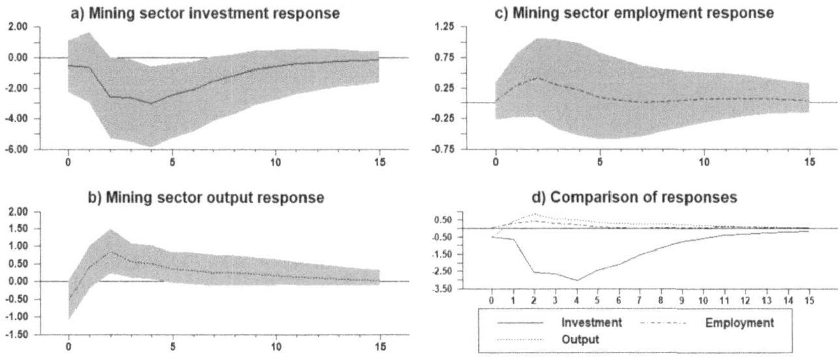

Fig. 15.4 Responses to positive overall exchange rate volatility shocks. (Note: The grey shaded area bands denote the 16th and 84th percentile confidence bands. Source: Authors' calculations)

ity components are included individually in the estimations. The sample spans the period 2000Q1 to 2016Q4. The VAR models are estimated with 2 lags and 10,000 Monte Carlo draws.

Figure 15.4 shows the responses to positive overall exchange rate volatility shocks. The results show that mining investment declines and remains depressed in response to positive overall exchange rate volatility shocks. But mining output and employment are transitorily affected by positive overall exchange rate volatility shocks.

The results in Fig. 15.4 contrast with those in Fig. 15.5 which show the responses to positive permanent exchange rate volatility shocks. Figure 15.5 shows that mining investment, output and employment growth are adversely affected by permanent exchange rate volatility. Mining investment and employment remain depressed over the forecast horizon. Thus, we conclude that the exchange rate volatility shocks lower the mining sector investment and output which in turn has negative effects on employment as shown in Fig. 15.2

Figure 15.6 shows a comparison of the mining investment, output and employment responses to positive overall and permanent exchange rate volatility shocks to assess which component exerts more adverse effects. Both overall and permanent exchange rate volatility shocks exert negative effects on mining investment, but permanent exchange rate volatility is especially bad for mining output and employment.

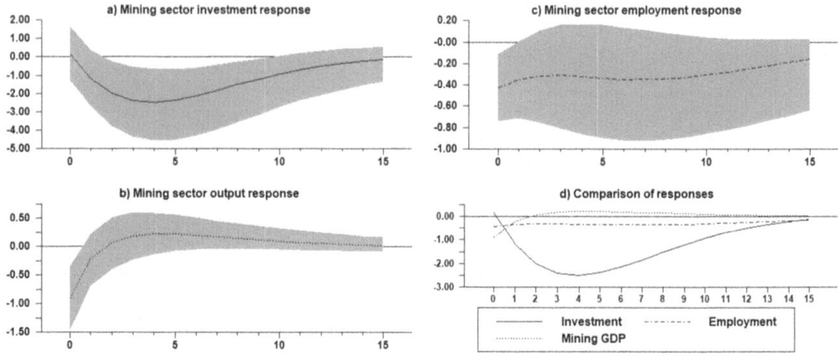

Fig. 15.5 Responses to permanent exchange rate volatility. (Note: The grey shaded area bands denote the 16th and 84th percentile confidence bands. Source: Authors' calculations)

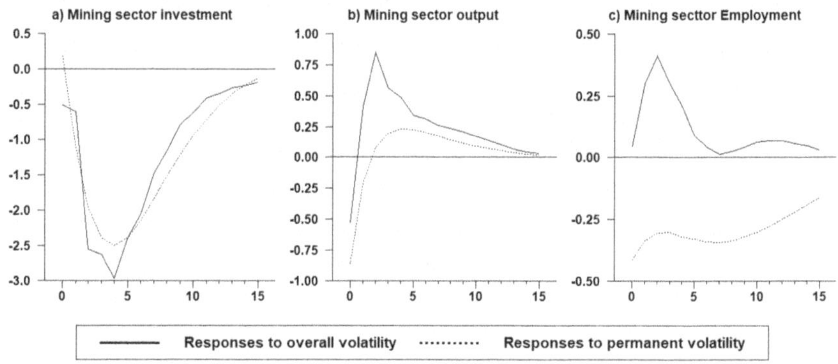

Fig. 15.6 Comparison of responses to positive overall and permanent exchange rate volatility shocks. (Source: Authors' calculations)

To conclude this section, we show the variance induced by positive overall and permanent exchange rate volatility shocks on mining investment, output and employment in Fig. 15.7. The results show that both volatilities explain a large share of variation in mining investment followed by output and employment.

Thus, we conclude that exchange rate volatility is bad for the mining sector. These results concur with earlier evidence in the preceding chapters that the exchange rate dynamics matter for the mining sector.

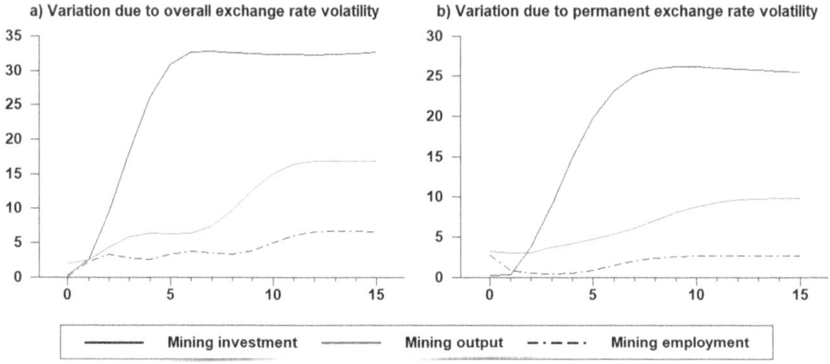

Fig. 15.7 Variance induced by positive overall exchange rate volatility shocks. (Source: Authors' calculations)

15.4.1 What Is the Impact of Exchange Rate Volatilities on Mining Exports?

We conclude the analysis of positive exchange rate volatility shocks by assessing their impact on exports. To this end, we replace mining investment in the earlier VAR estimations with mining exports. Figures 15.8 and 15.9 show that both overall and permanent exchange rate volatilities have an adverse effect on mining exports growth. The negative effects on mining exports are particularly pronounced due to the permanent component of the exchange rate volatility.

The results thus confirm that not only is the exchange rate volatility particularly bad for mining investment growth, it also has severe negative effects on mining exports growth.

15.5 The Threshold Effects on Mining Investment on Output and Employment

To conclude this chapter, we use the mining investment thresholds estimated in the earlier section to assess how positive shocks to mining investment in the low and high investment regimes impact mining output and employment growth. The South African Chamber of Mines (2018) shows

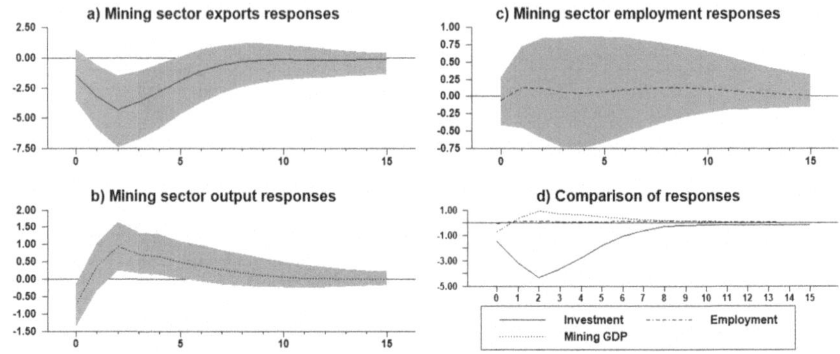

Fig. 15.8 Mining exports responses to positive overall exchange rate volatility. (Note: The grey shaded area bands denote the 16th and 84th percentile confidence bands. Source: Authors' calculations)

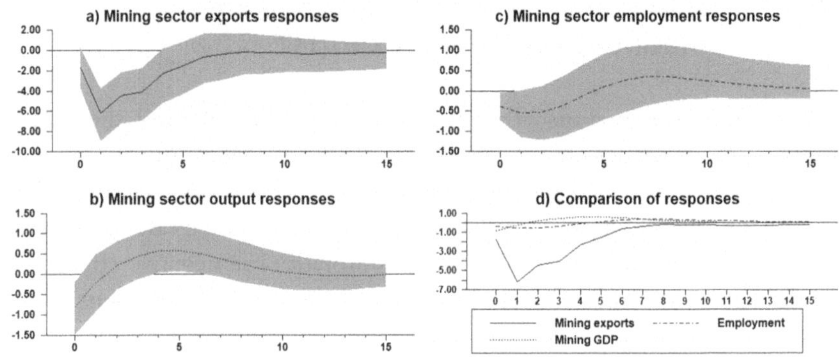

Fig. 15.9 Mining exports responses to positive permanent exchange rate volatility. (Note: The grey shaded area bands denote the 16th and 84th percentile confidence bands. Source: Authors' calculations)

that the mining sector is capital intensive. If gross operating surplus is used to represent the share of capital in the production process, the data reveals that the share of capital has historically accounted for almost 60 per cent in mining. But there are sectors such as the coal mining industry where output growth is mainly accounted for by increased labour productivity.[4] To capture the role and impact of investment regimes in the min-

[4] See http://www.chamberofmines.org.za/component/jdownloads/send/25-downloads/535-coal-strategy-2018.

ing sector, we create dummy variables that represent (i) *Dumm1* which takes on the value of mining investment as a ratio of nominal GDP for values above the estimated threshold and zero otherwise, (ii) *Dumm2* which takes on the value of mining investment as a ratio of total investment for values above the estimated threshold and zero otherwise and (iii) *Dumm3* which takes on the value of mining investment as a ratio of private sector investment for values above the estimated threshold and zero otherwise. These dummy variables are included separately in the estimation of the various VAR models. The VAR models include the dummy variable, mining output and employment growth. The models are estimated using 2 lags and 10,000 Monte Carlo draws.

The results in Fig. 15.10 show that irrespective of whether we use Dumm1, Dumm2 or Dumm3, positive shocks to mining investment during high mining investment episodes increase mining output and employment.

15.6 Conclusion and Policy Implications

What is the impact of positive exchange rate volatility shocks on mining exports, investment, output and employment growth? We estimate three components of the exchange rate volatility, namely, overall, permanent and transitory exchange rate volatility. Evidence shows that mining exports, investment, output and employment growth decline and remain depressed in response to overall and permanent exchange rate volatilities. Further, overall and permanent exchange rate volatilities explain a larger proportion of the variation in investment, output and employment growth. Overall and permanent exchange rate volatilities exert negative effects on mining investment, but permanent exchange rate volatility is especially bad for mining output and employment. Thus, we conclude that exchange rate volatility is bad for the mining sector. These results concur with earlier evidence in the preceding chapters that the direction and severe adverse shocks to the exchange rate matter for the mining sector.

Where do the thresholds for mining investment lie? We use the Balke (2000) threshold approach and establish that the (i) mining investment as a ratio of nominal GDP occurs at 1.9 and (ii) the thresholds for the mining investment as a ratio of total and private sector investment are

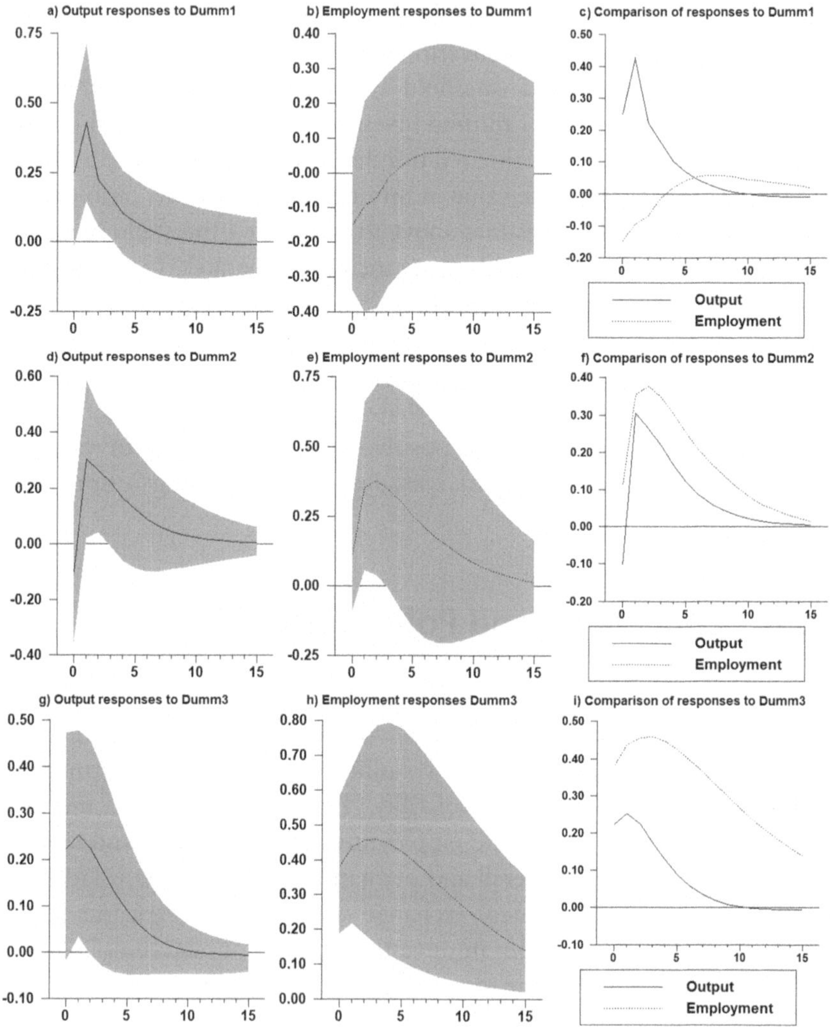

Fig. 15.10 Responses of mining output and employment to investment shocks in different regimes. (Note: The grey shaded area bands denote the 16th and 84th percentile confidence bands. *Dumm1* = the value of mining investment as a ratio of nominal GDP for values above the estimated threshold and zero otherwise, (ii) *Dumm2* = the value of mining investment as a ratio of total investment for values above the estimated threshold and zero otherwise, (iii) *Dumm3* = the value of mining investment as a ratio of private sector investment for values above the estimated threshold and zero otherwise. Source: Authors' calculations)

established at 11.6 and 17.8, respectively. All the estimated thresholds are above the long-term average levels of 1.9, 9.48 and 14.2 established in earlier chapters. In addition, all the ratios of mining investment are below the estimated investment ratio thresholds.

What are the implications of the estimated investment thresholds for mining output and employment? We use the thresholds that delineate the high and low investment regimes. Empirical evidence shows that positive shocks to mining investment during high mining investment episodes are positive for mining output and employment. High investment regimes are good for mining output and employment growth.

References

Arize, A.C. 1996. Real Exchange-Rate Volatility and Trade Flows: The Experience of Eight European Economies. *International Review of Economics and Finance*, 5(2), 187–205.

Bahmani-Oskooee, M., and Hanafiah Harvey, H. 2015. US–Indonesia Trade at Commodity Level and the Role of the Exchange Rate. *Applied Economics*, 46(18), 2154–66.

Balke, N.S. 2000. Credit and Economic Activity: Credit Regimes and the Nonlinear Propagation of Shocks. *Review of Economics and Statistics*, 82(2), 516–36.

Bonciani, D., and Van Roye, B. 2013. Uncertainty Shocks, Banking Frictions, and Economic Activity. *Journal of Economic Dynamics and Control*, 73(C), 200–19.

Cerra, V., and Saxena, S.W. 2008. Growth Dynamics: The Myth of Economic Recovery. *American Economic Review*, 98(1), 439–57.

Chamber of Mine South Africa. 2018. National Coal Strategy for South Africa. https://www.mineralscouncil.org.za/special-features/604-national-coal-strategy-for-south-africa

Chang, S.C. 2011. The Interrelationship between Exchange Rate Uncertainty and Unemployment for South Korea and Taiwan: Evidence from a Vector Autoregressive Approach. *International Economics*, 125, 65–82. January.

Grossmann, A., Love, I., and Orlov, A.G. 2014. The Dynamics of Exchange Rate Volatility: A Panel VAR Approach. *Journal of International Financial Markets, Institutions & Money*, 33, 1–27.

Hausmann, R., Hwang, J., and Rodrik, D. 2006. *What You Export Matters*. CEPR Discussion Papers 5444, CEPR Discussion Papers.
Ndou, E., Gumata, N., and Ncube, M. 2017. *Global Economic Uncertainties and Exchange Rate Shocks*. Palgrave Macmillan. ISBN 978-3-319-62279-8.

16

The Role of Policy Uncertainty, Low Confidence and the Mining Charter in the Transmission of Positive Shocks to Commodity Prices in the Mining Sector

Learning Objectives

- Explore the role of global and domestic policy uncertainty, low confidence and the mining charter in the transmission of positive shocks to commodity prices in the mining sector.
- Assess whether heightened domestic policy uncertainty and low confidence shocks reinforce each other to dampen the effects of positive commodity price shocks.

16.1 Introduction

Earlier chapters showed that investment growth in the mining sector has increased and consistently contributed above the long-term average of 10 per cent post-2009 but is lower than the estimated thresholds for investment ratios. The question explored in this chapter is premised on the observation that the contribution of mining investment growth to aggregate and private sector investment does not present a gloomy picture as expected in an industry reported to be plagued and paralysed by

N. Gumata, E. Ndou, *Accelerated Land Reform, Mining, Growth, Unemployment and Inequality in South Africa*, https://doi.org/10.1007/978-3-030-30884-1_16

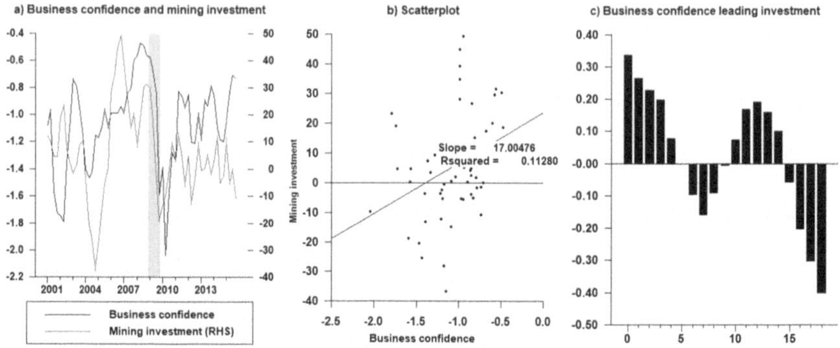

Fig. 16.1 Business confidence and mining investment growth. (Note: The grey shaded area denotes the South African recession. Source: South African Reserve Bank and authors' calculations)

heightened levels of policy uncertainty. This chapter asks: What is the impact of policy uncertainty, low confidence and the mining sector charter on mining investment, output and employment growth? Do they exert severe negative effects on mining investment, output and employment growth such that they neutralise the positive effects of commodity price shocks?

The scatterplot in Fig. 16.1 shows positive relationships between business confidence and the mining sector investment growth. The cross-correlations in Fig. 16.1(c) suggest that mining investment increases when led by business confidence. A similar trend is observed with respect to the association between mining sector gross operating surpluses and mining investment in Fig. 16.3. Increased profitability in the mining sector incentivises more investment in the sector. As expected, there is a negative association between policy uncertainty and mining sector investment in Fig. 16.2. Heightened policy uncertainty depresses investment in the mining sector.[1]

The R-squares and the lead relationships of business confidence and gross operating surpluses (proxy for profitability) indicate that the intensity of the association between the variables differs. Connolly and

[1] The South African policy uncertainty index is sourced from Hlatshwayo and Saxegaard (2016) https://www.imf.org/external/pubs/ft/wp/2016/wp16113.pdf.

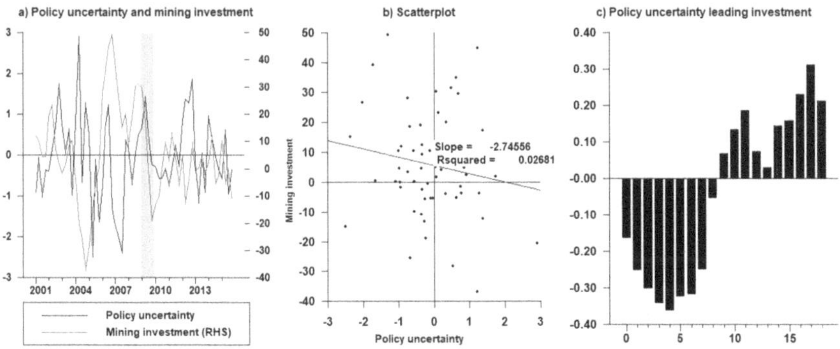

Fig. 16.2 Policy uncertainty and mining investment growth. (Note: The grey shaded area denotes the South African recession. Source: South African Reserve Bank, Hlatshwayo and Saxegaard (2016) and authors' calculations)

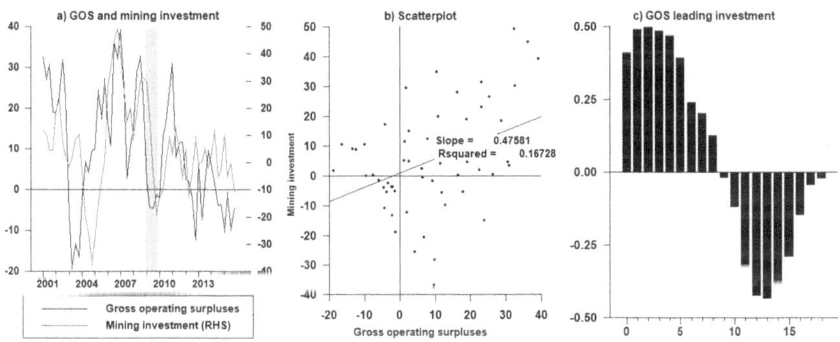

Fig. 16.3 Mining gross operating surpluses and mining investment growth. (Note: GOS = gross operating surpluses. Source: South African Reserve Bank and authors' calculations)

Orsmond (2011) observe that the prolonged period of low investment in the mining sector during the 1990s meant that the mining industry was not in a strong position to quickly increase supply when global demand for commodities finally picked up strongly in 2003. Earlier chapters showed that the ratio of mining investment to nominal GDP was below the long-term average of 1.76 per cent and only increased during 2005 but has since declined during 2014. A similar trend was observed with respect to the contribution of the mining sector investment to total investment.

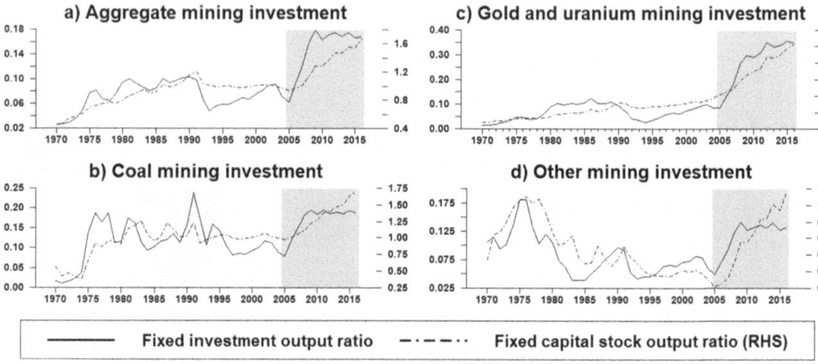

Fig. 16.4 Mining sector fixed capital stock and investment dynamics. (Note: The grey shaded area denoted the upward change in the observed trends. Source: The South African Chamber of Mines and authors' calculations)

Furthermore, the Chamber of Mines (2018) shows that mining sector is capital intensive. If gross operating surplus is used to represent the share of capital in the production process, the data reveals that the share of capital has historically accounted for almost 60 per cent in mining.

Furthermore, Fig. 16.4 shows that the trends in the mining sector fixed investment output ratio and fixed capital stock output ratio. The trends across the mining sector clearly show that there was trend break in 2005. This upward trend coincides with the commodity price boom episodes. In addition, there has been increased labour productivity across the board as shown in Fig. 16.5 post-2009.[2] The trends in these statistics help to anchor the debate and analysis around the role of uncertainty, the mining sector charter and the minimum wage in the mining sector.

It is against this background that we explore the role of the mining charter and policy uncertainty in the mining sector. The mining sector and commodity prices form an integral part of the economy, and the multiplier and spill-over effects to other economic sectors are important.

This is particularly the case when we consider the high unemployment level facing South Africa. It is common knowledge that the commodity

[2] The impact of the minimum wage is explored in detail in Chap. 12 where we assess the role of the prolonged labour unrest that was accompanied by the implementation of the wage floor for the sector.

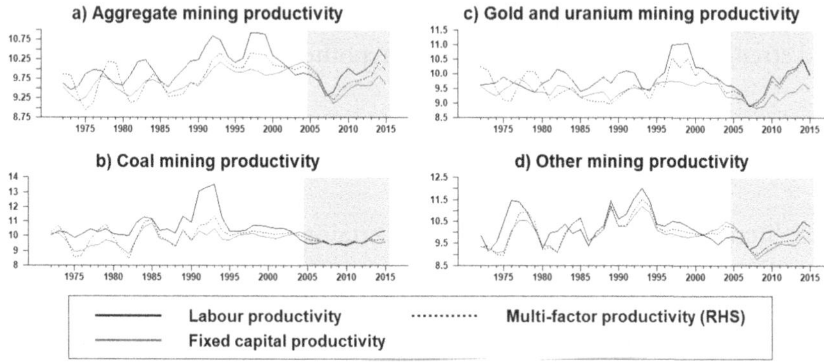

Fig. 16.5 Mining sector productivity growth trends. (Source: The South African Chamber of Mines and authors' calculations)

prices experienced what has been commonly referred to as the "*commodity prices super cycle*" during the period of the early 2000s to 2008 and the recent commodity price boom between 2009 and 2011.

The dominant narrative has been that South Africa, compared to other commodity exporters such as Australia and Canada, has squandered the opportunity to reap maximum benefits from the *commodity super cycle*, largely on account of domestic factors, hence, the so-called self-inflicted pain.[3] This chapter empirically tests the validity of this narrative and the largely untested anecdotal evidence on the mining sector. The introduction and implementation of various revised versions of the mining sector charter,[4] the domestic recession that was accompanied by the electricity outages, can be summarised under the policy uncertainty index as measured by Hlatshwayo and Saxegaard (2016).[5] Global uncertainty especially post-2009 can be captured via the global uncertainty index as measured by Baker et al. (2015).[6] We use these measures of domestic and

[3] Chapter 11 showed that South Africa did not miss out on the "commodity price boom". It may be the case that it could have performed far better given that it is well endowed with a broad basket on mineral resources.

[4] Also known as the Broad-Based Socio-Economic Empowerment Charter for the South African Mining and Minerals Industry.

[5] In cases where it is feasible because the dates are known such as, in the recession period, electricity outages, we create specific dummy variables to correctly identify the role and effect of these changes.

[6] See http://www.policyuncertainty.com/.

foreign policy uncertainties in the empirical section to test the validity and strength of the policy uncertainty hypothesis.

16.2 Literature Review

Vast literature has shown that policy certainty and confidence are key ingredients in the transmission of policy interventions into the real economy. Heightened levels of global and domestic uncertainties have a negative impact on consumer and business confidence and, in turn, investment and spending decisions. Empirical literature shows that uncertainty tends to adversely impact the domestic economy and there are spill-over effects of uncertainty within countries. Literature shows that risk and uncertainty shocks are distinct. Policy uncertainty, confidence and financial shocks, although different, are important drivers of economic fluctuations. Despite this, it is acknowledged that measuring economic policy uncertainty is very complex. But Bloom et al. (2013)[7] have developed new approaches to measure economic policy uncertainty. The authors measure policy uncertainty based on the frequency of certain economic indicators appearance in the media. These frequencies tend to be higher during periods of elevated economic uncertainty. These economic policy uncertainty indicators are then used to assess how policy uncertainty impacts economic activity.

Why should policymakers be concerned about heightened policy uncertainty and low levels of confidence? Do the effects of uncertainty depend on its source? Figure 16.6 starts by showing a schematic diagram of the transmission channels of uncertainty shocks.

Bernanke (1983a, b), Romer (1990) and Gilchrist et al. (2010) amongst others show that, when faced with high levels of uncertainty, the demand side of the economy may be dominated by firms that reduce investment expenditure. In some cases, firms may even postpone new projects as the environment may render such investment expenditure costly and non-profitable. Similarly, consumers might postpone their acquisition of durable goods as uncertainty increases. This is because uncertainty may

[7] See http://www.policyuncertainty.com/.

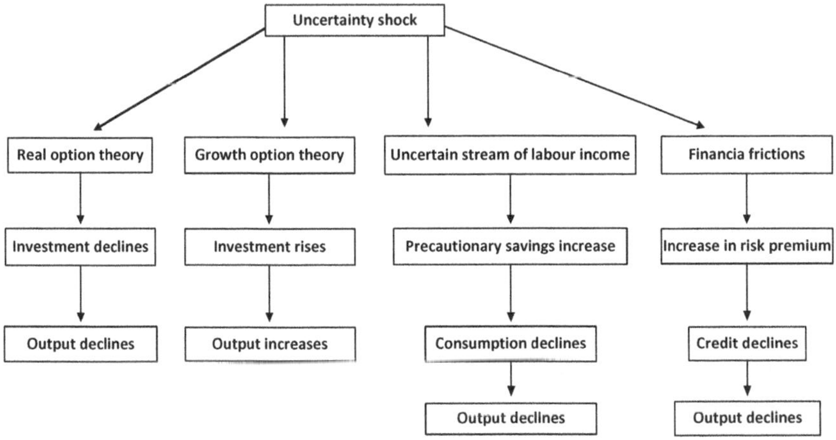

Fig. 16.6 Transmission channels of uncertainty shocks. (Source: Authors' drawing)

push up the cost of finance via an increase in risk premia. However, the effects of uncertainty are likely to vary across sectors in the economy due to varied levels of confidence that underlie stock market and other asset returns, investment and consumption decisions. Akerlof and Shiller (2009) allude to fact that the "*confidence multiplier*" played a meaningful role during and after the depression. This suggests that economic recoveries without sufficiently strong levels of confidence are highly unlikely to last and be robust, hence the conclusion that confidence is important.

Silvia and Iqbal (2011) identify two factors that play a key role in the decision-making process of economic agents, namely *ability* and *willingness*. Ability is defined as a quantitative factor, which consists of, among other factors, income, financial assets and loans. On the contrary, willingness is a qualitative factor, which includes expectations about the economy, earnings and future ability. These are part of the integral channels through which confidence can result in "recession-recovery" and "boom-bust" episodes. In addition, Barsky and Sims (2009) categorise the role of confidence in macroeconomics into two views. First, the animal spirits view which suggests autonomous fluctuations in beliefs that in turn have causal effects on economic activity. Second, the news view which regards the causal relationship between confidence and the subsequent macroeconomic activity. The news view is to be underpinned by the fact that confidence measures contain fundamental information about the current and future states of the economy. In most studies, the channel linking confidence and subsequent macroeconomic activity is changes in future productivity.

Several studies present evidence of the evolving nature of the transmission of policy uncertainty and confidence shocks. Chudik and Fratzscher (2012) show that the transmission of uncertainty shocks differed during the 2007–2008 financial crises and 2010–2011. They find that the flight-to-safety phenomenon due to the rise in risk and risk aversion characterised the pattern of capital flows in 2007–2008. The pattern of flows in 2010–2011 was different and investor decisions seemed to be informed by (i) a countries' sovereign rating, (ii) quality of institutions and (iii) financial exposure. Furthermore, Bloom et al. (2013) show that the recovery post-2009 has been different at least in one important dimension from the earlier ones, whether associated with financial crises or not, it has experienced bouts of elevated uncertainty. This suggests that there is a complementary explanation for the anaemic recovery—one that emphasises the roles played by macroeconomic and policy uncertainty in curtailing economic activity. On the other hand, Fornari and Stracca (2011) provide evidence that adverse financial shocks exert a significant influence on GDP and investment growth. This lack of full understanding of the channels of transmission of uncertainty may render policy decisions less effective and not achieve the desirable outcome; hence, they may accentuate or weaken intended purpose.

Caldara et al. (2014) shows that uncertainty shocks have a significant macroeconomic impact in situations where they elicit a tightening of credit and financial conditions. The authors show that increase in uncertainty is often associated with financial shocks which manifest in, for example, a widening of credit spreads and the depreciation of exchange rates. Collectively, the financial shocks can result in tightening in financial conditions. Farmer (2011) shows that not only do market participant's expectations or beliefs exert an independent influence on economic activity, they also select equilibrium. Consumer sentiment leads private activity, and it does not passively reflect the current state of the economy. Barsky and Sims (2012) find that consumer confidence results in an increase in GDP growth largely via changes in future productivity compared to the contribution of pure animal spirits. Nonetheless, the authors conclude that the contribution of animal spirits is non-negligible.

Hlatshwayo and Saxegaard (2016) construct a "news chatter" measure of policy uncertainty for South Africa. The authors then explore how this policy uncertainty index interacts with other supply-side constraints to impact exports performance. They find that increased policy uncertainty diminishes the responsiveness of exports to the REER and has short- and long-run level effects on export performance. They also show that a measure of competitiveness that adjusts for policy uncertainty and supply-side constraints greatly outperforms the REER in tracking exports performance.

Ndou et al. (2017) explore as to why South African growth has been volatile and weak following the recession in 2009. The subdued economic conditions have been characterised by high levels of uncertainty stemming from international and domestic events, such as macroeconomic policy uncertainty and the prolonged labour unrest in some key sectors of the economy. The authors establish foreign policy uncertainty shocks induce an unexpected trade decline in South Africa. The negative trade shock in turn induces heightened domestic economic policy uncertainty and exchange rate depreciation and these exert inflation pressures. At the same time, South African economic policy uncertainty amplifies the impact of foreign policy uncertainty on the domestic economy. For instance, domestic policy uncertainty amplifies the responses of domestic inflation and the exchange rate to UK economic policy uncertainty shocks and this is a risk to price stability. In addition, the domestic export demand channel in part explains why South African economic growth may not benefit to the maximum improvement in European GDP growth impulse.

16.3 Empirical Findings

This section conducts the empirical analysis of the role of global and domestic policy uncertainty, business confidence and commodity prices on key mining sector macroeconomic variables, namely, gross value added by the mining sector, investment, employment, mining imports and exports and the profitability of the mining sector.[8] The sample spans the period 2000Q1 to 2015Q4. The data is sourced for the South African Reserve Bank database. All growth rates are at annual rate. We create a dummy variable for the introduction and implementation of various revised versions of the mining sector charter; the domestic recession that was accompanied by the electricity outages can be summarised under the policy uncertainty index. We set the dummy to equal one in for the period post-2004Q1 when the mining charter was first introduced, and it is zero elsewhere. We use the Hlatshwayo and Saxegaard (2016) South African policy uncertainty to capture various aspects of domestic policy uncertainty. For global uncertainty especially post-2009, we use the global uncertainty index as measured by Baker et al. (2015). The structural shocks, namely, (i) the global uncertainty shock (GU), (ii) the domestic uncertainty shock (DU), (iii) the confidence shock, (iv) the commodity price shocks and (v) the mining sector charter shock, are included individually in the estimations of the VAR models. The VAR models are estimated using 2 lags and 10,000 Monte Carlo draws. The shocks are a one standard deviation shock.

We start by assessing the impact of structural shocks, namely, (i) heightened global uncertainty, (ii) heightened domestic uncertainty, (iii) the mining sector charter, (iv) negative domestic business confidence and (v) positive commodity prices on mining output, investment, exports and employment growth. The intention is to assess the validity of dominant narrative that compared to other commodity exporters such as Australia, Canada and South Africa squandered the opportunity to reap maximum benefits from the *commodity super cycle*, largely on account of domestic factors, hence, the so-called self-inflicted pain. We showed in earlier chapters that commodity prices experienced a boom post-2009 and that the mining sector investment grew since 2005 although it remained below the estimated thresholds. These shocks are estimated in different VAR models and their impact is compared thereafter.

---

[8] The impact of the minimum wage is explored in detail in Chap. 12 where we assess the role of the prolonged labour unrest that was accompanied by the implementation of the wage floor for the sector.

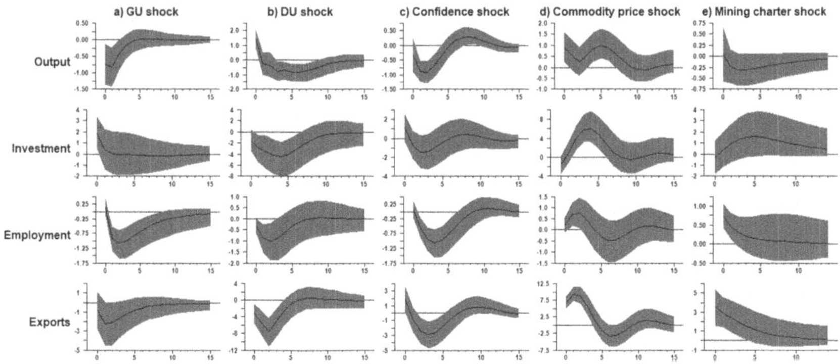

Fig. 16.7 Responses to various structural shocks. (Note: GU = global uncertainty, DU = domestic uncertainty. The responding variables are on the *y*-axis. The grey shaded area bands denote the 16th and 84th percentile confidence bands. Source: Authors' calculations)

Figure 16.7 shows the results of the five structural shocks. Column (a) shows that heightened global economic uncertainty (GU) shock lowers mining output, investment, employment and exports growth. The heightened domestic uncertainty (DU) shock also induces the same results in column (b). Similarly, we establish in column (c) that a negative shock to business confidence elicits the same response as that which is induced by heightened global and domestic uncertainty shocks. The mining sector charter in column (d) does not exert statistically significant negative effects on mining output.

In addition, we find that investment increases in response to mining sector charter shocks although the effects are not statistically significant. At the same time, we establish that employment and exports growth also increase significantly in the first two to four quarters following the mining sector charter shock. On the other hand, positive shocks to commodity prices result in an increase in mining output, investment, employment and exports growth.

However, we compare the effects of the shocks in Fig. 16.8 to establish the intensity of effects of different shocks. First, we establish that domestic uncertainty (DU) shocks in column (b) exert the most severe downward pressure on mining output compared to global uncertainty (GU) and the mining sector charter shocks. Second, domestic uncertainty

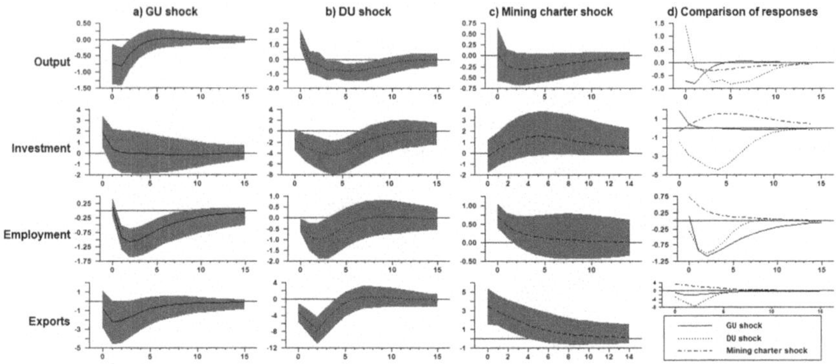

Fig. 16.8 Comparison of responses to heightened uncertainty and mining sector charter shocks. (Note: GU = global uncertainty, DU = domestic uncertainty. The responding variables are on the *y*-axis. The grey shaded area bands denote the 16th and 84th percentile confidence bands. Source: Authors' calculations)

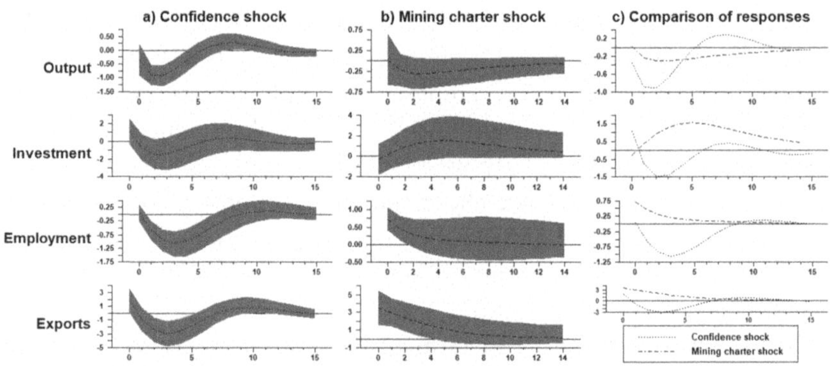

Fig. 16.9 Comparison of responses to low business confidence and mining sector charter shocks. (Note: GU = global uncertainty, DU = domestic uncertainty. The responding variables are on the *y*-axis. The grey shaded area bands denote the 16th and 84th percentile confidence bands. Source: Authors' calculations)

(DU) shocks lead to larger and persistent decline in mining investment compared to the global uncertainty (GU) and the mining sector charter shocks.

Third, mining exports and employment growth decline more due to domestic and global uncertainty shocks compared to the mining sector charter shock. Fourth, Fig. 16.9 shows that negative business confidence

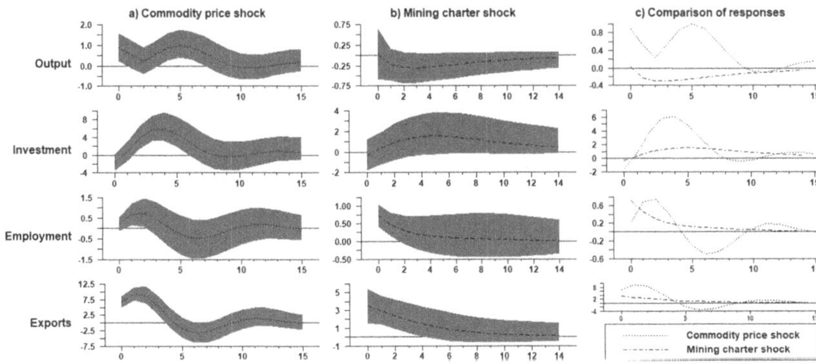

Fig. 16.10 Comparison of responses to positive commodity price and mining sector charter shocks. (Note: The responding variables are on the *y*-axis. The grey shaded area bands denote the 16th and 84th percentile confidence bands. Source: Authors' calculations)

shocks have potent negative effects on the mining sector compared to the mining sector shocks.

Last, Fig. 16.10 shows that positive commodity price shocks far outweigh the effects of the mining sector charter on the mining sector. Thus, we conclude that the mining sector charter does not exert any discernible and statistically significant negative effects on the mining sector.

The results show that heightened domestic uncertainty, low business confidence and positive commodity prices shocks play a major and statistically significant role in the mining sector compared to the mining sector charter. The policy implication is that lowering global and domestic policy uncertainty and policy measures that boost business confidence and commodity prices exert positive effects that far outweigh the idiosyncratic impact of the mining sector charter on the mining sector.

16.3.1 Historical Variance Decompositions

To examine the roles of domestic policy uncertainty, business confidence, commodity price and the mining sector charter shocks, we apply the historical variance decompositions approach. This approach decomposes the variance induced on the variables of interest by the shocks in the

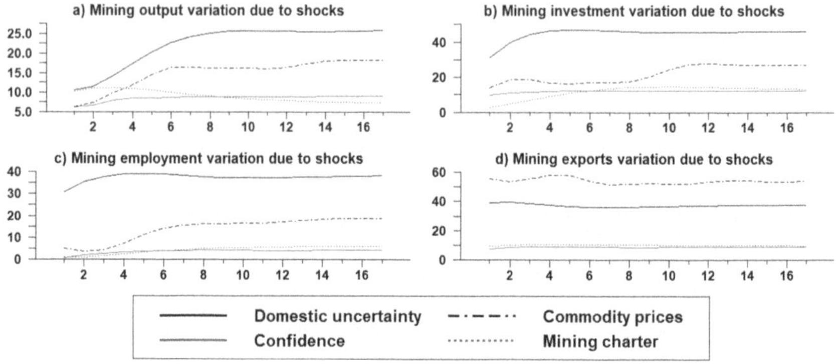

Fig. 16.11 Comparison of variances due to various structural shocks. (Source: Authors' calculations)

variables in the model. For ease of comparison, we present the variance decompositions of the same variables due to different structural shocks in the different VAR models. The results in Fig. 16.11 show that by and large domestic policy uncertainty and commodity prices explain a large proportion of the variation in mining sector output, investment, employment and exports growth compared to the role of the mining sector charter.

16.3.2 The Propagation of Positive Shocks to Commodity Prices by Various Shocks

To conclude this chapter, this section explores the role played by heightened domestic uncertainty, low business confidence and the mining sector in dampening or amplifying the effects of positive shocks to commodity prices. Like the previous chapters, we estimate a number of counterfactual VAR models which include the commodity prices, mining output, investment, employment and exports growth. We include the structural shocks, namely, domestic uncertainty, and business confidence separately in the estimations. The aim is to assess the role of these structural shocks as channels of transmission of positive shocks to commodity prices. We assess the role of the domestic policy uncertainty and business confidence channels in transmitting positive commodity price shocks. The propagation effects are measured as the difference between the actual and the counterfactual responses. The difference then gives the estimated role of the domestic policy uncertainty and business confidence channels in amplifying or dampening the role of positive commodity price shocks. The VAR models are estimated using 2 lags and 10,000 Monte Carlo draws.

Figures 16.12 and 16.13 show that positive commodity price shocks lead to an increase in mining output, investment, employment and exports growth. But the presence of heightened domestic policy uncertainty neutralises the full impact of positive commodity price shocks on the mining sector. The domestic uncertainty channel dampens the posi-

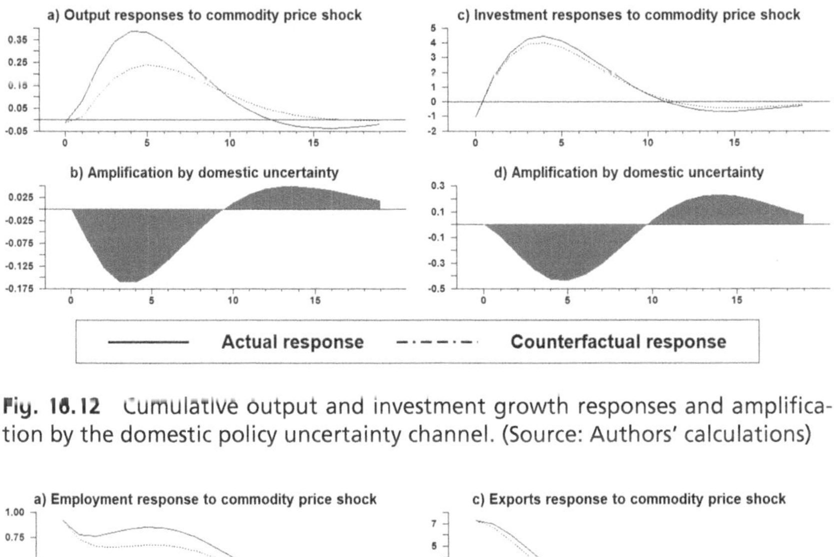

Fig. 16.12 Cumulative output and investment growth responses and amplification by the domestic policy uncertainty channel. (Source: Authors' calculations)

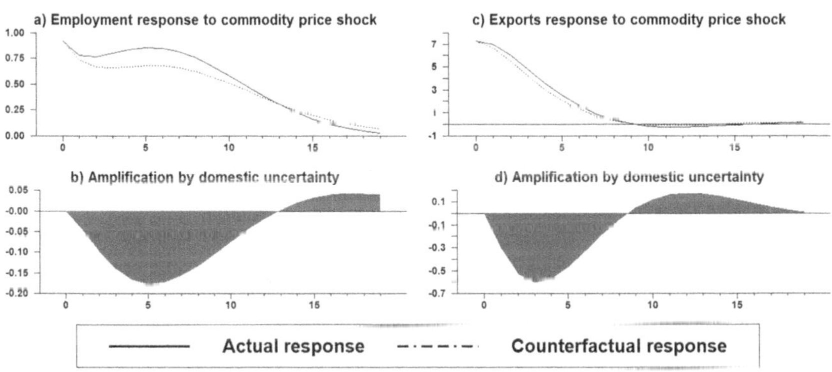

Fig. 16.13 Cumulative employment and exports growth responses and amplification by the domestic policy uncertainty channel. (Source: Authors' calculations)

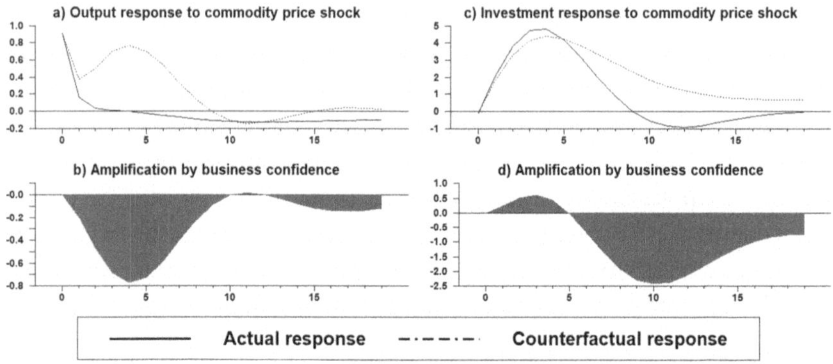

Fig. 16.14 Cumulative output and investment growth responses and amplification by the negative business confidence shocks. (Source: Authors' calculations)

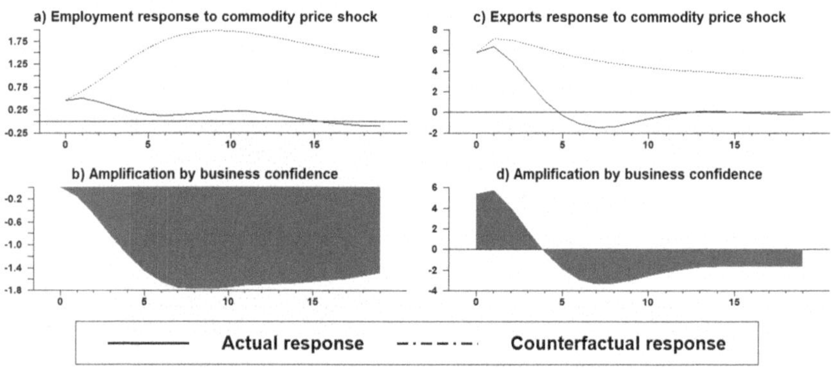

Fig. 16.15 Cumulative employment and exports growth responses and amplification by the negative business confidence shocks. (Source: Authors' calculations)

tive effects of commodity prices. These results further reinforce the findings in the earlier sections that lowering domestic policy uncertainty will benefit the mining sector from commodity price booms.

Similarly, Figs. 16.14 and 16.15 show that negative business confidence shocks dampen the positive effects of commodity price shocks on the mining sector.

The implication is that a combination of negative shocks to business confidence and heightened policy uncertainty deprives the mining sector from fully benefiting from positive commodity price shocks.

16.4 Conclusion and Policy Implications

What is the impact of global and domestic policy uncertainty, low confidence and the mining charter in the transmission of positive shocks to commodity prices on the mining sector output, investment, output and employment growth? Evidence in this chapter shows that heightened global and domestic economic uncertainty and low business confidence shocks lower mining output, investment, employment and exports growth. However, we fail to establish any statistically significant negative effects of the mining sector charter on mining the mining sector. Thus, we conclude that negative shocks global and domestic policy uncertainty and business confidence have potent negative effects on the mining sector compared to the mining sector shocks. The policy implication is that lowering global and domestic policy uncertainty and policy measures that boost business confidence and commodity prices exert positive effects that far outweigh the idiosyncratic impact of the mining sector charter on the mining sector.

Do they exert severe negative effects such that they neutralise the positive effects of commodity prices? We find that heightened domestic policy uncertainty and low confidence shocks reinforce each other in the same direction and dampen the effects of positive shocks to commodity prices on mining output, investment, employment and exports growth. Thus, we conclude that heightened domestic policy uncertainty and low business confidence dampen the positive effects of commodity prices on the mining sector. There is therefore evidence to support the hypothesis that South Africa did not fully maximise the opportunity presented by the recent commodity price booms to reap maximum benefits for the mining sector, largely on account of domestic factors, hence, the so-called self-inflicted pain.

References

Akerlof, G.A., and Shiller, R. 2009. *Animal Spirits: How Human Psychology Drives the Economy, and Why It Matters for Global Capitalism*. Princeton University Press: Princeton, NJ.

Baker, S.R., Bloom, N., and Davis, J.S. 2013. *Measuring Economic Policy Uncertainty*. Chicago Booth Research Paper.

Baker, S.R., Bloom, N., and Davis, J.S. 2015. *Measuring Economic Policy Uncertainty*. NBER Working Paper No. 21633. http://www.nber.org/papers/w21633.

Barsky, R.B., and Sims, E.R. 2009. *News Shocks*. NBER Working Paper No. 15312.

Barsky, R.B., and Sims, E.R. 2012. Information, Animal Spirits, and the Meaning of Innovations in Consumer Confidence. *American Economic Review*, 102, 1343–77.

Bernanke, B.S. 1983a. *Non-Monetary Effects of the Financial Crisis in the Propagation of the Great Depression*. NBER Working Paper 1054.

Bernanke, B.S. 1983b. Irreversibility, Uncertainty, and Cyclical Investment. *The Quarterly Journal of Economics*, 98(1), 85–106.

Bloom, N. 2014. Fluctuations in Uncertainty. *Journal of Economic Perspectives*, 28(2), 153–76.

Bloom, N., Floetotto, M., Jaimovich, N., Saporta-Eksten, I., and Terry, S. 2013. *Really Uncertain Business Cycles*. NBER WP 18245.

Caldara, D., Fuentes-Albero, C., Gilchrist, S., and Zakrajsek, E. 2014. *The Macroeconomic Impact of Financial and Uncertainty Shock*. Board of Governors of the Federal Reserve System International Finance Discussion Papers No. 1166.

Chamber of Mines. 2018. Facts and Figures. https://www.mineralscouncil.org.za/industry-news/publications/facts-and-figures

Chudik, A., and Fratzscher, M. 2012. *Liquidity, Risk and the Global Transmission of the 2007–08 Financial Crisis and the 2010–11 Sovereign Debt Crisis*. ECB Working Paper Series No. 1416.

Connolly, E., and Orsmond, D. 2011. The Mining Industry: From Bust to Boom. Reserve Bank of Australia. Reserve Bank of Australia Conference: The Australian Economy in the 2000s, pp. 111–56. https://www.rba.gov.au/publications/confs/2011/

Farmer, R.E.A. 2011. *Confidence, Crashes and Animal Spirits*. NBER Working Paper No. 14846.

Fornari, F., and Stracca, L. 2011. *What Does a Financial Shock Do? First International Evidence*. ECB Working Paper Series No. 1522.

Gilchrist, S., Sim, J., and Zakrajsek, E. 2010. *Uncertainty, Financial Frictions and Investment Dynamics*. 2010 Meetings Papers No. 1285. Society for Economic Dynamics.

Hlatshwayo, S., and Saxegaard, M. 2016. *The Consequences of Policy Uncertainty: Disconnects and Dilutions in the South African Real Effective Exchange Rate-Export Relationship*. IMF Working Paper WP/16/113.

Mohommad, A. 2017. *Labor Market Adjustment to Shocks in Australia*. IMF Working Paper WP/17/124.

Ndou, E., Gumata, N., and Ncube, M. 2017. *Global Economic Uncertainties and Exchange Rate Shocks*. Palgrave Macmillan. ISBN 978-3-319-62279-8.

Romer, P.M. 1990. Endogenous Technological Change. *The Journal of Political Economy*, 98(5), Part 2: The Problem of Development: A Conference of the Institute for the Study of Free Enterprise Systems, S71–S102. October.

Silvia, J., and Iqbal, A. 2011. Monetary Policy, Fiscal Policy and Confidence. *International Journal of Economics and Finance*, 3(4), 22–35.

17

What Are the Mechanisms and Channels Through Which the Mining Sector Adjusted to an Increase in the Binding Minimum Wage in 2014?

Learning Objectives

- Establish the main channels through which an increase in the binding minimum wage in the mining sector was transmitted.
- Whether the introduction of a higher binding minimum wage in the mining sector had a negative impact on employment and labour productivity growth.
- Establish which labour market theory and model best characterises the response of the mining sector to an increase in the binding minimum wage.

17.1 Introduction

The mining sector implemented a wage floor or minimum wage of R8000 across the board in 2014.[1] Figure 17.1 shows that remuneration in the mining sector increased from a low R2000 per month in 2001

[1] On 24 June 2014, a deal was reached and officially signed between the platinum companies and AMCU. The three-year agreement stated that workers who were currently earning less than

N. Gumata, E. Ndou, *Accelerated Land Reform, Mining, Growth, Unemployment and Inequality in South Africa*, https://doi.org/10.1007/978-3-030-30884-1_17

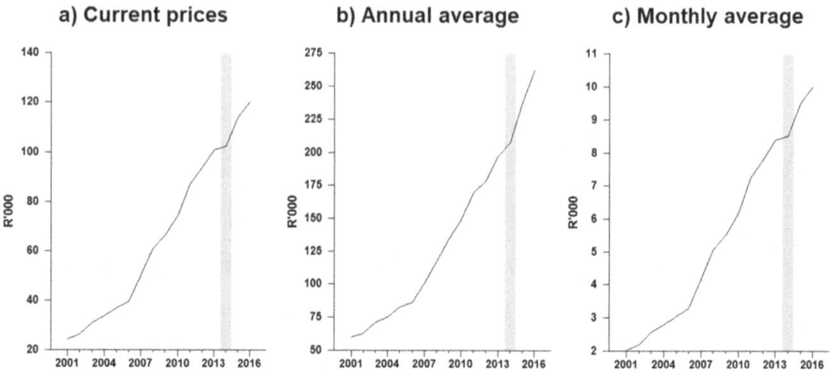

Fig. 17.1 Remuneration in the mining sector. (Note: The shaded area denotes the South African recession. Source: Chamber of Mines of South Africa Facts and Figures 2010)

to R10,000 per month in 2016 for the lowest paid worker. Earlier chapters showed that the non-gold mining sector's contribution to employment has been on a steady upward trend since 2000 and post the 2009 recession. At the same time, we showed that mining sector investment increased since 2005 in line with the recent commodity price booms. Figure 17.2 shows that the recent commodity price booms have had a positive effect on the fiscus. The mineral and petroleum resource royalty payments have been persistently high especially post-2009.[2] In addition, Fig. 17.3 shows that productivity growth in the mining sector increased post-2009 across the board and unit labour costs have stabilised around 10 per cent for a prolonged period in Fig. 17.4.

R12,500 will receive a R1000 increase in 2014 and in 2015. After the wage increases, the minimum salary would be R8000 a month. AMCU announced that it would continue to work to increase the minimum wage to R12,500 by the year 2017. Figure 17.13 in the Appendix compares other sectors and shows that at R8000 the mining sector minimum wage is more than double that of the national minimum of R3500. http://www.sahistory.org.za/article/2014-south-african-platinum-strike-longest-wage-strike-south-africa.

[2] The trend of mineral and petroleum resources royalty payments as a ratio of nominal GDP in Fig. 17.2 shows that the South African ratio is comparable to that in Australia. See Connolly and Orsmond (2011).

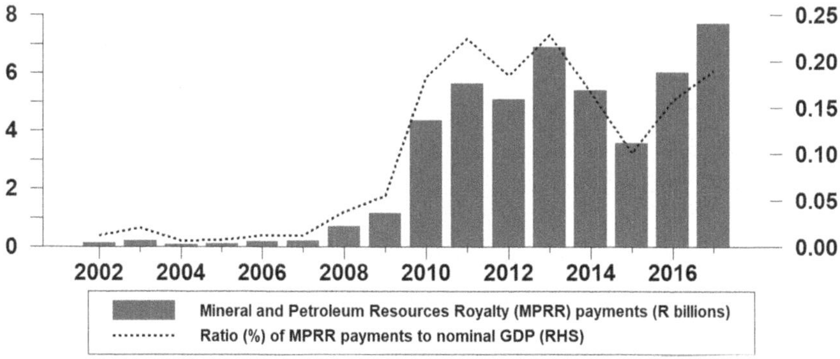

Fig. 17.2 Evolution of mineral and petroleum resources royalty (MPRR) payments. (Source: South African Reserve Bank and authors' calculations)

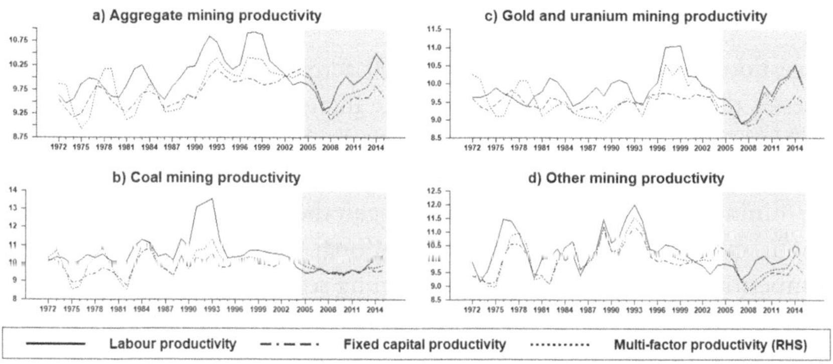

Fig. 17.3 Mining sector productivity growth trends. (Note: The grey shaded area denoted the upward change in the observed trends. Source: The South African Chamber of Mines and authors' calculations)

What could explain this momentum in the mining sector employment and investment growth despite the global financial crisis, domestic recession, heightened global and domestic policy uncertainty, including the rolling electricity outages, labour unrest and the implementation of a

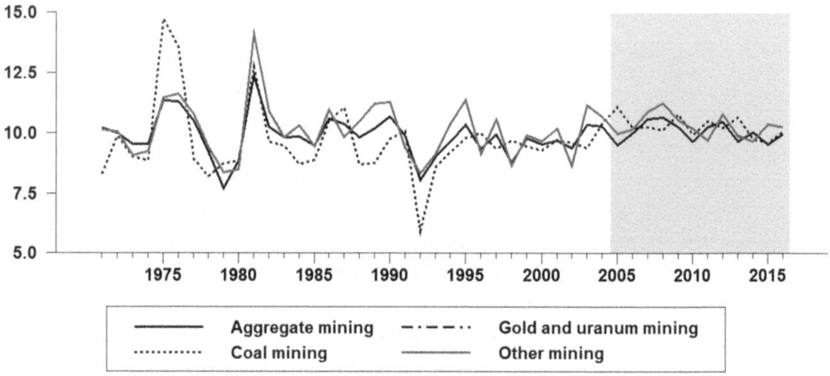

Fig. 17.4 Mining sector unit labour costs growth trends. (Note: The grey shaded area denoted the upward change in the observed trends. Source: The South African Chamber of Mines and authors' calculations)

wage floor or minimum wage of R8000 across the board? This chapter assesses the channels through which the increase in the minimum wage in the mining sector is transmitted through. What are the potent channels through which the increase in the minimum wage is transmitted in the mining sector? Does the evidence suggest the existence of a monopsony labour market structure or the institutional model as opposed to the competitive market structure in the mining sector?

The exact channels through which increases in the minimum wage affect the economy are still the subject of debate in the literature. The channels of adjustment range from (i) layoffs, (ii) cuts in hiring, (iii) price increases, (iv) cuts in non-labour costs, (v) wage rises for employees earning above the minimum wage and (vi) improvements in productivity.

Earlier chapters showed that the non-gold mining sector contribution to employment has been on a steady upward trend since 2000 and post the 2009 recession. Mining sector investment increased since 2005 in line with the recent commodity price booms. It is against this background that we explore the channels through which the mining sector adjusted to an increase in the minimum wage. This is particularly important given that the mining sector is largely export oriented and dependent on global demand and commodity price cycles. Furthermore, Bodnar et al. (2018) show that smaller, domestically owned, non-exporting firms and firms employing a higher proportion of low-skilled blue-collar workers tend to pay a higher share of their employees the minimum wage.

17.2 Literature Review

Basically, literature on the effect of changes in the minimum wage covers four main theoretical approaches, namely, (i) the competitive model, (ii) the dynamic monopsony model, (iii) the search and matching model and (iv) the institutional model. These theoretical approaches are based on different assumptions about how the labour market functions and the mechanisms for adjusting to binding minimum wages. In addition, these theoretical models provide evidence of other channels labour market adjustment to increases in the minimum wage other than just the employment channel.

The perfectly competitive labour model is based on the assumption that setting minimum wages above the market clearing level reduces the demand for labour and results in lower employment. Furthermore, if this assumption is relaxed to allow other channels of adjustment, firms adjustment by cutting working hours, reduce investment in training and other worker benefits, increases in prices as firms pass through the labour cost increase due to a higher minimum wage. Given that firms under perfect competitive labour markets already operate the assumptions of maximum productivity, this means that there is no room for any improvement in overall efficiency. Thus, the efficiency gains accruing to the increase in the minimum wage are not operational under the perfectly competitive labour model. Figure 17.5(a) presents the perfectly competitive labour market predictions about the impact of the minimum wage on employment. The competitive labour model assumes a downward sloping employment or labour demand curve and an upward-sloping labour supply or wage setting curve. Under the competitive labour market model, it is assumed that the labour force is homogenous; hence, the demand for labour by firms is a decreasing function of wages.

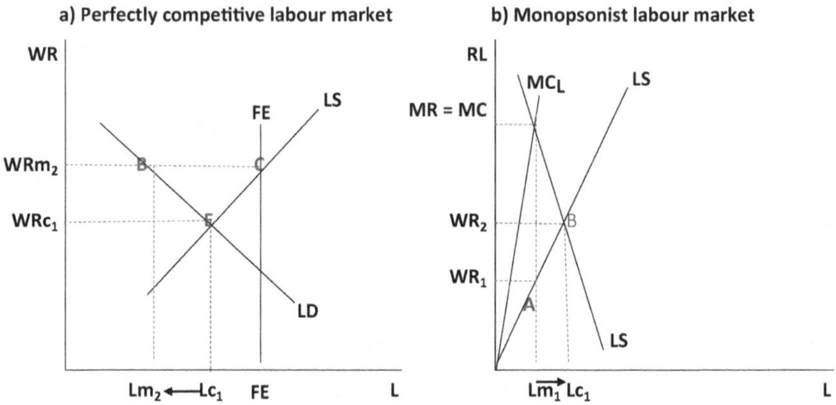

Fig. 17.5 Labour market models, minimum wage and active labour market policies. (Source: Authors' drawings)

The intersection of the labour demand and supply schedules at point E equilibrates the labour market at the wage rate WR_{c1} and employment rate L_{c1}. The introduction of the minimum wage (MW) WR_{m2} above the market clearing wage rate WR_{c1} and fixing the wage rate is expected to lead to a decline in the demand for labour and shift the employment rate lower from L_{c1} to L_{m2} but moves the labour market into a disequilibrium position B on the labour demand curve. The implication is that the introduction of the minimum wage creates disequilibrium in the labour market and employment loss. Full employment is given by the vertical line FE, and the amount of voluntary or involuntary unemployment is derived from the difference between FE and L_{C1}.

The monopsony labour market model assumes the presence of labour market frictions and market power that allow profit-targeting firms in cases where there is no binding minimum wage to hire less labour than the socially efficient amount. Firms in the monopsony labour market model set wages below the competitive market rate. As a result, the upward-sloping labour supply curve implies that employment is an increasing function of wages. The upward-sloping labour supply curve determines that employment and wages in monopsony labour market model increase in response to the binding minimum wage up to a competitive market level. The channels through which firms adjust to the increase in the minimum wage within the monopsonic market power include (i) passing through a portion of the increase in their production costs on to consumers by raising prices and (ii) positive spill-over effects of an increase in the minimum wage might attract new employees.

In Fig. 17.5(b) the monopsony or monopoly labour market is characterised by a single-buyer or seller of a commodity. As opposed to the competitive market, the monopsony market faces an upward-sloping and firms are price makers. The introduction of the minimum wage can lead to the increase in employment. This is because the introduction of the minimum wage that would prevail under the competitive means that the monopsonist can hire workers at a constant wage rate set by the minimum wage rate. For a monopsonist, the introduction of the minimum wage means that it faces a wage rate that is independent of how many workers it hires. As a result, the firm will employ until the value of the MP equals the minimum wage at point B in Fig. 17.5(b) which is the same rate as the competitive wage in the competitive labour market in Fig. 17.5(a).

The implication is that the wage floor set by the minimum wage for a monopsonist acts in the same way as the price ceiling for a monopolist and makes the firm move the demand for a factor in a similar fashion as that of a competitive firm. This is how the effects of the imposition of the minimum wage exert different effects in the competitive and monopsonist labour markets. Initially, without the minimum wage, a non-discriminating monopsonist employs fewer workers than would be employed if the market was competitive; hence there is underemployment. However, the introduction of the minimum wage results in an increase in the wage rate and employment. This means that a well-designed minimum wage can eliminate the market power of monopsonists and prevent the exploitation of workers.

The search and matching model assumes the existence of labour market frictions such as search frictions as unemployed workers search for jobs and firms driven by the profit maximisation objective search for employees to vacancies. This model assumes that the binding minimum wage can lead to a decline in unemployment especially in cases when an increase in the minimum wage leads to stronger job search efforts and improved matching process. The relationship between unemployment rate and vacancies known as Beveridge curve has implication for business cycle and inflation dynamics. The Beveridge curve (BC) describes the negative empirical relationship between the unemployment rate and the job vacancy rate. Bleakley and Fuhrer (1997) suggest that the BC can be used to assess the state of the labour markets relative to the business cycle phases. Figure 17.6 shows the business cycle effects on the Beveridge curve, the role of matching efficiency and government policy interventions such as training. Shifts of the BC inwards or outwards exhibit movement along the curve.

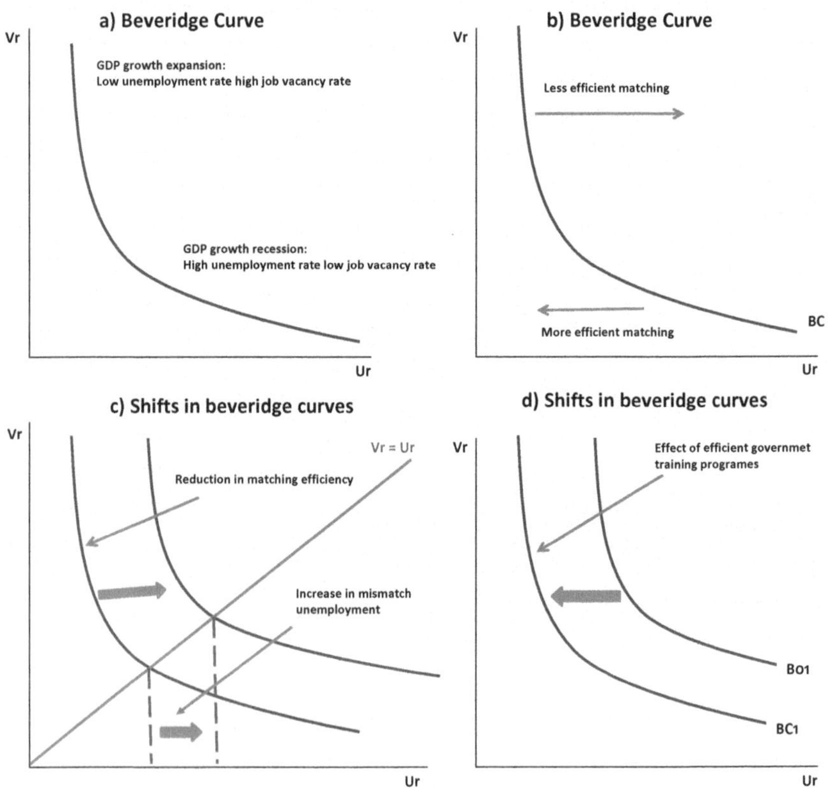

Fig. 17.6 Beveridge curve dynamics. (Source: Authors' drawings and adapted from Carlin and Soskice (2006) and Bleakley and Fuhrer (1997))

The business cycle matters for movements in the BC because in recessionary (expansionary) times, the economy moves towards a regime characterised by an increase (decrease) in the unemployment rate and a reduction (increase) in the vacancy rate. The BC can also shift outwards or inwards due to changes in factors such as matching efficiency, the implementation of effective training programmes by the government which reduce the skills mismatch between the readily available labour and the job openings. Thus, policies which tackle structural unemployment will shift the BC to the left in Fig. 17.6. The outward shift in the Beveridge curves in Fig. 17.6(c) is in line with an increasing skills mismatch and could be the result of a number of factors such as (i) the unemployed searching for jobs less effectively, (ii) being choosy in accepting jobs or (iii) firms become choosier in filling vacancies against long-term *U* or (iv) due to employment protection legislation.

The Beveridge curve can be used in conjunction with the wage-price setting curve to show the effects on wage growth and consumer price inflation in Fig. 17.7. The model postulates a positive relationship between wages and the number of vacancies in Fig. 17.7(a). Carlin and Soskice (2006) suggest that this means that an increase (decrease) in vacancies in the economy should increase (lower) the wages workers bargain for or that employers need to set to attract good workers.

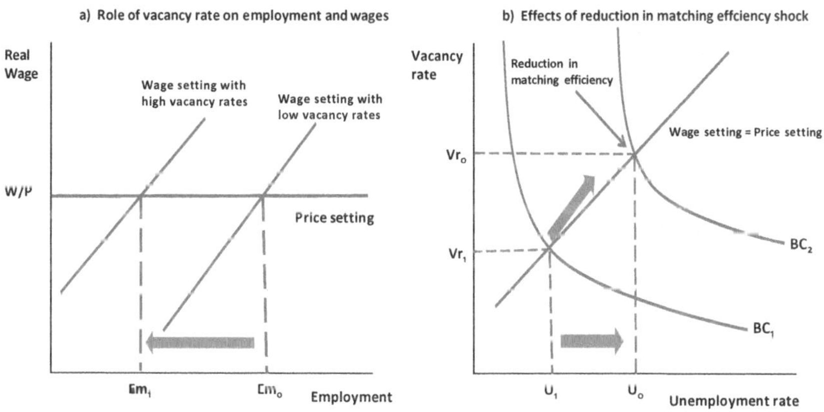

Fig. 17.7 The role of vacancy rates and efficiency in matching. (Source: Authors' drawings)

An outward shift in Beveridge curve can be a result of the inability of the economy to match workers to job, which leads to high unemployment and vacancy rates. The deterioration in matching occurs via the increase in the vacancy rate which pushes the wage-price-setting curve upwards thus raising inflationary pressures. Hence, the wage setting curve shifts up when the vacancy rates increase. This adjustment implies the inability of the economy to match workers to job vacancies which has implications for price stability and wage dynamics.

The institutional model assumes that (i) employees are heterogeneous; (ii) labour markets are imperfectly competitive, integrated and exposed to an excess labour supply; and (iii) firms operate under certain labour market institutions. Within the institutional model, firms respond to an increase in the minimum wage by improving their overall efficiency though two channels, namely, (i) reducing organisational inefficiencies or (ii) increasing the productivity of employees. The pass-through of an increase in the minimum wage and labour costs into higher prices is neutralised by the increase in efficiency. Figure 17.8 shows two scenarios (i) the effect of an increase in productivity and (ii) an effect of an increase in the labour force. The productivity shock shifts the labour demand schedule (LD) from LD1 outwards to LD2 and the wage setting curve (WS) shifts from WS1 inward to WS2 by the same amount.

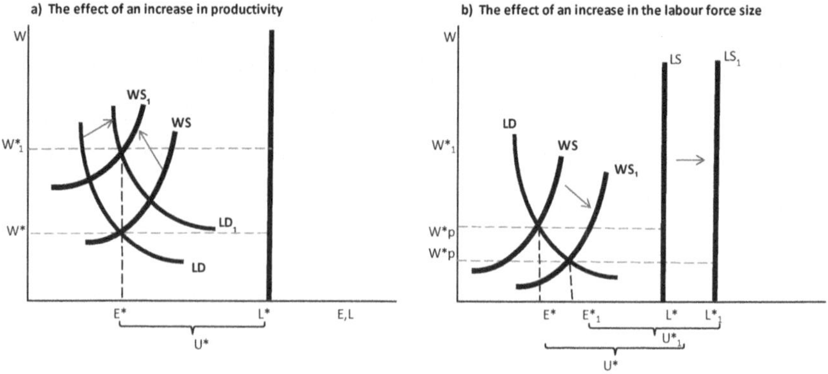

Fig. 17.8 Effects of productivity and labour force size shock. (Note: WS implies wage setting, LD implies labour demand, LS implies labour supply, U implies unemployment. Source: Authors' drawings)

Figure 17.7(b) shows the effects of an increase in the labour force on unemployment in the long run. A rise in the labour force shifts the labour supply curve (LS) from LS1 outwards to LS2 by same amount.

Thus, these theoretical models suggest that an increase in the minimum wage affects the demand and supply sides of the economy. On the demand side, the increase in binding minimum wages results in higher disposable income, which in turn boosts the demand for goods and services. This then supports growth in firm revenues and spills-over into demand for additional labour and higher wages. It is for this reason that firms have a number of strategies for reacting to the increase in the minimum wage. These adjustment strategies in turn mean that the increase in the minimum wage can have different specific effects on the cost components of firms. Various channels of adjustment to the increase in the minimum wage imply varying degrees of the pass-through of increased labour costs to prices.

Gumata and Ndou (2017) explored the channels through which the national minimum wage affects the South African economy from the monetary policy point of view. The authors establish evidence that rejects the predictions of perfectly competitive labour markets in favour of the monopsony labour market structure predictions in response to an increase in the minimum wage. The consumer price inflation and changes in the Gini coefficient decline, whereas wage growth, employment growth, GDP growth and gross operating surpluses growth increase in response to a positive shock to the minimum wage. Furthermore, the authors establish that a positive minimum wage growth shock leads to an increase in labour productivity growth, which is consistent with the wage efficiency hypothesis. At the same time, the responses of labour productivity and employment growth to a positive shock to the minimum wage tend to be significantly higher in the low inflation regime compared to the high inflation regime. This underscores the important role played by the low inflation regime as it accentuates efficiencies which leads and various adjustment channels to the increase in the minimum wage. These results concur with the monopsony and efficiency wage models which assume positive effects on employment and efficiency gains as workers and firms adjust to a higher binding minimum wage.

Hirsch et al. (2015) finds that increases in the minimum wage affect inflation significantly and Lemos (2008) concludes that an increase in the minimum wage is associated with a stronger increase in food prices but a weaker increase in overall prices. Similarly, Wadsworth (2010) finds that since the introduction of the minimum wage in the UK, prices increased significantly faster in several minimum wage-intensive sectors than in other sectors. But Katz and Krueger (1992) do not concur.

Bodnar et al. (2018) explore the transmission channels for increases in the minimum wage using a unique firm-level dataset from eight Central and Eastern European countries. They find that the rise in minimum wages is mostly transmitted into higher prices, cuts in non-labour costs and improvements in productivity. They establish that cuts in employment are less popular and occur mostly through reduced hiring rather than direct layoffs. Cutting employment is not a common reaction to a rise in the minimum wage but when it happens it is mostly through reduced hiring rather than direct layoffs. The most popular adjustment channels are the increase in product prices, the reduction of non-labour costs and productivity improvement. Similarly, in Levin-Waldman and McCarthy (1998), the imposition of a minimum wage does not necessarily destroy jobs but may hinder job creation.

In addition, Bodnar et al. (2018) establish the existence of potential spill-over effects that increases in the minimum wage can have on firms without minimum wage workers. Neumark and Wascher (2008) find that increases in the minimum wage compress the lower tail of the wage distribution and have positive spill-over effects on wages up to about 20 per cent above the minimum wage level. Hirsch et al. (2015) establish positive spill-over effects of the minimum wage for the US restaurant sector. In addition, the increase in minimum wages creates pressure on managers to increase labour productivity from the workforce by cross-training, multi-tasking and tighter work schedules.

17.3 Empirical Evidence

This section conducts the empirical estimations to assess the potent channels through which the mining sector adjusts to the increase in the minimum wage. Due to data availability for disaggregated unit labour costs

(ULCs), labour, capital and multifactor productivity, we only assess the coal, gold and uranium and the other mining sector. We create a dummy variable for the increase in the minimum wage which takes on the values of the minimum wage variable greater than R8000 and zero otherwise. We estimate several VAR models which include aggregate and disaggregated mining output, employment, unit labour costs, labour, capital and multifactor productivity for the aggregate mining sector and each mining commodity sector individually. All growth rates are at an annual rate. The data is quarterly (Q) and spans the period 2001Q1 to 2016Q4. The data is sourced from the South African Reserve Bank, Chamber of Mines and Statistics South Africa databases. The VAR models were estimated using 2 lags and 10,000 Monte Carlo draws. The shock is a one standard deviation shock.

First, Fig. 17.9 shows the responses of mining sector employment growth to an increase in the mining sector minimum wage above R8000 pm. The results show that there are differences in the responses at the aggregate and disaggregated mining sector. Employment growth declines across the sectors and the decline is severe at the aggregate level. Whereas, at the disaggregated level, the decline in other mining sectors employment is statistically insignificant compared to the gold and coal mining sectors.

On the other hand, Fig. 17.10 shows that unit labour costs decline across the sectors and this is on account of the increase in labour produc-

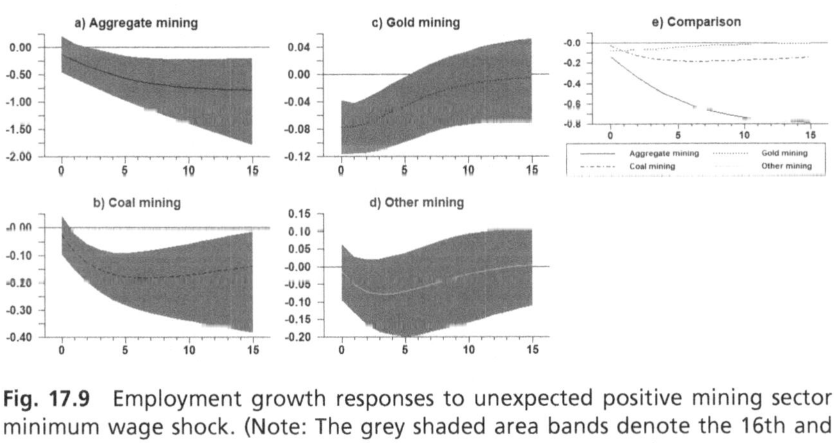

Fig. 17.9 Employment growth responses to unexpected positive mining sector minimum wage shock. (Note: The grey shaded area bands denote the 16th and 84th percentile confidence bands. Source: Authors' calculations)

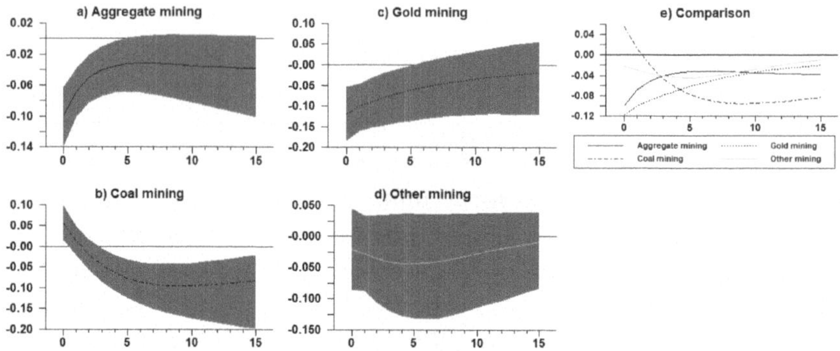

Fig. 17.10 Unit labour costs growth responses to unexpected positive mining sector minimum wage shock. (Note: The grey shaded area bands denote the 16th and 84th percentile confidence bands. Source: Authors' calculations)

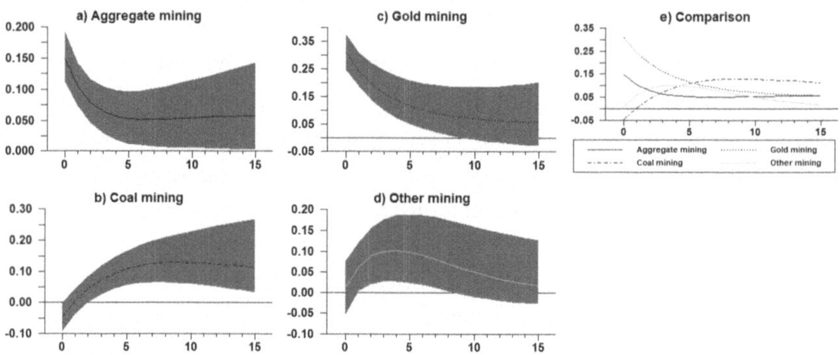

Fig. 17.11 Labour productivity growth responses to unexpected positive mining sector minimum wage shock. (Note: The grey shaded area bands denote the 16th and 84th percentile confidence bands. Source: Authors' calculations)

tivity in Fig. 17.11. Labour productivity increase in response to an increase in the minimum wage especially in the coal and other mining sectors.

In fact, Fig. 17.12 shows that an unexpected increase in the minimum wage in the mining sector pushes employment and labour productivity growth in different directions. Employment growth declines while labour productivity increases. This is especially the case for the coal mining and other mining sectors.

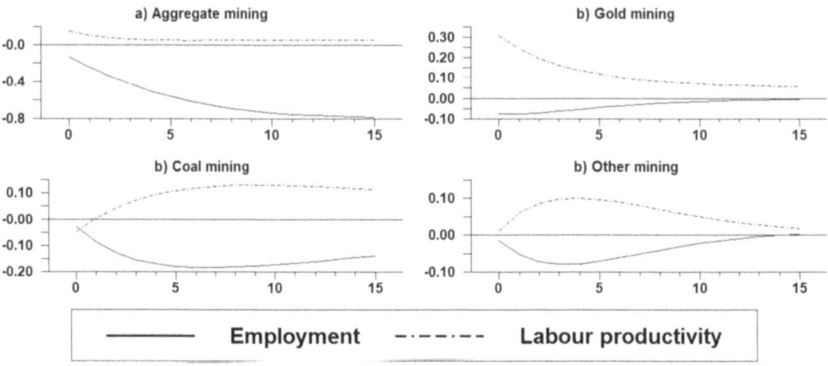

Fig. 17.12 Comparison of employment and labour productivity growth responses to an unexpected positive mining sector minimum wage shock. (Source: Authors' calculations)

The implication of the results is that the mining sector mainly adjusts via the employment and labour productivity growth. This means that the mining sector curtails employment growth and at the same time increases labour productivity to adjust and neutralise the impact of the increase in the minimum wage on employment growth. Alternatively, the mining sector employs less people than otherwise would have been the case in the absence of a binding increase in the minimum wage. Thus, the evidence contained in this chapter arrives at similar conclusions as those in Bodnar et al. (2018) and Levin-Waldman and McCarthy (1998) who find that the rise in minimum wages is mostly transmitted into higher product prices, cuts in non-labour costs and improvements in productivity. The imposition of a higher minimum wage in the mining sector does not necessarily destroy jobs but may hinder the intensity of job creation.

17.4 Conclusion and Policy Implications

What are the mechanisms and channels through which the mining sector adjusted to an increase in the binding minimum wage in 2014? Evidence shows that there are differences in the responses at the aggregate and disaggregated mining sector. First, employment growth declines across sectors and the decline is severe at the aggregate level. Whereas, at the disaggregated level, the decline in other mining sectors employment is statistically insignificant compared to the gold and coal mining sectors. Second, unit labour costs decline across sectors and this is on account of the increase in labour productivity. Labour productivity increases in response to an increase in the minimum wage especially in the coal and other mining sectors. Third, an increase in the minimum wage in the mining sector pushes employment and labour productivity growth in different directions. This is especially the case for the coal mining and other mining sectors.

Thus, we conclude that the impact of an increase in the binding minimum wage in the mining sector is best characterised by the institutional model which assumes that firms respond to an increase in the minimum wage by improving their overall efficiency though two channels, namely, (i) reducing organisational inefficiencies and or (ii) increasing the productivity of employees. The pass-through of an increase in the minimum wage and labour costs into higher prices is neutralised by the increase in efficiency.

The implication of the results is that the mining sector mainly adjusts via the employment and labour productivity growth channels. This means that the mining sector curtails employment growth, that is, the sector employs less people than otherwise would have been the case in the absence of a binding increase in the minimum wage. But at the same time, the mining sector increases labour productivity to adjust and neutralise the impact of the increase in the minimum wage on employment growth. The imposition of a higher minimum wage in the mining sector does not necessarily destroy jobs but may hinder the intensity of job creation. Labour productivity gains are used as the channel to neutralise and cushion employment losses (direct layoffs) in the sector.

From a policy perspective, policymakers have to pay attention to such idiosyncratic adjustment mechanisms to increases in the binding minimum wage especially when the mining sector is earmarked as a "sunrise industry" which is meant to contribute meaningfully to high and sustainable employment growth. In addition, setting up a sovereign wealth fund as an instrument for long-term planning and management of mineral resources will also assist the sector to adjust to such binding wage shocks. This is over and above broadening the scope of employee incentives beyond the reliance on just the binding minimum wages.

Appendix

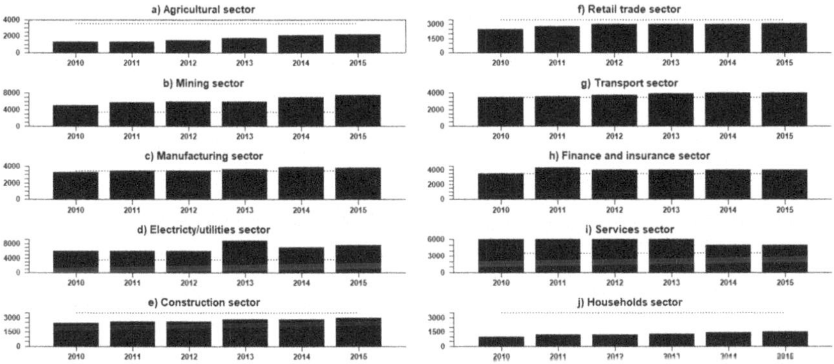

Fig. 17.13 Sector minimum wages relative to the national minimum wage. (Source: www.lrs.org.za/award)

References

Azar, J., Marinescu, I., and Steinbaum, M.I. 2017. *Labour Market Concentration*. NBER Working Paper 24147.

Bleakley, H., and Fuhrer, J.C. 1997. Shifts in the Beveridge Curve, Job Matching, and Labor Market Dynamics. *New England Economic Review*, September/October, pp. 3–19.

Bodnar, K., Fadejeva, L., Lordache, S., Malk, L., Paskaleva, D., Pesliakaite, J., Jemec, T.N., Toth, P., and Wyszynski, R. 2018. *How Do Firms Adjust to Rises in the Minimum Wage? Survey Evidence from Central and Eastern Europe*. ECB Working Paper No. 2122.

Carlin, W., and Soskice, D. 2006. *Macroeconomics: Imperfections, Institutions, and Policies*. Oxford University Press: Oxford, UK. ISBN 019-8-776-225.

Connolly, E., and Orsmond, D. 2011. *The Mining Industry: From Bust to Boom*. Discussion Paper 2011-08, Research Reserve Bank of Australia.

Gumata, N., and Ndou, E. 2017. *Bank Credit Extension and Real Economic Activity in South Africa: The Impact of Capital Flow Dynamics, Bank Regulation and Selected Macro-prudential Tools*. Palgrave Macmillan. ISBN 978-3-319-43550-3.

Hirsch, B., Kaufman, T., Bruce, E., and Zelenska, T. 2015. Minimum Wage Channels of Adjustment. *Industrial Relations: A Journal of Economy and Society*, 54(2), 199–239.

Katz, L.F., and Krueger, A.B. 1992. The Effect of the Minimum Wage on Fast Food Industry. *Industrial and Labor Relations Review*, 46(1), 1 October 1992, 6–21.

Krueger, A.B., and Posner, E.A. 2018. A Proposal for Protecting Low-Income Workers from Monopsony and Collusion. The Hamilton Project.

Lemos, S. 2008. A Survey of the Effects of the Minimum Wage on Prices. *Journal of Economic Surveys*, 22(1), 187–212, Wiley Blackwell.

Levin-Waldman, O.M., and McCarthy, G.W. 1998. Small Business and the Minimum Wage. Economics Policy Note Archive, Levy Economics Institute.

Manning, A. 2003. *Monopsony in Motion: Imperfect Competition in Labor Markets*. Princeton University Press.

Neumark, D., and Wascher, W. 2008. *Minimum Wages and Employment*. Institute for the Study of Labor (IZA) DP No. 2570.

Neumark, D., Salas J.M.I, and Wascher, W. 2014. Revisiting the Minimum Wage–Employment Debate: Throwing Out the Baby with the Bathwater? *Industrial & Labor Relations Review*, 67(3_suppl), 608–48.

Schmitt, J. 2013. *Why Does the Minimum Wage Have No Discernible Effect on Employment?* CEPR Reports and Issue Briefs, CEPR, No. 2013-4.

Steinbaum, Marshall. 2017. How Widespread Is Labor Monopsony? Some New Results Suggest It's Pervasive. Roosevelt Institute.

Wadsworth, J. 2010. Did the National Minimum Wage Affect UK Prices? *Fiscal Studies*, 31(1), March 2010, 81–120.

Wilson, M. 2012. *The Negative effect of Minimum Wage Laws*. Policy Analysis No. 701, Cato Institute. http://object.cato.org/sites/cato.org/files/pubs/pdf/PA701.pdf.

Part V

The Implications of the Policy of Accelerated Land Reform for Food Security and Affordability, Price Stability and the Agricultural Sector Output and Employment Growth

18

Land Reform, Redistribution and Agricultural Investment Growth: What Are Implications for the National Development Plan Output and Employment Targets?

Learning Objectives

- Assess what the implications of a lower growth rate in the agricultural sector GDP is for the agricultural sector employment growth and the National Development Plan (NDP) employment targets.
- Establish the aggregate and youth employment growth intensity induced by the agricultural sector GDP growth.
- Establish whether youth employment benefits from positive shocks to the agricultural sector GDP growth and employment growth.
- Examine the implications of an increase in the agricultural sector investment growth on the agricultural sector output growth and employment growth.
- Explore whether bringing underutilised land in the former homelands and communal areas make a meaningful difference in the agricultural sector output growth and employment growth.
- Compare the relative significance of only increasing agricultural sector investment growth versus bringing underutilised land in the former homelands and communal areas.

N. Gumata, E. Ndou, *Accelerated Land Reform, Mining, Growth, Unemployment and Inequality in South Africa*, https://doi.org/10.1007/978-3-030-30884-1_18

18.1 Introduction

The National Development Plan (NDP) targets to create an additional 1 million jobs in the agricultural sector by 2030.[1] In addition, the president has prioritised the agricultural sector as a key contributor to economic and employment growth. The president in his 2018 State of the Nation address reinforced the message by centralising the agricultural sector in economic activity and employment creation via the agricultural industrial revolution. At the same time, the resolution to expropriate land without compensation places the role of land for agricultural, housing, tourism and cultural proposes at the centre of economic activity and employment creation. This chapter contributes to this national topical policy issue by assessing the implications of the decline in the agricultural sector gross value added (output) growth, investment growth and area planted for the NDP agricultural sector output growth and employment targets. Furthermore, how employment intensive is the gross value added (output) in the agricultural sector? Does youth employment benefit from positive shocks to the agricultural sector GDP growth and employment growth? Are there meaningful differences between agricultural investment growth and accelerated land reform and redistribution?

Figure 18.1 shows the evolution of agricultural employment overtime. The trends show that the last time agricultural employment was around 2 million was in the 1960s. Although employment in the agricultural sector has turned around and increased since 2014Q3, the level remains below the 1 million mark as at 2018Q1.

Figure 18.2(a) shows that the average gross value added contribution by the agricultural sector was at 3.12 per cent in the 1960s compared to 2.67 per cent in the 2000s. Similarly, although gross fixed capital formation (investment) in the agricultural sector has been on a persistent decline since the 1960s in Fig. 18.2(b), it contributed more than 10 per cent to aggregate investment in the 1960s compared to an average of 3.24 per in the 2000s.

[1] The NDP aims to double the current level of people employed in the agricultural sector from the current 847,000 as at 2018Q1.

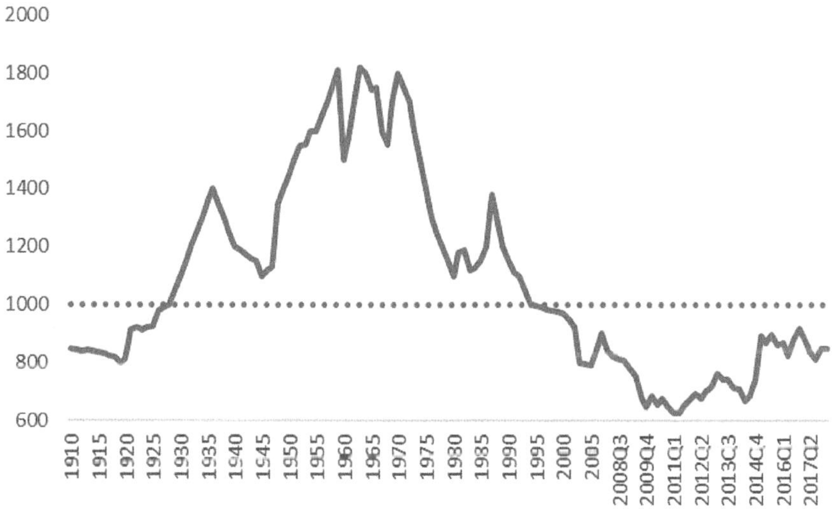

Fig. 18.1 Formal agricultural employment (regular and seasonal). (Source: BFAP (2011) and Statistics South Africa)

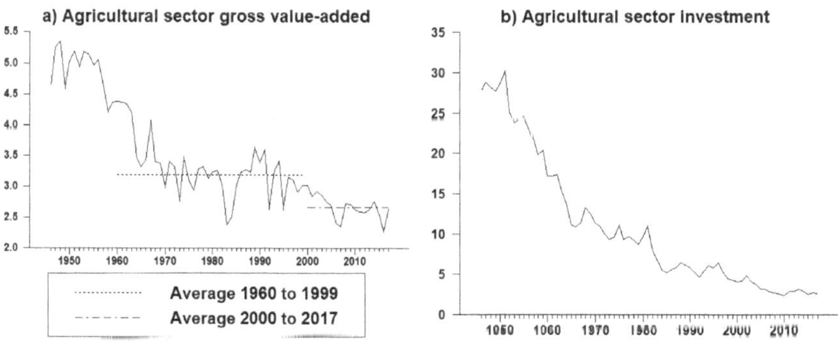

Fig. 18.2 Agricultural sector contribution to aggregate gross value added and investment. (Source: South African Reserve Bank and authors' calculations)

At the same time, Fig. 18.3 shows that the size of farms was on an increasing trend at the expense of the number of farms which was on a declining trend. Nonetheless, this change in the size and number of farms did not materially affect the area planted. In fact, Fig. 18.3 shows that the area planted is estimated to have remained largely unchanged since the

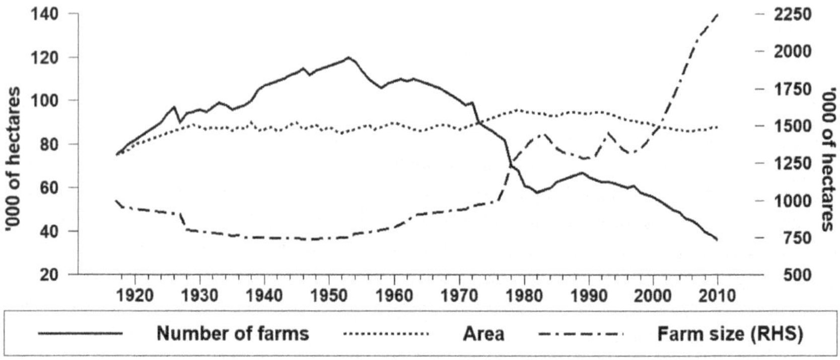

Fig. 18.3 Number, area and average size of farms in South Africa. (Source: Liebenberg (2013) and authors' calculations)

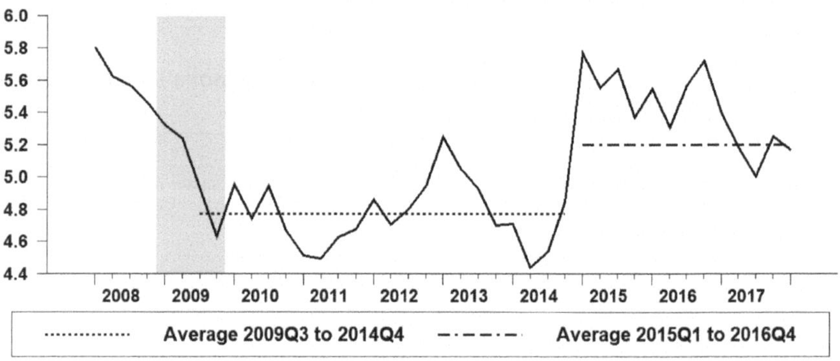

Fig. 18.4 Agricultural sector employment (2008Q1 to 218Q1). (Note: The grey shaded are denoted the South African recession. Source: Statistics South Africa and authors' calculations)

1940s. This trend corroborates the findings in earlier chapters showing that the estimated structural change indices indicate that structural changes in the agricultural sector have been on a decline since the early 1990s.

The objective of the NDP is to more than double the contribution of the agricultural sector employment from the current 5.2 per cent in Fig. 18.4(c) to almost 11 per cent. Table 18.1 shows that the agricultural sector last contributed around 12 per cent and 11 per cent in 1990 and

Table 18.1 Contribution of agricultural sector to total employment

	Total employment	Agriculture employment	Share of agriculture employment (%)
1990	10,403.0	1252.9	12.0
1991	10,799.7	1178.7	10.9
1992	11,247.3	1109.5	9.9
1993	11,696.1	1161.9	9.9
1994	12,185.7	992.5	8.1
1995	12,638.4	959.3	7.6
1996	13,131.4	982.9	7.5
1997	13,616.5	961.7	7.1
1998	14,121.4	922.7	6.5
1999	14,677.8	907	6.2
2000	15,232.8	968.5	6.4
2001	15,737.1	834	5.3
2002	16,145.2	986.8	6.1
2003	16,541.3	906.7	5.5
2004	16,863.5	921.4	5.5
2005	17,212.1	916	5.3
2006	17,594.0	981.8	5.6
2007	18,008.9	818.5	4.5
2008	18,699.3	905.2	4.8
2009	18,433.2	858.8	4.7
2010	18,163.0	832.3	4.6

Source: Liebenberg (2013)

1991, respectively, when the share of the gross value added by the agricultural sector was more than 3 per cent in Fig. 18.2(a).

BFAP (2011) contribute to this line of thought by the NDP and contend that the agricultural sector could potentially create a million employment opportunities. The authors argue that this could be achieved by expanding and investing in irrigation agriculture, bringing underutilised land in the communal areas under production, picking and supporting labour-intensive agricultural sectors and regions (provinces) as shown in Fig. 18.5 and supporting the creation of upstream and downstream industries.

To this end the authors recommend that land under intensive irrigation crops can be expanded by between 145,000 ha and 500,000 ha. Secondly, implied in the study is that the trends in area planted and the size of farms observed in Fig. 18.3 will have to change fundamentally. The authors argue that better utilisation of land in the former homeland

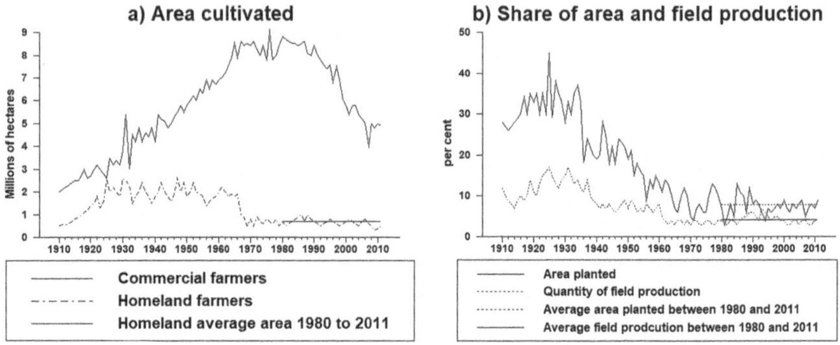

Fig. 18.5 Selected trends in commercial and homeland farmers. (Source: Liebenberg (2013) and authors' calculations)

areas can create 300,000 employment opportunities and an additional 326,500 employment opportunities via upstream and downstream value add in the agricultural sector.

In addition, BFAP (2011) contend that the bulk (64 per cent) of the small-holder schemes in the former homelands is geographically located in the ten districts, of which six were declared presidential poverty nodes.

Figure 18.5 shows the trends in area cultivated by commercial farmers and former homeland farmers and the contribution of the former homelands to area planted and production in field crops. It is evident that the area cultivated by both commercial and homeland farmers has declined. Whereas those planted by homeland farmers declined during the 1970s and 1980s and that planted by commercial farmers declined persistently post-1990 possibly coinciding with the period of democracy, large-scale market deregulation and consolidation in the agricultural sector.

The area planted by former homeland farmers has remained stable below 1 million hectares. At the same time, the share of former homeland farmers' area planted and quantity of field production persistently declined and has remained stable at long-term averages of 7.5 per cent and 4.3 per cent, respectively, since 1980.

Of the estimated 300,000 employment opportunities that can be created in the communal areas, BFAP (2011) suggests that small-scale farmers that have access to more than five hectares can be engaged in self-employment and a maximum of between two and three people thus

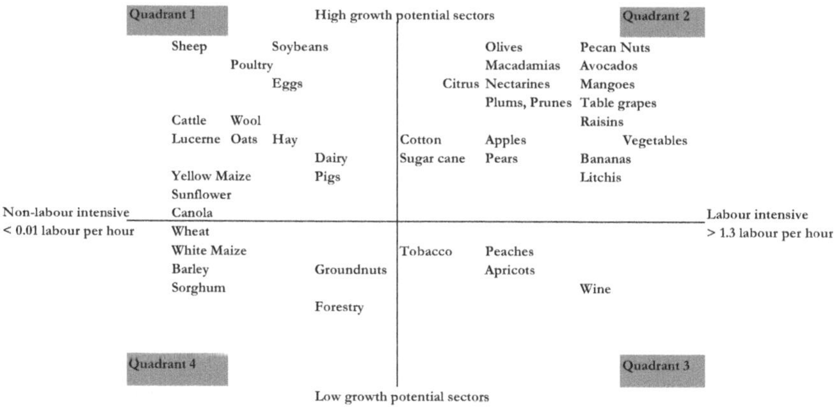

Fig. 18.6 Sector employment intensity and employment matrix. (Source: BFAP (2011))

contributing 75,000 job opportunities. In addition, between a half hectare and five hectares can contribute 165,000 job opportunities. Furthermore, subsistence farmers with access to less than half a hectare can contribute 83,000 job opportunities and better utilisation of land transferred though the land reform programme can contribute 70,000. Moreover, the study identifies the sectors shown in Fig. 18.6 as labour intensive. Lastly, McKinsey and Company (2015) and BFAP (2011) show that the Eastern Cape, KwaZulu-Natal and Limpopo provinces present significant opportunities for the agricultural sector.[2]

18.2 Further Stylised Facts on the Agricultural Sector

Prior to conducting the empirical analysis, this section extends the introductory analysis in the previous section by assessing the role of provinces in the agricultural sector. The contributions to the agricultural sector employment by province in Fig. 18.7 show that Limpopo, Western Cape

[2] See also Exhibit 45 of https://www.mckinsey.com/~/media/McKinsey/Global%20Themes/Middle%20East%20and%20Africa/South%20Africas%20bold%20priorities%20for%20inclusive%20growth/South_Africas_big_five_bold_priorities_for_inclusive_growth%20Full_report.ashx.

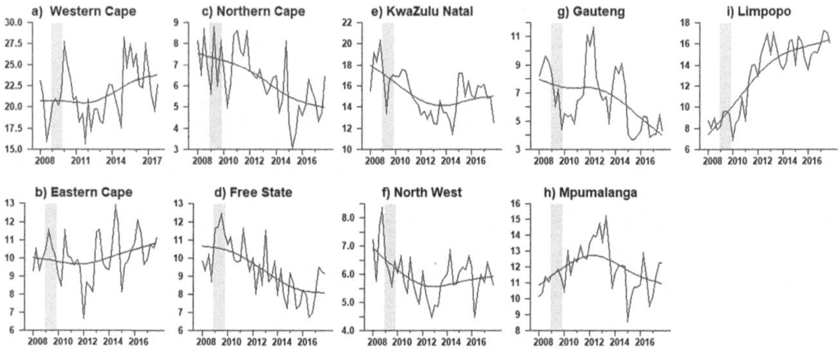

Fig. 18.7 QLFS employment. (Note: The grey shaded areas denote the South African recession. Source: Statistics South Africa and authors' calculations)

and Eastern Cape have registered an upward trend[3] in agricultural employment post-2009. This is particularly the case for Limpopo where the contribution to agricultural sector has been persistently upward trending and employment more than doubled and increased from just above 6 per cent to average 15.3 per cent between 2012Q1 and 2017Q2.

On the other hand, the Free State province, the traditional agricultural hub, has been on a prolonged downward trend since 2009. These trends bring to the fore the dynamics of the employment matrix presented in Fig. 18.6 and how they inform the process of land expropriation without compensation, land reform and redistribution to maximally benefit the agricultural sector, food production and security, provincial agricultural activity to impact rural-urban migration trends.

Figure 18.8 shows that the agricultural activities that contribute the largest share to the sector seem to have remained stable and broadly unchanged post-2009. For instance, the contribution of crop farming has remained stable around 58.92 per cent in Fig. 18.4(a), whereas animal farming has moved around the average of 23.48 per cent in Fig. 18.4(b) and mixed farming (i.e. growing of crops combined with animal farming) has contributed an average of 8.59 per cent in Fig. 18.4(c).

Thus, these trends indicate that the process of land reform so far has not impacted food security. These trends corroborate evidence from the

[3] The trends are based on the Hodrick-Prescott filter.

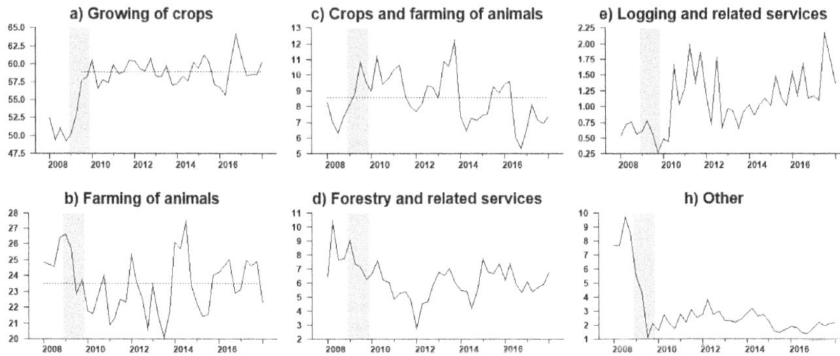

Fig. 18.8 QLFS employment by agricultural activity. (Note: Other includes agricultural and animal husbandry services, except veterinary activities, production of organic fertilisers, ocean and coastal fishing, fish hatcheries and fish farms and game hunting, trapping and game propagation, including related services. The grey shaded areas denote the South African recession. Source: Statistics South Africa and authors' calculations)

Economist Global Food Security Index (GFSI), showing that South Africa was ranked number 44th in 2017 out of 113 countries which was an improvement by 0.2 points. In addition, the GFSI shows that South Africa ranked 50th in the sub-component for food affordability, 37th of food availability and 53rd on food quality and safety.[4]

To assess the role of the so-called rural provinces in the South African labour market, we group the Eastern Cape, Northern Cape, Free State, Mpumalanga, Limpopo, North West and KwaZulu-Natal as constituting largely of rural areas and the Western Cape and Gauteng as constituting mostly urban areas. Figure 18.9 shows the proportion of the rural and urban provinces in the total labour force, employment, unemployment and not economical active working age population.

Largely due to the increase in the employment trend in the agricultural sector post-2014 (the grey shaded area), we concentrate the analysis on the labour market trends on this period so that we can better understand what informs the trends. The trends show that post-2014 the proportion of rural provinces in the labour force declined to lows of 53 per cent

[4] These rankings indicate that there is ample room for improvement for South Africa on a number of aspects related to the agricultural sector and food. We explore the role of land reform, redistribution and farm size and the impact it may have on poverty and inequality in later chapters.

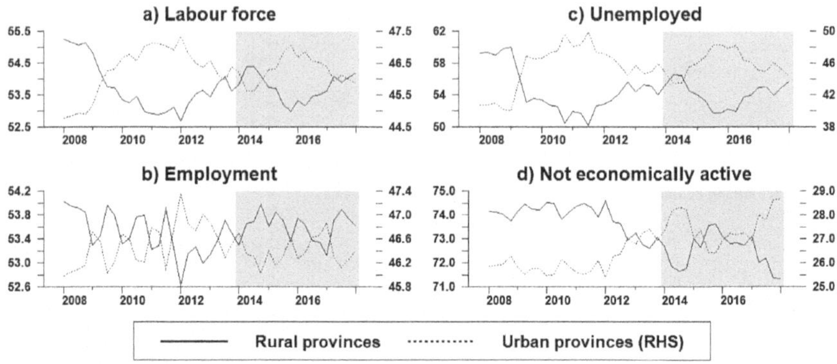

Fig. 18.9 Characteristics of rural and urban provinces' labour markets. (Note: The grey shaded area denotes developments in the trends post-2014. Source: Statistics South Africa and authors' calculations)

compared to those registered between 2010Q1 and 2011Q4 although the trend has reversed. The proportion of the labour force employed from rural provinces increased from 52.6 per cent in 2012Q1 and stabilised at an average of 53.8 per cent. In addition, the proportion of the labour force from the rural provinces that is unemployed declined from a high of 60 per cent in 2018Q4 to 50 per cent in 2011Q4 and later 52 per cent in 2016Q4 but has since increased to 55 per cent in 2018Q1. Last, the proportion of the not economically active population in the rural provinces declined to 71 per cent in 2018Q1 although it still remains at more than double that of the urban provinces. In summary, the rural provinces contribute more than 50 per cent to the labour force, the unemployed and the not economically active population in South Africa. Furthermore, there have been some changes post-2014 in line with the employment trends shown in Figs. 18.1 and 18.6.

To assess what the trends in Figs. 18.9, 18.7 and 18.8 imply for youth employment, we explore the nature of association between youth defined as (i) 15 to 24 years and (ii) 25 to 34 years in the labour market and aggregate agricultural sector employment. This is equivalent to assessing the preliminary evidence for Eq. (18.1).

The intention is to explore whether the upward trend in the agricultural sector employment post-2014 was associated with the absorption of youth labour. This is especially important because within the land expropriation

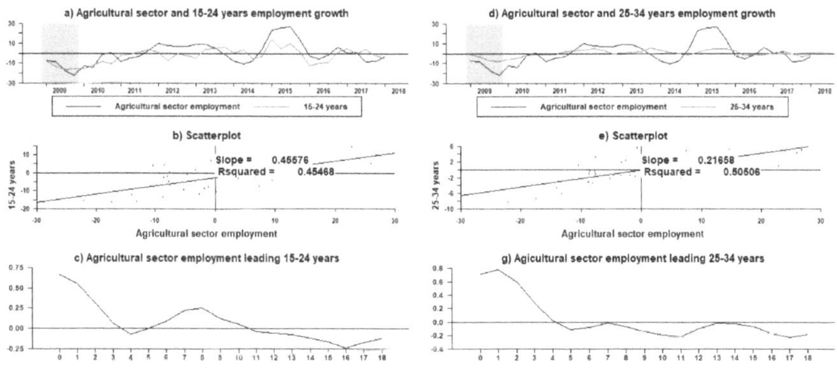

Fig. 18.10 Agricultural sector employment and youth employment growth. (Note: The grey shaded areas denote the South African recession. Source: Statistics South Africa and authors' calculations)

without compensation, redistribution and reform discourse. There has been much talk about the role of the agricultural sector in absorbing a large share of youth for gainful employment.[5] What does the data say about the association between youth and the agricultural sector employment growth? Figure 18.10 shows that there is a positive association between growth in employment in the agricultural sector and youth employment.

The bilateral relationships in Fig. 18.10(b) and (e) indicate that the variation in the agricultural sector employment is associated with an increase of 46 per cent in the 15 to 24 years and 51 per cent in the 25 to 34 years. At the same time, youth employment increases when led by increases in aggregate agricultural sector employment.

Furthermore, to assess the robustness of the stylised relationships in Fig. 18.10, we estimate four bilateral VAR models that include aggregate agricultural sector employment (i.e. 15 to 64 years) and the age-specific groups (i) 15 to 24 years, (ii) 25 to 34 years and (iii) 35 to 44 years agricultural employment growth. The sample size spans the period 2008Q1 to 2018Q1. All growth rates are at an annual rate. The VAR models are estimated using 2 lags and 10,000 Monte Carlo draws.

The responses of the bilateral VAR models in Fig. 18.11 show that employment growth for all age groups increases in response to a positive

[5] This has positive implications for the youth dividend.

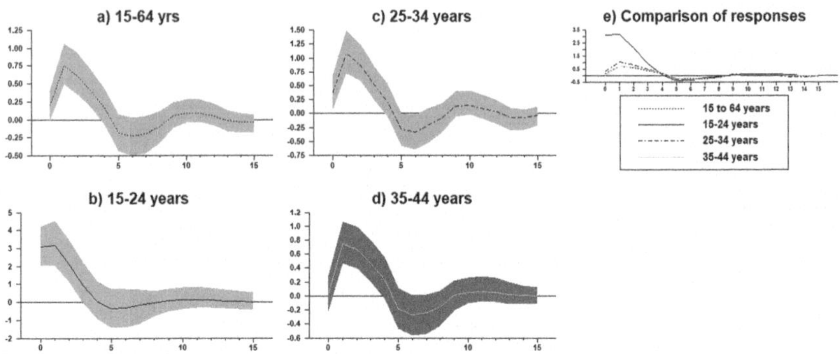

Fig. 18.11 Responses to positive agricultural sector employment shock. (Note: The grey shaded area bands denote the 16th and 84th percentile confidence bands. Source: Authors' calculations)

agricultural employment growth shock. But the agricultural employment growth for the age group 15 to 24 years increases more, followed by that of the 25 to 34 years age group. This implies that youth employment benefits from an unexpected increase in the agricultural sector. Thus, policies aimed at growing the agricultural sector such as land redistribution and reform, support for the agricultural sectors in various forms such as investment in irrigation, research and development will benefit employment creation especially the absorption and participation of youth (new entrants) in the labour markets. Such a policy strategy will also lead to increased rural labour absorption and participation and lower the unemployment rate in the so-called rural provinces.

18.3 How Employment Intensive Is the Agricultural Sector GDP Growth?

To answer this question, this section estimates the Okun's Law following the same approach as was the case in earlier chapters. We use the employment, unemployment and Okun's Law expressed in Eqs. (18.1) to (18.3)

$$E_t - E_t^* = \gamma\left(Y_t - Y_t^*\right) + D_{2014} \times \left(Y_t - Y_t^*\right) + \eta_t, \quad \gamma > 0 \quad \textit{employment equation.} \tag{18.1}$$

$$U_t - U_t^* = \delta\left(E_t - E_t^*\right) + D_{2014} \times \left(Y_t - Y_t^*\right) + \mu_t, \quad \delta < 0 \quad \textit{unemployment equation.} \tag{18.2}$$

$$U_t - U_t^* = \beta\left(Y_t - Y_t^*\right) + D_{2014} \times \left(Y_t - Y_t^*\right) + \varepsilon_t, \quad \beta < 0 \quad \textit{Okun's Law}, \tag{18.3}$$

where E_t in the *employment equation* Eq. (18.1) is the log of employment, Y_t is the log of output, U_t is the unemployment rate in the *unemployment equation* Eq. (18.2) and the $*$ signifies a long-run level. The coefficient β in the Okun's Law depends on the coefficients for:

1. γ is the response of employment to output.
2. δ is the response of unemployment to employment.
3. D_{2014} is the dummy variable which is equal to one from 2014Q3 to the end of the sample period.

The coefficients in the un(employment) relationships in Eqs. (18.1) and (18.2) underlie the Okun's Law. According to Ball et al. (2011), γ is affected by the decisions that firms take in adjusting labour and capital as inputs in the production function. Since it can be costly to adjust employment, firms tend to accommodate short run output fluctuations by, for example, adjusting the number of hours per worker and workers' productivity. On the other hand, the coefficient for δ is expected to be less than one in absolute value because unemployment moves less than one-for-one with employment. In addition, an increase in employment increases the returns to job search, which induces workers to enter the labour force (increase in the labour participation ratio). Hence, these pro-cyclical movements in the labour force tend to partly offset the effects of employment on the unemployment rate.

We use aggregate and youth agricultural employment, unemployment rate and agricultural gross value added. The sample spans the period 2008Q1 to 2018Q1. The data is sourced from the South African Reserve Bank and Statistics South Africa. To assess the dynamics induced by the structural upward shift post-2014Q3 shown in Fig. 18.1, we spilt the sample to 2014Q3 to 2018Q1. Figure 18.12 shows the evolution of γ, δ

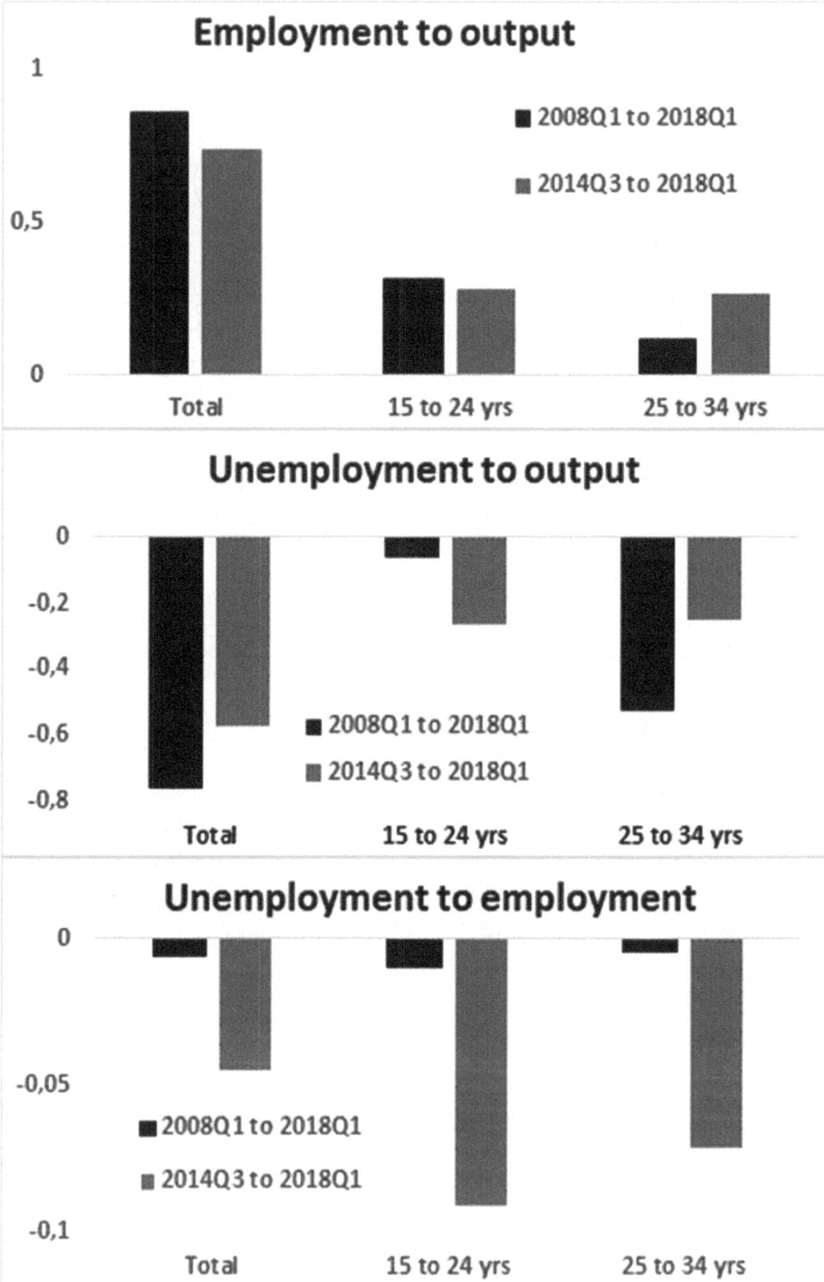

Fig. 18.12 The evolution of γ, δ and β coefficients in Eqs. (18.1), (18.2) and (18.3). (Source: Authors' calculations)

and β coefficients in Eqs. (18.1), (18.2) and (18.3) for the sample period 2008Q1 to 2018Q1 and 2014Q3 to 2018Q1.

The results show that indeed GDP growth in the agricultural sector leads to aggregate and youth employment growth. The gamma coefficients which show the response of employment to output in Eq. (18.1) indicate that agricultural sector GDP growth does lead to an increase in employment growth and youth employment benefits as well.

Similarly, the delta and beta coefficients for Eqs. (18.2) and (18.3) indicate that aggregate employment and GDP growth lead to a decline in the agricultural sector unemployment rate. Furthermore, the beta coefficients suggest that the agricultural sector GDP growth for the sub-sample period 2014Q3 to 2018Q1 was more beneficial and lowered the unemployment rate more.

Given that the coefficients presented in Fig. 18.12 are static and are point estimates over the entire sample and sub-sample, we estimate several VAR models including the same variables to determine how the variables vary overtime. We estimate VAR models that include the agricultural sector output, employment and the unemployment rate. Employment growth is further disaggregated into age groups to assess the sensitivity of the responses. The model is estimated using 2 lags and 10,000 Monte Carlo draws. The shock is a one standard deviation shock. The VAR results for the employment equation in Fig. 18.13 show that although the agricultural sector GDP growth leads to an increase in employment growth, this happens with a delay of about three quarters.

Furthermore, youth employment growth benefits across the board. At peak response, employment amongst the 15 to 25 years increases by around 4 percentage points, whereas that for the 25 to 34 years increases by almost 7 percentage points. This implies that agricultural GDP growth is good for youth employment growth.

In addition, Fig. 18.14 shows that the unemployment rate in the agricultural sector declines in response to an unexpected increase in employment growth. The positive effects of increased employment growth in the agricultural sector significantly lower the unemployment rate amongst the 25 to 34 years.

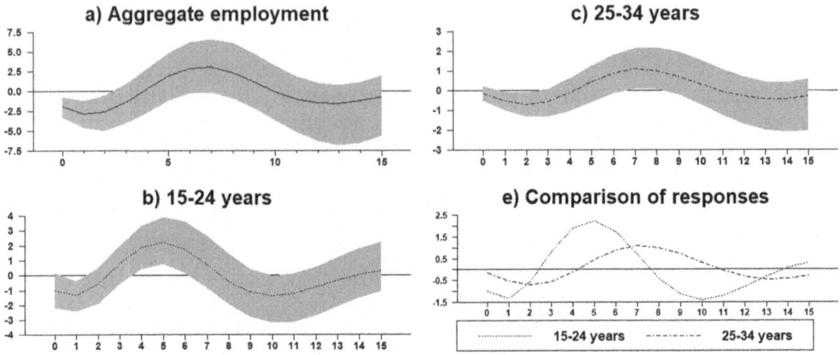

Fig. 18.13 Agricultural employment responses to positive output growth shock. (Note: The grey shaded area bands denote the 16th and 84th percentile confidence bands. Source: Authors' calculations)

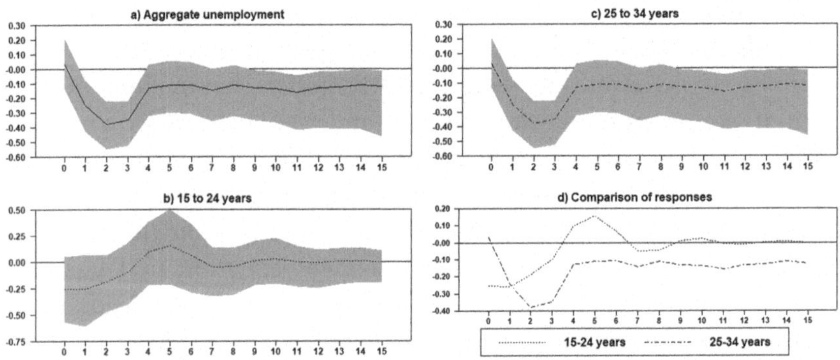

Fig. 18.14 Agricultural unemployment rate responses to positive employment growth shock. (Note: The grey shaded area bands denote the 16th and 84th percentile confidence bands. Source: Authors' calculations)

Last, the results for the Okun's Law in Eq. (18.3) shown in Fig. 18.15 indicate that the unexpected increase in agricultural GDP growth results in a decline in the unemployment rate. At peak response the unemployment rate amongst the 25 to 34 years declines by 0.75 percentage points, whereas that amongst the 15 to 24 years declines by around 0.5 percentage points. Thus, we conclude that not only is output and employment growth in the agricultural sector good for the economy, it is particularly

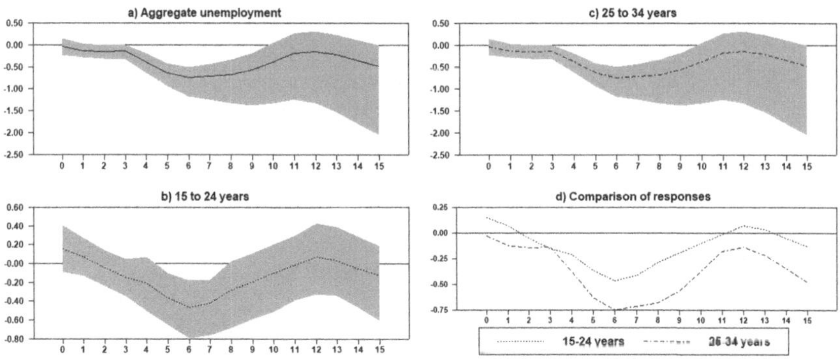

Fig. 18.15 Agricultural unemployment rate responses to positive GDP growth shock. (Note: The grey shaded area bands denote the 16th and 84th percentile confidence bands. Source: Authors' calculations)

an important policy intervention for the dealing decisively with youth unemployment.

18.4 What Happens to Agricultural GDP and Employment Growth When Investment Increases?

Earlier we stated that BFAP (2011) contend that expanding and investing in irrigation agriculture will improve the agricultural sector GDP and employment growth. This section tests the validity of this statement. We estimate a VAR model that includes gross fixed capital formation (investment), output and employment labour productivity growth in the agricultural sector. We estimate a VAR model which includes agricultural sector investment, output, employment and labour productivity growth. The growth rates are an annual rate. The model is estimated using 2 lags and 20,000 Monte Carlo draws. Figure 18.16 shows that output growth, employment growth and labour productivity growth increase in response to a positive investment growth shock.

The positive agricultural sector employment growth increases more than output growth implying that output growth tends to be labour

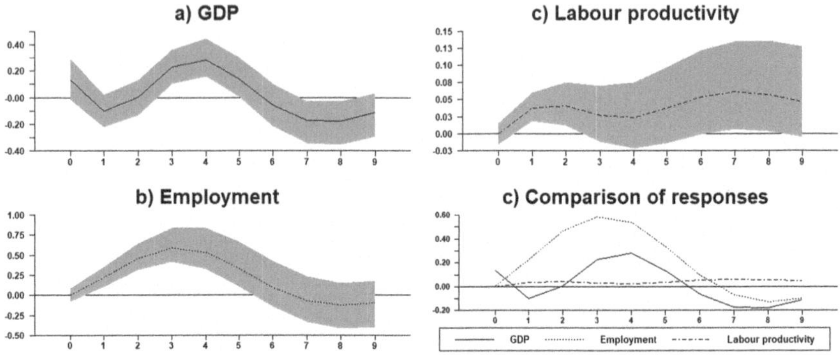

Fig. 18.16 Responses to positive agricultural sector investment growth shock. (Note: The grey shaded area bands denote the 16th and 84th percentile confidence bands. Source: Authors' calculations)

intensive (creates more employment). At the same time, labour productivity improves. Thus, we conclude that increasing investment growth and expanding investment in activities such as irrigation, research and development agriculture will improve the agricultural sector GDP growth and employment growth. Investment growth exerts effects similar to those of a technological change shock of productivity growth. The recommendations by BFAP (2011) are therefore valid.

18.5 Does Bringing Underutilised Land in the Former Homelands and Communal Areas Make a Meaningful Difference?

Figure 18.3 shows that the size of farms was on an increasing trend at the expense of the number of farms which was on a declining trend. Furthermore, the debate on land expropriation without compensation, land reform and redistribution implies that part of the policy intentions is to increase the area planted (farmland). The implication is that a strategy of picking and supporting labour-intensive agricultural sectors and regions (provinces) as shown in Fig. 18.5 and advocated by

BFAP (2011) will support the creation of upstream and downstream industries.

This section tests the validity of this statement by estimating several VAR models which include area cultivates by commercial and homeland farmers, agricultural output (GDP), employment growth and labour productivity. We shock the area cultivated in homelands and assess the responses of output growth, employment growth and labour productivity growth. For this exercise we use a VAR model as was the case in the earlier sections. In addition, because the trend shown in Fig. 18.5 indicated that even area cultivated by commercial farmers was on a declining trend, we add up the area cultivated by commercial and former homeland farmers and shock this aggregated cultivated area to assess the impact on output growth, employment growth and labour productivity growth. We compare the differences in the impact of a positive shock in the agricultural sector investment only as shown by the results in Fig. 18.16 and the impact on a positive shock to area cultivated. The aim is to show the different impact exerted by increasing investment only whilst keeping the area cultivated unchanged and increasing area cultivated and investment.

The results for a positive shock to area cultivated in the former homelands in Fig. 18.17 indicate that agricultural output, employment and labour productivity increase. This means that bringing underutilised land in the former homelands and communal areas will make a significant and meaningful difference in the agricultural sector contribution to growth, employment and labour productivity.

Furthermore, a comparison of the responses to just an increase in the agricultural sector investment growth in Fig. 18.16 and an increase in area under cultivation in the former homelands in Fig. 18.17 indicates that increasing investment alone is not sufficiently large enough to boost agricultural sector output growth, employment growth and labour productivity growth. In fact, the results in Fig. 18.18 show that bringing in underutilised land in the former homelands and communal areas more than doubles the response of the agricultural sector output growth, employment growth and labour productivity growth.

However, because the increase in total area cultivated (commercial and former homelands) implies varying degrees of increments in area cultivated, we use the Kilian and Vigfusson (2011) approach for the asymmetric transmissions of shocks. The approach uses a scenario approach in

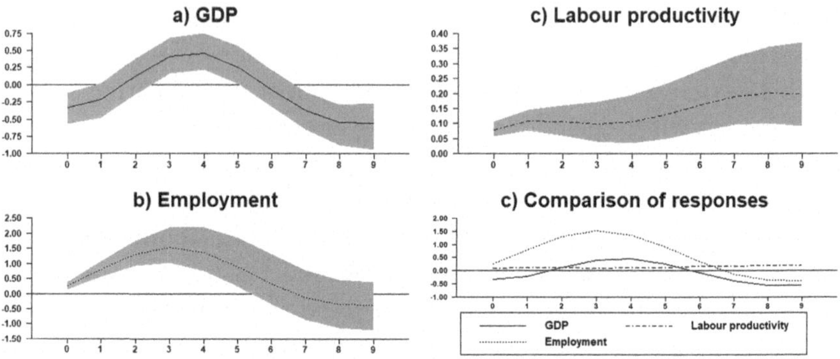

Fig. 18.17 Responses to positive shocks to area cultivated in former homelands. (Note: The grey shaded area bands denote the 16th and 84th percentile confidence bands. Source: Authors' calculations)

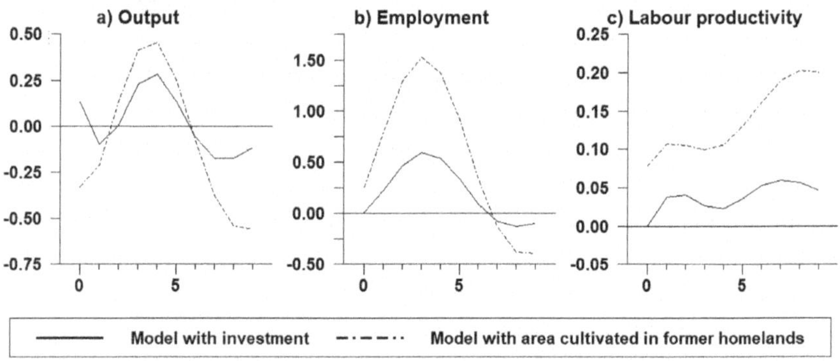

Fig. 18.18 Comparison of responses to an unexpected increase in investment growth and area cultivated in former homelands. (Source: Authors' calculations)

the analysis of asymmetric responses to different sizes and signs. Last, Fig. 18.19 shows increasing area cultivated by commercial and former homeland farmers under the scenarios of a positive one standard deviation, two standard deviations, four standard deviations and ten standard deviations shocks lead to asymmetric responses in agricultural sector output growth, employment growth and labour productivity.

The results imply varying degrees of increments induced by positive shocks to total area cultivated. Thus, we conclude that the implication of

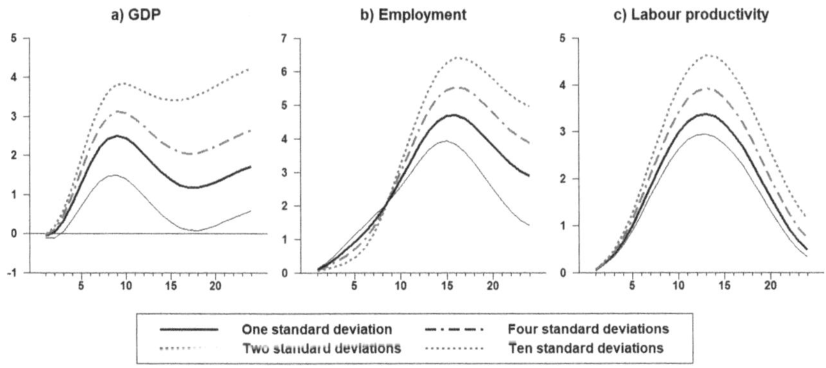

Fig. 18.19 Asymmetric transmission of shocks to total area cultivated. (Source: Authors' calculations)

a strategy of bringing in underutilised land in the former homelands and communal areas, increasing area cultivated under commercial farms, picking and supporting labour-intensive agricultural sectors and regions (provinces) as advocated by BFAP (2012) will support output, employment and labour productivity in the agricultural sector. Similarly, Leautier and Hanson (2013) contend that high economic growth has had differential impacts on job creation across countries in sub-Saharan Africa. The differences are attributable to the creative use of the agricultural sector, the success in growing market size and the level of innovation in the agricultural sector that support modernisation, attract the youth and enhance value added. The results support the authors' argument that the agricultural sector is well suited to play a crucial role in partly dealing with the unemployment problems.

18.6 Conclusion and Policy Implications

The NDP targets to create an additional 1 million jobs in the agricultural sector and double the contribution of the agricultural sector to growth by 2030. Furthermore, the debate surrounding the expropriation of land without compensation, accelerated land reform and redistribution has placed youth employment and food security as key objectives. This chapter contributes to the understanding of the role of the agricultural sector to the South African economy by empirically assessing a number of policy questions. First, we establish that Limpopo, Western Cape and Eastern Cape have registered an upward trend in agricultural employment post-2009. This is particularly the case for Limpopo where the contribution to agricultural sector has been persistently upward trending and employment more than doubled and increased from just above 6 per cent to average 15.3 per cent between 2012Q1 and 2017Q2. Second, these trends bring to the fore the dynamics of the employment matrix presented in BFAP (2011) and how they inform the process of land expropriation without compensation, land reform and redistribution to maximally benefit the agricultural sector, food production and security, provincial agricultural activity to impact rural-urban migration trends. This is especially important given the NDP objectives of doubling the current level of people employed in the agricultural sector from the current 847,000 as at 2018Q1 to 2 million by 2030. Needless to mention that such a strategy will also support the South African Reserve in attaining the expanded mandate of supporting sustainable growth and maximum employment growth.

Third, evidence in this chapter shows that the agricultural sector employment growth is associated with robust increased employment growth for the age group 15 to 24 years, followed by that of the 25 to 34 years age group. Thus, youth employment benefits from positive shocks to the agricultural sector. The policy implication is that policies aimed at growing the agricultural sector such as land redistribution and reform, support for the agricultural sectors in various forms such as investment in irrigation, research and development will benefit employment creation especially the absorption and participation of youth (new entrants) in the labour markets. In addition, such a policy strategy will also lead to increased rural labour absorption and participation and lower the unemployment rate in the so-called rural provinces.

Fourth, the unemployment rate in the agricultural sector declines in response to an increase in employment growth. Similarly, the agricultural GDP growth results in a decline in the unemployment rate. The positive effects of increased employment growth in the agricultural sector persist, especially for the unemployment rate amongst the 25 to 34 years. Thus, we conclude that not only is output growth and employment growth in the agricultural sector good for the economy, it is particularly an important policy intervention for the dealing decisively with youth unemployment.

Fifth, the results show that positive agricultural sector employment growth increases more than output growth in response to positive shocks to the agricultural investment growth, implying that output growth tends to be labour intensive (creates more employment). At the same time, labour productivity growth improves. Thus, we conclude that increasing investment growth and expanding investment in activities such as irrigation, research and development agriculture will improve the agricultural sector GDP growth and employment growth. Investment growth exerts effects similar to those of a technological change shock of productivity growth.

Furthermore, the results for a positive shock to area cultivated in the former homelands indicate that agricultural output growth, employment growth and labour productivity increase. This means that bringing underutilised land in the former homelands and communal areas will make a significant and meaningful difference in the agricultural sector contribution to output growth, employment growth and labour productivity growth. But increasing investment alone is not sufficiently large enough to boost agricultural sector output output, employment growth and labour productivity growth. In fact, the results show that bringing in underutilised land in the former homelands and communal areas more than doubles the response of the agricultural sector output growth, employment growth and labour productivity growth.

Last, we establish that a strategy of bringing in underutilised land in the former homelands and communal areas, increasing area cultivated under commercial farms, picking and supporting labour-intensive agricultural sectors and regions (provinces) as advocated by BFAP (2011) will support output, employment and labour productivity in the agricultural sector. This strategy is compatible with recommendations by Leautier and Hanson (2013) for creative use of the agricultural sector, growing market size, increasing the level of innovation in the agricultural sector that supports modernisation, attracts the youth and enhance value added.

Therefore, the results in this chapter indicate that the president's message in the State of the Nation address centralising the agricultural sector in economic activity and employment creation via the agricultural industrial revolution can be achieved. Periods during which the agricultural sector contribution was high and employment was above a million mark were associated with high levels of investment growth in the agricultural sector. However, as much as a higher level of investment is a necessary and important factor in the agricultural sector growth, it is insufficient on its own to achieve the targets set in the NDP. The current trends in area planted, size of farms, crops planted, investment, research and development will have to change fundamentally so as to realise the set objectives and targets in the NDP. Needless, to mention that such a structural change and policy objectives are compatible with dealing with the perennial societal ills associated with unemployment, poverty, income and wealth inequality.

References

Ball, L., Leigh, D., and Loungani, P. 2011. *Okun's Law: Fit at 50?* IMF Working Paper WP/11/10.

BFAP. 2011. The Contribution of the Agro-Industrial Complex to Employment in South Africa. Tech. Rep. June, The Bureau for Food and Agricultural Policy, Pretoria.

BFAP. 2012. Sustaining Agricultural Growth. Baseline Agricultural Outlook 2012–2021. Bureau for Food and Agricultural Policy.

Greyling, J.C. 2012. The Role of the Agricultural Sector in the South African Economy. Department of Agricultural Economics, University of Stellenbosch. https://agbiz.co.za/uploads/documents/careers/13_04-thesis_jan_c_greyling_published.pdf

Kilian, L., and Vigfusson, R.J. 2011. Are the Responses of the U.S. Economy Asymmetric in Energy Price Increases and Decreases? *Quantitative Economics*, 2(3), 419–53.

Leautier, F., and Hanson, K.T. 2013. Jobless Economic Growth in Africa: Is There a Role for Agriculture? *Journal of African Development*, 15(2), 1–17. African Finance and Economic Association (EFEA).

Liebenberg, F. 2013. South African Agricultural Production, Productivity and Research Performance in the 20th Century. Department of Agricultural Economics, Extension and Rural Development. University of Pretoria. https://repository.up.ac.za/handle/2263/24416.

McKinsey & Company. 2015. *South Africa's Big Five: Bold Priorities for Inclusive Growth*. McKinsey Global Institute: Johannesburg.

19

What Is the Role of Food Commodity Price Booms and Busts in the Agricultural Sector? Implications for Monetary Policy

Learning Objectives

- Establish dates during which food commodity price boom and bust episodes occurred.
- Establish the duration and amplitude of the food commodity price booms and busts.
- Assess the role of food commodity price booms and busts on food and consumer price inflation, the agricultural sector output growth, investment growth and employment growth.
- Establish the implications of food commodity price booms and busts for price stability and monetary policy.

19.1 Introduction

The trends presented in earlier chapters showed that on average the agricultural sector gross value added declined between 2000Q1 and 2018Q1 and yet the share of employment increased, especially post-2014Q3. What could explain these contradictory trends and dynamics? Is it

N. Gumata, E. Ndou, *Accelerated Land Reform, Mining, Growth, Unemployment and Inequality in South Africa*, https://doi.org/10.1007/978-3-030-30884-1_19

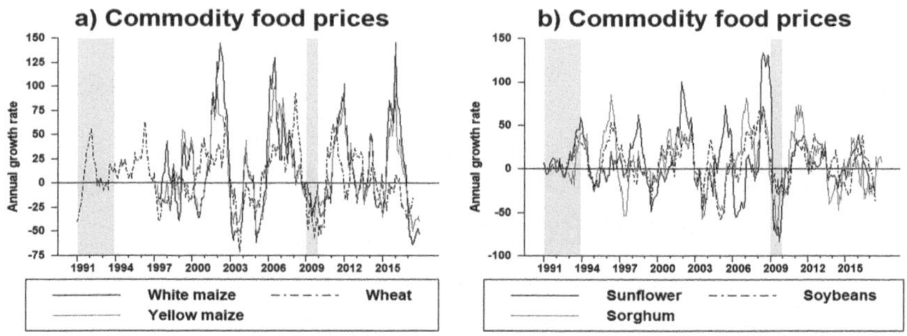

Fig. 19.1 Selected food commodity spot prices. (Note: The grey shaded areas denote the South African recessions. Source: Grain SA, Fred data and authors' calculations)

possible that food commodity price booms play a more important role in incentivising farmers to increase output, investment and employment? What is the role of food commodity price booms and busts on the agricultural sector? Do food commodity price booms and busts push food and consumer price inflation, agricultural sector output, investment and employment growth in different directions? If that is the case, what are the implications for the monetary policy response? This chapter explores the impact of food commodity price boom and bust episodes on inflation, the agricultural sector output, investment and employment growth.

First, Fig. 19.1 shows the evolution of selected food commodity prices, namely sorghum, soybeans, wheat sunflower seeds, white and yellow maize, and annual growth rates.[1] It is evident from Fig. 19.1 that the food commodity prices are highly cyclical, volatile and synchronised. For instance, the spot prices of food commodities more than doubled during 2014 and 2015 but have reversed the gains and declined by more than half (50 per cent). At the same time, the R/US$ exchange rate was on a prolonged and steady depreciation trend as shown in Fig. 19.2. Furthermore, the R/US$ exchange rate changes are positively associated

[1] The R'000 per ton prices are shown in Fig. 19.13 in the appendix. We note that the food commodity prices shown in Figs. 19.1 and 19.13 are not exhaustive. There are a number of other food commodity prices that influence the profitability and decisions of farmers.

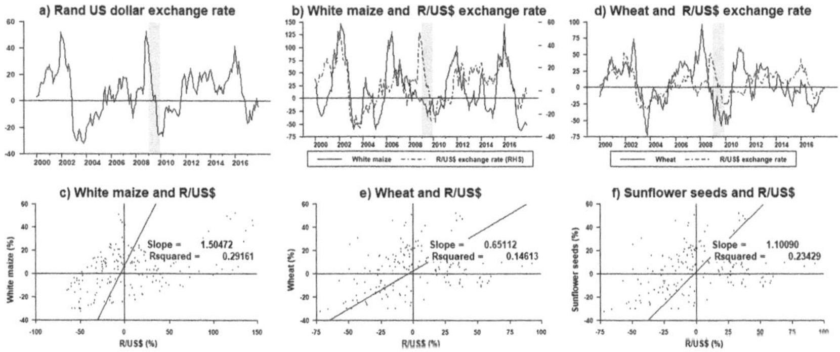

Fig. 19.2 Selected food commodity spot prices and the R/US$ exchange rate. (Note: The grey shaded areas denote the South African recession. Source: Grain SA, Fred data, South African Reserve Bank and authors' calculations)

with those in the key food commodity spot prices. So, it may be the case that the concurrence of sharp declines (increases) in food commodity prices and the R/US$ appreciation (depreciation) play a much larger role in the profitability of farmers. Thus, commodity prices, global demand and the exchange rate developments have a much more significant bearing on the farmers' decisions to produce, invest and employ more people.[2]

Furthermore, the agricultural sector has since the late 1990s been characterised by the reliance and the dominance of the parity pricing model, implying that the concurrence of drought episodes[3] which induce sharp and large shortages in food commodities tends to accentuate the impact of the R/US$ exchange rate movements on food commodity prices and the agricultural sector. Hence, this chapter explores whether food commodity price booms and busts push food and consumer price inflation, the agricultural sector output, investment and employment growth in different directions. If that is the case, what are the implications for monetary policy conduct?

[2] Later chapters explore the role of the export-led growth strategy, minimum wage, exchange rate appreciation, depreciation and volatility on the agricultural sector in detail.

[3] As was the case during 2001 and 2014.

19.2 The Identification of Food Commodity Price Booms and Busts

Similar to earlier, we use the (i) threshold techniques, namely, the Fatas et al. (2009) and Borgy et al. (2009), to date episodes of asset price booms and busts; and (ii) the Bry–Boschan Quarterly (BBQ) algorithm and Harding and Pagan (2002b) approaches to date turning points, calculate the amplitude, duration and synchronisation of cycles.

The Fatas et al. (2009) and Borgy et al. (2009) techniques use moving averages to define periods of booms and busts. Periods of booms (busts) are identified when the four-quarter or twelve-month moving average of the financial variable exceeds (is below) some growth rate threshold. Borgy et al. (2009) set the threshold for the boom (bust) at 15 (−15) per cent of the four-quarter moving average of the financial variable. Bordo and Jeanne (2002) set the thresholds for the boom (bust) at 20 (−20) per cent. The 20 (−20) per cent boom (bust) episodes are comparable to one positive (negative) standard deviation from the trend as done in some band-pass filter techniques.

The Harding and Pagan (2002a) dating cycle technique requires a search for maxima and minima over a given period. Then, it selects pairs of adjacent, locally absolute maxima and minima that meet certain censoring rules. The BBQ algorithm then develops a procedure for ensuring that peaks and troughs alternate. It imposes the rule that in the presence of a double trough, the lowest value is chosen, whereas, in the presence of a double peak, the highest value is chosen. The censoring rules are also imposed on the minimum duration of phases. The key features of the cyclical phases are their duration, amplitude and slope, as shown in Fig. 19.3.

The *duration* for recessions (downturns) is defined as the number of quarters (months) between *the peak and the trough*. In turn, the duration for upturns is defined as the time it takes to attain the level at the previous peak after the trough. Disruptions (booms) correspond to the bottom (top) 25 per cent of downturns (upturns) in terms of amplitude. Figure 19.4 and Table 19.1 to Table 19.6 show the periods during which boom and bust episodes occurred. We identify between five and six highly synchronised boom episodes post-2000 in all the commodity prices

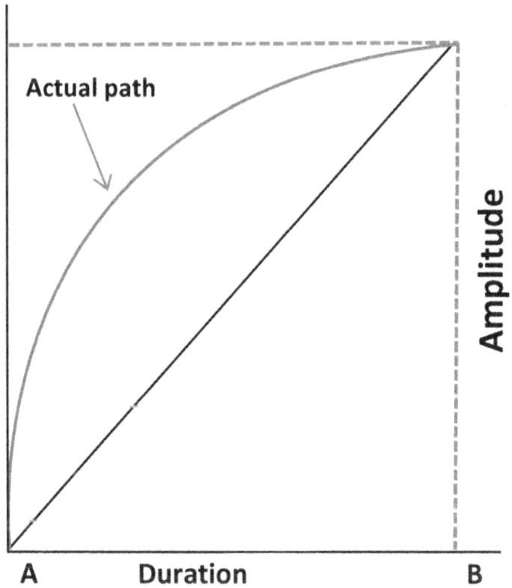

Fig. 19.3 Key features of the cyclical phases. (Source: Adapted from Harding and Pagan (2002a))

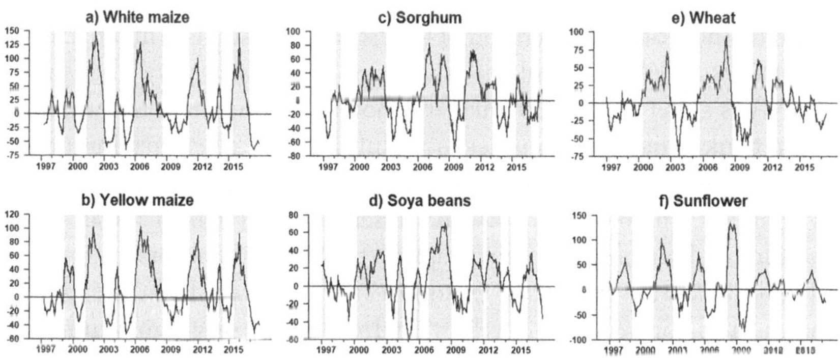

Fig. 19.4 Selected food commodity spot prices booms. (Note: The grey shaded areas denote food commodity spot prices booms. Source: Grain SA, Fred data and authors' calculations)

shown in Fig. 19.4. The longest boom episode occurred between 2004 and 2010 followed by the period 2012 to 2016, with amplitudes ranging between 179 per cent and 53 per cent, respectively, depending on the food commodity price.

The trends in Fig. 19.4 show that the food commodity price booms and busts are highly synchronised; hence we extract a common factor using the principal component analysis (PCA). Johnson and Wichern (1992) and Helbling et al. (2011) show that design factors extracted via PCA capture maximum variance and that the global factors obtained with a dynamic factor model are qualitatively similar to those derived via the first PCA. The PCA methodology extracts a common factor F_t that captures the greatest common variation in a group of P variables X_t. Furthermore, Forni et al. (2000), Bernanke et al. (2005) and Stock and Watson (2005) show that the factor-augmented vector autoregression (FAVAR) approach[4] provides a parsimonious and effective framework of analysis by incorporating information from many economic time series. Hence, FAVARs make it possible to introduce a higher amount of relevant information into economic estimations compared to standard VAR methods. In addition, FAVARs diminish the loss of degrees of freedom caused by the reduced dimension of the estimated systems. This characteristic enables FAVARs to deal with the "*curse of dimensionality*" that small-scale VARs suffer from. Bernanke and Boivin (2003) emphasise that the central bank is likely to consider more information when making policy decisions. Therefore, FAVAR models assist decision-making in a data-rich environment. In so doing, FAVARs lessen the problem of an arbitrary selection of observable series that capture theoretical concepts.

Figure 19.5 shows the first common factor derived from the annual growth rates for white and yellow maize, wheat, sorghum, sunflower seeds and soybeans. We use this first common factor in the empirical estimations to capture the common boom and bust episodes in these commodity prices. As stated earlier, FAVARs provide a parsimonious and effective framework of analysis by incorporating information from a large number of economic time series and make it possible to introduce a

[4] FAVARs extract common factors from a large set of data and use them in the vector autoregression (VAR) models.

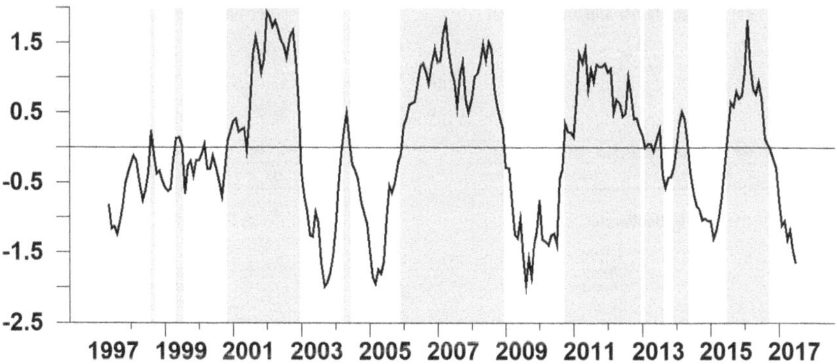

Fig. 19.5 First common factor for food commodity spot prices. (Note: The grey shaded areas denote food commodity spot prices booms. Source: Authors' calculations)

higher amount of relevant information into economic estimations compared to standard VAR methods. We use the first common factor to generate two dummy variables. The boom (bust) is equal to positive (negative) observations over the sample, and is zero otherwise.

19.3 How Reasonable and Plausible Is the First Common Food Commodity Price Factor?

Prior to the empirical estimations, this section conducts the reasonableness and plausibility tests for the estimated first common factor for food commodity prices. Faust (1998) and Uhlig (2005) show that a reasonable analysis of the identification schemes and validation of the structural shocks can also be conducted by extracting the shocks and assess whether their association with other macroeconomic variables produces reasonable relationships. Reasonableness is interpreted to mean that the relationships adhere to conventional theoretical predictions. We assess the plausibility and reasonableness of the first common factor in Fig. 19.5 by assessing how well associated it is with food and consumer price inflation. Figure 19.6 shows that the first common factor is positively associated with food and consumer price inflation although at varying degrees. This

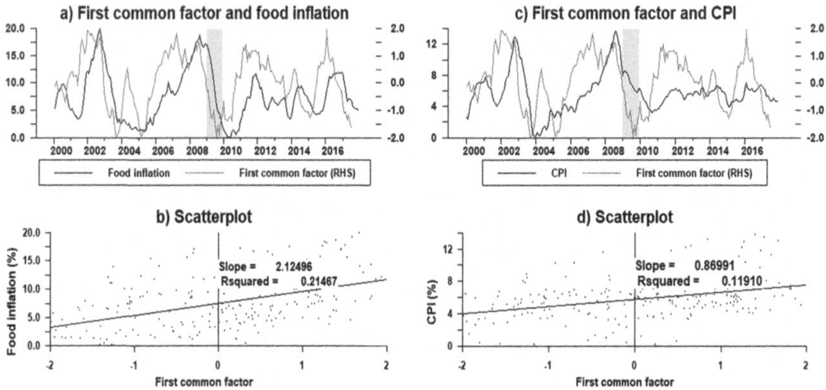

Fig. 19.6 Reasonableness and plausibility tests. (Note: The grey shaded areas denote the South African recession. Source: Authors' calculations)

is as expected, given that there are other factors beyond just food commodity prices that influence food and consumer price inflation.

The positive association in Fig. 19.6 indicates that episodes of booms (busts) in food commodity prices are expected to lead to an increase (decline) in food and consumer price inflation.

19.3.1 How Synchronised Are Domestic and Global Food Commodity Prices?

This section complements the previous section by assessing the lead–lag relationship between global and domestic food commodity prices. We use the cross-correlations to assess what happens when the IMF food and beverage price inflation leads the domestic first common factor for domestic food commodity prices in Fig. 19.5 and domestic food price inflation. Figure 19.7 shows that the domestic first common factor for domestic food commodity prices and the domestic food price inflation increase and remain elevated for 7 and 17 months, respectively, when led by increases in the intermediate moisture food (IMF) and beverage price inflation.

Thus, the results in Fig. 19.7 indicate that domestic food commodity prices are highly synchronised with global food prices. This means that shocks to global food commodity prices will be transmitted into the domestic economy.

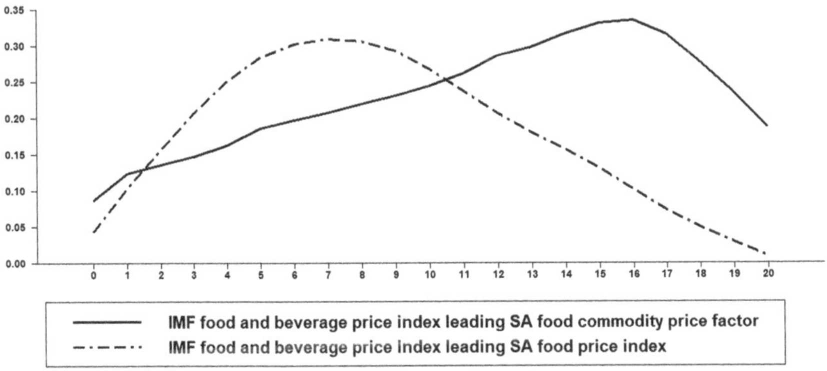

Fig. 19.7 Lead–lag relationship between global and domestic food commodity prices. (Source: IMF, SARB and authors' calculations)

19.4 What Is the Role of Food Commodity Price Booms and Busts in the Agricultural Sector?

This section conducts an empirical analysis. As stated earlier, we use the two-step FAVAR approach to conduct the empirical analysis. In the first step, common factors are computed and in the second stage, the system is estimated using standard time series methods and the extracted common factors are treated as other time series variables in the model. We create dummy variables based on the first common factor for food commodity prices shown in Fig. 19.5. The first (second) dummy takes on all positive (negative) values to capture boom (bust) food commodity price episodes.

We have stated that earlier chapters indicated that there are contradictory trends between the gross value added and employment in the agricultural sector. The agricultural sector gross value added has declined whereas employment levels have increased. What could explain these contradictory trends and dynamics? Is it possible that food commodity price booms play a more important role in incentivising farmers to increase output, investment and employment? What is the role of food commodity price booms and busts on the agricultural sector? Do food commodity price booms and busts push food and consumer price inflation, agricultural sector output, investment and employment growth in different directions? If that is the case, what are the implications for the monetary policy response? To answer these questions, we estimate a number of FAVAR models for the sample period 2000Q1 to 2017Q4. The FAVAR models are estimated using 2 lags and 10,000 Monte Carlo draws. The models include agricultural sector output, investment and employment growth. The first common factor is that boom and bust episodes enter the models individually. All growth rates reflect annual measurements.

First, Fig. 19.8 shows the responses of the agricultural sector output growth and employment growth to three models: (i) one that does not distinguish between boom and bust episodes; (ii) one that includes a dummy variable for food commodity price booms; and (iii) one that includes a dummy variable for food commodity bust episodes. It is evident that positive food commodity price shocks and boom episodes result in an increase in agricultural sector output growth and employment growth. On the other hand, food commodity price bust shocks result in the decline of output growth and employment growth. This is because food commodity price boom and bust episodes have an important bearing on the profitability of farmers.

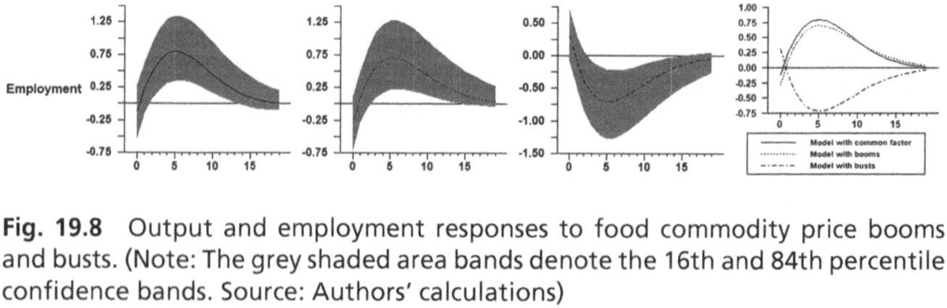

Fig. 19.8 Output and employment responses to food commodity price booms and busts. (Note: The grey shaded area bands denote the 16th and 84th percentile confidence bands. Source: Authors' calculations)

The results in Fig. 19.8 concur with the observed data trend that increases in commodity prices do not necessarily induce producers to increase area planted and quantities produced. On the other hand, commodity price booms induce farmers to increase employment. This is characteristic of (i) monopoly market structure; (ii) high reliance on volatile and cyclical food commodity prices; and (iii) very limited value added along the agricultural sector value chain. Monopoly market structures are characterised by market environments where producers possess market power to control either prices or quantities in order to maintain prices at elevated levels and even increase further.[5] In addition, the Bureau for Food and Agricultural Policy (BFAP 2011) contends that the expansion of the agricultural sector based on the labour intensity of crops should not only be driven by higher levels of productivity. The strategy must also be supported by domestic and international markets given that increased (excess/surplus) production will depress domestic prices, which is bad for output, investment and employment creation.

Hence, accelerated land reform and redistribution is an opportunistic policy intervention to change the agricultural market structure and allow more participants to participate and benefit in the market. At the same time, the policy intervention presents opportunities along the agricultural sector value chain and increases the value added by the sector as envisaged in the National Development Plan (NDP). It is against this background that the debate about the size and, alternatively, economies of scale in the agricultural market matters as well. Thus, we conclude that food commodity price boom episodes contribute to the employment intensity in the agricultural sector. Commodity price boom and bust episodes play an important role in the employment intensity of the agricultural sector.

19.4.1 What about Investment Growth in the Agricultural Sector?

To answer this question, we augment the VAR models estimated in the previous section and add the agricultural sector investment growth.

[5] See, for instance, https://saylordotorg.github.io/text_principles-of-microeconomics-v2.0/s13-monopoly.html. For further reading.

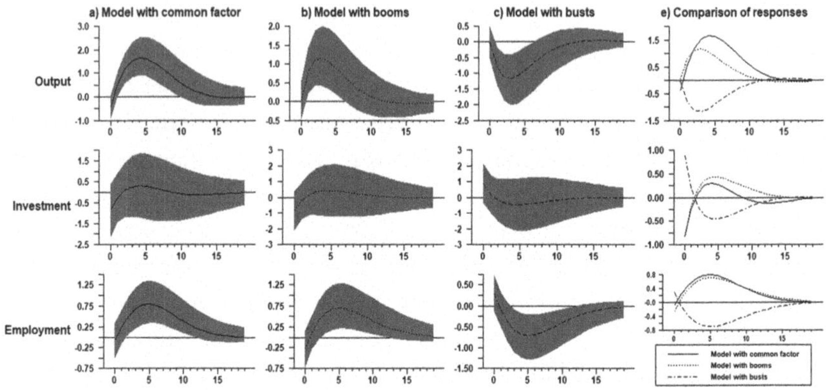

Fig. 19.9 Output, investment and employment responses to food commodity price boom and bust shocks. (Note: The grey shaded area bands denote the 16th and 84th percentile confidence bands. Source: Authors' calculations)

The results in Fig. 19.9 show that indeed food commodity price boom episodes induce farmers to increase investment growth. As expected, food commodity price bust shocks lead to a decline in investment growth.

19.4.2 Do Food Commodity Price Booms and Busts Push Food and Consumer Price Inflation, and Key Agricultural Sector Aggregates in Different Directions?

To conclude the analysis in this chapter, we consider the role of food commodity price boom and bust episodes on food and consumer price inflation. Do food commodity price booms and busts push food and consumer price inflation, and key agricultural sector aggregates in different directions? If that is the case, what are the implications for the monetary policy response? This question is important because the South African Reserve Bank is mandated to keep inflation and inflation expectations within the target range of 3 to 6 per cent. To answer this question, we include food and consumer price inflation separately in the VAR models estimated in the previous section.

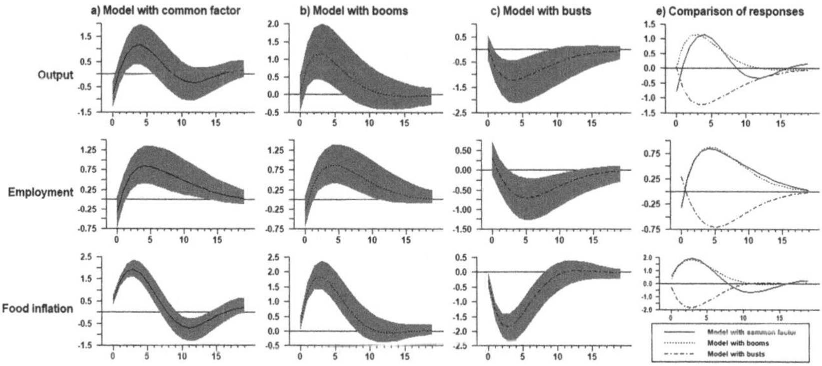

Fig. 19.10 Output, employment and food inflation responses to food commodity price boom and bust shocks. (Note: The grey shaded area bands denote the 16th and 84th percentile confidence bands. Source: Authors' calculations)

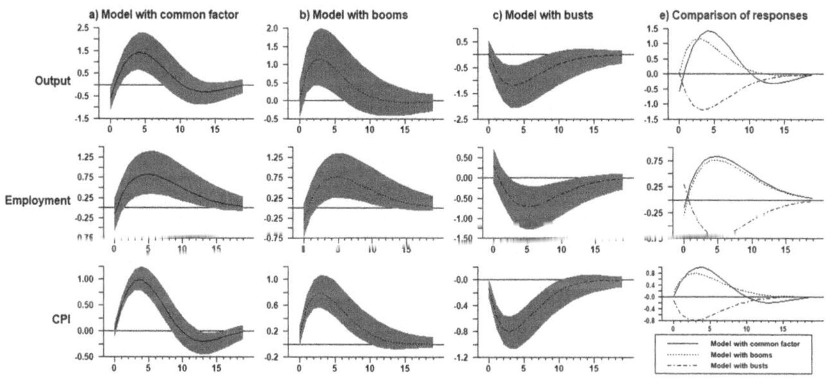

Fig. 19.11 Output, employment and consumer inflation responses to food commodity price boom and bust shocks. (Note: The grey shaded area bands denote the 16th and 84th percentile confidence bands. Source: Authors' calculations)

Figure 19.10 shows that food commodity price booms lead to an increase in food price inflation whereas busts dampen food inflation. The same effects are evident in the consumer price inflation in Fig. 19.11.

Thus, although food commodity price booms are good for the agricultural sector output and employment growth, they come at a cost of

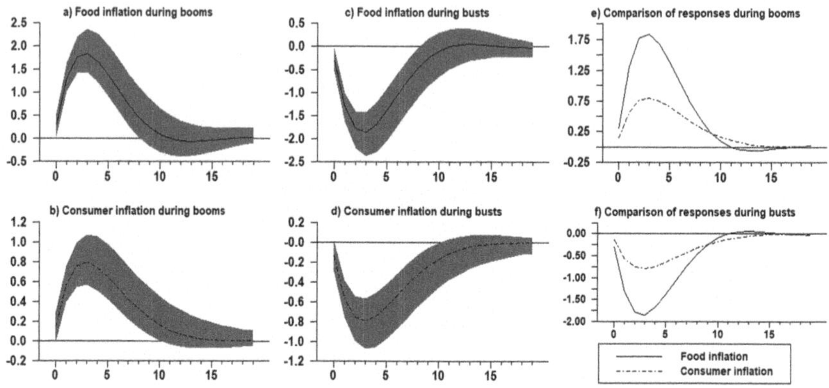

Fig. 19.12 Food and consumer price inflation responses to food commodity price boom and bust shocks. (Note: The grey shaded area bands denote the 16th and 84th percentile confidence bands. Source: Authors' calculations)

heightened food and consumer price inflation with implications for monetary policy. Thus, food commodity price booms and busts push food and consumer price inflation, and the agricultural sector output growth and employment growth in different directions. These movements imply opposing effects for monetary policy reaction.

In fact, Fig. 19.12 shows that food price inflation is highly responsive to food commodity price booms and busts. Figure 19.11(e) shows that food price inflation (decline) is more than double that of the consumer price inflation due to food commodity price booms and busts.

During episodes of food commodity price booms (busts) the increase in food price inflation implies elevated (muted) consumer price inflation. At the same time, the direction of food and consumer price inflation has a significant bearing on inflation expectations, wage settlements and the stability of inflation outcomes within the inflation target range of 3–6 per cent.[6] These results imply that there is a need for policy co-ordination, especially in cases where the fortunes of farmers in terms of elevated food commodity prices exert a negative impact on food and consumer price

[6] See Ndou and Gumata (2017) on the empirical analysis of the R/US$ exchange rate and food inflation on inflation expectations and outcomes.

inflation with implications for the price stability mandate and monetary policy response.[7]

19.5 Conclusion and Policy Implications

This chapter explored whether food commodity price booms play a more important role in incentivising farmers to increase output, investment and employment. Yes, evidence shows that food commodity price booms play a significant role in increasing output, investment and employment growth, albeit at differing intensities. First, we establish that domestic food commodity prices are highly cyclical, volatile and synchronised. In addition, domestic food commodity prices are highly synchronised with global food commodity prices. Domestic food commodity prices increase and remain elevated when led by increased global food commodity prices. Thus, shocks to global food commodity prices are transmitted into the domestic economy.

Second, evidence in this chapter shows that positive shocks to food commodity prices and boom (bust) episodes result in an increase (decline) in the agricultural sector output, investment and employment growth. The results indicate that increases and booms in food commodity prices do not necessarily induce producers to increase area planted and quantities produced. But food commodity price booms induce farmers to increase employment. This is characteristic of (i) monopolistic market structure; (ii) high reliance on volatile and cyclical food commodity prices; and (iii) very limited value added along the agricultural sector value chain. This is because food commodity price boom and bust episodes have an important bearing on the profitability of farmers. Thus, food commodity price booms and busts play a significant role in the agricultural sector.

Third, we establish that food commodity price booms and busts push food and consumer price inflation, agricultural sector output growth, investment and employment growth in different directions. Food price

[7] We explore the transmission of monetary policy via the balance sheet channel in later chapters of this book.

inflation is highly responsive to food commodity price booms and busts. In turn, food price inflation has a significant bearing on the duration and amplitude of consumer price inflation cycles. Thus, although food commodity price booms are good for the agricultural sector output growth and employment growth, they come at a cost of heightened food and consumer price inflation with implications for monetary policy. Food commodity price booms and busts push food and consumer price inflation, and the agricultural sector output growth and employment growth in different directions. These movements imply opposing effects for monetary policy.

The policy implications of the findings in this chapter concur with earlier findings that accelerated land reform and redistribution is also an opportunistic policy intervention and instrument to change the agricultural market structure and allow more participants to participate and benefit in the market. At the same time, the policy intervention presents opportunities along the agricultural sector value chain and increases the value added by the sector as envisaged in the NDP. It is against this background that the debate about size (economies of scale) in the agricultural market matters as well.

Furthermore, food commodity price boom episodes contribute to the employment growth intensity in the agricultural sector. But there is a need for policy co-ordination, especially in cases where the fortunes of farmers in terms of elevated food commodity prices and improved profitability exert a negative impact on food and consumer price inflation with implications for the price stability mandate and monetary policy response. The policy implications and trade-offs are especially binding in cases where the prevalence of the parity pricing model in the agricultural sector coincides with periods of droughts and severe exchange rate depreciations. In addition, the policy co-ordination becomes pertinent and binding when the South African Reserve Bank is also mandated with ensuring maximum employment over and above price and financial stability.

Appendix

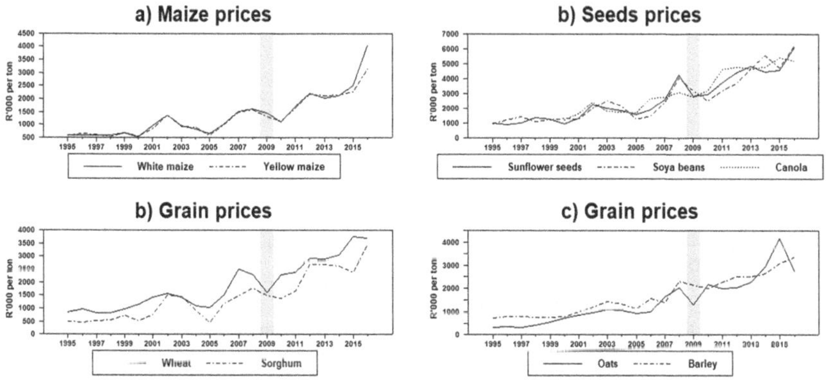

Fig. 19.13 Selected food commodity price spot prices. (Source: SAGIS)

Table 19.1 White maize price peaks, troughs and amplitude

Peak	Trough	Peak-to-Trough	Amplitude (%)
Jan 1998	Jan 1999	12	−61.53
Dec 1999	Jul 2000	7	−49.12
Mar 2002	Apr 2003	13	−152.93
Apr 2004	Feb 2005	10	−107.66
Jul 2006	Mar 2010	44	−23.77
Jan 2012	Jan 2013	12	−27.02
Feb 2014	Jan 2015	11	−57.65

Source: Authors' calculations

Table 19.2 Yellow maize price peaks, troughs and amplitude

Peaks	Troughs	Peak-to-Trough	Amplitude (%)
Apr 1999	Aug 2000	16	−57
Jan 2002	Aug 2003	19	−87.5
Apr 2004	Feb 2005	10	−83.21
Jul 2006	Jul 2009	36	0.38
Jan 2012	Aug 2013	19	−29.32
Feb 2014	Jan 2015	11	−57.22

Source: Authors' calculations

Table 19.3 Wheat price peaks, troughs and amplitude

Peaks	Troughs	Peak-to-Trough	Amplitude (%)
Jan 1999	Oct 1999	9	−24.06
Dec 2000	Sep 2001	9	2.87
Sep 2002	Oct 2003	13	−102.8
Apr 2004	Jan 2005	9	−30
Jun 2006	May 2007	11	29.29
Mar 2008	Mar 2010	24	−178.79
Feb 2011	Feb 2012	12	−19.42
Nov 2012	May 2015	30	−21.54
Jan 2016	Jan 2017	12	−44.67

Source: Authors' calculations

Table 19.4 Sunflower seeds price peaks, troughs and amplitude

Peaks	Troughs	Peak-to-Trough	Amplitude (%)
Dec 2001	Aug 2003	20	−79.46
Jun 2005	Apr 2006	10	−89.64
Jun 2008	Oct 2009	16	−142.56
Sep 2011	Feb 2012	5	−15.14
Mar 2013	Jun 2014	15	−13.2

Source: Authors' calculations

Table 19.5 Soybeans price peaks, troughs and amplitude

Peaks	Troughs	Peak-to-Trough	Amplitude (%)
Jul 1998	Jul 1999	12	−49.46
Dec 2000	May 2001	5	−8.72
Mar 2002	Aug 2003	17	−25.83
Mar 2004	Feb 2005	11	−101.24
Jun 2008	Jan 2010	19	−63.67
Feb 2011	Feb 2012	12	−4.34
Jul 2012	May 2015	34	−3.9

Source: Authors' calculations

Table 19.6 Sorghum price peaks, troughs and amplitude

Peaks	Troughs	Peak-to-Trough	Amplitude (%)
Jul 1998	Jul 1999	12	−32.63
Sep 2001	Aug 2003	23	−16.8
Apr 2004	Apr 2005	12	−63.13
Feb 2007	Nov 2007	9	−21.63
Jul 2008	Jul 2009	12	−112.6
Apr 2011	Apr 2012	12	1.14
Jul 2015	Jul 2016	12	−42.84

Source: Authors' calculations

References

BFAP. 2011. The Contribution of the Agro-Industrial Complex to Employment in South Africa. Tech. Rep. June, The Bureau for Food and Agricultural Policy, Pretoria.

Bernanke, B.S., and Boivin, J. 2003. Monetary Policy in a Data-Rich Environment. *Journal of Monetary Economics*, 50, 525–46.

Bernanke, B.S., Bovian, J., and Eliasz, P. 2005. Measuring the Effects of Monetary Policy: A Factor-Augmented Vector Autoregressive (FAVAR) Approach. *Quarterly Journal of Economics*, 120, 387–422.

Bordo, M.D., and Jeanne, O. 2002. Monetary Policy and Asset Prices: Does "Benign Neglect" Make Sense? *International Finance*, 5(2), 139–64.

Borgy, V., Laurent, C., and Jean-Paul, R. 2009. *Asset Price Boom Bust Cycles and Credit: What is the Scope of Macro Prudential Regulation?* Working Paper. Bank of International Settlements: Basel. December.

Fatas, A., Kannan, P., Rabanal, P., and Scott, A. 2009. Lessons from Asset Price Fluctuations for Monetary Policy. In *World Economic Outlook*. International Monetary Fund. September.

Faust, J. 1998. The Robustness of Identified VAR Conclusions about Money. *Carnegie-Rochester Conference Series on Public Policy*, 49(1), 207–44.

Forni, M., Hallin, M., Lippi, M. and Reichlin, L. 2000. The Generalized Factor Model: Identification and Estimation. *The Review of Economics and Statistics*, 82, 540–54.

Harding, D., and Pagan, A. 2002a. A Comparison of two Business Cycle Dating Methods. *Journal of Economics Dynamics and Control*, 27, 1681–90.

Harding, D., and Pagan, A. 2002b. Dissecting the Cycle: A Methodological Investigation. *Journal of Monetary Economics*, 49, 365–81.

Helbling, T., and Terrones, M. 2003. When Bubbles Burst. In *World Economic Outlook*, Chap. 2. IMF: Washington.

Helbling, T., Huidrom, R., Ayhan Kose, M., and Otrok, C. 2011. *Do Credit Shocks Matter? A Global Perspective*. IMF Working Paper.

Johnson, R.A., and Wichern, D.W. 1992. *Applied Multivariate Statistical Analysis*. Prentice Hall, Inc. ISBN 0-130-41146-9.

Kilian, L., and Vigfusson, R.J. 2011. Are the Responses of the U.S. Economy Asymmetric in Energy Price Increases and Decreases? *Quantitative Economics*, 2(3), 419–53.

McKinsey & Company. 2015. *South Africa's Big Five: Bold Priorities for Inclusive Growth*. McKinsey Global Institute: Johannesburg.

Ndou, E., and Gumata, N. 2017. *Inflation Dynamics in South Africa: The Role of Thresholds, Exchange Rate Pass-through and Inflation Expectations on Policy Trade-offs*. Palgrave Macmillan. ISBN 978-3-319-46701-6.

Stock, J.H., and Watson, M.W. 2005. *Implications of Dynamic Factor Models for VAR Analysis*. NBER Working Paper No. 11467.

Uhlig, H. 2005. What are the Effects of Monetary Policy on Output? Results from an Agnostic Identification Procedure. *Journal of Monetary Economics*, 52, 381–419.

20

What Is the Role of Trade Liberalisation and Food Commodity Price Booms in the Agricultural Sector? Implications for the Export-Led Growth Strategy

Learning Objectives

- Explore the impact of trade liberalisation and food commodity price booms on the agricultural sector.
- Assess the implications of food commodity price booms and busts for the export-led growth strategy in the agricultural sector.
- Understand the effects of the exposure to import competition in the agricultural sector and the role of import tariffs.

20.1 Introduction

Earlier chapters showed that food commodity price boom episodes induce farmers to increase employment growth more than they increase gross value added (GVA) or output growth. We stated that these market dynamics are characteristic of (i) monopoly market structure; (ii) high reliance on volatile and cyclical food commodity prices; and (iii) very limited value added along the agricultural sector value chain. This chapter extends the analysis by asking the following questions: Has trade liberalisation

N. Gumata, E. Ndou, *Accelerated Land Reform, Mining, Growth, Unemployment and Inequality in South Africa*, https://doi.org/10.1007/978-3-030-30884-1_20

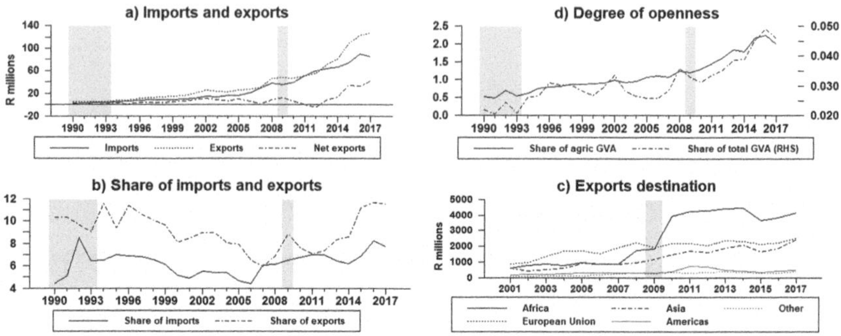

Fig. 20.1 Agricultural sector trade balance and degree of openness. (Note: The grey shaded areas denote the South African recessions. Source: Agri SA and authors' calculations)

benefitted the agricultural sector? What are the effects of food commodity price booms on exports growth? What are the implications of food commodity price booms for the export-led growth strategy in the agricultural sector? Figure 20.1 shows the evolution of the agricultural sector trade balance, exports and imports shares, export destinations and the degree of openness.

The trends show that the agricultural sector is a net exporter[1] largely to Africa at 42 per cent, the European Union at 25 per cent, Asia at 24 per cent, America at 5 per cent and other destinations at 4 per cent as of 2017. It is evident that the proportion of exports to Africa increased considerably post-2009. In addition, Fig. 20.1(b) shows that the share of exports accordingly increased, especially post-2014 and contributed around 12 per cent to the agricultural sector.[2] At the same time, Fig. 20.1(d) shows that the degree of openness (sum of imports and exports) measured as a proportion of the agricultural and aggregate gross value added increased post-1990 in line with the process of deregulating the sector.

[1] The implications for food security are that quantitatively and qualitatively, alternatively, in terms of food availability and quality, South Africa is doing relatively well. However, this does not directly imply food affordability.

[2] See also Fig. 20.15 in the Appendix.

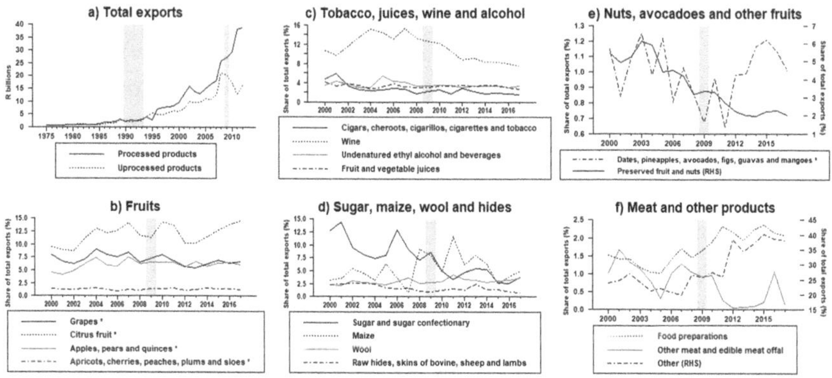

Fig. 20.2 Product breakdown of agricultural sector exports. (Note: * = fresh or dried. The grey shaded areas denote the South African recession. Source: Agri SA and authors' calculations)

The breakdown of exports by product in Fig. 20.2 shows that processed agricultural products constitute almost 70 per cent of exports.[3]

Figure 20.2(b) shows that as at 2017, total fruit exports contributed 30 per cent to total exports, with (i) citrus fruit at 14.59 per cent,[4] (ii) grapes at 6.67, (iii) apples, pears and quinces at 5.97, and (iv) apricots, cherries, peaches, plums and sloes at 1.29 per cent. The trends show that citrus fruits have consistently contributed more than 10 per cent to total exports since 2000 and have been on an upward trend since 2014. Furthermore, data indicate that the fruit sector contributes around 19 per cent to the agricultural sector employment.[5]

Figure 20.2(c) shows that tobacco, juices, wine and alcohol contributed 15 per cent to total exports with (i) wine at 7.47 per cent, (ii) cigars,

[3] See also Fig. 20.16 in the Appendix.

[4] South African citrus fruit production is forecast to continue its strong growth in the 2018/19 MY, due to expanded planted area, favourable weather conditions and strong demand. Trade is a key driver in the growth of South African citrus production, with total exports accounting for 79 per cent of the total citrus production. https://gain.fas.usda.gov/Recent%20GAIN%20Publications/Citrus%20Annual_Pretoria_South%20Africa%20-%20Republic%20of_2-5-2019.pdf.

[5] See for further reading https://www.businesslive.co.za/bd/opinion/2018-04-25-cherry-pick-high-value-exports-by-supporting-fresh-fruit-farmers/.

cheroots, cigarillos, cigarettes and tobacco at 1.61 per cent, (iii) undenatured ethyl alcohol and beverages at 3.25 per cent, and (iv) fruit and vegetable juices at 2.63 per cent as of 2017. The trends show that the contribution of wine declined from around 16 per cent pre-2009 to around 8 per cent post-2009. A similar trend is observed for sugar and sugar confectionary in Fig. 20.2(d) which declined from 16 per cent in 2001 to around 2.6 per cent in 2017. On the other hand, maize exports, although highly volatile, have increased to 5 per cent in 2017.

Wool exports contribution has doubled from around 2 per cent in 2000 to 4 per cent in 2017. The trends in Fig. 20.2(e) indicate that the contribution of preserved fruit and nuts has been on a persistent decline and their contribution has more than halved from around 6 per cent in 2000 to 2 per cent in 2017. On the other hand, having been on a persistently declining, albeit very volatile, trend, the contribution of dates, pineapples, avocados, figs, guavas and mangoes increased from just below 0.6 per cent pre-2009 to 1 per cent in 2017. This implies that there is indeed room for growth in these sectors in line with the potential and labour intensity as shown in earlier chapters.[6]

Thus, the trends presented so far about trade in the agricultural sector further contrast with those presented in earlier chapters showing that the contribution of the agricultural sector gross value added and investment have been on a persistent decline since the 1990s. Is it possible that a simultaneous occurrence of food commodity price booms and exports growth in part explains limited value added along the agricultural sector value chain? For instance, Vast literature shows that Africa's growth, while impressive, has been volatile and this can be largely explained by reliance on high commodity prices rather than by value added along the manufacturing value chains. To drive the point home, Adesina uses the cocoa market and demonstrates the economic effects of the trade imbalance. For example, Africa produces about 75 per cent of the world's cocoa but accounts for just 5 per cent of the nearly US$100 billion chocolate market.[7] We explore the policy implications of food commodity price booms and busts on the agricultural sector in later sections.

---

[6] See BFAP (2011) for further details.

[7] See for further reading https://www.project-syndicate.org/commentary/africa-industrialization-roadmap-by-akinwumi-adesina-2018-05.

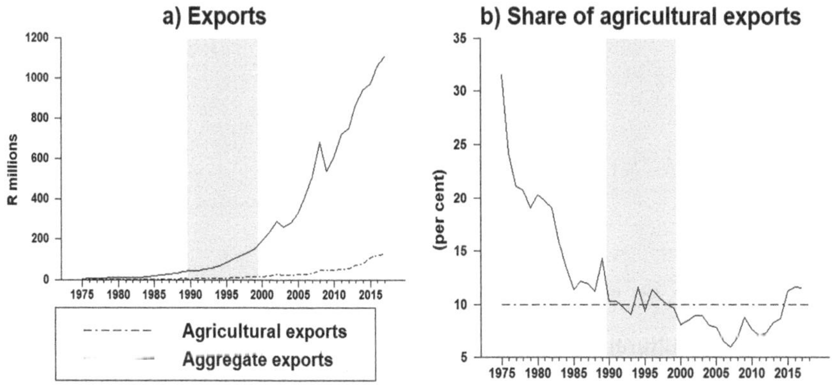

Fig. 20.3 Agricultural and aggregate exports. (Note: The grey shaded areas denote the South African recession. Source: Agri SA, South African Reserve Bank and authors' calculations)

20.2 How Has Trade Liberalisation Affected the Agricultural Sector?

This section assesses the role of trade liberalisation in the agricultural sector.[8] Trade liberalisation is founded on the premise that labour would benefit largely from export growth since production for exports is believed to be more labour-intensive than production for the domestic market (Leautier and Hanson 2013). This is because better and efficient allocation of resources based on the country's comparative or competitive advantage would stimulate economic and job growth as increased global demand for domestic exports induces an increase in domestic output and necessitates more labour.

Figure 20.1(a) has already shown that the agricultural sector is a net exporter largely to Africa, the European Union and Asia. In addition, Fig. 20.3(b) shows that the agricultural sector exports contributed 10 per

[8] In this section trade liberalisation refers to deregulation of the marketing system in the agricultural sector. At the end of 1996, the Marketing of Agricultural Products Act (Act No. 47 of 1996) was passed. By early 1998, all control boards ceased operation. Their assets were transferred to industry trusts which provide services such as market information, export advice and product development. Price controls were removed with the abolition of control boards. See for further reading http://www.dti.gov.za/economic_empowerment/docs/coops/legis_policy/coop-strategy.pdf.

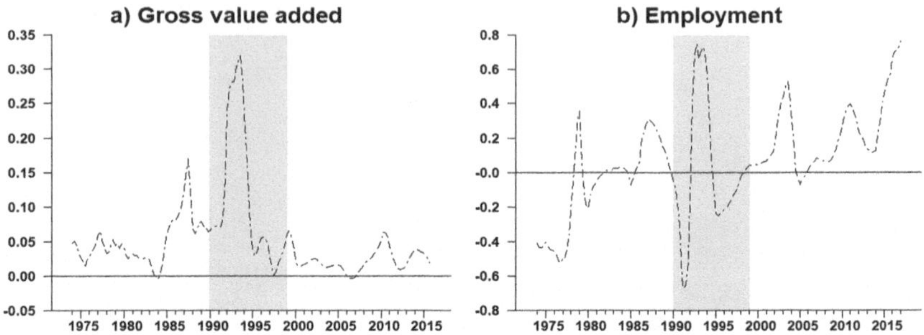

Fig. 20.4 Agricultural sector gross value added and employment rolling five-year window coefficients (1975Q1 to 2018Q4). (Note: The shaded area denotes the period of the trade liberalisation in the agricultural sector. Source: Authors' calculations)

cent on average during the 1990s, the period of trade liberalisation, but declined in the early 2000s. The recovery that started in 2007 has continued and the sector contributed 11.6 per cent to total exports as of 2017. We estimate the five-year rolling window elasticities for the agricultural sector gross value added (GVA) and employment with respect to the aggregate GVA and employment. The data are in levels.

Figure 20.4 shows that the five-year rolling coefficients (elasticities) for the agricultural sector gross value added and employment declined during the 1990s,[9] whereas the employment rolling coefficients increased significantly post-2000 and especially post-2014 in Fig. 20.4(b). The gross value added coefficient has largely remained flat and has moved sideways. The results indicate that indeed there has been a divergence between the contribution of the agricultural sector gross value added and employment to the aggregate economy. The employment intensity of the agricultural sector has increased whilst that of gross value added has remained weak. The implication is that the agricultural sector employment intensity had increased post-trade liberalisation, whereas gross value added has remained very weak. These are early indications that employment growth intensity of the agricultural sector has benefitted more from

[9] The five-year rolling window elasticities are estimated rolling coefficients of the agricultural sector gross value added and employment relative to the aggregate gross value added and employment. These are based on the linear regressions.

trade liberalisation of the agricultural sector compared to the gross value added (output growth) of the sector.

The next question we ask is whether the contrast in the effects has anything to do with the agricultural sector exports. How have the agricultural sector output and employment rolling elasticities evolved relative to the agricultural sector exports? We estimate the five-year rolling window elasticities for the agricultural sector output and employment with respect to the agricultural sector exports. The data are in levels. The results in Fig. 20.5 show that the elasticities for the agricultural sector gross value added and employment declined during the 1990s. They were even negative in the case of employment, indicating that agricultural exports did not benefit from employment growth. This, however, changed during the 2000s and especially exports post-2014.

To assess the robustness of the evolution of the relationships in the agricultural sector, shown in Fig. 20.6, we conduct cross-correlations and linear regressions between the agricultural sector output, exports and employment growth based on the subsamples: (i) 1970Q1 to 2017Q4, (ii) 1990Q1 to 2017Q4, and (iii) 2009Q1 to 2017Q4. The results reveal that the relationships have changed post-2009. Indeed, agricultural exports growth led to more employment growth in the agricultural sector

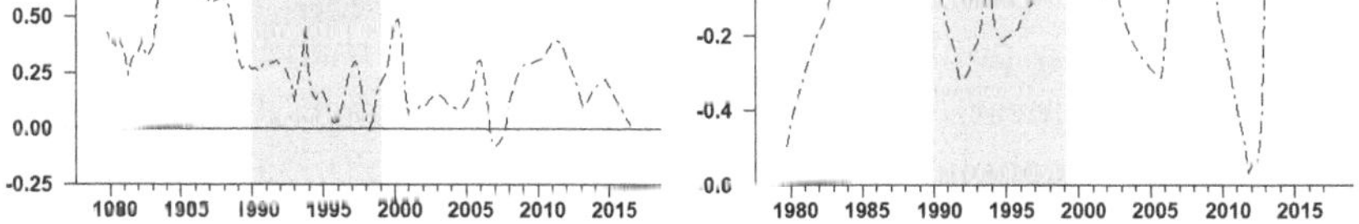

Fig. 20.5 Agricultural sector gross value added and employment rolling five-year window coefficients (1980Q1 to 2018Q4). (Note: The shaded area denotes the period of the trade liberalisation in the agricultural sector. Source: Authors' calculations)

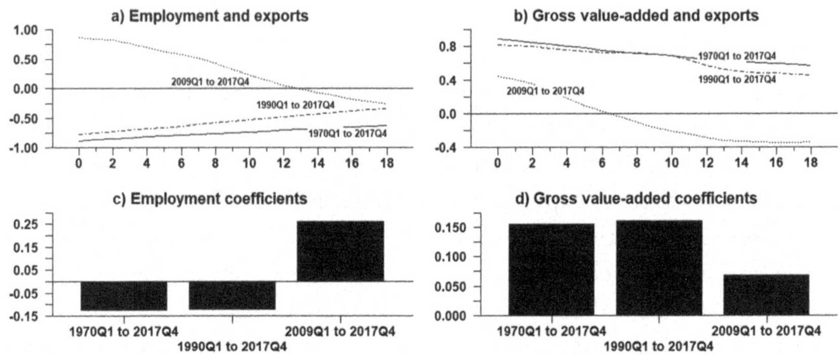

Fig. 20.6 Agricultural sector output, exports and employment relationships. (Source: Authors' calculations)

compared to output growth post-2009 in stark contrast to what was the case, for instance, during the 1990s.

At the same time, the relationships shown in Fig. 20.6 indicate that the intensity of the relationship between the agricultural sector gross value added and exports weakened post-2009. We explore the policy implications of the changes in the nature of the relationships for export growth–oriented strategies in the agricultural sector in the empirical section.

20.3 What Are the Effects of Exposure to Import Competition in the Agricultural Sector?

Figure 20.1 showed that the agricultural sector is a net exporter, but imports mostly rice, wheat, meat (as shown in Fig. 20.23 in the Appendix, largely poultry which accounts for more than 90 per cent of total imported meat), palm oil and alcoholic beverages (whisky, rum, gin and other alcoholic beverages), as shown in Fig. 20.7(a), (b) and (e). The breakdown of imports by country of origin shows the large share of imports originates from Argentina, Indonesia and Brazil. Collectively, the products shown in Fig. 20.7(a) and (b) and the countries of origin

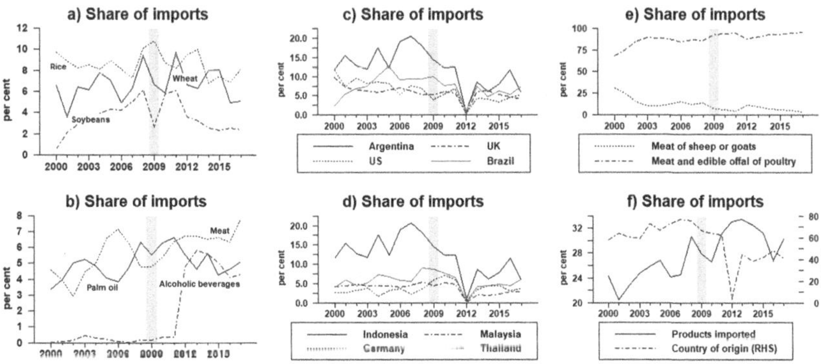

Fig. 20.7 Agricultural sector imports breakdown by product and country of origin. (Note: The shaded area denotes the South African recession. Source: Agri SA and authors' calculations)

shown in Fig. 20.7(c) and (d) account for 20 per cent of imports, respectively.[10]

To answer the question posed in this section, we concentrate on major imported products that South Africa can produce such as wheat, soybeans, meat and sunflower seeds.[11] We use the approach in Autor et al. (2016) to assess the impact of import competition due to the importation of wheat, soybeans, meat and sunflower seeds on the agricultural sector employment.

First, because of the trends shown in Fig. 20.7(e) where almost all the meat imported is poultry, we assess the evolution of chicken prices as collected by Statistics South Africa as part of the food price inflation basket.[12] Figure 20.22 shows the production and net consumption of white meat. The trends show that South Africa produces less white meat than is consumes. In addition, following appeals by the poultry industry, the Department of Trade and Industry increased import tariffs on poultry imports in 2013, anti-dumping measures were imposed in 2015 and a

[10] See Figs. 20.17 and 20.18 for the detailed breakdown of imports by product and country of origin.

[11] We use the grouping of the countries of origin based on the statistics from https://sapoultry.co.za/pdf-statistics/summary-imports-report.pdf and www.sagis.org.za.

[12] Data for frozen chicken portions is only available starting January 2018.

provisional safeguard duty on 15 December 2016.[13] In particular, we assess fresh (unfrozen) full birds and chicken portions which are produced domestically versus frozen portions which are largely imported. The trends in Fig. 20.7(a) show that the price of full fresh chicken has almost doubled from R25/kg in 2009 to R45.77/kg as of May 2018. On the other hand, the annual growth rate in Fig. 20.8(b) has averaged 5.59 per cent post-2009.

The trends that compare fresh portions which are largely domestically produced versus frozen portions which are mostly imported in Fig. 20.8(c) show that fresh domestically produced chicken portions retail at almost double the level of imported frozen chicken portions. For instance, in January 2013 during the imposition of the import tariff, fresh portions retailed at R44.67/kg compared to R24.79/kg for frozen portions. The

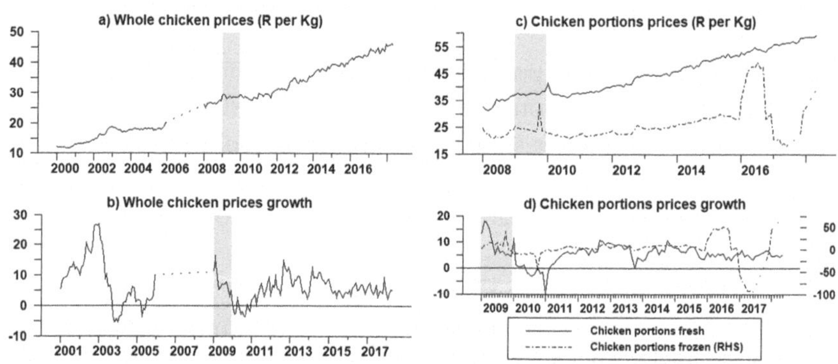

Fig. 20.8 Evolution of chicken prices. (Note: The shaded area denotes the South African recession. Source: Statistics South Africa and authors' calculations)

[13] For instance, import duties for chicken imports from countries like Brazil and the United States stand at 82 per cent for a whole bird, 31 per cent for carcasses, 12 per cent for boneless cuts, 30 per cent for offal and 37 per cent for "bone-in" portions. In 2015, anti-dumping measures ranging from 3.86 per cent to 73.33 per cent were imposed on frozen bone-in chicken pieces from Germany, the Netherlands and the United Kingdom. A provisional safeguard duty of 13.9 per cent was imposed on imports of frozen bone-in chicken pieces from the European Union on 15 December 2016 until 3 July 2017. See for further details https://www.iol.co.za/news/politics/dti-commits-to-helping-ailing-poultry-industry-7365462.

same trend is observed during 2015 when fresh portions retailed at R49.85/kg and frozen portions retailed at R28.28/kg.

The change is only observed in January 2016 when the price for frozen portions increases from R28.40/kg in December 2015 to R47.79/kg in September 2016. But that effect is short-lived as the price declines and the initial margin between fresh and frozen chicken portions is fully restored. In addition, it is at the same time that a widespread outbreak of deadly, highly pathogenic avian influenza in several EU countries has virtually stopped all EU poultry imports into South Africa.[14] This has placed serious doubt on the effectiveness of the imposed tariffs on the price of frozen chicken portions, especially taking into account the fact that a large proportion of imports originates from Denmark, Germany, Hungary, Ireland, the Netherlands, Spain and the UK, and South Africa imposes zero import tariffs on these countries, having signed a free trade agreement in 2001.[15] The import tariffs will most likely deter imports from Latin America whilst continuing to benefit those from Europe.[16]

Furthermore, the Competition Commission (2013) report on the poultry industry concluded on the findings that the oligopoly and vertically integrated market structure of the industry incentivised anti-competitive behaviour. Second, the oligopoly market structure has a bearing on input costs and is a huge barrier to new entrants. Third, the industry has no competition, no reason to improve on efficiency and no reason to reduce prices and the practices of vertical integration also promote tie-in and exclusivity. Fourth, marked allocation of geographical area and product sale concentration, particularly in the Western Cape, and marked tie-in, supply agreements and information exchange, which led to price setting and often industry associations, performed the

[14] See for further details https://m.fin24.com/Economy/sa-slaps-huge-import-tax-on-eu-chicken-legs-20161215.

[15] See Fourie (2013) for further details.

[16] See the evolution of domestic consumption and production of white meat in Fig. 20.22 in the Appendix. It also highlights the impact of imported chicken on the South African market. Chicken accounts for 65 per cent of South African meat production. While consumption has expanded rapidly, production growth has stagnated in recent years. Two main factors contributed to the stagnation, namely the high feed costs through a period which encompassed multiple years of severe drought and the rising volume of chicken imports. https://m.fin24.com/Companies/Agribusiness/sa-still-among-top-chicken-producers-for-cost-efficiency-report-20190410.

function of the secretariat of the cartel and coordinating anti-competitive outcomes.[17]

The South African Poultry association (2013) indicates that the poultry industry (i) contributes to almost a quarter of the agricultural sector gross domestic product (GDP); (ii) is the second biggest user of local maize and soybeans for feed; and (iii) employs more than 50,000 people directly and more than 60,000 indirectly across the industry value chain of which more than 18,000 are in the grain industry.[18]

With this background, this section uses the Autor et al. (2016) approach model in Eq. (20.1) to assess the impact of shifts in trade exposure on the agricultural sector employment:

$$\Delta L_{jr} = \alpha_r + \beta_1 \, \Delta IP_{jr} + \gamma \, X_{j0} + \mathrm{e}_{jr}, \tag{20.1}$$

where $\Delta\ L_{jr}$ is the annual log change in the agricultural sector employment depicted by j over the subperiod τ, ΔIP_{jr} is the annual change in import penetration from the major import countries in the South African agricultural sector depicted by j over the subperiod τ, β_1 is the estimated effect of exposure to import competition on industry employment, X_{j0} is a set of industry-specific start of period controls, α_r is a period-specific constant and e_{jr} is an error term. The estimation of the import penetration rates at a sectoral level helps in the identification of the labour-market consequences of trade shocks.

We use the agricultural sector gross value added and employment annual growth rates for the period 2000Q1 to 2017Q4 given that we do not have data for the sub-sector breakdown. As stated earlier, we use the country groupings to quantify the degree of import penetration that is used in the empirical estimations. The shock is one standard deviation increase in the imports growth or import penetration rate of the products from the selected countries. The import penetration ratio is measured as the ratio of the agricultural sector gross value added to selected import

[17] See for further details presentation by the Competition Commission: The Impact of Poultry Tariffs on Competition http://pmg-assets.s3-website-eu-west-1.amazonaws.com/130910impact.pdf and https://pmg.org.za/committee-meeting/16346/.

[18] See for further reading https://pmg.org.za/files/130910sapa.ppt.

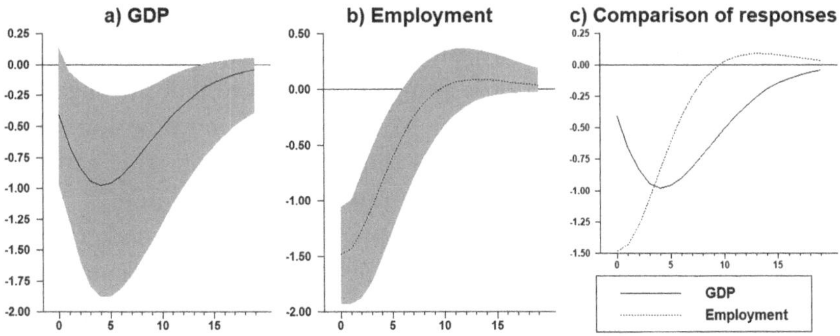

Fig. 20.9 The impact of selected agricultural sector imports penetration on gross value added and employment growth. (Note: The grey shaded area bands denote the 16th and 84th percentile confidence bands. Source: Authors' calculations)

products and countries as mentioned earlier. The vector autoregression (VAR) models are estimated using 10,000 Monte Carlo draws.

Figure 20.9 shows that a positive shock to import penetration leads to a decline in the agricultural sector gross value added (output growth) and employment growth. Employment growth declines more than output growth. The results are robust and the measurement of the impact of imports is shown in Fig. 20.18 in the Appendix. An increase in the imports of the selected products from the selected countries results in a decline in the agricultural sector gross value added and employment growth. Thus, a higher degree of import penetration has negative effects on the agricultural sector output and employment growth. Furthermore, the results in Fig. 20.21 in the Appendix show that the agricultural sector exports, output and employment growth decline in responses to food commodity price bust episodes.

However, the trends of the prices of fresh versus frozen chicken portions in Fig. 20.8[19] clearly indicate that the imposition of import tariffs is not the ideal and most effective tool to deal with prices, competition, output and employment growth in the agricultural sector. The divergence and the margin between the domestic and import price of chicken portions has continued to widen despite the various rounds of import tariffs imposed. A similar picture emerges in the case of wheat price, which is

[19] Refer to the evolution of wheat tariffs in Fig. 20.20 in the Appendix.

largely determined by international factors, and South Africa is a small player and cannot significantly affect prices. Indeed, in the case of the poultry sector, the competition commission is right in that the oligopoly and vertically integrated market structure are incentivising anti-competitive behaviour. In such cases there is a clear and wide gap that policy interventions via the land reform policy can help close.

Similar to the findings in earlier chapters of monopoly market structure in the agricultural sector, a well-structured and well-executed land reform policy strategy can help bring about competition in the poultry industry with benefits to the aggregate economy and consumers. We conclude that structural reforms and changes in the wheat and poultry market via land reform as a strategic tool can have the desired effect far better than what the import tariffs have been able to achieve. In addition, the strategy of using land reform and redistribution augers well with the argument that feed costs constitute 60 per cent of a chicken company's total costs. The findings concur with the recommendations of the Bureau for Food and Agricultural Policy (BFAP 2011) that substituting imports with locally produced commodities can trigger a range of upstream and downstream multipliers with positive effects on the intensity of job creation in the agricultural sector. But such import substitution initiatives must be accompanied by productivity gains to enhance the relative competitiveness of the agricultural sector and industries involved. This approach also deals with the well-documented negative long-term effects of the infant industry protection policies. In addition, BFAP (2011) identifies the poultry and eggs industries as high growth potential sectors as shown in earlier chapters. We explore the impact of exports growth on the labour productivity in later sections.

Furthermore, McMillan and Rodrik (2011) note that one important difference among countries is the degree to which they are able to manage the downside effects posed by the process of globalisation. The authors note that a distinguishing feature of the Asian-style globalisation process was that it had a two-track approach, where (i) many import-competing activities continued to receive support (ii) while new export-oriented activities were spawned. Hence, they conclude that whatever contribution the globalisation process made, its effects are also largely dependent on domestic circumstances, policy choices and domestic growth strategies.

20.4 Does Export Growth Cause Output Growth?

Leautier and Hanson (2013) contend that countries that did poorly in sustaining job creation in sub-Saharan Africa are those that are all highly dependent on the global economy for their export earnings. In addition, high economic growth has had differential impacts on job creation across countries in sub-Saharan Africa and the differences are attributable to the creative use of the agricultural sector, the success in growing market size and the level of innovation. For example, commodity-dependent economies such as Botswana, Lesotho and South Africa had high economic growth which was not job-intensive as their rates of unemployment were high despite achieving good GDP growth. The authors argue that the agricultural sector is well suited for playing a crucial role in dealing with Africa's unemployment problems. To this end, they recommend regional integration policies to expand markets, support modernisation and innovation in the agricultural sector that would attract the youth and enhance value added. Earlier chapters showed that the agricultural sector employment growth is associated with robust increased employment growth for the age group of 15 to 24 years, followed by that of the 25 to 34 years age group. Thus, youth employment benefits from positive shocks to the agricultural sector.

To test the merits of Leautier and Hanson (2013) argument for the agricultural sector, this section tests the hypothesis that agricultural sector export growth causes output growth. We adopt the same approach and analytical framework as in earlier chapters. Is there a prevalence of the "*exports led growth*" hypothesis over the "*growth-driven exports*" hypothesis in the agricultural sector? To answer these hypotheses, we estimate a number of VAR models which include the agricultural sector output, employment and exports growth. The sample spans the period 2000Q1 to 2018Q4. The model is estimated using 2 lags and 10,000 Monte Carlo draws. The shock is one standard deviation.

First, the results in Fig. 20.10 show that exports growth responds more to positive output growth shocks compared to the other way around. At peak response, the agricultural sector output growth increases by 1.63 percentage points compared to an increase of 2.36 percentage points in

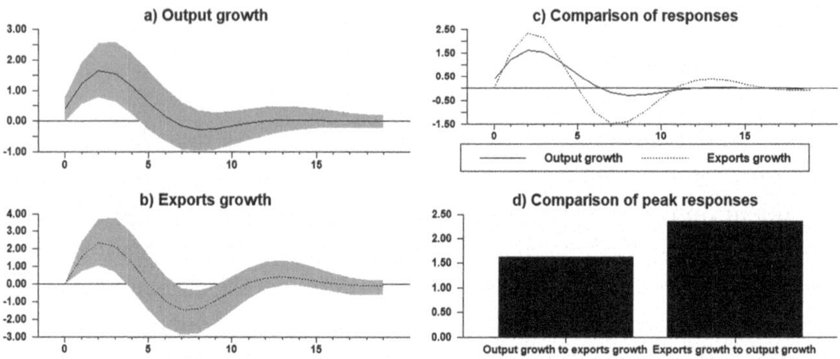

Fig. 20.10 Agricultural sector output and exports growth responses to shocks. (Note: The grey shaded area bands denote the 16th and 84th percentile confidence bands. Source: Authors' calculations)

exports growth. Thus, evidence indicates that exports growth responds more to output growth, hence the "*output growth-driven exports*" hypothesis and strategy best explain developments in the agricultural sector.

In addition, the assessment of whether exports growth versus output growth leads to more employment growth shows that the dominant effects are due to exports growth in Fig. 20.11(c). The results show that the agricultural sector employment growth responds more to positive exports growth shocks compared to output growth. Similarly, Fig. 20.12 labour productivity growth increases in response to positive export growth shocks. The results concur with those in in earlier chapters showing that farmers are more responsive to exports demand and this increases the employment growth intensity in the agricultural sector. The impact of selected agricultural sector imports growth on output and employment growth is shown in Fig. 20.19. The results show that the agricultural sector output growth and employment growth decline in response to a positive shock to the agricultural sector imports.

Thus, we conclude that the trade liberalisation and the "*output growth-driven exports*" hypothesis and strategy best explain developments in the agricultural sector. Trade openness and the export-oriented growth strategy auger well for the agricultural sector output and employment growth. The recommendation in Leautier and Hanson (2013) for the creative use of the agricultural sector, growing market size and innovation is valid for the South African agricultural sector.

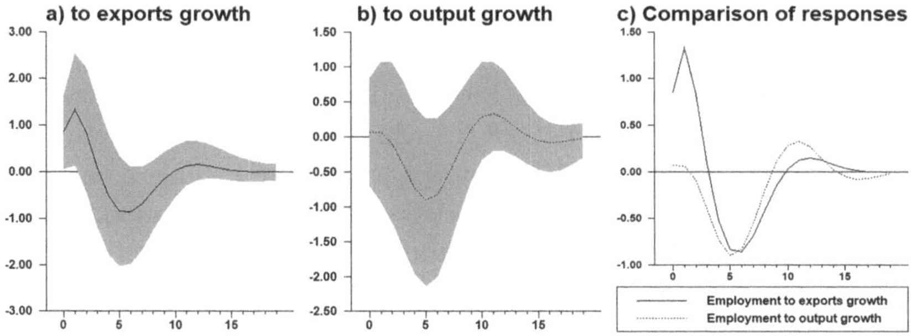

Fig. 20.11 Agricultural sector employment responses to output and export growth shocks. (Note: The grey shaded area bands denote the 16th and 84th percentile confidence bands. Source: Authors' calculations)

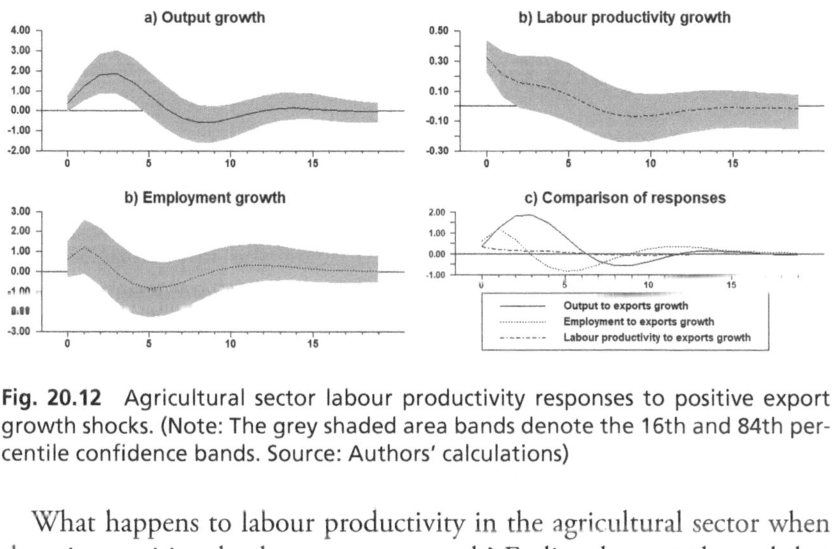

Fig. 20.12 Agricultural sector labour productivity responses to positive export growth shocks. (Note: The grey shaded area bands denote the 16th and 84th percentile confidence bands. Source: Authors' calculations)

What happens to labour productivity in the agricultural sector when there is a positive shock to exports growth? Earlier chapters showed that the level and relative share of the agricultural sector labour productivity increased.[20] These trends concur with a large body of empirical work on the productivity-enhancing effects of trade liberalisation. For instance, Auter et al. (2016) report that between 1998 and 2007 productivity in the Chinese manufacturing sector grew at an astounding pace of 8 per

[20] See Greyling (2012) and Liebenberg and Pardey (2010), who also report that a partial productivity analysis shows that trade liberalisation policies led to a significant increase in labour productivity in the agricultural sector.

cent per year. To answer this question, we estimate a VAR model with the agricultural sector exports growth, output growth, employment growth and labour productivity growth. The growth rates are at annual rates. The sample size spans the period 2000Q1 to 2015Q4 based on data availability for labour productivity. The model is estimated using 2 lags and 10,000 Monte Carlo draws. The shock is one standard deviation.

Figure 20.12 shows that the agricultural sector output growth increases to a positive exports growth shock. Similarly, employment growth and labour productivity growth increase. Thus, trade liberalisation and export-driven growth benefit labour productivity in the agricultural sector.

20.5 Do Food Commodity Price Booms Propagate the Demand Effects on Exports Growth?

The results in the earlier sections indicate that an increase in export demand and prices induce farmers to increase output growth and employment growth. What is the role of commodity price booms and busts? Do commodity price booms and busts propagate the impact of exports growth on the agricultural sector output and employment growth? To answer these questions, this section uses the first common factor constructed in earlier chapters. We use the first common factor for food commodity prices to generate two dummy variables. The boom (bust) dummy takes positive (negative) observations over the sample and zero otherwise. We estimate VAR models which include the dummy variable, exports growth, output growth and employment growth. The models are estimated using 2 lags and 10,000 Monte Carlo draws. The shock is one standard deviation. The results in Fig. 20.13 show that food commodity price booms result in an increase in exports growth, output growth and employment growth. On the other hand, busts result in a decline as shown in Fig. 20.22 in the Appendix.

Furthermore, Fig. 20.14 shows that food commodity price booms are not only positive for the agricultural sector, but they also propagate the effects of the positive and negative shocks throughout the sector.

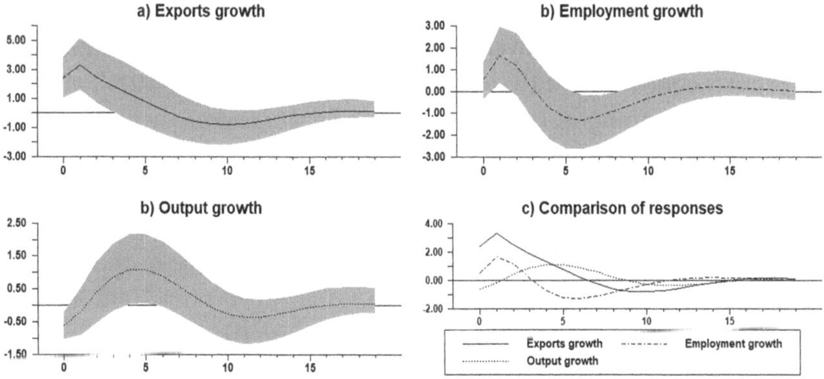

Fig. 20.13 Agricultural sector exports, output and employment responses to food commodity prices shocks. (Note: The grey shaded area bands denote the 16th and 84th percentile confidence bands. Source: Authors' calculations)

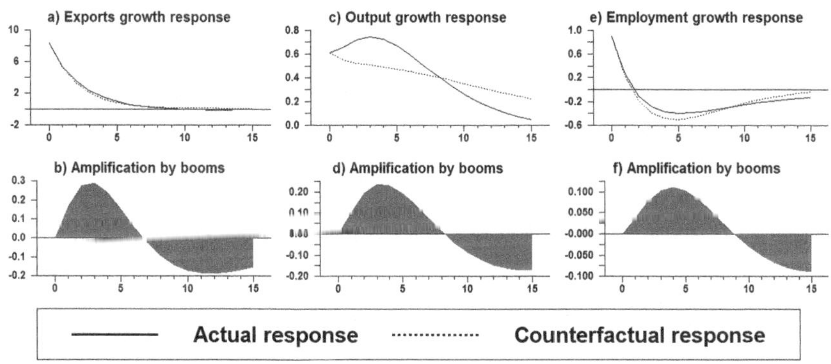

Fig. 20.14 Responses to food commodity price boom episode and the propagation effects of food commodity price boom episode. (Source: Authors' calculations)

20.6 Conclusion and Policy Implications

This chapter explored whether trade liberalisation benefitted the agricultural sector. First, evidence shows that the agricultural sector is a net exporter largely to Africa at 42 per cent, the European Union at 25 per cent, Asia at 24 per cent, America at 5 per cent and other destinations at 4 per cent as of 2017. Second, the breakdown of agricultural exports by product shows that fruit exports in total contributed 30 per cent to total exports, with citrus fruit covering almost half. Third, the agricultural sector exports contributed 11.6 per cent to total exports as of 2017, making the sector a meaningful contributor to aggregate export earnings. Thus, in terms of food availability and quality (quantitatively and qualitatively), South Africa is doing relatively well. However, this does not directly imply food affordability.

Fourth, exports growth leads to employment intensity in the agricultural sector compared to increased gross value added post-2009 in stark contrast to what was the case, for instance, during the 1990s. The assessment of whether exports growth versus output growth leads to more employment growth shows that the dominant effects are due to exports growth. The agricultural sector employment growth responds more to exports growth compared to output growth. The implication is that farmers are more responsive to exports demand and this increases the employment growth intensity in the agricultural sector. The "*output growth-driven exports growth*" hypothesis and strategy best explain developments in the agricultural sector. Trade openness and the export-oriented growth strategy auger well for the agricultural sector output, employment and labour productivity growth.

What are the effects of food commodity price booms on exports growth? The results show that food commodity price booms (busts) result in an increase (decline) in exports, output and employment growth. Furthermore, food commodity price booms propagate (amplify) the effects of the positive and negative shocks throughout the sector.

What are the effects of exposure to import competition in the agricultural sector? First, we establish that the agricultural sector mostly imports rice, wheat, meat (largely poultry which accounts for more than 90 per cent of total imported meat), palm oil and alcoholic beverages (whisky, rum, gin and other alcoholic beverages). Second, the breakdown of imports by country of origin shows that a large share of imports originates from Argentina, Indonesia and Brazil. Collectively, the products and the countries of origin account for 20 per cent of imports, respectively. Third, the results from the Autor et al. (2016) approach used to assess the impact of import competition due to the importation of wheat, soybeans, meat and sunflower seeds on the agricultural sector employment show that a higher degree of import penetration has negative effects on the agricultural sector output and employment growth.

However, the prices of, for instance, fresh versus frozen chicken portions and wheat clearly indicate that the imposition of import tariffs is not the ideal and effective tool to deal with prices, competition, output and employment growth in the agricultural sector. For instance, the divergence and the margin between the domestic and import price of chicken portions has continued to widen despite the various rounds of imports tariffs imposed. A similar picture emerges in the case of wheat price, which is largely determined by international factors, and South Africa is a small player and cannot significantly affect prices.

The policy implications of the findings in this chapter in the case of the poultry sector concur with those of the competition commission. Indeed, the poultry sector which is characterised by the oligopoly and vertically integrated market structure is incentivising anti-competitive behaviour. In such cases there is a clear and wide gap that policy interventions via the land reform policy can help close. Similar to the findings of the monopoly market structure in the agricultural sector, a well-structured and well-executed land reform policy strategy can help bring about competition in the poultry industry with benefits to the aggregate economy and consumers.

We conclude that structural reforms and changes in the wheat and poultry market via land reform policy as a strategic tool can produce the desired effects far better than what the import tariffs have been able to achieve. In addition, the strategy of using land reform and redistribution augers well with the argument that feed costs constitute 60 per cent of a chicken company's total costs. Substituting imports with locally produced commodities can trigger a range of upstream and downstream multipliers with positive effects on the intensity of job creation in the agricultural sector. But such import substitution initiatives have to be accompanied by productivity gains so as to enhance the relative competitiveness of the agricultural sector and industries involved. This approach also deals with the well-documented negative long-term effects of the infant industry protection policies.

Appendix

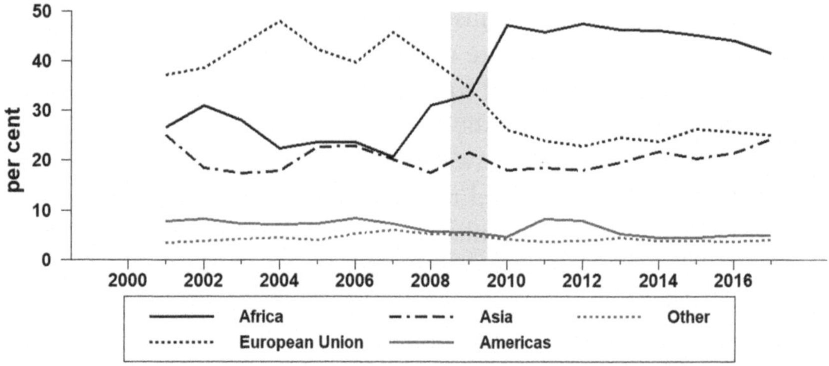

Fig. 20.15 Share of exports to various destinations. (Note: The grey shaded area denotes the South African recession. Source: Agri SA and authors' calculations)

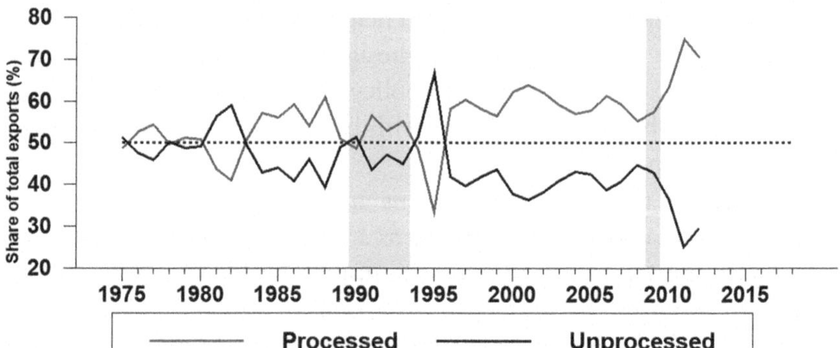

Fig. 20.16 Share of processed and unprocessed exports. (Note: The grey shaded area denotes the South African recessions. Source: Agri SA and authors' calculations)

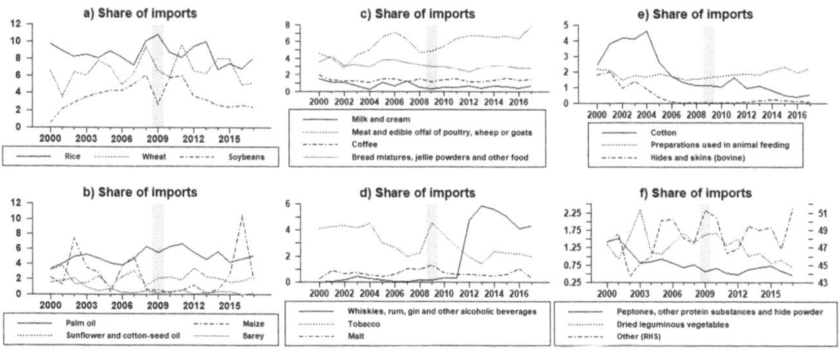

Fig. 20.17 Breakdown of agricultural sector imports by product. (Note: The grey shaded area denotes the South African recession. Source: Agri SA and authors' calculations)

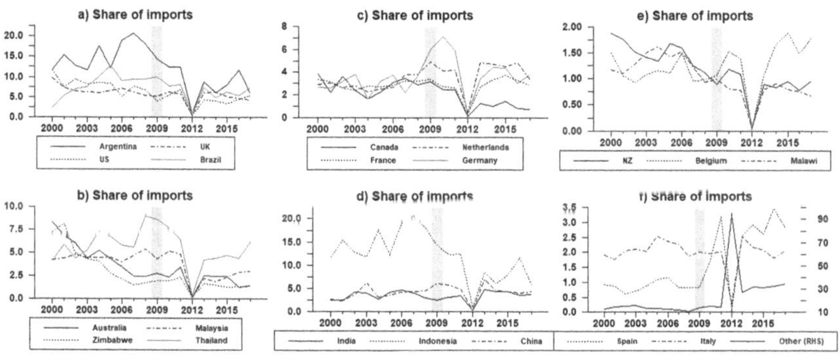

Fig. 20.18 Breakdown of agricultural sector imports by country of origin. (Note: The grey shaded area denotes the South African recession. Source: Agri SA and authors' calculations)

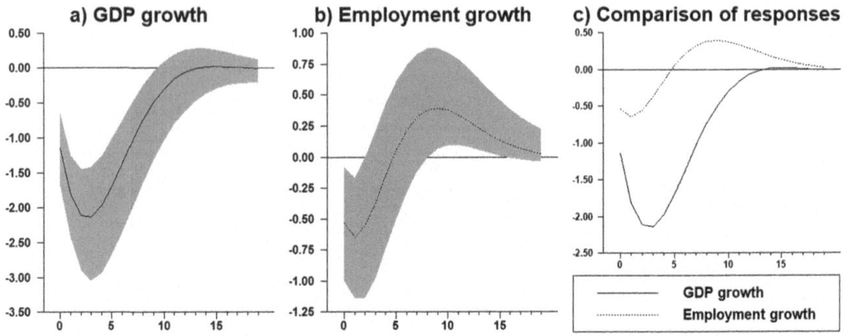

Fig. 20.19 The impact of selected agricultural sector imports growth on output and employment growth. (Note: The grey shaded area bands denote the 16th and 84th percentile confidence bands. Source: Authors' calculations)

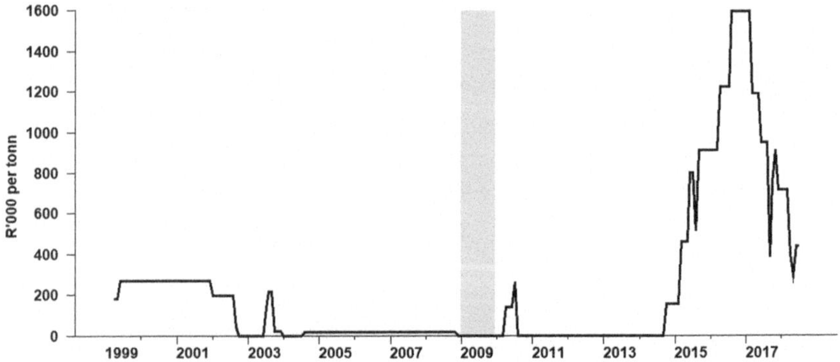

Fig. 20.20 Evolution of the wheat tariff. (Source: SAGIS http://www.sagis.org.za/Koringtarief-Historiese20180525.pdf)

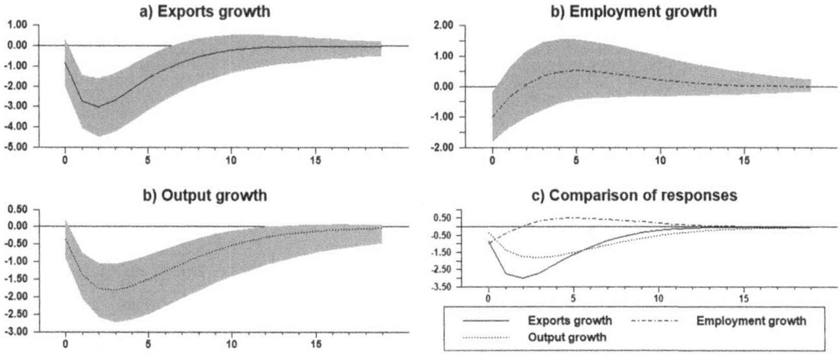

Fig. 20.21 Agricultural sector exports, output and employment responses to food commodity price bust episodes. (Note: The grey shaded area bands denote the 16th and 84th percentile confidence bands. Source: Authors' calculations)

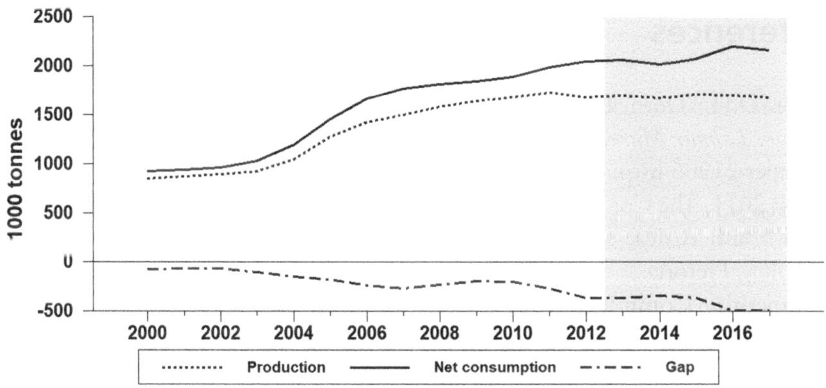

Fig. 20.22 Production and net consumption of white meat. (Note: The grey shaded area represents the period January 2013 to 3 July 2017 during which various imports tariffs were imposed on poultry products. Source: Agri SA and authors' calculations)

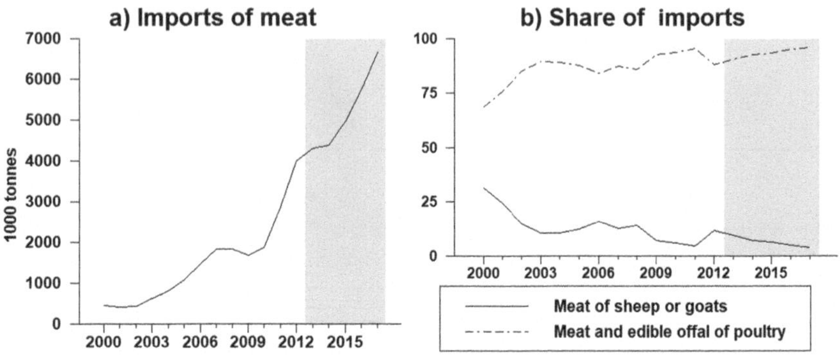

Fig. 20.23 Poultry imports. (Note: The grey shaded area represents the period January 2013 to 3 July 2017 during which various imports tariffs were imposed on poultry products. Source: Agri SA and authors' calculations)

References

Autor, D.H., Dorn, D., and Hanson, G.H. 2016. *The China Shock: Learning from Labour Market Adjustment to Large Changes in Trade*. NBER Working Paper 21906 http://www.nber.org/papers/w21906.

BFAP. 2011. The Contribution of the Agro-Industrial Complex to Employment in South Africa. Tech. Rep. June, The Bureau for Food and Agricultural Policy, Pretoria.

Competition Commission. 2013. The Impact of Poultry Tariffs on Competition Presentation to South African Parliament on the Status of Poultry tariffs in South Africa and the Impact of Proposed Tariff Increase for Poultry Imports: Input by Competition Commission, South African Poultry Association and Association of Meat Importers and Exporters. https://pmg.org.za/committee-meeting/16346/.

Fourie, H. 2013. Not a Free Lunch: The Implications of Increased Import Tariffs on South Africa's Chicken Market. https://econex.co.za/wp-content/uploads/2015/04/econex_researchnote_31.pdf

Greyling, J.C. 2012. The Role of the Agricultural Sector in the South African Economy. Department of Agricultural Economics, University of Stellenbosch. https://agbiz.co.za/uploads/documents/careers/13_04-thesis_jan_c_greyling_published.pdf

Leautier, F., and Hanson, K.T. 2013. Jobless Economic Growth in Africa: Is There a Role for Agriculture? *Journal of African Development*, 15(2), 1–17. African Finance and Economic Association (EFEA).
Liebenberg, F., and Pardey, P.G. 2010. South African Agricultural Production and Productivity Patterns. In J. Alston, B. Babcock, and P. Pardey (eds.) *The Shifting Patterns of Agricultural Production and Productivity Worldwide*, Chap. 13. Midwest Agribusiness Trade Research and Information Center: Ames.
Liebenberg, George Frederick (Frikkie). 2013. South African Production, Productivity, and Research Performance in the 20th Century.
McMillan, M.S., and Rodrik, D. 2011. *Globalisation, Structural Change and Productivity Growth*. NBER Working Paper 17143.
Sihlobo Blog. 2018. Structural Changes in the South African Agricultural Economy between 1910 and 2010. https://wandilesihlobo.com/2018/02/25/structural-changes-in-the-south-african-agricultural-economy-between-1910-and-2010/.
Vink, N., and Kirsten, J. 2002. Pricing Behaviour in the South African Food and Agricultural Sector. Tech. Rep. June, University of Stellenbosch, Stellenbosch.

21

Is the Agricultural Sector Sensitive to the Exchange Rate Depreciation and Volatility Shocks: Evidence from the Balance Sheet Channel

Learning Objectives

- Understand the impact of the R/US$ exchange rate volatility components and depreciation shocks on the importation of consumption, intermediate and capital goods in the agricultural sector.
- Establish the transmission of the R/US$ exchange rate appreciations and depreciations via the food prices and headline inflation channel of transmission.
- Explore the transmission of the R/US$ exchange rate, domestic poultry output, import duties and the import price channel in the poultry sector.
- Assess the relative impact of wheat tariffs, domestic wheat output and R/US$ exchange rate shocks on wheat imports.
- Determine the impact of the R/US$ exchange rate shocks on the components of the agricultural sector imports.

N. Gumata, E. Ndou, *Accelerated Land Reform, Mining, Growth, Unemployment and Inequality in South Africa*, https://doi.org/10.1007/978-3-030-30884-1_21

21.1 Introduction

Earlier chapters showed that food commodity price boom episodes significantly improve the fortunes of farmers in terms of elevated food commodity prices and improved profitability. This in turn contributes to the employment growth intensity in the agricultural sector. But food commodity price booms push prices (e.g. food and consumer price inflation) and the agricultural sector output growth and employment growth in different directions. These diverging responses have opposing effects for monetary policy decisions. This chapter extends the analysis on the agricultural sector by exploring the role of the exchange rate appreciation, depreciation and volatility shocks, and especially their effects via the balance sheet channel. This is because exchange rate shocks, like other financial and macroeconomic shocks, are transmitted into the real economy via a number of channels. In addition, the exchange rate can act as a conduit and an amplifier of other financial and macroeconomic shocks, especially in the presence of financial frictions largely embedded in balance sheets.

For instance, vast literature and empirical evidence shows that financial frictions can amplify the effects of financial shocks, such as the exchange rate and commodity prices. The channels of transmission operate via the working capital channel, which is sensitive to interest rate responses to exchange rate and commodity price shocks. These shocks are also transmitted via the financial accelerator channel which encompasses financial frictions due to credit supply shock responses to the balance sheet effects of leverage and collateral constraints induced by fluctuations in net worth. Furthermore, there is the balance sheet mismatch channel which is largely due to the currency composition and maturities of assets and liabilities on the balance sheet.

21.2 Why Is the Assessment of the Exchange Rate Balance Sheet Effects Important for the Agricultural Sector?

We established in earlier chapters that the "*output growth-driven exports growth*" hypothesis and strategy best explain developments in the agricultural sector. Trade openness and the export-oriented growth strategy auger well for the agricultural sector output growth, employment growth and labour productivity growth. In addition, earlier chapters showed that the Bureau for Food and Agricultural Policy (BFAP 2011a, b) recommended strategy of agricultural expansion that relies on the export-oriented strategy, that is, creating agro-processing industries which are export-oriented. Furthermore, evidence shows that the agricultural sector is a net exporter. Exporting industries compete in international markets and prices in international markets are largely determined by global demand and supply and the exchange rate. The BFAP (2011a, b) recommends a strategy of agricultural expansion which brings to the fore the role of multifactor productivity, infant industries[1] protection and the role of the exchange rate in the growth potential of the agricultural sector. Hence, this chapter explores the role of the exchange rate appreciation, depreciation and volatility shocks on the agricultural sector.

With respect to the role of the exchange rate in trade and development, McMillan and Rodrik (2011) find that countries that maintain competitive or undervalued currencies tend to experience more growth-enhancing structural change. This is in line with other work that documents the positive effects of undervaluation on modern, tradable industries. Rodrik (2008) establishes that undervalued exchange rates tend to act as a subsidy on those industries and facilitate their expansion. However, for the South African economy, Ndou and Gumata (2017) established that sharp, large and persistent exchange rate depreciations exert contractionary effects on the real economy. The contractionary effects due to sharp and persistent exchange rate depreciation shocks are largely due to the balance sheet effects induced by foreign debt and the importation of intermediate goods for investment and the production process.

We established contractionary exchange rate depreciation shock effects in the mining sector in earlier chapters. Evidence showed that the R/US$ exchange rate depreciation shock dividend is disproportionate on mining output growth and employment growth. This is because sharp R/US$ exchange rate depreciations do not incentivise the mining sector to improve size of gross value added (output growth).

[1] Alternatively, "micro crops" industries such as olives, macadamias, cherries and berries.

Sharp R/US$ exchange rate depreciation shock episodes are not good for the mining sector output growth. So, are there idiosyncratic elements in the agricultural sector that are at variance with the aggregate economy and the mining sector?

In addition, evidence in earlier chapters showed that food commodity price boom episodes and the prevalence of the parity pricing model in the agricultural sector tend to coincide with periods of droughts and severe exchange rate depreciation shocks. This occurrence has devastating effects on food and consumer price inflation. In addition, it has significant implications for the achievement of the price stability mandate and the monetary policy response to inflationary pressures. In such cases, the trade-offs are especially binding for the pursuit of the price stability mandate. In turn, the monetary policy decisions have a bearing on the sustainability and profitability of farmers. Hence, there is a need to understand the impact of the exchange rate shocks on the agricultural sector including food inflation.

21.3 The Balance Sheet Channel of the Monetary Policy Transmission

As stated earlier, this chapter explores the sensitivity of the agricultural sector to the exchange rate appreciation, depreciation and volatility shocks via the balance sheet channel. Without getting into a detailed analysis of all the channels of the monetary policy transmission, Fig. 21.3 shows those specifically related to the interest rate, exchange rate, the narrow and the broad credit channels of monetary policy transmission. The balance sheet channel or financial accelerator channel of monetary policy first argued by Bernanke and Gertler (1989) has a significant impact on the propagation of shocks into the real economy. We stated earlier that financial shocks such as the exchange rate can act as conduits and amplifiers of other financial and macroeconomic shocks, especially in the presence of financial frictions largely embedded in balance sheets. At the same time, financial shocks can be independent sources of shocks and amplifiers of other financial

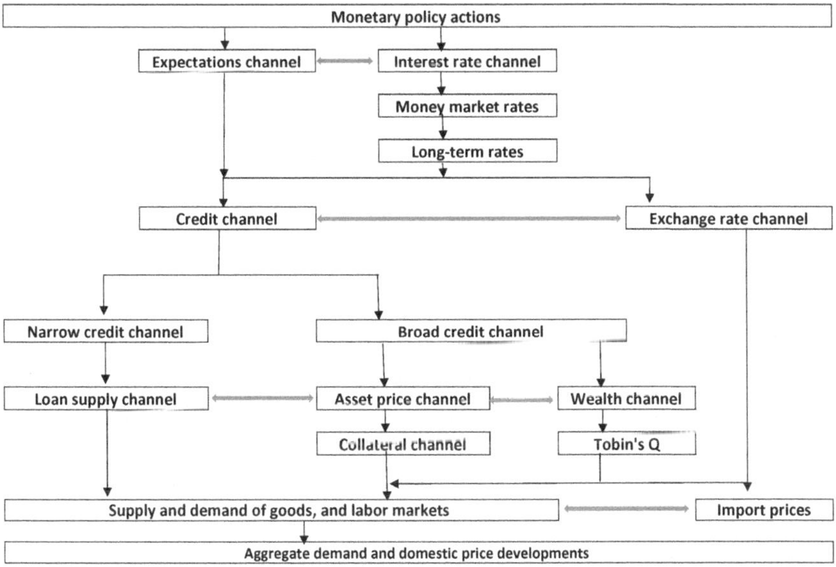

Fig. 21.1 The balance sheet channel of monetary policy. (Adapted from Kuttner and Mosser (2002) and European Central Bank. See https://www.ecb.europa.eu/mopo/intro/transmission/html/index.en.html)

and macroeconomic shocks. Bernanke and Gertler (1989) showed that the existence of information asymmetries implies that a firm's and household's net worth through the narrow and broad credit channels exert a significant impact on investment and spending decisions. In addition, the propagation effects of the balance sheet channel tend to be pro-cyclical largely because the credit and financial cycles are pro-cyclical.

The balance sheet channel starts with changes in the monetary policy stance in Fig. 21.1. Changes in the monetary policy decisions initiate interest rate and expectation changes. The interest rate channel operates through changes in the short-term and long-term interest rate to affect the credit and exchange rate. Through the broad and narrow credit channels, the interest rate channel affects bank credit conditions and asset prices. The ability of banks to extend credit (credit supply) is affected by the interest rate channel, which in turn affects the asset price and wealth channels. This has implications for bank-dependent borrowers, especially households and firms that do not have alternative sources of funding and strong collateral to back up loans. In this way, variations in the policy rates affect the financial position of households and firms via their balance sheets, cash flow and net worth. In addition, the health of the financial institutions balance sheet itself also affects the rate at which it can supply credit.[2]

Tobin's Q under the broad credit channel stems from the existence of an external funding premium, cost of capital and credit constraints faced by firms and their impact on investment spending by firms. Variations in the external financing premium affect borrowers' net wealth and, in turn, shocks to the borrower's net wealth affect the cost of external financing and the degree of capital expenditure and employment by firms. On the other hand, the exchange rate channel works through the credit channel and the import price channels to affect the supply and demand of goods, labour markets, aggregate demand and inflation.

The theoretical link between the exchange rate channel and the credit channel is derived from the identity in Eq. (21.1) showing that money supply can be decomposed into an identity made up of foreign exchange reserves and credit.[3]

$$\text{Money supply} = \text{Foreign exchange reserves} + \text{domestic credit} \quad (21.1)$$

Caves et al. (1996) show that in a floating exchange rate regime, reserves accumulation and foreign currency interventions if not sterilised increase the money supply and credit extension with ultimate inflationary effects.

Furthermore, depending on the assumptions of no and high capital mobility in Fig. 21.2(a) and (b), credit extension leads to a balance of payments deficit and different magnitudes of the exchange rate depreciation. In the theoretical model depicted in Fig. 21.2 the depreciation of the exchange rate is induced by the balance of payments deficit and not increased credit extension per se.

---

[2] We explore the interest rate channel of monetary policy in detail in *later chapters of the book.*

[3] See also Copeland (2005) for further details.

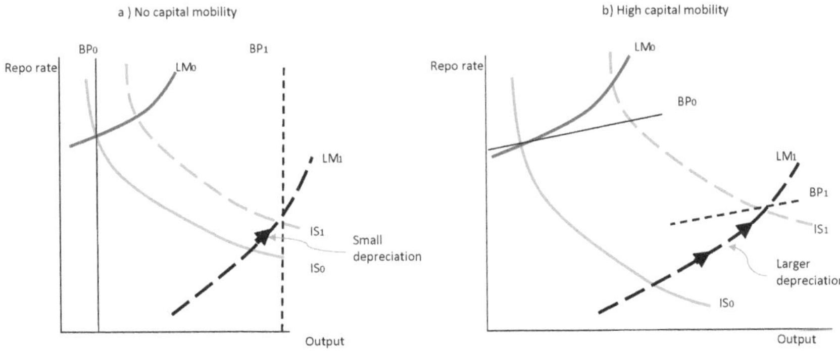

Fig. 21.2 Theoretical link between the credit and exchange rate channels. (Note: BP refers to the balance of payments schedule. IS refers to the investment-saving schedule. Source: Authors' drawings)

21.4 The Agricultural Sector Capital Assets on Commercial Farms

This section looks at the capital assets and the importation of goods in the agricultural sector. First, Fig. 21.3 shows the value of capital assets at the commercial firms and gross capital formation in the agricultural sector. Figure 21.3(b) shows that land and fixed improvements have grown at an annual growth rate of around 10 per cent post-2009.[4] We showed that various measures of nominal house prices recovered post-2009 and averaged just below 10 per cent as of 2017.

Similarly, Fig. 21.3(b) shows that the value of machinery, and livestock including game, has remained fairly buoyant at annual growth rates just below 10 per cent. On the other hand, Fig. 21.3(d) shows that gross capital formation in the agricultural sector is generally volatile. But since 2010 gross capital formation increased by an average of 12.67 per cent, with the investment rate in (i) fixed improvements and (ii) tractors, machinery and implements contributing an average of 7.67 per cent and 16.21 per cent, respectively.

[4] This trend concurs with our assertion in earlier chapters that nominal land prices shown in would have recovered from the slump in 2009Q1.

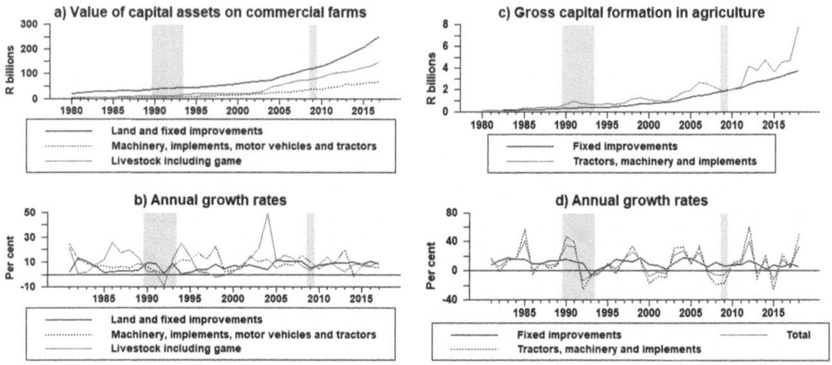

Fig. 21.3 Agricultural sector gross capital formation and the value of capital assets on commercial farms. (Note: The grey shaded areas denote the South African recession. Source: Agri SA, South African Reserve Bank and authors' calculations)

We classify total imports in the agricultural sector into (i) consumption goods; (ii) intermediate goods which include fertilisers, seeds, inputs to animal feed[5]; (iii) capital goods which include tractors, harvesting or threshing, straw or fodder balers, grass or hay mowers, forestry, poultry-keeping or bee-keeping machinery. The data are sourced from the United Nations trade statistics database, and are on an annual basis which spans the period 2001 to 2017. We are more interested on the impact of the exchange rate appreciations and depreciations shocks on the importation of consumption, intermediate and capital goods. To assess these effects, we create two dummy variables for the appreciation and depreciation. The dummy variables take on the values of the R/US$ appreciation and depreciation and zero otherwise. In this section we introduce the analysis of the impact of the exchange rate appreciations and depreciations shocks by looking at the lead relationships. In later sections, we conduct the empirical analysis through the estimation of various vector autoregression (VAR) models.

[5] In South Africa, 50 per cent of all maize and 90 per cent of all soybeans produced are used in chicken feed. Hence, if the chicken industry collapses, the knock-on effects will be dire. Agriculture is an essential value chain that must be defended. https://m.engineeringnews.co.za/article/poultry-association-says-importers-should-support-local-jobs-2019-04-25/rep_id:4433.

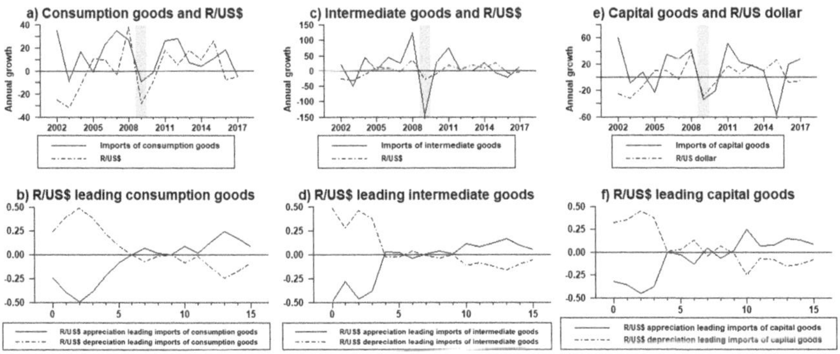

Fig. 21.4 Imports of R/US$ exchange rate, consumption, intermediate and capital goods. (Note: The grey shaded areas denote the South African recession. Source: United Nations trade statistics and authors' calculations)

Figure 21.4 shows that across all components of imported goods, the R/US$ exchange rate depreciation and appreciation lead to opposing effects. As expected, the R/US$ exchange rate depreciations (appreciation) is associated with the increase (decline) in the importation of agricultural sector goods. For instance, the persistent R/US$ exchange rate depreciation can result in a prolonged increase in the importation of goods of 4 to 6 years. The results in Fig. 21.4 are early indications of the asymmetric balance sheet effects of the exchange rate channel in the agricultural sector. These results have implications for the exchange rate policy within the context of the envisaged scale of the land reform policy and the agricultural revolution.

For instance, GrainSA (2011) shows that fertiliser as a production input contributes on average between 30 per cent and 50 per cent to a grain and oilseed producers' variable production costs in South Africa. In addition, the rate at which the domestic sector imports fertiliser increased from less than 20 per cent in 1990 to 40 per cent in 1999 and over 65 per cent in 2008. The domestic agricultural industry is a price taker and cannot completely pass-through high fertiliser prices up the value chain. Domestic fertiliser prices are highly correlated with international prices. As a result, international price trends spill over into the domestic market and tend to be asymmetrically transmitted into the domestic economy, meaning that fertiliser price increases and decreases are transmitted differently in the domestic economy. As such, the price that grain and oilseed producers pay for fertiliser is an important determinant of the profitability of grain and oilseed production in South Africa. This in turn can render the industry unprofitable in the long run with implications for food security and affordability. Key factors that influence the asymmetric transmission are (i) the exchange rate dynamics; (ii) deficiencies in the market largely caused by distortions induced by market power; (iii) physical and infrastructure factors related to transport and storage; (iv) commercial factors in relation to the transmission of market information; and (v) institutional arrangements related to credit, finance and regulations.

21.5 The Exchange Rate Channel of the Monetary Policy Transmission on the Agricultural Sector

This section assesses the significance of the exchange rate channel of the monetary policy transmission via (i) the food prices and headline inflation channel; (ii) import duties and the import price channel in the poultry sector; (iii) tariffs and wheat imports price; and (iv) the components of the agricultural sector imports, namely consumption, intermediate and capital goods.

21.5.1 The Food Prices and Headline Inflation Channel

We start with the analysis of the exchange rate channel via the food price and headline inflation channels. We showed in earlier chapters that the R/US$ exchange rate changes are positively associated with those in the key food commodity spot prices.[6] Food commodity price boom episodes

[6] In addition, evidence in earlier chapters showed that the concurrence of sharp declines (increases) in food commodity prices and the R/US$ appreciation (depreciation) play a much larger role in the profitability of farmers.

contribute to the employment growth intensity in the agricultural sector. But in most cases, the fortunes of farmers in terms of elevated food commodity prices and improved profitability exert a negative impact on food and consumer price inflation. This has implications for the price stability mandate and monetary policy response. This implies that policy trade-offs are especially binding in cases where the prevalence of the parity pricing model in the agricultural sector coincides with periods of drought and severe exchange rate depreciation. However, we did not show the impact of R/US$ exchange rate appreciations and depreciations on food price and headline inflation.

To show the impact of the exchange rate appreciations and depreciations shocks on food price and headline inflation we estimate a number of VAR models using monthly data (M) for the period 1997M1 to 2018M4. The model includes food price inflation, headline inflation, white and yellow maize prices, R/US$ exchange rate dummy variables for depreciation and appreciations. The appreciation (depreciation) dummy variables enter the models separately. The appreciation (depreciation) dummy variables equal negative (positive) R/US$ exchange rate changes only and are zero otherwise. The data are sourced from the South African Reserve Bank database. The shock is one positive standard deviation to the R/US$ exchange rate dummy variable for appreciation and depreciation. The model is estimated with 4 lags as chosen by Akaike's information criterion (AIC) and 10,000 Monte Carlo simulations.

Figure 21.5 shows the responses of white maize prices, food price and headline inflation to the R/US$ exchange rate appreciation and depreciation shocks. It is evident that the exchange rate depreciation and appreciation shocks result in differing degrees of increase in food prices along the value chain and on headline inflation, as shown in Fig. 21.5(c). The peak increases due to the R/US$ exchange rate appreciation are muted compared to those due to the depreciations, as shown in Fig. 21.5(c), (d) and (e).

Similarly, Fig. 21.6 shows that positive and negative white maize price shocks exert opposite effects on both food price and headline inflation. Negative (decline) white maize and food price shocks dampen inflationary pressures and thus headline inflation significantly.

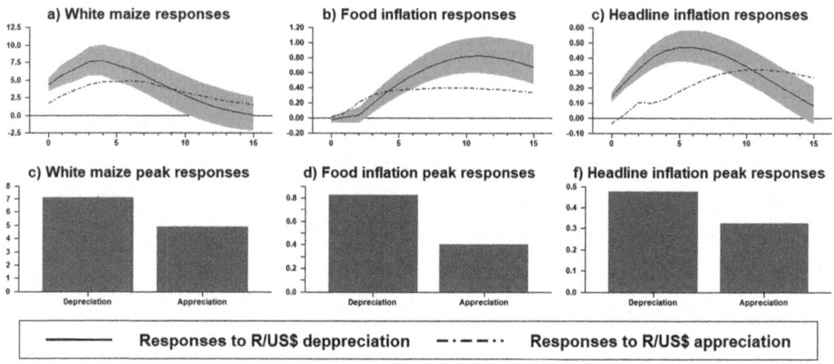

Fig. 21.5 Responses to R/US$ exchange rate depreciation and appreciation shocks. (Note: The grey shaded bands denote the 16th and 84th percentile confidence bands. Source: Authors' calculations)

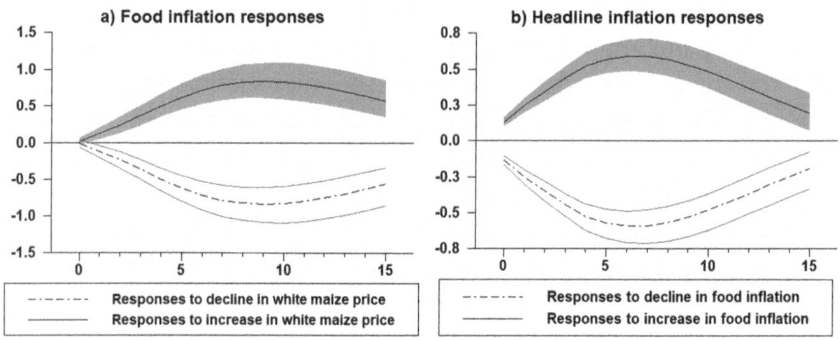

Fig. 21.6 Responses of food and headline inflation to white maize price shocks. (Note: The grey shaded bands denote the 16th and 84th percentile confidence bands. Source: Authors' calculations)

21.5.2 The Exchange Rate, Import Duties and the Import Price Channel in the Poultry Sector

The schematic chart of the balance sheet channel of monetary policy in Fig. 21.1 shows that the exchange rate also affects the import prices, supply and demand of goods and services, labour markets, aggregate demand and inflation. Despite the imposition of a number of import-deterring policies such as import tariffs, duties and anti-dumping measures at the time the R/US$ exchange rate was depreciating persistently for a prolonged period, poultry imports and prices did not respond.[7] In fact, the share of imported poultry increased even during the recession and the massive depreciation in 2009. Thus, it seems to be the case that there are instances in which the exchange rate depreciation of any magnitude fails to be a natural deterrent to import penetration. In such instances the market structure and failure to equilibrate supply and demand need to be dealt with via direct policy interventions.[8] Thus, these are early indications that the exchange rate depreciation alone cannot solve the structural market flaws and failures in the agricultural sector.

Vast literature, including recently Barattieri et al. (2018), shows that trade barriers including anti-dumping measures result in rising inflation and a decline in real economic activity regardless of the flexibility of the exchange rate in small open economies. In addition, Fig. 21.19 in the Appendix shows that there is a positive association between poultry and wheat tariffs with chicken and bread flour prices. These are early indications that tariffs and related anti-dumping measures on their own incur tax and exert inflationary pressures.

This section assesses the impact of various forms of import deterrents and the exchange rate depreciation effects on the production of poultry, importation of poultry and poultry prices. We estimate VAR models which include poultry production, poultry consumption, poultry imports and prices of poultry. We create three separate dummy variables for the imposition of imports tariffs in the poultry market, exchange rate appreciation and depreciation. The dummy variable for (i) the imposition of poultry tariffs takes on the value of 1 for the period 2013Q1 till the end of the sample and zero otherwise; (ii) the R/US$ exchange rate appreciation takes on the negative values of the exchange rate changes and zero otherwise; and (iii) the exchange rate depreciation takes on the negative values of the exchange rate changes and zero otherwise.

[7] Evidence in earlier chapters showed that despite the imposition of a number of import-deterring policies such as import tariffs, duties and anti-dumping measures at a time when the R/US$ exchange rate was depreciating persistently for a prolonged period, poultry imports and prices did not respond.

[8] See earlier chapters.

What is the association between poultry production, consumption, imports and prices? We explore this question because the imports of poultry have increased unabatedly. This is despite the imposition of tariffs and a persistent exchange rate depreciation. This trend indicates that domestic production and prices are not sufficient to meet domestic demand and clear the domestic market. There is persistently rising domestic demand that is not met by domestic producers. We project some stylised facts on the nature of the relationship between domestic production, which is the same as domestic supply, and consumption, which is the same as domestic demand, imports and prices of poultry.

Figure 21.7 shows that there is a negative association between an increase in the domestic production of white meat and the rate at which white meat is imported. An increase in the domestic production of white meat lowers white meat imports. This means that an increase in domestic production of white meat will curtail the rate at which white meat is imported. Then, there is a case for using increased domestic white meat production as a strategy to substitute the rate of poultry imports.

Figure 21.8(b) shows that although the R/US$ exchange rate changes are also negatively associated with the rate at which white meat is imported, the explanatory power is very weak compared to that of an increase in the domestic production of white meat shown in Fig. 21.8(b). Thus, these are preliminary indications that the R/US$ exchange rate on its own will have an insignificant impact on the rate at which white meat is imported. There is a need to invest and increase domestic white meat production to meaningfully deal with the impact of imports in the poultry sector.

To assess the empirical validity of the stylised facts presented in Figs. 21.7 and 21.8 we estimate a number of VAR models where we compare the impact of positive production of white meat shocks (white meat quantity produced domestically), the positive white meat tariffs shock and the R/US$ exchange rate depreciation shock as effective policy interventions to dampen the rate at which white meat is imported. We create a dummy variable which takes on the values of 1 for the period 2013Q1 onwards (in line with the increase in import tariffs on poultry imports in 2013, anti-dumping measures were imposed in 2015 and a provisional safeguard duty on 15 December 2016 by the Department of

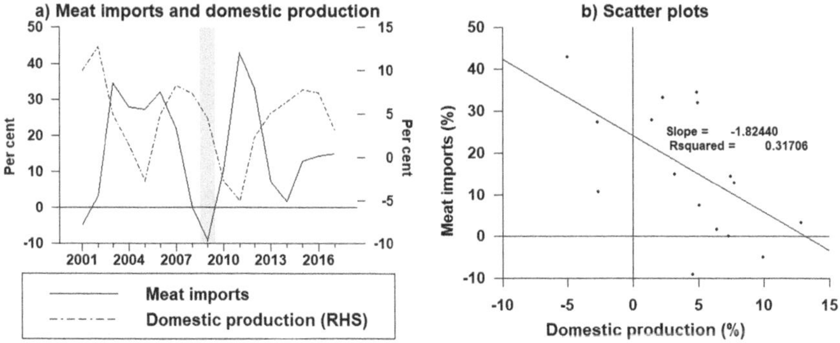

Fig. 21.7 Relationship between meat imports and domestic production. (Note: The grey shaded area denotes the South African recession. Source: Agri SA and authors' calculations)

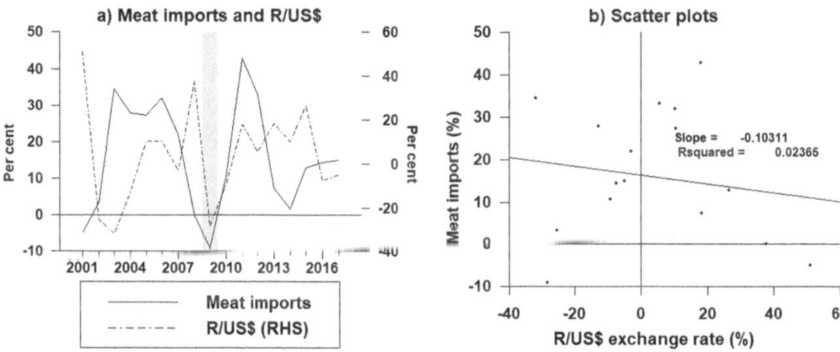

Fig. 21.8 Relationship between meat imports and R/US$. (Note: The grey shaded area denotes the South African recession. Source: Agri SA, South African Reserve Bank and authors' calculations)

Trade and Industry) and zero otherwise. The sample period for the estimations starts from 1999Q1 to 2017Q4. The growth rates are on an annual basis. The VAR model includes poultry imports, domestic white meat production, the import tariffs dummy and the R/US$ exchange rate depreciation dummy. The VAR models are estimated using 2 lags and 10,000 Monte Carlo simulations.

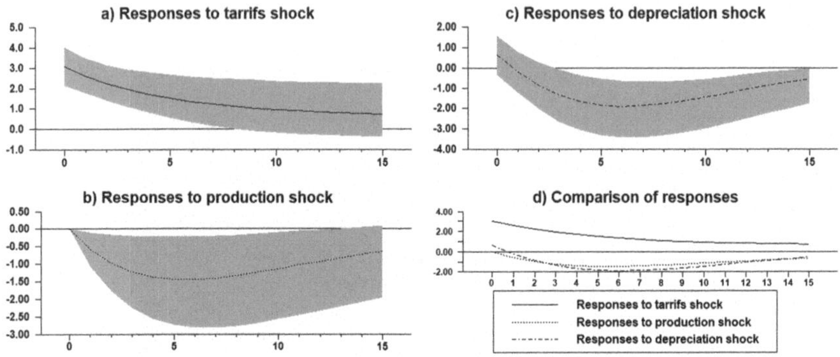

Fig. 21.9 Comparison of meat import responses to positive shocks to meat production, import tariffs and R/US$ depreciation shocks. (Note: The grey shaded bands denote the 16th and 84th percentile confidence bands. Source: Authors' calculations)

Figure 21.9 shows the comparison of the responses of white meat imports to the three positive shocks: (i) to white meat production, (ii) to white meat import tariffs and (iii) to the R/US$ depreciation. The results show that all the interventions have an effect of decreasing white meat imports, but the degree of effectiveness differs.

For instance, Fig. 21.9(a) shows that white meat imports do decline in response to an increase in tariffs, but they remain positive as opposed to the impact of the increase in domestic production and the R/US$ depreciation. The response to the tariff shock could mean that the import prices are lower from export destinations to neutralise the effects of tariffs so as to maintain market share in the importing country.[9]

The increase in the domestic production of white meat and the depreciation of the R/US$ result in a prolonged and pronounced decline in the

[9] Furthermore, the results of the impact of tariff shocks on the importation of white meat probably underscore the fact that the effectiveness of import tariffs is undermined by the fact that a large proportion of imports originates from Denmark, Germany, Hungary, Ireland, the Netherlands, Spain and the UK, and South Africa imposes zero import tariffs on these countries, having signed a free trade agreement in 2001. The decline in the rate of importation probably shows the effects of import tariffs on imports from Latin America.

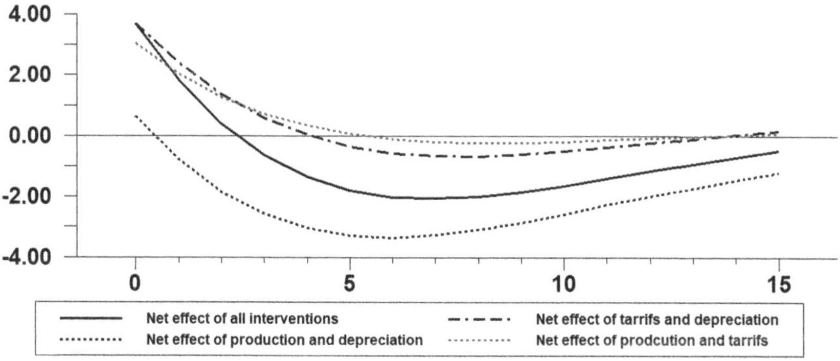

Fig. 21.10 Comparison of net effects of policy interventions on white meat imports. (Source: Authors' calculations)

importation of white meat. We determine the policy combinations that have a pronounced effect on the importation of white meat by netting out the effects of the shocks on poultry imports in Fig. 21.10. From a policy perspective, Fig. 21.10 shows that the policy interventions via the increase of domestic production and the R/US$ depreciation are superior in dampening the rate of the importation of white meat compared to the imposition of import tariffs and the R/US$ depreciation. The policy implication is that an increase in the production of domestic white meat works via the import substitution channel to dampen imports whereas the R/US$ depreciation works via the price channel to achieve the same effects.

Thus, we conclude that there is a compelling case to purse an import substitution strategy via the increase of domestic white meat production in the poultry industry to deal with the issues related to the distortions imposed by the increased degree of import penetration. In addition, the market structure in the poultry industry and the failure to equilibrate supply and demand need to be dealt with via direct policy interventions.[10] The imposition of tariffs and the exchange rate depreciation alone cannot solve structural market flaws and failures in the poultry industry sector.

[10] See earlier chapters.

21.5.3 What Is the Impact of Wheat Tariffs and R/US$ on Wheat Imports? Which One between Wheat Tariffs and R/US$ Depreciation Exerts Significant Effects?

Similar to the earlier section, we assess the impact of the unexpected increase in the area planted, R/US$ exchange rate depreciation and import tariffs in the wheat market. The intention is to assess which policy intervention has the most desired impact. First, Fig. 21.11 shows that the consumption of wheat has consistently surpassed domestic production since the late 1990s and the deficit is closed via the importation of wheat. Figure 21.11(c) shows that despite the imposition of wheat tariffs, wheat imports continued to rise as domestic production could not keep up with domestic consumption.

We assess the effectiveness of policy interventions in the wheat market by estimating various VAR models and explore the impact of three positive shocks on the importation of wheat. These are the unexpected increase in the import tariffs, domestic production and the R/US$ depreciation shocks. There is a positive association between bread flour prices and the R/US$ exchange rate in Fig. 21.12. Bread flour prices remain elevated when led by R/US$ exchange rate depreciation.

We estimate a number of VAR models which include wheat imports, domestic wheat production and the dummy variables that capture the

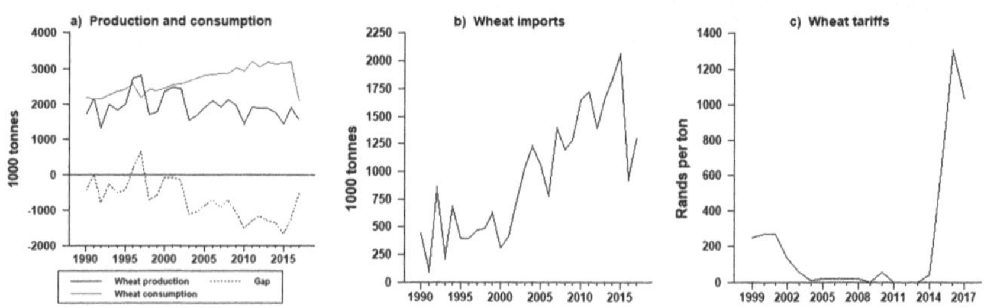

Fig. 21.11 Wheat production, consumption, imports and import tariffs. (Source: SAGIS and authors' calculations)

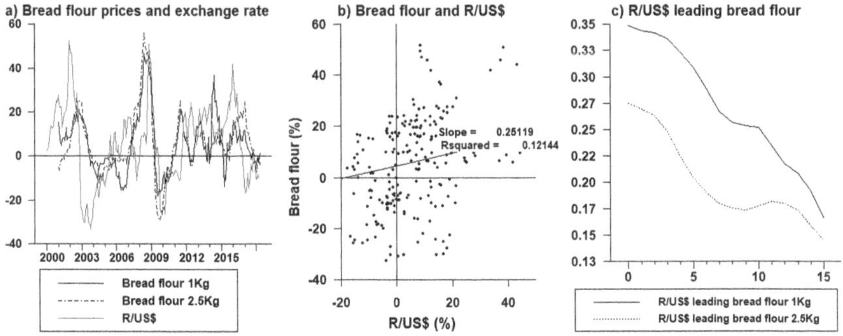

Fig. 21.12 Relationship between the R/US$ and bread flour prices. (Source: Statistics South Africa, South African Reserve Bank and authors' calculations)

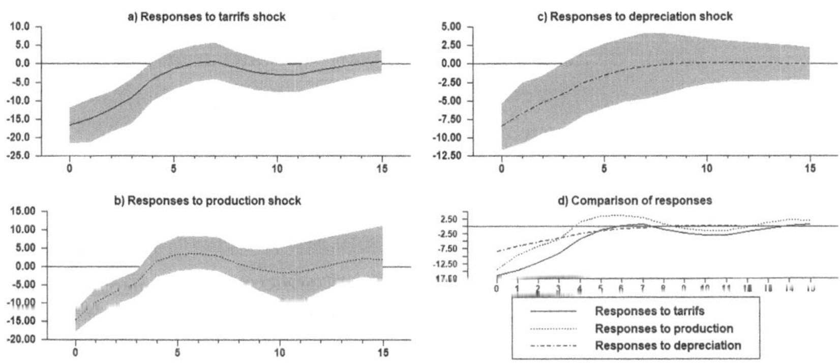

Fig. 21.13 Impact of positive shocks to import tariffs, domestic production and R/US$ depreciation on wheat import shocks. (Note: The grey shaded bands denote the 16th and 84th percentile confidence bands. Source: Authors' calculations)

wheat import tariffs and the R/US$ exchange rate depreciation. The wheat imports tariffs take on the value of 1 for the period during which imports are imposed and zero otherwise. The R/US$ exchange rate depreciation dummy takes on the positive values of the R/US$ exchange rate changes and zero otherwise. The VAR models are estimated using 2 lags and 10,000 Monte Carlo draws. The shock is one standard deviation. The results in Fig. 21.13 show that all policy interventions such as the

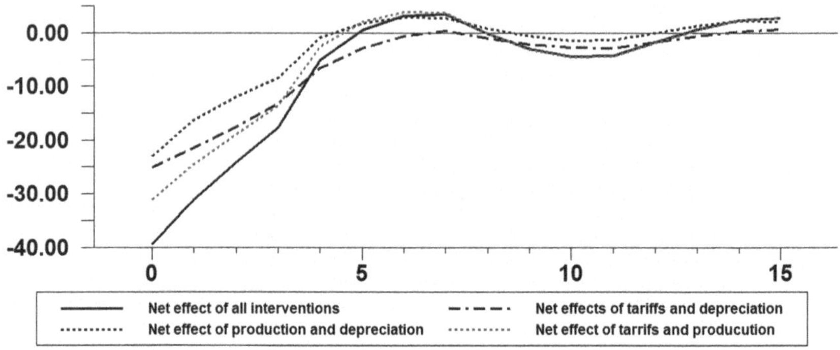

Fig. 21.14 Net effect of positive shocks to import tariffs, domestic production and R/US$ depreciation on wheat imports. (Source: Authors' calculations)

unexpected increase in import tariffs, domestic production and the R/US$ depreciation do result in a decline in the rate at which wheat is imported. But an unexpected increase in tariffs and domestic production have a greater impact in curbing wheat imports compared to the R/US$ depreciation.

We determine the policy combinations that have a pronounced effect on the importation of wheat by netting out the effects of the shocks on wheat imports in Fig. 21.14. However, Fig. 21.14 shows that the net effects of an increase in tariffs, domestic production and R/US$ depreciation can almost halve the rate at which wheat is imported. The combined net effects include the increase in (i) import tariffs and domestic production of wheat; (ii) import tariffs and the R/US$ depreciation; and (iii) domestic production of wheat and the R/US$ depreciation. These combinations result in a decline in the rate at which wheat is imported, albeit at a lesser rate compared to the net effects of the imposition of all interventions.

Nonetheless, on the scale of effectiveness, potency and persistence, the net effects of an increase in (i) tariffs and domestic wheat production and (ii) tariffs and R/US$ depreciation can exert similar effects on the rate of wheat importation. Thus, we conclude that on a cascading scale, the combined effects of an increase in the area planted for domestic wheat, imposition of tariffs and R/US$ depreciation deliver the desired effects of lowering the rate at which wheat is imported. As a very short-term measure, the combined net effects of an increase in the area planted for domestic wheat, imposition of tariffs and the R/US$ depreciation can be used as a policy intervention. But as a medium- to long-term policy intervention, an increase in the domestic area planted for wheat is the most effective policy to deter and substitute wheat imports. The results in these sections concur with the key message in the State of the Nation address in 2018. The President demonstrated and argued that the case for the import substitution approach to industrialisation is feasible and necessary.

21.5.4 The Impact of the Exchange Rate on the Components of the Agricultural Sector Imports

This section extends the analysis of the impact of the exchange rate depreciation shock effects to the import components of the agricultural sector. We also assess the impact of the exchange rate volatility components, namely, overall, permanent and transitory exchange rate volatility. Evidence in earlier chapters showed that mining exports growth, investment growth, output growth and employment growth decline and remain depressed in response to overall and permanent exchange rate volatilities. Overall and permanent exchange rate volatilities explain a larger proportion of the variation in investment growth, output growth and employment growth. Thus, we concluded that exchange rate volatility is bad for the mining sector. Is that the case for the agricultural sector as well?

In addition, we established that there is a balance sheet channel transmitting the negative shocks to commodity prices, demand for mining commodities and exchange rate depreciation into the mining sector investment growth, foreign debt and intermediate imports. Evidence indicated that mining investment declines and remains depressed in response to a real exchange rate depreciation shock. Foreign debt increases, and intermediate imports decline. The real exchange rate depreciation shocks are transmitted via the balance sheet items of foreign debt and the import of intermediate goods which are largely representative of inputs to the production process and investment. What does the evidence suggest are the main pertinent balance sheet channels in the agricultural sector?

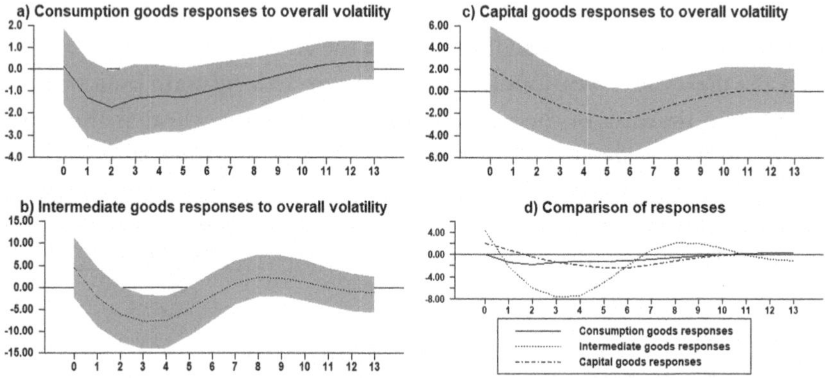

Fig. 21.15 Responses to positive overall R/US$ volatility shocks. (Note: The grey shaded bands denote the 16th and 84th percentile confidence bands. Source: Authors' calculations)

We use the exchange rate volatility components derived in earlier chapters to assess the impact of the exchange rate volatility on the balance sheet channel in the agricultural sector.[11] We use data for the period 2001Q1 to 2017Q4 due to data availability for the import components in the agricultural sector. The VAR models include the agricultural sector imports of consumption goods, intermediate goods, capital goods, R/US$ depreciation dummy, R/US$ exchange rate volatility components, namely, overall, permanent and transitory volatilities. The R/US$ depreciation dummy takes on the positive values of the exchange rate changes and zero otherwise. The R/US$ exchange rate dummy and the volatilities enter the VAR models separately. The models are estimated using 2 lags and 10,000 Monte Carlo draws. The shock is one standard deviation.

First, we present the results derived from the models estimating the effects of the R/US$ exchange rate volatility components in Figs. 21.15, 21.16 and 21.17. The results indicate that all R/US$ exchange rate volatility components exert negative effects on the imports in the agricultural sector. The impact is magnified especially on the intermediate goods. The transitory exchange rate volatility component in Fig. 21.17, as expected, exerts the least negative effects and they are insignificant. The comparison

[11] See earlier chapters.

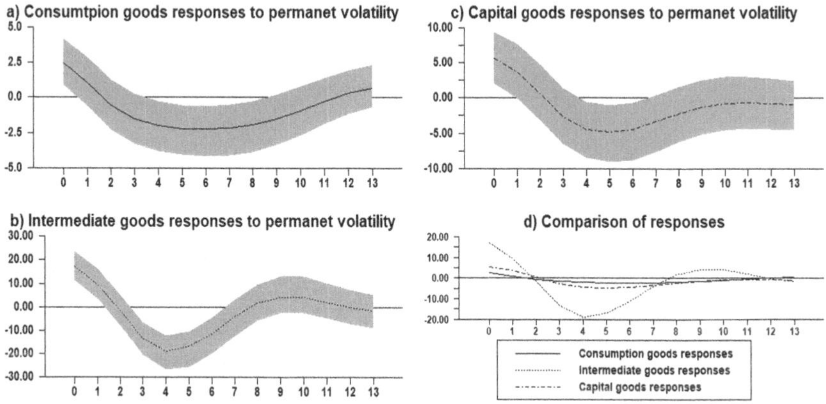

Fig. 21.16 Responses to positive permanent R/US$ volatility shocks. (Note: The grey shaded bands denote the 16th and 84th percentile confidence bands. Source: Authors' calculations)

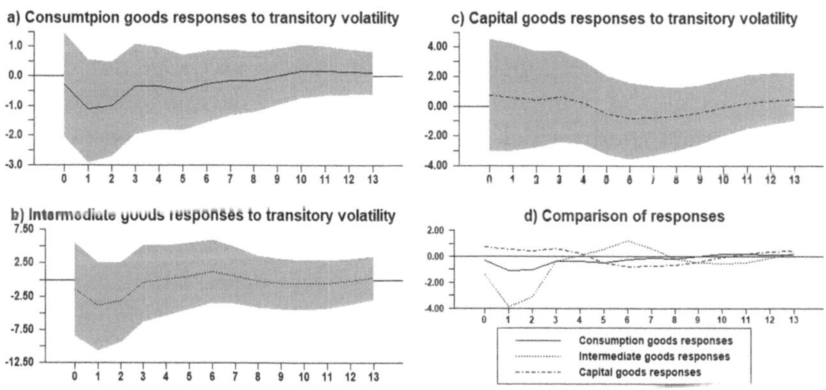

Fig. 21.17 Responses to positive transitory R/US$ volatility shocks. (Note: The grey shaded bands denote the 16th and 84th percentile confidence bands. Source: Authors' calculations)

of the responses in the fourth column shows that the imports of intermediate and capital goods are more responsive to the R/US$ exchange rate volatility compared to the consumption goods.

The results in Fig. 21.18 for the effects of the R/US$ exchange rate depreciation indicate that the importation of intermediate and capital

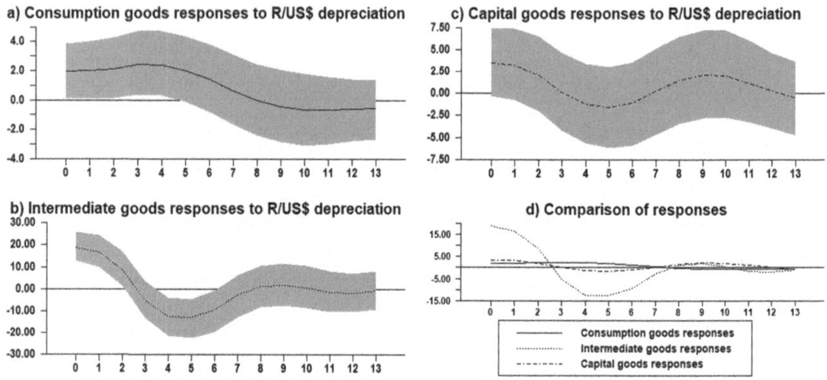

Fig. 21.18 Responses to positive R/US$ depreciation shocks. (Note: The grey shaded bands denote the 16th and 84th percentile confidence bands. Source: Authors' calculations)

goods declines more compared to consumption goods. These results concur with those derived from the R/US$ exchange rate volatility components. Thus, we conclude that the R/US$ exchange rate depreciation, overall and permanent volatility lead to a decline in intermediate and capital goods, which are key inputs in the production process. The results of the importation of intermediate goods, which include fertiliser, concur with the findings of GrainSA (2011) showing that domestic fertiliser prices respond more quickly to international fertiliser price increases and R/US$ exchange rate depreciation. GrainSA (2011) established the asymmetric transmission of international fertiliser prices into the domestic economy. Fertiliser companies react more quickly to increases (decreases) in international fertiliser prices that put their profit under pressure compared to international price changes that stretch their profits.

As a result, the study recommends that mechanisms to revitalise the local fertiliser industry to restrain sole dependence on imports, including the continuous monitoring of the fertiliser industry by the Competition Commission, be put in place. These policy interventions will support the agricultural revolution, competitiveness and ability of the agricultural sector to produce affordable food for the country. Thus, there is a need to rethink the short- and medium-term gains from trade, especially the rate at which we import consumption, intermediate and capital goods as it is related to the sustainability of the agricultural sector and the objectives that are set out in the National Development Plan (NDP).

Substituting imports with locally produced commodities can trigger a range of upstream and downstream multipliers with positive effects on the intensity of job creation in the agricultural sector.[12] But such import substitution initiatives have to be accompanied by productivity gains so as to enhance the relative competitiveness of the agricultural sector and industries involved. This approach also deals with the well-documented negative long-term effects of the infant industry protection policies. This is consistent with observations of McMillan and Rodrik (2011), who showed that whatever contribution globalisation has made in different countries, evidence shows that its effects depend heavily on local circumstances. Choices made by domestic policy makers and domestic growth strategies made the difference. The authors showed that one important difference among countries is the degree to which they are able to manage the downside effects posed by the process of globalisation.

21.6 Conclusion and Policy Implications

This chapter explored the role of the exchange rate appreciation, depreciation and volatility shocks in the agricultural sector. We find that the R/US$ exchange rate depreciations and appreciations exert asymmetric balance sheet effects. The R/US$ exchange rate depreciations (appreciations) are associated with the increase (decline) in the importation of agricultural sector goods. For instance, a persistent R/US$ exchange rate depreciation can result in a prolonged increase in the importation of consumption goods by 4 to 6 years.

What is the impact of the exchange rate on the agricultural sector including food inflation? The results show that the exchange rate depreciation (appreciation) shocks result in an increase (decline) in the food value chain with negative (positive) effects on headline inflation. In addition, positive and negative shocks to the white maize price exert

[12] The findings in earlier chapters also showed that the recommendations of BFAP (2011a, b) are valid.

opposite effects on food price and headline inflation. On a net basis, even though the R/US$ exchange rate appreciation dampens the grain price inflation, net effects do not result in immediate and significantly lower food and headline inflation. But they assist in containing inflationary pressures.

Are there idiosyncratic elements in the exchange rate balance sheet channel in the agricultural sector that are at variance with the aggregate economy and the mining sector? No, there is none. We find that the R/US$ exchange rate depreciation shock results in a sharper decline in the importation of intermediate and capital goods compared to consumption goods. In addition, imports of intermediate and capital goods are more responsive to the R/US$ exchange rate volatility shocks, in particular permanent volatility, compared to the consumption goods. Thus, the contractionary effects due to sharp and persistent exchange rate depreciation shocks are transmitted through the balance sheet effects. The contractionary effects induced by the importation of intermediate goods for investment and as input in the production process are present in the agricultural sector as well.

However, on a disaggregated (micro) level, we find that policy interventions via the increase of domestic production of poultry and wheat, and the R/US$ depreciation, are the most potent policy interventions in dampening the rate of the importation of white meat and wheat compared to the imposition of import tariffs and the R/US$ depreciation. The policy implication is that an increase in the production of domestic white meat and wheat by increasing the area planted works via the import substitution channel to dampen imports. On the other hand, the R/US$ depreciation works via the price channel to achieve the same effects. Thus, we conclude that there is a compelling case to purse an import substitution strategy via the increase of domestic white meat and wheat production to deal with the issues related to the distortions imposed by the increased degree of import penetration.

Such a strategy will have a significant impact on the rate of importation of consumption goods in the agricultural sector. We establish the same policy implications with respect to the importation of intermediate goods, especially fertilisers. The imposition of tariffs and the exchange rate depreciation alone cannot solve structural market flaws and failures in these industries. As a medium- to long-term policy intervention, an increase in the domestic production of white meat and fertiliser, and in the area planted for wheat is the most effective policy to deter and substitute imports. There is a need to pursue the import substitution strategies to industrialisation as envisaged in the State of the Nation, the land reform policy and agricultural revolution. This is consistent with the McMillan and Rodrik (2011) assertion that whatever contribution globalisation has made in different countries, evidence shows that its effects depend heavily on local circumstances. Choices made by domestic policymakers and domestic growth strategies made the difference. The authors show that one important difference among countries is the degree to which they are able to manage the downside effects posed by the process of globalisation. Evidence in this chapter clearly shows that the high degrees of import penetration exert downside effects of the process of globalisation on the agricultural sector. Policy interventions should be put in place to neutralise these adverse effects.

Appendix

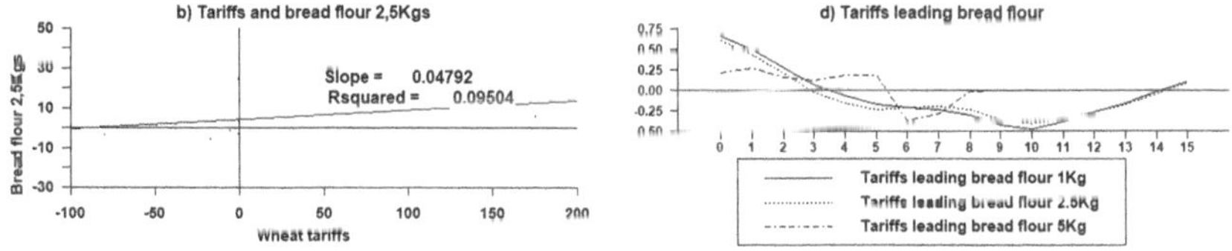

Fig. 21.19 Wheat tariffs and bread flour prices. (Source: Statistics South Africa, SAGIS and authors' calculations)

References

Aliber, M. 2009. Farmland Price Trends in South Africa, 1994–2008. Institute for Poverty, Land and Agrarian Studies (PLAAS). University of the Western Cape for the Directorate: Monitoring and Evaluation Department of Rural Development and Land Reform.

Angelopoulou, E., and Gibson, D.H. 2007. *The Balance Sheet Channel of Monetary Policy: Evidence from the UK*. Bank of Greece Working Paper No. 53.

Barattieri, A., Cacciatore, M., and Fabio Ghironi, F. 2018. Protectionism and the Business Cycle. https://voxeu.org/article/protectionism-and-business-cycle#.W27mDeKqh7M.twitter.

Bernanke, B.S., and Gertler, M. 1989. Agency Costs, Net Worth, and Business Fluctuations. *American Economic Review*, 79, 14–31.

Bernanke, B.S., and Gertler, M. 1995. Inside the Black Box: The Credit Channel of Monetary Policy Transmission. *Journal of Economic Perspectives, American Economic Association*, 9(4), 27–48.

BFAP. 2011a. The South African Agricultural Baseline. Bureau for Food and Agricultural Policy. https://www.sagis.org.za/BFAP_2011.pdf

BFAP. 2011b. The Contribution of the Agro-Industrial Complex to Employment in South Africa. Tech. Rep. June, The Bureau for Food and Agricultural Policy, Pretoria.

Caves, R., Frankel, J., and Jones, R. 1996. *World Trade and Payments*. Harper Collins: New York, NY.

Copeland, L. 2005. *Exchange Rates and International Finance*. 4th ed. Pearson Education: Harlow.

Van der Elst, H.J. 2007. *Post–settlement Support as Key Contribution to the Success of the South African Land Reform Program (1994–2007)*. North West University, UNISA Press. https://www.academia.edu/12075685/Post_settlement_support_as_key_contributor_to_the_success_of_the_South_African_land_reform_programme_1994-2007_.

Fourie, H. 2013. Not a Free Lunch: The Implications of Increased Import Tariffs on South Africa's Chicken Market. https://econex.co.za/wp-content/uploads/2015/04/econex_researchnote_31.pdf.

GrainSA. 2011. Grain SA Fertiliser Report. https://www.grainsa.co.za/upload/report_files/Kunsmisverslag-Volledig.pdf

Greenberg, S. 2010. Status Report on Land and Agricultural Policy in South Africa. Research Report. School of Government, UWC PLAAS Institute for

Poverty, Land and Agrarian Studies. http://www.plaas.org.za/sites/default/files/publications-pdf/RR40.pdf.

Hall, R., and Kepe, T. 2017. Elite Capture and State Neglect: New Evidence on South Africa's Land Reform. *Review of African Political Economy*. https://doi.org/10.1080/03056244.2017.1288615.

Jacobs, P., Lahiff, E., and Hall, R. 2003. Land Redistribution. Programme for Land and Agrarian Studies School of Government University of the Western Cape. http://www.plaas.org.za/sites/default/files/publications-pdf/ELARSA%2001.pdf.

Kiyotaki, N., and Moore, J. 1995. *Credit Cycles*. NBER Working Paper No. 5083.

Kuttner, K.N., and Mosser, P.C. (2002). The Monetary Transmission Mechanism: Some Answers and Further Questions. FRBNY Economic Policy Review.

McMillan, M.S., and Rodrik, D. 2011. *Globalisation, Structural Change and Productivity Growth*. NBER Working Paper 17143.

Moseneke, D.C.J. 2015. Reflections on South African Constitutional Democracy—Transition and Transformation. https://constitutionallyspeaking.co.za/dcj-moseneke-reflections-on-south-african-constitutional-democracy-transition-and-transformation/.

Ndou, E., and Gumata, N. 2017. *Inflation Dynamics in South Africa: The Role of Thresholds, Exchange Rate Pass-through and Inflation Expectations on Policy Trade-offs*. Palgrave Macmillan. ISBN 978-3-319-46701-6.

Ranwedzi, N. 2011. The Potential and Limits of the Proactive Land Acquisition Strategy (PLAS): Land Reform Implementation in Gauteng Province of South Africa. http://www.plaas.org.za/sites/default/files/publications-pdf/PP%2006.pdf.

Rodrik, D. 2008. The Real Exchange Rate and Economic Growth. *Brookings Papers on Economic Activity*, 39(2), 365–439.

Shousha, S. 2016. Macroeconomic Effects of Commodity Booms and Busts: The Role of Financial Frictions. Department of Economics, Columbia University. http://www.columbia.edu/~sfs2146/research.html.

Sihlobo, W. 2018. Fewer Farmers, More Milk. https://wandilesihlobo.com/2018/07/17/fewer-farmers-more-milk/.

Sihlobo, W., and Kirsten, J. Secret of Land-Reform Success Is to Learn Lessons from Experience. Business Day, 28 May 2018. https://www.businesslive.co.za/bd/opinion/2018-05-28-the-secret-of-land-reform-success-is-to-learn-lessons-from experience/.

22

What Is the Impact of a Binding Minimum Wage on the Agricultural Sector?

Learning Objectives

- Assess the impact of the binding minimum wage shock on the agricultural sector output growth and employment growth.
- Establish whether there is evidence that the capital-labour ratio dynamics are impacted by a positive shock to the minimum wage in the agricultural sector.
- Assess and compare the impact of food commodity prices, exports growth slump, monetary policy tightening and minimum wage shocks.
- Establish the effects of labour productivity growth and whether the hypothesis of the efficiency wage models holds in the agricultural sector.

22.1 Introduction

In Chap. 31 we argue that the South African Reserve Bank mandate be expanded to include the target of a low and stable unemployment rate (maximum employment growth), monitoring income and wealth inequality. We argue that a more comprehensive measure of welfare ought

N. Gumata, E. Ndou, *Accelerated Land Reform, Mining, Growth, Unemployment and Inequality in South Africa*, https://doi.org/10.1007/978-3-030-30884-1_22

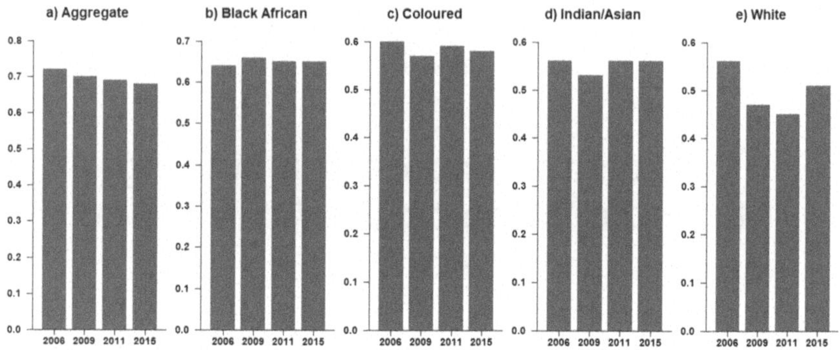

Fig. 22.1 Gini coefficient income per capita by race. (Source: Statistics South Africa)

to include the unemployment rate, income and wealth inequality. The rationale being that the assessment of income and wealth inequality encompass inclusive growth. Furthermore, the measures of income and wealth inequality are specific, in that they put a spotlight on the fact that economic growth can be inclusive and yet mask significant and growing income and wealth inequality. In addition, such an amendment to the mandate of the South African Reserve Bank is consistent with the National Development Plan's (NDP) overarching goal of eliminating poverty and reducing income inequality from the current aggregate level of 0.68 as shown in Fig. 22.1(a) to 0.6 by 2030.

This chapter extends the analysis on social welfare by exploring the impact of the binding minimum wage on the agricultural sector. The minimum wage at its core is a policy intervention aimed at minimising the effects of income inequality and *working poverty* that is largely driven by large wage differentials. Earlier chapters explored the channels through which changes in the binding minimum wages are transmitted in the mining sector. The mining sector implemented a wage floor or minimum wage of R8000 across the board in 2014. This resulted in remuneration in the mining sector increasing from a low R2000 per month for the lowest paid worker in 2001 to R10,000 per month in 2016. At this level, the mining sector wage floor is more than double the national minimum wage.[1] We established that an increase in the binding minimum wage in the mining sector pushes employment and labour productivity growth in different directions. This is especially the case for the coal mining and other mining sectors.

We concluded that evidence indicates that the impact of an increase in the binding minimum wage in the mining sector is best characterised by the institutional model. The institutional model assumes that firms respond to an increase in the minimum wage by improving their overall efficiency though two channels: (i) by reducing organisational inefficiencies and (ii) by increasing the productivity of employees. The pass-through of an increase in the minimum wage and labour costs into higher prices is neutralised by the increase in efficiency such as an increase in productivity. Is there evidence that the capital-labour ratio dynamics are impacted by positive minimum wage shocks in the agricultural sector? Do food commodity price busts, exports growth slumps and monetary policy tightening exert severe effects in comparison to the impact of the binding minimum wage? Do positive shocks to labour productivity growth matter? Alternatively, does the hypothesis of the efficiency wage models (EWMs) hold in the agricultural sector?

Theoretical economic models postulate that the implementation of the minimum wage can have substitution and scale effects. The two effects arise from the fact that an increase in the minimum wage leaves low-skilled workers worse off as employers substitute unskilled and low-skilled workers for more capital and higher-skilled labour. On the other hand, the scale or income effect implies that the firm takes advantage of the higher cost of labour and reduces the level of employment (labour) to produce goods and substitutes labour with capital. Thus, the substitution effects imply that firms take advantage of the wage increase and reallocate the mix of labour and capital in the production function. This will lead

[1] Briefly, the minimum wage law was published on 2 December 2002 and came into effect on 16 December 2002. The initial legislation for the farming sector was outlined in Sectoral Determination 8 and then later updated by Sectoral Determination 13. However, provisions related to the minimum wage only came into effect on 1 March 2003. Two separate wage levels are prescribed for full-time farmworkers, according to geographic location: a higher minimum wage of R800 per month for farmers working within urbanised municipal areas and a lower minimum wage of R600 per month for predominantly rural areas. The minimum wage is adjusted for inflation and updated through a formal government gazetting process by the Department of Labour. See Bhorat et al. (2014) and the Department of Labour publications for further reading.

to a decline in the demand for labour that reinforces the substitution of labour for capital. Bhorat et al. (2014) report that although farmers shed jobs after the minimum wage was introduced, hours worked did not change significantly. At the same time, Conradie (2004), Murray and Van Walbeek (2007) and Liebenberg and Pardey (2010) report that there was an element of adopting mechanisation to replace labour. Alternatively, farmers increasingly opted for labour-reducing practices where possible, such as chemical weed-killing over manual weeding practices. BFAP (2011a) states that producers of labour-intensive commodities are gradually shifting to become more mechanised. Despite the extremely steep capital investments in machinery, producers argue that they would rather take on the financial risk than the social risk of hiring labour under existing labour laws. Thus, we explore whether there is evidence that the capital-labour ratio dynamics are impacted by a positive shock to the minimum wage in the agricultural sector.

We argue that most of the studies exploring the impact of the minimum wage in the agricultural sector have largely ignored the concurrence of commodity price busts, large exchange rate depreciation and monetary policy tightening shock effects on the agricultural sector. In addition, these studies completely ignore the role of labour productivity growth and the impact of the minimum wage on the agricultural sector output growth. Needless to mention that a number of these studies are largely case studies based on the survey and qualitative data of local subsectors of the agricultural sector as opposed to time series data which we use in this chapter. For instance, Conradie (2004) studies the impact of the minimum wage on grape farms. He uses a survey of 190 wine and table grape farmers in the Western Cape. The authors finds that on average a wage increase of 10 per cent is likely to decrease employment by between 3 and 6 per cent. In addition, employment levels also appear to depend not only on the wage but also on the size of a farm's output, the price of inputs such as fuel, as well as the extent to which mechanisation can replace labour. In earlier chapters we showed that the share of exports of grapes and wine declined sharply and persistently since 2008. We argue that the exports channel because of the impact it has on the output growth and the revenue of farmers, is another factor to consider when assessing the impact of the minimum wage on the agricultural sector. The findings in earlier chapters showed that the exports growth channel is a potent channel through which global demand shocks are transmitted to the agricultural sector output growth and employment growth. Evidence shows that the agricultural sector employment growth responds more to adverse shocks to exports growth compared to output growth.

Similarly, Murray and Van Walbeek (2007) study the impact of the minimum wage on sugar cane farmers on the KwaZulu-Natal coast and find that job-shedding was disguised by the fact that farmers chose not to replace workers who left their jobs; in particular those who were unskilled were not replaced. In this regard, we showed in earlier chapters that the share of sugar exports has been on a persistent downward trend since the early 2000s and the world price for refined sugar has also been subdued since 2011. In addition, Bhorat et al. (2014) studied the effects of the minimum wage on the agricultural sector for the sample period 2003 to 2007 and found that the introduction of the minimum wage had a swift and large negative impact on employment in the agricultural sector. Employment fell in the year after the imposition of the minimum wage by close to 150,000 workers, representing a 17 per cent decline. We argue that this period was preceded by a severe drought in 2001 which coincided with a large exchange rate depreciation shock, increase in food commodity prices, food inflation and tightening in monetary policy to curb inflationary pressures as shown in Figs. 22.2 and 22.3.

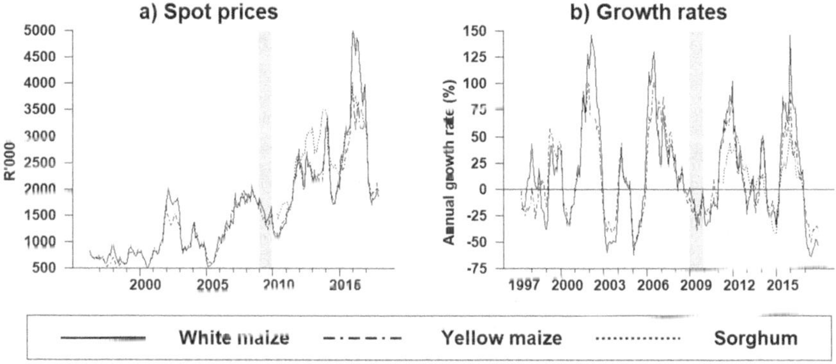

Fig. 22.2 Selected food commodity spot prices. (Note: The shaded areas denote the South African recessions. Source: Grain SA and authors' calculations)

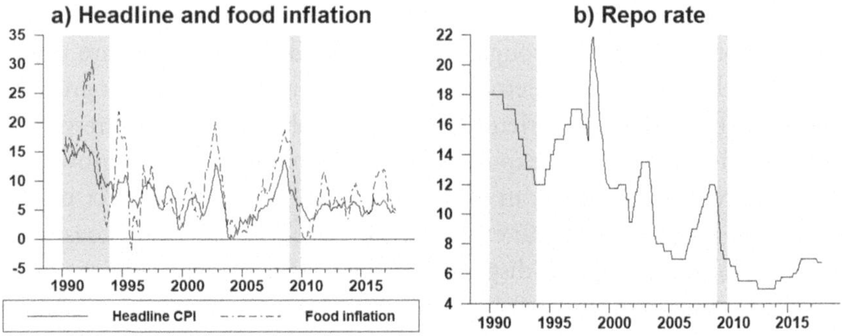

Fig. 22.3 Headline, food inflation and repo rate. (Note: The shaded areas denote the South African recessions. Source: South African Reserve Bank)

Figure 22.2 shows that the sorghum, white and yellow maize spot price and the annual growth rates in the prices declined by more than half (50 per cent). So it may be the case that the concurrence of the huge decline in the food commodity prices and the appreciation of the R/US$ exchange rate played a much larger role in the profitability of farmers compared to the introduction of the minimum wage per se, thus leading to a decline in employment growth in the agricultural sector. At the same time Fig. 22.3 shows that (i) food inflation had increased from 3.3 per cent in June 2001 to 19.9 per cent in September 2002; (ii) headline inflation had increased from 4 per cent in October 2001 to 12.9 per cent in November 2002; and (iii) the repo rate increased from 9.5 per cent in December 2001 to 13.5 per cent in May 2003.

Thus, there might have been some other balance sheet[2] effects induced by the adjustment to the increase in the lending rates on the profitability of farmers with adverse effects on employment growth in the agricultural sector. Similarly, there was a persistent increase in the food and headline inflation and the repo rate in 2006 which also falls within the sample period of the Bhorat et al. (2014) study. Results in earlier chapters showed that food commodity price booms (busts) result in an increase (decline) in

[2] We explored the role of the balance sheet effects in earlier chapters.

exports growth, output growth and employment growth. Evidence showed that food commodity price booms and busts propagate (amplify) the effects of the positive and negative shocks throughout the sector. At the same time, we established that food commodity price boom episodes contribute to the employment growth intensity in the agricultural sector. However, there is a need for policy co-ordination, especially in cases where the fortunes of farmers in terms of elevated food commodity prices and improved profitability exert a negative impact on food and consumer price inflation with implications for the price stability mandate and monetary policy response.

Thus, there are several other factors to consider when exploring the impact of the minimum wage. Hence, we contend that these studies are narrow and only focused on the minimum wage as the key determinant of job losses in the agricultural sector. In addition, given the successive increases in the minimum wage in the agricultural sector, what explains the increasing trend in the agricultural sector employment post-2014? What were the key factors driving the good performance of the agricultural sector employment during this period?

22.2 Summary of Recent Findings on the Impact of the Minimum Wage on the Agricultural Sector

Figure 22.4 shows the evolution of the employment levels in the agricultural sector. It is evident that the secular decline in the agricultural employment trends started in the late 1980s and continued right up to 2011. Since then, the employments trends have indeed turned, especially post-2014, although they remain below the million mark. We show these trends so that we can offer context to the analysis of the impact of the minimum wage in the agricultural sector conducted in this chapter.

Recent literature in this field shows that the introduction of the binding minimum wage has had a negative effect on employment growth and hours worked. But the introduction of the minimum wage legislation has been good for workers in that wages increased, and worker protection improved immensely. For instance, BFAP (2011a) state that

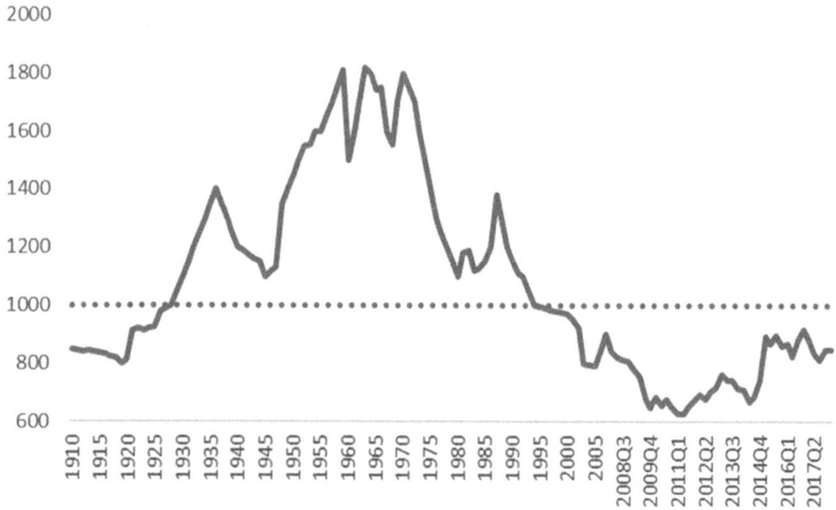

Fig. 22.4 Formal agricultural employment (regular and seasonal). (Source: BFAP (2011b) and Statistics South Africa)

producers of labour-intensive commodities are gradually shifting to become more mechanised. Despite the extremely steep capital investments in machinery, producers argue that they would rather take on the financial risk than the social risk of hiring labour under existing labour laws.

Liebenberg and Pardey (2010) report that the key drivers behind the long-term employment trends in the agricultural sector shown in Fig. 22.4 were uncertainties emanating from legislation in 1993 and 1997, particularly the Basic Conditions of Employment Act, No 147 of 1993 and the Extension of Security of Tenure Act, No 62 of 1997. More recently, the ongoing discussions about the national minimum wage have been the key driver behind the volatile labour market. Bhorat et al. (2014) find that the minimum wage had a swift and large negative impact on employment in the agricultural sector. Employment fell in the year after the imposition of the minimum wage by close to 150,000 workers, representing a 17 per cent decline. However, they establish that farm owners did not reduce hours worked to control higher wage costs. Hours worked after the minimum wage was introduced did not change significantly.

The authors estimate that farmworker wages in the post-law period increased on average by 17.6 per cent and worker protection improved, as the share of workers with a written employment contract rose sharply from 34 per cent in the pre-law period to reach 57 per cent by the end 2007.[3]

Conradie (2004) uses survey data of 190 grape farmers in the Western Cape to examine how labour practices have changed in response to increases in the minimum wage, in both the table grape and wine grape industries. The author finds that on average a wage increase of 10 per cent is likely to decrease employment by between 3 and 6 per cent, depending on the industry. The study established that farmers generally offset wage increases against non-wage benefits such as housing, electricity, clothing, transport and food. Employment levels also appear to depend not only on the wage but also on the size of a farm's output, the price of inputs such as fuel, as well as the extent to which mechanisation can replace labour.

Murray and Van Walbeek (2007) explore the effect of the sectoral determination among sugar cane farmers on the KwaZulu-Natal coast. The authors use qualitative data gathered from interviews with 103 farmers. They establish that farmers did not report mass retrenchments as a result of the minimum wage, and many farmers claimed not to be able to distinguish the impact of the minimum wage on their labour force from the impact of other labour laws. However, the authors note that job-shedding was disguised by the fact that farmers chose not to replace workers who left their jobs; in particular those who were unskilled were not replaced. In addition, some farmers reduced working hours in order to lower their total wage bill and approximately 40 per cent of growers had decreased in-kind benefits for their workers. Although the sugar cane industry remains relatively labour-intensive, farmers increasingly opted for labour-reducing practices where possible, such as chemical weed-killing over manual weeding practices.

---

[3] With respect to the impact of the minimum wage legislation on worker protection, Hertz (2005) and Dinkelman and Ranchhod (2012) examined the impact of the sectoral determination for domestic workers and found an immediate and significant increase in earnings and compliance with the requirement for employers to establish a written contract with employees.

22.3 Literature on the Channels of Adjustment to an Increase in the Binding Minimum Wage

The findings of the studies presented in the previous section indicate that there are a number of channels that farmers use to adjust to an increase in the binding minimum wage. In earlier chapters we showed that literature on the effect of changes in the minimum wage covers four main theoretical approaches: (i) the competitive model; (ii) the dynamic monopsony model; (iii) the search and matching model; and (iv) the institutional model. These theoretical approaches are based on different assumptions about how the labour market functions and the mechanisms for adjusting to binding minimum wages. In addition, these theoretical models provide evidence of other channels of labour market adjustment to increases in the minimum wage other than just the employment channel.

For instance, the perfectly competitive labour model is based on the assumption that setting minimum wages above the market clearing level reduces the demand for labour and results in lower employment. If this assumption is relaxed to allow other channels of adjustment, such as adjustment by cutting working hours, reducing investment in training and other worker benefits, increases in prices as firms pass through the labour cost become higher due to a higher minimum wage. Furthermore, given that firms under perfect competitive labour markets already operate under the assumptions of maximum productivity, this means that there is no room for any improvement in overall efficiency. Thus, the efficiency gains accruing to the increase in the minimum wage are not operational under the perfectly competitive labour model.

On the other hand, the monopsony labour market model assumes the presence of labour market frictions and market power that allows profit-targeting firms in cases where there is no binding minimum wage to hire less labour than the socially efficient amount. Firms in the monopsony labour market model set wages below the competitive market rate. The channels through which firms adjust to the increase in the minimum wage within the monopsonic market power include (i) passing through a portion of the increase in their production costs on to consumers by raising prices and (ii) positive spillover effects of an increase in the minimum wage, which might attract new employees.

As opposed to perfectly competitive markets, the monopsony or monopoly labour market is characterised by a single buyer or seller of a commodity. The monopsony market faces an upward slope and firms are price makers. The introduction of the minimum wage can lead to an increase in employment. This is because the introduction of the minimum wage that would prevail under the competitive markets means that the monopsonist can hire workers at a constant wage rate set by the minimum wage rate. For a monopsonist, the introduction of the minimum wage means that it faces a wage rate that is independent of how many workers it hires. As a result, the firm will employ workers until the value of the marginal product (MP) equals the minimum wage, which is the same rate as the competitive wage in the competitive labour market. This means that the wage floor set by the minimum wage for a monopsonist acts in the same way as the price ceiling for a monopolist and makes the firm move the demand for a factor in a similar fashion as that of a competitive firm.

Therefore, the imposition of the minimum wage exerts different effects in the competitive and monopsonist labour markets. Initially, without the minimum wage, a non-discriminating monopsonist would employ fewer workers than he would if the market was competitive; hence there is underemployment. However, the introduction of the minimum wage results in an increase in the wage rate and employment. This means that a well-designed minimum wage can eliminate the market power of monopsonists and prevent the exploitation of workers.

On the other hand, the search and matching model assumes the existence of labour market frictions such as search frictions as unemployed workers search for jobs and firms driven by the profit maximisation objective search for employees to fill vacancies. This model assumes that the binding minimum wage can lead to a decline in unemployment, especially in cases when an increase in the minimum wage leads to stronger job search efforts and improved matching processes. The relationship between unemployment rate and vacancies known as the Beveridge curve (BC) has implications for business cycle and inflation dynamics. The BC describes the negative empirical relationship between the unemployment rate and the job vacancy rate.

The institutional model assumes that (i) employees are heterogeneous; (ii) labour markets are imperfectly competitive, integrated and exposed to an excess labour supply; and (iii) firms operate under certain labour market institutions. Within the institutional model, firms respond to an increase in the minimum wage by improving their overall efficiency though two channels: (i) by reducing organisational inefficiencies and (ii) by increasing the productivity of employees. The pass-through of an increase in the minimum wage and labour costs into higher prices is neutralised by the increase in efficiency.

Theoretically, the implementation of a binding minimum wage can have substitution and scale effects. It is argued that an increase in the minimum wage affects low-skilled workers more as it leaves them worse off as employers when firms substitute unskilled and low-skilled workers for more capital and higher-skilled labour. The two effects are shown in Fig. 22.5. The minimum wage swivels the isocost line along the capital axis and points of intersection shift from point A to B to C. First, those firms that cannot easily substitute factor inputs will be forced to raise prices.

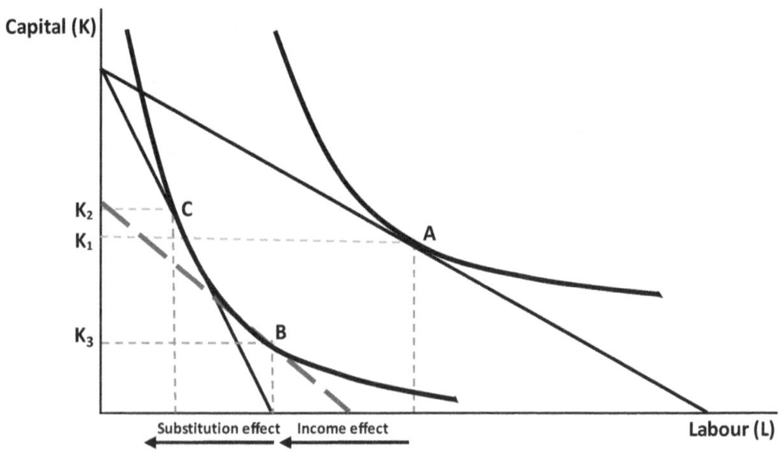

Fig. 22.5 Impact of the minimum wage on the firm's decision about labour and capital. (Source: Authors' drawing)

Second, firms that can substitute factor inputs will move from the optimal combination of capital and labour at point A in Fig. 22.5 to point C after the imposition of the minimum wage. The shift from point A to C is decomposed into the substitution and scale effect.

22.4 What Are the Dominant Channels of Adjustment to the Minimum Wage in the Agricultural Sector?

This section starts with the empirical analysis of the dominant channels of adjustment to a binding minimum wage in the agricultural sector. We explore the impact of a number of shocks over and above those on the minimum wage, namely food commodity prices, food commodity price booms and busts, and labour productivity in the agricultural sector. The food commodity price we use in the empirical estimations is based on the first common factor derived in earlier chapters. To construct the variables for food commodity price booms and busts, we create dummy variables for periods during which the first common factor is greater than one for booms and less than one for busts. We estimate a number of vector autoregression (VAR) models which include the food commodity price common factor, the food commodity price booms and busts dummy variable, the median minimum wage for low-paid workers, labour productivity in the agricultural sector, agricultural output, investment, employment and the repo rate. The repo rate is included to assess the impact of monetary policy tightening. Labour productivity growth is sourced from Productivity South Africa. The minimum wage for low-paid workers is sourced from the Labour Research Service (LRS) database.[4] The dummy variables for food commodity price booms (busts) take on the positive boom (negative bust) values of the food commodity prices, and are zero otherwise. The dummy variables enter the VAR models separately. All the other variables are sourced from Statistics South Africa, the South African Reserve Bank, Fred data and South African

[4] Data was accessed from the online database via the link www.lrs.org.za/award.

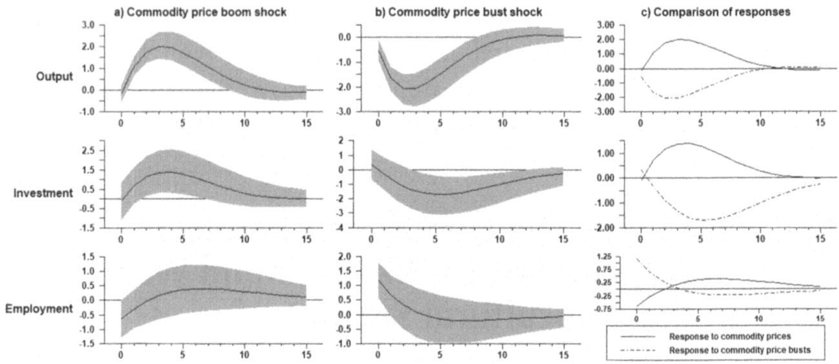

Fig. 22.6 Responses to food commodity price booms and busts shocks. (Note: The grey shaded area bands denote the 16th and 84th percentile confidence bands. Source: Authors' calculations)

Grain Information Services (SAGIS). All growth rates are calculated annually. The VAR models are estimated using 2 lags and 10,000 Monte Carlo simulations. The sample spans the period 2000Q1 to 2017Q4.

22.4.1 The Impact of Food Commodity Price Booms and Busts

First, we start by assessing the impact of food commodity price booms and busts on the agricultural sector output, investment and employment growth in Fig. 22.6. The results indicate that food commodity price booms and busts exert opposing effects on the agricultural sector output, investment and employment growth. Food commodity price booms (busts) are positive (negative) for the agricultural sector.

22.4.2 The Exports Growth Channel

What about the exports growth channel? We argued that the exports channel, because of the impact it has on the output growth and revenue of farmers is another factor to consider when assessing the impact of the minimum wage on the agricultural sector. Evidence in earlier chapters showed that

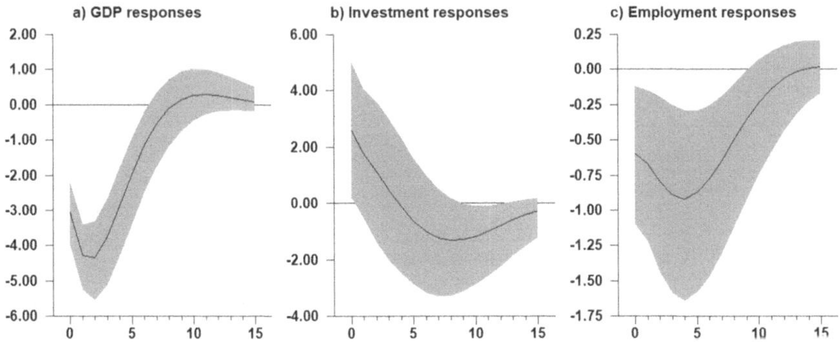

Fig. 22.7 Responses to an adverse agricultural sector exports growth shock. (Note: The grey shaded area bands denote the 16th and 84th percentile confidence bands. Source: Authors' calculations)

exports growth effects are potent on the agricultural sector employment growth. The agricultural sector employment growth responds more to exports growth compared to output growth. So how potent are the effects of an exports growth slump (adverse exports growth shock) on the agricultural sector? To estimate the VAR, we include the agricultural sector exports growth, output growth, investment growth and employment growth. The results in Fig. 22.7 indicate that an adverse shock to agricultural sector exports leads to a decline in investment growth and depresses output growth and employment growth.

22.4.3 Does the Hypothesis of the Efficiency Wage Hold in the Agricultural Sector?

What is the impact of agricultural sector labour productivity growth on the agricultural sector? For the estimation of the VAR model we change the specification to include the agricultural sector labour productivity growth, output growth, the minimum wage and employment growth. This specification is based on the theoretical framework that increases in labour productivity exert a positive impact on output, wages and employment. Thus, we are testing whether the hypothesis of the EWMs that worker productivity is a positive function of wages holds in the agricultural sector. Within the wage efficiency models, the wage rate plays a dual role. First, (i) it allocates jobs

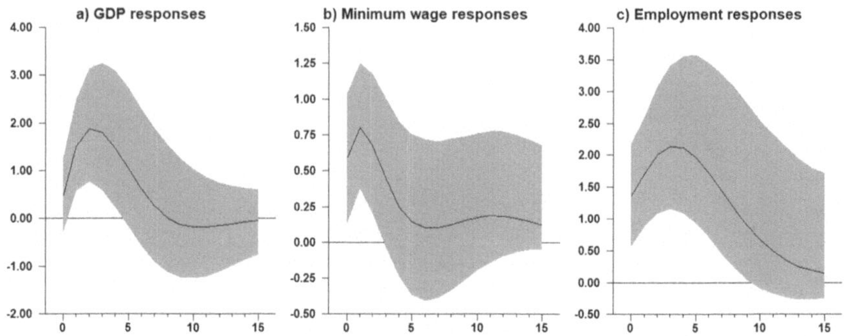

Fig. 22.8 Responses to positive shocks to labour productivity growth shocks. (Note: The grey shaded area bands denote the 16th and 84th percentile confidence bands. Source: Authors' calculations)

and then (ii) it affects the behaviour of workers by affecting physical productivity, work effort and morale, and determines the quality of the labour-hiring pool or the probability of acceptance of a firm's employment offer. Second, it offers insights into the channels of transmission of the efficiency wages hypothesis to increased productivity. These channels work via (i) reductions in turnover; (ii) reductions in absenteeism; (iii) higher morale which is associated with an increase in effort; and (iv) attraction of higher-productivity workers.

The results in Fig. 22.8 suggest that the agricultural sector output growth, the minimum wage and employment growth increase in response to positive labour productivity growth shocks. This implies that the agricultural sector conforms to the wage efficiency hypothesis. The increases in labour productivity growth are transmitted via an increase in output growth, wages and employment growth.

22.4.4 Do Tight Monetary Policy Shocks Matter for the Agricultural Sector?

We stated earlier that the period assessed by Bhorat et al. (2014), especially post-2003, was preceded by an increase in inflation which elicited tightening in monetary policy. Thus, we argue that the effects of tight monetary policy via the balance sheet channel might have impacted negatively on the profitability of farmers and the agricultural sector. To assess

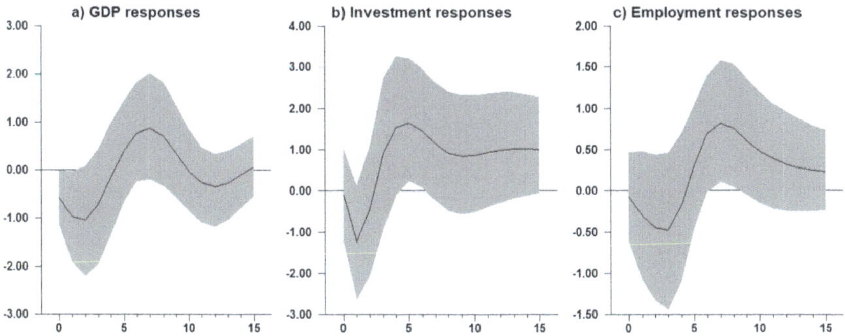

Fig. 22.9 Responses to monetary policy tightening shocks. (Note: The grey shaded area bands denote the 16th and 84th percentile confidence bands. Source: Authors' calculations)

the effects of a tightening in the repo rate, we estimate a VAR model that includes the repo rate, agricultural sector output growth, investment growth and employment growth. The results in Fig. 22.9 indicate that indeed tight monetary policy does negatively affect the agricultural sector as seen in the output growth, investment growth and employment growth declines.

22.4.5 How Does the Agricultural Sector Adjust to an Unexpected Increase in the Minimum Wage?

Having assessed all these other potential channel effects, how does the agricultural sector adjust to an increase in the minimum wage? Do the effects of a positive binding minimum wage shock dominate those caused by food commodity price busts, labour productivity and monetary policy tightening shock? To answer this question, we estimate a VAR model that includes the minimum wage, agricultural sector output growth and employment growth. The results in Fig. 22.10 show that positive minimum wage shocks exert similar effects as those of a food commodity price bust and monetary policy tightening on employment. However, the increase in the minimum wage does not result in a decline in the agricultural sector output as opposed to the effects exerted by the food commodity price bust and monetary policy tightening shocks.

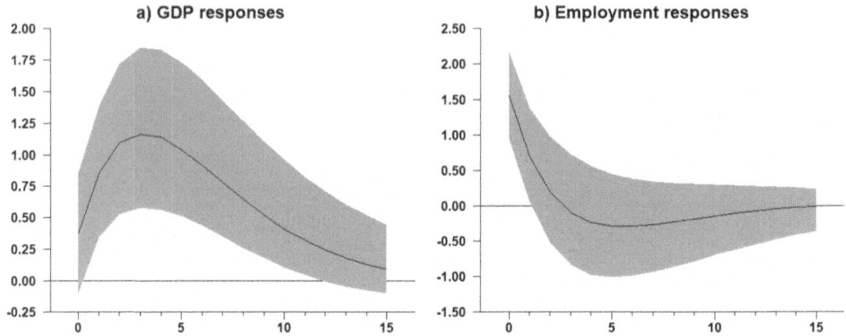

Fig. 22.10 Responses to positive minimum wage shocks. (Note: The grey shaded area bands denote the 16th and 84th percentile confidence bands. Source: Authors' calculations)

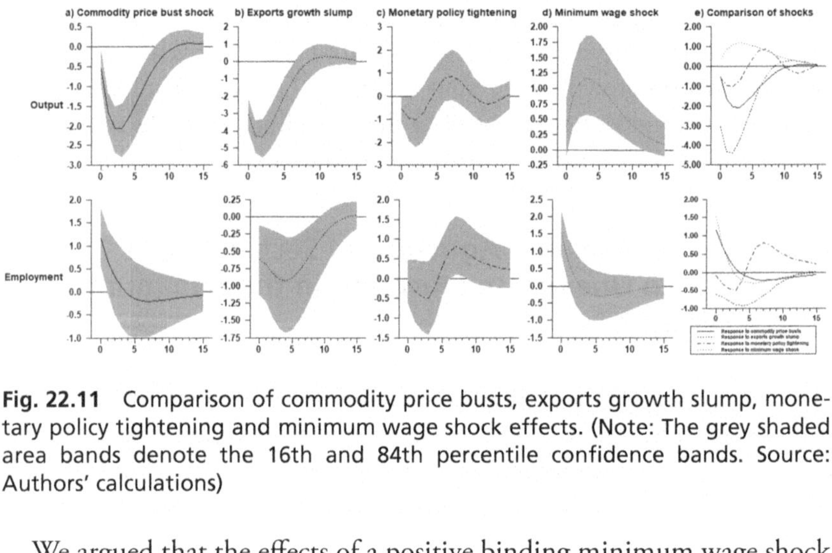

Fig. 22.11 Comparison of commodity price busts, exports growth slump, monetary policy tightening and minimum wage shock effects. (Note: The grey shaded area bands denote the 16th and 84th percentile confidence bands. Source: Authors' calculations)

We argued that the effects of a positive binding minimum wage shock have to be assessed alongside those of the food commodity price busts, slumps in exports growth and monetary policy tightening shocks that occurred during the sample period. Thus, we present a comparison of the shock effects and the net effects on employment growth in Figs. 22.11 and 22.12 to show the relative potency of the effects.

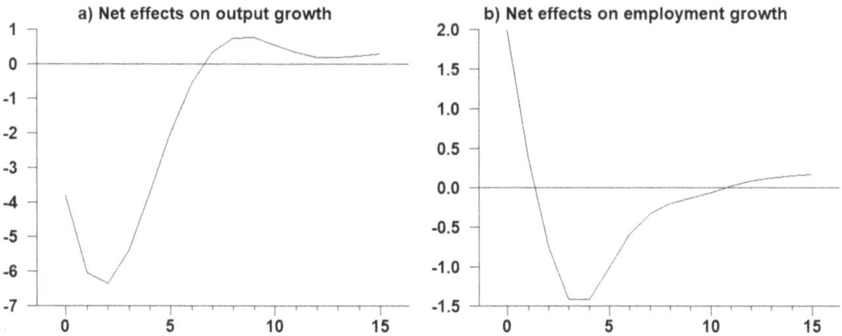

Fig. 22.12 The net effects of commodity price busts, exports growth slump, monetary policy tightening and minimum wage. (Source: Authors' calculations)

The comparison of the effects of the food commodity price busts, exports growth slumps, monetary policy tightening and the increase in the minimum wage indicates that exports growth slumps are the most potent channel through which the negative effects of factors such as a slowdown in global demand and droughts are transmitted to the agricultural sector. The employment growth decline due to a positive binding minimum wage shock is far more miniscule compared to that induced by a slump in exports growth and the monetary policy tightening shocks. Nonetheless, the effects of tight monetary policy shocks are transitory and correct after five quarters, whereas those due to exports growth slump depress employment growth for the entire forecast horizon.

The net effects of all the shocks in Fig. 22.12 indicate that the concurrence of all these shocks has a devastating effect on the agricultural sector output and employment growth. The implication is that the concurrence of the implementation of a binding minimum wage, commodity price busts, exports growth slump and monetary policy tightening shocks exerts severe and persistent negative effects on the agricultural sector. Employment losses do occur due to the increase in the binding minimum wage, but these are far muted compared to those due to exports growth slumps and monetary policy tightening shocks. Thus, global demand, food commodity prices and the balance sheet channel of the monetary policy transmission matter for the agricultural sector.

22.5 What Is the Role of Hours and the Capital-Labour Ratio Dynamics as Adjustment Channels to the Increase in the Minimum Wage?

We have established that the increase in the minimum wage exerts opposing effects on the agricultural sector output and employment. Does this mean that farmers produce more with less labour? Bhorat et al. (2014) report that although farmers shed jobs after the minimum wage was introduced, hours worked did not change significantly. At the same time, Conradie (2004), Murray and Van Walbeek (2007) and Liebenberg and Pardey (2010) report that there was an element of adopting mechanisation to replace labour. Alternatively, farmers increasingly opted for labour-reducing practices where possible, such as chemical weed-killing over manual weeding practices. BFAP (2011a) state that producers of labour-intensive commodities are gradually shifting to become more mechanised. Despite the extremely steep capital investments in machinery, producers argue that they would rather take on the financial risk than the social risk of hiring labour under existing labour laws. The implication is that there was an increase in the capital-labour ratio as an adjustment to the increase in the binding minimum wage in the agricultural sector. Therefore, is there evidence that the capital-labour ratio dynamics are impacted by a positive binding minimum wage shock in the agricultural sector?

We start exploring the role of hours worked as an adjustment mechanism to an increase in the binding minimum wage by farmers. We assess the evolution of hours worked across the five categories: (i) less than 15 hours; (ii) between 15 and 29 hours; (iii) between 30 and 39 hours; and (iv) between 40 and 45 hours. It is worth noting that there is no classification of hours worked by industry or sector in the time series data compiled by Statistics South Africa. Thus, there is no way of knowing exactly which industries or sectors are responsible for changes in the trends for hours worked. Figure 22.13 shows that the level of hours worked has by and large increased post-2009 recession, shown by the grey shaded area. The proportion of workers reporting to work

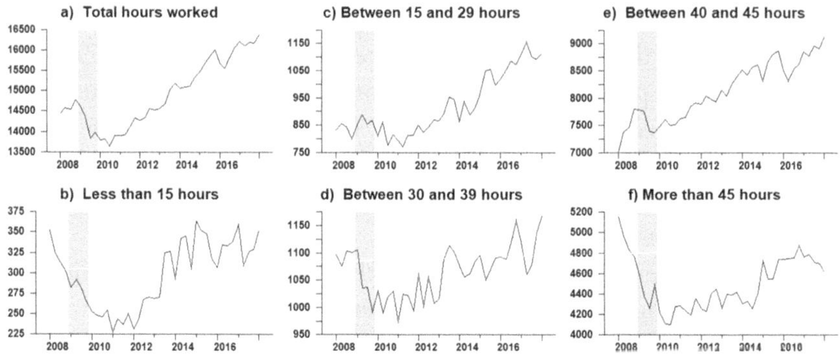

Fig. 22.13 Hours worked. (Note: The grey shaded areas denote the South African recession. Source: Statistics South Africa)

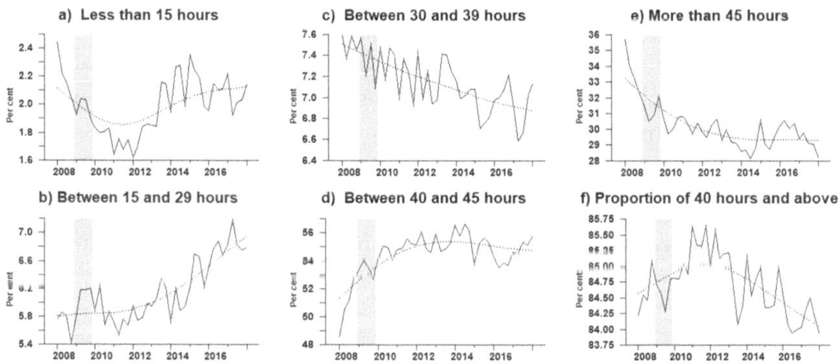

Fig. 22.14 Hours worked as a proportion of total. (Note: The grey shaded areas denote the South African recession. The dotted lines in the graphs represent the trends calculated using the Hodrick–Prescott filter. Source: Statistics South Africa and authors' calculations)

between 40 and 45 hours and more than 45 hours in total constitutes more than 85 per cent of hours worked in Fig. 22.14. The trends post 2009 in Fig. 22.14 show that the proportion of people reporting to be working more than 45 hours and between 30 and 39 hours a week has declined. Although the proportion of people reporting to work between 40 and 45 hours has increased, the combined total of 40 to 45 hours and more than 45 hours has declined persistently post-2009.

Whereas the proportion of those working less than 15 hours and between 15 and 29 hours has increased, it contributes less than 10 per cent of total hours worked. Nonetheless, the proportion of workers reporting to work less than 15 hours and between 15 and 29 increased significantly post-2014.

What could explain the increase in the trend of the proportion of workers reporting to be working between 15 and 29 hours per week, especially post-2014? Could this trend be associated with developments observed in the upward shift in the employment trend in the agricultural sector in Fig. 22.14? Could this trend in part explain and corroborate the findings in Bhorat et al. (2014) that although farmers shed jobs after the minimum wage was introduced, hours worked did not change significantly?

We use these categories of hours worked and estimate several VAR models that include the minimum wage, agricultural sector output growth and employment growth. Due to data availability for hours worked, we adjust the sample period for the estimations to 2008Q1 to 2018Q2. The results in Fig. 22.15 indicate that as we established earlier, output growth is unaffected by the increase in the minimum wage

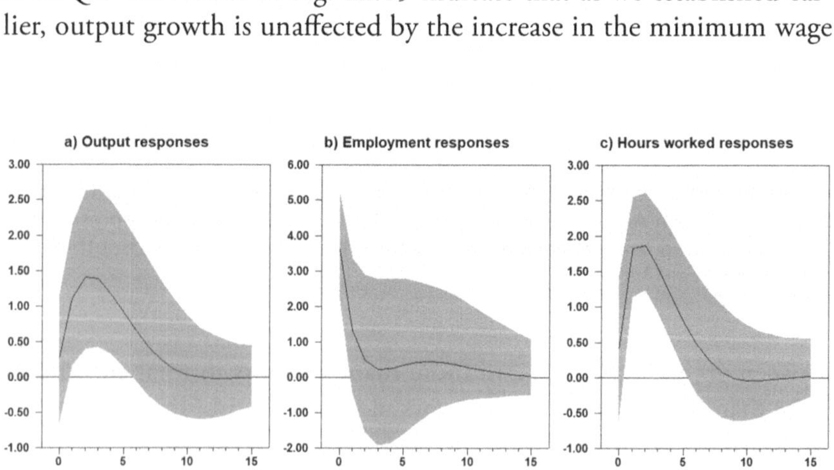

Fig. 22.15 Responses of hours worked to a positive shock to the minimum wage. (Note: The grey shaded area bands denote the 16th and 84th percentile confidence bands. Source: Authors' calculations)

as farmers decrease the rate of employment but increase the rate of hours worked. Thus, the data confirms the findings in Bhorat et al. (2014) that farmers shed jobs after the minimum wage was introduced but hours worked did not change significantly.

What about the role of the substitution effects between labour and capital in the agricultural sector? To assess the validity of the reports in response to the minimum wage, farmers increasingly opted for labour-reducing practices where possible as producers of labour-intensive commodities are gradually shifting to become more mechanised. To assess these effects of the minimum wage on the capital-labour ratio responses we use the average economy-wide capital-labour ratio as there is no other measure for the agricultural sector. We include the average capital-labour ratio, the minimum wage, agricultural sector output growth and employment growth in the VAR.

The results in Fig. 22.16 indicate that positive shocks to the minimum wage result in an increase in the capital-labour ratio. This implies that farmers not only increase hours worked in response to an increase in the binding minimum wage, but they also increase the rate at which the capital replaces labour in the production process. Hence there is no decline in output growth. Thus, hours worked and the introduction of labour-reducing practices explain how the agricultural sector adjusts to a binding minimum wage. These results are in line with the institutional model which

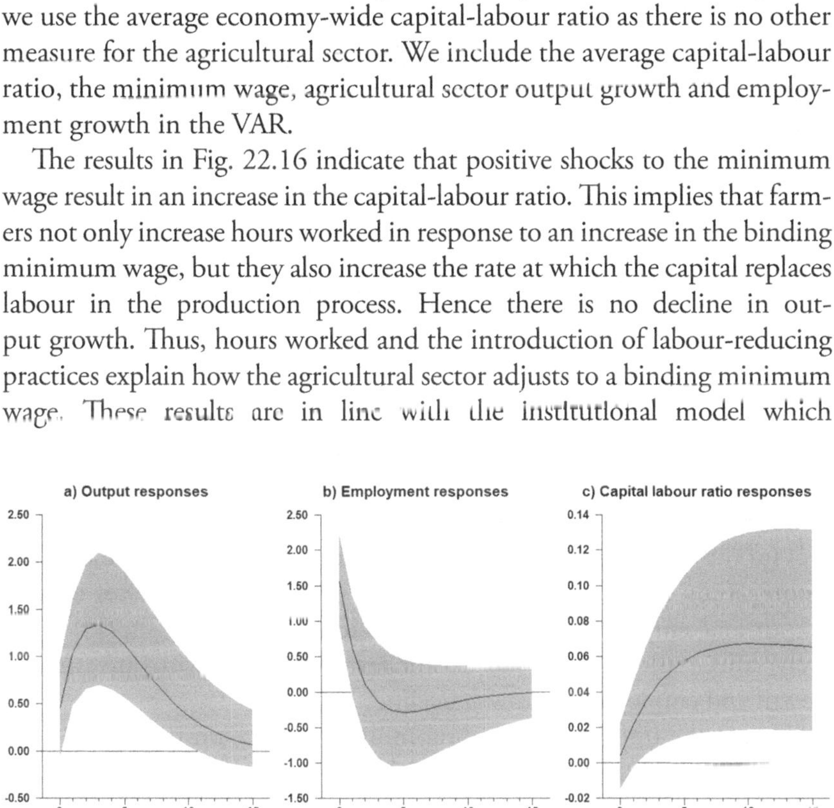

Fig. 22.16 Responses of the capital-labour ratio to a positive shock to the minimum wage. (Note: The grey shaded area bands denote the 16th and 84th percentile confidence bands. Source: Authors' calculations)

assumes that firms respond to an increase in the binding minimum wage by improving their overall efficiency through two channels: (i) by reducing organisational inefficiencies and (ii) by increasing the productivity of employees. The adjustment process also results in the substitution of workers with capital.

22.6 Conclusion and Policy Implications

Do positive shocks to labour productivity growth matter for the agricultural sector? Alternatively, does the hypothesis of the efficiency wage models (EWMs) hold in the agricultural sector? Yes, labour productivity growth matters for the agricultural sector. The results suggest that the agricultural sector output growth, the minimum wage and employment growth increase in response to positive shocks to labour productivity growth. This implies that the agricultural sector conforms to the wage efficiency hypothesis. The increases in labour productivity growth shocks are transmitted via an increase in output growth, wages and employment growth. Thus, labour productivity growth matters for the agricultural sector.

What is the impact of food commodity price booms and busts, exports growth slump and monetary policy tightening compared to the increase in the binding minimum wage in the agricultural sector? Evidence indicates that food commodity price booms and busts exert opposing effects on the agricultural sector output growth, investment growth and employment growth. Food commodity price booms (busts) are positive (negative) for the agricultural sector. An adverse shock to the agricultural sector exports leads to a decline in investment growth and depresses output growth and employment growth. Tight monetary policy shocks negatively affect the agricultural sector as output growth, investment growth and employment growth decline.

What is the impact of a binding minimum wage on the agricultural sector? We establish that positive shocks to the binding minimum wage exert similar effects as those of a food commodity price busts and monetary policy tightening on employment growth. However, the increase in the binding minimum wage does not result in a decline in the agricultural sector output growth. This contrasts with the effects exerted by the food commodity price busts and monetary policy tightening shocks. The agricultural sector output growth is unaffected by the increase in the binding minimum wage as farmers decrease the rate of employment growth but increase the rate of hours worked.

The comparison of the shock effects of the food commodity price busts, exports growth slumps, monetary policy tightening and the increase in the minimum wage indicates that exports growth slumps are the most potent channel through which the negative effects of factors such as a slowdown in global demand and droughts are transmitted to the agricultural sector. The employment growth decline due to the increase in the binding minimum wage is far more miniscule compared to that induced by a slump in exports growth and the monetary policy tightening shocks.

Furthermore, the net effects of all the shocks indicate that the concurrence of all these shocks has a devastating effect on the agricultural sector output growth and employment growth. The implication is that the concurrence of the implementation of a binding minimum wage, food commodity price busts, exports growth slump and monetary policy tightening shocks exert severe and persistent negative effects on the agricultural sector. Employment growth losses do occur due to the increase in the binding minimum wage, but these are far muted compared to those due to the exports growth slumps and monetary policy tightening shocks. Thus, global demand, food commodity prices and the balance sheet channel of the monetary policy transmission matter for the agricultural sector.

Is there evidence that the capital-labour ratio dynamics are impacted by a positive shock to the minimum wage in the agricultural sector? Yes, we establish that positive shocks to the binding minimum wage result in an increase in the capital-labour ratio. This implies that farmers not only increase hours worked in response to an increase in the binding minimum wage, but they also increase the rate at which the capital replaces labour in the production process; hence there is no decline in output. Thus, hours worked and the introduction of labour-reducing practices explain how the agricultural sector adjusts to a binding minimum wage. These results are in line with the institutional model which assumes that firms respond to an increase in the minimum wage by improving their overall efficiency through two channels: (i) by reducing organisational inefficiencies and (ii) by increasing the productivity of employees. The adjustment process also results in the substitution of workers with capital.

References

BFAP. 2011a. The South African Agricultural Baseline. Bureau for Food and Agricultural Policy. https://www.sagis.org.za/BFAP_2011.pdf

BFAP. 2011b. The Contribution of the Agro-Industrial Complex to Employment in South Africa. Tech. Rep. June, The Bureau for Food and Agricultural Policy, Pretoria.

Bhorat, H. 2013. A Tale of Two Impacts: Minimum Wage Outcomes in South Africa. http://blogs.worldbank.org/futuredevelopment/tale-two-impacts-minimum-wage-outcomes-south-africa.

Bhorat, H., Kanbur, R., and Stanwix, B. 2014. Estimating the Impact of Minimum Wages on Employment, Wages and Non-wage Benefits: The Case of Agriculture in South Africa. *American Journal of Agricultural Economics*, 96(5), 1402–19. October. https://doi.org/10.1093/ajae/aau049.

Conradie, B. 2004. *Wages and Wage Elasticities for Wine and Table Grapes in South Africa*. Working Paper 90, Centre for Social Science Research, University of Cape Town. http://www.cssr.uct.ac.za.

Dinkelman, T., and Ranchhod, V. 2012. Evidence on the Impact of Minimum Wage Laws in an Informal Sector: Domestic Workers in South Africa. *Journal of Development Economics*, 99(1), 27–45.

Hertz, T. 2005. *The Effect of Minimum Wages on the Employment and Earnings of South Africa's Domestic Service Workers*. Working Paper 05/099, Development Policy Research Unit. http://www.american.edu/cas/econ/workpap.htm.

Liebenberg, F., and Pardey, P.G. 2010. South African Agricultural Production and Productivity Patterns. In J. Alston, B. Babcock, and P. Pardey (eds.) *The Shifting Patterns of Agricultural Production and Productivity Worldwide*, Chap. 13. Midwest Agribusiness Trade Research and Information Center: Ames.

Mathae, T.Y., Millard, S., Rõõm, T., Wintr, L., and Wyszyński, R. 2019. *Shocks and Labour Cost Adjustment: Evidence from a Survey of European Firms*. Bank of England Staff Working Paper No. 791. https://www.bankofengland.co.uk/-/media/boe/files/working-paper/2019/shocks-and-labour-cost-adjustment-evidence-from-a-survey-of-european-firms.pdf?la=en&hash=90C59BCD4F9E4BF3F7CC02E54F81D02644EB04FB.

Murray, J., and Van Walbeek, C. 2007. *Impact of the Sectoral Determination for Farm Workers on the South African Sugar Industry: Case Study of the Kwazulu-Natal North and South Coasts*. Working Paper 181, Centre for Social Science Research, University of Cape Town. http://www.cssr.uct.ac.za.

23

Social Income Grants, Population Dynamics and Gender Distribution in the Agricultural Sector Employment

Learning Objectives

- Show the trends and distribution of social income grants.
- Present population changes over time.
- Show the gender distribution in the agricultural sector employment.
- Show the proportion of childcare grants to total social income grants by province.

23.1 Introduction

This chapter reviews the distribution of social income grants, population dynamics and the gender trends in the agricultural sector employment. The South Africa Household Survey (2019) shows that social income grants remain a vital safety net, particularly in the poorest provinces. The percentage of households and persons who benefitted from a social income grants has increased since 2002. The data trends show that in 2018, 31 per cent of South Africans benefitted from a social income grant and 44.3 per cent of households received one or more social income grants. A further

N. Gumata, E. Ndou, *Accelerated Land Reform, Mining, Growth, Unemployment and Inequality in South Africa*, https://doi.org/10.1007/978-3-030-30884-1_23

disaggregation by province shows that KwaZulu-Natal, the Eastern Cape, Gauteng and Limpopo provinces have the largest number of recipients for social income grants. Against this background, Aliber (2005) argues that the increase in the number of social income grant recipients coincided with a strong trend away from agriculture as a primary source of food and income. The expansion of social income grants seems to have replaced agriculture as a rural livelihood asset or safety net. We empirically explored the interaction of accelerated land reform, the minimum wage, social income grants, household consumption growth and the Gini coefficient in Chaps. 25 and 26. We established that an increase in the binding minimum wage and the social income grants reinforce each other, especially in cases where targeted part of the population is employed. An increase in a binding minimum wage exerts persistent reinforcing effects of the increase in social income on the Gini coefficient. An increase in social income grants has more persistent positive effects on the Gini coefficient when accompanied by an increase in the binding minimum wage.

Figure 23.1 shows that the number of total social income grants recipients increased from 2.5 million in 2000 to almost 17.5 million in 2017. The growth in the number of social income grants recipients was largely on account of the increase in the number of childcare grants as shown by the difference in Fig. 23.1. The number of recipients of childcare grants increased from 0.2 million in 2000 to 12.2 million in 2017, increasing the share of child support grants recipients to 70 per cent of the total in Fig. 23.1(b).

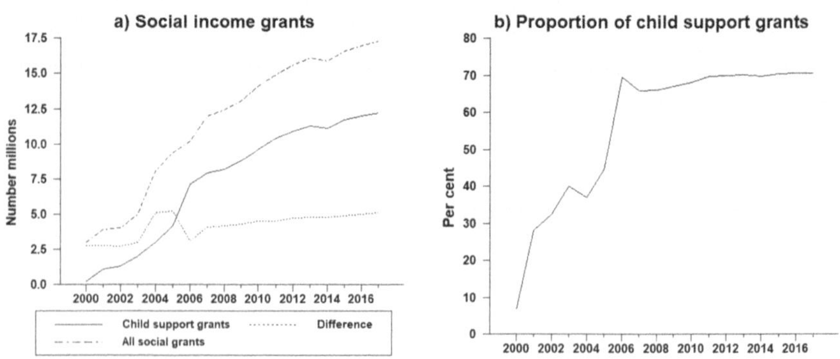

Fig. 23.1 Number of recipients of social income grants. (Source: Statistics South Africa and author's calculations)

23.2 Social Income Grants Trends and Studies on the Impact of the Social Income Grant System

The South Africa Household Survey (2019) shows that social income grants remain a vital safety net, particularly in the poorest provinces. A number of studies on the impact of the social income grant system show that social income grants, in particular the childcare grants, are well targeted at very poor households. Second, studies find that although social and childcare income grants have been an important part of the strategy to alleviate poverty, they have had little effect on overall inequality. Third, studies show that a quarter of the unemployed population derive income support exclusively from the social income grants of other members of their household. Fourth, the majority of childcare grants beneficiaries are women at 96 per cent. Fifth, the childcare grants have a positive impact on school attendance and healthcare. The number of children whose parents reported that their child had gone hungry declined from 31 per cent in 2002 to 23 per cent in 2005. This is largely due to the significant expansion of social income grants.[1] Neves et al. (2009) provide empirical research confirming that cash transfers in South Africa support consumption growth and improve the welfare of the recipients and their broader households. Their findings also suggest that social income grants facilitate investments in human capital (nutrition and schooling), along with investments in productive assets and activities.

Figure 23.1 showed that the number of recipients of social income grants increased mainly on account of childcare grants. A further disaggregation by province in Fig. 23.2 shows that KwaZulu-Natal, the Eastern Cape, Gauteng and Limpopo provinces have the largest number of recipients for social income grants. Statistics from the South Africa Household Survey (2019) show that the percentage of households and persons who benefitted from a social income grant has increased since 2002. In 2018, 31 per cent of South Africans benefitted from a social income grant and 44.3 per cent of households received one or more social income grants. Grants were the second most important source of income for households

[1] See for further reading https://africacheck.org/factsheets/separating-myth-from-reality-a-guide-to-social-grants-in-south-africa/.

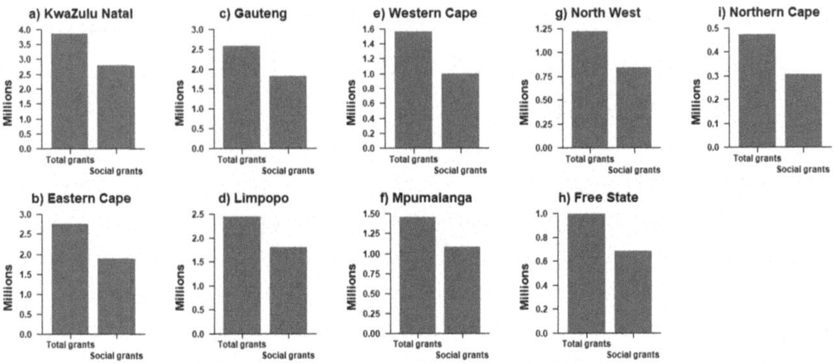

Fig. 23.2 Recipients of social income grants by province in 2017. (Source: Social Security (SASSA))

after salaries, and the main source of income for almost one-fifth of households nationally. A larger percentage of households received social income grants compared to salaries as a source of income in the Eastern Cape and Limpopo provinces. Social income grants were particularly important as a main source of income for households in the Eastern Cape, Limpopo and the Northern Cape.[2]

However, in all provinces the proportion of childcare grants was above 50 per cent as shown in Fig. 23.3, further indicating the significant contribution of childcare grants to total social income grants. This means that more than 60 per cent of the social welfare safety net spending in terms of social income grants was directed to childcare. These trends of the social and childcare income grants are a precursor to understanding whether the data supports the Aliber (2005) hypothesis that there has been a strong trend away from agriculture as a primary source of food and income since 2000 in favour of social income and childcare grants. In addition, data presented so far provides early evidence of how widespread and pervasive income and wealth inequality, unemployment and poverty are across the country. The evidence also gives credence to a statement by Hall (2019) that the debate about land reform and redistribution speaks to the intergenerational transfer of poverty and privilege.

[2] See Statistics South Africa Household Survey 2019, page 30 http://www.statssa.gov.za/publications/P0318/P03182018.pdf#page16.

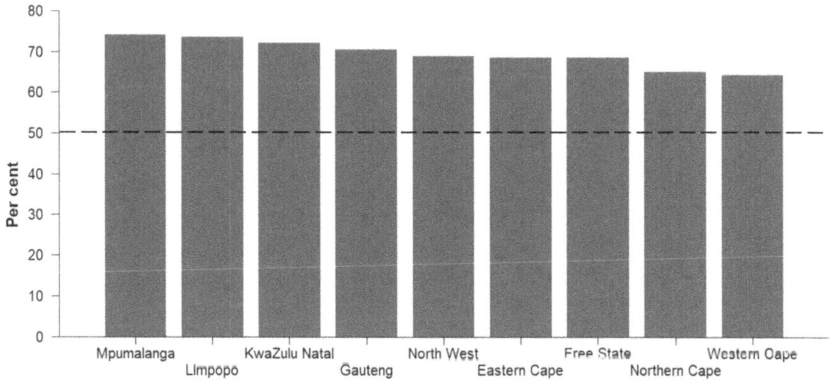

Fig. 23.3 Proportion of childcare grants to total social income grants by province in 2017 (Source: Social Security (SASSA) and authors' calculations)

In addition, the process of land reform and redistribution is trying to address a multigenerational processes of dispossession that has impacted on people's access to education and the acquisition of assets.

23.3 Population and Gender Dynamics

Another key question related to the policy of accelerated land reform and the debate on expropriation without compensation is whether they can help reduce the degree of gender inequality and disparities in South Africa. To contextualise these discussions, Fig. 23.4(a) shows that the proportion of women in the population has increased from 50 per cent in the 1960s to just below 51 per cent in 2015, whereas rural population growth and its proportion has declined persistently since the 1980s, as shown in Fig. 23.4(b) and (c), indicating the rapid increase in the rate of rural urban migration and urbanisation.

In addition, the gender labour dynamics shown in Fig. 23.5 indicate that the female unemployment rate on average constitutes more than 26 per cent of the labour force. In the case of youth, the young women unemployment rate accounts for more than 50 per cent of the labour

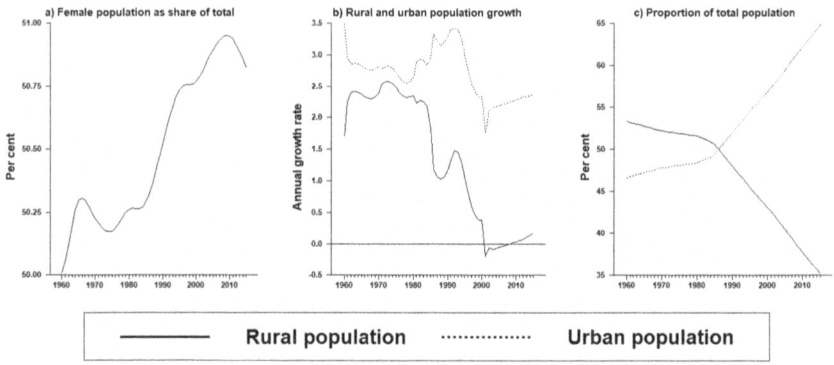

Fig. 23.4 Female population as a share of total population. (Source: World Bank)

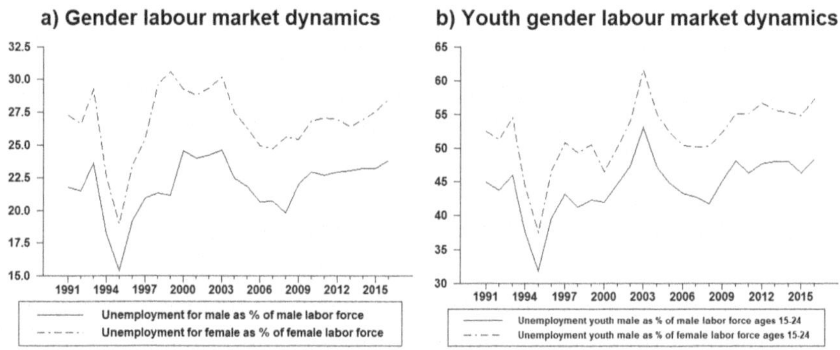

Fig. 23.5 Gender and youth labour force dynamics. (Source: World Bank)

force. Thus, whichever way we analyse the statistics, women constitute a larger share of the population and the unemployment rate.

With respect to the agricultural sector, Fig. 23.6 shows that men still dominate the agricultural labour market. The upward movement in the agricultural sector employment post-2014 did not result in any significant shift in the gender distribution in employment trends. In fact, Fig. 23.6(b) shows that although rate employment for women did increase more than that of men during 2014Q3 and 2016Q1 it was not enough to meaningfully change the gender distribution. Hence, the

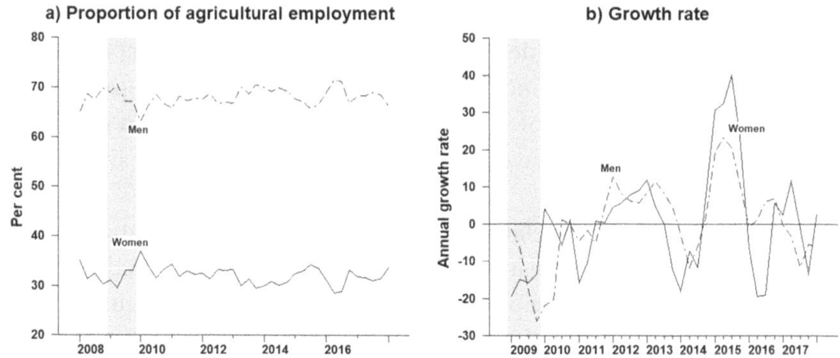

Fig. 23.6 Gender distribution in the agricultural sector employment. (Source: Statistics South Africa and authors' calculations)

employment shares shown in Fig. 23.6(a) indicate that improvements in the agricultural sector employment post-2014Q3 were positive for the men's share of employment.

23.4 Conclusion

This chapter reviews the distribution of social income grants, population dynamics and gender trends in the agricultural sector employment. The South Africa Household Survey (2019) shows that social income grants remain a vital safety net, particularly in the poorest provinces. The percentage of households and persons who benefitted from a social income grant has increased since 2002. The data trends show that in 2018, 31 per cent of South Africans benefitted from a social income grant and 44.3 per cent of households received one or more social income grants. A further disaggregation by province shows that KwaZulu-Natal, the Eastern Cape, Gauteng and Limpopo provinces have the largest number of recipients for social income grants. However, in all provinces the proportion of childcare grants was above 50 per cent in 2017, indicating the significant contribution of childcare grants to total social income grants. More than 60 per cent of the social welfare safety net spending in terms of social income grants was directed to childcare. Against this background, Aliber (2005) argues that the increase in the number of social income grant recipients coincided with a strong trend away from agriculture as a primary source of food and income. The expansion of social income grants seems to have replaced agriculture as a rural livelihood asset or safety net.

Another key question related to the policy of accelerated land reform and the debate on expropriation without compensation is whether these policy interventions can help reduce the degree of gender inequality and disparities in South Africa. Long-term trends show that the proportion of women in the population has increased from 50 per cent in the 1960s to just below 51 per cent in 2015. Rural population growth and its proportion have declined persistently since the 1980s, indicating the rapid increase in the rate of rural urban migration and urbanisation. With respect to the agricultural sector, data trends show that men still dominate the agricultural labour market. The upward movement in the agricultural sector employment post-2014 did not result in any significant shift in the gender distribution in employment trends.

References

Aliber, M. 2005. Synthesis and Conclusions. In M. Aliber, et al. (eds.) *Trends and Policy Challenges in the Rural Economy*. Cape Town: HSRC Press, pp. 87–110

Greenberg, S. 2010. *Status Report on Land and Agricultural Policy in South Africa, 2010*. PLAAS Research Report 40, University of the Western Cape, Institute for Poverty, Land and Agrarian Studies.

Hall, R. 2019. The Land is Ours: Insights from the Land Forum. Gordon Institute of Business Science, University of Pretoria. https://www.gibs.co.za/news-events/news/Pages/The-Land-is-Ours-_-Insights-from-the-land-forum.aspx

Institute for Poverty, Land and Agrarian Studies (PLAAS). 2018. Submission to the Constitutional Review Committee. University of the Western Cape.

Jacobs, P., Lahiff, E., and Hall, R. 2003. Land Redistribution. Programme for Land and Agrarian Studies School of Government University of the Western Cape.

Leibbrandt, Murray, Finn, Arden, and Woolard, Ingrid. 2012. Describing and Decomposing Post-apartheid Income Inequality in South Africa. *Development Southern Africa*, 29(1), 19–34. https://doi.org/10.1080/0376835X.2012.645639.

Netshipale, A.J., Oosting, S.J., Raidimi, E.N., Mashiloane, M.L., and De Boer, I.J.M. 2007. Land reform in South Africa: Beneficiary Participation and Impact on Land Use in the Waterberg District. *NJAS Wageningen Journal of Life Sciences*, 83, 57–66.

Neves, D., Samson, M., Van Niekerk, I., Hlatshwayo, S. (EPRI), and Du Toit, A. 2009. The Use and Effectiveness of Social Grants in South Africa. Institute for Poverty, Land and Agrarian Studies (PLAAS). http://repository.uwc.ac.za/xmlui/bitstream/handle/10566/4672/The_use_and_effectiveness_of_social_gran.pdf?sequence=1&isAllowed=y.

24

Land Redistributed between 1994 and 2017, the Production Function and the Evolution of Area Planted in Various Agricultural Sector Commodities

Learning Objectives

- Assess progress on land redistributed between 1994 and 2017 and the beneficiaries.
- Explore the trend of women beneficiaries in land reform between 1994 and 2016.
- Discuss land as a primary factor in the production function.
- Assess selected long-term trends in commercial and homeland farmers.
- Review the evolution of area planted, tonnes per hectare produced and yield per hectare planted in selected field crops.

24.1 Introduction

Land plays a central role in the production function and economic devel opment. Land enters the production function as a primary input into the production process together with labour, capital, technical change and entrepreneurship. Land is a significant asset and agricultural products make up a large portion of national income (Azadi and Vanhaute 2019).

N. Gumata, E. Ndou, *Accelerated Land Reform, Mining, Growth, Unemployment and Inequality in South Africa*, https://doi.org/10.1007/978-3-030-30884-1_24

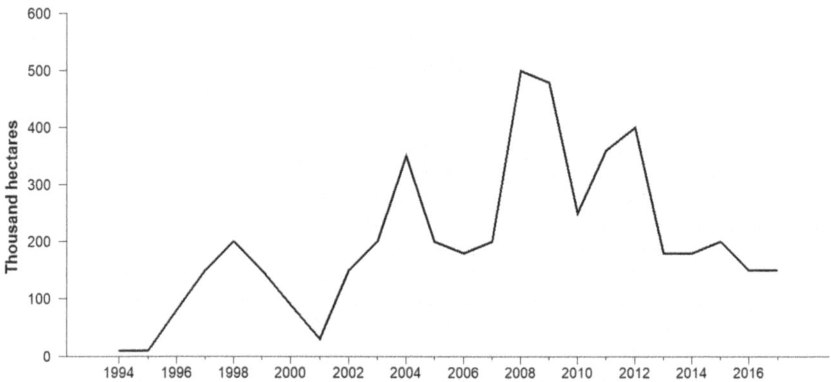

Fig. 24.1 Hectares of land redistributed between 1994 and 2017. (Source: PLAAS (2018))

Furthermore, the authors indicate that the major challenge in developing poor countries lies in the rural sector, which suffers from chronic poverty, high levels of unemployment, widening income and wealth inequality, low levels of education and poor health. As such, land and how it is distributed plays a central role in theories and policy interventions that try to change the development patterns, shift the production possibilities frontier and raise incomes over the long run. Restuccia and Rogerson (2008) resource misallocation theory states that frictions and barriers due to various factors can prevent the efficient use of resources, resulting in low aggregate factor productivity. Ando and Nassar (2017) provide evidence showing that education as a proxy for skills is necessary to help reduce structural distortions and can enhance labour mobility, innovation and improved labour participation and absorption.

This chapter reviews land redistributed between 1994 and 2017, the role of land in the production function and the evolution of area planted in various agricultural sector commodities. Figure 24.1 shows the evolution of hectares of land redistributed between 1994 and 2017. The trend shows that the land reform programme has failed to meet the set target of redistributing 30 per cent (85 million hectares) of agricultural land by 2014 by a wide margin. Furthermore, the breakdown of the land redistributed by province in Table 24.1 shows that more than a quarter of the land redistributed is in the Northern Cape. The Northern Cape and KwaZulu-Natal have been the biggest beneficiaries of land reform and restitution in terms

Table 24.1 Land transferred and beneficiaries

	Redistribution and tenure			Restitution			Total	
Province	Number	Hectares	Beneficiaries	Claims	Hectares	Beneficiaries	Hectares	Beneficiaries
Eastern Cape	675	353,357	25,633	16,201	94,834	215,201	448,191	240,834
Free State	799	350,291	7,721	2,662	47,615	40,893	397,906	48,614
Gauteng	286	34,513	7,328	13,159	9,476	70,179	43,989	77,507
KwaZulu-Natal	690	547,414	67,761	14,752	642,447	433,168	1,189,861	500,929
Limpopo	291	91,235	7,403	3,382	513,024	220,227	604,259	227,630
Mpumalanga	444	322,839	13,950	2,694	399,876	225,877	722,715	239,827
Northern Cape	271	952,744	2,773	3,682	539,620	100,554	1,492,364	103,327
North West	300	268,566	40,539	3,709	373,642	172,963	642,208	213,502
Western Cape	223	122,304	12,750	15,546	3,769	118,165	126,073	130,915
Total	3979	3,043,263	185,853	75,787	2,624,303	1,597,227	5,667,566	1,783,085

Source: Greenberg (2010)

of hectares. Has land reform in these provinces impacted their contribution to the agricultural sector output growth and employment growth?

Earlier chapters showed that Limpopo, Western Cape and Eastern Cape have registered an upward trend in agricultural employment post-2009. This is particularly the case for Limpopo, where the contribution to the agricultural sector has been persistently upward-trending and employment has more than doubled. The agricultural sector employment growth in Limpopo increased from just above 6 per cent to an average of 15.3 per cent between 2012Q1 and 2017Q2. On the other hand, the Free State province, the traditional agricultural hub, has been on a prolonged downward trend since 2009.

These trends bring to the fore the key question explored in earlier chapters, namely, can the policies of accelerated land reform and expropriation of land without compensation help reduce unemployment, poverty and inequality? If the Northern Cape and KwaZulu-Natal have been the biggest beneficiaries of land reform and restitution in terms of hectares as shown in Table 24.1, but are lagging behind Limpopo, Western Cape and Eastern Cape in terms of the contribution of the agricultural sector activity and the economy at large, then, is accelerated land reform on it own a sufficient condition to reduce unemployment, poverty and inequality?

Greenberg (2010) and other vast literature in this area of land reform and restitution show that there are two major interlinked challenges that face the land reform policy: speeding up of the transfer of land and the post-settlement support for productive use of transferred land. For instance, Sepaela (2006a) shows that many of the beneficiaries of the land reform process in rural areas are unskilled and lack the experience and expertise to develop and utilise acquired land to its full potential. To this end, Sepaela (2006b) argues that the government has been ineffective in ensuring that the majority of land reform beneficiaries in rural areas are empowered to ensure that they can pursue sustainable livelihoods by the effective utilisation of the redistributed land. Samayende (2005) shows that the current land reform programme has failed to contribute to economic growth in the country, specifically in terms of creating sustainable livelihoods, rural employment and poverty alleviation. The failure rate of post-settlement support projects since 1994 has been as high as 90 per cent due to the lack of, among other things, farm management knowledge, marketing skills and adequate access to development credit.

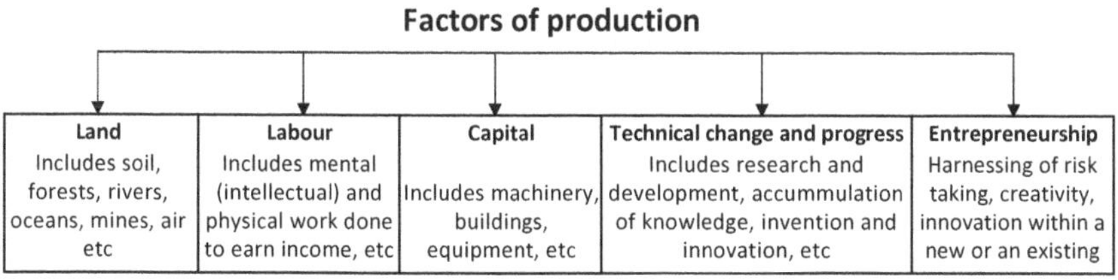

Fig. 24.2 Factors of production (Source: Author's drawing)

24.2 Land as a Primary Factor in the Production Function and the Evolution of Land Reform in South Africa

From an economic perspective, land is a part and parcel of the production function. As shown in Fig. 24.2, land enters the production function as a primary input into the production process together with labour, capital, technical change and entrepreneurship.[1] In addition, positive shocks to the factors contained in the production function affect potential output. Therefore, from a theoretical point of view there is a strong case for accelerated land reform as part of the policies aimed at dealing with resource misallocation at the sector level and raising potential output growth.

Evidence in earlier chapters showed that increasing area (hectares) cultivated in the former homelands results in an increase in agricultural output growth, employment growth and labour productivity growth. This means that bringing underutilised land in the former homelands and communal areas will make a significant and meaningful difference in the agricultural sector contribution to aggregate output growth, employment growth and labour productivity growth. Evidence shows that bringing in underutilised land in the former homelands and communal areas more than doubles the response of the agricultural sector output growth, employment growth and labour productivity growth. To complement this strategy, later chapters in this book argue and present a robust case for changes in the financial landscape and the use of financial regulatory and macro-pruden-

[1] All these inputs into the production function are well captured in the primary objectives of the Land Bank. See for further reading http://www.treasury.gov.za/legislation/acts/2002/a15-02.pdf.

tial tools to support funding to the agricultural sector. In these chapters, we establish robust evidence that (i) an increase in the balance sheet of the Land Bank; (ii) the use of macroprudential and financial regulation tools to support and increase funding directed to the agricultural sector; (iii) changes to the banking and financial regulations to open up space for the Postbank, mutual and co-operatives banks will largely benefit and diversify the supply of credit to the agricultural sector. The benefits of these is policy initiatives will also contribute to making the policy of accelerated land reform a success. We concluded that a multi-institutional approach to funding the policy of accelerated land reform and the agricultural sector is a prudent risk based long-term approach to make sure that the agricultural sector and the value chain are sustainable for the long haul.

Furthermore, evidence in earlier chapters showed that the dominant effects in the agricultural sector are due to exports growth. The agricultural sector employment growth responds more to exports growth compared to output growth. The implication is that farmers are more responsive to exports demand and earnings growth. In turn, this increases the employment growth intensity of output growth in the agricultural sector. We established that the "*output growth-driven exports growth*" hypothesis and strategy best explains developments in the agricultural sector. Trade openness and the export-oriented growth strategy auger well for the agricultural sector output growth, employment growth and labour productivity growth. Thus, favourable trade and active policies that increase access to new markets for the agricultural sector will support and make a success of the accelerated land reform policy.

Therefore, we have provided robust empirical evidence that the policies of accelerated land reform and expropriation of land without compensation on their own are necessary but insufficient conditions to reduce unemployment, poverty and inequality. The policies of accelerated land reform and expropriation of land without compensation must be accompanied by the productive utilisation of land as captured in the Land and Agricultural Development Bank Act (2002), a holistic approach to post-settlement support and favourable trade and access to markets policies.[2] Data contained in the high-level panel on the assessment of key

[2] We showed that these supportive policy interventions include, for example, provision of persistent investment in supportive infrastructure, ample funding for housing, sanitation, agricultural development and revolution, innovation, productivity, profitability and so on.

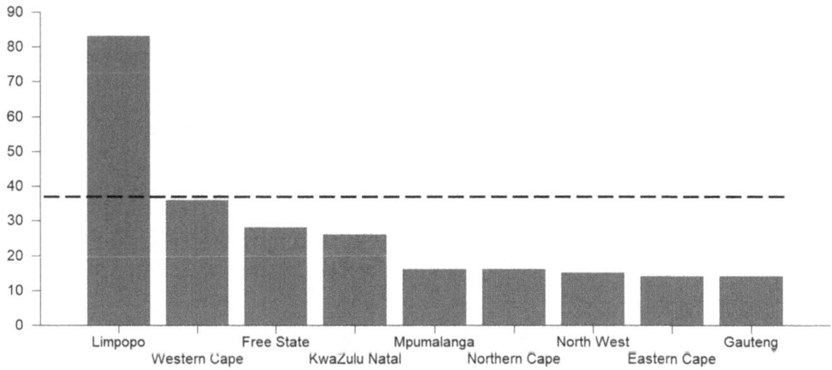

Fig. 24.3 Percentage of women beneficiaries in land reform between 1994 and 2016. (Source: Umrabulo No. 43 (2018). See for further reading http://www.anc.org.za/sites/default/files/pubs/umrabulo43.pdf)

legislation and the acceleration of fundamental change showed that nationally women constituted only 23 per cent of land redistribution beneficiaries between 1994 and 2016. Women are a minority of beneficiaries in a majority of provinces and make up less than one quarter of beneficiaries as shown in Fig. 24.3.[3] In addition, Bureau for Food and Agricultural Policy (BFAP 2011a) contends that the bulk (64 per cent) of the small-holder schemes in the former homelands is geographically located in ten districts. Six of these ten districts were declared presidential poverty nodes. The majority of rural households in these districts rely and are headed by women. In addition, these rural households largely consist mainly of children and the elderly.

In later chapters of the book, we thus argued that there is a case to be explicit and clear as to what "*equitable basis*" in section 25(5) of the constitution means, especially when it comes to redressing gender imbalances within the accelerated land redistribution policy and expropriation of land without compensation. At the same time, at the policy level, the ownership of land and the participation of women in the agricultural sector should be encouraged, enforced and supported via legislation as stated in the Land and Agricultural Development Bank Act. Such legislation and laws should

[3] See for further reading https://www.parliament.gov.za/storage/app/media/Pages/2017/october/High_Level_Panel/HLP_Report/HLP_report.pdf.

be complemented by setting up mechanisms through which the implementation is monitored and evaluated against the set objectives and targets.

Furthermore, vast literature in this area indicates that different forms of approaches to land reform have had different effects in addressing gender, class and poverty. Literature shows that various approaches to land acquisition and the choice of land for redistribution models have implications for the impact of land reform policies on gender, class and poverty. For instance, Netshipale et al. (2007) present evidence showing that the changes in land redistribution policies over time resulted in significant differences in beneficiary participation among land redistribution models. The implementation outcomes of land redistribution indicate that the Settlement Land Acquisition Grant (SLAG) model benefited the poor while the Land Redistribution for Agricultural Development Phase 1 (LRAD1), Land Redistribution for Agricultural Development Phase 2 (LRAD2) and Proactive Land Acquisition Strategy (PLAS) models benefitted mostly other social classes. Therefore, the approach to accelerated land redistribution has to pay attention not only to gender but also to class, which is a proxy for poverty. Furthermore, evidence shows that poverty is also disproportionately distributed along racial lines.

What should policymakers do to make sure that the gains in the gender distribution in the agricultural employment are accelerated? Jacobs et al. (2003a, b) state that the LRAD programme was designed and promoted as the flagship programme through which a class of black commercial farmers, the so-called *emerging black farmers* would emerge and thrive. We argue that with respect to addressing the gender and class imbalances in landownership and participation in the agricultural sector, intentional policies and programmes such as these must be designed and implemented. Policies and programmes that are intentionally designed to increase the participation *of women, especially from rural and poor* backgrounds have to be designed, implemented and evaluated to assess their success rate. Evidence in earlier chapters showed that McKinsey & Company (2015) and BFAP (2011b) indicate that the Eastern Cape, KwaZulu-Natal and Limpopo provinces present significant opportunities for the agricultural sector.[4] Thus, policies and programmes that are

[4] See also Exhibit 45 of https://www.mckinsey.com/~/media/McKinsey/Global%20Themes/Middle%20East%20and%20Africa/South%20Africas%20bold%20priorities%20for%20inclusive%20growth/South_Africas_big_five_bold_priorities_for_inclusive_growth%20Full_report.ashx.

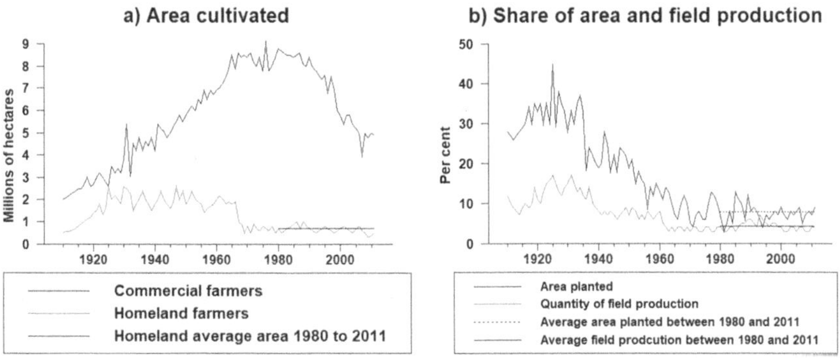

Fig. 24.4 Selected trends in commercial and homeland farmers. (Source: Liebenberg (2012) and authors' calculations)

intentionally designed to increase the participation of women, especially from rural and poor backgrounds can be guided by the areas identified and the employment matrix presented in BFAP (2011b). Such an approach to accelerated land reform and redistribution will also address aspects related to size and scale for the involvement of targeted beneficiaries.

The BFAP (2011b) argues that the trends in area planted and the size of farms observed in Fig. 24.4 will have to change fundamentally. Better utilisation of land in the former homeland areas, especially communal areas, can create 300,000 employment opportunities and an additional 326,500 employment opportunities via upstream and downstream value added in the agricultural sector. This could be achieved by (i) expanding and investing in irrigation agriculture; (ii) picking and supporting labour-intensive agricultural sectors and regions (provinces) as shown in the employment matrix presented in earlier chapters; and (iii) supporting the creation of upstream and downstream industries. The BFAP (2011b) study shows that this can result in the improvement of the livelihoods of close to 70,000, 40,000 and 27,000 people, respectively, if these policy initiatives are implemented.

The trends observed in Fig. 24.4 showing that area planted and the share of area and field production in the former homelands declined since the 1980s in part answer the hypothesis put forward by Aliber (2015).[5] Similarly, Fig. 24.5 shows that non-commercial maize hectares planted

[5] See earlier chapters.

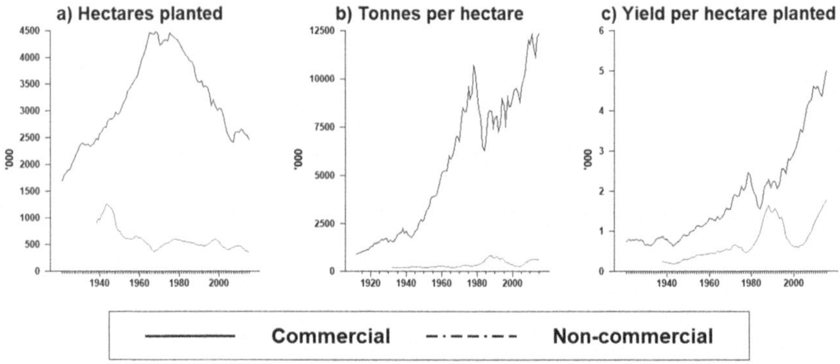

Fig. 24.5 Commercial and non-commercial maize hectares planted and yields. (Source: SAGIS and authors' calculations)

have been on a declining trend since the 1980s. The data trends show that the phenomenon of less reliance on agricultural income in the rural areas preceded the expansion of social income grants in 2000. However, it may be the case that the expansion of social income grants exacerbated the shift away from agriculture as the main source of income in the rural areas. Thus, as a policy intervention to alleviate lack of sufficient income and poverty in rural areas, the expansion of social income grants further entrenched the negative effects of other factors that explain a strong trend away from agriculture as a primary source of food and income.

24.3 The Evolution of Area Planted, Tonnes per Hectare Produced and Yield per Hectare Planted in Selected Field Crops

In this section, we place the impact of the increase in the area (hectares) planted in the former homelands and by commercial farmers and the tonnes produced per hectare into context by presenting the evolution of these variables over time. The presentation of the variables over time also serves to argue the case that there is potential in a number of crops as recommended by the BFAP (2011b) employment matrix shown in earlier chapters.

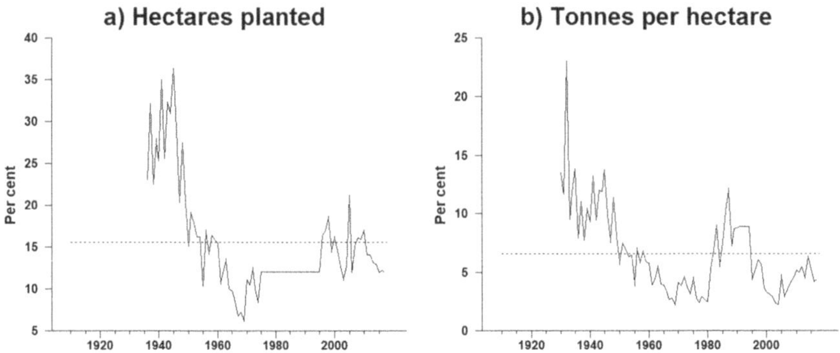

Fig. 24.6 Share of non-commercial maize hectares planted, and tonnes produced. (Source: SAGIS and authors' calculations)

The trends in Fig. 24.5 show that hectares planted for maize by commercial famers peaked in the 1960s. As of 2017, area planted by both commercial and non-commercial farmers is half the size of what it used to be pre-1980s. The decline in the area planted is in stark contrast to the tonnes produced per hectare, shown in Fig. 24.5(b), and the increase in the yield per hectare planted, shown in Fig. 24.5(c). These diverging trends indicate the role played by technological advances and innovation in the agricultural sector.

The share of non-commercial maize famers' area planted and production averaged 15.6 per cent and 6.6 per cent for the sample period shown in Fig. 24.6. These trends present an opportunity in the maize market, especially in the context of accelerated land reform and agricultural revolution. The policy implications based on the recommendations of the BFAP (2011b) sector employment intensity and employment matrix, indicate that there is a large potential and opportunity for yellow maize where there is also a case for the strategy of import substitution.

Figure 24.7 shows that similar to the commercial farmers' maize, the area planted for wheat also declined in the 1960s to less than half as of 2017. The same trend is visible for sorghum.

Earlier chapters showed that the consumption of wheat has consistently surpassed domestic production since the late 1990s resulting in the need to close the deficit via the importation of wheat. We argued

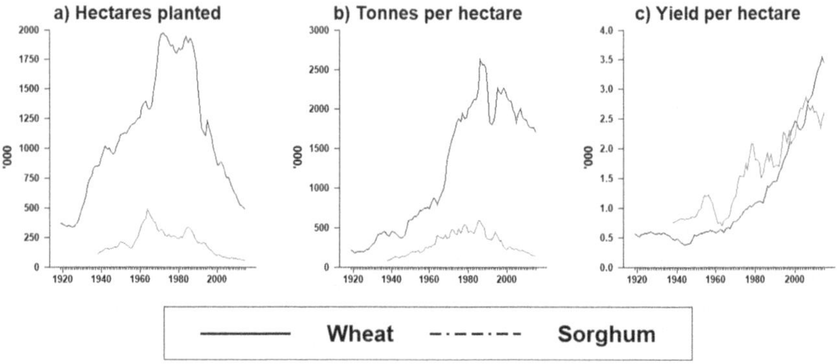

Fig. 24.7 Wheat and sorghum hectares planted and yields. (Source: SAGIS and authors' calculations)

that there is a case to pursue a strategy of increasing domestic area planted as opposed to relying only on the imposition of wheat tariffs to stem or neutralise the impact of wheat imports. The results in earlier chapters showed that on a cascading scale, and as a very short-term measure, the combined net effects of an increase in the area planted for domestic wheat, imposition of wheat tariffs and the R/US$ depreciation can be used as a policy interventions to neutralise the degree of import penetration whilst fully catering to domestic demand for wheat. But as a medium- to long-term policy intervention, an increase in the domestic area planted for wheat is the most effective policy intervention to deter and substitute wheat imports, whilst satisfying domestic demand. In the BFAP (2011b) sector employment intensity and employment matrix, white maize, wheat and sorghum are in Quadrant 4, whereas yellow maize is in Quadrant 1. Based on the interpretation of the BFAP (2011b) employment intensity and employment matrix, this means that the expansion of yellow maize has high growth potential as an agricultural commodity sub-sector.

Furthermore, in terms of international food commodity prices which are a proxy for export earnings, the international prices in US$ terms for these crops have increased significantly in recent years, indicating that that there are benefits for South African producers to enter and expand in these food commodity markets. Evidence in earlier chapters showed that exports growth leads to employment intensity in the agricultural sector. In addition, food commodity price booms (busts) result in an increase (decline) in exports, output and employment growth. Food commodity price booms propagate (amplify) the effects of the positive and negative shocks throughout the sector.

Thus, the classification of the crops in Quadrant 4 of the employment intensity and employment matrix by BFAP (2011b) should be interpreted alongside the impact of food commodity prices and exports growth in the agricultural sector. At the same time, we should not lose sight of the need to make food not only available but also affordable in South Africa. With respect to the evolution of canola and sunflower seed, Fig. 24.8 shows that the area planted has been increasing, although it is evident that canola production is still in its very early stages. At the same time, the international prices for canola and sunflower seed have increased in recent years, indicating the positive impact on the agricultural sector exports earnings growth, output growth and employment growth. The BFAP (2011b) sector employment intensity and employment matrix puts canola and sunflower seeds in Quadrant 1 and these are among the agricultural sector industries with high potential for growth. In addition, yields per hectare are still very low when compared to maize, wheat and sorghum, indicating that there is high potential in these crops for the agricultural sector.

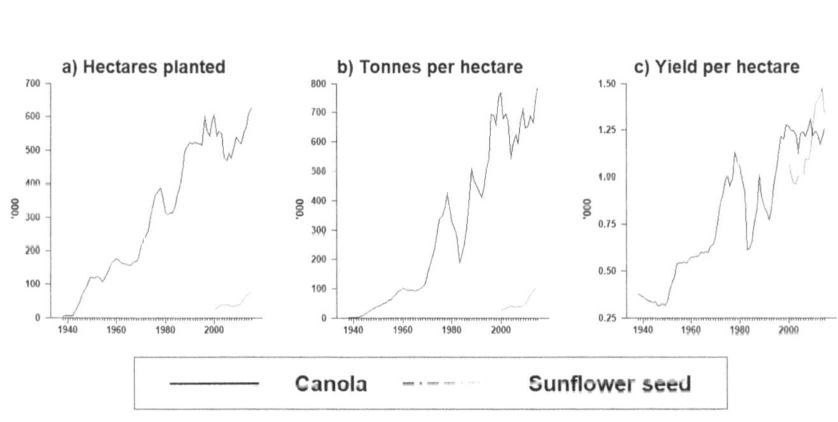

Fig. 24.8 Canola and sunflower seed hectares planted and yields. (Source: SAGIS and authors' calculations)

Figure 24.9 shows that the area planted for groundnuts declined and is less than 100,000 hectares as of 2017, whilst that of soybeans increased as well as tonnes per hectare. Soybeans are in Quadrant 1, groundnuts are in Quadrant 4; and macadamia and pecan nuts are in Quadrant 2 of the BFAP (2011b) employment intensity and employment matrix. What are the policy implications? These agricultural sector commodity industries present high potential growth sectors which are also labour intensive. Furthermore, recent research shows that there is a boom in the nut market and prices in recent years as consumers are opting for healthier foods. This has increasingly persuaded farmers to replace their crops with nut trees.

The saturated production in the world's largest production regions presents South African farmers with an unbeatable opportunity to enter the international markets.[6] Sihlobo (2013) also provides evidence that there is potential to increase production and reach new export markets.[7]

The area planted for barley shown in Fig. 24.10 also declined from peak levels of 120,000 hectares planted in the mid-1980s to less than

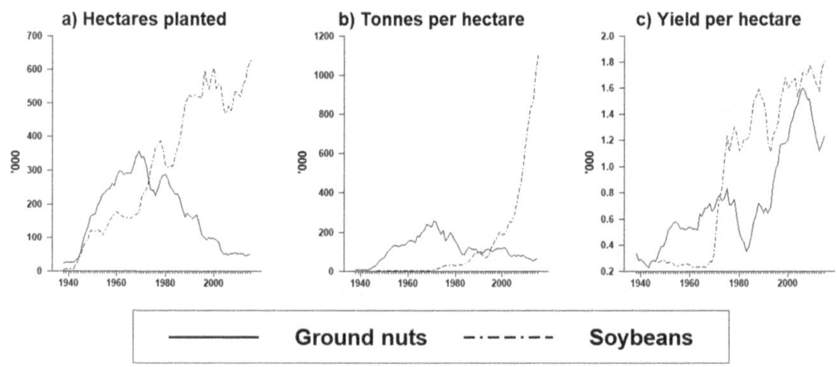

Fig. 24.9 Groundnut and soybean hectares planted and yields. (Source: SAGIS and authors' calculations)

[6] See for further reading https://www.farmersweekly.co.za/opinion/by-invitation/cracking-into-the-almond-business/, https://www.farmersweekly.co.za/crops/fruit-nuts/pecan-nut-farming-high-cost-big-returns/.

[7] See for further reading http://www.grainsa.co.za/an-overview-of-potential-export-markets-for-south-african-groundnuts.

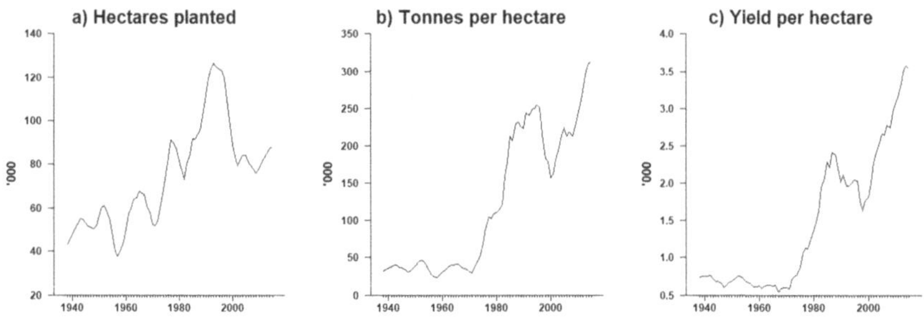

Fig. 24.10 Barley hectares planted and yields. (Source: SAGIS and authors' calculations)

100,000 hectares in 2017. Nonetheless, yields and tonnes per hectare produced increased. Barley is in Quadrant 4 together with wheat, white maize and groundnuts in the BFAP (2011b) sector employment intensity and employment matrix.

24.4 Conclusion and Policy Implications

Land plays a central role in the production function and economic development. Land enters the production function as a primary input into the production process together with labour, capital, technical change and entrepreneurship. Land is a significant asset and agricultural products make up a large portion of national incomes. This chapter reviewed land redistributed between 1994 and 2017, the role of land in the production function and the evolution of area planted in various agricultural sector commodities. The trends show that the land reform programme has failed to meet the set target of redistributing 30 per cent (85 million hectares) of agricultural land by a wide margin. The breakdown of the land redistributed by province shows that more than a quarter of the land redistributed is in the Northern Cape. The Northern Cape and KwaZulu-Natal have been the biggest beneficiaries of land reform and restitution in terms of hectares. In addition, women are a minority of beneficiaries of the land redistribution policy in a majority of provinces. Data shows that women make up less than one quarter of beneficiaries of land redistribution. However, the Northern Cape and KwaZulu-Natal contribute less to the agricultural sector and the economy. Hence, we argue that accelerated land reform is a necessary but insufficient condition to reduce unemployment, poverty and inequality. Post-settlement support should be an integral part of the policy output in order to achieve long-term sustainable development outcomes. Thus, policy interventions should be designed to ensure that post-settlement support cuts across all major land reform programmes, namely, redistribution, land tenure and restitution. In addition, policy interventions should provide a comprehensive post-settlement reconstruction and development programme plan.

Therefore, the policies of accelerated land reform and expropriation of land without compensation must be accompanied by productive utilisation of land as captured in the Land and Agricultural Development Bank Act (2002), a holistic approach to post-settlement support and favourable trade policies. The policy of accelerated land reform and an increase in hectares planted, can create a class of entrepreneurs and self-employed people through the formation of co-operatives, and small and medium enterprises. This is another channel through which employment growth can be created in the agricultural sector. Accelerated land reform and an increase in hectares planted might not have a direct and instantaneous impact on poverty and inequality per se but may work via a number of channels to affect output growth, investment growth, exports growth and employment growth, lower poverty and inequality. Furthermore, accelerated land reform and an increase in hectares planted contribute to food security and affordability. In turn, this can be channelled to support sustainable school nutrition systems to offer more alternative nutritious foods and further alleviate poverty. Thus, all these policy interventions are ultimately aimed at lowering poverty and inequality, but they will have different impacts on growth in output, investment, exports, employment, labour participation and absorption.

References

Adamopoulos, T., and Restuccia, D. 2019. *Land Reform and Productivity: A Quantitative Analysis with Micro Data*. NBER Working Paper No. 25780. https://www.nber.org/papers/w25780.pdf.

Aliber, M. 2015. Unravelling the Willing Buyer/Willing Seller Question. In B. Cousins, and C. Walker (eds.) *Land Divided: Land in South African Society in 2014 and Beyond*, Jacana: Johannesburg.

Ando, A., and Nassar, K. 2017. *Indexing Structural Distortions: Sectoral Productivity, Structural Change and Growth*. IMF Working Paper WP/17/205.

Azadi, H., and Vanhaute, E. 2019. Mutual Effects of Land Distribution and Economic Development: Evidence from Asia, Africa, and Latin America. *MDPI Journal for Land*, 8, 96.

BFAP. 2011a. The South African Agricultural Baseline. Bureau for Food and Agricultural Policy. https://www.sagis.org.za/BFAP_2011.pdf

BFAP. 2011b. The Contribution of the Agro-Industrial Complex to Employment in South Africa. Tech. Rep. June, The Bureau for Food and Agricultural Policy, Pretoria.

Greenberg, S. 2010. Status Report on Land and Agricultural Policy in South Africa. Research Report. School of Government, UWC PLAAS Institute for Poverty, Land and Agrarian Studies. http://www.plaas.org.za/sites/default/files/publications-pdf/RR40.pdf

Jacobs, P., Lahiff, E., and Hall, R. 2003a. *Evaluating Land and Agrarian Reform in South Africa Series; No. 1: Land Redistribution*. PLAAS, University of the Western Cape: Cape Town.

Jacobs, P., Lahiff, E., and Hall. R. 2003b. Who Will Benefit from Land Reform?[online]. *The Star*, October 10. Available on the Internet at: http://www.thestar.co.za/index.php?fSectionId=129&fArticleId=258159 (29 June 2004).

Liebenberg, F. 2012. South African Agricultural Production, Productivity and Research Performance in the 20th Century. Department of Agricultural Economics, Extension and Rural Development Faculty of Natural and Agricultural Sciences, University of Pretoria.

McKinsey & Company. 2015. South Africa's Big Five: Bold Priorities for Inclusive Growth. McKinsey Global Institute. https://www.mckinsey.com/~/media/mckinsey/featured%20insights/Middle%20East%20and%20Africa/South%20Africas%20bold%20priorities%20for%20inclusive%20growth/South_Africas_big_five_bold_priorities_for_inclusive_growth%20Full_report.ashx

Netshipale, A.J., Oosting, S.J., Raidimi, E.N., Mashiloane, M.L., and De Boer, I.J.M. 2007. Land Reform in South Africa: Beneficiary Participation and Impact on Land Use in the Waterberg District. *NJAS Wageningen Journal of Life Sciences*, 83, 57–66.

PLAAS (Institute for Poverty, Land and Agrarian Studies). 2018. Submission to the Constitutional Review Committee. University of the Western Cape.

Restuccia, D., and Rogerson, R. 2008. Policy Distortions and Aggregate Productivity with Heterogeneous Establishments. *Review of Economic Dynamics*, 11(4), 707–20.

Samayende, S. 2005. Land Reform a 'Dismal Failure'. *City Press*, July 14, p. 7.

Sepaela, P. 2006a. Summit's Resolutions to go Public. In *DLA: Land News*. Government Printer, Pretoria, South Africa, pp. 6–10.

Sepaela, P. 2006b. Nkuzi Has Its Say. In *DLA: Land News*. Government Printer, Pretoria, South Africa, pp. 14–16.

Sihlobo, W. 2013. An Overview of Potential Export Markets for South African Groundnuts. *Grain SA*. https://www.grainsa.co.za/an-overview-of-potential-export-markets-for-south-african-groundnuts

Umrabulo. 2018. Lets' Talk. Umrabulo No. 43, August 2018. https://www.anc1912.org.za/umrabulo-43-2018.

25

The Interaction between the Minimum Wage, Social Income Grants, Household Consumption and the Gini Coefficient

Learning Objectives

- Explore the interaction between an increase in social income grants and the binding minimum wage on household expenditure for non-durable goods and the Gini coefficient.
- Establish whether an increase in social income grants and the binding minimum wage reinforce each other's effects on household expenditure for non-durable goods and the Gini coefficient.
- Assess whether the expansion in social income grants contributed to the decline in the reliance on the agricultural sector as a key source of income.

25.1 Introduction

This chapter assesses the impact of an increase in social income grants compared to that of the binding minimum wage on household consumption and the Gini coefficient. Social income grants are part of the social

N. Gumata, E. Ndou, *Accelerated Land Reform, Mining, Growth, Unemployment and Inequality in South Africa*, https://doi.org/10.1007/978-3-030-30884-1_25

safety net, aimed at and received by, for example, population groups in old age, affected by disability, veterans or childcare. The common thread being the inability to work and thus in unemployment. As such, social income grants are narrow in focus compared to a policy of accelerated land redistribution, an increase in hectares (area) planted and the binding minimum wage.[1] Furthermore, the policies of accelerated land reform, an increase in hectares (area) planted and social income grants have an element of fiscal stimulus involved. But they also speak to the composition and nature of fiscal spending. Fiscal stimulus via an increase in social income grants is not expected to have an impact on employment growth or on output growth or investment growth. But it is expected to improve the spending capacity of the affected population groups, especially the unemployed and those with low income. Thus, social income grants are largely part of the demand side policy interventions.

On the other hand, a binding minimum wage is aimed at those already in employment and those who might enter the labour market. At its core, it is aimed at curbing *working-class poverty*, *compressing the wage gaps* and *directly lowering income inequality*. Thus, an increase in the binding minimum wage and the social income grants are expected to affect expenditures, especially on basic needs as they are policy interventions aimed on the demand side of the economy. As policy interventions, an increase in the binding minimum wage and social income grants are likely to reinforce each other by improving the capacity of populations in unemployment and low-income categories to spend. But they are funded differently, and the employment status is a key differentiator. For the unemployed, an increase in social income grants provides much needed reprieve. However, the social income grants do not deal with the fact that the status of unemployment is the worst state to be in, as workers are least productive (McMillan and Rodrik 2011).

[1] We explore the role of accelerated land redistribution, increase in hectares planted and the Gini coefficient in earlier chapters.

25.2 Do Positive Shocks to the Minimum Wage and Social Income Grants Lead to an Increase in Household Consumption and a Decline in the Gini Coefficient?

For the empirical analysis, we compare the effects of positive social income grants and a binding national minimum wage of R3500 shocks on the Gini coefficient to assess which shock exerts the most pronounced and persistent effects. The estimated vector autoregression (VAR) models include the Gini coefficient, the value of social income grants and the national minimum wage. Largely due to the fact that the value of social income grants paid out sourced from the South African Social Security Agency is only available from 2004, we adjust the sample size in the estimations by using deposits in the Postbank as proxy social income grants.[2] The median minimum wage for low-paid workers is sourced from the Labour Research Service (LRS) database,[3] the Gini coefficient is sourced from Statistics South Africa and household consumption is sourced from the South African Reserve Bank database.

We start the empirical analysis by estimating small models which are specified in the same way to assess the direct impact of these policy interventions on household consumption and the Gini coefficient. Model one includes social income grants, households' consumption of non-durable goods and the Gini coefficient. Model two includes the minimum wage, households' consumption of non-durable goods and the Gini coefficient. The VAR models in this section are estimated for the sample period 2004Q1 to 2017Q4 largely due to the availability of data for the value of social income grants. The VAR models are estimated using 2 lags and 10,000 Monte Carlo draws. All growth rates are calculated annually. The shock is one standard deviation.

[2] Data for the values of social income grants paid out are sourced from the South African Social Security Agency http://www.sassa.gov.za/index.php/knowledge-centre/annual-reports?start=6.

[3] Data were accessed from the online database via the link www.lrs.org.za/award.

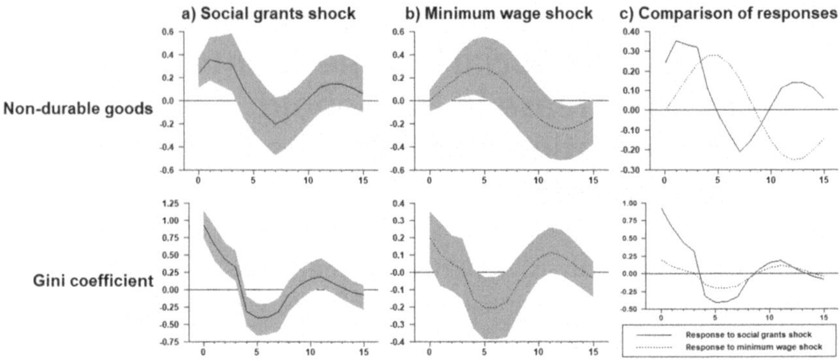

Fig. 25.1 Non-durable goods consumption and Gini coefficient responses to various positive shocks. (Note: The grey shaded areas denote the 16th and 84th percentile confidence bands. Source: Authors' calculations)

The results in Fig. 25.1 show that indeed positive shocks to social income grants and the minimum wage result in an increase in household consumption of non-durable goods and a decline in the Gini coefficient, albeit at differing magnitudes. The comparison of the impulse responses to the shocks shows that increases in the social income grants result in a contemporaneous increase in households' non-durable consumption expenditure and a decline in the Gini coefficient. But the positive effects are very transitory as they dissipate within three quarters. The positive effects of the minimum wage are far more persistent on non-durable goods consumption. In addition, although they are muted on the Gini coefficient, they are far more persistent.

These results are consistent with the findings of Gumata and Ndou (2017), who show that persistent positive shocks to the minimum wage growth have a pronounced impact in lowering the Gini coefficient compared to small-sized non-persistent shocks. Furthermore, the authors showed that the Gini coefficient declined more due to large and persistent positive shocks to the minimum wage in a low inflation regime compared to a high inflation regime. The authors show that high and robust GDP growth rates are also necessary conditions to ensure a sustained lower Gini coefficient. Similarly, firm profitability measured by gross operating surplus plays an important role in reducing the Gini coefficient in responses to minimum wage increases. Firm profitability and GDP growth are the biggest propagators of the transmission of positive shocks to the minimum wage in lowering the decline in the Gini coefficient.

In addition, Neves et al. (2009) provide empirical research confirming that cash transfers in the form of social income grants in South Africa support household consumption and improve the welfare of recipients and their broader households. Their findings also suggest that social income grants facilitate investments in human capital (nutrition and schooling), along with investments in productive assets and activities. On the other hand, Cooper et al. (2019) find that minimum wage increases are associated with reduced total debt among households with low credit scores, higher auto debt and increased the households' access to credit.

25.3 Do Positive Shocks to the Minimum Wage and Social Income Grants Reinforce Each Other's Effects on Household Consumption and the Gini Coefficient?

This section concludes the analysis in this chapter by assessing whether an increase in the minimum wage and the social income grants reinforce each other, especially in cases where a targeted part of the population is employed. We use the counterfactual VAR approach, where we shut off the role of the social income grants and compare them to those that occur in the absence of such shocks. To assess the amplification effects of the minimum wage, we shut off the role of the minimum wage and compare the impulse responses to those that occur in the absence of such shocks. The estimated VAR models include the value of social income grants, the national minimum wage, the Gini coefficient and household consumption expenditure on non-durable goods. The models are estimated using 2 lags and 10,000 Monte Carlo draws. The shocks are a one standard deviation.

The results in Figs. 25.2 and 25.3 show that indeed the minimum wage and social income grants reinforce each other. However, as shown in Fig. 25.2, an increase in the binding minimum wage has a persistent

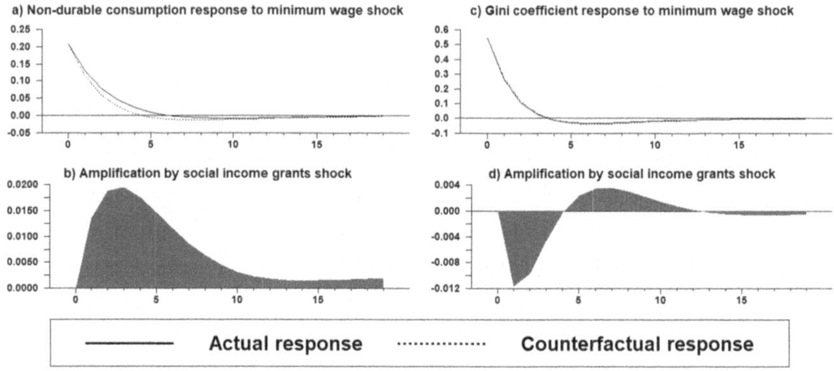

Fig. 25.2 Responses to positive shocks to the minimum wage and amplifications by social income grants. (Source: Authors' calculations)

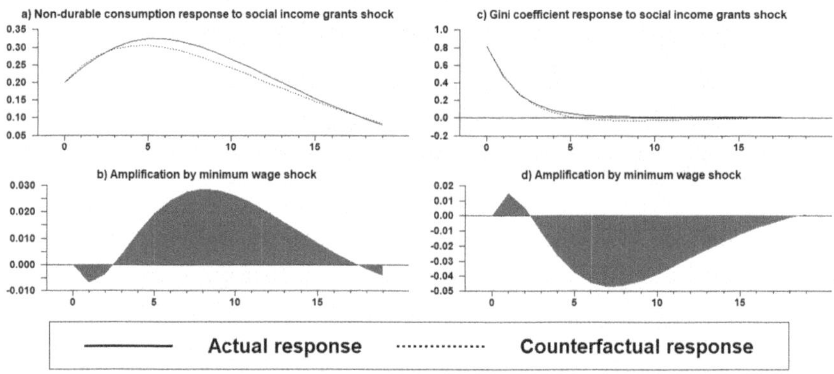

Fig. 25.3 Responses to positive shocks to social income grants and amplifications by the minimum wage. (Source: Authors' calculations)

effect in reinforcing the effects of the increase in social income on the Gini coefficient.

The results imply that an increase in social income grants has more persistent positive effects when accompanied by an increase in the binding minimum wage. Thus, a desirable policy intervention is that which complements an increase in social income grants with employment opportunities. An increase in social income grants does help to increase household consumption expenditure and alleviates poverty but it needs to be accompanied by job opportunities that pay a minimum wage to have more persistent effects. As demand side policy interventions, an increase in the minimum wage and social income grants achieve the set objectives of increasing household consumption expenditure and improving the capacity of households to spend. We showed in earlier chapters that recipients of child income support grants constitute almost 70 per cent of people receiving social income grants. At the same time, the recipients of child support grants are more than 70 per cent across all provinces. Thus, despite being smaller in value of payout, it means that an increase in social income grants will disproportionality benefit recipients of child support grants.

25.4 Is There Evidence of a Direct Impact of Social Income Grants on the Agricultural Sector in the Rural Areas?

To conclude this chapter, we test the Aliber (2005) hypothesis that the shift of reliance on agricultural income in the rural areas can be largely attributed to the expansion of social income grants since 2000. We showed in earlier chapters that there is more to the decline in the quality of the livelihoods of people living in rural areas than just the expansion of social income grants. We observed that post-settlement support must be accelerated and be persistent in order to make a success of the accelerated land redistribution policy. As a result, a significant portion of funding to the agricultural sector across all tiers of the banking sector has to be directed to support investment in this sector. Furthermore, earlier evidence shows that a desirable policy intervention is that which complements an increase in social income grants with employment opportunities.

Nonetheless, to assess the direct impact of the expansion of social income grants on the agricultural sector in the rural areas we use data on the area (hectares) planted in the former homelands and non-commercial farmers. We estimate several VAR models that include area (hectares) planted in the former homelands or by non-commercial farmers, the value of social income grants and employment growth in the agricultural

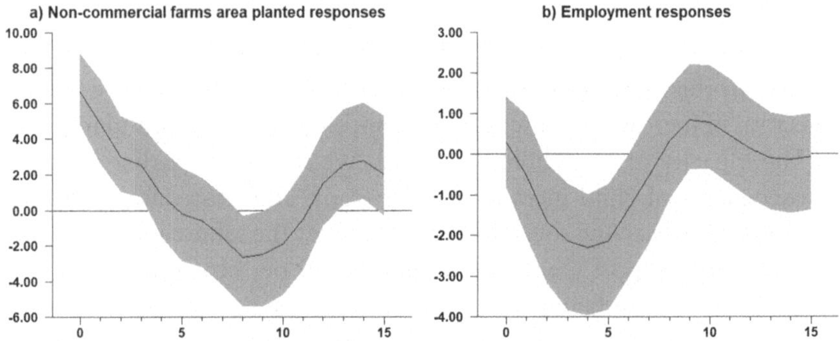

Fig. 25.4 Responses of non-commercial farmers' area planted to positive social income grants shocks. (Note: The grey shaded areas denote the 16th and 84th percentile confidence bands. Source: Authors' calculations)

sector. Due to lack of data we use the area planted in the former homelands or by non-commercial farmers as a proxy for rural area agriculture. The results in Fig. 25.4 show that indeed positive shocks to social income grants result in a decline in the area (hectares) planted by non-commercial farmers and employment growth. These results corroborate the findings in the earlier section that an increase in social income grants has to be accompanied by employment opportunities.

Thus, the data confirms the hypothesis by Aliber (2005) that the expansion in social income grants contributed to the decline in the reliance on the agricultural sector as a key source of income in rural areas. However, social income grants as a demand side policy intervention achieve their set objective of increasing household consumption expenditure and improving the capacity of households to spend. But they fail dismally in terms of solving the long-term effects of low output growth, high unemployment rate, high poverty rates and diversifying sources of income for rural communities.

25.5 Conclusion and Policy Implications

What is the nature of the interaction between the binding minimum wage, social income grants, household consumption and the Gini coefficient? We find that increases in the social income grants result in a contemporaneous increase in households' non-durable consumption expenditure and a decline in the Gini coefficient. But the positive effects are very transitory as they dissipate within three quarters. On the other hand, the positive effects of the binding minimum wage are far more persistent on non-durable goods consumption. Thus, an increase in social income grants has the desired effect of an increase in consumption expenditure, and increasing the capacity to spend is achieved. But the effects are very transitory compared to those associated with, for instance, an increase in the binding minimum wage.

Furthermore, an increase in the binding minimum wage and the social income grants reinforce each other, especially in cases where a targeted part of the population is employed. However, an increase in the binding minimum wage has a persistent effect of reinforcing effects of the increase in social income grants on the Gini coefficient. An increase in social income grants has more persistent positive effects when accompanied by an increase in the binding minimum wage. Thus, a desirable policy intervention is that which complements an increase in social income grants with employment opportunities that pay a minimum wage. An increase in social income grants does help to increase household consumption expenditure and it alleviates poverty but it needs to be accompanied by job opportunities that pay a minimum wage to have more persistent effects on the Gini coefficient. Social income grants as a demand side policy intervention achieve their set objective of increasing household consumption expenditure and improving the capacity of households to spend. But they fail dismally in terms of solving the long-term effects of low output growth, high unemployment rate, high poverty rates and diversifying sources of income for rural communities.

References

Aliber, M. 2005. Synthesis and Conclusions. In M. Aliber, et al. (eds.) *Trends and Policy Challenges in the Rural Economy*. Cape Town: HSRC Press, pp. 87–110.

Cooper, Daniel, Luengo-Prado, María José, and Parker, Jonathan A. 2019. *The Local Aggregate Effects of Minimum Wage Increases*. NBER Working Paper No. 25761.

Greenberg, S. 2010. *Status Report on Land and Agricultural Policy in South Africa, 2010*. PLAAS Research Report 40, University of the Western Cape, Institute for Poverty, Land and Agrarian Studies.

Gumata, N., and Ndou, E. 2017. *Bank Credit Extension and Real Economic Activity in South Africa: The Impact of Capital Flow Dynamics, Bank Regulation and Selected Macro-prudential Tools*. Palgrave Macmillan. ISBN 978-3-319-43551-0.

Institute for Poverty, Land and Agrarian Studies (PLAAS). 2018. Submission to the Constitutional Review Committee. University of the Western Cape.

Jacobs, P., Lahiff, E., and Hall, R. 2003. Land Redistribution. Programme for Land and Agrarian Studies School of Government University of the Western Cape.

Leibbrandt, Murray, Finn, Arden and Woolard, Ingrid. 2012. Describing and Decomposing Post-apartheid Income Inequality in South Africa. *Development Southern Africa*, 29(1), 19–34. https://doi.org/10.1080/0376835X.2012.645639.

McMillan, M.S., and Rodrik, D. 2011. *Globalisation, Structural Change and Productivity Growth*. NBER Working Paper 17143.

Netshipale, A.J., Oosting, S.J., Raidimi, E.N., Mashiloane, M.L., and De Boer, I.J.M. 2007. Land Reform in South Africa: Beneficiary Participation and Impact on Land Use in the Waterberg District. *NJAS Wageningen Journal of Life Sciences*, 83, 57–66.

Neves, D., Samson, M., Van Niekerk, I., Hlatshwayo, S. (EPRI), and Du Toit, A. 2009. The Use and Effectiveness of Social Grants in South Africa. Institute for Poverty, Land and Agrarian Studies (PLAAS). http://repository.uwc.ac.za/xmlui/bitstream/handle/10566/4672/The_use_and_effectiveness_of_social_gran.pdf?sequence=1&isAllowed=y

26

Can Accelerated Land Reform and The Increase in Hectares Planted Policy Tools Help Increase Employment Growth and Reduce Income Inequality?

Learning Objectives

- Assess the impact of accelerated land reform and redistribution on household consumption expenditure and income inequality as measured by the Gini coefficient.
- Understand the impact of accelerated land reform and redistribution on the agricultural sector output growth, investment growth, employment growth and income inequality.
- Explore whether land redistribution and an increase in area planted are complementary policy tools.

26.1 Introduction

This chapter assesses whether accelerated land reform and an increase in area (hectares) planted policy tools can help increase output growth, employment growth and reduce income inequality (Gini coefficient). The intention is to establish whether there is robust evidence that these two policy tools complement one another for agricultural sector output growth,

N. Gumata, E. Ndou, *Accelerated Land Reform, Mining, Growth, Unemployment and Inequality in South Africa*, https://doi.org/10.1007/978-3-030-30884-1_26

employment and income inequality. Accelerated land redistribution and increase in hectares (area) planted are broader supply side policy interventions aimed at dealing with the problem of perennial poverty, income and wealth inequality at a much broader level. They are supply side policy interventions aimed at unleashing potential gross domestic product (GDP) as shown in the production function in earlier chapters, changing the ownership patterns in the economy, increasing participation in the economy, labour absorption and economic inclusion. We showed that land enters the production function as a primary resource with multi-factor effects. In addition, it is not only the agricultural sector that stands to benefit from accelerated land reform and an increase in area (hectares) planted, but a number of sectors such as manufacturing, exports, transport, wholesale and retail trade, catering, accommodation and tourism, finance and insurance services, community and social services as well.

At the same time, the policy of accelerated land reform and an increase in hectares planted, because they are aimed at creating a class of entrepreneurs and self-employed people through the formation of co-operatives, and small and medium enterprises (SMMEs), also presents a channel through which employment can be created. Accelerated land reform and an increase in hectares planted might not have a direct and instantaneous impact on poverty and inequality as such but may work via a number of channels to affect output growth, investment growth, exports growth and employment growth, poverty and inequality. This, therefore, implies that there are additional channels, such as the exchange rate, asset price, collateral and wealth effects, as well as Tobin's Q involved in the transmission of shocks to accelerated land reform and increase in hectares planted into the real economy. Furthermore, accelerated land reform and increase in hectares planted contribute to food security and affordability, which in turn can be channelled to support sustainable school nutrition systems to offer more alternative nutritious foods and further alleviate poverty. For instance, Gordon and Ruffini (2018) show that the impact of school-based child nutrition services extends beyond academic gains. It has a potential to improve a range of student outcomes extending beyond test scores. Thus, accelerated land reform and an increase in hectares planted policy interventions are ultimately aimed at lowering poverty and inequality, but they are expected to have a different impact on growth in output, investment, exports, employment, labour participation and absorption.

26.2 Do Positive Shocks to Area Planted and Land Redistribution Lead to an Increase in Household Consumption and the Gini Coefficient?

To generate the variable for area planted we sum up the hectares planted for maize, wheat, sorghum, canola and sunflower seeds, groundnuts, soybeans and barley to get the total. We are aware that largely due to data availability this is not a comprehensive picture of the agricultural sector as it does not include several other variants of field crops, fruit farming, livestock farming, game farming, tourism and fishing as shown in the Bureau for Food and Agricultural Policy (BFAP) (2011) sector's employment intensity and employment matrix shown in earlier chapters. Nonetheless, it presents an opportunity to assess the impact of positive shocks to the potential output of the agricultural sector. To assess the robustness of the results based on the positive shocks of area (hectares) planted, we assess the impact of positive land redistributed shocks based on data in earlier chapters, which is a much broader definition compared to area (hectares) planted.

We start the empirical analysis by estimating small models which include land redistribution, area (hectares) planted, household consumption and the Gini coefficient. The vector autoregression (VAR) models in this section are estimated for the sample period 2001Q1 to 2017Q4. The VAR models are estimated using 2 lags and 10,000 Monte Carlo draws. All growth rates are at calculated annually. The shock is one standard deviation. Figure 26.1 shows that positive hectares (area) planted and accelerated land redistribution result in an increase in household consumption of non-durable goods and a decline in the Gini coefficient.

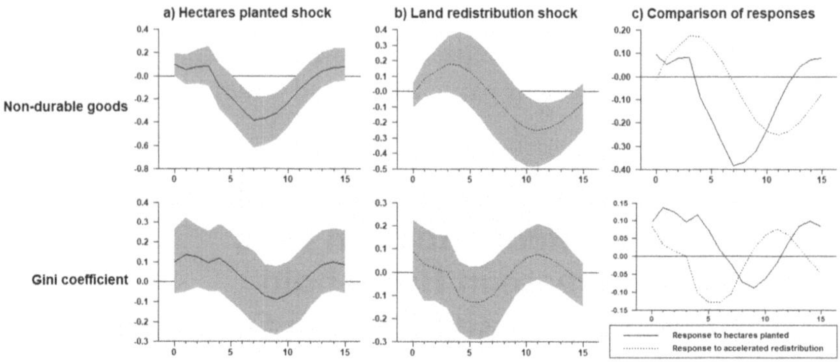

Fig. 26.1 Non-durable goods consumption and Gini coefficient responses to area planted and land redistribution positive shocks. (Note: The grey shaded area bands denote the 16th and 84th percentile confidence bands. Source: Authors' calculations)

26.3 Can Accelerated Land Reform and Increase in Hectares Planted Policy Tools Help Increase Employment Growth and Reduce Income Inequality?

This section assesses whether accelerated land reform and an increase in hectares panted can help increase the agricultural sector output growth, investment growth, employment growth and decrease inequality. Accelerated land reform policy and increase in the hectares (area) planted are supply side policies aimed at unlocking potential output. These are different from demand side policies, such as the binding minimum wage policy and social income grants. We estimate a number of VAR models that include the agricultural sector output growth, investment growth, employment growth, hectares (area) planted, land redistributed and the Gini coefficient.

The results in Figs. 26.2 and 26.3 show that indeed an increase in hectares planted and land redistribution lead to an increase in the agricultural sector output growth, investment growth and employment growth and they lower the Gini coefficient. Thus, there is also a strong economic case for the policy of accelerated land reform. These results concur with those

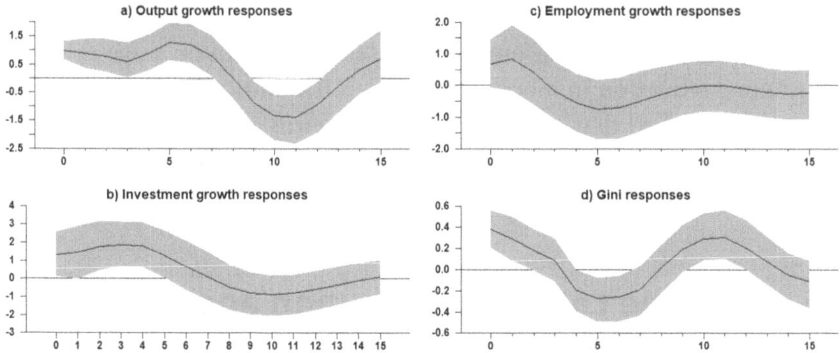

Fig. 26.2 Responses to positive area planted shocks. (Note: The grey shaded area bands denote the 16th and 84th percentile confidence bands. Source: Authors' calculations)

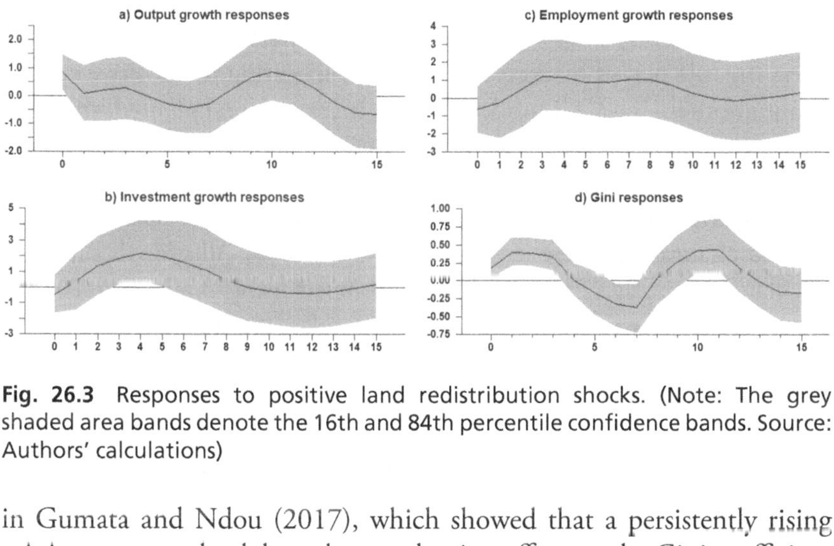

Fig. 26.3 Responses to positive land redistribution shocks. (Note: The grey shaded area bands denote the 16th and 84th percentile confidence bands. Source: Authors' calculations)

in Gumata and Ndou (2017), which showed that a persistently rising minimum wage shock has a large reduction effect on the Gini coefficient but a low inflation regime. In addition, high and robust GDP growth rates are also necessary conditions to ensure a sustained lower Gini coefficient. Similarly, firm profitability measured by gross operating surplus plays an important role in reducing the Gini coefficient in responses to minimum wage increases. Firm profitability and GDP growth are the biggest propagators of the transmission of positive shocks to the minimum wage in lowering the decline in the Gini coefficient.

We need robust GDP growth, firm profitability and a low inflation regime to ensure that persistent increases in the minimum wage result in a sustained reduction in income inequality. The authors also showed that the results implied that profit-sharing schemes to allow workers to share in the firm's profitability can be a useful tool as a means of income redistribution and lowering income inequality.

26.4 Do the Land Redistribution and Increase in Hectares Planted Policies Complement Each Other?

This section concludes the analysis by assessing whether the accelerated land redistribution and an increase in hectares (area) planted policies are complementary tools. We estimate two counterfactual VAR models to assess the role played by each channel in propagating the positive shocks to one another. The VAR models include hectares (area) planted, the Gini coefficient and agricultural sector employment and redistributed land. In Model one we shut off the role of the land redistributed channel to assess its counterfactual effects. In Model two we shut off the hectares (area) planted channel to assess its counterfactual effects. All growth rates are calculated annually. The models are estimated using 2 lags and 10,000 Monte Carlo draws. The shocks are one standard deviation.

Figure 26.4 shows that the Gini coefficient declines and remains depressed across horizons in response to a positive hectares (area) planted shock and the agricultural sector employment growth remains positive. In addition, the positive land redistribution shock amplifies the decline in the Gini coefficient and the increase in the agricultural sector employment growth. Similarly, a positive land redistribution shock to land redistribution increases employment growth and lowers the Gini coefficient in Fig. 26.5, and these effects are propagated by an increase in hectares (area) planted.

Thus, we conclude that land redistribution and increase in hectares planted policies are tools that complement each other. A combination of these supply side policy tools exerts the desired effects on the agricultural sector employment growth and leads to a decline in the Gini coefficient.

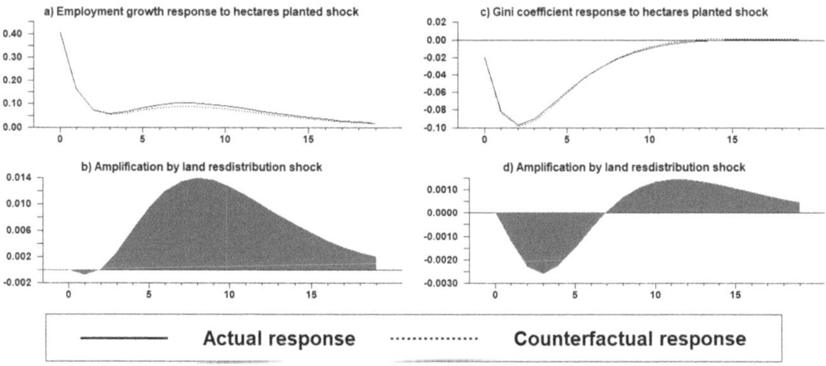

Fig. 26.4 Responses to positive hectares (area) planted and employment growth and propagation by land redistribution shocks. (Source: Authors' calculations)

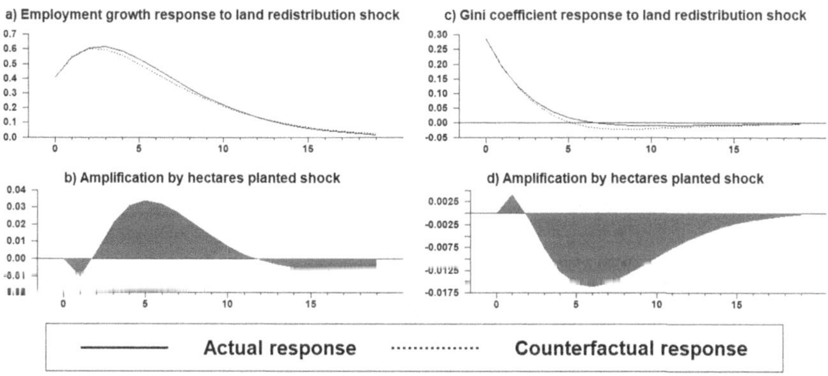

Fig. 26.5 Responses to positive land redistribution and propagation by hectares (area) planted shocks. (Source: Authors' calculations)

26.5 Conclusion and Policy Implications

Can accelerated land reform and an increase in hectares (area) planted policy tools help increase employment growth and reduce income inequality? Evidence shows that as supply side policy interventions, increase in hectares (area) planted and accelerated land redistribution lead to an increase in the agricultural sector output growth, investment growth and employment growth and lower the Gini coefficient. Thus, there is also a strong socioeconomic case for the policy of accelerated land reform. Furthermore, land redistribution and an increase in hectares (area) planted policies are tools that complement each other. A combination of these supply side policy tools exerts the desired effects on the agricultural sector employment growth and leads to a decline in the Gini coefficient.

References

BFAP. 2011. The Contribution of the Agro-Industrial Complex to Employment in South Africa. Tech. Rep. June, The Bureau for Food and Agricultural Policy, Pretoria.

Gordon, Nora E., and Ruffini, Krista J. 2018. *School Nutrition and Student Discipline: Effects of Schoolwide Free Meals*. NBER Working Paper No. 24986.

Gumata, N., and Ndou, E. 2017. *Bank Credit Extension and Real Economic Activity in South Africa: The Impact of Capital Flow Dynamics, Bank Regulation and Selected Macro-prudential Tools*. Palgrave Macmillan. ISBN 978-3-319-43551-0.

Part VI

The Interaction Between the Financial Sector Regulatory Framework, Property Rights Clause and the South African Reserve Mandate

27

The Transmission of Shocks to Farmland Prices, Interest Rates and the Confidence Channels in the Agricultural Sector

Learning Objectives

- Understand the evolution and association between farmland prices and house prices in relation to the housing price boom of 2004 to 2008.
- Explore the transmission of positive interest rates, farmland prices and the agricultural sector business confidence shocks to the agricultural sector.
- Determine whether positive agricultural sector business confidence shocks amplify the role of positive farmland price shocks.
- Understand other factors that are idiosyncratic to farmland prices, such as changes in the land redistribution models and policies over time.
- Learn more about the impact of the Settlement Land Acquisition Grant (SLAG) model, Proactive Land Acquisition Strategy (PLAS) model and Land Redistribution for Agricultural Development (LRAD) on farmland prices, beneficiary participation and social classes.

N. Gumata, E. Ndou, *Accelerated Land Reform, Mining, Growth, Unemployment and Inequality in South Africa*, https://doi.org/10.1007/978-3-030-30884-1_27

27.1 Introduction

This chapter assesses the role of farmland prices, interest rate and confidence channels in the agricultural sector in transmitting shocks to the agricultural sector. We explore the role of farmland prices and relate them to the housing price boom of 2004 to 2008, interest rate and the agricultural sector business confidence developments. Greenberg (2010) shows that average prices of farmland adjusted for inflation did not grow significantly until 2001, after which they increased rapidly alongside increases in the broader property market. This implies that there is a higher degree of association and spillover effects of housing prices to farmland prices. We explore the role of farmland prices and property prices largely because there is a lot of debate and anecdotal evidence that under the "*willing buyer:willing seller*" model of land reform, prices may be inflated artificially, especially in cases where the seller does not really want to sell. Thus, in such cases sellers use the inflated selling prices as a deterrent to buyers with negative effects on the set objectives of the land and agrarian reform programme (LARP).

Furthermore, the growth rate in farmland prices and property prices has a significant bearing on how far the budgets allocated for land reform can be stretched and how much can be achieved. For instance, Aliber and Kleinbooi (2009) estimated that an allocation of R74 billion more would be required to realise the 30 per cent government target of redistributing an additional 17 million hectares by 2014. Sihlobo and Kirsten (2018) attest to the fact that the land reform process has been too slow, bureaucratic and costly.[1] In addition, Greenberg (2010) shows that the land reform programme failed to meet its delivery targets of 30 per cent by a wide margin. The target year of 1999 by which 30 per cent of agricultural land was to have been transferred to black farmers was shifted from 1999 to 2014 and again to 2025. By the end of September 2009, just 5.67 million hectares of which 6.9 per cent is agricultural land had been transferred

[1] The land reform programme needs to be fast-paced, otherwise a combination of excessive bureaucracy, centralisation of the process and legal challenges are likely to render the programme ineffective (Sihlobo and Kirsten, Business Day, 28 May 2018).

to 1.78 million beneficiaries. More than a quarter, that is 26 per cent of the redistributed land, is in the arid Northern Cape.[2]

27.2 The "*Willing Buyer:Willing Seller*" Model and the Funding Requirement for Land Reform

At the core of the debate about the pace of land reform under the "*willing buyer:willing seller*" model is the funding requirement, at the centre of which are farmland and property prices. This is over and above the necessary financial support required to make a success of the redistributed land (post-settlement funding). For instance, Greenberg (2010) states that many of the beneficiaries, especially of the restitution programme, have been unable to settle on the land or to use it productively. This is either because of (i) the agreements they were compelled to sign with strategic partners or (ii) lack of infrastructure, input or technical and financial support. This brings to the fore the design and role of the financial landscape and institutions that will support the intended objectives and outcomes of changes to section 25 of the constitution.[3]

Scrapping the "*willing buyer:willing seller*" approach to land and agrarian reform and the clarity of cases under which expropriation without compensation will be used is intended and expected to speed up the transfer of land whilst releasing much needed funding to support the most important second leg of the transactions of the productive use of transferred land. Vast literature in this area attests to the role that lack of comprehensive post-settlement support plays in the rate of success of land reform projects. For instance, Van der Elst (2007) and Hall (2004) identified financial support, agricultural training support programmes, mentorship programmes and environmental support structures as critical areas for any meaningful post-settlement support. Jacobs et al. (2003)

[2]We explored in detail the role that accelerated land reform can play in reducing poverty, and income and wealth inequality in South Africa in earlier chapters.

[3]We explore the role of the Land Bank, lower-tier banks, financial regulation and macroprudential tools in earlier chapters of this book.

pointed out that post-transfer support is crucial for the overall success of land redistribution, yet it has been neglected by virtually all the key role players. The authors show that there is an intricate relationship between land redistribution and post-settlement support as part of land reform. Support services, or complementary development support, include assistance with productive and sustainable land use, infrastructure support, farm credit, agricultural inputs and access to markets for farm outputs.

Largely due to the lack of post-settlement support, the majority of beneficiaries including communities and individuals who obtained ownership and access to land in rural areas through either restitution, redistribution or tenure reform have been unable to utilise the land to its full potential. Thus, the ideal of achieving sustainable development and improved quality of life, especially in terms of agricultural development, has not been realised. Furthermore, evidence shows that the current land reform programme has failed to contribute to economic growth in the country, specifically in terms of creating sustainable livelihoods, rural employment and poverty alleviation. Compared to the earlier Settlement Land Acquisition Grant (SLAG) programme, the Land Redistribution for Agricultural Development (LRAD) model was intended to introduce a significant shift in the area of post-transfer support.

27.3 Idiosyncratic Factors Related to Farmland Prices

With respect to other factors that are idiosyncratic to farmland prices, Aliber (2009) identifies the role of (i) the land redistribution model effect on the farmland prices; (ii) the impact of speculative sales; and (iii) interest rates. For instance, Aliber (2009) shows that between 2002 and 2008 during the farmland and house price boom episode, disaggregated data indicate that prices of land reform and restitution projects were on an upward trend whereas the price per hectare for redistribution projects was below that of farmland prices. Aliber (2009) suggests that the growing use of the Proactive Land Acquisition Strategy (PLAS) and the shift in the nature of farmland transactions in favour of larger properties as opposed to smaller properties certainly contributed to the rapid increase in land reform, redistribution and restitution prices during the boom episode.

Furthermore, Netshipale et al. (2007) present evidence showing that the changes in the land redistribution policy over time resulted in significant differences in beneficiary participation among land redistribution models. The changes in the land redistribution policy over time resulted in significant differences in the extent of land use among the land redistribution models. For instance, the SLAG programme had the lowest beneficiary participation level at 19 per cent per farm. The Proactive Land Acquisition Strategy (PLAS) model had the highest beneficiary participation at 100 per cent per farm. On average, redistribution farms under the SLAG and the Land Redistribution for Agricultural Development (LRAD2) models used 70 per cent or more of the farmland, while farms under LRAD1 and PLAS models used more than 90 per cent of the farmland. However, the implementation outcomes of land redistribution indicate that the SLAG model benefited the poor while the LRAD1, LRAD2 and PLAS models benefitted mostly other social classes.

27.4 A Brief Discussion of the Models of Land Reform since 1994

Netshipale et al. (2007) show that amendments and adjustments of the land redistribution programme have led to four distinguishable models:

1. Settlement Land Acquisition Grant (SLAG), which was active from 1995 until 2000. Ranwedzi (2011) shows that under this model, the value of the grant was limited to the purchase of, and did not extend to, production inputs and other necessary post-settlement support.
2. Land Redistribution for Agricultural Development Phase 1 (LRAD1), which was active from 2001 until 2007.
3. Land Redistribution for Agricultural Development Phase 2 (LRAD2), which was active from 2008 until 2010. Ranwedzi (2011) shows that both LRAD models were characterised by delayed and/or cancelled

transactions due to the applicants' inability to secure supplementary funds to complete the purchase of the land. These effects were compounded by the high land prices and the lack of post-settlement support.

4. Proactive Land Acquisition Strategy (PLAS), which started from 2006 to date. Ranwedzi (2011) states that the intention of the model is to accelerate the land redistribution process, ensure that land is acquired in the areas of high agricultural potential, improve the identification and selection of beneficiaries and ensure maximum productive use of land acquired. In addition, Hall and Kepe (2017) indicate that the PLAS model is a guide to the state leasehold model and empowers state officials to buy farms in the open market and allocate them to selected beneficiaries.

Overall, Netshipale et al. (2007) show that all the models differed especially on the funds allocated to targeted beneficiaries. The grant amounts allocated to qualifying beneficiaries increased overtime from the SLAG model to the LRAD2 model with beneficiaries gaining landownership. However, under the PLAS model, the state does not allocate grants. Beneficiaries have to make lease payments to access land with the possibility of becoming future landowners. The basis for grant allocation over the years of the implementation of these land redistribution models shifted from the demonstration of a business plan viability under the SLAG model to prospects of economic viability of the business plan under the LRAD model, to signing of a lease or caretaker agreement under the PLAS model. Thus, the PLAS model removed the requirement of the grant on the part of the beneficiaries.

Under the PLAS model the state is responsible for identifying and buying land. The beneficiaries must just apply for access to the land.[4] By so doing, the PLAS model releases the primary condition of purchasing of land by the beneficiaries over and above making sure that (i) the land is acquired in the areas of high agricultural potential; (ii) the identification and selection of beneficiaries are improved; and (iii) there is maximum productive use of land acquired.

[4] Under the SLAG and LRAD models beneficiaries were responsible for the identification of the land and for making applications. The state would thereafter provide funds to purchase the land.

However, Ranwedzi (2011) and Hall and Kepe (2017) show that the PLAS model has a major drawback in that the lease under the model was initially for a three-year test period after which the title would be transferred to "emergent farmers" who had proven themselves to be successful. But after widespread non-payment of rent, the promise of the eventual title has been abandoned. As a result, there has been no provision of support to projects under the PLAS model largely because of a lack of long-term leases. Furthermore, under the PLAS model from the moment of transfer, when farms become state property, all commercial operations cease, with profound impacts on farmworkers, who are usually also residents on the farm. When government buys farms, farmworkers lose their jobs and often their only sources of cash income. They conclude that, without rights, access to land does not translate into opportunities for development. In addition, special consideration may be needed to treat farm dwellers differently from other beneficiaries, especially to avoid the pattern of farmworkers losing their jobs as a result of state acquisition. Furthermore, Kepe and Hall (2018) argue that the PLAS model of land reform, where the state remains the landowner, is no longer consistent with the project of decolonisation. These authors are of the view that land redistribution in South Africa has drifted away from the ideal of social justice as it increasingly displays symptoms of the colonial present and recolonisation.

Nonetheless, Jacobs et al. (2003) show that all these models of land redistribution are heavily dependent on the "*willing buyer:willing seller*" strategy and are thus highly dependent on market forces where the supply of land is largely driven by a combination of economic and political factors such as land speculation, inflated land prices, changes in land use, conditions in product markets, the indebtedness of the sellers and interest rates. Hence, there has been lack of significant contribution to the development of semi-commercial and commercial black farmers, and limited impact on rural employment, development and transformation of agricultural landholdings.

On the impact of speculative sales on farmland prices, Aliber (2009) used the farmland transactions data to identify all cases where a given property was bought and then later sold by the buyer within the time-frame of the dataset (repeat sales). Thereafter, the purchase and reselling price at the time the property was held are compared so as to gauge the potential magnitude of speculative sales on farmland prices. Aliber (2009) finds that the share of farms bought and resold is quite high. For example, he established that of the farm properties for which the purchase agreement was struck in 1995, 26.7 per cent was resold by the end of 2008, representing 21.6 per cent of all farmland purchased in 1995 by area. Furthermore, farms that were resold within three years (12 quarters) yielded positive returns and more than 40 per cent of farm sold realised a real return of 20 per cent, especially between 1999 and 2005 in line with the boom episode. Aliber (2009) concludes that the proportion of farm resales during this period implies that speculative sales also impacted on farmland prices.

In addition, Aliber (2009) contends that the land reform projects and market activity in terms of the amount of land transacted in hectares were also impacted by the movements in the prime interest rate, especially the sizeable decline in 1998. In essence, Aliber (2009) is arguing for the presence of the interest rate and narrow credit (credit supply) channels in the farmland market. To this end, Van der Elst (2007) and Sihlobo and Kirsten (2018) contend that the redistribution of land is a necessary but not sufficient condition to bring about real economic empowerment and poverty alleviation. Post-settlement support should be an integral part of the policy output in order to achieve long-term sustainable development outcomes. Policy interventions should be designed to ensure that post-settlement support cuts across all major land reform programmes, namely, redistribution, land tenure and restitution. In addition, post-settlement policy interventions should provide a comprehensive reconstruction and development programme plan.

27.5 The Relationship between Farmland Prices and Selected House Price Indicators

We start the empirical analysis by doing some preliminary analysis between farmland and house prices, the prime rate and mortgage advances as a proxy of the rate of transactions in the property market. The data are

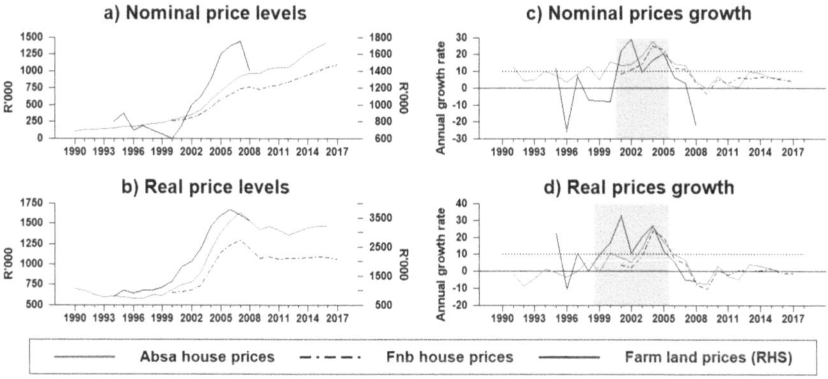

Fig. 27.1 Nominal and real farmland and house prices. (Note: Grey shaded area shows periods during which annual growth rates exceeded 10 per cent. Source: Aliber (2009), Greenberg (2010), South African Reserve Bank and authors' calculations)

gathered on an annual (A) basis between 1990 and 2017. However, data for farmland prices are only available from 1994 to 2008. The data for the First National Bank (FNB) house price index start in 2000. We present data for Amalgamated Banks of South Africa (ABSA) and FNB house price indices alongside the farmland price index to assess the association of the trends.[5] In addition, a comparison of these trends will enable the assessment of what the trend of farmland price would have looked like post-2008 if the data were available. Thus, using house price time series in the empirical analysis will not bias the results.

Figure 27.1 shows the evolution of nominal and real farmland and house prices. Real house prices are deflated using the consumer price index. We present the farmland prices alongside the house prices due to limited data availability. The nominal prices in Fig. 27.1(a) and (c) show that the boom period in farmland and house prices coincided and were synchronised during the period 2000 to 2006 when all these property prices increased above 10 per cent. The boom episode lasted for two more

[5]The sample size for nominal and real farmland prices spans the period 1994 to 2008, whereas that for the ABSA house prices spans 1966 to 2016 and the time series for the First National Bank (FNB) house prices starts in 2000 up to date.

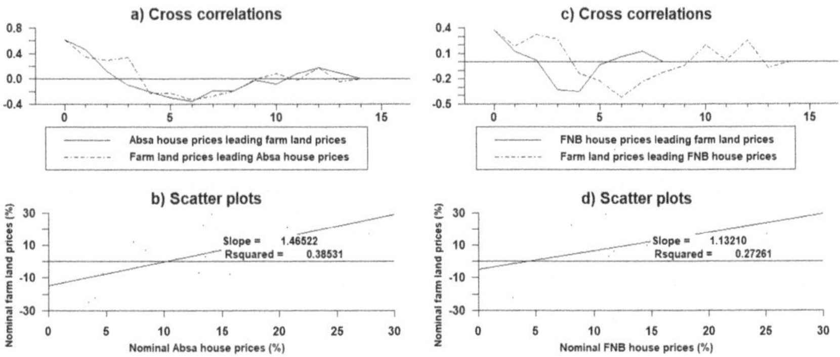

Fig. 27.2 Lead relationship between farmland and house prices. (Source: Authors' calculations)

years until 2008 for house prices. Thereafter, farmland prices entered a recessionary period, whereas house prices have remained subdued below 10 per cent.

The same trend is observed with respect to real farmland and house prices in Fig. 27.1(b) and (d) showing that the boom episodes were highly synchronised for the period 1999 to 2005, after which real prices have remained very depressed. Furthermore, the lead relationships in Fig. 27.2(a) and (c) show that there is bidirectional causality between nominal farmland and house prices. At the same time, ABSA and FNB nominal house price growth explains 39 per cent and 27 per cent of the variation in farmland price growth.

Thus, these trends indicate that although farmland and house price are synchronised and there are bidirectional causality effects, there are other factors that influence farmland prices over and above house prices. In addition, it is very likely that nominal farmland prices would have corrected post-2008 and more or less followed a similar trend as that of house prices.

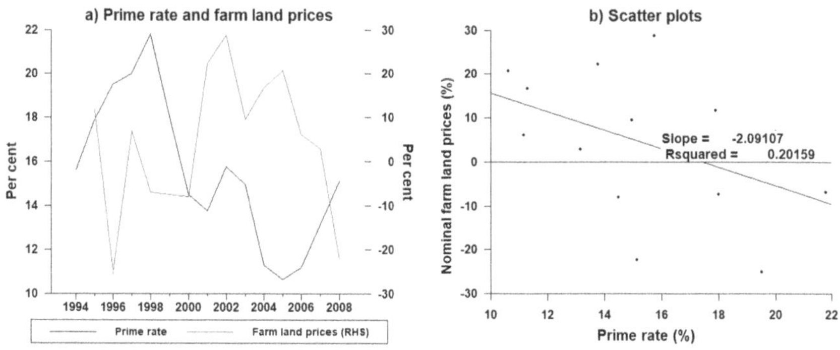

Fig. 27.3 Relationship between nominal farmland and the prime rate. (Source: Aliber (2009), South African Reserve Bank and authors' calculations)

27.6 The Relationship between Prime Rate and Nominal Farmland Prices

Figure 27.3 shows that there is a negative association between the prime rate and nominal farmland prices. For the sample period, the variation in the prime rate explains around 20 per cent of the changes in nominal farmland prices in Fig. 27.3(b). This means that farmland prices decline (increase) when the prime rate increases (declines). Therefore, the data confirm that the prime rate has negative impact on farmland prices as argued by Aliber (2009).

This evidence shows early indications of the presence of the interest rate and narrow credit (credit supply) channels in the farmland market.

27.7 The Channels of Transmission of Interest Rate Shocks in the Agricultural Sector

This section conducts the empirical analysis and assesses the role of the interest rate channels on the broad credit channels: (i) wealth; (ii) asset price; (iii) collateral channel; and (iv) Tobin's Q in the agricultural sector.

To assess the impact of these channels on the agricultural sector, we estimate vector autoregression (VAR) models that include farmland prices, repo or prime rate, agricultural sector gross value added (output) growth, investment growth, exports growth and employment growth. We compare the impact of positive interest rate and farmland price shocks on the agricultural sector output growth, investment growth and employment growth. The VAR models are estimated for the sample period 1994 to 2008. All growth rates are calculated on an annual basis. The VAR models were estimated with 2 lags and 10,000 Monte Carlo draws. The shock is a unit shock.

27.7.1 The Asset Price Channel Operating Via Farmland Prices in the Agricultural Sector

The results in Fig. 27.4 show that the agricultural sector output growth, investment growth and employment growth increase in response to positive farmland price shocks. However, it is evident that the responses for investment growth are significant on impact and become insignificant thereafter. A comparison of the responses in Fig. 27.2(d) indicates that the agricultural sector output growth is very responsive to positive farmland price shocks compared to investment and employment growth.

These results are consistent with the effects of asset prices operating via the wealth, collateral and Tobin's Q channels. This means that the broad credit channel of the monetary policy transmission mechanism is operational in the agricultural sector. Furthermore, the results in Fig. 27.5 indicate that the interest rate channel of the monetary policy transmission mechanism is also operational in the agricultural sector. The agricultural sector output growth, investment growth and employment growth decline in response to an increase in the prime rate. Thus, we conclude that similar to other sectors of the macroeconomy, the interest rate and broad credit channels of the monetary policy transmission mechanism are operational in the agricultural sector. Changes in farmland prices and

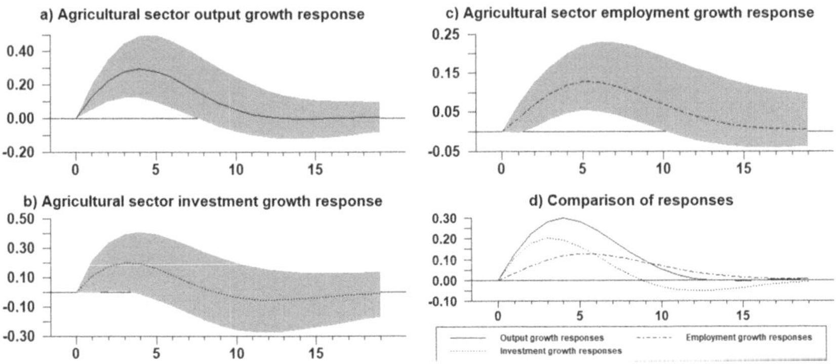

Fig. 27.4 Responses to positive farmland price shocks. (Note: The grey shaded area bands denote the 16th and 84th percentile confidence bands. Source: Authors' calculations)

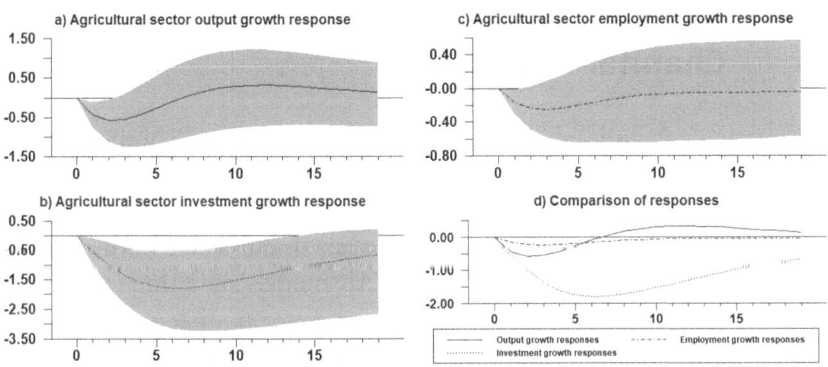

Fig. 27.5 Responses to positive prime rate shocks. (Note: The grey shaded area bands denote the 16th and 84th percentile confidence bands. Source: Authors' calculations)

interest rate have a significant effect on the agricultural sector. The security of tenure (ownership of land) in the land reform and redistribution process is important as the asset price channel also operates via the wealth and collateral channels of transmission to affect the agricultural sector.

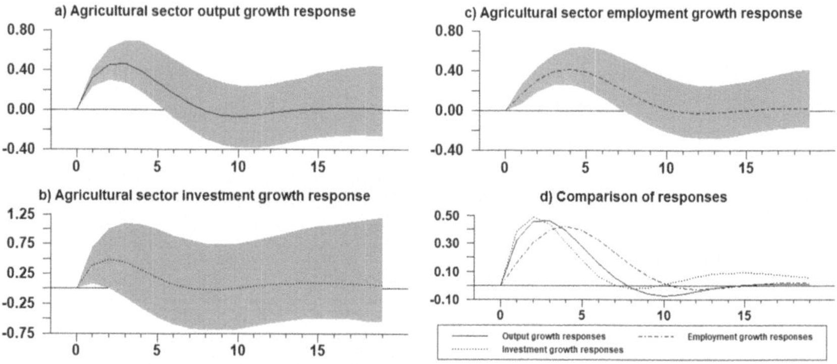

Fig. 27.6 Responses to positive business confidence shocks. (Note: The grey shaded area bands denote the 16th and 84th percentile confidence bands. Source: Authors' calculations)

27.8 The Role of the Business Confidence Channel

This section concludes the analysis by considering the role of the agricultural sector business confidence channel. We estimate a VAR model with farmland prices, agricultural sector gross value added (output) growth, investment growth, exports growth, the agricultural sector business confidence and employment growth. The VAR models are estimated for the sample period 2000 to 2008. All growth rates are at an annual rate. The VAR models were estimated with 1 lag and 10,000 Monte Carlo draws. The shock is a unit shock. The results in Fig. 27.6 show that positive business confidence shocks in the agricultural sector result in an increase in output growth, investment growth and employment growth.

27.8.1 Does the Agricultural Sector Business Confidence Channel Propagate Positive Shocks to Farmland Prices?

To answer this question, we estimate counterfactual VAR models which include farmland prices, agricultural sector gross value added (output) growth, investment growth, exports growth, the agricultural sector

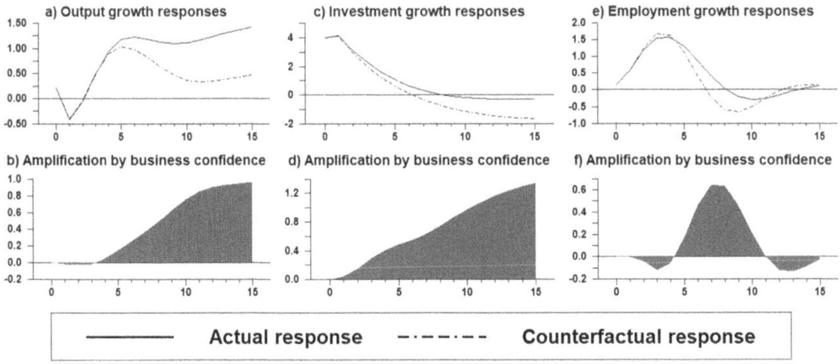

Fig. 27.7 The role of the agricultural sector business confidence channel. (Source: Authors' calculations)

business confidence and employment growth. The differences between the actual and counterfactual responses are used to assess whether the agricultural sector business channel propagates or neutralises the effects of positive farmland prices. The counterfactual responses are those in which the role of the business confidence channel is not active in the model. The VAR models are estimated with 1 lag and 10,000 Monte Carlo draws. The results in Fig. 27.7 show that the agricultural sector business confidence amplifies the responses of output growth, investment growth and employment growth to positive farmland price shocks.

27.9 Conclusion and Policy Implications

This chapter assessed the role of farmland prices, interest rate and confidence channels in the agricultural sector in transmitting shocks to the agricultural sector. At the core of the debate about the pace of land reform under the "*willing buyer:willing seller*" model is the funding requirement. In turn, at the centre of which are farmland and property prices. This is over and above the necessary financial support required to make a success of the redistributed land. The scrapping of the "*willing buyer:willing seller*" approach to land and agrarian reform is intended and expected to speed up the transfer of land whilst releasing much needed funding to support the most important second leg of the transactions of the productive use of transferred land. Vast literature in this area attests to the role that lack of comprehensive post-settlement support plays in the rate of success of land reform projects.

Evidence in this chapter establishes that the boom period in farmland and house prices coincided with the period of 2000 to 2006 when all these property prices increased above 10 per cent. However, there are other factors that are idiosyncratic to farmland prices. For instance, changes in the land redistribution models and policies over time resulted in significant differences in beneficiary participation and farmland prices. We find that the agricultural sector output growth, investment growth and employment growth increase in response to positive farmland price shocks. These results are consistent with the effects of asset prices operating via the wealth, collateral and Tobin's Q channels. This means that the broad credit channel of the monetary policy transmission mechanism is operational in the agricultural sector. Furthermore, the results indicate that the interest rate channel of the monetary policy transmission mechanism is also operational in the agricultural sector. The agricultural sector output growth, investment growth and employment growth decline in response to an increase in the prime rate. In addition, positive shocks to the agricultural sector business confidence amplify the responses of output growth, investment growth and employment growth to positive farmland price shocks.

On the approaches to land reform, evidence shows that the SLAG had the lowest beneficiary participation level at 19 per cent per farm. The PLAS model had the highest beneficiary participation at 100 per cent per farm. However, the implementation outcomes of land redistribution indicate that the SLAG model benefited the poor while the LRAD1, LRAD2 and PLAS models benefitted mostly other social classes. Although the PLAS model released the primary condition of purchasing of land by the beneficiaries, after widespread non-payment of rent, the promise of an eventual title has been abandoned. As a result, there has been no provision of support to projects under the PLAS model largely because of a lack of long-term leases. Thus, the redistribution of land is a necessary but not sufficient condition to bring about real economic empowerment and poverty alleviation. Post-settlement support should be an integral part of the policy output in order to achieve sustainable long-term development outcomes. Policy interventions should be designed to ensure that post-settlement support cuts across all major land reform programmes, namely, redistribution, land tenure and restitution. The post-settlement policy interventions should provide a comprehensive reconstruction and development programme plan.

References

Aliber, M. 2009. Farmland Price Trends in South Africa, 1994–2008. Institute for Poverty, Land and Agrarian Studies (PLAAS). University of the Western Cape for the Directorate: Monitoring and Evaluation, Department of Rural Development and Land Reform.

Aliber, M. 2015. Unravelling the Willing Buyer/Willing Seller Question. In B. Cousins and C. Walker (eds.) *Land Divided: Land in South African Society in 2014 and Beyond*, Jacana: Johannesburg.

Aliber, M., and Kleinbooi, K. 2009. Land Budget Update. *Umhlaba Wethu* 7, p. 4.

Amaral, P. 2017. *Monetary Policy and Inequality*. Economic Commentary 01, Federal Reserve Bank of Cleveland.

Barnett, Alina, and Thomas, Ryland. 2013. *Has Weak Lending and Activity in the United Kingdom Been Driven by Credit Supply Shocks?* December 20. Bank of England Working Paper No. 482.

Bernanke, B.S., and Gertler, M. 1989. Agency Costs, Net Worth, and Business Fluctuations. *American Economic Review*, 79, 14–31.

Dolado, J., Motyovszki, G., and Pappa, E. 2018. Monetary Policy and Inequality: A New Channel. VOX CEPR Portal.

Domanski, D., Scatigna, M., and Zabai, A. 2016. Wealth Inequality and Monetary Policy. *BIS Quarterly Review*, March 2016.

Furceri, D., Loungani, P., and Zdzienicka, A. 2016. *The Effects of Monetary Policy Shocks on Inequality*. IMF Working Paper WP/16/245.

Gambetti, L., and Musso, A. 2014. Loan Supply Shocks and the Business Cycle. ECB Conference Paper, November 20, 2014.

Greenberg, S. 2010. Status Report on Land and Agricultural Policy in South Africa. Research Report. School of Government, UWC PLAAS Institute for Poverty, Land and Agrarian Studies. http://www.plaas.org.za/sites/default/files/publications-pdf/RR40.pdf

Hall, R. 2004. Land and Agrarian Reform in South Africa: A Status Report 2004. PLAAS: Cape Town.

Hall, R., and Kepe, T. 2017. Elite Capture and State Neglect: New Evidence on South Africa's Land Reform. *Review of African Political Economy*. https://doi.org/10.1080/03056244.2017.1288615.

Jacobs, P., Lahiff, E., and Hall, R. 2003. Land Redistribution. Programme for Land and Agrarian Studies School of Government University of the Western Cape. http://www.plaas.org.za/sites/default/files/publications-pdf/ELARSA%2001.pdf.

Kepe, T., and Hall, R. 2018. Land Redistribution in South Africa: Towards Decolonisation or Recolonisation? *South African Journal of Political Studies*, 45(1): Decolonisation after Democracy. https://www.tandfonline.com/doi/full/10.1080/02589346.2018.1418218.

Kganyago, L. 2018. Inequality and Monetary Policy in South Africa. A public lecture at the Nelson Mandela University, Port Elizabeth, 1 August 2018.

Mersch, Y. 2014. Speech at Corporate Credit Conference, Zurich, 17 October 2014.

Netshipale, A.J., Oosting, S.J., Raidimi, E.N., Mashiloane, M.L., and De Boer, I.J.M. 2007. Land Reform in South Africa: Beneficiary Participation and Impact on Land Use in the Waterberg District. *NJAS Wageningen Journal of Life Sciences*, 83, 57–66.

Ranwedzi, N. 2011. The Potential and Limits of the Proactive Land Acquisition Strategy (PLAS): Land Reform Implementation in Gauteng Province of South Africa. http://www.plaas.org.za/sites/default/files/publications-pdf/PP%2006.pdf.

Sihlobo, W. 2018. Fewer Farmers, More Milk. https://wandilesihlobo.com/2018/07/17/fewer-farmers-more-milk/.

Sihlobo, W., and Kirsten, J. 2018. Secret of Land-Reform Success is to Learn Lessons from Experience. *Business Day*, May 28. https://www.businesslive.co.za/bd/opinion/2018-05-28-the-secret-of-land-reform-success-is-to-learn-lessons-from-experience/.

Van der Elst, H.J. 2007. Post Settlement Support as Key Contributor to the Success of the South African Land Reform Programme (1994–2007). *The Journal of School of Basic Sciences*, 26(3), 287–305. North–West University.

28

The Land Bank Balance Sheet and the Transmission of Shocks to the Agricultural Sector

Learning Objectives

- Understand the institutional evolution and breakdown of farm and agricultural sector debt.
- Assess the position of the Land Bank balance sheet relative to commercial banks.
- Explore the composition of the Land Bank balance sheet relative to its mandate. Furthermore, what the implications of the accelerated land reform policy mean for its balance sheet.
- Assess the impact of non-performing loans (credit risk) on the Land Bank balance sheet and activity in the agricultural sector.
- Explore the transmission of adverse credit risk and loans supply shocks to the agricultural sector.

N. Gumata, E. Ndou, *Accelerated Land Reform, Mining, Growth, Unemployment and Inequality in South Africa*, https://doi.org/10.1007/978-3-030-30884-1_28

28.1 Introduction

Does the Land Bank balance sheet transmit adverse credit risk and credit (loan) supply shocks to the agricultural sector? What is the role of the agricultural sector non-performing loans (credit risk)? This chapter extends the analysis of the balance sheet channel of the monetary policy transmission mechanism by assessing the transmission of adverse loan supply shocks and agricultural sector non-performing loans via the Land Bank balance sheet. Theoretically, the interest channel is also transmitted via the narrow and broad credit channels which consist of the loan supply, asset price, collateral and wealth channels. Literature shows that the balance sheet channel or financial accelerator channel of monetary policy, first argued by Bernanke and Gertler (1989), has a significant impact in the propagation of shocks into the real economy. Furthermore, financial shocks can be independent sources of shocks, conduits and amplifiers of other financial and macroeconomic shocks. Bernanke and Gertler (1989) showed that the existence of information asymmetries implies that a firm's and household's net worth through the narrow and broad credit channels exert a significant impact on investment and spending decisions. In addition, the propagation effects of the balance sheet channel tend to be procyclical largely because the credit and financial cycles are procyclical.

Furthermore, the procyclicality of the credit and financial cycles and the balance sheets tend to propagate and amplify the amplitude of economic cycles in both directions. Vast literature such as Kiyotaki and Moore (1995), Bernanke and Gertler (1995), and Angelopoulou and Gibson (2007) show that through the financial accelerator mechanism, credit and collateral constraints interact with aggregate economic activity over the business cycle, implying that even small shocks can have large macroeconomic effects.[1] The dynamic interaction between credit limits and asset prices tends to be a powerful transmission mechanism through which the effects of shocks persist, are amplified, and spill over to other

[1] In such instances, durable assets such as land, buildings and machinery play a dual role as factors of production and collateral for loans, such that there is bidirectional causality between the credit limits and the prices of the collateralised assets of borrowers.

sectors of the economy. Hence, small and temporary shocks to, for example, technology or income distribution can generate large, persistent fluctuations in output and asset prices.

28.2 The Evolution and Structure of the Agricultural Sector Debt

Figure 28.1 shows the evolution of total farm debt. Of note is the divergence between the commercial banks, agricultural co-operatives and Land Bank shares of farm debt during the 1990s, which coincides with the period of deregulation, financial and trade liberalisation in the agricultural sector. The level of farm debt increased from R64 billion at the end of 1999 to R158 billion at the end of 2017. Almost 60 per cent of farm debt is with commercial banks, 30 per cent is with the Land Bank and the remainder is held by agricultural co-operatives, the Department of Agriculture, private persons and other financial institutions. Therefore, these trends suggest that commercial banks and the Land Bank are highly exposed to the agricultural sector.

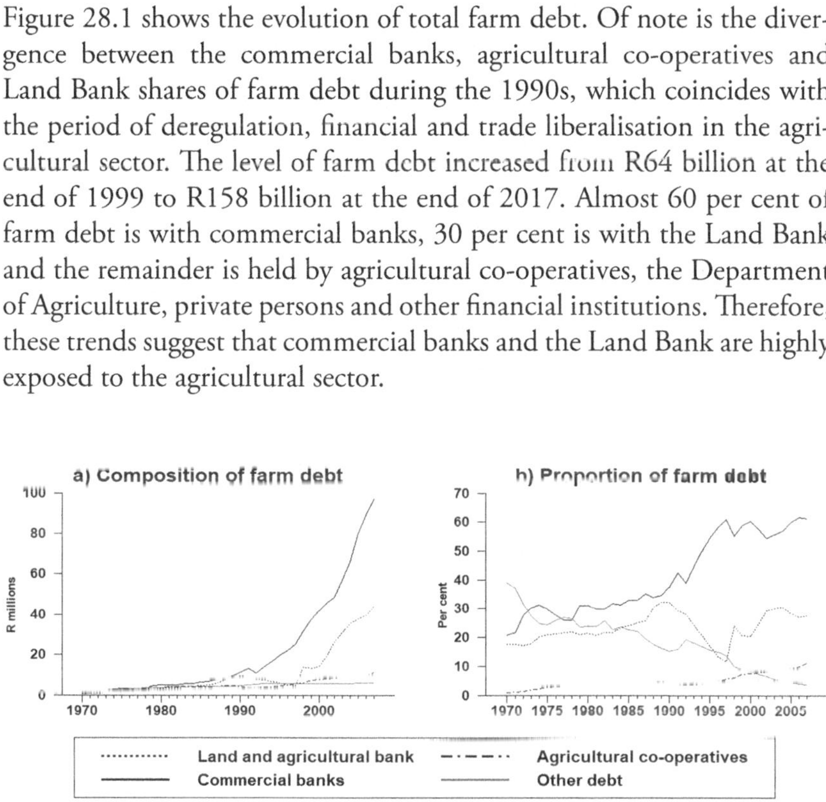

Fig. 28.1 The evolution and structure of farm debt in South Africa. (Note. Other debt consists of the Department of Agriculture, private persons, other financial institutions and other debt. Other financial institutions include discount houses; merchant banks; other monetary institutions; insurance companies; pension funds; trust companies; non-monetary banks and trust assets; and participation mortgage bond holders. Source: Agri SA and authors' calculations)

However, Fig. 28.3 shows that the commercial banks' exposure to the agricultural sector constitutes less than 2 per cent of their balance sheet. This means that only 2 per cent of the commercial banks' balance sheet is dedicated to finance the agricultural sector. With respect to the size of the Land Bank relative to commercial banks, Fig. 28.2 shows that commercial banks hold R6 trillion worth of assets compared to the Land Bank's R50 billion as of March 2018. Figure 28.2(b) shows that the relative size of the Land Bank declined from around 5 per cent in the 1990s to below 1 per cent since 2006. Thus, the scale of funding dedicated to and available for land reform and agricultural development through the Land Bank as a vehicle for finance constitutes less than 1 per cent of the commercial banking sector.

Figure 28.1 showed that bank credit contributes around 60 per cent to farm debt. But data based on the exposure of banks to different sectors of the economy in Fig. 28.3 shows that even though banks are responsible for 60 per cent of loans to the agricultural sector, bank credit to the agricultural sector constitutes less than 2 per cent of the total balance sheet of banks. This means that the credit exposure (risk) posed by the agricultural sector to the banking sector is less than 2 per cent. The 2 per cent bank credit exposure to the agricultural sector compares with almost 45 per cent and 17 per cent dedicated to private households, and financial intermediation and insurance sectors, respectively. However, Fig. 28.3 shows that the banking sector exposure to the agricultural sector increased from 1.2 per cent in 2008 and stabilised around 2 per cent thereafter. As the banks' credit exposure to, for instance, private households declined sharply post-2009 they shifted part of their business to the agricultural sector.[2]

28.3 What about the Land Bank Exposure?

Figure 28.1 showed that the Land Bank constitutes 30 per cent of the agricultural sector debt. At the same time Fig. 28.2 shows that the relative size of the Land Bank declined from around 5 per cent in the 1990s to

[2] We show the exposure to other sectors of the economy in Fig. 28.12 in the Appendix.

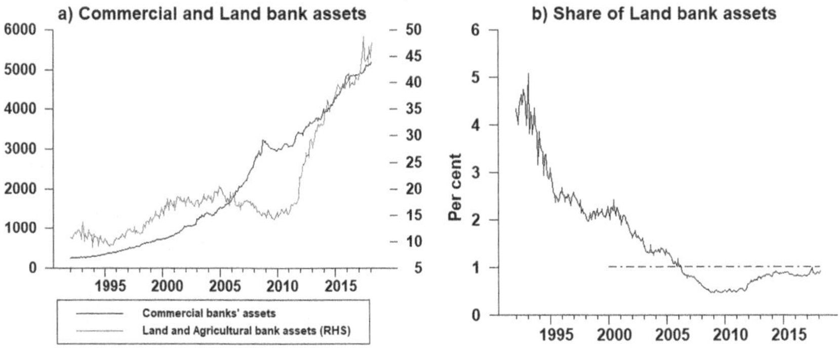

Fig. 28.2 Commercial banks' and Land Bank assets. (Source: South African Reserve Bank and authors' calculations)

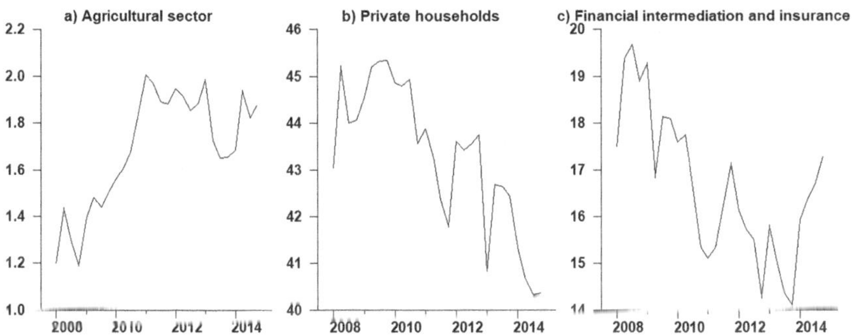

Fig. 28.3 Banks' credit exposure to the agricultural, private households, finance and insurance sectors. (Source: South African Reserve Bank and authors' calculations)

below 1 per cent since 2006. Thus, the scale of funding dedicated and available to the land reform and agricultural development through the Land Bank as a vehicle for finance constitutes less than 1 per cent of the commercial banking sector. This magnitude is almost the same as the size of the commercial banks' exposure to the agricultural sector. This means that, in total, the financial sector dedicates almost 2 per cent of available funding to the agricultural sector. Furthermore, Fig. 28.4(a) shows that the Land Bank loan book more than doubled and increased from around R15 billion in 2009 to R40 billion in 2017. Thus, over a period of almost

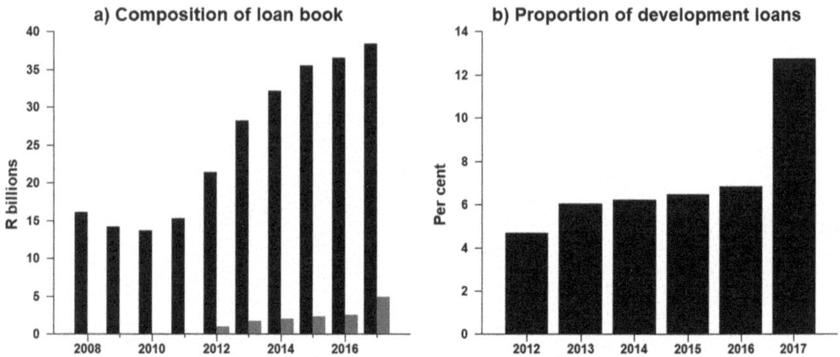

Fig. 28.4 Land Bank loan book. (Source: Land Bank and authors' calculations)

ten years, the Land Bank managed to double the size of its loan book. But this did not result in any meaningful increase in the size of the Land Bank balance sheet relative to that of commercial banks; nor did it meaningfully increase the exposure of the financial sector to the agricultural sector.

In addition, Fig. 28.4(b) shows that the Land Bank started extending development loans to farmers in 2012. Development loans increased from R1 billion in 2012 to R4.9 billion in 2017 and the share of these loans increased from 4 per cent to 12.8 per cent over the same period. The core mandate of the Land Bank is (i) to ensure the sustainability, productivity, competitiveness, investment, innovation and profitability of famers; (ii) to support agricultural entrepreneurship and job creation; and (iii) to develop thriving rural financial systems. The Land Bank states that it currently supports approximately 1500 black farmers and that it has relinquished approximately R100 million of its profits to subsidise the interest rates to these farmers.[3] This is because the agricultural loans funded by the Land Bank are at interest rates comparable to those charged by commercial banks at the prime rate. At the same time, the funding model of the Land Bank is very similar to that of the commercial banks. Furthermore, the Land Bank states that it achieved increased participation in development funding by reallocating funding using its balance

[3] See 2016/17 Land Bank annual report http://docs.wixstatic.com/ugd/ab09f3_c4ab5e61816640af97dc3a4b39cf4519.pdf.

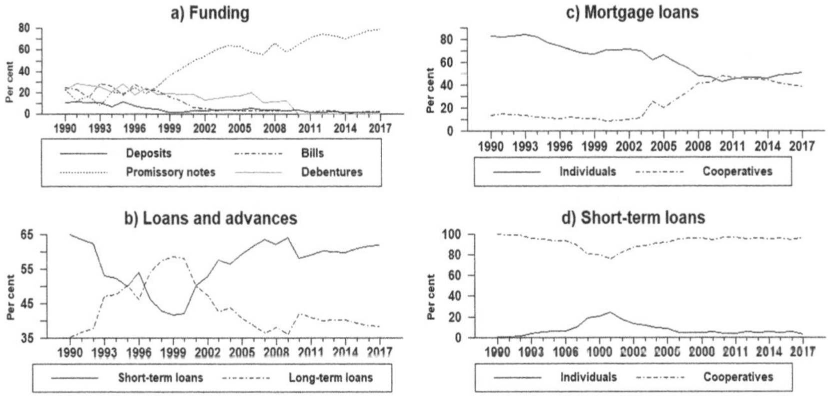

Fig. 28.5 Composition of Land Bank liabilities and assets. (Source: Land Bank and authors' calculations)

sheet to bridge gaps where the perceived risk of transactions exceeds the appetite of commercial funders such as development projects, financing farmers with limited assets to offer as security. One of the key contributing factors to the increase in development finance is that average transaction values increased from approximately R0.7 million in 2016 to more than R2.0 million in 2017.

Further analysis of the Land Bank balance sheet in Fig. 28.5(a) shows that 80 per cent of the Land Bank funding is sourced via the issuance of Promissory Notes (PNs) or Negotiable Certificates of Deposit (NCDs). Retail deposits account for less than 2 per cent as a source of funding.

In fact, combined, retail deposits and bills account for 5 per cent of total liabilities of the Land Bank.[4] On the other hand, debentures used to account for 20 per cent of total liabilities but are no longer issued since 2009. The implication of the trends shown in Fig. 28.5(a) is that a large portion of the Land Bank liabilities are funded at the PN or NCD rates, which are priced at a few basis points above the repo rate depending on the maturities.[5] The Land Bank funds a large proportion of its liabilities from the wholesale funding market as opposed to the retail deposit market.

[4] We note that this funding model is also informed by the regulatory environment governing the Land Bank.

[5] See Fig. 28.13 in the Appendix for the evolution of NCD rates of various maturities.

Furthermore, Fig. 28.5(b) shows that short-term loans account for 60 per cent of total loans and advances by the Land Bank. This means that the bulk of funding is directed at funding the working capital needs of borrowers, especially those of agricultural co-operatives in Fig. 28.5(d). The large share of mortgage advances by the Land Bank used to go to individuals but has since 2000 been directed to agricultural co-operatives. The period of the increase in the share of mortgage advances to agricultural co-operatives coincided with the acceleration in house prices.

In addition, the Land Bank started extending development loans to farmers in 2012 and the share of these loans increased from 4 per cent to 12.8 per cent over the same period.

28.3.1 The Quality of the Land Bank Loan Book

Figure 28.6 shows the evolution of the Land Bank and commercial banks' non-performing loans as a percentage of total loans and advances. The intention of this section is to assess the degree of the association and synchronisation of the quality of the loan books. Cognisant of the vast differences in the loan portfolios and business models, the trends show that both the Land Bank and commercial banks' non-performing loans (NPLs) increased post-2006 following the housing price boom and the

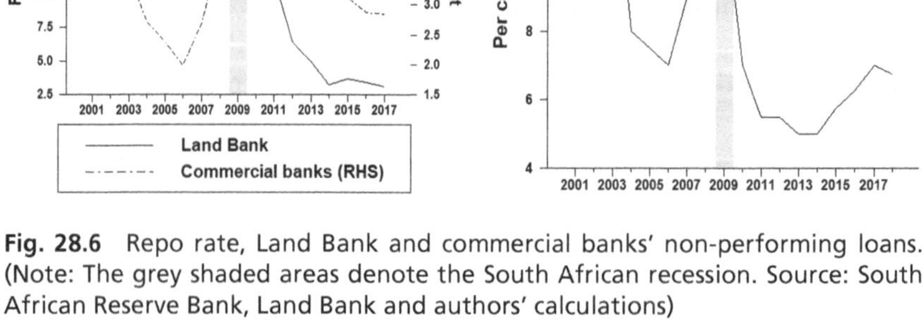

Fig. 28.6 Repo rate, Land Bank and commercial banks' non-performing loans. (Note: The grey shaded areas denote the South African recession. Source: South African Reserve Bank, Land Bank and authors' calculations)

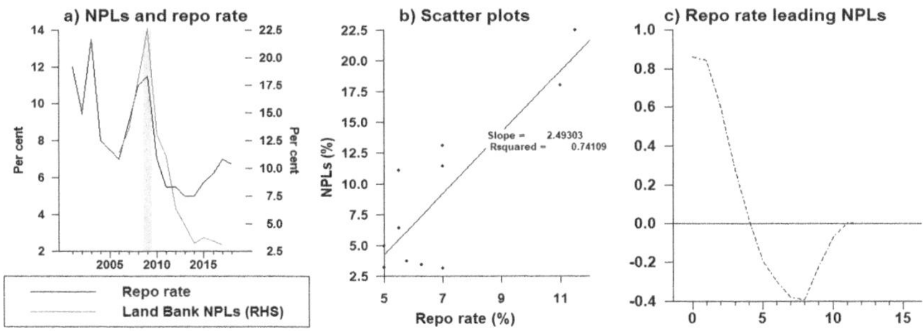

Fig. 28.7 Land Bank's non-performing loans and the repo rate. (Note: The grey shaded areas denote the South African recession. Source: South African Reserve Bank, Land Bank and authors' calculations)

subsequent increase in the repo rate. Due to data limitations, the data for the Land Bank NPLs used is on annual (A) basis from 2006 to 2017. The non-performing loans of the Land Bank peaked at 22.5 per cent versus 6 per cent of the commercial banks in 2009.

The trends pre-2009 show the impact of land and property prices on the performance of the banks' loan books. Of note and importance is the trend of the Land Bank's non-performing loans during and post-2015 following the severe drought and despite tight monetary policy conditions between 2014 and 2017.[6] It is interesting to note that the proportion of non-performing loans did not increase to the degree that was experienced following the property prices slump and tight monetary policy in Fig. 28.6(b) pre-2009. This is early indication of the balance sheet effects, severity and persistent nature of property price slumps and tight credit conditions.

To conclude this section, we complement the analysis presented in Fig. 28.6 by showing the stylised facts between the Land Bank's non-performing loans and the repo rate. Figure 28.7 shows that the repo rate explains 74 per cent of the variation in the Land Bank's non-performing loans. An increase in the repo rate leads to an increase in non-performing loans and they only start to be negative after 5 years. The implication of the results presented in this section is that there is indeed credible

[6] This probably shows the impact of insurance for risks faced by farmers such as drought and floods.

preliminary evidence of the significant effects of the interest rate and balance sheet effects of the monetary policy transmission in the agricultural sector. We explore the robustness of these results by conducting empirical analysis in the following sections.

Based on the facts established so far, there is not much differentiation between the Land Bank and other commercial bank funding models and loan rates.[7] The interest rate margin of the Land Bank is around 3 per cent, which is comparable to that of commercial banks and the margin of the prime lending rate to the repo rate. In fact, we can draw conclusions that it seems that the Land Bank is unable to meet its developmental mandate of bridging the gaps where the perceived risk of transactions exceeds the appetite of commercial bank funders such as development projects, financing farmers with limited assets to offer as security (collateral) under the current funding model and institutional design. To this effect, the Land Bank had to relinquish profits and use direct lending channels in order to subsidise the interest rates to emerging farmers.

28.4 How Are Loan Supply Shocks Transmitted Via the Land Bank Balance Sheet?

This section explores the transmission of the narrow credit (loan supply) channel to the agricultural sector via the Land Bank balance sheet. The results in earlier chapters showed that a contractionary monetary policy shock which leads to an increase in the prime lending rate results in the decline in output growth, investment growth and employment growth. So what distinguishes an adverse loan supply to a contractionary monetary policy shock? An adverse credit (loan) supply shock is similar to an adverse (contractionary) monetary policy shock. Both shocks result in an increase in lending rates but can have a different effect on the quantities of credit.

[7] It is also notable that the agricultural debt market structure and the balance sheet of the Land Bank have changed fundamentally since the mid-1990s when the Agricultural Credit Board was disbanded.

Table 28.1 Identification scheme for adverse monetary policy and loan supply shocks

	Monetary policy	Aggregate supply	Aggregate demand	Loan supply
Policy rate	+	+	–	+
Prime rate	+	+	–	+
Investment	–	+	–	?
Credit growth	?	?	?	?
GDP growth	–	–	–	–
Employment	–	–	–	?

Barnett and Thomas (2013) show that credit supply shocks tend to be associated with quantity-rationing effects which are absent under a monetary policy shock. Gambetti and Musso (2014) find that loan supply shocks appear to have a significant effect on economic activity, inflation and credit market variables in the Euro Area, the UK and the US from 1980 to 2011. In addition, the impact of loan supply shocks seems to be particularly important during recessions. The policy implication of these findings is that insufficient provision of loans to the private sector by banks caused by balance sheet constraints affecting financial intermediaries requires a different policy response compared to the case of declining loan growth due to declining demand from households and enterprises. Thus, for a central bank it is essential to know the factors driving credit growth so that in cases where credit growth is driven by credit supply shocks affecting the balance sheets of banks, measures to support the banking system may be needed. Whereas, in cases where credit growth is driven by credit demand shocks, policy intervention measures to support the real economy must be prioritised. Therefore, in cases of loan supply shocks different policy responses are needed compared to, for example, when there is a loan demand shock.

To distinguish a loan supply shock from a monetary policy shock we use the identification scheme shown in Table 28.1. The simultaneous identification of structural shocks ensures that the loan supply shock captures the exogenous shifts of the loan supply curve rather than any endogenous reaction of the loan supply to one of the other shocks.[8]

[8] See Hristov et al. (2012) and Barnett and Thomas (2013) for further reading.

Table 28.1 shows that a contractionary monetary policy shock leads to an unexpected rise of the policy rate, and short-term and lending interest rates. This has a negative effect on output growth, investment growth, employment growth and credit growth. To distinguish between a contractionary monetary policy shock and an adverse aggregate supply shock, inflation is expected to decline following a negative monetary policy shock. Furthermore, although an adverse credit supply and monetary policy shocks result in an increase in lending rates, they can have a different effect on the quantities of credit. Credit supply shocks tend to be associated with quantity-rationing effects, which are absent under a monetary policy shock.

To identify the loan supply shock via the Land Bank balance sheet, we use credit extended by the Land Bank as shown in Fig. 28.5. We estimate a vector autoregression (VAR) model which includes credit extended by the Land Bank, farmland or house prices, repo, prime rate, agricultural sector output growth, investment growth and employment growth. We use the sign-restricted approach VAR model by Uhligh (2005). The VAR model is estimated using 2 lags and 10,000 Monte Carlo simulations. The sample spans the period 2000Q1 to 2017Q4. All growth rates are measured on an annual basis.

The results in Fig. 28.8 show that the agricultural sector credit growth, output growth, investment growth and employment growth decline in response to an adverse loan supply shock. A comparison of the responses

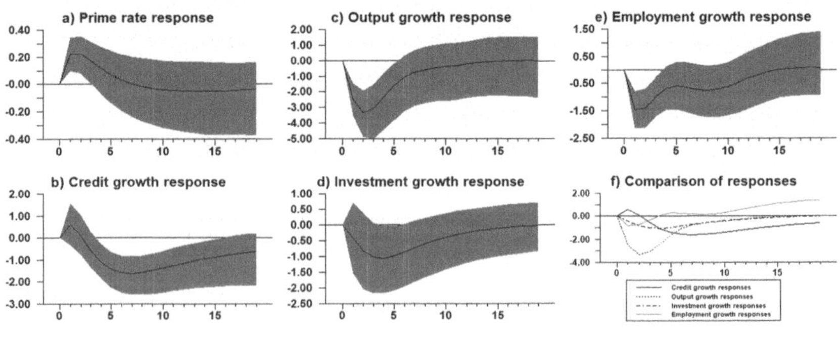

Fig. 28.8 Responses to loan adverse supply shocks. (Note: The grey shaded area bands denote the 16th and 84th confidence bands. Source: Authors' calculations)

in Fig. 28.8(d) shows that output growth declines more followed by investment and employment growth. These results concur with those in earlier chapters showing that asset prices operate via the wealth, collateral and Tobin's Q channels to affect activity in the agricultural sector. The policy implication of the results is that the interest rate, narrow and broad credit channels of the monetary policy transmission are operational in the agricultural sector. The Land Bank balance sheet plays an important and significant role in transmitting shocks to the agricultural sector.

Furthermore, adverse loan supply shocks and interest rate shocks exert significantly severe negative effects on the agricultural sector. We stated earlier that vast literature including Gambetti and Musso (2014) indicates that in cases where the slowdown in credit is largely driven by credit supply shocks affecting the balance sheets of banks, measures to support the banking system may be needed. The Land Bank reported that in order for it to effectively pursue its developmental mandate of supporting emerging black farmers it had to relinquish a substantial portion of its profits to subsidise the interest rates and other risks associated due to farmers in this category. This therefore means that policy interventions to capacitate the Land Bank are needed over and above the diversification of funding sources to deal with the cost of funds. A different model to fund the Land Bank will also deal with the management of risks associated with new entrants in this market, thus enabling the bank to fully pursue its developmental mandate.

28.5 Asymmetric Effects of Positive Land Bank Balance Sheet Shocks

We stated earlier that the scale of the agricultural sector and rural development implied by the accelerated land reform policy is large and long-term in nature. Hence in this section we explore what happens when the share of the Land Bank balance sheet is increased, for instance, by 5, 10, 15 or 20 per cent of the banking sector over the next 12 years or by 2030 in line with the agricultural sector targets in the National Development Plan (NDP). Furthermore, we showed earlier that the Land Bank funding model is not different from that of commercial banks. At the same time, we showed that the Land Bank largely extends short-term loans to fund the working capital needs of borrowers, especially those of agricultural co-operatives and a large share of mortgage advances is directed to agricultural co-operatives.

Thus, given the set objective of accelerated land reform aimed at changing the distorted patterns of rural–urban development and supporting agricultural revolution, how does the expansion of the Land Bank balance sheet affect the agricultural sector credit growth, output growth, investment growth and employment growth? This is particularly important given the scale of the accelerated land reform and the entry of new farmers into the agricultural sector. We showed earlier that the balance sheet of the Land Bank is highly constrained to the degree to which it can handle the demands and scale of the land reform policy and agricultural revolution it envisages. Even though expropriation without compensation relieves funding to some degree (fewer financial resources dedicated to acquiring land), the fulfilment of the mandate of the Land bank requires dedicated long-term funding. Sihlobo and Kirsten (2018) and various other researchers in this area argue that land reform is only one part of a comprehensive programme of economic reconstruction and development. Accelerated land reform and redistribution are necessary but not sufficient to bring about real economic empowerment and poverty alleviation. Additional services, including infrastructure, markets and social services, amongst others, have to be provided as part of a comprehensive reconstruction and development programme. These factors are already provided for in the Land and Development Bank Act (2002).

The Land Bank is a state bank. This means that the expansion of its balance sheet implies that government will have to capacitate the Land Bank in various ways so that the set objectives in the Land and Development Bank Act are fully achieved. In addition, the Land Bank regulatory framework will have to be changed to allow it to access funding at the central bank discount window or, alternatively, to allow it to participate in the central bank open market operations. Another way in which the Land Bank can be capacitated is via a persistent and incremental injection of cash over a prolonged period. These policy interventions are over and above the implementation and enforcement of a rigorous financial and prudential regulatory environment to make sure that the

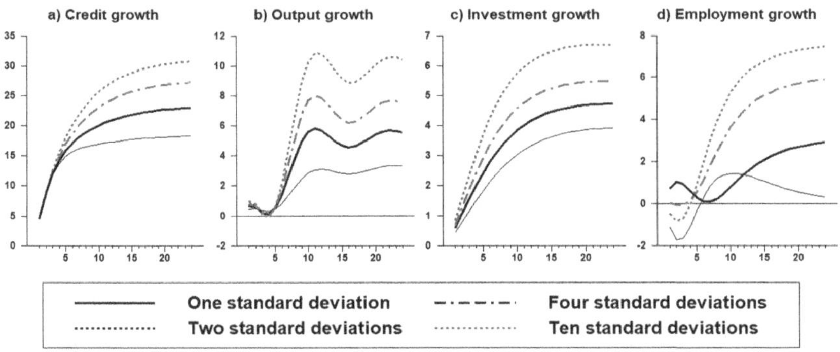

Fig. 28.9 Asymmetric responses to Land Bank balance sheet shocks. (Source: Authors' calculation)

risks faced by the bank are well managed and that the new business model to support the accelerated land reform policy, rural development and agricultural revolution is sustainable over the long run.[9]

So what happens when the share of the Land Bank balance sheet is increased, for instance, by 5, 10, 15 or 20 per cent of the banking sector over the next ten years? To assess the impact of different sizes of increases in the size of the Land Bank balance sheet and credit growth on various aspects of the agricultural sector, we use the Kilian and Vigfusson approach for asymmetric transmissions of shocks. We estimate several VAR models which include credit growth by the Land Bank, agricultural sector output growth, investment growth and employment growth. The models are estimated for the period 2000Q1 to 2017Q4. The VAR models are estimated with 2 lags and 10,000 Monte Carlo draws. All growth rates are measured on an annual basis.

The results in Fig. 28.9 show that credit growth by the Land Bank will have to go beyond 10 per cent (double-digit growth rates) so as to have

[9] The Land Bank is part of the monetary sector. The increase in its balance sheet will affect the size of the banking sector, the allocation and distribution of financial risks in the economy, private sector credit and thus the price and financial stability mandates over and above the objective maximum employment, low and sustainable unemployment and inequality. Currently the Land Bank is regulated under a different supervisory regime, and the changes to its business model imply that this will have to change significantly so that the bank is given access to other open market operation facilities available to commercial banks. The change in the regulatory environment for the Land Bank is the responsibility of the Prudential Authority and the monetary policy authorities.

significant and meaningful impact on the agricultural sector output growth, investment growth and employment growth.

28.6 Quality of the Balance Sheet: The Case of Land Bank Non-performing Loans

To conclude the analysis on the Land Bank balance sheet we assess the impact of the deterioration in its balance sheet as proxied by an increase in the non-performing loans as a ratio of total loans. Do positive shocks to the non-performing loans in the Land Bank book constrain its ability to lend to farmers? What is the impact of an impaired Land Bank balance sheet on the agricultural sector output, investment and employment growth? Non-performing loans are also a proxy bank's credit risk and vast recent literature has shown that there is a negative feedback between contractionary monetary policy shocks, increase the lending rate spreads on new loans due to the deterioration in collateral values, borrowers' net worth and credit risk.

To answer these questions, we estimate a VAR model which includes non-performing loans, agricultural sector output growth, investment growth and employment growth. The VAR model is estimated with 1 lag and 10,000 Monte Carlo draws. Due to data limitations for the Land Bank non-performing loans, the sample spans 2005Q1 to 2017Q4. The shock is one standard deviation.

The results in Figs. 28.10 and 28.11 show that an increase in the Land Bank non-performing loans results in depressed credit growth by the Land Bank, agricultural sector output growth, investment growth and employment growth.

The impact of positive shocks to non-performing loans (credit risk) is similar to those due to loan supply shocks. Thus, we establish robust evidence that adverse loan supply and credit risk shocks operating via the Land Bank balance sheet exert significantly large and persistent negative effects on the agricultural sector.

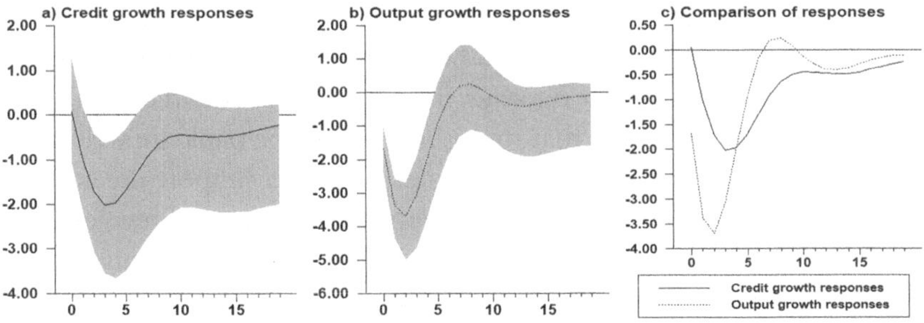

Fig. 28.10 Credit and output growth responses to positive non-performing loans shocks. (Note: The grey shaded area bands denote the 16th and 84th confidence bands. Source: Authors' calculations)

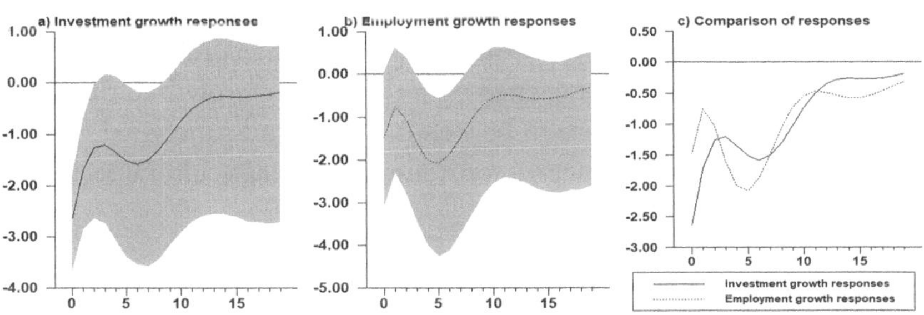

Fig. 28.11 Investment and employment growth responses to positive non-performing loan shocks. (Note: The grey shaded area bands denote the 16th and 84th confidence bands. Source: Authors' calculations)

28.7 Conclusion and Policy Implications

How are adverse loan supply shocks and credit risk transmitted to the agricultural sector via the Land Bank balance sheet? We find that adverse loan supply shocks and credit risk shocks as proxied by positive shocks to non-performing loans exert downward pressure on the agricultural sector credit growth, output growth, investment growth and employment growth. In addition, credit extended by the Land Bank will have to increase at double-digit rates so that its balance sheet increases more than the current 1 per cent as a share of the banking sector. Thus, the scale of funding dedicated to and available for land reform and agricultural development through the Land Bank as a vehicle for development finance has to double overtime. This has to be accompanied by the implementation and enforcement of a rigorous financial and prudential regulatory environment to make sure that the risks faced by the bank are well managed. Furthermore, that the new business model to support the accelerated land reform policy, rural development and agricultural revolution is sustainable over the long run. The main objective of these changes is to enable and enact the constitutional objectives or, alternatively, what Moseneke (2015) refers to as the democratic consolidation of achieving urban and rural land equity.

The policy implication of the results is that in order to support the accelerated land reform policy, new entrants in the agricultural sector and agricultural revolution, the Land Bank balance sheet and credit growth will have to persistently grow at double-digit levels for a prolonged period. However, the credit risks associated with this kind of growth in the Land Bank balance sheet will have to be well managed and supervised as they can end up imposing the biggest constraints on the agricultural sector.

Appendix

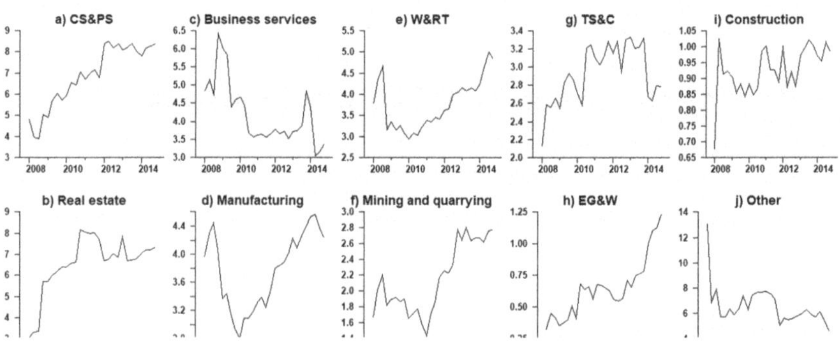

Fig. 28.12 Banks' credit exposure to selected sectors of the economy. (Note: TS&C = Transport, storage and communication, EG&W = Electricity, gas and water, W&RT = Wholesale and retail trade, CS&PS = Community, social and personal services. Source: South African Reserve Bank)

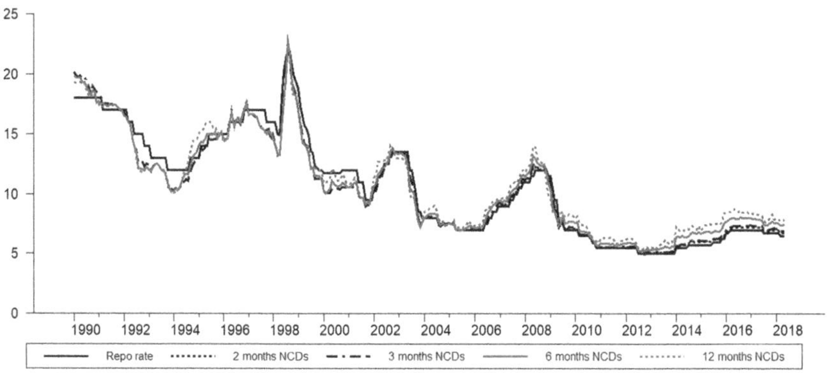

Fig. 28.13 Funding rates. (Source: South African Reserve Bank)

References

Amaral, P. 2017. *Monetary Policy and Inequality*. Economic Commentary 01, Federal Reserve Bank of Cleveland.

Angelopoulou, E., and Gibson, D.H. 2007. *The Balance Sheet Channel of Monetary Policy: Evidence from the UK*. Bank of Greece Working Paper No. 53.

Barnett, Alina, and Thomas, Ryland. 2013. *Has Weak Lending and Activity in the United Kingdom Been Driven by Credit Supply Shocks?* December 20. Bank of England Working Paper No. 482.

Bernanke, B.S., and Gertler, M. 1989. Agency Costs, Net Worth, and Business Fluctuations. *American Economic Review*, 79, 14–31.

Bernanke, B.S., and Gertler, M. 1995. Inside the Black Box: The Credit Channel of Monetary Policy Transmission. *Journal of Economic Perspectives, American Economic Association*, 9(4), 27–48.

Borio, C., Disyatat, P., Juselius, M., and Rungcharoenkitkul, P. 2018. *Monetary Policy in the Grip of a Pincer Movement*. BIS Working Papers No. 706.

Dolado, J., Motyovszki, G., and Pappa, E. 2018. Monetary Policy and Inequality: A New Channel. VOX CEPR Portal.

Domanski, D., Scatigna, M., and Zabai, A. 2016. Wealth Inequality and Monetary Policy. *BIS Quarterly Review*, March 2016.

Drehmann, Mathias, and Juselius, Mikael. 2012. Do Debt Service Costs Affect Macroeconomic and Financial Stability? *BIS Quarterly Review*, September (Basel: Bank for International Settlements).

Drehmann, Mathias, and Juselius, Mikael. 2013. *Evaluating Early Warning Indicators of Banking Crises: Satisfying Policy Requirements*. BIS Working Paper Series No. 421 (Basel: Bank for International Settlements).

Furceri, D., Loungani, P., and Zdzienicka, A. 2016. *The Effects of Monetary Policy Shocks on Inequality*. IMF Working Paper WP/16/245.

Gambetti, L., and Musso, A. 2014. Loan Supply Shocks and the Business Cycle. ECB Conference Paper, November 20, 2014.

Hristov, N., Hülsewig, O., and Wollmershäuser, T. 2012. Loan Supply Shocks during the Financial Crisis: Evidence for the Euro Area. *Journal of International Money and Finance*, 31, 569–92. http://www.buseco.monash.edu.au/depts/ebs/pubs/wpapers/

Jacobs, P., Lahiff, E., and Hall, R. 2003. Land Redistribution. Programme for Land and Agrarian Studies School of Government University of the Western Cape. http://www.plaas.org.za/sites/default/files/publications-pdf/ELARSA%2001.pdf.

Kganyago, L. 2018. Inequality and Monetary Policy in South Africa. A Public Lecture at the Nelson Mandela University, Port Elizabeth 1 August 2018.

Kiyotaki, N., and Moore, J. 1995. *Credit Cycles*. NBER Working Paper No. 5083.

Kuttner, K.N., and Mosser, P.C. 2002. The Monetary Transmission Mechanism: Some Answers and Further Questions. *FRBNY Economic Policy Review*, Vol. 8, No. 1, May 2002.

Mersch, Y. 2014. Speech at Corporate Credit Conference, Zurich. 17 October 2014.

Moseneke, D.C.J. 2015. Reflections on South African Constitutional Democracy—Transition and Transformation. https://constitutionallyspeaking.co.za/dcj-moseneke-reflections-on-south-african-constitutional-democracy-transition-and-transformation/.

Sihlobo, W. 2018. Fewer Farmers, More Milk. https://wandilesihlobo.com/2018/07/17/fewer-farmers-more-milk/.

Sihlobo, W., and Kirsten, J. 2018. Secret of Land-Reform Success Is to Learn Lessons from Experience. *Business Day*, May 28. https://www.businesslive.co.za/bd/opinion/2018-05-28-the-secret-of-land-reform-success-is-to-learn-lessons-from-experience/.

Uhlig, H. 2005. What are the Effects of Monetary Policy on Output? Results from an Agnostic Identification Procedure. *Journal of Monetary Economics*, 52, 381–419.

Van der Elst, H.J. 2007. Post–settlement Support as Key Contribution to the Success of the South African Land Reform Program (1994–2007). North West University: UNISA Press. https://www.academia.edu/12075685/Post_settlement_support_as_key_contributor_to_the_success_of_the_South_African_land_reform_programme_1994-2007_.

29

Is There a Role that Lower-Tier Banks Can Play in Complementing the Land Bank Development Mandate of the Agricultural Sector Value Chain?

Learning Objectives

- Explore the role lower-tier banks such as the mutual banks, Postbank, co-operative banks and co-operative financial institutions must play in a changing financial landscape guided by the objectives of innovation, alleviation of poverty, income and wealth inequality, inclusion and the development of rural and township economies.
- Understand the historical role of co-operative banks, control and marketing boards in the agricultural sector.
- Assess the effects of positive credit extension shocks by the Postbank, co-operative banks and mutual banks.
- Explore the financial implications of increasing the size of the Postbank, co-operative banks and mutual banks.

N. Gumata, E. Ndou, *Accelerated Land Reform, Mining, Growth, Unemployment and Inequality in South Africa*, https://doi.org/10.1007/978-3-030-30884-1_29

29.1 Introduction

Do lower-tier banks and agricultural co-operatives have a role to play in complementing the Land Bank's development mandate of the agricultural sector value chain? This chapter extends the analysis, covering necessary changes to the banking and financial landscape in order to support and make a success of the accelerated land reform and redistribution. We stated in the earlier chapters that lack of post-settlement support has been identified as a major setback and impediment in the productive use of redistributed land and the agricultural revolution policy. The analysis in this chapter is important given the fact that specialised institutions to serve the agricultural sector can be better organised to price and manage the risks posed by new entrants into the agricultural sector at the scale envisaged by the accelerated land reform policy and the agricultural (green) revolution. In this chapter we argue that over and above the Land Bank and commercial banks as financial vehicles to support the accelerated land reform policy and the agricultural revolution, there is a case for the increased participation of co-operative banks, mutual banks and the Postbank in the agricultural, manufacturing and other sectors related to the value chain that supports the agricultural revolution.

29.2 The Historical Role of Co-operative Banks, Control and Marketing Boards in the Agricultural Sector

It is a well-known and established fact that the co-operative sector in South Africa started with the establishment of the predominantly white agricultural co-operatives.[1] The agricultural co-operatives were agents of the control boards. This policy strategy was aimed at developing and building a successful white farming community in South Africa. Later, these co-operatives eventually developed into powerful business ventures, which controlled agricultural production, marketing and processing in

[1] For further reading, see agricultural and finance co-operatives http://www.dti.gov.za/economic_empowerment/docs/coops/legis_policy/coop-strategy.pdf.

rural areas. These co-operatives succeeded mainly through massive government support in the following forms:

1. The Land Bank was established in 1912 to provide these co-operatives with access to finance.
2. The 1912 Land Settlement Act and the 1913 and 1936 Land Acts were enacted to support the co-operatives.
3. The Co-operatives Societies Acts of 1922 and 1939, and the Natives Administration Act of 1936 were also enacted.
4. The Marketing Boards were established through the promulgation of the 1937 Agricultural Marketing Act. The Marketing Boards were tasked with fixing the prices of agricultural commodities and acted as secondary co-operatives that purchased produce from co-operatives and marketed it locally and internationally.
5. The state also provided subsidies and tax exemptions to these agricultural co-operatives.
6. In February 1952, the Minister of Agriculture announced a long-term loan scheme for constructing infrastructure to support the agricultural sector such as grain silos. The infrastructure was financed by the Land Bank under the supervision of the Grain Silo Committee.[2]
7. The control boards also played an important role in the way agricultural produce, especially grain products were transported. During the regulated agricultural sector era the control boards were essentially the only entities that transported agricultural produce on a large scale in South Africa. They mainly used rail transport, which was provided only by the government's Railways and Harbour Administration. This approach and strategy made it easier to co-ordinate the transport needs to the interior of the country as well as to and from the harbours. The transportation of grain products by road increased rapidly in the 1990s as the agricultural sector was deregulated. Statistics show that as at 2019 about 85 per cent of all agricultural produce in South Africa was estimated to be transported by road compared to just 15 per cent in 1990.

[2] See for further reading http://www.grainsa.co.za/ebook/eng/GSA-HistoryBook-H1/files/assets/common/downloads/publication.pdf.

29.3 The Land and Agricultural Bank Act and the Agricultural Sector Development

The following are the objectives of the Land and Development Bank:

1. Sustainability, productivity, competitiveness, investment, innovation and profitability of famers.
2. Support and development of agricultural entrepreneurship and job creation.
3. Development of thriving rural financial systems at the core of land reform.

Guided by these stated objectives of the Land and Agricultural Bank Act (2002), we are of the opinion that the role of agricultural marketing and credit boards is equivalent to that which can be performed through policies aimed at the protection of infant industries as per the recommendations of the Bureau for Food and Agricultural Policy (BFAP 2011), import substitution policies and strategies, changes in the financial landscape to allow for greater participation of commercial banks, mutual banks, Land Bank and other lower-tier banks for co-ordinated support of entrepreneurship and small, medium and micro enterprises (SMMEs). In addition, changes to the banking, financial landscape and institutional design argued for in this section do not preclude the establishment of a land reform fund at the Land Bank. Sihlobo and Kirsten (2018) argue that a land reform fund and its roll-out through one-stop shops where acquisition grants, subsidised loans and subsidies for on-farm improvements can be accessed is also necessary to make a success of land reform. The authors also argue for the consolidation of the funds currently sitting with the Department of Agriculture, Forestry and Fisheries for the comprehensive agricultural support programme (CASP), the Ilima/Letsema conditional grant and funds earmarked for land acquisition, land reform and post-settlement support at the Department of Rural Development and Land Reform to the land reform fund at the Land Bank. Vast literature and empirical studies in this area also note that the budget allocation for land reform (acquisition of land) is disproportionate in relation to the

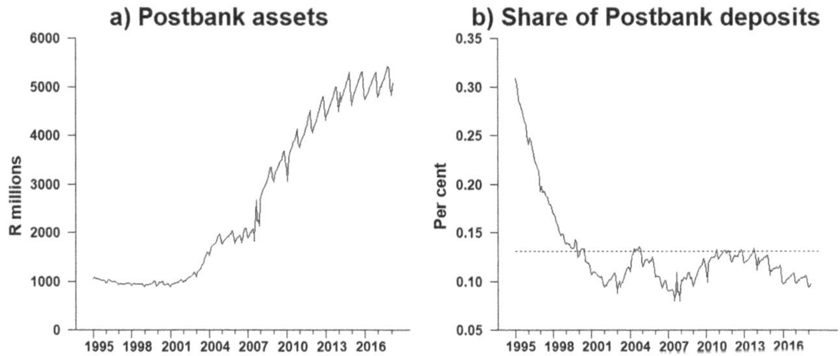

Fig. 29.1 Postbank deposits and size relative to the banking sector. (Source: South African Reserve Bank and authors' calculations)

post-settlement support. It is this aspect of the land reform debate that speaks to the role that expropriation without compensation can play in correcting such an imbalance.[3]

29.4 Stylised Facts of the Balance Sheets of Lower-Tier Banks in South Africa

29.4.1 The Postbank Balance Sheet

The Postbank is a fully fledged bank which, based on the Postbank Limited Act of 2010, is mandated to offer a range of financial services, in particular, to rural and low-income communities that have little or no access to banking facilities and financial services.[4] Based on data in Fig. 29.1 the Postbank had R5 billion worth of deposits at end of 2018

[3] For example, the funds currently sitting with the department of agriculture, forestry and fisheries for the comprehensive agricultural support programme (CASP) (R5.6 billion over the medium-term budget period 2018/2021), Ilima/Letsema conditional grant (R1.6 billion) and funds earmarked for land acquisition (R4.2 billion), land reform (R8.7 billion) and post-settlement support (R1.5 billion) at the department of rural development and land reform, https://www.businesslive.co.za/bd/opinion/2018-08-13-how-private-sector-can-supply-land-in-a-way-that-makes-reform-work/.

[4] It was in 2010 that legislation was promulgated that made it possible for Postbank to change from a deposit-taking institution to a full-fledged bank, opening up the possibility for any South African to save, transact, and invest with minimal hassle and ultimate reward. See Postbank Act https://

M12. This translated to an average of 0.13 per cent of the share of total banking sector assets for the sample period 1995 M1 to 2018 M12 as shown in Fig. 29.1(b).

The Postbank reports that over and above offering banking and financial services to social income grants recipients, in 2005 it became the leading provider of Mzansi accounts in South Africa. According to the Postbank, it has more Mzansi account holders than any other bank, which includes the four big banks. This is financial inclusion[5] and in part the fulfilment of the mandate of financial innovation and the development of thriving rural financial systems which is at the core of accelerated land reform. In addition, the Postbank reports that it has over 2000 Post Offices across the country. This is a massive footprint which should be leveraged on to fundamentally change the rural and township economies.

In terms of credit extension, the Postbank reports that all its deposits are lent out as claims on the private sector (credit extended to the private sector). Figure 29.2 shows growth in credit extended by the Postbank. The trends show that there were spikes of growth above 10 per cent associated with the following: (i) the launch of the Paymaster by the Postbank, where recipients of social income grants were able to open a Postbank account in 2003; (ii) in 2005 when the Postbank became the leading provider of Mzansi accounts in South Africa; and (iii) in 2010 when the Postbank changed from being just a deposit-taking institution to a fully-fledged bank. However, it is evident that since 2012 growth in the Postbank credit extension has slowed down to below 10 per cent.

The trends presented in this section mean that based on the size of deposits, the Postbank is bigger than the three current mutual banks. Thus, the Postbank is a significant player in the banking and financial system. Furthermore, it provides essential financial services to households in the lower-income categories. This means that there is a case to change the regulatory environment it operates in. The change in the regulatory

www.postbank.co.za/PostbankAct.pdf for further details and https://www.postbank.co.za/history.html for the key milestones of the Postbank.

[5] With the unbanked spaza shop market valued at an estimated R40 billion a year, and at least 90% of the transactions conducted in cash, there is a lot of potential to be unlocked through offering credit lines for the shops to stock up. https://city-press.news24.com/Business/meet-the-entrepreneurs-solving-the-biggest-headache-for-spaza-shops-20190328.

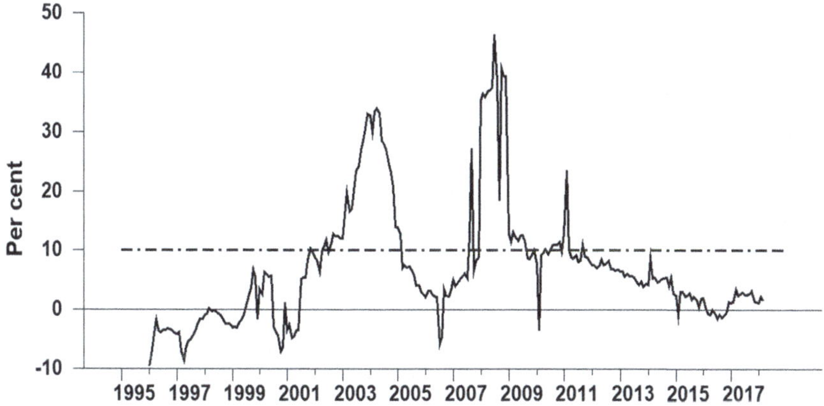

Fig. 29.2 Postbank credit extension. (Source: South African Reserve Bank and authors' calculations)

environment is particularly important if we take into account the fact that majority of the Postbank clients are social income grants recipients. We argue that the rigorous financial regulation of the Postbank will also deal with reckless (and even predatory) lending with known devastating consequences for financial stability and severe social welfare costs.

29.4.2 The Mutual Banks' Balance Sheet

Based on data sourced from the South African Reserve Bank (SARB) Prudential Authority, there were three mutual banks at the end of 2017.[6] Figure 29.3 shows that the rand-denominated deposits at mutual banks were R4 billion and this translated to an average of 0.05 per cent relative to the banking sector assets. As we stated earlier, this means that based on the size of rand-denominated deposits, the Postbank is bigger compared to the three current mutual banks. Nonetheless, both the Postbank and mutual banks are miniscule compared to commercial banks.

[6] See South African Reserve Bank annual report https://www.resbank.co.za/Lists/News%20and%20Publications/Attachments/8507/01%20BankSupAR2017.pdf.

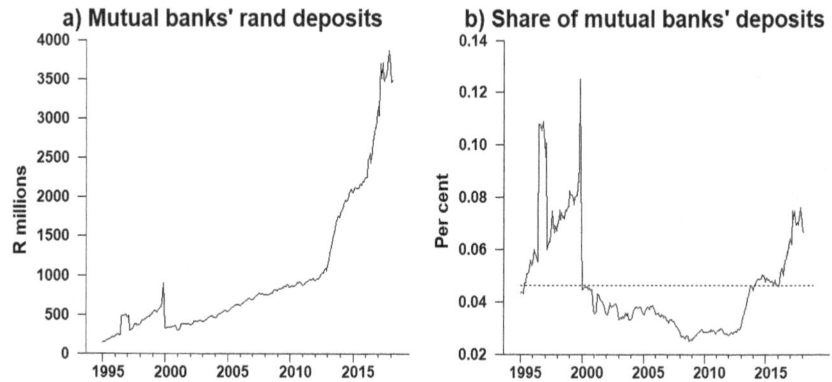

Fig. 29.3 Mutual banks' deposits and size relative to the banking sector. (Source: South African Reserve Bank and authors' calculations)

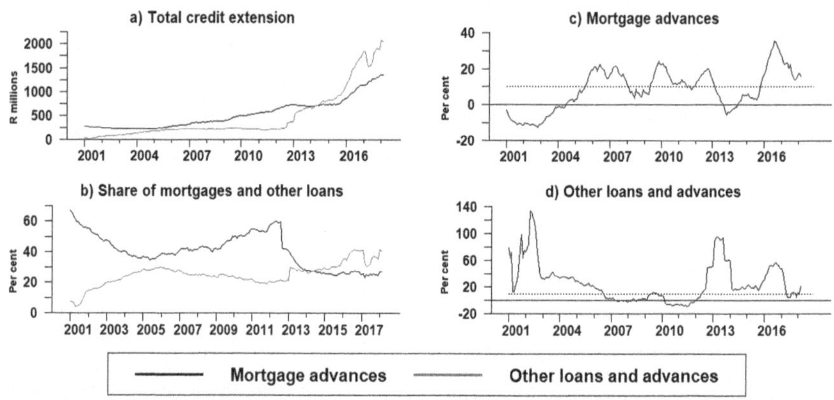

Fig. 29.4 Mutual banks' credit extension. (Source: South African Reserve Bank and authors' calculations)

However, compared to the Postbank, mutual banks have a considerable mortgage book. For mutual banks, Fig. 29.4 shows that mortgage advances and other loans and advances account for a greater proportion of credit extended. In addition, mutual banks increased the level of mortgage advances and other loans and advances to more than R1 billion in 2014. As a result, the annual growth rates have been above 10 per cent as shown in Fig. 29.4(c) and (d).

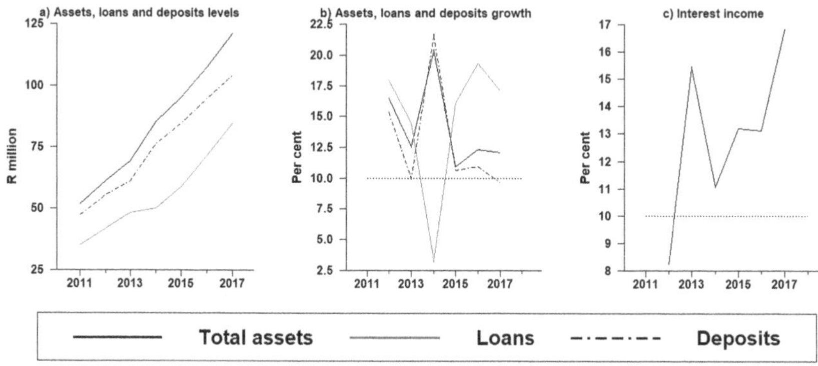

Fig. 29.5 Co-operative bank assets, loans, deposits and interest income. (Source: South African Reserve Bank and authors' calculations)

29.4.3 The Co-operative Banks' Balance Sheet

Data sourced from the South African Reserve Bank Prudential Authority shows that there were three co-operative banks at end of 2017.[7] Figure 29.5 shows that co-operative banks held R104 million deposits and R121 million in assets at end of February 2017.[8] Figure 29.5(a) shows that the co-operative banks extended R85 million is credit.[9] Data trends show that assets, loans and deposits growth in Fig. 29.5(b) and (c) have remained above 10 per cent since 2012. The co-operative banks earned R12.7 million in interest income and the growth rate has been persistently above 10 per cent as shown in Fig. 29.5(c). The trends in Fig. 29.5 show that although few and small, co-operative banks are growing and are very profitable.

Thus, we have shown that the lower-tier banks (i.e. the Postbank, mutual banks and the co-operative banks) although small and few provide meaningful banking and financial service to other sectors of the South African

[7] See South African Reserve Bank annual report https://www.resbank.co.za/Lists/News%20and%20Publications/Attachments/8507/01%20BankSupAR2017.pdf.

[8] See South African Reserve Bank Cooperatives banks annual report https://www.resbank.co.za/Lists/News%20and%20Publications/Attachments/7928/Cooperative%20Banks%202016_2017.pdf.

[9] Data for co-operative banks are only available on an annual basis from 2011.

population. In addition, data from the South African Reserve Bank Prudential Authority shows that there were 24 co-operative financial institutions (CFIs) across the country, with assets to the tune of R142 million, R115 million deposits and extended loans amounting to R94 million.[10]

These trends indicate that co-operative financial institutions subject to the necessary regulatory requirements have the potential to become fully fledged co-operative banks. They are the feeding pipeline to expanding lower-tier banks across the country. This means that with full adherence to the financial regulatory requirements and enough support, the number of co-operative banks can easily grow to more than ten spread across the country. In turn, the sustainable growth of co-operative banks will contribute to the growth and increase of the number of mutual banks. Hence, we argue that to bridge the gaps where the perceived risk of transactions exceeds the appetite of commercial funders for entrepreneurs, SMMEs and housing to clients with limited assets to offer as collateral, the Postbank, co-operative banks, co-operative financial institutions and mutual banks have a big role to play.

29.5 What Are the Effects of Positive Credit Extension Shocks by the Postbank, Co-operative Banks and Mutual Banks?

Given the mandate of (i) financial innovation and the development of thriving rural financial systems which are at the core of accelerated land reform and (ii) changing the patterns of rural-urban migration, development of township economies, inclusion and poverty alleviation, what are the financial implications of increasing the size of the Postbank, co-operative banks and mutual banks balance sheets? To answer this question, we aggregate credit extended by the Postbank, mutual banks and co-operative banks to assess the impact of varying degrees of positive credit growth shock extended by these institutions. We note that except for the mutual banks, it is unclear as to what credit extended by the

[10] See for further reading https://www.resbank.co.za/Lists/News%20and%20Publications/Attachments/6854/Cooperative%20Banks%202014.pdf.

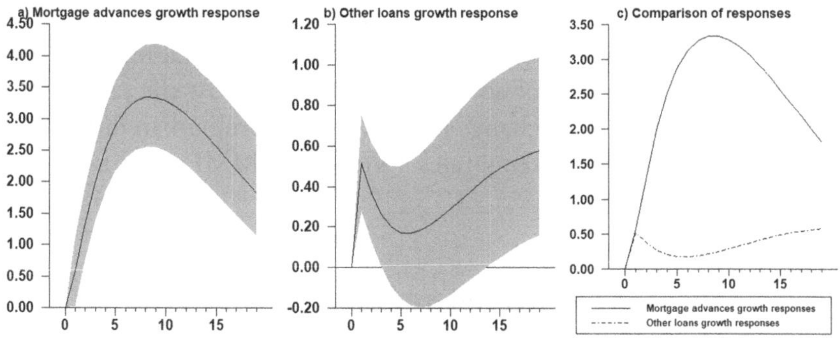

Fig. 29.6 Responses to positive credit growth shocks by lower-tier banks. (Source: Authors' calculations. Note: The grey shaded areas denote the 16th and 84th percentile confidence bands)

Postbank and the co-operative banks is for.[11] Thus, in our analysis we assume that loans extended by the Postbank and the co-operative banks are largely consumer credit.

We estimate a VAR model which includes total credit growth, other loans growth and mortgage advances growth by mutual banks, Postbank and the co-operative banks. The intention is to assess what happens when there are positive aggregate credit shocks extended by these financial institutions to mortgage advances and other loans in this tier of banks. The sample is on a monthly (M) basis and starts in 1995 M1 up to 2018 M12. The VAR models are estimated with 4 lags and 10,000 Monte Carlo draws. All growth rates are measured on an annual basis. The shock is a unit shock.

The results in Fig. 29.6 show that mortgage advances growth increases more than other loans growth in response to a positive total credit shock extended by the Postbank, mutual banks and co-operative banks. The results imply that lower-tier banks can have a meaningful impact in financing housing and SMMEs within the policy of accelerated land

[11] We contend that this presents an opportunity for the reporting requirements by the Postbank and co-operative banks to change and be disaggregated. Furthermore, regulations have to be put in place to enforce a requirement that the loan books of lower-tier banks are geared towards the financing of productive assets that contribute to the objectives of financial innovation, development of thriving rural financial systems, rural-urban migration, township economies and poverty alleviation.

reform. As we stated, this is particularly important given the mandate of financial innovation and the development of thriving rural financial systems which is at the core of accelerated land reform. At the same time, there is an urgent need to change the patterns of rural–urban migration, development of township economies, funding of SMMEs, inclusion and poverty alleviation.

29.6 What Are the Financial Implications of Increasing the Size of the Postbank, Co-operative Banks and Mutual Banks?

To conclude this section, we explore the financial implications of increasing the size of credit extended by lower-tier banks by 5, 10 and 20 per cent? Similar to the analysis on the Land Bank balance sheet in Chap. 28, we use the Kilian and Vigfusson approach for asymmetric transmissions of shocks to the credit extended by lower-tier banks. Figure 29.7 shows that the varying magnitudes of shocks to the credit extended by lower-tier banks will result in double-digit growth in mortgage advances and other loans. Similar to shocks to the Land Bank balance sheet, this means that growth in aggregate credit extension will rise by double digits as all the institutions are included in the monetary sector.

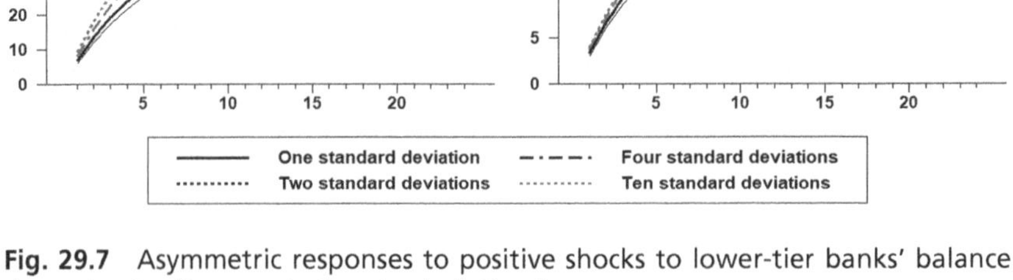

Fig. 29.7 Asymmetric responses to positive shocks to lower-tier banks' balance sheet shocks. (Source: Authors' calculations)

The results imply that the financial regulatory and reporting environment must change and be aligned to the changing banking and financial landscape. To this effect, the provision for the South African Reserve Bank to be the sole supervisor of lower-tier banks including primary and secondary co-operative banks is in accordance with the rigorous financial regulation of the banking and financial sectors. Furthermore, such an institutional arrangement is in line with the objective of maintaining and achieving the financial stability mandate.[12] Such regulatory changes include agricultural co-operatives that are interested in establishing banking services for their members using their existing branch networks, especially in rural areas. As shown in earlier chapters, agricultural co-operatives held almost 10 per cent of farm debt in 2017.

The regulatory interventions aimed at encouraging co-operative banks and co-operative financial institutions to adapt to risk-based approaches, adherence to appropriately designed and sophisticated capital/adequacy requirements are consistent with the observations of Corbae and Levine (2018). These authors show that economies can avoid the fragility costs of competition by enhancing bank governance and tightening leverage requirements. In addition, the authors find that the monetary transmission mechanism is materially shaped by bank competition because bank lending responds more aggressively to central bank–induced changes in interest rates in more competitive environments. Thus, regulations that improve bank governance boost efficiency and support the financial stability mandate.

Furthermore, an approach that nurtures co-operative financial institutions to become fully fledged co-operative banks can contribute to the decentralisation of the distribution of banks and concentration of the banking system. Ndou et al. (2019) find that the interest rate pass-through increases (declines) in the high (low) competition regimes, whereas the loan intermediation markup declines (increases) in the high (low) competition regime. These results indicate that greater market concentration and low competition decreased the size of the interest rate pass-through

[12] The tiering of co-operative financial institutions (CFIs) is based on their classification by asset size: (i) CFIs with deposits of R20 million or more are considered to be very large; (ii) CFIs with deposits between R1 million and R20 million are considered to be large; (iii) CFIs with deposits between R150,000 and R1 million are considered to be small; and (iv) CFIs with deposits less than R150,000 are considered to be very small. See for further reading https://www.resbank.co.za/Lists/News%20and%20Publications/Attachments/5099/Cooperative%20Banks%202012.pdf.

and increased the loan intermediation markup. Increases in banking sector competition raise the interest rate pass-through and lower the loan intermediation markup. Furthermore, Flogel and Gartner (2018) show that Germany has a decentralised system not only regarding the distribution of banks, but also its financial and political system more generally. The authors show that decentralised banks, which are predominantly regional savings banks and co-operative banks account for most lending to business and have extended lending compared to centralised big banks.

Thus, evidence in this chapter shows that over and above the Land Bank as a financial vehicle to support the accelerated land reform policy and the agricultural revolution, there is a case to change the financial institutional arrangements and regulations to allow for greater participation of lower-tier banks. We have shown that increased participation of lower-tier banks can benefit the housing sector, development of rural and township economies and SMMEs. These sectors of the economy are intricately linked to the agricultural, manufacturing and other sectors related to the value chain that supports the agricultural revolution. The main objective is to enable and enact the constitutional objectives of the democratic consolidation in achieving urban and rural land equity.

29.7 Conclusion and Policy Implications

Is there a role that mutual banks, Postbank, co-operative banks and co-operative financial institutions can play in complementing the Land Bank, especially in development funding for the agricultural sector value chain? Yes, evidence in this chapter shows that they have a role to play. Evidence in this chapter shows that mortgage advances growth increases more than other loans growth in response to a positive total credit shock extended by the Postbank, mutual banks and co-operative banks, collectively referred to as lower-tier banks. Furthermore, as the size of lower-tier banks increases over time, this will result in double-digit growth in mortgage advances and other loans. This means that lower-tier banks can have a meaningful impact in financing housing and SMMEs within the policy of accelerated land reform, alleviation of poverty, reducing income and wealth inequality, facilitating inclusion and the development of rural and township economies.

Thus, there is a case to change the financial institutional arrangements and regulations to allow for greater participation of lower-tier banks. Increased participation of lower-tier banks can benefit the housing sector, development of township and rural economies and SMMEs. These sectors of the economy are intricately linked to the agricultural, manufacturing and other sectors related to the value chain that supports the agricultural revolution. The main objective of changes to the financial regulations is to enable and enact the constitutional objectives of the democratic consolidation in achieving urban and rural land equity. Furthermore, changes to the financial landscape imply that there is a case to change the regulatory environment lower-tier banks operate in. The change in the regulatory environment is particularly important if we take into account the fact that there is going to be an increase in credit extension. This requires rigorous regulation of lower-tier banks in order to deal with reckless (and even predatory) lending with known devastating consequences for financial stability and severe social welfare costs. In addition, co-operative financial institutions subject to some rigorous regulatory requirements have the potential to become fully fledged co-operative banks. Therefore, they are the feeding pipeline to expanding lower-tier banks across the country.

With full adherence to the regulatory requirements and sufficient support, the number of co-operative banks can easily grow to more than ten spread across the country. In turn, the sustainable growth of co-operative banks will contribute to the growth and increase in the number of mutual banks. Hence, lower-tier banks have a role to play in bridging the gaps where the perceived risk of transactions exceeds the appetite of commercial funders for entrepreneurs, SMMEs and housing to clients with limited assets to offer as collateral. Furthermore, an approach that nurtures co-operative financial institutions to become fully fledged co operative banks can contribute to the decentralisation of the distribution of banks and concentration of the banking system.

References

Amaral, P. 2017. *Monetary Policy and Inequality*. Economic Commentary 01, Federal Reserve Bank of Cleveland.

Barnett, Alina, and Thomas, Ryland. 2013. *Has Weak Lending and Activity in the United Kingdom Been Driven by Credit Supply Shocks?* December 20. Bank of England Working Paper No. 482.

BFAP. 2011. The Contribution of the Agro-Industrial Complex to Employment in South Africa. Tech. Rep. June, The Bureau for Food and Agricultural Policy, Pretoria.

Corbae, D., and Levine, R. 2018. Competition, Stability, and Efficiency in Financial Markets. Paper Presented at the Annual Economic Symposium in Jackson Hole, Wyo. https://www.kansascityfed.org/~/media/files/publicat/sympos/2018/papersandhandouts/825180810corbaelevinepaper.pdf?la=en

Dolado, J., Motyovszki, G., and Pappa, E. 2018. Monetary Policy and Inequality: A New Channel. VOX CEPR Portal.

Domanski, D., Scatigna, M., and Zabai, A. 2016. Wealth Inequality and Monetary Policy. *BIS Quarterly Review*, March 2016.

Flogel, F., and Gartner, S. 2018. *The Banking Systems of Germany, the UK and Spain from a Spatial Perspective: The German Case*. IAT Discussion Paper 18/02. https://www.econstor.eu/bitstream/10419/180381/1/1026705681.pdf#page=2

Furceri, D., Loungani, P., and Zdzienicka, A. 2016. *The Effects of Monetary Policy Shocks on Inequality*. IMF Working Paper WP/16/245.

Kganyago, L. 2018. Inequality and Monetary Policy in South Africa. A public lecture at the Nelson Mandela University, Port Elizabeth, 1 August 2018.

Kiyotaki, N., and Moore, J. 1995. *Credit Cycles*. NBER Working Paper No. 5083.

Mersch, Y. 2014. Speech at Corporate Credit Conference, Zurich, 17 October 2014.

Moseneke, D.C.J. 2015. Reflections on South African Constitutional Democracy—Transition and Transformation. https://constitutionallyspeaking.co.za/dcj-moseneke-reflections-on-south-african-constitutional-democracy-transition-and-transformation/.

Ndou, E., Gumata, N., and Tshuma, M.M. 2019. *Exchange Rate, Second Round Effects and Inflation Processes: Evidence from South Africa*. Palgrave Macmillan.

Sihlobo, W. 2018. Fewer Farmers, More Milk. https://wandilesihlobo.com/2018/07/17/fewer-farmers-more-milk/.

Sihlobo, W., and Kirsten, J. 2018. Secret of Land-Reform Success Is to Learn Lessons from Experience. *Business Day*, May 28. https://www.businesslive.co.za/bd/opinion/2018-05-28-the-secret-of-land-reform-success-is-to-learn-lessons-from-experience/.

30

The Impact of Financial Regulations and Macroprudential Tools on the Funding of the Agricultural Sector Growth

Learning Objectives

- Explore the impact of excess capital adequacy ratio (CAR) and risk-weighted assets (RWAs) on the share of the agricultural sector credit.
- Assess the impact of the increase of the agricultural sector credit share on the agricultural sector output growth, investment growth and employment growth.

30.1 Introduction

Is the lowering of the banks' excess capital adequacy ratio (CAR) another channel through which the banking and financial regulations can be used to support the accelerated land reform policy and the agricultural revolution as envisaged in the National Development Plan (NDP)? Figure 30.1 shows that banks have consistently held CAR in excess of the minimum required and excess CAR holding increased post-2009. In addition, Fig. 30.1(c) shows that excess CAR is negatively associated with risk-weighted assets (RWAs). This implies that heightened excess CAR leads

N. Gumata, E. Ndou, *Accelerated Land Reform, Mining, Growth, Unemployment and Inequality in South Africa*, https://doi.org/10.1007/978-3-030-30884-1_30

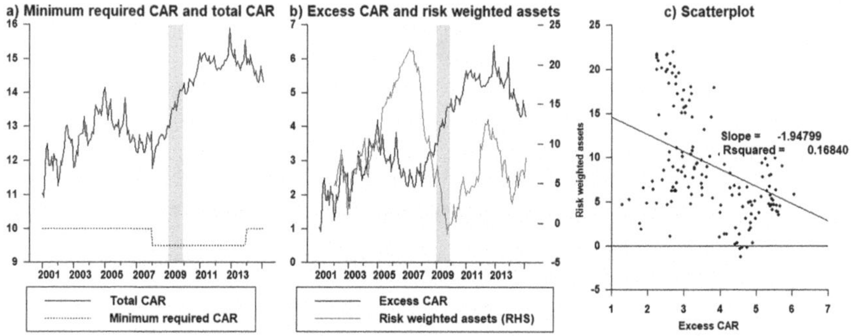

Fig. 30.1 Risk-weighted assets, total and excess capital adequacy ratio. (Note: The grey shaded area denotes the South African recession. Source: South African Reserve Bank and authors' calculations)

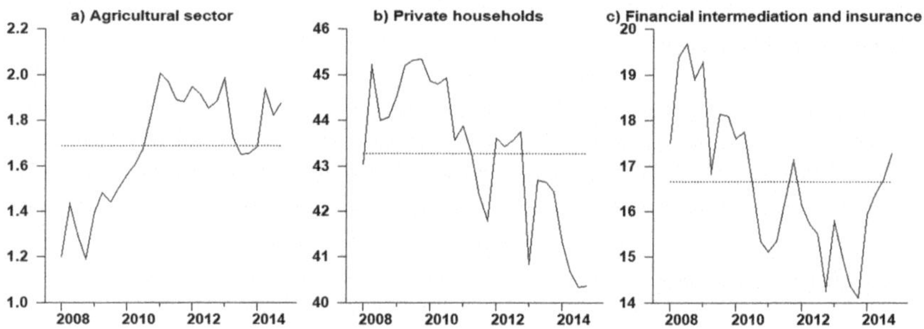

Fig. 30.2 Sectoral distribution of bank credit. (Source: South African Reserve Bank and authors' calculations)

to a decline in risk-taking by banks, which manifests in tighter lending criteria, a decline in credit growth and an increase in the lending rate margins.

This chapter assesses whether the loosening of excess CAR and an increase in the share of the agricultural sector credit leads to an increase in the agricultural sector output growth, investment growth and employment growth. Figure 30.2 shows that on average between 2008Q1 and 2014Q4, banks extended 1.69 per cent of total bank credit to the agricultural sector compared to 43.28 per cent to the households' sector and 16.65 per cent to the financial intermediation and insurance sectors.

Thus, is there scope to use financial regulations and macroprudential tools in the funding of the agricultural sector growth?

We fill the academic and policy research gaps by showing that excess CAR or, alternatively, the countercyclical capital buffer (CCyB) can be loosened and used as an effective financial regulatory and macroprudential tool to support agricultural sector growth. Gumata and Ndou (2017) provided evidence showing that macroprudential tools such as loan-to-value ratios (LTVs) and repayment-to-income ratios (RTIs) are complementary tools to monetary policy tools. The repo rate and LTV and RTI tightening shock effects reinforce each other. At the same time, the transmission of the LTV and RTI shocks occurs through the same channels as those that are impacted by tight or loose monetary policy shocks.

30.2 What Is the Impact of a Decline in Excess CAR on RWAs and the Share of the Agricultural Sector Credit by the Banking Sector?

This section starts by assessing the response of RWAs and the share of the agricultural sector credit by the banking sector to a decline in excess CAR. We estimate a vector autoregression (VAR) model that includes excess CAR, RWAs and the share of the agricultural sector credit extended by banks. The data used in the model are on a quarterly (Q) basis and span the period 2008Q1 to 2014Q4. The VAR model is estimated using 1 lag and 10,000 Monte Carlo draws. The shock is a unit shock.

The results in Fig. 30.3 show that RWAs and the credit share of the agricultural sector by the banking sector increase in response to a negative shock to excess CAR. Thus, the loosening of the CCyB is effectively an accommodative monetary policy stance and the injection of liquidity into the real economy to support investment spending, output and employment growth. This is another channel through which the banking and financial regulations can be used to support the accelerated land reform policy and the agricultural revolution as envisaged in the NDP. In

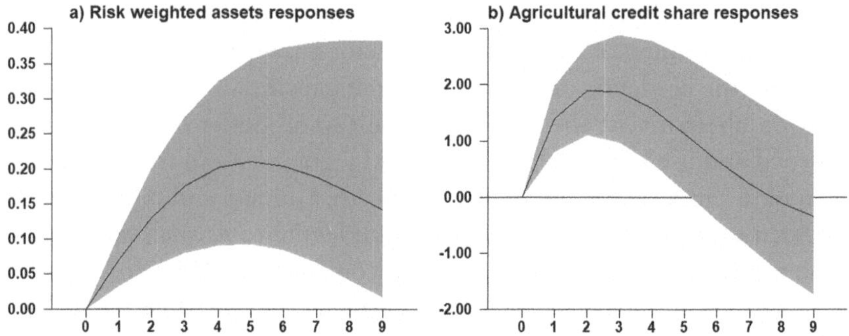

Fig. 30.3 Risk weighted assets and credit share responses to a negative shock to excess capital adequacy ratio. (Note: The grey shaded area bands denote the 16th and 84th percentile confidence bands. Source: Authors' calculations)

addition, the use of banking regulations and macroprudential tools can assist in the redistribution of risk and bank lending from being largely concentrated on private households, financial intermediation and insurance sectors as shown in Fig. 30.3.

30.3 What Is the Impact of a Decline in Excess CAR on the Agricultural Sector Growth?

To answer this question, we estimate a VAR model that includes excess CAR, the share of the agricultural sector credit extended by banks, the agricultural sector output growth, investment growth and employment growth. The VAR model is estimated using 1 lag and 10,000 Monte Carlo draws. The shock is a unit shock. The results in Fig. 30.4 show that lowering excess CAR leads to an increase in the credit share of the agricultural sector by commercial banks, which has a positive effect on the agricultural sector output growth, investment growth and employment growth. The results imply that loosening excess CAR and increasing the credit share allocated to the agricultural sector benefit the agricultural sector growth.

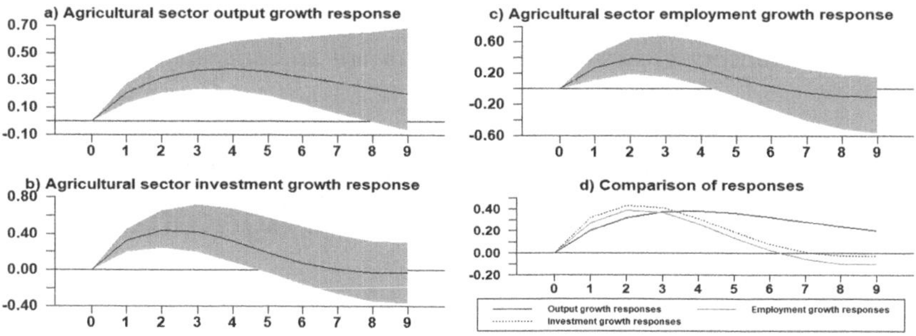

Fig. 30.4 Responses to negative shocks to excess capital adequacy ratio. (Note: The grey shaded area bands denote the 16th and 84th percentile confidence bands. Source: Authors' calculations)

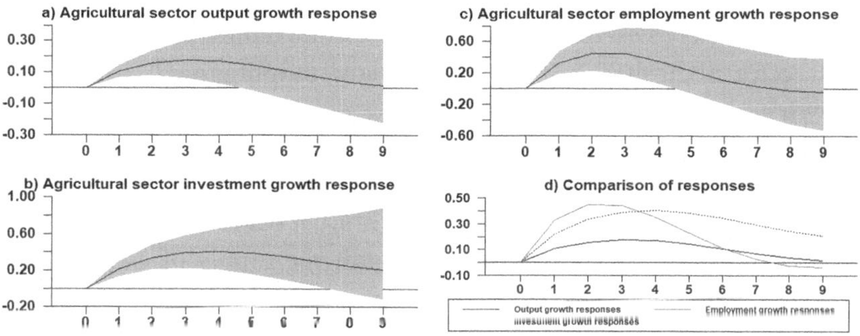

Fig. 30.5 Responses to positive shocks to risk-weighted assets. (Note: The grey shaded area bands denote the 16th and 84th percentile confidence bands. Source: Authors' calculations)

30.4 Robustness Analysis: Inferences for the Impact of Positive RWAs Shocks

Because the loosening of excess CAR also implies changes to risk weights on corporate sector credit, we estimate another VAR model where we replace excess CAR with RWAs to assess the responses of the agricultural sector. We assess the impact of positive shocks to the RWAs on the share of the agricultural sector credit extended by commercial banks, output, investment and employment growth. The results in Fig. 30.5 show that the share of the agricultural sector credit increases alongside the agricultural sector output growth, investment growth and employment growth.

30.5 Do Negative Excess CAR Shocks Exert Asymmetric Effects on the Agricultural Sector?

To conclude the analysis in this chapter, this section conducts a scenario analysis of the effects of different magnitudes of negative shocks to excess CAR on the agricultural sector credit extended by commercial banks. We use the Kilian and Vigfusson approach for asymmetric transmissions of shocks. The results in Fig. 30.6 show that the different magnitudes of negative shocks to excess CAR have incremental benefits for the agricultural sector credit share by the banking sector, output growth, investment growth and the employment growth.

Thus, we have established robust evidence that an increase in the balance sheet of the Land Bank, changes to the banking and financial regulations to open up space for the Postbank, mutual banks and co-operatives banks (lower-tier banks) will largely benefit the supply of credit to the agricultural sector and to benefits that accrue to accelerated land reform. This means that a multi-institutional approach to funding accelerated land reform and the agricultural sector is a prudent risk based on a long-

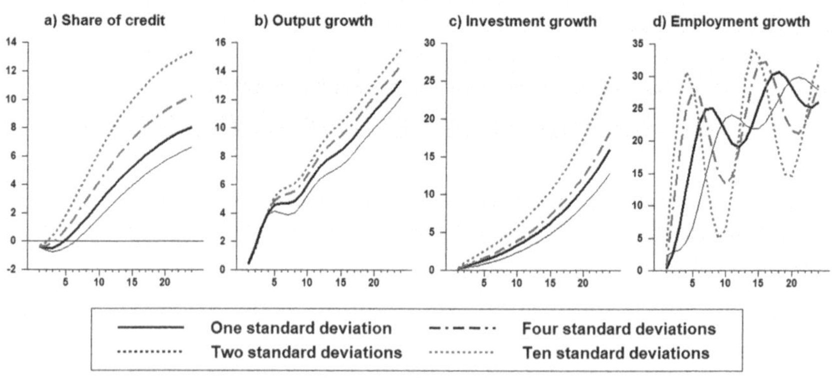

Fig. 30.6 Asymmetric responses to negative shocks to excess capital adequacy ratios. (Source: Authors' calculations)

term approach to make sure that the agricultural sector and the value chain are sustainable for the long haul.[1]

30.6 Conclusion and Policy Implications

Is the lowering of the banks' excess CAR another channel through which the banking and financial regulations can be used to support the accelerated land reform policy and the agricultural revolution as envisaged in the NDP? Yes, it is. We establish that RWAs and the credit share of the agricultural sector by the banking sector increase in response to a negative (decline) shock to excess CAR. Thus, the loosening of the CCyB is effectively an accommodative monetary policy stance and the injection of liquidity into the real economy to support investment spending, output and employment growth. This is another channel through which the banking and financial regulations can be used to support the accelerated land reform policy and the agricultural revolution as envisaged in the NDP.

Furthermore, lowering excess CAR leads to an increase in the credit share of the agricultural sector by commercial banks, which has a positive effect on the agricultural sector output growth, investment growth and employment growth. Thus, loosening excess CAR and increasing the credit share allocated to the agricultural sector benefit agricultural sector growth. In addition, different magnitudes of negative shocks to excess CAR have incremental benefits for the agricultural sector credit share by the banking sector, output growth, investment growth and employment growth. Thus, we have established robust evidence that an increase in the balance sheet of the Land Bank, changes to the banking and financial regulations to open up space for the Postbank, mutual banks and co-operatives banks (lower-tier banks) will largely benefit the supply of credit to the agricultural sector and to benefits that accrue to accelerated land

[1] In this case and as stated by the Agricultural Development Bank the agricultural sector value chain includes water supply infrastructure, bore holes, main line and irrigation equipment, all pumping requirements for irrigation, dams, internal or external fencing, electricity supply by any supplier, silos; and roads to access farming areas, developing the rural financial system, providing export and import financial services, agricultural entrepreneurship, small and medium-size enterprises (SMEs), support programmes that enhance productivity, profitability, investment and innovation in the agricultural sector, programmes that contribute to rural development, food security and affordability, and job creation in the agricultural sector and rural economies.

reform. This means that a multi-institutional approach to funding accelerated land reform and the agricultural sector is a prudent risk based on a long-term approach to make sure that the agricultural sector and the value chain are sustainable for the long run.

References

Angelopoulou, E., and Gibson, D.H. 2007. *The Balance Sheet Channel of Monetary Policy: Evidence from the UK.* Bank of Greece Working Paper No. 53.

Bernanke, B.S., and Gertler, M. 1989. Agency Costs, Net Worth, and Business Fluctuations. *American Economic Review*, 79, 14–31.

Bernanke, B.S., and Gertler, M. 1995. Inside the Black Box: The Credit Channel of Monetary Policy Transmission. *Journal of Economic Perspectives, American Economic Association*, 9(4), 27–48.

Borio, C., Disyatat, P., Juselius, M., and Rungcharoenkitkul, P. 2018. *Monetary Policy in the Grip of a Pincer Movement.* BIS Working Papers No. 706.

Corbae, D., and Levine, R. 2018. Competition, Stability, and Efficiency in Financial Markets. https://www.kansascityfed.org/~/media/files/publicat/sympos/2018/papersandhandouts/825180810corbaelevinepaper.pdf?la=en.

Domanski, D., Scatigna, M., and Zabai, A. 2016. Wealth Inequality and Monetary Policy. *BIS Quarterly Review*, March 2016.

Drehmann, Mathias, and Juselius, Mikael. 2012. Do Debt Service Costs Affect Macroeconomic and Financial Stability? *BIS Quarterly Review*, September (Basel: Bank for International Settlements).

Drehmann, Mathias, and Juselius, Mikael. 2013. *Evaluating Early Warning Indicators of Banking Crises: Satisfying Policy Requirements.* BIS Working Paper Series No. 421 (Basel: Bank for International Settlements).

Flogel, F., and Gartner, S. 2018. The Banking Systems of Germany, the UK and Spain from a Spatial Perspective: The German Case. https://www.econstor.eu/bitstream/10419/180381/1/1026705681.pdf#page=2.

Furceri, D., Loungani, P., and Zdzienicka, A. 2016. *The Effects of Monetary Policy Shocks on Inequality.* IMF Working Paper WP/16/245.

Gumata, N., and Ndou, E. 2017. *Bank Credit Extension and Real Economic Activity in South Africa: The Impact of Capital Flow Dynamics, Bank Regulation and Selected Macro-prudential Tools.* Palgrave Macmillan. ISBN 978-3-319-43551-0.

IMF. 2014. *Staff Guidance Note on Macroprudential Policy—Detailed Guidance on Instruments*. IMF Policy Papers. http://www.imf.org/external/np/pp/eng/2014/110614a.pdf.

Kganyago, L. 2018. Inequality and Monetary Policy in South Africa. A public lecture at the Nelson Mandela University, Port Elizabeth, 1 August 2018.

Kiyotaki, N., and Moore, J. 1995. *Credit Cycles*. NBER Working Paper No. 5083.

31

The Interaction Between the Financial Sector Regulatory Framework, Property Rights Clause and the South African Reserve Bank Mandate

Learning Objectives

- Understand how section 25 of the constitution is linked with section 224 of the constitution.
- Assess what the changes to section 25 of the constitution imply for the current mandate of the South African Reserve Bank (SARB) and the framework in which monetary policy is conducted in South Africa.
- Understand how section 25(5) of the constitution can be redrafted to protect gender equity.
- Explore whether there is a case to redraft and expand the criteria set out in 25(3) of the constitution to decide what is fair, just and equitable compensation.

31.1 Introduction

This chapter assesses the interaction between the property rights clause, the South African Reserve Bank (SARB) mandate and the framework in which monetary policy is conducted in South Africa. We are of the

N. Gumata, E. Ndou, *Accelerated Land Reform, Mining, Growth, Unemployment and Inequality in South Africa*, https://doi.org/10.1007/978-3-030-30884-1_31

opinion that the proposed changes to section 25 of the constitution have a significant bearing on the current mandate of the SARB. We treated the proposed changes to section 25 of the constitution as an empirical question in earlier chapters of this book. In addition, as an empirical question, we argue that the balance sheet channel of the monetary policy transmission anchors the debate about how section 25 of the constitution is linked with section 224 of the constitution. Irrespective of what the changes to section 25 of the constitution are, especially when (i) the "*willing buyer:willing seller*" land and agrarian reform model is scrapped; (ii) the wording of the constitution is changes to be explicit as to what is meant by "*expropriation of land without compensation*" and under what circumstances the policy is to be implemented; and (iii) the definition of what "*equitable access*" and "*just and equitable*" are, we argue that there are significant financial implications that have a bearing on the macroeconomy and welfare of South Africans, the mandate of the SARB and the framework of the conduct of monetary policy in South Africa.

Against the background of the proposed changes to section 25 of the constitution, this chapter contributes to the academic and policy research gaps exploring how section 25(5) of the constitution can be redrafted to protect gender equity. We also explore whether there is a case to redraft and expand the criteria set out in section 25(3) of the constitution to decide what is fair, just and equitable compensation. Last, we explore the interaction between sections 25 and 224 of the constitution, especially against the background of the objectives of the Land and Development Bank:

1. Sustainability, productivity, competitiveness, investment, innovation and profitability of famers
2. Agricultural entrepreneurship and job creation
3. Development of thriving rural financial systems, at the core of accelerated land reform, agricultural funding and development.

31.2 How Can Section 25(5) of the Constitution Be Redrafted to Protect Gender Equity?

This section starts by reviewing how changes in section 25 of the constitution impact on section 224 dealing with the SARB and the Reserve Bank Act. First, the Land and Agricultural Development Bank Act 2002 explicitly states that the Land bank is established in recognition that racially discriminatory practices and laws of the past and apartheid deprived historically disadvantaged people of land, resulting in their exclusion from the agricultural sector and racially skewed patterns of landownership in South Africa. The Land Bank was therefore established in order to fulfil the following objectives:

1. To effect a change in the patterns of landownership by promoting greater participation in the agricultural sector by historically disadvantaged persons
2. To increase ownership of agricultural land by such persons through the provision of appropriate financial services

In addition, the Land Bank Act is specific and explicit about the objectives of the Land Bank:

1. To redress the race and gender imbalance in the agricultural sector
2. To enhance productivity, profitability, investment and innovation in the agricultural sector and rural financial systems
3. Implement agrarian reform, land redistribution and development programmes aimed at historically disadvantaged persons or groups for the development of farming enterprises and agricultural purposes
4. To support programmes that stimulate growth of the agricultural sector and better use of land
5. To support programmes that lead to job creation
6. To promote a competitive and profitable agricultural sector

Gender equality should feature strongly in the redrafting of section 25. The high-level panel on the assessment of key legislation and the accelera-

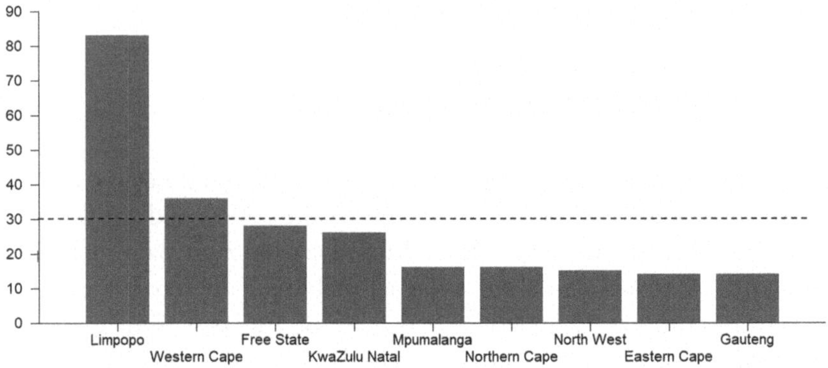

Fig. 31.1 Percentage of women beneficiaries in land reform between 1994 and 2016. (Source: Umrabulo No. 43 (2018). See for further reading http://www.anc.org.za/sites/default/files/pubs/umrabulo43.pdf)

tion of fundamental change shows that, nationally, women constitute only 23 per cent of land redistribution beneficiaries.[1] Women are a minority of beneficiaries in a majority of provinces and make up less than one quarter of beneficiaries as shown in Fig. 31.1.

In addition, the Bureau for Food and Agricultural Policy (BFAP 2011) finds that the bulk (64 per cent) of the smallholder schemes in the former homelands is geographically located in the ten districts, of which six were declared presidential poverty nodes. The majority of these rural households rely and are headed by women and largely consist of children and the elderly.

Earlier chapters presented evidence from studies showing that land acquisition and the choice of land for redistribution have implications for the impact of land reform on gender, class and poverty. Netshipale et al. (2007) present evidence showing that the changes in land redistribution policy over time have resulted in significant differences in beneficiary participation among land redistribution models. The implementation outcomes of land redistribution indicate that the Settlement Land Acquisition Grant (SLAG) model benefited the poor while the Land Redistribution for Agricultural Development (LRAD1, LRAD2) and

[1] See for further reading https://www.parliament.gov.za/storage/app/media/Pages/2017/october/High_Level_Panel/HLP_Report/HLP_report.pdf.

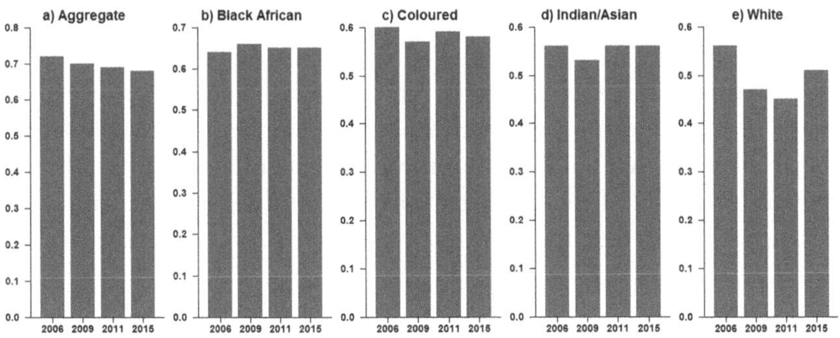

Fig. 31.2 Gini coefficient Income per capita by race. (Source: Statistics South Africa)

Proactive Land Acquisition Strategy (PLAS) models benefitted mostly other social classes. Therefore, the approach to accelerated land redistribution has to pay attention not only to gender but also to class, which is a proxy for poverty. Figure 31.2 shows that poverty and inequality are disproportionately distributed along racial lines.

The legislation that clearly seeks to redress gender and class imbalance in landownership and participation in the agricultural sector such as that contained in the Land and Agricultural Development Bank should be enforced and monitored to evaluated progress. Section 25(5) states that the state must take reasonable legislative and other measures, within its available resources, to foster conditions which enable citizens to gain access to land on an equitable basis. This can be achieved by clearly defining, stating and being explicit in section 25(5) of the constitution as to what is meant by and what constitutes "equitable access".

As Ngcukaitobi says, "the constitution is a fundamentally disruptive, revolutionary, liberating document. Today we take for granted the idea of equality because it is embedded in the constitution". Hence the need to be explicit and clear in terms of gender equity in the redrafting of the section 25(5) of the constitution so that all is embedded in the constitution and that is what also informs policy, regulations and laws for execution of mandates. Similarly, Madonsela states that guaranteeing these socioeconomic rights for women in the constitution will assure democracy by not leaving it to politicians and political entrepreneurship to determine what's good for the people. Socioeconomic rights primarily place a responsibility on the state to create an environment that frees everyone's potential, so that people can improve the quality of their own lives while contributing to the well-being of their communities.[2] In addition, Hall states that land is about the intergenerational transfer of poverty and privilege.[3] Thus, gender disparities on their own demand that they be safeguarded in the constitution as they form part and parcel of the bill of rights.[4]

31.2.1 What Are the Implications for Communal Land?

We showed in earlier chapters that a positive shock to area cultivated in the former homelands indicates that agricultural output, employment and labour productivity increase. This means that bringing underutilised land in the former homelands and communal areas will make a significant and meaningful difference in the agricultural sector's contribution to growth, employment and labour productivity. But increasing investment alone is not sufficient to boost agricultural sector output, employment and labour productivity. In fact, the results show that bringing in underutilised land in the former homelands and communal areas more than doubles the response of the agricultural sector output growth, employment and labour productivity growth. This means that all the legislation and laws that inhibit, place barriers and make it difficult for women to own land and property and participate in the agricultural sector should be resolved. Such legislation and laws are not only incompatible with the constitution but are also a binding constraint on the realisation of the full potential of women and value added to the economy at large.

---

[2] See for further reading https://www.businesslive.co.za/fm/opinion/on-my-mind/2018-06-21-thuli-madonsela-the-making-of-a-strong-constitution/.

[3] See for further reading buff.ly/2xaxqpw.

[4] We explore in detail the role that accelerated land redistribution can play in reducing poverty and inequality in earlier chapters.

31.3 What about the Criteria Set Out in 25(3) of the Constitution to Decide What Is Fair, Just and Equitable Compensation? Is There a Case to Redraft and Expand Criteria in Making Decisions about the Trade-Offs?

This section expands on the earlier section arguing for the redrafting of section 25(5) to be explicit as to what "*equitable access*" means in relation to gender. Is there a case to redraft and expand criteria in section 25(3) in making decisions about the trade-offs of what constitutes fair, just and equitable compensation? First, section 25(2) states that property may be expropriated only in terms of law of general application (a) for a public purpose or in the public interest; and (b) subject to compensation, the amount of which and the time and manner of payment of which have either been agreed to by those affected or decided or approved by a court.

31.3.1 What Is in the Public Interest and What Is for a Public Purpose?

In part, section 25(4) gives us a glimpse of what this means as it states that for the purposes of section 25(4), the public interest includes the nation's commitment to land reform, and to reforms to bring about equitable access to all of South Africa's natural resources. This implies that land reform is a national constitutional mandate and section 25(3) sets out the five key criteria which underpin the decision of how to execute this mandate for land reform and redistribution.

Section 25(3) states that the amount of the compensation and the time and manner of payment must be just and equitable, reflecting an equitable balance between the public interest and the interests of those affected, having regard to all relevant circumstances, including

(a) The current use of the property
(b) The history of the acquisition and use of the property

(c) The market value of the property
(d) The extent of direct state investment and subsidy in the acquisition and beneficial capital improvement of the property
(e) The purpose of the expropriation

To this effect Moseneke (2015) states that the compensation must be just and equitable and not necessarily the market value of the land. Market price is but one of five criteria that section 25(3) of the constitution lists for a court to set for fair compensation. In addition, Moseneke (2015) argues that the property clause does not carry the phrase "*willing buyer:willing seller*", which is often blamed for an inadequate resolution of a land question. The state's power to expropriate does not depend on the willingness of the landowner. The compensation may be agreed but, if not, a court must fix it.

31.3.2 How Does the Court Fix It and What Is Fair Compensation?

In fixing the issues related to fair compensation, the court starts from the basis of what the valuation is of the asset in question by the market. So, yet again, we are unable to escape the role of market forces in dictating the starting point of resolving the question of what compensation is fair. In interpreting fair compensation which is just and equitable the court will yet again be guided by the market price as a starting point or a point of departure. The "*willing buyer:willing seller*" aspect in the land reform policy is a direct outcome of the fact that valuation of land and property are dependent on the valuations derived from markets. The land and housing markets which equilibrate demand and supply are the starting point.

The constitution, by being explicit and including the market value of property as one of the criteria to decide what *fair, just and equitable compensation* is, has legitimised and constitutionalised the market price irrespective of whether the price derived from that market structure is fair or not. And yet the economics discipline has ample cases in which it shows that markets can fail dismally to determine the fair value of the underlying asset. At any given point, the asset in question can be highly over- or undervalued depending on the factors driving the market at that particular point in time.

For instance, in the case of the land market, it is evident that a large buyer such as government entering this market of a limited and scarce resource such as valuable and usable farmland can immediately distort the price discovery process (price formation) in favour of the sellers. The distortion in the price formation process when government enters such a market can be compounded by the perception that is has unlimited financial resources and thus can afford to settle at highly inflated farmland and property prices. This is especially the case given the objective for which the land is bought or acquired. In such cases, a large player such as government entering the land and property markets and the implied demand can easily distort the market and the price formation process, rendering the farmland and property prices highly unfair.

The five criteria to decide what is fair and equitable in section 25(3) speak to the variables that have to be taken into account when deciding what fair, just and equitable compensation is. The "*willing buyer:willing seller*" model of land reform and redistribution might not be carried in the property clause, as Moseneke (2015) argues. And yet by specifically and explicitly including the market value of the property as one of the criteria or variables to resolve the trade-offs involved in solving the problem of what is *fair, just and equitable compensation*, the constitution has legitimised and constitutionalised the market forces as one of the key pillars that solve the problem of land reform and redistribution in South Africa. The market value of farmland and property forms the basis on which the constitution has chosen to start the resolution of the land question. In the absence of any other valuation approaches to determine the value of the asset in question, the constitution, effectively, has overwhelming bias regarding the settling of the question of what is deemed to be *fair, just and equitable compensation* according to the market price.

Thus, in the absence of other valuation approaches to determine the value of the asset in question, we argue that the most important questions that the redrafting of section 25 must contend with are the following: What weights do we allocate to the five criteria? Are they allocated equal weights in the decision-making about what is *fair, just and equitable compensation*? If that is not the case, at what point does discretion kick in and what informs such a judgement call? Can a price of zero be *fair, just and equitable compensation* for an asset in question? In other words, what anchors or constrains the discretion and judgement by the courts? It is our view that in this current form section 25(3) leaves the courts with too many degrees of freedom in their decision of what is fair, just and equitable compensation.

There must be a constraining factor in the judgement of what is fair, just and equitable compensation. In this case, the preamble of the constitution itself is a guide in that it states the fact that

> *we the people of South Africa acknowledge the injustices of our past, honour those who suffered for justice … Hosi katekisa Africa*

31.3.3 What Constrains and Anchors the Application of Discretion and Judgement on What Is Fair, Just and Equitable Compensation?

The constraining factor in the application of discretion and judgement must be anchored by justice, the need to reform landownership patterns and nation-building. At the same time, the definition of *fair, just and equitable compensation* must take into account the huge funding demands of post-transfer support on the fiscus to make a success of land reform and redistribution. What is the balance that should be struck in terms of the funding of the first leg of the transaction versus the second leg of the transaction? This is the trade-off that the criteria set out in section 25(3) must answer. This must guide how far below the fair or market value compensation can be set. Under what circumstances is it constitutionally *fair, just and equitable to set compensation to zero*. This is what expropriation without compensation effectively means. The case for expropriation without compensation is strengthened as it releases funds and prioritises the second leg of the transaction. Expropriation without compensation loosens the government budgetary or financial constraint. Policy trade-offs and difficult choices have to be made.

As the preamble states,

adopt this Constitution as the supreme law of the Republic so as to heal the divisions of the past.

The language in section 25 can be redrafted to prize *justice, healing the injustices of the past and building a new nation.* There has to be clarity that the market price of the land and property is subject to the convergence of a number of valuation approaches and this does not preclude a zero valuation of the asset. The inclusion of zero valuation of the property in question also guards against other market failures that can be induced by collusion. In addition, the definition of the purposes of expropriation has to be expanded and it has to be made explicit that it is not only confined to land reform as is the case currently. There are cases where the development needs of the country rank higher, such as with the development of new towns or cities which also caters for housing, transportation and industrial bases, which can be causes for expropriation of land. We already argued that "*equitable access*" must be clearly defined to cater for gender, which in turn addresses the issues of class and race.

Furthermore, there is nothing in section 25 that refers explicitly to private ownership of land and property. The property clause is silent on the private ownership of land and property, and yet this is the principle that underlies property contracts, legislation, laws and policies. We have shown that the asset price, collateral and wealth channels of the monetary policy transmission mechanism play an important role in the financial and macroeconomy. Thus, in redrafting section 25, private ownership of land and property must be made explicit and constitutional. In so doing, we are of the opinion that the proposed amendments to section 25 (the property clause) of the constitution do not abrogate or destroy the basic structure of the constitution. Alternatively, these constitutional amendments are not unconstitutional. They can be read consistently with the balance of the constitution.

Lastly, section 25(6) property is not limited to land. No provision of this section may impede the state from taking legislative and other measures to achieve land, water and related reform, in order to redress the results of past racial discrimination, provided that any departure from the provisions of this section is in accordance with the provisions of section 36(1).

Thus, we conclude that, if section 25 is anchored on the constitutionality of justice, equitable access to land, property and resources, equitable redress of the injustices of people or communities dispossessed of land and property after June 1913 as a result of racially discriminatory laws and practices, then the weight allocated to the market price as one of the key criteria for *fair, just and equitable compensation* should be redrafted so that it can be inclusive of the interpretation that there are cases where this can be zero. In cases where justice trumps the market price, fair, just and equitable compensation can be zero. This should be made clear and explicit in the constitution. Similarly, the definition of "*equitable access*" has to be clearly defined to cater for gender, which in turn addresses the issues of class and race. Furthermore, in redrafting section 25, private ownership of land and property can be made explicit and constitutional. The process of redrafting and amending section 25 will also inform the land reform and redistribution policy to the effect that the "willing buyer:willing seller" model is not the only determinant of accelerated land reform policy.[5]

31.4 What Are the Implications for Section 223 of the Constitution for the Monetary Policy Framework of the South African Reserve Bank?

How then does the country quantitatively measure, evaluate and monitor the progress of developing the rural financial system, food security and affordability and job creation? We argue that in order to align and coordinate policies, and quantitatively measure, evaluate and monitor the progress, the SARB will play a much more meaningful role. This has implications for the mandate of the SARB. In its current form, section 224(1) states that the mandate of the SARB

[5] This is consistent with Aliber's (2015) conclusions that the majority of participants in the Summit rejected the notion that the land reform process should be based solely on the notion of "willing seller: willing buyer".

is to protect the value of the currency in the interest of balanced and sustainable economic growth in the Republic.

31.4.1 The Price Stability Mandate

As it currently stands, section 224 makes no reference to price and financial stability. Rather, it refers to the protection of the value of the currency in the interest of balanced and sustainable growth in the Republic. We argue that the wording of section 224 is characteristic of the time preceding that during which it was drafted, when the country was isolated under the apartheid political regime and prone to balance of payments crisis. As such, the wording is very outdated and bears no resemblance to the vision encapsulated in the constitution itself.[6] In what follows in this section, we lay out the areas and wording that can be considered in the redrafting of section 224 and changes to the monetary policy framework.

We started this section by asking: How then does the country quantitatively measure, evaluate and monitor the progress of developing the rural financial system, food security and affordability, and job creation? We argue that all these elements are contained in the current mandates of the SARB for price and financial stability, although this is not explicit in the current wording of section 224. The price stability mandate captures the social welfare imperative to make sure that general domestic prices are not only stable between 3 and 6 per cent but are low and sustainable.[7]

But we are of the opinion that at an operational level the definition for low and stable must be made explicit. In this regard, we argue that lowering the inflation target range to between 2 and 4 per cent is numerically explicit and consistent with the mandate of low and stable inflation. Ndou and Gumata (2017) have shown that this target range is compatible with asymmetries induced by low and high inflation regimes on the

[6] In fact, Borio et al. (2018) argue that the mandates enshrined in the central bank law are typically written in very general terms and provide plenty of scope for interpretation. They tend to be very vague and are largely a product of the time when they were written.

[7] Thus, the aspect of affordability over and above food security is well captured in the price stability mandate, and can be enforced and evaluated.

domestic financial and macroeconomic variables over and above the exchange rate pass-through to inflation.[8]

31.4.2 The Financial Stability Mandate

Although the financial stability mandate captures the development of the rural financial system in as far as the financial regulations and macroprudential tools can be used to achieve these goals, we contend that we have to be explicit as to how we will quantitatively measure, monitor and evaluate the achievement of these objectives at the operational level.[9] Because monetary policy cannot achieve financial stability, it follows that it should not have financial stability as a goal. Monetary policy has a strong and systematic effect on inflation and employment but normally a small and unsystematic effect on financial stability. On the other hand, macroprudential policy has a strong and systematic effect on financial stability. Nonetheless, there is interaction between the policies because financial regulation also has income and wealth distribution effects, including intergenerational effects. As such, Hammond (2017) argues that macroprudential policy needs to have a secondary goal, such as in the case of the Bank of England's Financial Policy Committee of "supporting the economic policy of Her Majesty's Government, including its objectives for growth and employment". As such, we argue that the amendment of section 223 gives the opportunity to clearly define what the financial stability mandate actually means and how its achievement is to be measured, monitored and evaluated. In this regard, we are of the opinion that the explicit wording to the following effect can be adopted:

> *To increase the resilience of the domestic financial system, to counter instability in the domestic financial system arising from exchange rate, long-term interest*

[8] The assessment of the inflation target range suitable for the domestic economy conducted in Ndou and Gumata (2017) provides robust empirical evidence beyond the normal argument to the effect of aligning the domestic inflation target to our key trading partners. Furthermore, in earlier chapters we presented the argument for the inflation targeting monetary policy framework and a lower inflation target range.

[9] See for further reading https://www.ecb.europa.eu/pub/pdf/other/ecb.futurecentralbankingcolloquiumconstancio201812.en.pdf.

rates, credit, asset price and liquidity shocks, and to promote, maintain a safe, sound and efficient payments system.[10]

The efficient financial system also captures the argument raised by Cecchetti and Kharroubi (2012) that a financial system is supposed to reduce transaction costs, raise investment directly, as well as improve the distribution of capital and risk across the economy. These two channels, operating through the level and composition of investment, are the mechanisms through which financial development improves growth.

Hammond (2017) states that the most important aspect of the definition of financial stability is that the financial system can fulfil its three main functions of transforming saving into financing, allowing risk management and transmitting payments with sufficient resilience[11] to disturbances that threaten these functions. The crucial part of the definition is sufficient resilience to disturbances, so as to limit the probability and magnitude of financial crises, because there will be unavoidable disturbances and shocks to the financial system from unanticipated directions. Furthermore, the resilience of the financial system is broad and does not only mean the resilience of lenders, banks and other financial intermediaries. It also implies the resilience of borrowers, including households and firms in all sectors of the economy. Financial regulation has benefits to the extent that it remedies negative effects of market failures, such as externalities, correcting for the costs associated with less competition and less efficient resource allocation.

To increase the resilience of the financial system implies that there are threshold effects and asymmetries induced by low and high regimes in the financial and real economies. Thus, we must elaborate at the financial regulatory, policy implementation and operational level on the effects of

[10] See also the constitutional mandates of the Bank of New Zealand, Unites States Federal Reserve Bank, Bank of Canada, Reserve Bank of Australia, Norges Bank and Sveriges Riksbank among other central banks.

[11] Resilience is about the structural side of the financial system. The intention is to make sure that the system is resilient enough to withstand shocks. See for further reading https://www.ecb.europa.eu/pub/pdf/other/ecb.futurecentralbankingcolloquiumconstancio201812.en.pdf.

these thresholds, regulations and policies to show, for instance, the following[12]:

1. What level of nominal house and land prices, and mortgage advances induces instability to the financial system?
2. What level of lending rate margins in selected credit extension categories induces instability to the financial system?
3. What level of Treasury Bill rates and bond yields induces financial instability?
4. What level of indebtedness (aggregate and sectoral) induces financial instability?
5. What level of LTVs, RTIs and DSTIs induces financial stability?
6. What level of the household's total debt-to-income (DSTI) ratio induces financial instability? This is especially important given the evidence presented in earlier sections showing the extent to which the Land Bank, Postbank, co-operative banks and co-operative financial institutions (CFIs) are exposed to the economic participants. Evidence presented in earlier sections indicated that the scale of credit extension beyond the current monetary system is large and must be effectively measured, regulated and evaluated.
7. Be explicit to the fact that LTVs, RTIs and DSTI ratios are three key policy tools and pillars aimed at dealing with household debt cycles, housing credit and house price cycles, the prevalence of reckless lending (even predatory lending) and building the resilience of households to indebtedness. To this effect, as the Land Bank, Postbank, co-operative banks and CFIs become institutions directly regulated by the SARB's Prudential Authority (PA), we strongly recommend that a comprehensive and coordinated database be developed within the statistics division of the PA to facilitate the understanding, analysis and evaluation of household debt so as to assist with the development of appropriate policy interventions. The analysis and evaluation

[12] The case of being explicit on the use of macro-prudential tools is further strengthened by empirical evidence showing that the use of monetary policy and the leaning against the wind (LAW) approach tends to be costly. Evidence shows that the case for leaning against the wind is limited, as in most circumstances costs outweigh benefits. See for further reading https://www.ecb.europa.eu/pub/pdf/other/ecb.futurecentralbankingcolloquiumconstancio201812.en.pdf.

of household debt extends to stress tests under different interest rates and income scenarios.[13] Furthermore, these ratios including the nature of provisioning requirements for risk-weighted assets also apply to the corporate sector, especially with respect to commercial real estate business.

Furthermore, vast literature such as Basten and Koch (2015) and Benetton et al. (2018) shows that at an individual loan level, banks charge increasingly higher interest rates, which spread a higher LTV ratio in order to compensate for the greater risk of default (individual lending supply curve). For instance, they show that a 20-percentage point smaller down payment is associated with a 22-basis point higher interest rate at origination, and a higher ex-post default rate. They argue that this suggests that lenders see down payment as a signal for unobservable risk. Hence, a combination of the LTV, RTI and DSTI ratios as macroprudential tools for housing can also assist in mitigating and pricing borrower risks and assist in lowering the level and spreads of various lending rates. Therefore, the combined use of the LTV, RTI and DSTI ratios will assist in mitigating factors that induce instability in the financial system over and above dealing with the lending rate margins.

8. The household's DSTI ratio and limits is the ultimate tool to help restrict the borrower debt servicing cost relative to the income. This is based on the recognition that over-indebtedness of households emanates from additional secured or unsecured borrowings from multiple sources and these tend to induce instability into the financial system. The debt/service ratio and the sectoral credit-GDP gap also play a complementary role to these three macroprudential tools.
9. What level of foreign exchange reserves is sufficient to cover trade commitments and associated liquidity and exchange rate volatility shocks that induce financial instability?
10. What level of the exchange rate (currency or external value of the currency) level and volatility is compatible with pursuing the best

[13] Nonetheless, it is possible that such aspects fall within the National Credit Regulator, in which case there will have to be co-ordination and information-sharing.

financial and economic interests of South Africans in support of the financial and price stability?[14]

31.4.3 The Expanded Monetary Policy Mandate

We are of the opinion that the current mandate of the SARB as stated earlier is silent on the policy objectives to achieve maximum employment growth and low and sustainable unemployment rate. There is therefore no compelling constitutional mandate to pursue this important social welfare objective. Simply put, there is no institution that is constitutionally mandated to ensure that the price and financial stability mandates translate to maximum employment and a low and sustainable unemployment rate.[15] In this current form, the price and financial stability mandates of the SARB "*exist in order to exist*" and are not anchored on other broader social welfare objectives. We are of the opinion that for the mandates of low and stable inflation or, alternatively, for price stability and financial stability to be well aligned and attuned to the objectives of the South African constitution, Section 224 of the constitution has to be amended. In addition, at the operational level it should be made explicitly clear what the social welfare objectives mean[16]:

1. The unemployment rate below 5 per cent by 2030 as captured in the National Development Plan. It will be left to the SARB at the opera-

[14] For instance, the Bank of Canada mandate is explicit about how it views the external value of the national monetary unit and to mitigate the influence of its fluctuations in the general level of production, trade, prices and employment. See also Bank of Brazil for the manner in which it implements the exchange rate policy and how banks' reserve requirements are used as a monetary and macroprudential tool to contribute to the financial system's liquidity, capital flows during capital flow surge episodes and the financial stability mandate https://www.bcb.gov.br/conteudo/homeen/FAQs/FAQ%2011Central%20Bank%20of%20Brazil%20Functions.pdf.

[15] Calls for a coordinated federal effort to attain full employment https://amp.businessinsider.com/civil-rights-movement-had-major-impact-on-us-economic-policy-2017-7.

[16] The objective of monetary policy can be expressed as price stability and full employment, without prejudice to the objective of price stability. Possible alternatives to "full employment" are "maximum sustainable employment", "minimum sustainable unemployment", "maximum sustainable output", "full resource utilization", "real stability" and so on, which, with the appropriate explanation, will have the same meaning for practical purposes. See for further reading https://www.ecb.europa.eu/pub/pdf/other/ecb.futurecentralbankingcolloquiumconstancio201812.en.pdf.

tional level to articulate what that means in terms of short- and medium-term targets, how to integrate the unemployment target within its price and financial stability mandates, or how to conduct monetary and financial policies to achieve the unemployment target. In addition, the communication of measures such as differentiation in terms of the various definitions of unemployment as it relates to the inclusion and exclusion of discouraged work seekers, gender, age and geographical location will be left to the Reserve Bank to decide, especially as they relate to the conduct of monetary and financial policies over and above the evaluation of the effectiveness of other macroeconomic policy interventions.

2. Income and wealth inequality should also feature prominently and strongly in the definition of social welfare. Recent literature has shown that the low and stable price, financial and unemployment mandates can be achieved and yet this can come at the expense of growing and wider income and wealth inequality.[17] In some instances, the conduct of monetary and financial policies itself can propagate income and wealth inequality.[18] Again it must be left to the Reserve Bank to decide which measure of income and wealth inequality—alternatively, different measures of the Gini coefficient—it will monitor, evaluate and communicate to the public in relation to its conduct of monetary and financial policy. The main objective is to strengthen the foundation for policies through explicit mandates, the analytical framework used to implement and evaluate them, and, lastly, the accountability mechanisms.

[17] A similar realisation became evident during the 2007 global financial crisis, namely, that low and stable inflation can mask the build-up of severe and systemic financial imbalances and risks. Hence, the decision to explicitly state the mandate of financial stability, redesign institutions and regulations in order to appropriately measure, monitor and evaluate financial risks and make appropriate policy interventions thereof.

[18] See, for instance, a recent speech by Kganyago on how monetary policy and selected channels of transmission such as borrowing costs, asset prices, employment growth, output growth and inflation impact income and wealth inequality https://www.resbank.co.za/Lists/Speeches/Attachments/530/Nelson%20Mandela%20University%20Public%20Lecture%2001%20August%202018.pdf. See also Furceri et al. (2016), Domanski et al. (2016) and Mersch (2014) amongst others.

Inequality measured as both income and wealth inequality encompasses inclusive growth. But at the same time, these are specific in that they put a spotlight on the fact that economic growth can be inclusive and yet mask significant and growing inequality. Hence, we strongly recommend that inequality be specified in the mandate of the SARB. Such an amendment to the mandate is consistent with the National Development Plan's (NDP) overarching goal of eliminating poverty and target to reduce inequality from current levels, shown in Fig. 31.2, to 0.6 by 2030.[19] Thus, in part low income and wealth inequality form part and parcel of how we ought to measure social welfare.

We suggest that section 224(1) be amended to

> *low and stable inflation and financial stability that facilitates, supports and generates sustainable output growth, trade and maximum employment for the social welfare*[20] *of the citizens of the Republic*

The rationale behind this is as follows:

1. Price stability is too general and not specific enough as to what it means. Yet low and stable inflation is specific that inflation should not only be within the target range of 4–2 per cent but it should be low and stable within the target range.
2. Facilitates, supports and generates speak to the earlier argument that in this current form, the conduct of price and financial stability mandates of the SARB "exist in order to exist" and are not anchored on other broader social welfare objectives.
3. Sustainable clarifies the fact that it is the baseline or the long-term or base financial regime below which you have to avoid operating with respect to inflation, whereas, with respect to the unemployment rate target and the Gini coefficient for income and wealth inequality, it means the desirable long-term unemployment, income and wealth inequality regimes to operate in.

[19] See Poverty Trends in South Africa: An examination of absolute poverty between 2006 and 2015. Statistics South Africa (2017) for further reading http://www.statssa.gov.za/publications/Report-03-10-06/Report-03-10-062015.pdf.

[20] Alternatively, the socioeconomic conditions.

4. Trade speaks to the role of the SARB as the executor of the exchange rate mandate. The SARB has at its disposal the numerous regulations and policy tools to ensure that the current flexible exchange rate regime is robust, functions efficiently and maintains a competitive exchange rate that supports the mandate as stated earlier.
5. Maximum employment is the highest level of employment growth that the low and stable inflation environment and sustainable growth can generate. It is the maximum job creation intensity that output growth generated by low and stable inflation and financial stability can create.
6. Balanced and sustainable economic growth speaks to the pursuit of the internal and external balances that are key to the achievement of the mandate as stated earlier.

Section 224(2) states that the SARB in pursuit of its primary object must perform its functions independently and without fear, favour or prejudice, but there must be regular consultation between the Bank and the Cabinet members responsible for national financial matters.

31.5 Conclusion and Policy Implications

How can section 25(5) of the constitution be redrafted to protect gender equity? What are the implications for communal land? This chapter presented evidence showing that, nationally, women constitute only 23 per cent of land redistribution beneficiaries. Thus, women are a minority of beneficiaries in a majority of provinces and make up less than one quarter of beneficiaries. This contrasts with evidence showing that the bulk (64 per cent) of the smallholder schemes in the former homelands is geographically located in the ten districts, of which six were declared presidential poverty nodes. The majority of rural households rely and are headed by women and largely consist of children and the elderly. In addition, land acquisition and the choice of land for redistribution model have implications for the impact of land reform on gender, class and poverty. In turn, poverty and inequality are disproportionately distributed along racial lines.

We argue that this can be achieved by clearly defining, stating and being explicit in section 25(5) of the constitution as to what is meant by and what constitutes equitable access. What about the criteria set out in section 25(3) of the constitution to decide what is fair, just and equitable compensation? Is there a case to redraft and expand criteria in making decisions about the trade-offs? We argue that by specifically and explicitly including the market value of the property as one of the criteria or variables to resolve the trade-offs involved in solving the problem of what is *fair, just and equitable compensation*, the constitution has legitimised and constitutionalised the market forces as one of the key pillars that solve the problem of land reform and redistribution in South Africa. We argue that the constraining factor in the application of discretion and judgement must be anchored by *justice, the need to reform landownership patterns and nation-building*.

How then does the country quantitatively measure, evaluate and monitor the progress of developing the rural financial system, food security and affordability and job creation? We argue that in order to align and coordinate policies, and quantitatively measure, evaluate and monitor the progress, the SARB will have to play a much more meaningful role. In the current form, the price and financial stability mandates of the SARB "*exist in order to exist*" and are not anchored on other broader social welfare objectives. This has implications for the mandate and the monetary policy framework of the SARB. In its current form, section 224(1) must change and the monetary policy framework under which the SARB operates must also change.

References

Aliber, M. 2009. Farmland Price Trends in South Africa, 1994–2008. Institute for Poverty, Land and Agrarian Studies (PLAAS). University of the Western Cape for the Directorate: Monitoring and Evaluation Department of Rural Development and Land Reform.

Aliber, M. 2015. Unravelling the Willing Buyer/Willing Seller Question. In B. Cousins and C. Walker (eds.) *Land Divided: Land in South African Society in 2014 and Beyond*, Jacana: Johannesburg.

Amaral, P. 2017. *Monetary Policy and Inequality*. Economic Commentary 01, Federal Reserve Bank of Cleveland.

Barnett, Alina, and Thomas, Ryland. 2013. *Has Weak Lending and Activity in the United Kingdom Been Driven by Credit Supply Shocks?* December 20. Bank of England Working Paper No. 482.

Basten, C., and Koch, C. 2015. *Higher Bank Capital Requirements and Mortgage Pricing: Evidence from the Countercyclical Capital Buffer (CCB)*. BIS Working Papers No 511.

Benetton, M., Bracke, P., and Nicola Garbarino, N. 2018. *Down Payment and Mortgage Rates: Evidence from Equity Loans*. Bank of England Staff Working Paper No. 713.

BFAP. 2011. The Contribution of the Agro-Industrial Complex to Employment in South Africa. Tech. Rep. June, The Bureau for Food and Agricultural Policy, Pretoria.

Borio, C., Disyatat, P., Juselius, M., and Rungcharoenkitkul, P. 2018. *Monetary Policy in the Grip of a Pincer Movement*. BIS Working Papers No. 706.

Cecchetti, S.G., and Kharroubi, E. 2012. *Reassessing the Impact of Finance on Growth*. BIS Working Papers No. 381.

Corbae, D., and Levine, R. 2018. Competition, Stability, and Efficiency in Financial Markets. https://www.kansascityfed.org/~/media/files/publicat/sympos/2018/papersandhandouts/082518081 0corbaelevinepaper.pdf?la=en.

Dolado, J., Motyovszki, G., and Pappa, E. 2018. Monetary Policy and Inequality: A New Channel. VOX CEPR Portal.

Domanski, D., Scatigna, M., and Zabai, A. 2016. Wealth Inequality and Monetary Policy. *BIS Quarterly Review*, March 2016.

Drehmann, Mathias, and Juselius, Mikael. 2012. Do Debt Service Costs Affect Macroeconomic and Financial Stability? *BIS Quarterly Review*, September (Basel: Bank for International Settlements).

Drehmann, Mathias, and Juselius, Mikael. 2013. *Evaluating Early Warning Indicators of Banking Crises: Satisfying Policy Requirements*. BIS Working Paper Series No. 421 (Basel: Bank for International Settlements).

Elst van der, H.J. 2007. Post–settlement Support as Key Contribution to the Success of the South African Land Reform Program (1994–2007). North West University: UNISA Press. https://www.academia.edu/12075685/Post_settlement_support_as_key_contributor_to_the_success_of_the_South_African_land_reform_programme_1994-2007_.

Flogel, F., and Gartner, S. 2018. The Banking Systems of Germany, the UK and Spain from a Spatial Perspective: The German Case. https://www.econstor.eu/bitstream/10419/180381/1/1026705681.pdf#page=2.

Functions of the Central Bank of Brazil. October 2016. https://www.bcb.gov.br/conteudo/home-en/FAQs/FAQ%2011Central%20Bank%20of%20Brazil%20Functions.pdf.

Furceri, D., Loungani, P., and Zdzienicka, A. 2016. *The Effects of Monetary Policy Shocks on Inequality*. IMF Working Paper WP/16/245.

Gambetti, L., and Musso, A. 2014. Loan Supply Shocks and the Business Cycle. ECB Conference Paper, November 20, 2014.

Greenberg, S. 2010. Status Report on Land and Agricultural Policy in South Africa. Research Report. School of Government, UWC PLAAS Institute for Poverty, Land and Agrarian Studies. http://www.plaas.org.za/sites/default/files/publications-pdf/RR40.pdf.

Hall, R., and Kepe, T. 2017. Elite Capture and State Neglect: New Evidence on South Africa's Land Reform. *Review of African Political Economy*. https://doi.org/10.1080/03056244.2017.1288615.

Hammond, P. 2017. Remit and Recommendations for the Financial Policy Committee. Letter to Mark Carney, March 8, 2017, HM Treasury, www.bankofengland.co.uk.

IMF. 2014. *Staff Guidance Note on Macroprudential Policy—Detailed Guidance on Instruments*. IMF Policy Papers. http://www.imf.org/external/np/pp/eng/2014/110614a.pdf.

Jacobs, P., Lahiff, E., and Hall, R. 2003. Land Redistribution. Programme for Land and Agrarian Studies School of Government University of the Western Cape. http://www.plaas.org.za/sites/default/files/publications-pdf/ELARSA%2001.pdf.

Kganyago, L. 2018. Inequality and Monetary Policy in South Africa. A public lecture at the Nelson Mandela University, Port Elizabeth, 1 August 2018.

Mersch, Y. 2014. Speech at Corporate Credit Conference, Zurich, 17 October 2014.

Moseneke, D.C.J. 2015. Reflections on South African Constitutional Democracy—Transition and Transformation. https://constitutionallyspeaking.co.za/dcj-moseneke-reflections-on-south-african-constitutional-democracy-transition-and-transformation/.

Ndou, E., and Gumata, N. 2017. *Inflation Dynamics in South Africa: The Role of Thresholds, Exchange Rate Pass-through and Inflation Expectations on Policy Trade-offs*. Palgrave Macmillan. ISBN 978-3-319-46702-3.

Netshipale, A.J., Oosting, S.J., Raidimi, E.N., Mashiloane, M.L., and De Boer, I.J.M. 2007. Land Reform in South Africa: Beneficiary Participation and Impact on Land Use in the Waterberg District. *NJAS Wageningen Journal of Life Sciences*, 83, 57–66.

Ranwedzi, N. 2011. The Potential and Limits of the Proactive Land Acquisition Strategy (PLAS): Land Reform Implementation in Gauteng Province of South Africa. http://www.plaas.org.za/sites/default/files/publications-pdf/PP%2006.pdf.

Umrabulo. 2018. Lets' Talk. Umrabulo No. 43, August 2018. https://www.anc1912.org.za/umrabulo-43-2018.

Index[1]

[1] Note: Page numbers followed by 'n' refer to notes.

N. Gumata, E. Ndou, *Accelerated Land Reform, Mining, Growth, Unemployment and Inequality in South Africa*, https://doi.org/10.1007/978-3-030-30884-1

N

The manufacturer's authorised representative in the EU is Springer Nature Customer Service Centre GmbH, Europaplatz 3, 69115 Heidelberg, Germany. If you have any concerns regarding our products, please contact ProductSafety@springernature.com

Printed and bound by CPI Group (UK) Ltd, Croydon, CR0 4YY
25/09/2026
02222881-0011